A History of Russia

A History of Russia

Volume 2: Since 1855

SEVENTH EDITION

Nicholas V. Riasanovsky
University of California, Berkeley

Mark D. Steinberg
University of Illinois, Urbana-Champaign

New York   Oxford
OXFORD UNIVERSITY PRESS
2005

Oxford University Press

Oxford   New York
Auckland   Bangkok   Buenos Aires   Cape Town   Chennai
Dar es Salaam   Delhi   Hong Kong   Istanbul   Karachi   Kolkata
Kuala Lumpur   Madrid   Melbourne   Mexico City   Mumbai
Nairobi   São Paulo   Shanghai   Taipei   Tokyo   Toronto

Published by Oxford University Press, Inc.
198 Madison Avenue, New York, New York, 10016
http://www.oup.com

Oxford is a registered trademark of Oxford University Press

Text design by Cathleen Elliott.
Maps prepared by Vaughn Gray and Bill Nelson.

Library of Congress Cataloging-in-Publication Data
Riasanovsky, Nicholas Valentine, 1923–
    A history of Russia / by Nicholas V. Riasanovsky and Mark D. Steinberg.—7th ed.
        p. cm.
    Includes bibliographical references and index.
    ISBN-13: 978-0-19-515392-7 (v. 1)—ISBN-13: 978-0-19-515393-4 (v. 2)
    ISBN-10: 0-19-515392-8 (v. 1)—ISBN-10: 0-19-575393-6 (v. 2)
        1. Russia—History. 2. Soviet Union—History. 3. Russia (Federation)—History. I.
    Steinberg, Mark D., 1953– II. Title.
    DK40.R5 2004
    947—dc22
                                                                                    2004049594

Printing number: 9 8 7 6 5 4 3 2 1

Printed in the United States of America
on acid-free paper

To Our Students

Contents

Maps ix

Illustrations xi

Prefaces xv

Introduction xxv

29 The Reign of Alexander II, 1855–81 341

30 The Reign of Alexander III, 1881–94, and the First Part
of the Reign of Nicholas II, 1894–1905 362

31 The Last Part of the Reign of Nicholas II: The Revolution
of 1905 and the Constitutional Period, 1905–17 377

32 The Economic and Social Development of Russia from
the "Great Reforms" until the Revolutions of 1917 396

33 Russian Culture from the "Great Reforms" until the
Revolutions of 1917 415

34 The Revolutions of 1917 439

Part VI *Soviet Russia*

35 Soviet Russia: An Introduction 451

36 War Communism, 1917–21, and the New Economic
Policy, 1921–28 460

37 The First Three Five-Year Plans, 1928–41 482

38 Soviet Foreign Policy, 1921–41, and the Second World
War, 1941–45 501

39 Stalin's Last Decade, 1945–53 517

40 The Soviet Union after Stalin, 1953–85 529

41 Soviet Society and Culture 556

42 The Gorbachev Years, 1985–91, and the Collapse of the
Soviet Union 584

Part VII Russian Federation

43 Russia after Communism: Yeltsin, 1991–99,
    and Putin, 2000– 609

44 Society and Culture since 1991   641

    Appendix tables
      1–4 Russian Rulers   A-2
      *5 Political Subdivisions of the U.S.S.R. as of
        January 1, 1976*   A-6
    Bibliography   B-1
    A Select List of Readings in English on Russian History   SR-1
    Index   I-1

Maps

1. The Balkans, 1877–1878   359
2. Russo-Japanese War, 1904–1905   375
3. Russia in World War I—1914 to the Revolution of 1917   393
4. Industry and Agriculture—19th Century   401
5. Revolution and Civil War in European Russia, 1917–1922   468
6. Industry and Agriculture—1939   491
7. Russia in World War II, 1939–1945   509
8. Population Growth   560
9. Contemporary Russia   611

Illustrations

1. Alexander II (*Tsarstvyuiushchii dom Romanovykh*). 342
2. Alexander III in 1889 (*Treasures of Russia Exhibition*). 364
3. Nicholas II in seventeenth-century costume, 1903 (*New York Public Library*). 368
4. Nicholas II blessing troops leaving for the front in the Russo-Japanese War, 1905 (*Sunset of the Romanov Dynasty* [Moscow: Terra Publishers, 1992]). 373
5. Social Democrats demonstrate in 1905 (*Russian State Archive of Film and Photographic Documents*). 380
6. Peter Stolypin (*Central State Archive of Film, Photographic, and Sound Documents of St. Petersburg*). 387
7. Gregory Rasputin (Rene Fülöp-Miller, *Rasputin: The Holy Devil* [Leipzig: Grethlein and Co, 1927]). 394
8. Count Sergei Witte in St. Petersburg in 1905 (*Sunset of the Romanov Dynasty*). 399
9. Aleksei Medvedev (*Moskovskie pechatniki v 1905 godu* [Moscow: Izd. Moskovskogo gubotdela, 1925]). 403
10. A meeting of the *mir* (*Victoria and Albert Museum*). 409
11. The *Passazh* on Nevsky prospect, 1901 (*Central State Archive of Film, Sound, and Photographic Documents, St. Petersburg*). 412
12. Fedor Dostoevsky (*New York Public Library*). 421
13. Leo Tolstoy (*New York Public Library*). 422
14. Anton Chekhov (*New York Public Library*). 425
15. Anna Akhmatova (*Zephyr Press, Brookline, MA*). 427
16. Modest Mussorgsky (*Sovfoto*). 429
17. Peter Tchaikovsky (*New York Public Library*). 429
18. Vaslav Nijinsky (*New York Public Library*). 430
19. Kazimir Malevich, "0.10: Last Futurist Painting Exhibition," Petrograd, 1915 (*Steinberg Collection*). 431
20. Provisional Government (*Russian State Archive of Film and Photographic Documents*). 442

21. Soldiers at funeral for fallen in revolution (*Russian State Archive of Film and Photographic Documents*). **448**

22. V. I. Lenin in 1917 (*Vladimir Il'ich Lenin: Biografiia* [Moscow: Gosizdat, 1960]). **453**

23. "A Specter Is Haunting Europe—The Specter of Communism" (*Victoria Bonnell*). **462**

24. "The Struggle of the Red Knight against the Dark Force," 1919 (*Gosizdat*). **471**

25. Nicholas Bukharin (*Stephen Cohen*). **478**

26. Leon Trotsky (*New York Public Library*). **479**

27. Joseph Stalin (*Sovfoto*). **480**

28. "Full Speed Ahead with Shock Tempo: The Five Year Plan in Four Years," 1930 (*Lenizogiz*). **487**

29. "Long Live Our Happy Socialist Motherland, Long Live Our Beloved Great Stalin," 1935 (*Victoria Bonnell*). **490**

30. Soviet Communist Party and "deviationists" (*Mark Steinberg*). **494**

31. "Any Peasant Can Now Live Like a Human Being," 1934 (*Victoria Bonnell*). **498**

32. "Avenge Us," 1942 (*Sovetskoe iskusstvo*). **515**

33. "Under the Leadership of the Great Stalin," 1951 (*Victoria Bonnell*). **523**

34. Stalin's funeral (*Sovfoto*). **530**

35. Nikita Khrushchev (*Sovfoto*). **533**

36. Soviet leaders, 1967 (*World Wide Photos*). **535**

37. Brezhnev on a skimobile (*V. Musaelyan*). **537**

38. Kustodiev, "Bond between City and Country," 1925 (*Gosizdat*). **562**

39. Young women on a Moscow street in the 1980s (*I. Moukhin*). **565**

40. Literacy poster, 1920 (*Gosizdat*). **569**

41. Vladimir Tatlin, Monument to the Third International, 1919–20 (Nikolai Punin, *Pamiatnik III Internatsionala* [Petrograd: Otd. izobrazitel'nykh iskusstv N. K. P., 1920]). **577**

42. Moscow State University (*World Wide Photos*). **580**

43. The seventeenth-century Simeon Stolpnik church in front of Soviet housing project (*Sovfoto*). **582**

44. Leaders of the communist world, 1986 (*World Wide Photos*). **588**

45. "We shall look at things realistically" (*Sovetskii khudozhnik*). **590**

46. Patriarch Alexei II blessing Yeltsin (*World Wide Photos*). **596**

47. Children playing on toppled statue of Lenin, August 1991. **605**

48. Boris Yeltsin on tank in August 1991 (*Associated Press*). **612**

49. Vladimir Putin speaking with American journalists, 2001 (*Alexander Zemlianichenko, Associated Press*).   626

50. Demonstration against *prikhvatizatsiia,* Moscow 1992 (*Mark Steinberg*).   643

51. Sales booth in Moscow, 1994 (*Mark Steinberg*).   645

52. Small business in Moscow, 1994 (*Mark Steinberg*).   646

53. Communists demonstrate in Moscow, 1992 (*P. Gorshkov*).   652

54. Woman in church under reconstruction, 1991 (*M. Rogozin*).   656

55. Christ the Savior cathedral in Moscow being rebuilt, 1997 (*Mark Steinberg*).   658

56. Viacheslav Mikhailov, "Metaphysical Icon," 1994 (*V. Mikhailov*).   663

Preface to the First Edition

For a student of Russian history to write a complete history of Russia is, in a sense, to give an account of his entire intellectual and academic life. And his indebtedness to others is, of course, enormous. I know at least where to begin the listing of my debts: my father, Valentin A. Riasanovsky, made a huge contribution to this *History of Russia* both by his participation in the writing of the book and, still more important, by teaching me Russian history. Next I must mention my teachers of Russian history at Harvard and Oxford, notably the late Professor Michael Karpovich, the late Warden B. H. Sumner, and Professor Sir Isaiah Berlin. A number of colleagues read sections of the manuscript and made very helpful comments. To name only those who read large parts of the work, I thank Professors Gregory Grossman, Richard Herr, and Martin Malia of the University of California at Berkeley, my former teacher Professor Dimitri Obolensky of Oxford University, Professor Richard Pipes of Harvard University, and Professor Charles Jelavich of Indiana University.

I wish, further, to thank the personnel of the Oxford University Press both for great help of every kind and for letting me have things my own way. I am also indebted to several University of California graduate students who served as my research assistants during the years in which this work was written and prepared for publication; in particular, to Mrs. Patricia Grimsted and Mr. Walter Sablinsky, who were largely responsible for the Bibliography and the Index, respectively. Nor will I forget libraries and librarians, especially those in Berkeley. The publication of this volume can be considered a tribute to my wife and my students: my wife, because of her persistent and devoted aid in every stage of the enterprise; my students, because *A History of Russia* developed through teaching them and has its main *raison d'être* in answering their needs.

I would also like gratefully to acknowledge specific contributions of material to my *History of Russia*. The following publishers allowed me to quote at length from the works cited.

Harvard University Press for Merle Fainsod, *How Russia Is Ruled* (Cambridge, 1954), pp. 372–73.

American Committee for Liberation for *News Briefs on Soviet Activities*, Vol. II, No. 3, June 1959.

Houghton Mifflin Company for George Z. F. Bereday, William W. Brickman, and Gerald H. Read, editors, *The Changing Soviet School* (Boston, 1960), pp. 8–9.

Further, I am deeply grateful to the Rand Corporation and to Harvard University Press for their permission to use Table 51 on page 210 of Abram Bergson, *The Real National Income of Soviet Russia Since 1928* (Cambridge, 1961). A condensed version of that table constitutes an appendix to my history. Professor Bergson not only gave his personal permission to use this material but advised me kindly on this and certain related matters.

Several people have been most generous in lending material for the illustrations. I should like to thank Mr. George R. Hann for making available to me prints of his superb collection of icons: Mrs. Henry Shapiro, who lent photographs taken by her and her husband during recent years spent in Russia; Professor Theodore Von Laue, who took the pictures I have used from our trip to Russia in 1958; Miss Malvina Hoffman, who lent the pictures of Pavlova and Diaghilev; and the Solomon R. Guggenheim Museum, which permitted reproduction of a painting in their collection, *Winter* by Vasily Kandinsky.

As every writer—and reader—in the Russian field knows, there is no completely satisfactory solution to the problems of transliteration and transcription of proper names. I relied on the Library of Congress system, but with certain modifications: notably, I omitted the soft sign, except in the very few cases where it seemed desirable to render it by using *i*, and I used *y* as the ending of family names. A few of these names, such as that of the composer Tchaikovsky, I spelled in the generally accepted Western manner, although this does not agree with the system of transliteration adopted in this book. As to first names, I preferred their English equivalents, although I transliterated the Russian forms of such well-known names as Ivan and used transliterated forms in some other instances as well, as with Vissarion, not Bessarion, Belinsky. The names of the Soviet astronauts are written as spelled in the daily press. I avoided patronymics. In general I tried to utilize English terms and forms where possible. I might have gone too far in that direction; in any case, I feel uneasy about my translation of *kholopy* as "slaves."

As with transliteration, there is no satisfactory solution to constructing an effective bibliography to a general history of a country. I finally decided simply to list the principal relevant works of the scholars mentioned by name in the text. This should enable the interested reader who knows the required languages to pursue further the views of the men in question, and it should provide something of an introduction to the literature on Russian history. The main asset of such a bibliography is that it is manageable. Its chief liability lies in the fact that it encompasses only a fraction of the works on which this volume is based and of necessity omits important authors and studies.

I decided to have as appendixes only the genealogical tables of Russian rulers, which are indispensable for an understanding of the succession to the throne in the eighteenth century and at some other times, and Professor Bergson's estimate of the growth of the gross national product in the U.S.S.R.

NICHOLAS V. RIASANOVSKY

Berkeley, California
September 24, 1962

Preface to the Second Edition

The second edition of my *History of Russia* follows in all essentials the first. Still, the passage of time and the continuous development of scholarship resulted in many additions and modifications. In particular, the Soviet period was expanded both to encompass the last six years and to devote a little more attention to certain topics. A dozen additional authors proved important enough to be cited by name in the second edition, and thus enter the bibliography. Numerous other researchers in the field, some of equal importance to me, received no personal citation. In addition to the text and the bibliography, changes were made in the maps and the illustrations. In the appendixes, the table of the U.S.S.R. gross national product was brought up to date and a table of the administrative divisions of the U.S.S.R. was added. Moreover, a new appendix containing a select list of readings in English on Russian history was included in the second edition.

Again, I have very many people to thank. In the first place, I want to thank my students and students throughout the United States who have used my *History* and have thus given it its true test. I have tried to utilize their experience and their opinions. I am also deeply grateful to very numerous colleagues who used *History of Russia* in their courses, or simply read it, and made corrections or comments. While it is not feasible to list all the appropriate names, I must mention at least Professor Gregory Grossman of the University of California at Berkeley, without whom the gross national product table would not have been possible and who, in addition, paid careful attention to the entire section on the Soviet Union, and the Soviet scholar V. B. Vilinbakhov, who has subjected my presentation of the early periods of Russian history to a thorough and searching criticism. Needless to say, as I thank these and other scholars for their help, I must state that they are not responsible for the opinions or the final form of my book. I am further indebted to my research assistants Mrs. Victoria King and Mr. Vladimir Pavloff and, most especially, to my wife.

NICHOLAS V. RIASANOVSKY

Berkeley, California
December 19, 1968

Preface to the Third Edition

No attempt has been made in this third edition of *A History of Russia* to alter the character and basic design of previous editions. The passage of time since the completion of the second edition in 1968 has brought us from the occupation of Czechoslovakia to the Twenty-fifth Party Congress in 1976 and the current Tenth Five-Year Plan. Numerous changes have therefore been made in the text as a consequence of recent events and of recent scholarship as well. The bibliography and especially the English reading list have been expanded. The section on the Soviet period has grown slightly in proportion to the whole, although the aim remains to present a single balanced volume.

Many people deserve my special gratitude. Professor Gregory Grossman of the University of California at Berkeley again brought up to date the gross national product table and, moreover, was of invaluable help in updating the entire Soviet section. Other Berkeley colleagues generously contributed their knowledge and wisdom in regard to subjects which preoccupied me during the preparation of this third edition. Colleagues elsewhere were equally helpful as they used *A History of Russia* as a textbook and informed me of their experience or simply commented on the work. I would like to thank particularly many conscientious reviewers, such as Professor Walter Leitsch of Vienna. Mr. Gerald Surh and Mr. Jacob Picheny proved to be excellent research assistants, who aided me in every way and most notably in the preparation of the English reading list and the index. The mistakes and other deficiencies that remain after all that help are, I am afraid, mine, and, taking into account the scope of the book, they may well be considerable. My most fundamental gratitude goes to my constant helper, my wife, and to the students for whom this textbook was written and who have been using it. May the group of students who recently called me across the continent from Brown University to discuss my *History of Russia* and whose names I do not know accept the thanks I extend to them, as the representatives of students everywhere.

NICHOLAS V. RIASANOVSKY

Berkeley, California
March 12, 1976

Preface to the Fourth Edition

The death of Leonid Ilich Brezhnev on November 10, 1982, and Iurii Vladimirovich Andropov's prompt succession to the leadership of the Soviet Union have provided a striking terminal point to this fourth edition of my *History of Russia*. The new material in the book covers the last seven years of the Brezhnev regime. It includes also additions and changes in all previous parts of Russian and Soviet history as well as the updating of the two bibliographies.

Acknowledging my overall fundamental and grateful indebtedness to the scholarship in the field, I must record special thanks to my colleagues, particularly Berkeley colleagues, who contributed directly to the preparation of this edition. Professor Gregory Grossman again updated the population and gross national product table and, beyond that, offered invaluable help based on his matchless knowledge of the Soviet economy and of the Soviet Union in general. Other colleagues, such as Professor George Breslauer, whose notable book *Khrushchev and Brezhnev as Leaders: Building Authority in Soviet Politics* came out just as Brezhnev died, were also generous with their time and expert advice. For checking, rechecking, typing, preparing the index, and much else, I was blessed with an excellent research assistant, Mr. Maciej Siekierski, who also contributed his special knowledge of Poland and Lithuania, and an excellent secretary, Ms. Dorothy Shannon. And, once more, I must emphasize my indebtedness to my students and my wife: the students have been using *A History of Russia*, often both enthusiastically and critically, for some twenty years; my debt to my wife is even more basic as well as of a still longer duration.

NICHOLAS V. RIASANOVSKY

Berkeley, California
September 1983

Preface to the Fifth Edition

I ended the first four editions of *A History of Russia* with a comment on the contemporary Soviet conundrum. I wrote that the Soviet Union was neither a stable nor a happy country, but that the problem of change, either by revolution or by evolution, was, in its case, an extremely difficult one, which I could not clearly foresee. The last sentences were,

> To conclude, the Soviet system is not likely to last, not likely to change fundamentally by evolution, and not likely to be overthrown by a revolution. History, to be sure, has a way of advancing even when that means leaving historians behind.

Shortly after this assessment appeared in print, an author of a generally kind and even flattering review wrote in exasperation that Professor Riasanovsky, unfortunately, terminated 710 lucid pages with a murky sentence. In response to my critic, I have considered and reconsidered my conclusion throughout the years and with every edition, but always retained it. To be sure, it was not distinguished by perspicacity or precision, but it was the best I could offer. Now, however, I am moving it from the conclusion to the preface. Historians, and all others as well, have been left behind. The first part of my commentary, on the instability and unhappiness in the Soviet Union, needs no elaboration. The second, on the difficulty of change, is something the citizens of the former Soviet Union and even other people in the world are living through day by day.

To be sure, as many friends have advised me, it would be wiser to wait with a new edition of *A History of Russia*. I am not waiting for two reasons: I have always been in favor of writing contemporary history, no matter how contemporary, as well as other kinds, and Oxford University Press has provided me with an excellent determined editor with whom I have been working for many years. Let us hope that the next edition will be lucid in its final as well as its earlier pages. (And, incidentally, that it will bring reliably up to date Tables 5 and 6 of the Appendix, an impossibility at present.)

The next edition may also be richer in historiography. *Glasnost* has been perhaps the most striking substantive change in the Soviet Union in the past few years. It does represent the breaking out from a totalitarian straight jacket so characteristic of Soviet society and culture. It may be irreversible. But so far, because of the shortage of time and other reasons, it has not transformed Soviet historiography. Having participated in the conference, held in Moscow in April 1990, on rewriting Soviet history, having read Soviet publications, and having talked with Soviet historians, I must conclude that the change has been slow. I do not want to minimize the work of such revisionist historians as

Evgeny Viktorovich Anisimov, all the more so because to them probably belongs the future, but I have been on the whole impressed and depressed by the difficulty of change. Understandably, if often unfortunately, people who have spent many years or a lifetime at hard work try to retain at least some of their accomplishment rather than sweep it away. Bolder and more important historiographical developments should appear in the coming years.

In the preparation of this new edition, I made the usual additions and changes throughout the manuscript, and considered or introduced at least fifty-seven emendations in Soviet history prior to 1985. If not always minor— the figure of Soviet casualties in the Second World War was raised from 20 million to 27 million, and that is 7 million more dead—they were brief and precise. The last narrative chapter was, of course, written anew, and the "Concluding Remarks" underwent considerable change.

As always, I am deeply indebted to many people: my colleagues at the University of California, Berkeley; other colleagues whom I met at the Wilson Center and the Kennan Institute in Washington, D.C., where I spent the 1989–1990 academic year; still other American colleagues elsewhere as well as extremely numerous Soviet scholars and other Soviet visitors. I must emphasize my gratitude to Professor Gregory Grossman, whose help has been, again, invaluable in the treatment of the Soviet economy in the volume and, moreover, whom I consider in general to be our best specialist on the Soviet Union. I am grateful to Nancy Lane and her colleagues at Oxford University Press; to my secretary, Nadine Ghammache; and to my research assistants, Theodore Weeks, John W. Randolph, Jr., and Ilya Vinkovetsky, who had the major responsibility for revising the index. More generally, I am grateful for the continuing response to my *History* abroad as well as in the United States. Since the publication of the fourth American edition, there appeared another and different Italian edition, a French edition, and even a pirated Korean edition in South Korea of the imperial part of my volume (I was told that the earlier part is being prepared for publication). But as usual, in these fluid times, too, my main indebtedness is to my students and my wife.

NICHOLAS V. RIASANOVSKY

Berkeley, California
April 1992

Preface to the Sixth Edition

The seven years that passed since the last edition of my *A History of Russia* proved to be less definitive for that country than many specialists, as well as the general public, had expected. Russia is still in transition and under great stress and strain. Its economy continues to decline. Indeed, the financial collapse of August 1998 delivered a major blow even to those groups in society which had formerly prospered because of the transformation. Still, grim as numerous forecasts of the Russian future are, they do not include a return to the Union of Soviet Socialist Republics. For well or ill the country has entered a new historical period, that of Russian Federation. The great importance attached to the forthcoming elections is one clear indication that the scenario has changed.

As with earlier editions, and probably more so, I tried to keep up with the latest developments, especially for the new chapter on "Yeltsin's Russia," and also to profit by the opening of the Russian archives, particularly for the Soviet period. Fortunately some of the best work based on these archives has been done by our Berkeley Ph.D.s and Ph.D. candidates. I used opportunities to go to Russia, attend scholarly conferences, and engage in discussion with many Russian scholars (as well as with many more when they came to Berkeley or to international or our national conferences), and I lectured in Moscow (in the Kremlin, no less). I want to thank here warmly my Russian hosts and interlocutors. I am also deeply grateful to American colleagues and helpers. Professor Gregory Grossman, as before, was invaluable in the area of economics, but also for his unsurpassed knowledge of the Soviet Union in general. Other colleagues who usefully read and criticized parts of the manuscript included Professors Robert Middlekauff, Alexander Vucinich, and Reginald Zelnik. Dr. John Dunlop of the Hoover Institution provided some very valuable newly-available source material. My research assistant, Ilya Vinkovetsky, demonstrated again his marvelous acquaintance with the Soviet and contemporary Russian scene, and he also worked on the index. Ms. Nadine Ghammache supplied once more fine and eager secretarial help. Further, I want to acknowledge the prompt and effective work of what is for me a new Oxford University Press "team" of Ms. Gioia Stevens, Ms. Stacie Caminos, and Mr. Benjamin Clark. Our daughter Maria helped me with the photographs and in certain other matters. Finally, I am most in debt, for reasons too long to list here, to my wife Arlene.

NICHOLAS V. RIASANOVSKY

Berkeley, California
May 1999

Preface to the Seventh Edition

Every historian knows that time marches on. In the words of a recent bilingual immigrant: "Vremia-to goes idët." Therefore, the seventh edition of *A History of Russia* has two authors rather than a single one. Professor Mark Steinberg received his doctorate in 1987 at the University of California at Berkeley and has previously taught at Harvard and Yale universities. He is professor of history at the University of Illinois at Urbana-Champaign, where for a number of years he was also director of the Russian and East European Center. Steinberg's research has centered on the cultural and social history of Russia in the late nineteenth and early twentieth centuries. Like Riasanovsky, though, he is interested in many other periods and themes in Russian and comparative history. The result of this new collaboration is this intrinsically joint volume, which has been substantially revised, especially for the years from 1855 to the present. Both authors remain active as writers and especially as teachers. With this in mind, the seventh edition of *A History of Russia* remains dedicated to our students.

We want to express deep gratitude to numerous colleagues in our two universities and elsewhere, especially to Professor Gregory Grossman, to our editor Peter Coveney and his colleagues at Oxford University Press, and, in particular, to our wives, Arlene Riasanovsky and Jane Hedges.

NICHOLAS V. RIASANOVSKY
Berkeley, California

MARK D. STEINBERG
Urbana, Illinois

Introduction:
The Historical Background

It could be argued, and often has been, that the modern age in Russia was only fully underway in the wake of Alexander II's "great reforms," which ended serfdom, created new forms of rural and urban self-government, gave the universities greater autonomy, replaced a backward legal system characterized by arbitrariness and confusion with one of the most progressive and open judicial orders in Europe, replaced a system of bureaucratic censorship of books and journals with a system grounded in law, and restructured the military on the modern European model of limited years of service and a regular reserve. The chapters that follow provide plenty of evidence that Russia was traveling along a path of common European modernity—though the particularities of Russia's modern path will also be apparent (modernity, it bears remembering, even in Europe, has not been a singular phenomenon that was everywhere the same). Scholars still debate how modernity should be defined. But the most persuasive and useful definitions, at least of its European history, keep in play its contradictory faces: both rationalistic and scientific modernization (including a driving will to order, control, and improve the physical environment and social and economic relationships) and a spirit of disruption, iconoclasm, flux, and uncertainty. Modern faith in the forward march of progress has similarly been accompanied, it is argued, by no less modern anxiety, unease, doubt, and resistance. This picture of modernity is useful for thinking about the history of Russia since the mid-nineteenth century. But the story began earlier. As the preceding volume describes, much was already changing in Russia before the "great reforms."

In the seventeenth century, the Muscovite state (which came into being as the princes of Moscow, starting in the fifteenth century, fought against both Mongol rule and the fragmentation of power among numerous princes) embarked on policies of political and social ordering of the nation. These years saw increasing bureaucratic centralization, the systematization of administration and law, the weakening of aristocratic authority (especially by making landholding conditional on state service and keeping the noble estate open to newcomers by rewarding servitors with land and noble status), and increasing control over the rural laboring population (especially by ending all rights to flee from the estate and its lord, thus establishing complete rural serfdom but also setting in motion a long history of peasant rebellion). This increasingly powerful nation-state also continued to expand its borders in the seventeenth century, westward to encompass what is now Belarus and Ukraine (which meant uniting to the Moscow state lands that had been the historic center of pre-Mongol "Rus," or Kievan Russia), into the southern steppe to the Caspian sea, and eastward into the vast expanses of Siberia. By the end of the seventeenth century, Russia was already becoming a multi-ethnic empire with an increasingly modern, if highly authoritarian, state.

The seventeenth century also saw an acceleration of Russia's cultural links with western Europe. To be sure, connections to the rest of Europe already had a long history. Many of Russia's ruling elites traced their origins to the Scandinavian invaders who established the Kievan Russian state. Commercial and dynastic ties to Greece began even before Russia's rulers converted the nation to Orthodox Christianity in the tenth century. Thereafter, Russia felt the cultural influences of Orthodox Byzantium in many areas, including politics and the arts. At the same time, however, Italian architects were invited to design the grand new stone churches in the Moscow Kremlin in the fifteenth century. The seventeenth century, especially the reign of Alexis (1645–76), saw a change in the degree and depth of Western influence in Russia. An effort to bring Church ritual more in line with Greek practices—by a patriarch who viewed Russia's Orthodoxy in universal not national terms—was supported by the state, though it provoked a schism among believers. In Kiev and other cities, Slavonic-Latin-Greek academies were established as centers of intellectual exchange with the West. And large numbers of foreigners from all over Europe entered the tsar's service, served as officers in the Russian army, or played key roles in foreign trade and in setting up factories. Western manners and ideas became influential among many Russians, including the heir to the throne, tsar Alexis's restless son Peter.

Under Peter I (1682–1725), the pace of Russia's modernization and Westernization accelerated. With enormous energy and drive, and plenty of authoritarian brutality, Peter took to the task of remaking a Russia he saw as still backward and isolated in relation to the West. While continuing to expand the reach of Russia's empire—officially recognized as such when Peter accepted the added title of *imperator* as well as "Great" in 1721—he devoted himself to bringing still more rational systematization and centralization to government and administration, creating a new system of ministries called colleges, a senate, and a political police, among other agencies; reorganizing the empire by dividing the country into provinces and establishing provincial administrations; and putting the Church under state control. Parallel to these reforms were changes meant to transform society as well as the state. Peter established a single "Table of Ranks," which merged old and new nobilities into one hierarchical class based on promotion through service; organized the urban population into guilds and corporations; founded factories and other industries; modernized the army and created a navy; reformed the tax structure (to make it more effective); and stimulated a Westernized intellectual life by opening schools and Russia's first academy of higher education, creating a new secular alphabet, organizing the first printing presses in Russia, and even redesigning the calendar so that Russians could count years, as in western Europe, from the birth of Christ rather than the creation of the world.

Historians have seen in Peter's reign the strong presence of a leitmotif that extends through the whole of Russian history—what Wortman has called the idea of the "civilizing role of force exerted from above." Like many Russian rulers, Peter used the power of the state to ensure Russia's progress. But under Peter, more than ever before, it was precisely "Western civilization" that was to be the aim. This was signaled most strongly in two symbolic acts for which his reign is best remembered: insisting that his elite wear Western dress and cut off their beards and building a Western capital with an entirely Western name, Sankt Peterburg (at first, Sankt Piter Burkh). For Peter, western European modernity was defined above all as the rationalization and regularization of administration, laws, and social structure. He sought for Russia clear laws, rules, and procedures, improved technologies, and a more modern economy. Appropriately, Russia's new capital was a geometric city—a city of lines, squares, grids, and triangles imposed on an unruly, swampy, flood-prone terrain.

Peter's successors in the eighteenth century, notably Elizabeth (1741–61) and Catherine II (1762–96), were mainly women, made possible by Peter's revision of the law of succession to allow the sovereign to choose any appropriate heir regardless of class, gender, or blood line. Peter's daughter Elizabeth did much to continue Peter's legacy: she led further efforts to routinize and rationalize government institutions; encouraged higher education and cultural development; stimulated the economy (for example, by abolishing custom barriers and encouraging entrepreneurship); and, in foreign policy, continued efforts to demonstrate that Russia was a European great power, even defeating Prussia in the Seven Years' War and briefly occupying Berlin in 1760. But she is perhaps best remembered for her promotion of a new spirit of culture and beauty in Russian life. She brought Italian architects to build a series of gorgeous palaces and parks. And she promoted what has been called a "cult of happiness" in Russian public life. Odes about the ruler spoke of the "love" and "kindness" with which she ruled. She herself, in her quite public private life, pursued a life devoted to the virtues of pleasure.

Catherine II—named "the Great" for her conquests in war and further expansion of the empire—was inspired by ambitious desires to continue Russia's modernization. She tried again to codify Russia's laws. Her purpose, however, was not only systematization but also political-cultural modernization. She summoned representatives of various classes to an unprecedented national Legislative Commission in 1767 and charged the deputies, in her famous *Nakaz*, or *Instruction*, with creating a new law code in keeping with the principles that Russia was "a European State," that the purpose of monarchy is "not to deprive people of their natural liberty but to correct their actions in order to attain the supreme good," that the state should be ruled according to law, and that every person must be equal and subject to the same laws. This idealistic vision, strongly influenced by Enlightenment philosophy, remained unrealized, though Catherine achieved a great deal during her reign to promote Russia's modernization. She restructured the central administration to make procedures and departments more efficient. She accepted one of the few popular decisions of her late husband, emperor Peter III (who had been overthrown and killed by guards officers): ending required state service for all nobles, evidently hoping to encourage them to become more active in local affairs and in the management of their estates. She initiated major reforms in how localities were administered: reorganizing the provinces to make them more logical, creating new urban institutions to run the growing cities, establishing noble assemblies, and creating a new provincial court system. She promoted education and culture, including allowing private publishing and printing for the first time and establishing free public primary and high schools. She worked to develop the economy with various loans and other incentives to noble farmers and business owners. And she continued to expand the empire, bringing large numbers of Poles, Ukrainians, Lithuanians, Jews, and others under Russian rule. This too, it was believed, enhanced Russia's status as a great power in the world.

Emperor Paul's efforts to undo many of his mother's, Catherine II's, reforms were cut short by his overthrow and murder. Talk of enlightened reform resumed in the reign of Alexander I (1801–25). At the very outset of his reign, Alexander established an Unofficial Committee to discuss major political and social reforms, including a constitution and the end of serfdom. These he did not achieve, though he did reform the central state by giving the Senate greater influence in coordinating policy and as a supreme court, replacing inefficient and often corrupt colleges with more efficient and responsible ministries, and creating an appointed body of experts to advise the tsar on legislation, the State Council, modeled on Napoleon's Conseil d'etat. He also enacted legislation to mitigate some of the more brutal conditions in serfs' lives (such as the sale of individual serfs), to encourage the economy by allowing non-nobles to own estates, and to stimulate culture by establishing new universities and schools. He also continued to expand Russia's role in the world, especially in the war against Napoleon in 1805–7 and in the war of 1812, which began with Napoleon's invasion of Russia and concluded with Russian troops marching into Paris in 1814, a powerful symbol of Russia's status as a European power.

At the same time, like his predecessors, Alexander carefully guarded his absolute power. Many reasons have been suggested for why he failed to give Russia a constitution or abolish serfdom, ranging from his distraction with international affairs to the influence of European conservatives like Prince von Metternich to his own growing anxieties about the dangers of liberalization to sheer duplicity. Even had he granted Russia a constitution, however, it should be kept in mind that his notions of constitutionalism were not especially democratic. Alexander and his allies, recent scholars have emphasized, understood a constitution to mean not balancing and limiting the power of the executive with an elected legislative and a powerful judiciary but an orderly system of administration and law, free from arbitrariness and tyranny. In a word, they wanted clarity, order, efficiency—a *Rechtsstaat*—not democracy. Like most of his enlightened predecessors, Alexander believed that a strong state was essential for Russia's modern progress.

In the reign of Nicholas I (1825–55), emphasis shifted more toward the necessity for order and power than toward ideas about the progress that power could bring. Order, often ruthlessly imposed, was a leitmotif. Nicholas I's struggles against European revolutions earned him the nickname "Gendarme of Europe." At home, he took aim at education, the press, scholarship, literature, and even science with policies designed to seek out and silence dissent. A leading official in Nicholas I's government, Count Sergei Uvarov, remarked that he would die with a sense of duty fulfilled if he could succeed in "pushing Russia back some fifty years from what is being prepared for her by the theories." This effort to halt the influence of new ideas of government and society—"the theories"—was remarkably successful. In the view of one contemporary, Nicholas imposed on Russia "the quiet of a graveyard, rotting and stinking, both physically and morally." The debacle of the Crimean War (1854–55) made abundantly clear Russia's relative backwardness in relation to modern Western states. Efforts to stop Russia's development as a Western nation appeared to be harmful not only for its reputation in the world but also for its power and even survival.

Nicholas was not the first ruler to try to avert the march of modernizing change in Russia. Similar efforts were made by Peter III (1762) and Paul I (1796–1801) especially. But in Nicholas I's reign, reaction to reform and reformist ideas was newly linked to an explicit ideology, termed by historians "Official Nationality." This ideology, most fully elaborated by Count Uvarov, contained three principles: Orthodoxy, Autocracy, and Nationality. Orthodoxy referred not only to the large public role of the established Church but also to the true faith as the ultimate source of meaning and value in life. In particular, Orthodoxy here stood in opposition to the prime place given in Enlightenment thought to human reason and human capacities. Autocracy meant that the absolute power of the sovereign was both sacred and necessary for the good of Russia. Nationality—*narodnost* in Russian—referred to the special nature of Russia and the Russian people as loving and obedient subjects of the tsar and as both needing and desiring strong and caring guidance.

Meanwhile, society and culture in Russia were changing at an increasing pace. These changes reflected both faces of the modern—rationalizing and scientific progress as well as instability, flux, and challenges to established institutions and ideas. We have already noted the growing influence of European culture and ideas in Russia, especially from the seventeenth century on. These years saw the growing influence in Russian life of modern science, secular education, Enlightenment ideas about reason and progress, and foreign languages. New genres of literature, influenced by classicism, sentimentalism, and other European trends, bourgeoned in eighteenth-century Russia. The early nineteenth century, the age of Pushkin and Gogol among others, has been called the beginning of Russia's literary "golden age." Secular music, theater, painting, and architecture also appeared in the eighteenth century and thrived in the early nineteenth. Quite simply, Russian culture by 1800 looked very little like that of 1700, and the pace of development was continually accelerating. Also, simple borrowing gave way to much creative adaptation and originality.

Perhaps the most unsettling cultural development in the late eighteenth and early nineteenth centuries was the rise of an "intelligentsia." This term, which has entered English from the Russian, denoted not simply educated people or even people devoted to a life of ideas but educated and intellectually

engaged individuals (men until the 1860s) who, in the name of absolute principles, influenced first by the Enlightenment and then by Romanticism, stood
against what they saw as a repressive and restrictive political and social order.
Although the term "intelligentsia" would not be used until the 1860s, its history began earlier. During the reign of Catherine the Great, such critics of the
established order as Nicholas Novikov chastised the pervasive "weakness,
imperfection, and vice" with harsh satire and advocated a society and policy
based on a view of human beings as sacred creations equal in dignity and
rights, while the more radical Alexander Radishchev openly criticized serfdom
in the name of the equal dignity of all human beings. Both were eventually
imprisoned for their daring by Catherine—who grew increasingly anxious
about the dangers of too much freedom, especially after the French Revolution.
In the early 1800s, a movement of secret political societies among noble youths
appeared that would later be known as the "Decembrist Movement," after an
attempted armed uprising against the new emperor Nicholas I in December
1825. In the name of Enlightened reason and belief in individual dignity and
rights, they advocated replacing the autocracy with either a constitutional
monarchy or a republic, guaranteeing basic civil rights (freedom of speech,
press, assembly, and religion), and abolishing serfdom. After their attempted
coup, the leaders of the movement were arrested and tried. Many were exiled
to Siberia. Five young noblemen, leaders of the movement, were hanged.

    A still greater revival of intelligentsia dissidence—though a movement
more cautious about public action—developed in the 1830s and 1840s. This was
also a time when the intelligentsia split into two competing ideological currents.
"Westernizers" like Alexander Herzen, Vissarion Belinsky, and Michael
Bakunin opposed autocracy, serfdom, and the lack of civil rights in Russia as
violations of the central principle of human dignity and began to speak of
"socialism" as the only order that ensured all individuals a life of dignity.
"Slavophiles" like Alexis Khomiakov, Ivan Kireevsky, and George Samarin also
opposed serfdom, the lack of civil freedom, and government intrusion into private life, but they did so in the name of the principle of "spiritual community"
(*sobornost*), according to which society and polity must be united by free will
and shared moral and spiritual values, such as had existed, they maintained,
before Peter the Great introduced alien and mechanistic principles of power
and social order into Russia. For all their differences, the intelligentsia of the
1830s and 1840s shared a common spirit. They all felt a passion for ideas (their
favorite philosophers were German idealists), a powerful sense of wrong in the
world, and a pathos for change. They sought to discover the destiny of their
nation and to make it their mission to bring this future into being. These were
not the only intellectual currents of the age, of course. Varieties of conservatism
were also becoming more developed and explicit. Nicholas Karamzin, for
example, during the reign of Alexander I, made vigorous arguments, grounded
in a careful review of Russia's entire historical development, about the necessity for a state absolute in its power though also virtuous in purpose.

    In social and economic matters, which attracted growing attention among
the educated, much had already changed even before the abolition of serfdom
in 1861 opened up new possibilities for social and economic growth and transformation in Russia. Agriculture in many parts of the country had become

more market oriented. And manufacturing and domestic and international commerce grew steadily, creating new occupations and growing urban populations. These developments undermined a social order still viewed in terms of the traditional social estates. Still, the majority of the population remained peasants, and serfdom, fully established in the mid-seventeenth century, was the dominant fact of social life. But it was proving less and less stable. Not only did many educated Russians view serfdom as both an economic liability and a moral stain on the nation, but peasants themselves were resisting it.

Peasants found various ways of coping with the material hardships and uncertainties of their life. They formed strong peasant communities, managed by communal assemblies of the heads of households (the *mir*), to ensure order in the community and their collective survival. Peasants held to a deeply religious view of the world as inhabited by spiritual forces but manageable with the help of prayer and Christian rituals as well as with older magical practices. Peasants sometimes rebelled in the face of a system of serfdom that amounted to a type of slavery—serfs were forbidden to move elsewhere and obliged to deliver some combination of labor and money dues to their landlord, who might be paternally kind or who might make unbearable demands and allow cruel punishment. Most commonly, peasants resisted in small ways: with apparent laziness and sloppy work, especially when working estate lands as labor service (as opposed to the lands left to them to raise their own food or even products to market); petty theft from estate fields or other seigniorial or state property; and such forms of "cultural resistance" as holding to religious beliefs and practices that the Church told them were backward and ignorant, ranging from "pagan" practices to Old Belief (the dissident form of Orthodoxy that emerged in reaction to the seventeenth-century reform of Church rites) to non-Orthodox "sectarianism." Peasants also sometimes petitioned the government for help against, for example, higher labor or cash dues or brutal beatings. Periodically, especially in the late eighteenth and early nineteenth centuries, the government recorded local "disturbances" (*volnenie*) by peasants acting collectively to protest particular conditions. Sometimes, mass uprising broke out, as in the Stenka Razin rebellion during the reign of Alexis, the Bulavin rebellion during Peter I's rule, and the Pugachev uprising under Catherine II—rebellions named after their leaders, all of whom were Cossacks, once freebooting tribes of frontiersmen whose freedoms and autonomy were curtailed by the expanding Muscovite and Petrine states. The Pugachev rebellion—Pugachev claimed to be Peter III, miraculously saved from the murderous hands of the nobles who overthrew him, but failed to kill him, when he allegedly decided to free the serfs—attracted serfs and state peasants, peasants "ascribed" to labor in foundries and mines, lower-class town dwellers, Old Believers, disgruntled Cossacks, and many non-Russians to a violent (and violently suppressed) movement to distribute all the land to peasants and to free peasants of noble authority. When the rebellion was suppressed, Pugachev was captured, placed in a cage for transport to Moscow, and publicly decapitated and quartered, his head and body parts displayed around the city as a warning. Catherine the Great, on reading Pugachev's proclamations, dismissed these as "castles in the air." Such "castles"—dreams of a completely free and happy society—would long remain a presence in Russian life.

A History of Russia

Chapter 29

The Reign of Alexander II, 1855–81

However, sounds of music reached our ears, and we all hurried back to the hall. The band of the opera was already playing the hymn, which was drowned immediately in enthusiastic hurrahs coming from all parts of the hall. I saw Baveri, the conductor of the band, waving his stick, but not a sound could be heard from the powerful band. Then Baveri stopped, but the hurrahs continued. I saw the stick waved again in the air; I saw the fiddle-bows moving, and musicians blowing the brass instruments, but again the sound of voices overwhelmed the band. . . . The same enthusiasm was in the streets. Crowds of peasants and educated men stood in front of the palace, shouting hurrahs, and the Tsar could not appear without being followed by demonstrative crowds running after his carriage. . . . I was in Nikolskoe in August, 1861, and again in the summer of 1862, and I was struck with the quiet, intelligent way in which the peasants had accepted the new conditions. They knew perfectly well how difficult it would be to pay the redemption tax for the land, which was in reality an indemnity to the nobles in lieu of the obligations of serfdom. But they so much valued the abolition of their personal enslavement that they accepted the ruinous charges—not without murmuring, but as a hard necessity—the moment that personal freedom was obtained. . . . When I saw our Nikolskoe peasants, fifteen months after the liberation, I could not but admire them. Their inborn good nature and softness remained with them, but all traces of servility had disappeared. They talked to their masters as equals talk to equals, as if they never had stood in different relations.

KROPOTKIN

The abolition of serfdom signified the establishment of capitalism as the dominant socio-economic formation in Russia.

ZAIONCHKOVSKY

Alexander II succeeded his father, Nicholas I, on the Russian throne at the age of thirty-seven. He had received a rather good education as well as considerable practical training in the affairs of state. Alexander's teachers

Alexander II   (Tsarstvuiushchii dom Romanovykh)

included the famous poet Zhukovsky, who has often been credited with developing humane sentiments in his pupil. To be sure, Grand Duke Alexander remained an obedient son of his strong-willed father and showed no liberal inclinations prior to becoming emperor. Indeed he retained an essentially conservative mentality and attitude throughout his life. Nor can Alexander II be considered a strong or a talented man. Yet, forced by the logic of the situation, the new monarch decided to undertake, and actually carried through, fundamental reforms unparalleled in scope in Russian history since Peter the Great. These reforms, although extremely important, failed to cure all the ills of Russia and in fact led to new problems and perturbations, which resulted, among other things, in the assassination of the "Tsar-Liberator."

The Emancipation of the Serfs

The last words of Alexander II's manifesto announcing the end of the Crimean War promised reform, and this produced a strong impression on the public.

The new emperor's first measures, enacted even before the termination of hostilities, included the repeal of some of the Draconian restrictions of Nicholas I's final years, such as those on travel abroad and on the number of students attending universities. All this represented a promising prologue; the key issue, as it was for Alexander I, the last ruler who wanted to transform Russia, remained serfdom. However, much had changed in regard to serfdom during the intervening fifty or fifty-five years. Human bondage, as indicated in an earlier chapter, satisfied less and less effectively the economic needs of the Russian Empire. With the growth of a money economy and competition for markets, the deficiencies of low-grade serf labor became ever more obvious. Many landlords, especially those with small holdings, could barely feed their serfs; and the gentry accumulated an enormous debt. As we know, free labor, whether really free or merely the contractual labor of someone else's serfs, became more common throughout the Russian economy during the first half of the nineteenth century. Moreover, the serfs perhaps declined in absolute number in the course of that period, while their numerical weight in relation to other classes certainly declined: from 58 percent of the total population of Russia in 1811 to 44.5 percent on the eve of the "great reforms," to cite Blum's figures again. Interpretations of the Russian economic crisis in mid-nineteenth century range from Kovalchenko's emphatic restatement, with the use of quantitative methods, of the thesis of the extreme and unbearable exploitation of the serfs to Ryndziunsky's stress on the general loosening of the social fabric. Economic liberals at the time, and generations of historians since, have agreed that serfdom was becoming increasingly anachronistic. But this was likely not the main reason for reform. First, some scholars recently have questioned the evidence behind arguments about the economic failure of serfdom or the decline in peasant living standards. In any case, perception and opinion are usually more determining than facts alone. Whatever the economic facts, it is clear that the majority of government officials and most of the landowning nobility did not share the view that serfdom must be abolished for economic reasons. So we must consider other reasons.

The fear of peasant rebellion has often been identified as a key reason the state finally acted to end serfdom. Oppressed and exasperated beyond endurance, the serfs kept rising against their masters. While no nineteenth-century peasant insurrection could at all rival the Pugachev rebellion, the uprisings became more frequent and on the whole more serious. Semevsky, using official records, had counted 550 peasant uprisings in the nineteenth century prior to the emancipation. A Soviet historian, Ignatovich, raised the number to 1,467 and gave the following breakdown: 281 peasant rebellions, that is, 19 percent of the total, in the period from 1801 to 1825; 712 rebellions, 49 percent, from 1826 to 1854; and 474 uprisings, or 32 percent, in the six years and two months of Alexander II's reign before the abolition of serfdom. Ignatovich emphasized that the uprisings also increased in length, in bitterness, in the human and material losses involved, and in the military effort necessary to restore order. Okun and other Soviet scholars further expanded Ignatovich's list of uprisings. Moreover, Soviet scholarship claimed that peasant rebellions played the decisive role in the emancipation of the serfs, and that on the eve of the "great reforms" Russia experienced in effect a revolutionary situation. Although exaggerated, this view cannot be entirely dismissed. Interestingly, it was the Third Department, the gendarmery, that had stressed the danger of serfdom during the reign of Nicholas I. Besides rising in rebellion, serfs ran away from their masters, sometimes by the hundreds and even by the thousands. On occasion large military detachments had to be sent to intercept them. Pathetic mass flights of peasants, for example, would follow rumors that freedom could be obtained somewhere in the Caucasus, while crowds of serfs tried to join the army during the Crimean War, because they mistakenly believed that they could thereby gain their liberty.

A growing sentiment for emancipation, based on moral grounds, also contributed to the abolition of serfdom. The Decembrists, the Slavophiles, the Westernizers, the Petrashevtsy, some supporters of Official Nationality, together with other thinking Russians, all wanted the abolition of serfdom. As education developed in Russia, and especially as Russian literature came into its own, humane feelings and attitudes became more widespread. Such leading writers as Pushkin and particularly Turgenev, who in 1852 published in book form his magnificent collection of stories, *Sportsman's Sketches*, where serfs were depicted as full-blown, and indeed unforgettable, human beings, no doubt exercised an influence. In fact, on the eve of the abolition of serfdom in Russia—in contrast to the situation with slavery in the American South—virtually no one defended that institution; the arguments of its proponents were usually limited to pointing out the dangers implicit in such a radical change as emancipation.

Finally, the Crimean War provided additional evidence of the deficiencies and dangers of serfdom which found reflection both in the poor physical condition and listlessness of the recruits and in the general economic and technological backwardness of the country. Besides, as Rieber emphasized, Russia had essentially to rely on a standing army without a reserve, because the government was afraid to allow soldiers to return to villages.

At the time of the coronation, about a year after his assumption of power, Alexander II, addressing the gentry of Moscow, made the celebrated statement that it would be better to begin to abolish serfdom from above than to wait until it would begin to abolish itself from below, and asked the gentry to consider the matter. Although the government experienced great difficulty in eliciting any initiative from the landlords on the subject of emancipation, it finally managed to seize upon an offer by the gentry of the three Lithuanian provinces to discuss emancipation without land. The ensuing imperial rescript made it clear that emancipation was indeed official policy and, furthermore, that emancipation would have to be with land.

A remarkable aspect of the coming of emancipation was the publicity and public discussion that surrounded this process. The government announced its plans and invited discussion and suggestions—a process of openness and publicity known as *glasnost*. Noble assemblies were asked to discuss how the reform should be implemented, and they sometimes opened their sessions to non-nobles. Restrictions on discussing the abolition of serfdom in the press were lifted. At the same time, Alexander asked the police to submit weekly reports on the public's attitude and mood, and warnings and even arrests could result when overly critical opinion was voiced. Some historians have argued that the government, at least its more liberal members, deliberately wished to "awaken public opinion," since nurturing a modern civil society was the deeper goal of the "great reforms." Others have insisted that the government really had no choice—the public was already aroused and had to be recognized. In any case, a wave of expectation and enthusiasm swept the country after the publication of the rescript. Even Herzen exclaimed to Alexander II: "Thou hast conquered, O Galilean!"

Eventually, in 1858, gentry committees were established in all provinces to consider emancipation, while a bureaucratic Main Committee of nine members was set up in St. Petersburg. Except for a few diehards, the landlords assumed a realistic position and accepted the abolition of serfdom once the government had made its will clear, but they wanted the reform to be carried out as advantageously for themselves as possible. The gentry of southern and south-central Russia, with its valuable, fertile soil, wanted to retain as much land as possible and preferred land to a monetary recompense; the gentry of northern and north-central Russia, by contrast, considered serf labor and the resulting obrok as their main asset and, therefore, while relatively willing to part with much of their land, insisted on a high monetary payment in return for the loss of serf labor. Gentry committees also differed on such important issues as the desirable legal position of the liberated serfs and the administration to be provided for them.

The opinions of provincial committees went to the Editing Commission—actually two commissions that sat together and formed a single body—created at the beginning of 1859 and composed of public figures interested in the peasant question, such as the Slavophiles George Samarin and Prince Vladimir Cherkassky, as well as of high officials. After twenty months of work the Editing Commission submitted its plan of reform to the Main Committee, whence it went eventually to the State Council. After its quick consideration by the State Council, Alexander II signed the emancipation manifesto on March 3, 1861—February 19, Old Style. Public announcement followed twelve days later.

Throughout its protracted and cumbersome formulation and passage the emancipation reform faced the hostility of conservatives in government and society. That a far-reaching law was finally enacted can be largely credited to the determined efforts of so-called "enlightened bureaucrats" and "liberals," including officials such as Nicholas Miliutin, the immediate assistant to the minister of the interior and the leading figure in the Editing Commission, and participants from the public like George Samarin. Two members of the imperial family, the tsar's brother Grand Duke Constantine and the tsar's aunt Grand Duchess Helen, belonged to the "liberals." More important, Alexander II himself repeatedly sided with them, while his will became law for such devoted bureaucrats as Jacob Rostovtsev—a key figure in the emancipation—who cannot be easily classified as either "conservative" or "liberal." The emperor in effect forced the speedy passage of the measure through an antagonistic State Council, which managed to add only one noxious provision to the law, that permitting a "pauper's allotment," which will be mentioned later. Whereas the conservatives defended the interests and rights of the gentry, the "liberals" were motivated by their belief that the interests of the state demanded a thoroughgoing reform and by their views of what would constitute a just settlement.

The law of the nineteenth of February abolished serfdom. Thenceforth human bondage was to disappear from Russian life. It should be noted, however, that, even if we exclude from consideration certain temporary provisions that prolonged various serf obligations for different periods of time, the reform failed to give the peasants a status equal to that of other social classes: they had to pay a head tax, were tied to their communes, and were judged on the basis of customary law. In addition to landowners' serfs, the new freedom was extended to peasants on the lands of the imperial family and to the huge and complex category of state peasants.

Together with their liberty, serfs who had been engaged in farming received land: household serfs did not. While the detailed provisions of the land settlement were extremely complicated and different from area to area, the peasants were to obtain roughly half the land, that part which they had been tilling for themselves, the other half staying with the landlords. They had to repay the landlords for the land they acquired and, because few serfs could pay anything, the government compensated the gentry owners by means of treasury bonds. Former serfs in turn were to reimburse the state through redemption payments spread over a period of forty-nine years. As an alternative, serfs could take one-quarter of their normal parcel of land, the so-called "pauper's allotment," and pay nothing. Except in Ukraine and a few other areas, land was given not to individual peasants, but to a peasant commune—called an *obshchina* or *mir*, the latter term emphasizing the communal gathering of peasants to settle their affairs—which divided the land among its members and was responsible for taxes, the provision of recruits, and other obligations to the state.

The emancipation of the serfs can be called a great reform, although an American historian probably exaggerated when he proclaimed it to be the greatest legislative act in history. It directly affected the status of some fifty-two million peasants, over twenty million of them serfs of private land owners. That should be compared, for example, with the almost simultaneous liberation of four million black slaves in the United States, obtained as a result of a huge Civil War, not by means of a peaceful legal process. The moral value of the emancipation was no doubt tremendous, if incalculable. It might be added that the arguments of Pokrovsky and some other historians attempting to show that the reform was a clever conspiracy between the landlords and the government at the expense of the peasants lack substance: they are contradicted both by the actual preparation and passage of the emancipation legislation and by its results, for it contributed in a major manner to the decline of the gentry. By contrast, those specialists who emphasize the importance of the abolition of serfdom for the development of capitalism in Russia stand on much firmer ground. The specific provisions of the new settlement have also been defended and even praised, especially on the basis of the understanding that the arrangement had to be a compromise, not a confiscation of everything the gentry owned. Thus, the emancipation of serfs in Russia has been favorably compared to that in Prussia at the beginning of the nineteenth century, and land allotments of Russian peasants, to allotments in several other countries.

And yet the emancipation reform also deserves thorough criticism. The land allotted to the former serfs turned out to be insufficient. While in theory they were to retain the acreage that they had been tilling for themselves prior to 1861, in fact they received 18 percent less land. Moreover, in the fertile southern provinces their loss exceeded the national average, amounting in some cases to 40 percent or more of the total. Also, in the course of the partitioning, former serfs often failed to obtain forested areas or access to a river with the result that they had to assume additional obligations toward their onetime landlords to satisfy their needs. Khodsky estimated that 13 percent of the former serfs received liberal allotments of land; 45 percent, allotments sufficient to maintain their families and economies; and 42 percent, insufficient allotments. Liashchenko summarized the settlement as follows: "The owners, numbering 30,000 noblemen, retained ownership over some 95 million dessyatins of the better land immediately after the Reform, compared with 116 million dessyatins of suitable land left to the 20 million 'emancipated' peasants." Other scholars have stressed the overpopulation and underemployment among former serfs, who, at least after a period of transition, were no longer obliged to work for the landlord and at the same time had less land to cultivate for themselves. State peasants, although by no means prosperous, received, on the whole, better terms than did the serfs of private owners.

The financial arrangement proved unrealistic and impossible to execute. Although liberated serfs kept meeting as best they could the heavy redemption payments, which were not related to their current income, the arrears kept mounting. By the time the redemption payments were finally abolished in 1905, former serfs paid, counting the interest, 1.5 billion rubles for the land initially valued at less than a billion. It should be noted that while officially the serfs were to redeem only the land, not their persons, actually the payments included a concealed recompense for the loss of serf labor. Thus, more had to be paid for the first unit of land, the first desiatina, than for the following units. As a whole the landlords of southern Russia received 340 million rubles for land valued at 280 million; those of northern Russia, where obrok prevailed, 340 million rubles for land worth 180 million rubles. The suspect Polish and Polonized landlords of the western provinces constituted an exception, for they were given slightly less money than the just price of their land.

The transfer of land in most areas to peasant communes rather than to individual peasants probably represented another major error, although this is an extremely complex issue. Arguments in favor of the commune ranged from the Slavophile admiration of the moral aspects of that institution to the desire on the part of the government to have taxes and recruits guaranteed by means of communal responsibility and to the assertion that newly liberated peasants would not be able to maintain themselves but could find protection in the commune. While some of these and other similar claims had a certain validity— indeed, as a practical matter the government could hardly have been expected to break up the commune at the same time the serfs were being freed and peasants themselves were deeply attached to the commune as both a practical necessity for survival and a moral value in defining proper social relationships in the village—the economic disadvantages of the commune may have outweighed its advantages. Of most importance was the fact that the commune sustained a subsistence ethos (whereby community survival stands above all other values), which perpetuated low productivity, resistance to innovation, and overpopulation in the countryside precisely when Russian agriculture drastically needed improvement and modernization.

The emancipation reform disappointed Russian radicals, who considered it inadequate. More important, it disappointed peasants who evidently believed that they had a right to all the land they worked without payment. A rash of agrarian disturbances followed the abolition of serfdom, and the misery, despair, and anger in the countryside remained a powerful threat to imperial Russia until the very end of imperial rule.

Other "Great Reforms"

The emancipation of the serfs made other fundamental changes much more feasible. Alexander II and his assistants turned next to the reform of local government, to the establishment of the so-called zemstvo system. For centuries local government had remained a particularly weak aspect of Russian administration and life. The arrangement that the "Tsar-Liberator" inherited dated from Catherine the Great's legislation and combined bureaucratic management with some participation by the local gentry; the considerable manorial jurisdiction of the landlords on their estates formed another prominent characteristic of the pre-reform countryside. The new law, enacted in January 1864, represented a strong modernization and democratization of local government, as well as a far-reaching effort on the part of the state to meet the many pressing needs of rural Russia and to do this largely by stimulating local initiative and activity. Institutions of self-government, zemstvo assemblies and boards, were created at both the district and provincial levels—the word zemstvo itself connotes land, country, or people, as distinct from the central government. The electorate of the district zemstvo assemblies consisted of three categories: the towns, the peasant communes, and all individual landowners, including those not from the gentry. Representation was proportional to landownership, with some allowance for the possession of real estate in towns. The elections were indirect. Members of district assemblies, in turn, elected from their own midst, regardless of class, delegates to their provincial assembly. Whereas the district and provincial zemstvo assemblies, in which the zemstvo authority resided, met only once a year to deal with such items as the annual budget and basic policies, they elected zemstvo boards to serve continuously as the executive agencies of the system and to employ professional staffs. A variety of local needs fell under the purview of zemstvo institutions: education, medicine, veterinary service, insurance, roads, the establishment of food reserves for emergency, and many others.

The zemstvo system has legitimately been criticized on a number of counts. For example, for a long time it encompassed only the strictly Russian areas of the empire, some thirty-four provinces, not the borderlands. Also, it possessed a limited, many would say insufficient, right to tax. In broader terms, it represented merely a junior partner to the central government, which retained police and much administrative control in the countryside; a governor could in various ways interfere with the work of a zemstvo, but not vice versa. The smallest zemstvo unit, the district, proved too large for effective and prompt response to many popular needs, and the desirability of further zemstvo subdivision soon became apparent. The democracy of the system too had its obvious limitations: because they owned much land, members of the gentry were very heavily represented in the district assemblies, and even more so in the provincial assemblies and the zemstvo boards, where education, leisure, and means to cover the expenses incurred favored gentry delegates. Thus, according to one count, the gentry generally held 42 percent of the district assembly seats, 74 percent of the seats in the provincial assemblies, and 62 percent of the positions on the zemstvo boards. Yet, even such a system constituted a great step toward democracy for autocratic and bureaucratic Russia. It might be added that the zemstvo institutions functioned effectively also in those areas, such as large parts of the Russian north, where there were no landlords and where peasants managed the entire system of local self-government.

Yet, in spite of its deficiencies—and it should be noted that most of the aforementioned criticisms refer in one way or another to the insufficient extent of the reform and not to substantive defects in it—the zemstvo system accomplished much for rural Russia from its establishment in 1864 until its demise in 1917. Especially valuable were its contributions to public education and health. In effect, Russia obtained a kind of socialized medicine through the zemstvo long before other countries, with medical and surgical treatment available free of charge. As G. Fischer and other scholars have indicated, the zemstvo system also served, contrary to the intentions of the government, as a school for radicalism and especially liberalism which found little opportunity for expression on the national, as distinct from local, scene until the events of 1905 and 1906.

In 1870 a municipal reform reorganized town government and applied to towns many of the principles and practices of the zemstvo administration. The new town government, which was "to take care of and administer urban economy and welfare," consisted of a town council and a town administrative board elected by the town council. The town council was elected by all property owners or taxpayers; but the election was according to a three-class system, which gave the small group on top that paid a third of the total taxes a third of the total number of delegates, the middle taxpayers another third, and the mass at the bottom that accounted for the last third of taxes the remaining third of delegates.

At the end of 1864, the year that saw the beginning of the zemstvo administration, another major change was enacted into law: the reform of the legal system. The Russian judiciary needed reform probably even more than the local government did. Archaic, bureaucratic, cumbersome, corrupt, based on the class system rather than on the principle of equality before the law, and relying entirely on a written and secret procedure, the old system was thoroughly hated by informed and thinking Russians. Butashevich-Petrashevsky and other radicals attached special importance to a reform of the judiciary. A conservative, the Slavophile Ivan Aksakov, reminisced: "The old court! At the mere recollection of it one's hair stands on end and one's flesh begins to creep!" The legislation of 1864 fortunately marked a decisive break with that part of the Russian past.

The most significant single aspect of the reform was the separation of the courts from the administration. Instead of constituting merely a part of the bureaucracy, the judiciary became an independent branch of government. Judges were not to be dismissed or transferred, except by court action. Judicial procedure acquired a largely public and oral character instead of the former bureaucratic secrecy. The contending parties were to present their cases in court and have adequate legal support. In fact, the reform virtually created the class of lawyers in Russia, who began rapidly to acquire great public prominence. Two legal procedures, the general and the abbreviated one, replaced the chaos of twenty-one alternate ways to conduct a case. Trial by jury was introduced for serious criminal offenses, while justices of the peace were established to deal with minor civil and criminal cases. The courts were organized into a single unified system with the Senate at the apex. All Russians were to be equal before the law and receive the same treatment. Exceptions to the general system were the military and ecclesiastical courts, together with special courts for peasants who lived for the most part by customary law.

The reform of the judiciary, which was largely the work of the Minister of Justice Dmitrii Zamiatnin, his extremely important assistant Serge Zarudny, and several other enlightened officials, proved to be the most successful of the "great reforms." Almost overnight it transformed the Russian judiciary from one of the worst to one of the best in the civilized world. Later the government tried on occasion to influence judges for political reasons; and, what is more important, in its struggle against radicalism and revolution it began to withdraw whole categories of legal cases from the normal procedure of 1864 and to subject them to various forms of the courts-martial. But, while the reform of the judiciary could be restricted in application, it could not be undone by the imperial government; and, as far as the reform extended, modern justice replaced arbitrariness and confusion. Russian legal reform followed Western, especially French, models, but, as Kucherov and others have demonstrated, these models were skillfully adapted to Russian needs. It might be added that the courts, as well as the zemstvo institutions, acquired political significance, for they served as centers of public interest and enjoyed a somewhat greater freedom of expression than was generally allowed in Russia.

A reorganization of the military service in 1874 and certain changes within the army have usually been grouped as the last "great reform." Inspired by military needs and technically complex, the reform nevertheless exercised an important general impact on Russian society and contributed to the modernization and democratization of the country. It was executed by Minister of War Dmitrii Miliutin, Nicholas Miliutin's brother, who wanted to profit by the example of the victorious Prussian army. He introduced a variety of significant innovations, of which the most important was the change in military service. The obligation to serve was extended from the lower classes alone to all Russians, while at the same time the length of active service was drastically reduced—from twenty-five years in the beginning of Alexander II's reign to six after the reform of 1874—and a military reserve was organized. Recruits were to be called up by lot; different exemptions were provided for hardship cases; and, in addition, terms of enlistment were shortened for those with education, a not unwarranted provision in Russian conditions. Miliutin also reformed military law and legal procedure, abolished corporal punishment in the army, strove to improve the professional quality of the officer corps and to make it somewhat more democratic, established specialized military schools, and, a particularly important point, introduced elementary education for all draftees. Measures similar to Miliutin's were carried out in the navy by Grand Duke Constantine.

Other reforms under Alexander II included such financial innovations as Valery Tatarinov's establishment of a single state treasury, publication of the annual budget, and the creation in 1866 of the State Bank to centralize credit and finance, as well as generally liberalizing steps with regard to education and censorship.

The "great reforms" went a long way toward transforming Russia. To be sure, the empire of the tsars remained an autocracy, but it changed in many other respects. Vastly important in themselves, the government's reforms also helped to bring about sweeping economic and social changes, which will be discussed in a later chapter. The growth of capitalism in Russia, the evolution of the peasantry, the decline of the gentry, the rise of the middle class, particularly the professional group, and also of the proletariat, and the development of a public sphere—all were affected by Alexander II's legislation. Indeed, Russia began to take long strides on the road to becoming a modern nation. Nor could the changes be undone: there was no return to serfdom or to pre-reform justice.

The Difficult Sixties

However, although the government could not return to the old ways, it could stop advancing on the new road and try to restrict and limit the effectiveness of the changes. And in fact it attempted to do so in the second half of Alexander II's reign, under Alexander III, and under Nicholas II until the Revolution of 1905. While the need for reforms had been apparent, the rationale of reaction proved less obvious and more complicated. For one thing, the reforms, as we know, had their determined opponents in official circles and among the Russian gentry, who did their best to reverse state policy. Special circumstances played their part, such as peasant uprisings, student disturbances, the unexplained fires of 1862, the Polish rebellion of 1863, and Dmitrii Karakozov's attempt to assassinate the emperor in 1866. More important was the fact that the government failed to resolve the fundamental dilemma of change: where to stop. The "great reforms," together with the general development of Russia and the intellectual climate of the time, led to pressure for further reform.

Possibly the granting of a constitutional monarchy and certain other concessions would have satisfied most of the demand and provided stability for the
empire. But neither Alexander II nor certainly his successors were willing to go
that far. Instead they turned against the proponents of more change and fought
to preserve the established order. The "great reforms" had come only after the
Crimean War had demonstrated the total bankruptcy of the old system, and
they owed little to any far-reaching liberalism or vision on the part of Alexander II and his immediate associates. The sequel showed how difficult it was for
the imperial government to learn new ways.

After the political stillness and immobility of Nicholas I's reign, and stimulated by the "great reforms," the early 1860s in Russia were loud and active.
Peasant riots occurred with great frequency and on a large scale. In 1861 and
1862 disturbances, provoked largely by the clumsy and authoritarian policies
of the new minister of education, Count Admiral Evfimii Putiatin, swept Russian universities. In 1862 the provincial assembly of the Tver gentry, led by
Alexis Unkovsky, renounced its gentry privileges and demanded the convocation of a constituent assembly representing the entire people to establish a new
order in Russia. And in the same year of 1862 a series of mysterious fires broke
out in St. Petersburg and in a number of towns along the Volga. Also, in 1861
and 1862 leaflets urging revolution began to appear in different Russian cities.
In 1863 Poland erupted in rebellion.

In Poland, too, Alexander II had instituted a liberal policy. Thus in 1862
much of the former Polish autonomy was restored. The change in the Russian
attitude found favorable response among Polish moderates, led by Marquis
Alexander Wielopolski, but failed to satisfy the nationalists, who wanted complete independence and the historic "greater Poland." Recent successes of Italian unification, the sympathy of Napoleon III and influential French circles,
and the general nationalistic spirit of the age encouraged Polish extremists.
Following a series of disorders, the government took steps to draft the unruly
element, students in particular, into the army. A rebellion followed in January
1863. Although this time, in contrast to the situation in 1831, the Poles possessed no regular army and had to fight for the most part as guerrilla bands,
the insurrection spread to Lithuanian and White Russian lands and was not
finally suppressed until May 1864. Great Britain, France, and Austria tried to
aid the Polish cause by diplomatic interventions, but were rebuffed by Russia.
As a result of the rebellion, Poland again lost its autonomous position and
became fully subject to Russian administration. Nicholas Miliutin, Samarin,
and Cherkassky were dispatched to conquered Poland to study the conditions
there and propose appropriate measures. Of their recommendations, however,
only those referring to the emancipation of the serfs and land settlement were
adopted. Peasants in Poland obtained a more favorable arrangement than
those in Russia, while the Polish landlords fared much worse than their Russian counterparts. Otherwise the government chose to rely on centralization,
police control, and Russification, with the Russian language made compulsory
in Polish schools. A still more intense Russification developed in the western
borderlands of Russia, where every effort was made to eradicate the Polish
influence. A 10 percent assessment was imposed there on Polish estates, the use

of the Polish language was forbidden, and the property of the Catholic Church was confiscated. In 1875 the Uniates in Poland proper were forcibly reconverted to Orthodoxy.

In spite of the serious troubles of the early 1860s, Alexander II and his associates continued to reform Russia, and the future course of state policy appeared to hang in the balance. For example, while the authorities penalized disaffected Russian students and punished severely—sometimes, as in the case of Nicholas Chernyshevsky, rather clearly on insufficient evidence—those connected with the revolutionary agitation, a considerably more liberal official, Alexander Golovnin, replaced Admiral Putiatin in 1862 as minister of education, and a new and much freer University Statute became law in 1863. Even the Polish rebellion, while it resulted in oppression of the Poles, did not seem to affect the course of reform in Russia. The decisive change away from reform came, in the opinion of many historians, in 1866, following an attempt by an emotionally unbalanced student, Dmitrii Karakozov, to assassinate the emperor. In that year the reactionary Count Dmitrii Tolstoy took charge as minister of education, and the government proceeded gradually to revamp schooling in Russia, intending that stricter controls and heavy emphasis on the classical languages would discipline students and keep their attention away from the issues of the day. Over a period of years reaction also expressed itself in the curbing of the press, in restrictions on the collection of taxes by the zemstvo and on the uses to which these taxes could be put, in the exemption of political and press cases from regular judicial procedure, in continuing Russification, in administrative pressure on magistrates, and the like. On the other hand, despite the reactionary nature of the period, the municipal reform took place in 1870 and the army reform as late as 1874.

New Radicalism and the Revolutionary Movement

Russian history came increasingly to be dominated by a struggle between the government Right and the radical and revolutionary Left, with the moderates and the liberals in the middle powerless to influence the fundamental course of events. The government received unexpected support from the nationalists. It was in 1863, at the time of the Polish rebellion and diplomatic pressure by Great Britain, France, and Austria on behalf of Poland, that the onetime Westernizer, Anglophile, and liberal, journalist Michael Katkov, came out emphatically in support of the government and Russian national interests. Katkov's stand proved very popular during the Polish war. In a sense Katkov and his fellow patriots who enthusiastically defended the Russian state acted much like the liberals in Prussia and Germany when they swung to the support of Bismarck. Yet, in the long run, it proved more characteristic of the situation in Russia that, although the revolutionaries remained a small minority, they attracted the sympathy of broad layers of the educated public.

While the intellectual history of Russia in the second half of the nineteenth century will be summarized in a later chapter, some aspects of Russian radicalism of the 1860s and 1870s must be mentioned here. Following Turgenev, it has become customary to speak of the generation of the sixties as "sons" and "nihilists" and to contrast these "sons" with the "fathers" of the forties. A powerful contrast does emerge. The transformation in Russia formed part of a broader change in Europe which has been described as a transition from romanticism to realism. In Russian conditions the shift acquired an exaggerated and violent character.

Whereas the "fathers" grew up on German idealistic philosophy and romanticism in general, with its emphasis on the metaphysical, religious, aesthetic, and historical approaches to reality, the "sons," led by such young radicals as Nicholas Chernyshevsky, Nicholas Dobroliubov, and Dmitrii Pisarev, hoisted the banner of utilitarianism, positivism, materialism, and especially "realism." "Nihilism"—and also in large part "realism," particularly "critical realism"—meant above all else a fundamental rebellion against accepted values and standards: against abstract thought and family control, against lyric poetry and school discipline, against religion and rhetoric. The earnest young men and women of the 1860s wanted to cut through every polite veneer, to get rid of all conventional sham, to get to the bottom of things. What they usually considered real and worthwhile included the natural and physical sciences—for that was the age when science came to be greatly admired in the Western world—simple and sincere human relations, and a society based on knowledge and reason rather than ignorance, prejudice, exploitation, and oppression. The casting down of idols—and there surely were many idols in mid-nineteenth-century Russia, as elsewhere—emancipation, and freedom constituted the moral strength of nihilism. Yet few in our age would fail to see the narrowness of its vision, or neglect the fact that it erected cruel idols of its own.

It has been noted that the rebels of the sixties, while they stood poles apart from the Slavophiles and other idealists of the 1830s and 1840s, could be considered disciples of Herzen, Bakunin, and to some extent Belinsky, in their later, radical, phases. True in the very important field of doctrine, this observation disregards the difference in tone and manner: as Samarin said of Herzen, even the most radical Westernizers always retained "a handful of earth from the other shore," the shore of German idealism and romanticism, the shore of their youth; the new critics came out of a simpler and cruder mold. Socially too the radicals of the sixties differed from the "fathers," reflecting the progressive democratization of the educated public in Russia. Many of them belonged to a group known in Russian as *raznochintsy*, that is, people of mixed background below the gentry, such as sons of priests who did not follow the calling of their fathers, offspring of petty officials, or individuals from the masses who made their way up through education and effort. The 1860s and the 1870s with their iconoclastic ideology led also to the emancipation of a considerable number of educated Russian women—quite early compared to other European countries—and to their entry into the arena of radical thought and revolutionary politics. The word and concept "intelligentsia," which came to be associated with a critical approach to the world and a protest against the existing Russian order, acquired currency during that portentous period. Finally, the consecutive history of the Russian revolutionary movement—which, to be sure, had such early and isolated forerunners as the Decembrists—began in the years following the "great reforms."

The Russian revolutionary movement can be traced to the revolutionary propaganda and circles of the 1860s. It first became prominent, however, in the 1870s. By that time the essentially individualistic and anarchic creed of nihilism, with its stress on a total personal emancipation, became combined with and in part replaced by a new faith, populism—*narodnichestvo*—which gave the "critical realists" their political, social, and economic program. While populism also has a broad meaning which could include as adherents Dostoevsky, Tolstoy, certain ideologists of the Right, and other diverse Russian figures, in the narrow sense it came to be associated with the teachings of such intellectuals as Herzen, Bakunin, Nicholas Chernyshevsky, Peter Lavrov, and Nicholas Mikhailovsky—who will be discussed in a later chapter—and the main trend of the Russian radical and revolutionary movement in the last third of the nineteenth century. If nihilists gloried in their emancipation, independence, and superiority to the rotten world around them, populists felt compelled to turn to the masses, which in Russia meant the peasants. They wanted to repay their debt for acquiring education—which had brought the precious emancipation itself—at the expense of the sweat and even the blood of the *muzhik*, and to lead the people to a better future. The intellectuals, it must be added, desired to learn as well as to teach. In particular, following Herzen and Bakunin, they believed in the unique worth and potential of the peasant commune, which could serve as an effective foundation for the just social order of the future. In one way or another most populists hoped to find in the people that moral purity and probity—truth, if you will—which their own environment had denied them. Whether their search stemmed from critical realism or not represents another matter. Venturi, Itenberg, and others, with all their determined erudition, cannot quite convince the reader that reason ruled the populist movement.

The climax came in 1873, 1874, and the years immediately following. When in 1873 the imperial government ordered Russian students to abandon their studies in Switzerland—where Russians, especially women, could often pursue higher education more easily than in their fatherland—and return home, a considerable number of them, together with numerous other young men and women who had stayed in Russia, decided to "go to the people." And they went to the villages, some two and a half thousand of them, to become rural teachers, scribes, doctors, veterinarians, nurses, or storekeepers. Some meant simply to help the people as best they could. Others nurtured vast radical and revolutionary plans. In particular, the followers of Bakunin put their faith in a spontaneous, elemental, colossal revolution of the people which they had merely to help start, while the disciples of Lavrov believed in the necessity of gradualism, more exactly, in the need for education and propaganda among the masses before they could overturn the old order and establish the new.

The populist crusade failed. The masses did not respond. The only uprising that the populists produced resulted from an impressive but forged manifesto, in which the tsar ordered his loyal peasants to attack his enemies, the landlords. Indeed the muzhiks on occasion handed over the strange newcomers from the cities to the police. The police, in turn, were frantically active, arresting all the crusaders they could find. Mass trials of the 193 and of the 50 in 1877 marked the sad conclusion of the "going to the people" stage of populism. The peasants, to repeat, would not revolt, nor could satisfactory conditions be established to train them for later revolutionary action.

Yet, one more possibility of struggle remained: the one advocated by another populist theoretician, Peter Tkachev, and by an amoral and dedicated revolutionist, Serge Nechaev, and given the name "Jacobin" in memory of the Jacobins who seized power to transform France during the great French Revolution. If the peasants would not act, it remained up to the revolutionaries themselves to fight and defeat the government. Several years of revolutionary conspiracy, terrorism, and assassination ensued. The first instances of violence occurred more or less spontaneously, sometimes as countermeasures against brutal police officials. Thus, early in 1878 Vera Zasulich shot and wounded the military governor of St. Petersburg, General Theodore Trepov, who had ordered a political prisoner to be flogged; a jury failed to convict her, with the result that political cases were withdrawn from regular judicial procedure. But before long an organization emerged which consciously put terrorism at the center of its activity. The conspiratorial revolutionary society "Land and Freedom," founded in 1876, split in 1879 into two groups: the "Black Partition," or "Total Land Repartition," which emphasized gradualism and propaganda, and the "People's Will," which mounted an all-out terroristic offensive against the government. Members of the "People's Will" believed that, because of the highly centralized nature of the Russian state, a few assassinations could do tremendous damage to the regime, as well as provide the requisite political instruction for the educated society and the masses. They selected the emperor, Alexander II, as their chief target and condemned him to death. What followed has been described as an "emperor hunt" and in certain ways it defies imagination. The Executive Committee of the "People's Will" included only about thirty men and women, led by such persons as Andrew Zheliabov who came from the serfs and Sophia Perovskaia who came from Russia's highest administrative class, but it fought the Russian Empire. Although the police made every effort to destroy the revolutionaries and although many terrorists perished, the "People's Will" made one attempt after another to assassinate the emperor. Time and again Alexander II escaped through sheer luck. Many people were killed when the very dining room of his palace was blown up, while at one time the emperor's security officials refused to let him leave his suburban residence, except by water!

After the explosion in the Winter Palace and after being faced by strikes, student disturbances, and a remarkable lack of sympathy on the part of the educated public, as well as by the dauntless terrorism of the "People's Will," the emperor finally decided on a more moderate policy which could lead to a *rapprochement* with the public. He appointed General Count Michael Loris-Melikov first as head of a special administrative commission and several months later as minister of the interior. Loris-Melikov was to suppress terrorism, but also to propose reforms. Several moderate or liberal ministers replaced a number of reactionaries. Loris-Melikov's plan called for the participation of representatives of the public, both elected and appointed, in considering administrative and financial reforms—not unlike the pattern followed in the abolition of serfdom. On March 13, 1881, Alexander II indicated his willingness to consider Loris-Melikov's proposal. That same day he was finally killed by the remaining members of the "People's Will."

Foreign Policy

The foreign policy of Alexander II's reign, while perhaps not quite as dramatic as its internal history, also deserves careful attention. It began with the termination of the Crimean War and the Treaty of Paris, possibly the nadir of the Russian position in Europe in the nineteenth century, and it did much to restore Russian prestige. Notably, the Russians fought a successful war against Turkey and largely redrew the map of the Balkans. Also, in the course of the reign, the empire of the Romanovs made a sweeping expansion in the Caucasus, Central Asia, and the Far East. But not everything went well. Russia experienced important diplomatic setbacks as well as victories. Moreover, the changing pattern of power relations in Europe—fundamentally affected by the unification of Germany, which the tsarist government helped more than hindered—was in many ways less favorable to the state of the Romanovs in 1881 than it had been fifty years earlier.

The Crimean War meant the collapse of the world of Nicholas I, the world of legitimism with himself as its leader. Specifically, it left the Russian government and public bitterly disappointed with Austria, which, in spite of the crucial Russian help in 1849, did everything to aid Russia's enemies short of actually fighting. As Tiutchev insisted, no "Austrian Judas" could be allowed to pay last respects to Nicholas I on behalf of the Hapsburgs! It is worth noting that when the new minister of foreign affairs, Prince Alexander Gorchakov, surveyed the situation, he turned to France as a possible ally, and Napoleon III indicated reciprocal interest. Yet at that time—in contrast to what happened thirty years later—the Franco-Russian *rapprochement* foundered on the Polish rebellion of 1863. As already mentioned, both the French ruler and his people sympathized with the Poles, and, as in the case of Great Britain and Austria, France intervened diplomatically on behalf of the Poles, arguing that from the time of the Congress of Vienna and the creation of the Kingdom of Poland the fate of that country was of international concern and not simply an internal Russian affair. The imperial government could reject the argument of these powers and rebuff their intervention only because of the strong support that it obtained from the Russian public and also from Prussia. Bismarck, who realized the danger of Polish nationalism for Prussia and wanted to secure the goodwill of the tsar, sent Count Constantine Alvensleben to promise the Russians cooperation against the Polish rebels and to sign a convention to that effect. Bismarck's astute handling of the Russians contributed, no doubt, to the rather benevolent attitude on the part of the tsarist government toward the unification of Germany under Prussia, which involved the defeat of Austria in 1866 and of France in 1870. In retrospect, the fact that Russia did nothing to prevent the emergence of Germany as the new continental giant has been called the worst mistake that tsarist diplomacy ever made. To qualify that charge, it should at least be noted that Russian statesmen were not the only ones in that crucial decade totally to misjudge the situation and prospects in Europe. Also, Russia did obtain some compensation through the abrogation of the Black Sea provisions of the Treaty of Paris: at a time when European attention centered on the Franco-Prussian war, Gorchakov, with Bismarck's backing, repudiated the vexatious obligation not to have a warfleet or coastal fortifications on the Black Sea that Russia had assumed under the Treaty. The British protested and an international conference was held in London in March 1871, but the Russian action was allowed to stand, although the principle of general consent of the signatories as against unilateral action was reaffirmed.

When in the 1870s the tsarist government looked again for allies, it once more found Prussia, or rather Germany, and Austria, which had become Austria-Hungary. For a century the Hohenzollerns had remained, on the whole, the best friends of the Romanovs; as to the Hapsburgs, the Russian rancor against them, generated by their behavior at the time of the Crimean War, had somewhat subsided in the wake of Austrian defeats and other misfortunes. The new alliance, the so-called Three Emperors' League, was formed in 1872 and 1873. Russia's part in it involved a military convention with Germany, according to which each party was to assist with 200,000 troops if its partner were attacked by a European power, and a somewhat looser agreement with Austria-Hungary. The League could be said to represent a restoration of the old association of conservative eastern European monarchies determined to preserve the established order. But, in contrast to earlier decades when Alexander I and Nicholas I led the conservative coalition, the direction of the new alliance belonged to Bismarck. In fact, the Russian government was grateful to be admitted as a partner. Moreover, Russian and German interests did not correspond in some important matters. The lack of harmony became obvious in 1875 when Russia and Great Britain exercised strong pressure on Germany to assure that it would not try a preventive war against France.

The Three Emperors' League finally collapsed over the issue of Turkey and the Balkans, which in the 1870s led to a series of international crises and to war between Russia and the Ottoman Empire. Beginning with the insurrection against Turkish rule in Herzegovina and Bosnia in July 1875, rebellion swept the Balkans. The year 1876 witnessed a brutal Turkish suppression of a Bulgarian uprising, as well as fighting and massacres in other parts of the peninsula, and the declaration of war on the Porte by Serbia and Montenegro. The Russian public reacted strongly to these developments. Pan-Slavism—hitherto no more than a vague sentiment, except for certain small circles of intellectuals—for the first time became an active force. Pan-Slav committees sent up to five thousand volunteers, ranging from prominent members of society to simple peasants and including about eight hundred former Russian army officers, to fight in the Serbian army, which had been entrusted to another Russian volunteer, General Michael Cherniaev. But the Turks defeated the Serbs; hence the last hope of Balkan nationalities in their uneven contest with the Ottomans rested on Russian intervention. The imperial government considered intervention carefully and without enthusiasm. The international situation, with Great Britain and Austria-Hungary hostile to Russia, argued against war; and so did the internal conditions, for reforms were in the process of enactment, notably in the military

The Balkans 1877–1878

Boundary of Ottoman Empire, 1877
Proposed boundary of Bulgaria by Treaty of San Stefano, 1878
Boundaries after Treaty of Berlin, 1878

0   Miles   300

and financial domains, and there was populist unrest. Besides, Gorchakov and other responsible tsarist officials did not believe at all in Pan-Slavism, the exception being the Russian ambassador to Constantinople, Count Nicholas Ignatiev. However, as the Balkan struggle continued, as international diplomacy failed to bring peace, and as Russia became gradually more deeply involved in the conflict, the tsarist government, having come to an understanding with Austria-Hungary, declared war on Turkey on April 24, 1877.

The difficult, bitter, and costly war, highlighted by such engagements as the Russian defense of the Shipka pass in the Balkan mountains and the Turkish defense of the fortress of Plevna, resulted in a decisive Russian victory. The tsarist troops were approaching Constantinople when the fighting ceased. The Treaty of San Stefano, signed in March 1878, reflected the thorough Ottoman defeat: Russia obtained important border areas in the Caucasus and southern Bessarabia; for the latter, Romania, which had fought jointly with Russia at Plevna and elsewhere, was to be compensated with Dobrudja; Serbia and Montenegro gained territory and were to be recognized, along with Romania, as fully independent, while Bosnia and Herzegovina were to receive some autonomy and reform; moreover, the treaty created a large autonomous Bulgaria reaching to the Aegean Sea, which was to be occupied for two years by Russian troops; Turkey was to pay a huge indemnity.

But the Treaty of San Stefano never went into operation. Austria-Hungary and Great Britain forced Russia to reconsider the settlement. Austria-Hungary was particularly incensed by the creation of a large Slavic state in the Balkans, Bulgaria, which Russia had specifically promised not to do. The reconsideration took the form of the Congress of Berlin. Presided over by Bismarck and attended by such senior European statesmen as Disraeli and Gorchakov, who was still the Russian foreign minister, it met for a month in the summer of 1878 and redrew the map of the Balkans. While, according to the arrangements made in Berlin, Serbia, Montenegro, and Romania retained their independence and Russia held on to southern Bessarabia and most of her Caucasian gains, such as Batum, Kars, and Ardakhan, other provisions of the Treaty of San Stefano were changed beyond recognition. Serbia and Montenegro lost some of their acquisitions. More important, the large Bulgaria created at San Stefano underwent division into three parts: Bulgaria proper, north of the Balkan mountains, which was to be autonomous; Eastern Rumelia, south of the mountains, which was to receive a special organization under Turkish rule; and Macedonia, granted merely certain reforms. Also, Austria-Hungary acquired the right to occupy, although not to annex, Bosnia, Herzegovina, and the Sanjak of Novi Bazar, while Great Britain took Cyprus. The diplomatic defeat of Russia reflected in the Berlin decisions made Russian public opinion react bitterly against Great Britain, Austria-Hungary, and, less justifiably, Bismarck, the "honest broker" of the Congress.

Expansion in Asia

Whereas Russian dealings with European powers in the reign of Alexander II brought mixed results, the empire of the tsars continued to expand in Asia, turning the already multinational Russian Empire into a truly colonial power. Indeed, many scholars assert the existence of a positive correlation between Russian isolation or rebuffs in the west and the eastward advance. In turn, Russia's colonial expansion made England and other colonial powers increasingly nervous. Be this as it may, there can be no doubt that the third quarter of the nineteenth century witnessed enormous Russian gains in Asia, notably in the Caucasus, in Central Asia, and in the Far East. Also, in 1867, the tsarist government withdrew from the Western hemisphere by selling Alaska to the United States for $7,200,000.

As mentioned earlier, Georgian recognition of Russian rule and successful wars against Persia and Turkey in the first decades of the nineteenth century had brought Transcaucasia and thus all of the Caucasus under the sway of the tsars. But imperial authority remained nominal or nonexistent as far as numerous mountain tribes were concerned. The determination to subdue the mountaineers produced a series of wars against Circassians, Abkhazians, Osetians, Chechens, and others, beginning in the 1810s. The mountaineers, mostly Muslims, responded to attempts at Russian domination by uniting in a prolonged jihad, or holy war, in defense of their freedom and faith. The complete "pacification" of the Caucasus, therefore, took decades, and military service in that majestic land seemed for a time almost tantamount to a death warrant. Beginning in 1857, however, Russian troops commanded by Prince Alexander Bariatinsky, using a new and superior rifle against the nearly exhausted mountaineers, staged another, this time decisive, offensive. In 1859 Bariatinsky captured the legendary Shamil, who for twenty-five years had been the military, spiritual, and political leader of Caucasian resistance to Russia. That event has usually been considered as the end of the fighting in the Caucasus, although more time had to pass before order could be fully established there. A large number of Muslim mountaineers chose to migrate to Turkey.

The conquest of Central Asia began in earnest only during the reign of Alexander II, with a series of daring military expeditions in the period from 1865 to 1876. Led by such able and resourceful commanders as Generals Constantine Kaufmann and Michael Skobelev, Russian troops, in a series of converging movements in the desert, encircled and defeated the enemy. Thus in the course of a decade the Russians conquered the khanates of Kokand, Bokhara, and Khiva, and finally, in 1881, also annexed the Transcaspian region. Russian expansion into Central Asia bears a certain resemblance both to colonial wars elsewhere and to the American westward movement. Ideologically as well, these years saw the development of thinking that much resembled Western imperialism, especially the view that Russia, as a civilized nation, had the duty to control backward peoples and bring them order. Central Asia proved attractive for commercial reasons, for the peoples of that area could supply Russia with raw materials, for example, cotton, and at the same time provide a market for Russian manufactured goods. Also, Russian settlements had to be defended against predatory neighbors, and that led to further expansion. More important, it would seem that the fluid Russian frontier simply had to advance in one way or another, at least until it came up against more solid obstacles than the khanates of Bokhara and Khiva. While natives of Central Asia were viewed as alien and inferior "others"—literally, *inorodtsy*—the establishment of Russian rule usually interfered little with the native economy, society, law, religion, or customs. Russia's imperial approach in Central Asia, as in the Caucasus, was still focused on control more than on assimilation.

The Russian Far Eastern boundary remained unchanged from the Treaty of Nerchinsk drawn in 1689 until Alexander II's reign. In the intervening period, however, the Russian population in Siberia had increased considerably, and the Amur river itself had acquired significance as an artery of communication. In 1847 the energetic and ambitious Count Nicholas Muraviev—known later as Muraviev-Amursky, that is, of the Amur—became governor-general of Eastern Siberia. He promoted Russian advance in the Amur area and profited from the desperate plight of China, at war with Great Britain and France and torn by a rebellion, to obtain two extremely advantageous treaties from the Celestial Empire: in 1858, by the Treaty of Aigun, China ceded to Russia the left bank of the Amur river and in 1860, by the Treaty of Peking, the Ussuri region. The Pacific coast of the Russian Empire began gradually to be settled: the town of Nikolaevsk on the Amur was founded in 1853, Khabarovsk in 1858, Vladivostok in 1860. In 1875 Russia yielded its Kurile islands to Japan in return for the southern half of the island of Sakhalin.

Chapter 30

The Reign of Alexander III, 1881–94, and the First Part of the Reign of Nicholas II, 1894–1905

The natural conclusion is that Russians live in a period which Shakespeare defined by saying, "The time is out of joint."

M. KOVALEVSKY

Politically, the reign of Alexander III and the reign of Nicholas II until the Revolution of 1905 formed a period of deepening crisis and intensifying efforts to preserve the traditions of autocratic monarchical power. In the eyes of many, this was nothing less than an age of continuous reaction. In fact, as has been indicated, reaction had started earlier when Alexander II abandoned a liberal course in 1866 and the years following. But the "Tsar-Liberator" did enact major reforms early in his rule, and, as the Loris-Melikov episode indicated, progressive policies constituted a feasible alternative for Russia as long as he remained on the throne. Alexander III and Nicholas II saw no such alternative. Convinced of the sacredness and necessity of unlimited personal power remaining in the hands of the tsar, they not only rejected further reform, but also did their best to limit the effectiveness of many changes that had already taken place. Thus they instituted what have come to be known in Russian historiography as "counterreforms." The official estimate of Russian conditions and needs became increasingly unreal. The government relied staunchly on the gentry, although that class was in decline. It held high the banner of "Orthodoxy-autocracy-nationality," in spite of the fact that Orthodoxy could hardly cement together peoples of many faiths in a multinational empire or unite even the many formally Orthodox Russians for whom religion was no longer central to their lives and identities or had become a more personal and variable form of sacred belief and value; that autocracy was bound to be even more of an anachronism and obstacle to progress in the twentieth than in the nineteenth century; and that a nationalism still grounded in a paternalistic ideal of the mystical bond of love and devotion between tsar and people little satisfied the political and social desires of ordinary Russians and, to the extent that it had come to include Russification, could only split a multinational state. Whereas the last two Romanovs to rule Russia agreed on principles and policies, they differed in character: Alexander III was a strong man, Nicholas II a weak one; under Nicholas confusion and indecision complicated further the government's fundamentally wrong-headed efforts.

Alexander III, born in 1845, was full of strength and vigor when he ascended the Russian throne after the assassination of his father. The new ruler was determined to suppress revolution and to maintain autocracy, a point that he made clear in a manifesto of May 11, 1881, which led to the resignation of Loris-Melikov, Dmitrii Miliutin, Grand Duke Constantine, and the minister of finance, Alexander Abaza. Yet it took a number of months and further changes at the top before the orientation represented by Loris-Melikov was entirely abandoned and the government embarked on a course away from all reform. The promoters of reaction included Constantine Pobedonostsev, formerly a noted jurist at the University of Moscow, who had served as tutor to Alexander and had become in 1880 the Ober-Procurator of the Holy Synod; Dmitrii Tolstoy, who returned to the government in 1882 to head the Ministry of the Interior; and Ivan Delianov, who took charge of the Ministry of Education in the same year. Pobedonostsev, the chief theoretician as well as the leading practitioner of reaction in Russia in the last decades of the nineteenth century, characteristically emphasized the weakness and viciousness of man and the fallibility and dangers of human reason, hated the industrial revolution and the growth of cities, and even wanted "to keep people from inventing things." The state, he believed, had as its high purpose the maintenance of law, order, stability, and unity among men. In Russia that aim could be accomplished only by means of autocracy and the Orthodox Church.

"Temporary Regulations" to protect state security and public order, issued late in the summer of 1881, gave officials in designated areas broad authority in dealing with the press and with people who could threaten public order. Summary search, arrest, imprisonment, exile, and trial by courts-martial became common occurrences. The "Temporary Regulations" were aimed primarily at the "People's Will," which lasted long enough to offer the new ruler peace on conditions of political amnesty and the convocation of a constituent assembly! Although the "People's Will" had been largely destroyed even before the assassination of the emperor and although most of its remaining members soon fell into the hands of the police, the "Temporary Regulations" were not rescinded, but instead applied, as their vague wording permitted, to virtually anyone whom officials suspected or simply disliked. For many years after the demise of the "People's Will," terrorism died down in Russia, although occasional individual outbreaks occurred. Yet the "Temporary Regulations," introduced originally for three years, were renewed. Indeed, the tsarist government relied on them during the rest of its existence, with the result that Russians lived under something like a partial state of martial law.

Alexander III's government also enacted "counterreforms" meant to curb the sweeping changes introduced by Alexander II and to buttress the centralized, bureaucratic, and class nature of the Russian system. New press regulations made the existence of radical journals impossible and the life of a mildly liberal press precarious. The University Statute of 1884, which replaced the more liberal statute of 1863, virtually abolished university autonomy and also emphasized that students were to be considered "individual visitors," who had no right to form organizations or to claim corporate representation. In fact most policies of the Ministry of Education—which will be summarized in a later chapter—whether they concerned the emphasis on classical languages in secondary schools, the drastic curtailment of higher education for women, or the expansion of the role of the Church in elementary teaching, consciously promoted the radically conservative aims of the regime.

The tsar and his associates used every opportunity to help the gentry and to stress their leading position in Russia, as, for example, by the creation in 1885 of the State Gentry Land Bank. At the same time they imposed further restric-

Alexander III in 1889. Known for his strength of conservative conviction, as well as physical strength, Alexander III was described as a "mountain of stone." He was the first Russian ruler since Peter the Great to grow a beard.   (Peterhof palace)

tions on the peasants, whom they considered essentially wards of the state rather than mature citizens. The policies of bureaucratic control of the peasants and of emphasizing the role of the gentry in the countryside found expression in the most outstanding "counterreform" of the reign, the establishment in 1889 of the office of *zemskii nachalnik,* zemstvo chief, or land captain. That official—who had nothing to do with the zemstvo self-government—was appointed and dismissed by the minister of the interior following the recommendation of the governor of the land captain's province. His assigned task consisted in exercising direct bureaucratic supervision over the peasants and, in effect, in managing them. Thus the land captain confirmed elected peasant officials as well as decisions of peasant meetings, and he could prevent the officials from exercising their office, or even fine, arrest, or imprison them, although the fines imposed by the land captain could not exceed several rubles and the prison sentences, several days. Moreover, land captains received vast judicial powers, thus, contrary to the legislation of 1864, again combining administration and justice. In fact, these appointed officials replaced for the peasants, that is, for the vast majority of the people, elected and independent justices of peace. The law of 1889 stipulated that land captains had to be appointed from members of the local gentry who met a certain property qualification. Each district received several land captains; each land captain administered several volosti, that is, townships or cantons. Russia obtained in this manner a new administrative network, one of land captaincies.

The following year, 1890, the government made certain significant changes in the zemstvo system. The previous classification of landholders, that of 1864, had been based on a form of property that did not distinguish members of the gentry from other Russians who happened to hold land in individual ownership. In 1890 the members of the gentry became a distinct group—and their representation was markedly increased. Peasants, on the other hand, could thenceforth elect only candidates for zemstvo seats, the governor making appointments to district zemstvo assemblies from these candidates, as recommended by land captains. In addition, the minister of the interior received the right to confirm chairmen of zemstvo boards in their office, while members of the boards and zemstvo employees were to be confirmed by their respective governors. In 1892 the town government underwent a similar "counterreform," which, among other provisions, sharply raised the property requirement for the right to vote. After its enactment, the electorate in St. Petersburg decreased from 21,000 to 8,000, and that in Moscow from 20,000 to 7,000.

The reign of Alexander III also witnessed increased pressure on non-Orthodox denominations and a growth of the policy of Russification. Even Roman Catholics and Lutherans, who formed majorities in certain western areas of the empire and had unimpeachable international connections and recognition, had to face discrimination: for instance, children of mixed marriages with the Orthodox automatically became Orthodox, and all but the dominant Church were forbidden to engage in proselytizing. Old Believers and Russian sectarians suffered greater hardships. The government also began to oppose non-Christian faiths such as Islam and Buddhism, which had devoted adherents among the many peoples of the empire.

Russification went hand in hand with militant Orthodoxy, although the two were by no means identical, for peoples who were not Great Russians such as the Ukrainians and the Georgians belonged to the Orthodox Church. Although Russification was practiced earlier against the Poles, especially in the western provinces following the rebellions of 1831 and 1863 and to a somewhat lesser extent in Poland proper, and was also apparent in the attempts to suppress the budding Ukrainian nationalism, it became a general policy of the Russian government only late in the nineteenth century. It represented in part a reaction against the growing national sentiments of different peoples of the empire with their implicit threats to the unity of the state and in part a response to the rising nationalism of the Great Russians themselves. Alexander III has often been considered the first nationalist on the Russian throne. Certainly, in his reign measures of Russification began to be extended not only to the rebellious Poles, but, for example, to the Georgians and Armenians in Transcaucasia and even gradually to the loyal Finns.

The Jews, who were very numerous in western Russia as a result of the invitation policy of late medieval Polish kings, were bound to suffer in the new atmosphere of aggressive Orthodoxy and Russification. And indeed old limitations came to be applied to them with a new force, while new legislation was enacted to establish additional curbs on them and their activities. Thus, in contrast to the former lax enforcement of rules, Jews came to be rigorously restricted to residence in the "Pale of Jewish Settlement," that is, the area in western Russia where they had been living for a long time, with the added proviso that even within the Pale they could reside only in towns and smaller settlements inhabited by merchants and craftsmen, but not in the countryside. Educated or otherwise prominent Jews could usually surmount these restrictions, but the great bulk of the poor Jewish population was tied to its location. In 1887 the government established quotas for Jewish students in institutions of higher learning: 10 percent of the total enrollment within the Pale of Jewish Settlement, 5 percent in other provinces, and 3 percent in Moscow and St. Petersburg. In 1881, pogroms—the sad word entered the English language from the Russian—that is, violent popular outbreaks against the Jews, occurred in southwestern Russian towns and settlements, destroying Jewish property and sometimes taking Jewish lives. They were to recur sporadically until the end of imperial Russia. Local authorities often did little to prevent pogroms and on occasion, it is rather clear, even encouraged them. As Pobedonostsev allegedly remarked, the Jewish problem in Russia was to be solved by the conversion to Orthodoxy of one-third of the Russian Jews, the emigration of one-third, and the death of the remaining third. It should be added that the Russian government defined Jews according to their religion; Jews converted to Christianity escaped the disabilities imposed on the others.

Yet even under Alexander III state policies could not be limited to curbing the "great reforms" and generally promoting reaction. Certain more constructive measures were enacted in the domains of finance and national economy where the government had to face a difficult and changing situation, and where it profited from the services of several able ministers. While the development of the Russian economy and of society after the "great reforms" will be discussed in a later chapter, it should be noted here that Nicholas Bunge, who headed the Ministry of Finance from 1881 to 1887, established a Peasant Land Bank, abolished the head tax, introduced the inheritance tax, and also began labor legislation in Russia. His pioneer factory laws included the limitation of the working day to eight hours for children between twelve and fifteen, the prohibition of night work for children and for women in the textile industry, and regulations aimed at assuring the workers proper and regular pay from their employers, without excessive fines or other illegitimate deductions. Factory inspectors were established to supervise the carrying out of the new legislation. It is significant that Bunge had to leave the Ministry of Finance because of the strong opposition to his measures and accusations of socialism. His successors, Ivan Vyshnegradsky, 1887–92, and Serge Witte, 1892–1903, strove especially to develop state railways in Russia and to promote heavy industry through high tariffs, state contracts and subsidies, and other means.

Nicholas II

Nicholas II, Alexander III's eldest son, who was born in 1868, became the autocratic ruler of Russia after his father's death in 1894. The last tsar possessed personal qualities that many have admired, such as modesty, self-discipline, faith, patriotism, a deep sense of duty, and devotion to his family. But these virtues mattered little in a situation that demanded strength, adaptability, and vision. It may well be argued that another Peter the Great could have saved the Romanovs and imperial Russia. There can be no doubt that Nicholas II did not. In fact, he proved unable to remove his traditionalist political blinders even when circumstances forced him into entirely new situations with great potentialities, and at the same time unable to manage even reaction effectively. Everything about Nicholas II's upbringing, experience, intellect, and personality led him to believe deeply in a polity based on the most traditional notions of power (often deriving from a nostalgic image of pre-Petrine Russia). Nicholas believed explicitly that the unrestricted personal power of the tsar was the only assurance of Russia's might, stability, and even progress as a nation. This was, however, a moral power. This was autocracy linked with Orthodoxy and nationality. The ruler, Nicholas believed, was blessed and guided by God. Typically, he loved the traditional saying, "the heart of the tsar is in the hand of God." And the Russian ruler enjoyed, he believed, a special bond of almost mystical love of the people. Even when forced, reluctantly, to respond to massive public unrest in 1905 by agreeing to demands for a national representative assembly, he continued to cast his vision of even a reformed political order in traditionalist terms: "Let there be established as in olden time, the union between Tsar and all Rus', the communion between Me and the people of the land, which lies at the foundation of an order that corresponds to unique Russian principles." At the same time, Nicholas loved orderliness and discipline. His model and inspiration was the military, whose rituals he always loved. At the same time, complicating these convictions, he revealed what many saw as signs of deeper uncertainty and even weakness. The emperor struck many observers as peculiarly automatic in his attitudes and actions, without the power of spontaneous decision. Various, often unworthy, ministers made crucial decisions that the sovereign failed to understand fully or to evaluate. Later in the reign the empress, Alexandra, a German-born convert to Orthodoxy whose devotion to old Russian traditions, moral conservatism, mysticism, and contempt for the reformist ideas of intellectuals were perhaps even more stubborn than Nicholas's, became the tsar's closest confident and advisor. Perhaps the most notorious sign of Nicholas's poor judgment, and Alexandra's baneful influence, was that such an incredible person as Rasputin could rise to the position of greatest influence in the state. On top of all this, Nicholas was notably fatalistic. He was often quoted as saying, "God knows what is good for us, we must bow down our heads and repeat the sacred words 'Thy will be done.'" It has been argued that Nicholas may have been a good man, even a saintly one (indeed, he has recently been canonized by the Ortho-

Nicholas II in seventeenth-century dress for a masked ball at the Winter Palace in 1903. Nicholas admired what he viewed as a more national and healthy spirit in Russia before Peter the Great.   (New York Public Library)

dox church in Russia), but that he was a miserable ruler lost in the moment of crisis. At a time when so much was changing in Russia and the world and so many Russians were convinced that the time had come for new political relationships based on limited central government, civil rights, democratic participation, and the rule of law, it appears that the autocracy was retreating into a stubborn, even blind, faith in Russia's ancient political traditions: the ideal of absolute personal rule by a divinely anointed and inspired monarch bound to his people through mystical love rather than modern democratic institutions. Trotsky and other determinists have insisted that the archaic, rotten Russian system, which was about to collapse, could not logically produce a leader much different from that ineffective relic of the past. Or, as an old saying has it, the gods blind those whom they want to destroy.

Reaction under Nicholas II

In the face of expectations that he would relax the restrictive policies of his father and possibly embark on needed reforms, Nicholas II hastened to make clear to society where he stood politically. Addressing a gathering of representatives of the gentry, zemstvos, and cities in January 1895, he bluntly declared (in words widely reported in the press), "It is known to Me that voices have been heard of late, in some zemstvo assemblies, by persons carried away by senseless dreams of participation of representatives of the zemstvos in the affairs of internal administration. Let all know that, in devoting all my strength to the people's well-being, I will preserve the principles of autocracy as firmly and unswervingly as did my late unforgettable father." Policy followed accordingly. Himself a former pupil of Pobedonostsev, Nicholas relied on the Ober-Procurator of the Holy Synod and on other reactionaries such as his ministers of interior Dmitrii Sipiagin and Viacheslav Plehve. The government continued to apply and extend the "Temporary Regulations," to supervise the press with utmost severity, and as best it could to control and often restrict education. The zemstvo and municipal governments experienced further curtailments of their jurisdictions. For example, in 1900 the limits of zemstvo taxation were strictly fixed and the stockpiling of food for emergency was taken away from zemstvo jurisdiction and transferred to that of the bureaucracy. Moreover, the authorities often refused to confirm elections of zemstvo board members or appointments of zemstvo employees, trying to assure that only people of unimpeachable loyalty to the regime would hold public positions of any kind.

Official Russian nationalism, closely linked to these conservative political values, meant both constant talk about the "loving communion" of the tsar and his true Russian people and restrictions and persecution for those defined as outside the national fold. These policies were not without some ambiguity. The state sometimes celebrated, as in the ceremonies marking Nicholas's accession, the variety of the empire's subjects (though emphasizing Russian leadership), tolerated local customs and native languages, and even encouraged a circumscribed role in administration or education for non-Russians themselves, though all in the pursuit of the integration of diverse peoples into a common imperial polity. But intolerance for difference was also quite evident and brutal. Religious persecution grew. Russian sectarians suffered the most, in particular those groups that refused to recognize the state and perform such state obligations as military service. Many of them were exiled from central European Russia to the Caucasus and other distant areas. It was as a result of the policies of the Russian government that the Dukhobory and certain other sects—helped, incidentally, by Leo Tolstoy—began to emigrate in large numbers to Canada and the United States. The state also confiscated the estates and charity funds of the Armenian Church and harassed other denominations in numerous ways. The position of the Jews too underwent further deterioration. Additional restrictions on them included a prohibition from acquiring real estate anywhere in the empire except in the cities and settlements of the Jewish Pale, while new pogroms erupted in southwest Russia, including the horrible one in Kishinev in 1903.

But the case of Finland represented in many respects the most telling instance of the folly of Russification. As an autonomous grand duchy from the time it was won from Sweden in 1809, Finland received more rights from the Russian emperor, who became the Grand Duke of Finland, than it had had under Swedish rule, and remained a perfectly loyal, as well as a relatively prosperous and happy, part of the state until the very end of the nineteenth century and the introduction of a policy of Russification. Finnish soldiers helped suppress the Poles, and in general the Finns participated actively and fruitfully in almost every aspect of the life of the empire. Yet the new nationalism demanded that they too be Russified. While some preliminary measures in that direction had been enacted as early as in the reign of Alexander III, real Russification began with the appointment of General Nicholas Bobrikov as governor-general of Finland and of Plehve as state secretary for Finnish affairs in 1898. Russian authorities argued that Finland could remain different from Russia only as far as local matters were concerned, while it had to accept the general system in what pertained to the entire state. With that end in view, a manifesto concerning laws common to Finland and Russia and a new statute dealing with the military service of the Finns were published in 1899. Almost overnight Finland became bitterly hostile to Russia, and a strong though passive resistance developed: new laws were ignored, draftees failed to show up, and so on. In 1901 freedom of meetings was abrogated in Finland. In 1902 Governor-General Bobrikov received the right to dismiss Finnish officials and judges and to replace them with Russians. In 1903 he was vested with extraordinary powers to protect state security and public order, which represented a definitive extension of the "Temporary Regulations" of 1881 to Finland. In 1904 Bobrikov was assassinated. The following year the opposition in Finland became part of the revolution that spread throughout the empire.

Witte and the Ministry of Finance

However, under Nicholas II, as in the reign of Alexander III, the Ministry of Finance pursued a more intelligent and far-sighted policy than did the rest of the government; and this affected many aspects of the Russian economy and life. The minister, Serge Witte, was an economic planner and manager of the type common in recent times in the governments of western Europe and the United States, but exceedingly rare in the high officialdom of imperial Russia. Witte devoted his remarkable energy and ability especially to the stabilization of finance, the promotion of heavy industry, and the building of railroads. In 1897, after accumulating a sufficient gold reserve, he established a gold standard in Russia, a measure which did much to add stability and prestige to Russian economic development, and in particular to attract foreign capital. Witte encouraged heavy industry by virtually every means at his command, including government orders, liberal credits, unceasing efforts to obtain investments from abroad, tariff regulations, and improved transportation. As to railroads, the minister, who had risen to prominence as a railroad official, always retained a great interest in them: the Russian railroad network doubled in mileage between 1895 and 1905, and the additions included the enormous Trans-Siberian line, built between 1891 and 1903—except for a section around Lake Baikal completed later—the importance of which for Siberia can be compared to the importance of the Canadian Pacific Railroad for Canada. Witte's activities, as we shall see presently, affected foreign policy as well as domestic affairs.

Russian Foreign Policy after the Congress of Berlin

Russian foreign policy had been undergoing important changes in the decades that followed the Congress of Berlin. The most significant developments were the final rupture with Austria-Hungary and Germany and the alliance with France. Although the Three Emperors' League had foundered in the Balkan crisis, a new Alliance of the Three Emperors was concluded in June 1881 for three years and renewed in 1884 for another three years. Its most essential provision declared that if one of the contracting powers—Germany, Austria-Hungary, or Russia—engaged in war with a fourth power, except Turkey, the other two were to maintain friendly neutrality. But, because of their conflicting interests in the Balkans, it proved impossible for Russia and Austria-Hungary to stay in the same alliance. The next major crisis occurred over Bulgaria where—as Charles Jelavich and other specialists have demonstrated—Russia destroyed a great amount of popularity and goodwill by an overbearing and stupid policy. The Russian quarrel with the Bulgarian ruler, Alexander of Battenberg, and the Russian refusal to sanction the unification of Bulgaria and Eastern Rumelia in 1885 failed to stop the unification but resulted in the abdication of Alexander of Battenberg and the election by the Bulgarian Assembly of the pro-Austrian Ferdinand of Saxe-Coburg to the Bulgarian throne. Bulgaria abandoned the Russian sphere of influence and entered the Austrian, leaving the empire of the tsars virtually without Balkan allies. At the same time tension in relations between Russia and Austria-Hungary increased almost to the breaking point. However, Germany, by contrast with Austria-Hungary and despite the fact that in 1879 it had become a close partner of the Hapsburg state, tried at first to retain the Russian connection. Thus when the Alliance of the Three Emperors expired in 1887, Germany and Russia concluded in secret the so-called Reinsurance Treaty, Bismarck's "wire to St. Petersburg" and a veritable *tour de force* of diplomacy: each party was to remain neutral in case the other fought a war, with the exception of an aggressive war of Germany against France or of Russia against Austria-Hungary—the exception making it barely possible for Germany to square the Reinsurance Treaty with its obligations to Austria-Hungary. Nevertheless, following Bismarck's forced resignation in 1890, Germany discontinued the Reinsurance Treaty and thus severed its connection with Russia.

The Russian rupture with the Germanic powers and the general isolation of Russia appeared all the more ominous because of Anglo-Russian tension over the expansion of the Russian Empire in Central Asia, which, the British felt, threatened India. That tension attained its high point in 1885 when the Russians, having reached as far south as the vague Afghan border, clashed with the soldiers of the amir. Although an Anglo-Russian war was avoided and the boundary settled by compromise, Great Britain and Russia remained hostile to each other well past the turn of the century as they competed for influence and control in vast lands south of Russia, especially in Iran.

Political realities pointed to a Franco-Russian alliance—Bismarck's nightmare and the reason behind the Reinsurance Treaty—for France was as isolated as Russia and more threatened. Alexander III, his cautious foreign minister Nicholas Giers, and other tsarist high officials reached that conclusion reluctantly, because they had no liking for the Third Republic and no confidence in it, and because the traditional German orientation in Russian foreign policy died hard. Yet France remained the only possible partner, and it had much to offer. In particular, Paris alone provided a great market for Russian state loans—the Berlin financial market, it might be added, was closed to Russia in 1887—and thus the main source of foreign financial support much needed by the imperial government. In fact, Frenchmen proved remarkably eager to subscribe to these loans as well as to invest directly in the Russian economy. Economics thus joined politics, although it would be fair to say that politics led the way. The alliance was consolidated in several stages, beginning with the diplomatic understanding of 1891 and ending with the military convention of December 1893–January 1894. B. Nolde, Langer, and other scholars have indicated how through the drawn-out negotiations the French pressed for an ever firmer and more binding agreement, gradually forcing the hand of the hesitant Russians. In its final form the alliance provided that if France were attacked by Germany, or by Italy supported by Germany, Russia would employ all available forces against Germany; and if Russia were attacked by Germany, or by Austria-Hungary supported by Germany, France would employ all available forces against Germany. Additional articles dealt with mobilization, the number of troops to be contributed, and other specific military plans. The Franco-Russian agreement was to remain in force for the duration of the Triple Alliance of Germany, Austria-Hungary, and Italy.

Nicholas II approved Alexander III's foreign policy on the whole and wanted to continue it. However, as we shall see, the new emperor proved to be less steady and more erratic than his father in international relations as in domestic affairs. Also, while Alexander III relied on the careful and experienced Giers throughout his rule, Nicholas II had several foreign ministers whose differences and personal preferences affected imperial diplomacy. In addition, the reign of the last tsar witnessed more than its share of court cliques

Nicholas II blessing troops leaving for the front in the Russo-Japanese War, 1905. Nicholas often spoke of the Russian common people's traditional love and devotion for their tsar and described moments like these as deeply moving. (Terra Publishers)

and cabals which on occasion exercised a strong and at the same time irresponsible influence on the conduct of Russian foreign policy.

Nicholas II appeared prominently on the international scene in 1899, when he called together the first Hague Peace Conference attended by representatives of twenty-six states. Although instigated by Russian financial stringency and in particular by the difficulty of keeping up with Austrian armaments, this initiative was in accord with the emperor's generally peaceful views. While the Conference failed to agree on disarmament or compulsory arbitration of disputes, it did pass certain "laws of war"—later often disregarded in practice, as in the case of the temporary injunction against the use of "projectiles thrown from balloons"—and set up a permanent court of arbitration, the International Court of Justice at the Hague. More important, it became the first of a long series of international conferences on disarmament and peace, on which the hopes of humankind ride today. The Second Hague Peace Conference, in 1907, was also attended by Russian representatives, but again it could not reach agreement on the major issues under discussion.

The Russo-Japanese War

Nicholas II's own policy, however, did not always contribute to peace. Aggressiveness and adventurous involvement characterized Russian behavior in the Far East around the turn of the century, which culminated in the Russo-Japanese War of 1904–5. The construction of the Trans-Siberian railroad between 1891 and 1903, entirely justified in terms of the needs of Siberia, served also to link Russia to Manchuria, China, Korea, and even, indirectly, to Japan. Japan had just gone through a remarkable modernization and in 1894–95 it fought and defeated China, obtaining by the Treaty of Shimonoseki the Chinese territories of Formosa, the Pescadores Islands, and the Liaotung Peninsula, together with other gains, including the recognition of full independence for Korea. Before Japan could profit from the Liaotung Peninsula, Russia, France, and Germany forced her to give it up. Next Russia concluded a secret agreement with China, whereby in return for guaranteeing Chinese territory against outside aggression, it obtained the right to construct a railroad through Manchuria to the coast. Although the new railroad, the East China Railway, belonged nominally to a private company with a large Chinese participation, it marked in effect the establishment of a Russian sphere of influence in northern Manchuria, an influence centered in Harbin and extending along railroad tracks and properties guarded by a special Russian railroad guard.

While Russia had legitimate commercial and other interests in Asia—for one thing, selling the products of its factories in the East when they could not compete in the West—and while up to that point Russian imperialism in the Far East had limited itself to peaceful penetration, the situation became increasingly tense. Moreover, Russia responded to new opportunities more and more aggressively. Thus, when the murder of two German missionaries in November 1897 led to the German acquisition of Kiao-chow through a ninety-nine year lease, Nicholas II demanded and obtained a twenty-five year lease of the southern part of the Liaotung Peninsula with Port Arthur—in spite of Witte's opposition to that move and in flagrant disregard of the Russian treaty with China. Witte in turn proceeded to make the most of the situation and rapidly develop Russian interests in southern Manchuria. Following the so-called Boxer rebellion of the exasperated Chinese against foreigners in 1900–1901, which Russian forces helped to suppress, tsarist troops remained in Manchuria on the pretext that local conditions represented a threat to the railroad. In addition, a group of adventurers with strong connections at the Russian court began to promote a scheme of timber concessions on the Yalu River meant to serve as a vehicle for Russian penetration into Korea. Witte, who objected energetically to the dangerous new scheme, had to leave the Ministry of Finance; the Foreign Office failed to restrain or control Russian policy in the Far East; and Nicholas II himself sided cheerfully with the adventurers, apparently because he believed in some sort of Russian mission in Asia and, in common with almost everyone else, grossly underestimated Japan. Russian policy could hardly be defended in terms of either justice or wisdom, in spite of the efforts of such able scholars as Malozemoff.

Japan proved to be the more skillful aggressor, notwithstanding the contempt often expressed in the boulevard press for the Japanese as "yellow monkeys." Offering partition, which would give the Russians northern Manchuria and the Japanese southern Manchuria and Korea, the Japanese gauged the futility of negotiating, chose their time well, and on February 8, 1904, attacked successfully the unsuspecting Russian fleet in the outer harbor of Port Arthur—thus accomplishing the original Pearl Harbor. What followed turned

Russo-Japanese War 1904–1905

out to be a humiliating war for the Russians. The Russian colossus suffered defeat after defeat from the Japanese pigmy. This outcome, so surprising at the time, resulted from ample causes: Japan was ready, well-organized, and in effect more modern than Russia, while Russia was unprepared, disorganized, troubled at home, and handicapped by a lack of popular support and even by some defeatism; Japan enjoyed an alliance with Great Britain and the favor of world public opinion, Russia found itself diplomatically isolated; Japan used short lines of communication, Russian forces had to rely on the enormously long single-track Trans-Siberian railroad, with the section around Lake Baikal still unfinished. In any case, although Russian soldiers and sailors fought with their usual courage and tenacity, the Japanese destroyed the Russian navy in the Far East, besieged and eventually captured Port Arthur, and gradually, in spite of bitter engagements near Mukden and elsewhere, pushed the main Russian army north in Manchuria. Finally, on May 27–29, 1905, in the battle of Tsushima Strait, they annihilated Admiral Zinovii Rozhdestvensky's antique fleet which had been sent to the Far East all the way from the Baltic. That fleet, it might be added, had caused a serious international incident when on its journey to the Far East it had fired by mistake at some English fishing vessels on the Dogger Bank, inflicting casualties.

An armistice followed soon after Tsushima. The Russians had suffered numerous defeats, and the government had to cope with revolutionary unrest at home. The Japanese had exhausted their finances and, despite their victories, could not destroy the main Russian army or force a conclusion. In response to a secret Japanese request, President Theodore Roosevelt arranged a peace conference at Portsmouth, New Hampshire, in August 1905. The provisions of the Treaty of Portsmouth reflected the skillful diplomacy of Witte, who headed the Russian delegation, and represented, everything considered, a rather satisfactory settlement for Russia: Russia acknowledged a paramount Japanese interest in Korea and ceded to Japan its lease of the Liaotung Peninsula, the southern part of the railroad up to Chang-chun, and the half of the island of Sakhalin south of the fiftieth degree of latitude; both countries agreed to restore Manchuria to China; in spite of strong Japanese insistence, there was no indemnity.

The Russian government ended the war against Japan none too soon, for, as fighting ceased, the country was already in the grip of what came to be known as the Revolution of 1905.

Chapter 31

The Last Part of the Reign of Nicholas II: The Revolution of 1905 and the Constitutional Period, 1905–17

Russia at the dawn of the twentieth century knew no more magic word than "revolution." The idea of revolution was viewed with fear and hatred by the propertied classes of the population, and was loved and revered by all who dreamed of liberty. To the Russians who longed for a new life, there was enchantment in the very sound of the word. Even as they conceived it, even as they pronounced the sacred words, "Long Live the Revolution," Russians felt obscurely that they were already halfway to liberation.

ISAAC STEINBERG

There is an easier and more convincing explanation for the failure of the constitutional monarchy: it puts the blame primarily on the king himself. Although Louis was well-meaning and showed occasional flashes of insight, his narrow mind had a stubborn and devious quality about it, too. The king did little to consolidate the new system, even though it left him a role of real importance. . . .

. . . The explanation may lie in the constant pressure of the queen and her advisers, which weakened Louis's resolution and changed his flabby mind. Or it may be that this pious king had serious pangs of conscience at some of the reforms built into the new system. . . . Or again, perhaps the course of events brought out his own true character as an irritable, small-minded, stubborn man who built up a neurotic resentment at his loss of initiative after 1789. It is true that even if Louis XVI had been ideally suited to his new role, the system might have broken down nevertheless.

WRIGHT

Whereas actually the main weakness of the Russian monarchy of the imperial period consisted not at all in representing the interests of a *"minority,"* restricted in this or that manner, but in the fact that it represented *no one* whatsoever.*

FLOROVSKY

---

*Italics in the original.

M. Kovalevsky and many other Russians hoped that the period of blind reaction, "the time out of joint," which descended upon Russia in the second half of Alexander II's reign and was certainly present in the reigns of Alexander III and Nicholas II, would give way to a new wave of sweeping liberal reforms. But the government refused to change its course. Instead the country finally exploded into the Revolution of 1905.

The Background of the Revolution of 1905

The Revolution of 1905 could occur because of the social transformation that had been going on in the empire of the tsars and because of the concomitant growth of opposition to the regime. In the decades that followed the "great reforms," capitalism at last became prominent in Russia. In fact, the 1880s and 1890s witnessed rapid industrialization of the country with resulting social changes and tensions. While the Russian society of that period will be discussed in the following chapter, no special exposition is needed to make the point that the growth of capitalism led to the rise of two social groups, a bourgeoisie and a working class. The middle class, traditionally weak in Russia at least after the times of Kiev and Novgorod, began finally to come into its own. Even though the Russian commercial and industrial bourgeoisie remained still relatively underdeveloped and inarticulate, professional people seemed eager and ready to participate in politics. These professional groups—whether they should be classified as part of the middle class or as a separate adjoining stratum is of no consequence here—had profited especially from the "great reforms": thus, the judicial reform of 1864 had virtually created the lawyers, while the introduction of the zemstvo system provided numerous openings for doctors, veterinarians, teachers, statisticians, and many other specialists, the so-called "third element" of the zemstva. Liberalism found particularly propitious circumstances for development among the professionals, as well as among some gentry landlords of the zemstva. The rise of the working class and the emergence of a labor movement pointed in their turn to a more radical trend in Russian opposition. And, of course, behind dissatisfied bourgeois, critical intellectuals, and bitter workers there spread the human ocean of destitute and desperate peasants—an ocean that had risen in uncounted storms through centuries of Russian history.

The opposition began to organize. The frightful famine of 1891–92 marked the end of a certain lull in Russia and the resumption of social and political activity with emphatic criticism of the regime. The liberals, who could boast of many prominent names in their ranks and who represented at that time the elite of the opposition, eventually formed the Union of Liberation in 1903, with its organ, *The Liberation*, published abroad by the noted economist Peter Struve. In 1905 they organized the Constitutional Democratic Party—or "Cadet," a word based on the two initial letters in the Russian name—led by the historian Paul Miliukov and encompassing liberals of different kinds, both constitutional monarchists and republicans.

The radicals formed two important parties around the turn of the century: the Social Democratic, or "SD," and the Socialist Revolutionary, or "SR." The

Social Democrats were Marxists, and the creation of their party represented a landmark in the development of Marxism in Russia. Propounded by George Plekhanov and other able intellectuals, Marxism became prominent in the empire of the tsars in the 1880s and especially in the 1890s. Its close association with the labor movement dated at least from 1883, when Plekhanov organized the Emancipation of Labor Group; but a Marxist political party, the Social Democratic, appeared only in 1898. In fact, the convention of 1898—although commemorated in the USSR as the first and founding congress—proved abortive, and most of its few participants were shortly arrested. The party became a reality only after the second convention held in Brussels and London in 1903. At that time the Social Democrats also split into the Bolsheviks, led by Vladimir Ulianov, better known as Lenin, who wanted a tightly knit organization of professional revolutionaries, and the Mensheviks, who preferred a somewhat broader and looser association. In time the ramifications of that relatively slight initial difference acquired great importance. The Socialist Revolutionaries, who engaged in a running debate with the Marxists concerning the nature of Russian society and its future, represented essentially the older populist tradition of Russian radicalism, even though they too were influenced by Marxism. They formed their party in 1901 and had Victor Chernov as their most noted leader.

As the twentieth century opened, Russia was in turmoil. Workers' demonstrations and strikes spread throughout the country. Student protests and disturbances became more frequent, constituting an almost continuous series from 1898 on. Sporadic peasant disturbances kept the tension high in rural areas and offered increased opportunities to the Socialist Revolutionaries, just as the growth of the labor movement encouraged the Social Democrats. In 1902, 1903, and early 1904, committees dealing with the national economy, conferences of teachers and doctors, and other public bodies all demanded reforms. Moreover, the Socialist Revolutionaries resumed the terrorist tactics of their predecessors such as the "People's Will." Their "Battle Organization" assassinated a number of important officials, including the two especially reactionary ministers of the interior, Sipiagin in 1902 and Plehve in 1904, and early in 1905 Grand Duke Serge, commanding officer of the Moscow military region and Nicholas II's second cousin and brother-in-law. The war against Japan and resulting defeats added fuel to the fire. The government was not entirely unresponsive. Plehve was replaced as minister of the interior by Prince Dmitrii Sviatopolk-Mirsky, who spoke openly as few tsarist officials had before of finding ways for the voice of "society" to be heard, initiating what many expectantly called a political "spring" in relations between state and society. But this only further stimulated civic demands for reform. In November and December 1904, liberals staged a "banquet campaign," inspired by the French example of 1847–48, featuring fervent speeches and resolutions calling for democratizing political change. In November, a zemstvo congress, meeting in St. Petersburg, demanded a representative assembly and civil liberties. The same demands were made with increasing frequency by numerous other public bodies. In particular, professional organizations, such as unions of doctors and teachers, and other associations spread rapidly throughout Russia and made their voices heard.

The Revolution of 1905

On January 22, 1905 (January 9 on the Russian calendar), the police of the capital fired on a huge demonstration of workers marching toward the Winter Palace with a petition for the tsar, killing, according to the official estimate, one hundred and thirty persons and wounding several hundred. "Bloody Sunday," as it came to be known in Russian history, set in motion an unprecedented political and social upheaval throughout the empire. The march had been led by George Gapon, a charismatic priest who had organized workers throughout the city into an "Assembly of Russian Factory Workers." Ironically, Gapon's union had begun in 1904 as part of a police effort to lure workers away from socialists and nurture their loyalty to autocracy through inexpensive tearooms, edifying lectures, and concern for their everyday material needs. What resulted was an organization whose meetings were marked by a mixture of social criticism, moral fervor, and sacred purpose, and which began to act with increasing vigor to help and defend workers. Ironically too, the workers were converging on the Winter Palace—ignorant of the fact that Nicholas II was not there—with icons and the tsar's portraits, as faithful subjects, nay, children, of their sovereign, begging him for redress and help. The entire ghastly episode thus testified to official incompetence in more ways than one. The massacre led to a great outburst of indignation in the country and gave another boost to the revolutionary movement. In particular, as many authorities assert, it meant a decisive break between the tsar and those numerous workers who had until that "Bloody Sunday" remained loyal to him.

Social Democrats demonstrate in 1905. Banners read "Proletarians of All Countries, Unite!" "Russian Social-Democratic Workers' Party," "We Demand a Constituent Assembly," "Down with Autocracy."   (Russian State Archive of Film and Photographic Documents)

Under ever-increasing pressure, Nicholas II declared early in March his intention to convoke a "consultative" assembly; in further efforts toward pacification, he proclaimed religious tolerance and repealed some legislation against ethnic minorities; nevertheless, the revolutionary tide kept rising. The revolution had many faces: workers' and students' strikes, demonstrations stretching through city streets, vandalism and other periodic violence, naval mutinies (most famously the rebellion on the battleship *Potemkin* on the Black Sea), peasant unrest in many provinces, and nationalist movements in the imperial borderlands. On August 19 an imperial manifesto created an elective Duma with consultative powers, but that too failed to satisfy the educated public or the masses. The revolutionary movement culminated in a mammoth general strike which lasted from the twentieth to the thirtieth of October and has been described as the greatest, most thoroughly carried out, and most successful strike in history. Russians seemed to act with a single will, as they made perfectly plain their unshakable determination to end autocracy. To bolster their demands, society had become more organized than ever before. In May, fourteen professional unions united to form a huge Union of Unions led by the liberal Cadets. Industrial workers established, without seeking official approval, trade unions, in which socialist workers and intellectuals often played leading roles. During strikes, factory-based and industry-wide strike committees proliferated, and business owners also began to organize. In addition, many organizations began to publish their own newspapers. During the October general strike, and in order to direct it, workers and socialists in St. Petersburg organized a *soviet*, or council—a harbinger of the then unknown future. Paralyzed in their essential activities and forced at last to recognize the immensity of the opposition, Nicholas II and his government finally capitulated. On October 30, the emperor, as advised by Witte, issued the October Manifesto. That brief document guaranteed civil liberties to the Russians, announced a Duma with the true legislative function of passing or rejecting all proposed laws, and promised a further expansion of the new order in Russia. In short, the October Manifesto made the empire of the Romanovs a constitutional monarchy.

Also, it split the opposition. The liberals and moderates of all sorts felt fundamentally satisfied. The radicals, such as the Social Democrats, on the contrary, considered the tsar's concession entirely inadequate and wanted in any case a constituent assembly, not handouts from above. Thus divided, the opposition lost a great deal of its former power. In the middle of December the government arrested the members of the St. Petersburg Soviet. The Soviet's appeal for revolution found effective response only in Moscow where workers and some other radicals fought bitterly against the police and the soldiers, including a guards' regiment, from the twenty-second of December until the first of January.

The year 1905 thus ended in Russia in bloody fighting. However, the revolution had spent itself with that last effort. In the course of the winter, punitive expeditions and summary courts-martial restored order in many troubled areas. The extreme Right joined the army and the police; Rightist active squads, known as the "Black Hundreds," beat and even killed Jews, liberals, and other intellectuals. Proto-fascist in nature, this newly awakened Right throve on ethnic and religious hatreds and appealed especially to wealthy peasants and to members of the lower middle class in towns. More important, the great bulk of the people was tired of revolution and longed for peace. It might be added that Witte further strengthened the hand of the government by obtaining a large loan from France.

The Fundamental Laws

On May 6, 1906, virtually on the eve of the meeting of the First Duma, the government promulgated the Fundamental Laws. These laws provided the framework of the new Russian political system; the October Manifesto had merely indicated some of its guiding lines. According to the Fundamental Laws, the emperor retained huge powers. He continued in complete control of the executive, the armed forces, foreign policy—specifically making war and peace—succession to the throne, the imperial court, imperial domains, and so forth. He maintained unchanged his unique dominating position in relation to the Russian Church. And he even retained the title of autocrat. He was to call together the annual sessions of the Duma and to disband the Duma, in which case, however, he had to indicate the time of the election and of the meeting of the new Duma. He had the power of veto over legislation. Moreover, in case of emergency when the Duma was not in session, he could issue *ukazes* with the authority of laws, although they had to be submitted for approval to the next session of the Duma no later than two months after its opening.

The Duma, to be sure, received important legislative and budgetary rights and functions by the Fundamental Laws, but these rights were greatly circumscribed. Notably, almost 40 percent of the state budget, encompassing such items as the army, the navy, the imperial court, and state loans, stayed outside the purview of the Duma, while the remainder, if not passed by the Duma, was re-enacted in the amounts of the preceding year. Ministers and the entire executive branch remained responsible only to the emperor, although the Laws did contain complicated provisions for interpellation, that is, questioning of ministers by the Duma. Furthermore, the State Council, which had functioned since its creation by Alexander I as an advisory body of dignitaries, became rather unexpectedly the upper legislative chamber, equal in rights and prerogatives to the Duma and meant obviously as a conservative counterweight to it. "No more than half" of the membership of the upper house was to be appointed by the emperor—appointed not even for life but by means of annual lists—and the other half elected by the following groups: 56 with very high property standing by the provincial zemstva, 18 by the gentry, 12 by commerce and industry, 6 by the clergy, 6 by the Academy of Sciences and the universities, and 2 by the Finnish Diet. Legislation also extended the October Manifesto's promises of reform into social policy. Unions and even strikes were legalized—it was at this point that employers began to organize—though police retained extensive authority to monitor union activities and to close unions for engaging in illegal political activities. Greater press freedom was guaranteed, but in practice the press was carefully monitored and subject to punitive fines and even closure for overstepping the bounds of tolerated free speech.

Personally, Nicholas II increasingly regretted the power he ceded in 1905–6, and he would do what he could in the coming years to undo the concessions he had made under duress. Nicholas's letters and conversations in the months and years following 1905 make it clear that he had taken Witte's advice to issue the October Manifesto out of desperation, but that he had not and never would compromise his fundamental political values. He refused to accept as a principle, as distinct from an expedient for the sake of stability, limitations on the tsar's personal authority—hence his insistence that his title as autocrat be preserved and that so much power remain in his hands. But this had perilous consequences. It has been argued that Nicholas II, along with prominent conservative figures who supported and advised him, ultimately became a source of instability in the emerging political order of late Imperial Russia. While ministers like Witte and Stolypin and the legislators of the Duma worked to construct a stable polity around the ideal of a modernized autocracy ruling, however firmly, according to law and over a society of citizens, Nicholas II was at the forefront of those embracing a political vision that insisted on situating legitimate state power in the person of the emperor. As R. Wortman has argued, "rather than accommodating the monarchy to the demands for a civic nation," Nicholas II clung tenaciously to a tradition, established most strongly with Nicholas I, that "redefined the concept of nation to make it a mythical attribute of the monarch." The tsar's insistent attachment to this increasingly archaic political vision, it has been argued, could only have harmful consequences for Russia.

The First Two Dumas

Whereas the Fundamental Laws introduced numerous restrictions on the position and powers of the Duma, the electoral law emphasized its representative character. The electoral system, despite its complexities and limitations, such as the grouping of the electorate on a social basis, indirect elections, especially in the case of the peasants, and a gross underrepresentation of urban inhabitants, allowed almost all Russian men to participate in the elections to the Duma, thus transforming overnight the empire of the tsars from a country with no popular representation to one which practiced virtually universal manhood suffrage. The relatively democratic nature of the electoral law resulted partly from Witte's decision in December 1905, at the time when the law received its final formulation, to make concessions to the popular mood. More significantly, it reflected the common assumption in government circles that the peasants, the simple Russian people, would vote for their tsar and for the Right. After a free election, the First Duma convened on May 10, 1906.

Contrary to its sanguine expectations, the government had suffered a decisive electoral defeat. According to Walsh, the 497 members of the First Duma could be classified as follows: 45 deputies belonged to parties of the Right; 32 belonged to various national and religious groups, for example, the Poles and the Muslims; 184 were Cadets; 124 were representatives of different groups of the Left; and 112 had no party affiliation. The Cadets with 38 percent of the deputies thus emerged as the strongest political party in the Duma, and they had the added advantage of an able and articulate leadership well-versed in parliamentary procedure. Those to the Left of the Cadets, on the other hand, lacked unity and organization and wanted mainly to fight against the regime, purely and simply. The cause of the Left in the First Duma had been injured by the fact that both the Socialist Revolutionaries and the Social Democrats had largely boycotted the election to the Duma. The deputies with no political affiliation were mostly peasants who refused to align themselves permanently with any of the political groupings, but belonged in a general sense to the opposition. The government received support only from the relatively few members of the unregenerate Right and also from the more moderate Octobrists. The Octobrists, as their name indicates, split from the Cadets over the October Manifesto, which they accepted as a proper basis for Russian constitutionalism, while the Cadets chose to consider it as the first step on the road to a more democratic system.

Not surprisingly, the government and the Duma could not work together. The emperor and his ministers clearly intended the Duma to occupy a position subordinate to their own, and they further infuriated many deputies by openly favoring the extreme Right. The Duma, in its turn, also proved quite intractable. The Left wanted merely to oppose and obstruct. The Cadets, while much more moderate and constructive, seem to have overplayed their hand: they demanded a constituent assembly, they considered the First Duma to be, in a sense, the Estates-General of 1789, and they objected to the Fundamental Laws, thus in effect telling the government to abdicate. Similarly, while they insisted on a political amnesty, they refused to proclaim their opposition to terrorism, lest their associates to the Left be offended. But the most serious clash came over the issue of land: the Duma wanted to distribute to the peasants the state, imperial family, and Church lands, as well as the estates of landlords in excess of a certain maximum, compensating the landlords; the government proclaimed alienation of private land inadmissible, even with compensation. The imperial regime continued to the last to stand on the side of the landlords. After seventy-three days and forty essentially fruitless sessions, Nicholas II dissolved the First Duma.

The dissolution had a strange sequel. Some two hundred Duma deputies, over half of them Cadets, met in the Finnish town of Viborg and signed a manifesto that denounced the government and called for passive resistance by the people. It urged them not to pay taxes or answer the draft call until the convocation of a new Duma. Although the Viborg Manifesto cited as its justification certain irregularities in the dissolution of the First Duma, in itself it constituted a rash and unconstitutional step. And it turned out to be a blunder as well, for the country failed to respond. The Viborg participants were sentenced to three months in jail. More important, they lost the right to stand for election to the Second Duma which was thus deprived of much of its potential leadership.

In contrast to the first election, the government exerted all possible pressure to obtain favorable results in the election to the Second Duma, and it was assisted by the fact that much of Russia remained in a state of emergency. But the results again disappointed the emperor and his associates. Although—as one authoritative calculation has it—the Duma opposition, including mainly the Cadets and the Left, might have declined from 69 to 68 percent of the total number of deputies, it also became more extreme. In fact, a polarization of political opinion, with both wings gaining at the expense of the center, constituted the most striking aspect of the election. More specifically, the Cadet representation declined from 184 to 99 deputies, while the Social Democrats and the Socialist Revolutionaries, who this time participated fully in the election, gained respectively 64 and 20 seats. The entire Left membership in the Duma rose from 124 to 216 deputies. Significantly, the Duma personnel underwent a sweeping change, with only 31 members serving both in the First Duma and in the Second, a result not only of the penalties that followed the Viborg Manifesto, but also of a preference for more extreme candidates. Significantly too, the number of unaffiliated deputies declined by about 50 percent in the Second Duma.

The Second Duma met on March 5, 1907, and lasted for a little more than three months. It also found itself promptly at an impasse with the government. Moreover, its special opponent, the prime minister, was no longer the nonentity Ivan Goremykin—who had replaced the first constitutional prime minister, Witte, early in 1906—but the able and determined Peter Stolypin. Before it could consider Stolypin's important land reform, he had the Second Duma dissolved on the sixteenth of June, using as a pretext its failure to comply immediately with his request to lift the immunity of fifty-five, and particularly of sixteen, Social Democratic deputies whom he wanted to arrest for treason.

The Change in the Electoral Law and the Last Two Dumas

On the same day, June 16, 1907, Nicholas II and his minister arbitrarily and unconstitutionally changed the electoral law. The tsar mentioned as justification his historic power, his right to abrogate what he had granted, and his intention to answer for the destinies of the Russian state only before the altar of God who had given him his authority! The electoral change was, of course, meant to create a Duma that would co-operate with the government. The peasant representation was cut by more than half and that of the workers was also drastically cut, whereas the gentry gained representation quite out of proportion to its number. Also, Poland, the Caucasus, and some other border areas lost deputies; and the representation of Central Asia was entirely eliminated on the ground of backwardness. At the same time the election procedure became more indirect and more involved, following in part the Prussian model. In addition, the minister of the interior received the right to manipulate electoral districts. It has been calculated that the electoral change of June 1907 produced the following results: the vote of a landlord counted roughly as much as the votes of four members of the upper bourgeoisie, or of sixty-five average middle-class people, or of 260 peasants, or of 540 workers. To put it differently, 200,000 members of the landed gentry were assured of 50 percent of the seats in the Duma.

The electoral change finally provided the government with a co-operative Duma. And indeed, by contrast with the first two Dumas which lasted but a few months each, the Third Duma served its full legal term of five years, from 1907 to 1912, while the Fourth also continued for five years, from 1912 until the revolution of March 1917, which struck just before the Fourth Duma was to end. In the Third Duma the government had the support of some 310 out of the total of 442 deputies: about 160 representatives of the Right and about 150 Octobrists. The opposition, reduced to 120 seats, encompassed 54 Cadets, smaller numbers of other moderates, and only 33 deputies of the former Left. The Socialist Revolutionaries, it might be noted, boycotted the Third and Fourth Dumas. To indicate another aspect of the change, it has been calculated that whereas non-Great Russians had composed almost half of the member-ship of the First Duma, in the Third there were 377 Great Russians and 36 rep-resentatives of all the other nationalities of the empire.

In the election of 1912 the government made a determined effort to obtain a Right majority that would eliminate its dependence on the Octobrist vote, but it could not quite accomplish its purpose. The Fourth Duma contained approx-imately 185 representatives of the Right, 98 Octobrists, and 150 deputies to the left of the Octobrists. Because of their crucial central position, the Octobrists continued to play a major role in the Duma, although their number had been drastically diminished. For the rest, the gain of the Right found a certain coun-terbalance in the gain of the Left.

The Octobrists, who had replaced the Cadets after the electoral change of June 1907 as the most prominent party in the Duma, represented both the less conservative country gentry and business circles. While their Left wing touched the Cadets, Right Octobrists stood close to the old-fashioned Right. The party enjoyed the advantages of skillful leadership, in particular the lead-ership of Alexander Guchkov, and operated well in a parliament. The Octobrist deputies, it might be noted, were the wealthiest group in the last two Dumas. The Cadets, who became the loudest voice of the Duma opposition, were, above all, the party of professional people, although their influence extended to large layers of the middle class, especially perhaps of the upper middle class, as well as to some landlords and other groups. The Right, which consisted of more than one party, defended to the limit the interests of the landlords, although it also made demagogic efforts to obtain broader support and paraded some priests and peasants in the Dumas. Bitter dissatisfaction, wide-spread among the Russian masses, found a modicum of expression in the Duma Left.

Stolypin's Policy

With the Duma under control, the government could develop its own legisla-tive program. The architect of the program, Stolypin, has been described as the last truly effective and important minister of imperial Russia. Indeed, historian A. Asher has argued that Stolypin's "drive and persistence" and "command-ing presence" were decisive in shaping the government's policies in the years 1906–11. Stolypin's aim consisted of "pacification" and reform. "Pacification" meant an all-out struggle against the revolutionaries, for, although the mass opposition movements characteristic of 1905 no longer threatened the regime,

Prime Minister Peter Stolypin. Contemporaries and historians have viewed Stolypin variously as the Russian leader doing the most to avert revolution through reform in the years after 1905 and as undermining progress by weakening the Duma and brutally repressing dissent. (Central State Archive of Film, Photographic, and Sound Documents of St. Petersburg)

terrorism continued on a large scale. Practiced especially by the Battle Organization of the Socialist Revolutionaries and by the Socialist Revolutionaries-Maximalists who had split from the main party, terrorism caused some 1,400 deaths in 1906 and as many as 3,000 in 1907. The victims included police officers and agents, various officials, high and low, and numerous innocent bystanders. In August 1906, for example, the Maximalists blew up Stolypin's suburban residence, killing 32 persons and wounding many others, including the prime minister's son and daughter, but not the prime minister himself.

Stolypin acted with directness and severity. By the end of 1906, 82 areas in the Russian Empire had been placed under different categories of special regulations; also, the publication of 206 newspapers had been stopped, and over 200 editors had been brought to court. Moreover, Stolypin introduced sum-

mary courts-martial, consisting of officers without juridical training, which
tried those accused of terrorism and rebellion. The trials and the execution of
sentences were carried out within a matter of some two days or even a few
hours. Although the special courts-martial lasted only several months—
because Stolypin never submitted the law creating them to the Duma and it
expired two months after the Second Duma had met—they led to the execution
of well over a thousand persons. "Stolypin's necktie"—the noose—became
proverbial in Russia. The policy of "pacification" succeeded on the whole. The
Maximalists and many other terrorists were killed or executed, while numerous revolutionaries escaped abroad. A relative quiet settled upon the country.

It should be added that Stolypin continued to sponsor police infiltration of
the revolutionary movement and an extremely complex system of agents and
informers. Such police practices led, among other things, to the emergence of
remarkable double agents, the most notorious of whom, the unbelievable Evno
Azeff, successfully combined the roles of the chief informer on the Socialist
Revolutionaries and of leader of their Battle Organization. In the latter capacity he arranged the assassination of Plehve and other daring acts of terrorism.

Stolypin intended his "pacification" to constitute a prelude to important
changes, especially to a fundamental agrarian reform. That reform, introduced
by an imperial legislative order in the autumn of 1906, approved by the Third
Duma in the summer of 1910, and developed by further legislative enactments
in 1911, aimed at a break-up of the peasant commune and the establishment of
a class of strong, independent, individual farmers—Stolypin's so-called wager
on the strong and the sober. The emergence of a large group of prosperous and
satisfied peasants would, presumably, transform the Russian countryside from
a morass of misery and a hotbed of unrest into a conservative bulwark of the
regime.

The new legislation divided all peasant communes into two groups: those
that did not and those that did engage in land redistribution. In the first type
all peasants simply received their landholdings in personal ownership. In the
communes with periodic redistribution every householder could at any time
request that the land to which he was entitled by redistribution be granted to
him in personal ownership. He could also press the commune to give him the
land not in scattered strips, but in a single location; the commune had in effect
to comply with this request if separation occurred at the time of a general communal redistribution of land, and it had to meet the request "in so far as possible" at other times. Similarly, the commune had to divide its land into consolidated individual plots if requested to do so by not less than one-fifth of the
total number of householders. Moreover, separated peasants invariably
retained rights to common lands, meadows, forests, and the like. Indeed a partitioning even of pastures and grazing lands was permitted in 1911. Finally, the
commune could be entirely abolished: by a majority vote in the case of non-
repartitional communes, and by a two-thirds vote in the case of those that
engaged in a redistribution of land. It is significant that the reform made the
household elder the sole owner of the land of the household, replacing the former joint family ownership which remained only in the case of households
containing members other than the elder's lineal descendants.

Stolypin's major agrarian reform—the impact of which on Russian economy and society will be discussed in a later chapter—received support from a number of related government policies and measures. Notably, the Peasant Land Bank became much more active in helping peasants to buy land, while considerable holdings of the state and the imperial family were put up for sale to them. Also, reversing its earlier attitude, the government began finally to encourage and help peasant migration to new lands in Siberia and elsewhere in the empire. Stolypin's reform, it should be added, made peasants more equal legally to other classes, not only by reducing the power of the commune, but also by limiting that of land captains, and by exempting peasants from some special restrictions. In a different field of action, the ministers and the Dumas worked together to develop education, which made important advances during the last years of the imperial regime. In fact a law of 1908 foresaw schooling for all Russian children by 1922. The government also broadened labor legislation, worked to strengthen the army and national defense, and engaged in a variety of other useful activities.

However, all this fell short of fundamental reform. Only Stolypin's controversial agrarian legislation attempted a sweeping change in the condition of the Russian people, and even that legislation had perhaps too narrow a scope, for Stolypin was determined not to confiscate any gentry land, even with recompense. Moreover, progressive measures remained intertwined with reaction. Thus constitutional Russia witnessed a terrorism of the Right—for example the assassinations in 1906 and 1907 of two Cadet deputies to the First Duma—as well as a terrorism of the Left, and the terrorism of the Right usually went unpunished. Stolypin, himself from the Western borderlands, acted as a nationalist and a Russificator, for one thing reviving the ill-fated policy of trying to Russify Finland. Besides, the government lacked stability. The prime minister, who was after all something of a constitutionalist, antagonized much of the Right in addition to the Left. He managed to have one important piece of legislation enacted only by having the emperor prorogue the legislature for three days and suspend two leading members of the State Council; his high-handed tactics made the Octobrist leader Guchkov resign as chairman of the Third Duma. On September 14, 1911, Stolypin was fatally shot by a police agent associated with a revolutionary group. Stolypin's successor, Count Vladimir Kokovtsov, possessed intelligence and ability, but not his predecessor's determination or influence within the government. After a little more than two years he was replaced by the weak and increasingly senile Goremykin, who thus became prime minister for the second time. Goremykin assumed the leadership of the government in early 1914; in a matter of a few months he and Russia had to face the devastating reality of the First World War.

Russian Foreign Policy, 1905–14

Like the other powers, Russia stumbled into the First World War. The tsarist government contributed its share to international alignments, tensions, and crises, and in the fateful summer of 1914 it decided to support Serbia and thus resort to arms. Yet its part of the infamous "war guilt" should not be exaggerated or singled out. Russian ambitions and eagerness for war were no greater than those of other countries, while Russian preparedness for an armed conflict proved to be less. The empire of the tsars took no part in the race for colonies overseas which constituted an important aspect of the background of the First World War. Russian interests and schemes in the Balkans and the Near East were paralleled by those of Austria-Hungary and eventually also to some extent by those of Germany. The Pan-Germans were authentic cousins of the Pan-Slavs; and—a point which Fay and many others failed to appreciate—it was the German government, not the Russian, which enjoyed widespread popular support in its own country for a strong national policy. The fatal conflict erupted first between Austria-Hungary and Serbia, and both states can be charged with a responsibility for its tragic outcome which preceded Russia's. Even the early Russian mobilization found its counterpart in the Austrian. Besides, it deserves to be noted that in the summer of 1914 only Austria-Hungary, of all the powers, desired war, although it thought merely of a quick destruction of Serbia, not of a continental conflagration.

In the course of a personal meeting shortly before the opening of the Portsmouth Peace Conference, Emperor William II of Germany talked Nicholas II into signing a defensive alliance, known as the Treaty of Björkö. However, that agreement proved to be stillborn, because leading officials in both governments expressed strong objections to it and especially because France refused cooperation and held Russia to its obligations under the treaty of 1891–94. The years that followed the Russo-Japanese War witnessed an alienation of Russia from Germany, a virtual breakdown of Russo-Austrian relations, and at the same time a further *rapprochement* between Russia and France as well as the establishment of an Anglo-Russian Entente. The agreement with Great Britain, signed on August 31, 1907, was a landmark in Russian foreign policy, for it transformed a relationship of traditional and often bitter hostility into one of cordiality. That result was achieved through compromise in those areas where the interests of the two countries clashed: in Persia, Russia was assigned a large sphere of influence in the northern part of the country, and Great Britain a smaller one in the southeastern section, while the central area was declared neutral; Russia agreed to consider Afghanistan outside its sphere of influence and to deal with the Afghan ruler only through Great Britain, Great Britain in turn promising not to change the status of that country or interfere in its domestic affairs; both states recognized the suzerainty of China over Tibet. Because Great Britain and France had reached an agreement in 1904, the new accord marked the emergence of the Triple Entente of France, Russia, and Great Britain, poised against the Triple Alliance of Germany, Austria-Hungary, and Italy. On the Russian side, the Entente meant an effective military and political alliance with France and only a vague understanding with Great Britain. Yet, as already indicated, that understanding represented a major reorientation of Russian, as well as British, foreign policy, and it helped to group Europe into two camps. It should be added that the alignment with France and Great Britain gained in popularity in Russia in the years preceding the First World War. It attracted the support of liberals, of many radicals, of business circles closely linked to French and British capital, and also of numerous conservatives who veered toward Pan-Slavism or suffered from tariff wars with Germany and objected to tariff arrangements with that country as detrimental to Russian agriculture.

Alexander Izvolsky, the Russian minister of foreign affairs from 1906 to 1910, not only made an agreement with Great Britain, but also developed an active policy in the Balkans and the Near East. In fact he, his successor Serge Sazonov who headed the ministry from 1910 to 1916, and their various subordinates have been described as a new generation of Russian diplomats eager to advance Russian interests against Turkey and Austria-Hungary after a quarter-century of quiescence. To be sure, as early as 1896 the Russian ambassador in Constantinople, Alexander Nelidov, had proposed to his government that Russia seize the Straits, but that proposal was never implemented. Izvolsky devised a different scheme. In September 1908, in Buchlau, Moravia, he came to an agreement with the Austrian foreign minister, Count Alois von Aehrenthal: Russia would accept the Austrian annexation of Bosnia and Herzegovina, which Austria had been administering according to a decision of the Congress of Berlin; Austria-Hungary in turn would not object to the opening of the Straits to Russian warships. Austria-Hungary proceeded to annex Bosnia and Herzegovina before Russia could prepare diplomatically the desired reconsideration of the status of the Straits—a betrayal of the mutual understanding, according to Izvolsky, but not according to Aehrenthal. Betrayed or not, Russia was left holding the bag, because other powers, especially Great Britain, proved unwilling to see Russian warships in the Straits. The tsarist government experienced further humiliation when it hesitated to endorse the Austrian coup but was finally forced to do so after receiving a near-ultimatum from Germany.

The years following the annexation of Bosnia and Herzegovina witnessed repeated tensions, crises, and conflicts in the Balkans and the Near East. Like Austria-Hungary and Russia, Germany also pursued a forward policy in that area. William II visited Constantinople and made a point of declaring his friendly feelings for Turkey and the Muslims; German interests pushed the construction of the Berlin-Baghdad railway—a project they had initiated as early as 1898—and more German military experts came in 1913 to reorganize the Ottoman army. Two important Balkan wars were fought in 1912 and 1913. First Bulgaria, Serbia, Greece, and Montenegro combined to defeat Turkey and expand at Turkish expense. Next, the victors quarreled and the Bulgarians suffered a defeat by the Serbians, the Greeks, and the Montenegrins, as well as by the Romanians and by the Turks, who resumed hostilities to regain some of their losses. The Balkan wars left a legacy of tensions behind them, in particular making Bulgaria a dissatisfied and revisionist state and further exacerbating the relations between Austria-Hungary and Serbia.

When the heir to the Habsburg throne, Archduke Francis Ferdinand, was assassinated by Serbian patriots on June 28, 1914, and Austria delivered a crushing ultimatum to Serbia, the Russian government decided to support Serbia—the alternative was another, and this time complete, defeat in the Balkans. With the alliances operating almost automatically, Germany backed Austria-

Hungary, while France stood by Russia. Austria-Hungary declared war on Serbia on July 28, Germany on Russia on August 1 and on France on August 3. The German attack on Belgium brought Great Britain to the side of France and Russia on August 4. Europe entered the First World War.

Russia in the First World War

From the summer of 1914 until its collapse during the months that followed the overthrow of the imperial regime in 1917, the Russian army fought tenaciously and desperately under most difficult circumstances. The improvised offensive into East Prussia, which opened the hostilities and helped France at the most critical moment, ended in a shattering defeat of the Russians in the battles of Tannenberg and the Masurian Lakes. This offensive, General Michael Alekseev's epic retreat in Poland in 1915, the repeated offensives and counteroffensives in Galicia, and heavy fighting in numerous other sectors of the huge and shifting Eastern front cost the Russians enormous casualties. Quickly the Russian army ran out of its supply of weapons and ammunition, and for a period of time in 1915 up to 25 percent of Russian soldiers were sent to the front unarmed, with instructions to pick up what they could from the dead. Although later the Russian supply improved, the Russian forces remained vastly inferior to the German and the Austrian in artillery and other weapons.

The Allies could help little, for the German navy controlled the Baltic, and approaches through the Black Sea were cut off when Turkey joined the Central Powers in the autumn of 1914. The so-called Gallipoli campaign of the Allies, which aimed to break the Turkish hold on the Straits, failed in 1915. Bulgaria joined the Central Powers in October 1915 to help crush Serbia. The Romanian entry into the war on the side of the Entente at the end of August 1916 led to a catastrophic defeat of the Romanians and served to extend the Russian front. Yet the Russian troops went on fighting. In fact, they generally outfought the Austrians, and they also scored successes on the Caucasian front against Turkey. More important, in spite of many defeats and the necessity of retreating, they continued to force Germany to wage a major war on two fronts at the same time. As a British historian put it: "Despite all defects and difficulties, the Russians fought heroically, and made a decisive contribution to the course of the war." In the field of diplomacy, devoted during those years to the prosecution of the war and the formulation of war aims, the Russian government made a striking gain when in the spring of 1915 Great Britain and France agreed to the Russian acquisition of Constantinople, the Straits, and the adjoining littoral at the peace settlement. Italy, which joined the Entente at the end of August 1916, acquiesced in the arrangement.

While the Russian command made its share of military mistakes, the political mistakes of the Russian government proved to be both greater and more damaging. Nicholas II and his ministers failed to utilize the national rally that followed the outbreak of the war. In fact, they continued to rely on exclusively bureaucratic means to mobilize the resources of the nation, and they proceeded to oppress ethnic and religious minorities in the areas temporarily won from Austria as well as in home provinces. In particular, they failed to make

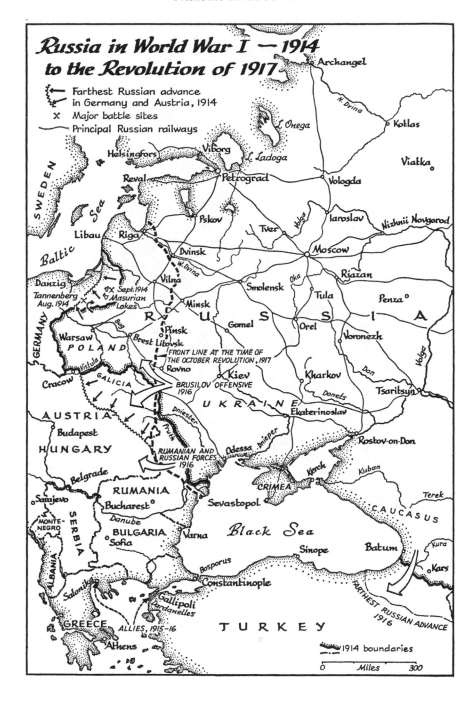

Russia in World War I — 1914 to the Revolution of 1917

Farthest Russian advance in Germany and Austria, 1914
x   Major battle sites
Principal Russian railways

Gregory Rasputin. A contemporary caricature, titled "The Russian Ruling House," portray-
ing Rasputin as controlling Nicholas and Alexandra as puppets. Many such images were in
circulation, often in the form of postcards—including some suggesting an immoral intimate
relationship between Rasputin and Alexandra.   (Fülöp-Miller, Rasputin)

the necessary concessions to the Poles. Russian defeats, the collapse of Russian
supply, and the utter incompetence of the war minister, General Vladimir
Sukhomlinov, as well as of some other high officials, did lead, to be sure, to certain adjustments. The Duma was finally called together in August 1915 for a
short session, Sukhomlinov and three of his colleagues had to resign, and the
government began to utilize the efforts of society to support the army. These
efforts, it should be added, which were led by public figures and industrialists
such as Guchkov, had developed on a large scale, ranging from work in the
Red Cross to widespread measures to increase production of military matériel.
The Zemstvo Union and the Union of Towns, which joined forces under the
chairmanship of Prince George Lvov, and the War Industry Committee, led by
Guchkov, became especially prominent.

But the *rapprochement* between the government and the public turned out to be slight and fleeting. Nicholas II would not co-operate with the newly created, moderate Progressive Bloc led by Miliukov, which included the entire membership of the Duma, except the extreme Right and the extreme Left, and which won majority support even in the State Council. Instead he came to rely increasingly on his wife Empress Alexandra and on her extraordinary advisor, the peasant Gregory Rasputin. Moreover, in spite of the protests of ten of his twelve ministers, the sovereign unwisely took personal command of the armed forces, which had been commanded by his relative Grand Duke Nicholas, leaving Alexandra and Rasputin in effective control in the capital. Thus a narrow-minded, reactionary, hysterical woman and an ignorant, weird peasant—who apparently made decisions simply in terms of his personal interest, and whose exalted position depended on the empress's belief that he could protect her son from hemophilia and that he had been sent by God to guide her, her husband, and Russia—had the destinies of an empire in their hands. Ministers changed rapidly in what has been described as a "ministerial leapfrog," and each was more under Rasputin's power than his predecessor. Eventually, after Rasputin's assassination, one of them claimed communion with Rasputin's spirit! That assassination, long and gruesome, took place at the end of December 1916. It was engineered by a leader of the extreme Right, a member of the imperial family, and another aristocrat related to the imperial family by marriage, who each tried to save the dynasty and Russia. As the year 1917 began, there were rumors of a palace coup that would restore sanity and leadership to the imperial government. But a popular revolution came first.

Chapter 32

The Economic and Social Development of Russia from the "Great Reforms" until the Revolutions of 1917

The last sixty years of Imperial Russia are not only in themselves a period of great historical interest: they are significant for other countries and other periods. The pattern of this period in Russia has repeated and is repeating itself elsewhere. It is not only in Russia, and not only in Europe, that the impact of the nineteenth- or twentieth-century West on a backward country has caused distortions and frustrations, has released revolutionary forces. New countries have been drawn into the world capitalist economy, into the rapid exchange of goods and ideas. The loss of centuries has to be made up in a few years. Improved communications, public order and sanitation increase population faster than output. The impoverished masses become more impoverished. The new ways create a new intelligentsia. The shrieking contrast between the old and the new drive a part of the intelligentsia to revolutionary ideas, and if political conditions make this necessary, to conspiratorial organization. The force which keeps such societies together is the bureaucracy. It holds the power, the privileges and the means of repression. From it and through it come such reforms as are permitted. It is outwardly impressive. It weighs heavily on the backs of the people. But like cast iron, though heavy it is also brittle. A strong blow can shatter it to pieces. When it is destroyed there is anarchy. Then is the moment for a determined group of conspiratorial revolutionary intellectuals to seize power.

H. SETON-WATSON

Whether the general well-being of the peasantry had shown improvement or decline—whether there had been within the peasant mass a tendency to draw together or to draw apart—still, as the day of revolt approached, there was no doubt of the existence in the countryside of a morass of penury sufficiently large, an antithesis between poverty and plenty sufficiently sharp, to give rise to what-

ever results might legitimately be bred and born of economic misery
and economic contrast.

ROBINSON

Who lives joyfully,
Freely in Russia?
NEKRASOV

T he "great reforms" made a division in the economic and social development of Russia. Even if we disregard the peculiar Soviet periodization, which
considers Russia as feudal from the late Kievan era until the emancipation of
the serfs and capitalistic from the emancipation of the serfs until 1917, the crucial significance of the "great reforms" must still be emphasized. In particular,
these reforms contributed immensely to the economic changes and the concomitant social shifts which characterized the empire of the Romanovs during
its last five or six decades and culminated in its downfall.

Every social class felt the impact of the "great reforms" and of their aftermath. The gentry, to be sure, remained the dominant social group in the country. In fact, as already indicated, both Alexander III and Nicholas II made every
effort to strengthen the gentry and to support its interests. Court circles consisted mainly of great landlords. The bureaucracy that ran the empire was
closely linked on its upper levels to the landlord class. The ministers, senators,
members of the State Council, and other high officials in the capital and the
governors, vice-governors, and heads of various departments in the provinces
belonged predominantly to the gentry. With the establishment in 1889 of land
captains to be appointed from the local gentry, Russia obtained a new network
of gentry officials who effectively controlled the peasants. A year later the zemstvo "counterreform" greatly strengthened the role of the gentry in local self-
government and emphasized the class principle within that government. In
the army most high positions were held by members of the landlord class,
while virtually the entire officer corps of the navy belonged to the gentry. The
government supported gentry agriculture by such measures as the establishment in 1885 of the State Gentry Land Bank which provided funds for the landlords on highly favorable terms.

Nevertheless, the gentry class declined after the "great reforms." Members
of the gentry owned 73.1 million *desiatin** of land according to the census of
1877, 65.3 million according to the census of 1887, 53.2 in 1905 according to a
statistical compilation of that year, and only 43.2 million desiatin in 1911
according to Oganovsky's calculations. At the same time, to quote Robinson:
"The average size of their holdings also diminished, from 538.2 *desiatinas* in
1887 to 488 in 1905; and their total possession of work horses from 546,000 in
1888–1891, to 499,000 in 1904–1906—that is, by 8.5 percent." Although the
emancipation settlement was on the whole generous to the gentry, it should be
kept in mind that a very large part of the wealth of that class had been mort-

---

*A *desiatina* equals 2.7 acres.

gaged to the state before 1861 and that, therefore, much of the compensation that the landlords received as part of the reform went to pay debts, rather little remaining for development and modernization of the gentry economy. Moreover, most landlords failed to make effective use of their resources and opportunities. Deprived of serf labor and forced to adjust to more intense competition and other harsh realities of the changing world, members of the gentry had little in their education, outlook, or character to make them successful capitalist farmers. A considerable number of landlords, in fact, preferred to live in Paris or Nice, spending whatever they had, rather than to face the new conditions in Russia. Others remained on their estates and waged a struggle for survival, but, as statistics indicate, frequently without success. Uncounted "cherry orchards" left gentry possession. The important fact, much emphasized by Soviet scholars, that a small segment of the gentry did succeed in making the adjustment and proceeded to accumulate great wealth in a few hands does not fundamentally change the picture of the decline of a dominant class.

The Industrialization of Russia

If the "great reforms" helped push the gentry down a steep incline, they also led to the rise of a Russian middle class, and in particular of industrialists, businessmen, and technicians—both results, to be sure, were not at all intentional. It is difficult to conceive of a modern industrial state based on serfdom, although, of course, the elimination of serfdom constituted only one prerequisite for the development of capitalism in Russia. Even after the emancipation the overwhelmingly peasant nature of the country convinced many observers that the empire of the tsars could not adopt the Western capitalist model as its own. The populists argued that the Russian peasant was self-sufficient, producing his own food and clothing, and that he, in his egalitarian peasant commune, did not need capitalism and would not respond to it. Perhaps more to the point, the peasant was miserably poor and thus could not provide a sufficient internal market for Russian industry. Also the imperial government, especially the powerful Ministry of the Interior, preoccupied with the maintenance of autocracy and the support of the gentry, for a long time in effect turned its back on industrialization.

Nevertheless, Russian industry continued to grow—a growth traced in detail by Goldsmith and others—and in the 1890s it shot up at an amazing rate, estimated by Gerschenkron at 8 percent a year on the average. Russian industrialists could finally rely on a better system of transportation, with the railroad network increasing in length by some 40 percent between 1881 and 1894 and doubling again between 1895 and 1905. In addition to Russian financial resources, foreign capital began to participate on a large scale in the industrial development of the country: foreign investment in Russian industry has been estimated at 100 million rubles in 1880, 200 million in 1890, and over 900 million in 1900. Most important, the Ministry of Finance under Witte, in addition to building railroads and trying to attract capital from abroad, did everything possible to develop heavy industry in Russia. To subsidize that industry Witte increased Russian exports, drastically curtailed imports, balanced the budget,

Count Sergei Witte in St. Petersburg in 1905.   (Terra Publishers)

introduced the gold standard, and used heavy indirect taxation on items of everyday consumption to squeeze the necessary funds out of the peasants. Thus, in Russian conditions, the state played the leading role in bringing large-scale capitalist enterprise into existence.

Toward the end of the century Russia possessed eight basic industrial regions, to follow the classification adopted by Liashchenko. The Moscow industrial region, comprising six provinces, contained textile industries of every sort, as well as metal processing and chemical plants. The St. Petersburg region specialized in metal processing, machine building, and textile industries. The Polish region, with such centers as Lodz and Warsaw, had textile, coal, iron, metal processing, and chemical industries. The recently developed south Russian Ukrainian region supplied coal, iron ore, and basic chemical products. The Ural area continued to produce iron, non-ferrous metals, and minerals. The Baku sector in Transcaucasia contributed oil. The southwestern region specialized in beet sugar. Finally, the Transcaucasian manganese-coal region supplied substantial amounts of its two products.

The new Russian industry displayed certain striking characteristics. Because Russia industrialized late and rapidly, the Russians borrowed advanced Western technology wholesale, with the result that Russian factories were often more modern than their Western counterparts. Yet this progress in certain segments of the economy went together with appalling backwardness in others. Indeed, the industrial process frequently juxtaposed complicated machinery and primitive manual work performed by a cheap, if unskilled, labor force. For technological reasons, but also because of government policy, Russia acquired huge plants and large-scale industries almost overnight. Before long the capitalists began to organize: a metallurgical syndicate was formed in 1902, a coal syndicate in 1904, and several others in later years. Russian entrepreneurs and employers, it might be added, came from different classes—from gentry to former serfs—with a considerable admixture of foreigners. Their leaders included a number of old merchant and industrialist families who were Old Believers, such as the celebrated Morozovs. As to markets, since the poor Russian people could absorb only a part of the products of Russian factories, the industrialists relied on huge government orders and also began to sell more abroad. In particular, because Russian manufactures were generally unable to compete successfully in the West, export began on a large scale to the adjacent Middle Eastern and Asian countries of Turkey, Persia, Afghanistan, Mongolia, and China. Again Witte and the government helped all they could by such means as the establishment of the Russo-Persian Bank and the Russo-Chinese Bank, and the building of the East China Railway, not to mention the Trans-Siberian. As already indicated, Russian economic activity in the Far East was part of the background of the Russo-Japanese War.

The great Russian industrial upsurge of the 1890s ended with the depression of 1900, produced by a number of causes, but perhaps especially by the "increasing weakness of the base," the exhaustion of the Russian peasantry. The depression lasted several years and became combined with political unrest and finally with the Revolution of 1905. Still, once order had been restored and the Russians returned to work, industrialization resumed its course. In fact, the last period of the economic development of imperial Russia, from the calling of the First Duma to the outbreak of the First World War, witnessed rapid industrialization, although it was not as rapid as in the 1890s, with an annual industrial growth rate of perhaps 6 percent compared to the 8 percent of the earlier period. The output of basic industries again soared, with the exception of the oil industry. Thus, counting in millions of *pudy** and using 1909 and 1913 as the years to be compared, the Russian production of pig iron rose from 175 to 283, of iron and steel from 163 to 246, of copper from 1.3 to 2.0, and of coal from 1,591 to 2,214.

The new industrial advance followed in many ways the pattern of the previous advance, for instance, in the emphases on heavy industry and on large plants. Yet it exhibited some significant new traits as well. With the departure

---

*A *pud* equals 36 pounds.

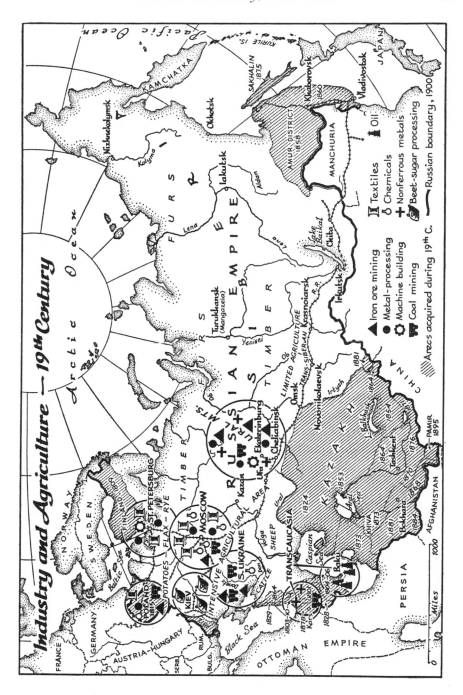

Industry and Agriculture — 19th Century

of Witte, the government stopped forcing the pace of industrialization, decreased the direct support of capitalists, and relaxed somewhat the financial pressure on the lower classes. Russian industry managed to make the necessary adjustments, for it was already better able to stand on its own feet. Also, industry often had the help of banks, which began to assume a guiding role in the economic development of the country. But, financial capital aside, Russian industrialists themselves were gradually gaining strength and independence. Also, it can well be argued that during the years immediately preceding the First World War Russian industry was becoming more diversified, acquiring a larger home market, and spreading its benefits more effectively to workers and consumers.

To be sure, the medal had its reverse side. In spite of increasing production in the twentieth century, imperial Russia was falling further behind the leading states of the West—or so it is claimed by many analysts. Just as the Russian government relied on foreign loans, Russian industry remained heavily dependent on foreign capital, which rose to almost two and a quarter billion rubles in 1916/17 and formed approximately one-third of the total industrial investment. The French, for example, owned nearly two-thirds of the Russian pig iron and one-half of the Russian coal industries, while the Germans invested heavily in the chemical and electrical engineering industries, and the British in oil. On the basis of investment statistics some analysts have even spoken of the "semi-colonial" status of Russia. More ominously, Russian industry rose on top of a bitter and miserable proletariat and a desperately poor peasant mass.

The Peasant Question

Peasants constituted the vast majority of the Russian people, at least three-quarters of the total population according to the census of 1897. In a sense, they were the chief and the most direct beneficiaries of the "great reforms," particularly since the serfs received their freedom and the state peasants escaped some of their bondage to the state. Yet, after the reforms, their condition remained the largest and the gravest problem in Russia. As mentioned, the emancipation provisions proved to be insufficient to develop a healthy peasant economy—whether any provisions would have sufficed is another matter—and some of these provisions were shown to be entirely unrealistic: at the time of the partition former serfs received considerably less than their half of the land, and they simply could not meet the redemption payments. Peasants themselves, scholars have argued, felt not only the impossibility of their new situation but also its injustice. The widespread belief among peasants that the land ought to belong to those who work it made any settlement that left in place large private land owners using hired labor likely disappointing. But it especially grated that the emancipation did not even give to peasants all of the land that they had formerly been farming for themselves. Moreover, the emancipation took a long time and followed an uneven course throughout Russia, with periods of transition and other delays to the peasants' full acquisition of their new status. And even that status, when finally attained, did not make the peasants equal to other social groups. Thus they possessed a separate administration and courts and, besides, were tied to the peasant commune in most of European Russia.

A staged photograph taken around 1900 by British photographer Netta Peacock of a meeting of the peasant commune (the mir), comprising heads of households. The mir has been interpreted variously as an instrument of the state for taxing and controlling peasants, a means of collective survival, an expression of peasant notions of moral order and justice, a form of primitive socialism on which basis a socialist society could be created in Russia, a backward hindrance to modern rural economic development, and a means for male patriarchs to exercise domination in the village. (Victoria and Albert Museum)

The communes, which received the land at the time of the emancipation, were made responsible for taxes and recruits and were in general intended to serve as bulwarks of order and organized life in the countryside. As a result, the commune became more important than ever in the lives of peasants. Acting through the periodic assembly of male heads of household, the commune made the major decisions about land use—what work should be done in each field, when it should be done, and by which methods—and periodically, according to tradition, redistributed the holdings, which were divided into scattered strips among peasant families on the basis of a calculus of hands to work and mouths to feed. The commune also carried out a wide range of administrative functions to sustain the village community. In addition to collecting taxes and designating military recruits, the commune controlled who had permission to work away from the village, investigated and punished petty crimes, maintained roads and bridges, kept up the local church or chapel, and cared for needy members of the community, especially widows and orphans without kin and the aged. No doubt they helped many peasants keep their bearings in post-reform Russia, and they usually provided at least minimal security for their members.

The price of communal life was high, however. In the view of many contemporaries (and historians have tended to agree, though debate continues), the commune tended to keep productivity low—and hence peasant need for more land high—by perpetuating backward, indeed archaic, agricultural production. To be sure, some circumstances were beyond the peasants' control, such as shortages in draft animals and fertilizer, the continued use of less efficient equipment such as wooden plows, and the lack of investment capital. But, it has been argued, low productivity was also the "fault" of communal agriculture. Since the land a peasant family worked might eventually belong to some other family through redistribution, individuals had little incentive to improve their soil through modern techniques such as fertilization, deep plowing, or crop diversification. The division of land into small strips in each field, in order that each household would receive land of every quality, resulted in much unused land between strips, led to inefficient use of time, and compelled conformity with the practices of one's neighbors. More generally, the heads of household who dominated the commune tended to see custom, not innovative scientific advice, as the best guide. At the same time communes greatly hampered peasant mobility and promoted ever-increasing overpopulation in the countryside. Members of a commune frequently found it difficult to obtain permission to leave, because their departure would force the commune to perform its set obligations to the state with fewer men. Also, where communes periodically redivided the land among the households, the head of the household could prevent the departure of one of its members on the ground that that would result in a smaller allotment of land to the household at the next reapportionment. As Gerschenkron commented: "Nothing was more revealing of the irrational way in which the village commune functioned than the fact that the individual household had to retain the abundant factor (labor) as a precondition for obtaining the scarce factor (land)."

Population in Russia grew rapidly after the emancipation: from over 73 million in 1861 to over 125 million according to the census of 1897 and almost 170 million in 1917. Land prices more than doubled between 1860 and 1905, and almost doubled again between 1905 and 1917. In spite of the fact that peasants purchased much of the land sold over a period of time by the gentry, individual peasant allotments kept shrinking. Russian economic historians have calculated that 28 percent of the peasant population of the country could not support itself from its land allotments immediately after the emancipation, and that by 1900 that figure had risen to 52 percent. That the allotments still compared reasonably well with the allotments of peasants in other countries proved to be cold comfort, for with the backward conditions of agriculture in Russia they plainly did not suffice. The average peasant ownership of horses also declined sharply, with approximately one-third of peasant households owning no horses by 1901. The peasants, of course, tried a variety of ways to alleviate their desperate plight, from periodic employment in the cities to migration, but with limited success at best. They worked as hard as they could, exhausting themselves and the land, and competing for every bit of it. In this marginal economy droughts became disasters, and the famine of 1891 was a shattering catastrophe. But even without outright famine peasants died rapidly. At the beginning of the twentieth century, the annual death rate for European Russia, with the countryside leading the cities, stood at 31.2 per thousand, compared to 19.6 in France and 16 in England. Naturally, conditions differed in the enormous Russian Empire, with Siberian peasants, for example, reasonably prosperous. On the other hand, perhaps the worst situation prevailed in the thickly populated provinces of central European Russia—caused by the so-called "pauperization of the center." How the peasants themselves felt about their lot became abundantly clear in the agrarian disturbances culminating in the massive upheavals of 1905–7.

To appreciate the burden that the Russian peasant had to carry, we should take further note of the fiscal system of the empire. Thus, an official inquiry indicated that after the emancipation the peasants paid annually to the state in taxes, counting redemption payments, ten times as much per desiatina of land as did members of the gentry. And even after the head tax was abolished in 1886 and the redemption payments were finally canceled in 1905, the impoverished masses continued to support the state by means of indirect taxes. These taxes, perennially the main source of imperial revenue, were levied on domestic and imported items of everyday consumption such as vodka, sugar, tea, tobacco, cotton, and iron. The tax on alcohol, which Witte made a state monopoly in 1894, proved especially lucrative. While relentless financial pressure forced the peasants to sell all they could, the government, particularly Witte, promoted the export of foodstuffs, notably grain, to obtain a favorable balance of trade and finance the industrialization of Russia. Foodstuffs constituted almost two-thirds in value of all Russian exports in the first years of the twentieth century compared to some two-fifths at the time of the emancipation.

However, the last years of imperial Russia, the period from the Revolution of 1905 to the outbreak of the First World War, brought some hope and improvement—many authorities claim much hope and great improvement—into the lives of the Russian peasants, that is, the bulk of the Russian people. The upswing resulted from a number of factors. As already indicated, the industrialization of Russia no longer demanded or obtained the extreme sacrifices characteristic of the 1890s, and the new Russian industry had more to offer to the consumer. The national income in fifty provinces of European Russia rose, according to Prokopovich's calculation, from 6,579.6 million rubles in 1900 to 11,805.5 million in 1913. In 1913 the per capita income for the whole Russian Empire amounted to 102.2 rubles, a considerable increase even if highly inadequate compared to the figures of 292 rubles for Germany, 355 for France, 463 for England, or 695 for the United States. Luckily, the years preceding the First World War witnessed a series of bountiful harvests. Russian peasants profited, in addition, from a remarkable growth of the co-operative movement, and from government sponsorship of migration to new lands. Co-operatives multiplied from some 2,000 in 1901 and 4,500 in 1905 to 33,000 at the outbreak of the First World War, when their membership extended to 12 million people. Credit and consumers' co-operatives led the way, although some producers' co-operatives, such as Siberian creamery co-operatives, also proved highly successful. As to migration, the government finally began to support it after the Revolution of 1905 by providing the necessary guiding agencies and also by small subsidies to the migrants, suspension of certain taxes for them, and the like. In 1907 over half a million people moved to new lands and in 1908 the annual number of migrants rose to about three-quarters of a million. After that, however, it declined to the immediate pre-war average of about 300,000 a year. Land under cultivation increased from 88.3 million desiatin in 1901–5 to 97.6 million in 1911–13. Also as mentioned earlier, the Peasant Land Bank became much more active, helping peasants to purchase over 4.3 million desiatin of land in the decade from 1906 to 1915, compared to 0.96 million in the preceding ten years. State and imperial family lands amounting to about a million and a quarter desiatin were offered for sale to the peasants.

Stolypin's land reform could well be considered the most important factor of all in the changing rural situation, because it tried to transform the Russian countryside. Stolypin's legislation of 1906, 1910, and 1911—outlined in the preceding chapter—aimed at breaking up the peasant commune and at creating a strong class of peasant proprietors. These peasant proprietors were to have their land in consolidated lots, not in strips. In a relatively brief span of years, the reform had considerable impact, though historians still debate how deep the changes went and what the precise effects of the changes were. Most agree that by January 1, 1916, only 24 percent of formerly communal households completed their legal withdrawal from the commune, thus transforming their lands into personal ownership. But many scholars emphasize greater spread and potentiality of the reform. Although only 470,000 households in non-repartitional communes had time to receive legal confirmation of their new independent status, the law of 1910 made in effect all householders in such communes individual proprietors. Two million would thus be a more realistic figure than 470,000. If we make this adjustment and if we add to the newly established independent households the three million or more hereditary tenure households in areas where communal ownership had never developed, we obtain for European Russia at the beginning of 1916 over seven million individual proprietary households out of the total of thirteen or fourteen million. In other words, peasant households operating within the framework of the peasant commune had declined to somewhat less than half of all peasant households in Russia. Consolidation of strips, a crucial aspect of the reform, proceeded much more slowly than separation from the commune, but it too made some progress. One important set of figures indicates that of the almost two and a half million households that had left communes somewhat more than half had been provided with consolidated farms by 1916.

Still, these impressive statistics do not necessarily indicate the ultimate wisdom and success of Stolypin's reform. True, Stolypin has received much praise from many specialists, including post-Soviet Russian historians and such American scholars as Treadgold, who believe that the determined prime minister was in fact saving the empire and that, given time, his agrarian reform would have achieved its major objective of transforming and stabilizing the countryside. But critics have also been numerous and by no means limited to populists or other defenders of the commune as such. They have pointed, for example, to the limited scope of Stolypin's reform, which represented, in a sense, one more effort to save gentry land by making the peasants redivide what they already possessed, and to the element of compulsion in the carrying out of the reform. They argued that the reform had largely spent itself without curing the basic ills of rural Russia. Moreover, it added new problems to the old ones, in particular by helping to stratify the peasant mass and by creating hostility between the stronger and richer peasants whom the government helped to withdraw from the commune on advantageous terms and their poorer and more egalitarian brethren left behind.

While strong communal life in the village preserved much that was traditional in the everyday peasant experience, much was changing in peasant experiences and expectations, especially in the early years of the twentieth century. With enormous consequence, peasants were becoming less and less a "world apart." Partly, this resulted from the policies of the government, which began, after the turn of the century, to remove some of the disabilities that marked peasants as a distinct and legally inferior social estate. Collective responsibility for tax payment was ended in 1903, corporal punishment was abolished in 1904, and Stolypin's reforms aimed at freeing peasants from the rule of the commune. In addition, various outsiders to the village (educated reformers, teachers, clergy, and others) were an increasing presence, organizing cooperatives, mutual assistance organizations, lectures and readings, theaters, and temperance societies. The expansion of schooling and literacy (discussed in the next chapter) and the huge rise in newspapers and literature directed at common people (which even the illiterate could hear read and discussed in village taverns and tearooms) exposed peasants in unprecedented ways to knowledge of the larger world. Perhaps most important, Russia's continuing economic development made it possible for many peasants to leave the village for industrial and urban work. This experience affected the lives of millions of peasants—not only the migrants themselves but also their kin and fellow villagers when these individuals returned to the countryside after seasonal or temporary industrial or commercial work, on holidays, or after becoming sick or aged. In quite tangible ways, peasant everyday life was changing. Many peasants, especially younger men and women who had been to the city, demonstrated new social values (for example, in personal and sexual relations), began wearing urban-style clothing, and purchased, or at least desired, commodities such as clocks, urban furniture, stylish boots and hats, porcelain dishes, and cosmetics. Raised expectations and stimulated desire, of course, could also bring greater frustration.

Labor

The industrialization of Russia created, of course, a considerable working class. While Russians began to work in factories in the Urals and elsewhere far back in history, as mentioned in previous chapters, a sizeable industrial proletariat grew in Russia only toward the end of the nineteenth century. Russian industrial workers numbered over 2 million in 1900 and perhaps 3 million out of a population of about 170 million in 1914. Not impressive in quantity in proportion to total population, the proletariat was more densely massed in Russia than in other countries. Because of the heavy concentration of Russian industry, over half the industrial enterprises in Russia employed more than 500 workers each, with many employing more than 1,000 each. The workers thus formed large and closely knit groups in industrial centers, which included St. Petersburg and Moscow.

True, the term "worker" may be too definitive and precise as applied to the Russian situation. Populists, Marxists, and scholars of other persuasions, as well as Western specialists such as Zelnik and Johnson, have debated the extent to which Russian workers remained—or ceased to be—peasants. These workers usually came from the village. Often they belonged to the village commune, left their families behind in the village, and spent a part of every year there, gathering harvest and performing other peasant tasks. For them the village remained their home, while the factory became a novel way to earn obrok, so to speak. When a close relationship with the village ceased, many factory hands still maintained their membership in it and sought to retire to it to end their days in peace. And even after all important ties with the countryside were broken and workers were left entirely and permanently on their own in towns and cities, they could not shed overnight their peasant mentality and outlook. The Russian proletariat tended to be not only the pride but also the despair of the Marxists both before and after 1917. In fact, in the years following the October Revolution much of it vanished into the countryside. Nevertheless, the Marxists were right in their argument with the populists to the extent that they emphasized the continuing growth of capitalism and the proletariat in Russia. With all due qualifications, from the 1880s on, an industrial working class constituted a significant component of Russian population, an essential part of Russian economy, and a factor in Russian politics.

As noted in an earlier chapter, the government initiated modern labor legislation in the 1880s, when Minister of Finance Bunge tried to eliminate or curb certain glaring abuses of the factory system and established factory inspectors to supervise the carrying out of new laws. More legislation followed later, with a law in 1897 applicable to industrial establishments employing more than 20 workers that limited day work of adults to eleven and a half hours and night work to ten hours. The ten-hour day was also to prevail on Saturdays and on the eve of major holidays, while no work was allowed on Sundays or the holidays in question. Adolescents and children were to work no more than ten and nine hours a day respectively. A pioneer labor insurance law, holding the employers responsible for accidents in connection with factory work, came out in 1903, but an improved and effective labor insurance act, covering both accidents and illness, appeared only in 1912. Unions were finally allowed in 1906, and even then exclusively on the local, not the national, level.

However, in spite of labor legislation, and also in spite of the fact that wages probably increased in the years preceding the First World War, Russian workers remained in general in miserable condition. Workers endured overcrowded housing with often deplorable sanitary conditions, an exhausting workday (ten hours a day, six days a week, even after the reforms of the late nineteenth century), widespread disease (notably tuberculosis) and high rates of premature mortality (made worse by pervasive alcoholism), constant risk of injury from poor safety conditions, harsh workplace discipline, and inadequate wages. The proletariat of imperial Russia represented in effect an excellent example of a destitute and exploited labor force, characteristic of the early stages of capitalist development and described so powerfully by Marx in *Capital*. The positive benefits of urban industrial life also affected the lives of urban workers, though these could be just as dangerous to the social and political status quo. Acquiring new skills and learning to cope with city life often gave workers a new sense of self-respect and confidence, which in turn tended to raise desires and expectations. The expanding array of consumer goods could

Aleksei Medvedev, a compositor, around 1903. A worker in a Moscow printing house, Medvedev was one of the organizers of a printers' strike in 1903 and of an illegal trade union, one of the first in Russia. Dressing in "bourgeois" fashion was a common gesture among "conscious" workers, meant to signal respectability and a recognition of their own human dignity, the violation of which was a central theme in workers' protests. (Moskovskie pechatniki v 1905 godu)

provide new pleasures and hope, but with very limited incomes workers were just as likely to feel envy and anger. As urban workers were more likely than peasants to become literate, they were also more readily exposed to new ideas and possibilities.

Not surprisingly, workers began to organize to better their lot. Indeed, they exercised at times sufficient pressure to further labor legislation, notably in the case of the law of 1897, and they were not deterred by the fact that unions remained illegal until after the Revolution of 1905 and were still hampered and suspected by the government thereafter. The first significant strikes occurred in St. Petersburg in 1878 and 1879 and at a Morozov textile factory near Moscow in 1885. The short-lived but important Northern Workers' Union, led by a worker and populist, Stephen Khalturin, helped to organize the early labor movement in the capital. Major strikes took place in the '90s, not only in St. Petersburg, but also in Riga, in industrial areas of Russian Poland, and in new plants in the Ukraine. In addition, railwaymen struck in several places. The strike movement again gathered momentum in the first years of the twentieth century, culminating, as we know, in the Revolution of 1905. Strikes broke out in almost every industry and every part of the country. Trade unions and soviets proliferated. The government legalized strikes in December 1905 and unions in March 1906, clearly hoping that legalizing strikes and unions and allowing workers to vote for representatives to the new State Duma would lead the labor movement onto a more peaceful path. Initially, this appeared to be precisely what happened. Thousands of workers joined the legal unions and concentrated on attaining better economic conditions. For their leaders, workers tended to choose activists from the more moderate wing of Social Democrats, the Mensheviks, who emphasized, at least for the short term, legal struggle for realizable and mainly liberal-democratic gains. This moderation of the labor movement did not continue, however. The fault was partly the government's. Although trade unions were authorized by law, they remained under very close surveillance and control by the police, who regularly closed meetings, arrested leaders, and shut down union papers. Meanwhile, employers formed their own strong organizations and endeavored, often with success, to take back economic gains workers had made in 1905. When the strike movement revived in 1910–14, workers' frustrations were sharply visible, not only in the stubborn persistence of strikers and the revival of political demands, but also in the growing popularity of the more radical Bolsheviks. Many unions elected Bolshevik majorities to their governing boards. And in the fall of 1912, Bolsheviks won a majority of workers' votes to the Duma in almost all industrial electoral districts. Strikes became especially frequent after the massacre of workers in the Lena gold fields in April 1912, when police fired into a crowd of protesting workers killing and wounding more than a hundred of them. In 1912, 725,000 workers went out on strike, 887,000 in 1913, and over a million and a quarter from January to July in 1914. In July 1914, only days before the outbreak of war, a large and sometimes violent strike broke out in St. Petersburg, echoing a strike in the Baku oil fields.

Workers' strike demands often combined the economic with the political, but they also very often included what historians have called moral demands for decent treatment that respected workers' "dignity." At the same time, labor protest could contain a great deal of bitter resentment and anger, even violence. Of course, evidence of labor protest is not the whole of the story of working-class mentalities. Many activists among workers, and many "conscious" workers themselves, regularly complained that the average working-class man lived most of the time a debased life marked by drunkenness, passivity before fate, and crass tastes in boulevard fiction, the music hall, and (by the eve of the war) low-brow popular cinema. Working-class women, in turn, were viewed as victims—of men's lies about wages spent on drink or of men's fists—and as lost in even deeper "backwardness" than most male workers.

Civil Society

One of the most consequential developments in Russian life after the Great Reforms, recent scholarship has emphasized, was the expansion of the public sphere in the late 1800s and early 1900s. The growth of a civic space in which organized associations mediate between the individual and the state, citizens communicate with one another on matters of general interest, and public opinion takes shape dramatically altered the social terrain in Russia, with enormous implications for politics. A major site for the development of civil society were voluntary associations, which proliferated in the late 1800s and after. These included learned societies, literacy and temperance societies, business and professional associations, philanthropic and service organizations, workers' mutual assistance funds, and varied cultural associations and circles. Already before the de facto press freedom of 1905 and the official freeing of the press from preliminary censorship in 1906, newspapers (including a mass circulation daily press), magazines, journals, and books had become pervasive and powerful media for disseminating and exchanging information and ideas. In addition, universities, public schools, law courts, organizations of local rural and urban self-government, and even the Church stood on the uncertain boundaries of being at once state and civil institutions, though offering an important space for individuals to be involved in the emerging public life. The Revolution of 1905, as we have seen, unleashed civic opinion and organization as never before. The increase of civil rights resulting from 1905 gave these further impetus, including enabling the formation of legal political parties and other new types of civic associations. While most of these organizations concerned themselves with everyday secular matters, religion also thrived in this expanding public sphere, though often running outside the official channels of the established Church. For example, a series of Religious-Philosophical Meetings in St. Petersburg, begun at the end of 1901, brought together prominent intellectuals and clergy to discuss the meaning of religion in public life. After 1905, religious associations such as the Spiritualist Society and the Russian Theosophical Society formed. We also see a revival of religious enthusiasm and organization among the urban middle and lower classes, including gatherings in taverns to talk about religion, the charismatic movement known as the "Brethren," Tolstoyans, and growing and increasingly visible congregations of religious dissenters, ranging from Baptists to well-established Russian groups

The Passazh *on Nevsky prospect, St. Petersburg, 1901. Palaces of commerce, department stores were not only economically central to the rise of a consumer life in Russia but characteristically modern locations as sites for public display (of both products and people) and desire.* (Central State Archive of Film, Photographic, and Sound Documents of St. Petersburg)

like the Molokany ("milk drinkers") or Skoptsy ("castrates") to new sectarian groups.

These years also saw the rise of public movements to extend rights to disadvantaged groups. We have already described the rise of the labor movement. Also in these years arose organized efforts to promote women's rights and emancipation. During 1905, women were often heard at meetings appealing for respect as human beings and for equal rights as citizens. A series of women's organizations and publications emerged to promote the cause, such as the All-Russian Union for Women's Equality, and feminist and women's groups joined together in a series of women's congresses (on women's rights, the struggle against prostitution, and women's education). In the non-Russian areas of the empire, but also among ethnic and religious minorities living in the major Russian cities, these were years of widespread nationalist activism. Many groups—Poles, Ukrainians, Finns, Balts, Jews, Georgians, Armenians, Muslims, and others—defined themselves as "nations" (a modern concept gaining increasing resonance), and activists organized movements seeking cultural autonomy and perhaps an independent nation state. Changes in the lives and expectations of non-Russians, however, were not limited to the history of political and nationalist movements. For many non-Russian communities, these were also years of exploring new possibilities and new identities—likely more than we know, as historians are still only beginning to research this non-Russian side of Russian history. Among Jews, for example, we see the rise around the turn of the century and after of schools promoting Hebrew or Yiddish along with growing numbers of Russian-educated Jews, the emergence of a new Jewish literature and a Jewish periodical press, increasing secular studies in traditional Jewish schools, and organized political movements of both Jewish socialism, which sought a transformed Russian Empire, and Zionism, which sought salvation in a new land. We see similar movements of national revival and organization, especially after 1905, among Russia's Muslims—Tatars, Azeris, Central Asians, and others. Muslim organizations proliferated—including libraries, charities, credit unions, national congresses, and political unions and parties—expressing ideologies ranging from liberalism and socialism to Pan-Islamism and Pan-Turkism.

The daily newspaper, itself an institution at the center of Russia's increasingly vital civic life, reminded readers of how deeply contradictory this life was. On the one hand, newspapers reported the best of what modern life produced: scientific and technical knowledge, opportunities for upward mobility, increasing numbers of institutions of culture (museums, schools, libraries, exhibitions, theaters), and civic organizations of all sorts. Regular ads as well as daily reportage pointed to Russia's emerging consumer life, most evident in the rise of department stores, like Moscow's famous Muir and Merrilies, and glass-covered arcades like the St. Petersburg "Passage," which displayed goods designed not only to cater to material needs but to stimulate new notions of being visibly fashionable and respectable. The papers also kept readers informed about the many public entertainments available to those with at least some disposable income (though even workers saved for such pleasures), such as music halls, nightclubs, outdoor summer "pleasure gardens," and theaters at all price levels. At the same time, the press reminded readers of the dark sides of modern public life: the egoistic and predatory practices of some merchants and employers, frightening attacks on respectable citizens and civic order by irrational "hooligans," the pervasive dangers and depredations of con-artists, thieves, and burglars, sexual licentiousness and debauchery, murder and suicide, widespread public drunkenness, neglected and abandoned children (who often turned to street crime and vice), and the spread of diseases such as syphilis, tuberculosis, and cholera that were seen as nurtured by the very conditions of urban public life.

Conclusion

Various evaluations have been given of Russia's social and economic development in the last years of the empire. Whereas Gerschenkron, Karpovich, Pavlovsky, and other scholars have emphasized progress and grounds for optimism, Soviet authorities, as well as such Western specialists as Von Laue, concluded that in spite of all efforts—perhaps the maximum efforts possible under the old regime—Russia was not solving its problems either in terms of its own requirements or by comparison with other countries. Most close students of the period have come out with the feeling—so pronounced in Robinson's valuable work on rural Russia—that, whether the conditions of life in Russia improved or declined on the eve of the First World War, they remained desperately hard for the bulk of the population.

It has been said that revolutions occur not when the people are utterly destitute, oppressed beyond all measure, and deprived of hope—crushing conditions lead only to blind and fruitless rebellions—but when there is growth, advancement, and high expectation, hampered, however, by an archaic and rigid established order. Such a situation existed in Russia in the early twentieth century: in economic and social matters as well as in politics.

Chapter 33

Russian Culture from the "Great Reforms" until the Revolutions of 1917

There is only one evil among men—ignorance; against this evil there is only one medicine—learning; but this medicine must be taken not in homeopathic doses, but by the pail and by the forty-pail barrel.

PISAREV

The three points where the new man thought he had made himself most secure were: first, his liberation from all the values and institutions of the *status quo*; second, his complete faith in human reason and the principles it made known to him; and finally, his assurance that he was the personal instrument of the historical process.... They were convinced that they had found the path to a state of personal engagement which could sustain them in their struggle with the tsarist system, because they believed in the justice of their assault and in the inevitability of its ultimate issue. But if we view it critically we note that it rested on an "adjustment" that was composed in large part of hostility to existing institutions, and in equally large part of commitment to a world that had not yet come into being. Described so, its precariousness becomes obvious.

MATHEWSON

Various forces were at work in the 1890s in opposition to the Gorky-Andreyev school, and particularly to the dominance of social significance and nihilistic thought in literature. There was a definite turning away from civic morality to aestheticism, from duty to beauty, and cultural and individual values were stressed at the expense of political and social values. Most of the participators in this movement were brilliant intellectuals, and their efforts represented a lofty degree of cultural refinement that had never been achieved by any literary group in Russia hitherto.

SIMMONS

T he Decades that elapsed between the emancipation of the serfs and the revolutions of 1917 constituted an active, fruitful, and fascinating period in the history of Russian culture. Education continued to grow at all levels, in spite of obstacles and even governmental "counterreforms"; in the twentieth century the rate of growth increased sharply. Russian science and scholarship, already reasonably well-established at the time of Nicholas I's death, developed further and blossomed out. In a word, Russia became a full-fledged contributor to and partner in the intellectual and academic efforts of the Western world. Russian literature continued its "golden age," although primarily in prose rather than in poetry and largely through the achievements of several isolated individuals, such as Turgenev, Tolstoy, and Dostoevsky. Later, when the giants died or, as in the case of Tolstoy, stopped writing fiction and the "golden age" came to its end, Chekhov, Gorky, and some other outstanding authors maintained the great tradition of Russian prose. Moreover, the very end of the nineteenth century and the first part of the twentieth witnessed another magnificent literary and artistic revival, designated sometimes as the "silver age." In literature that renaissance meant the appearance once again of superb poetry, especially Alexander Blok's, the introduction of a wide variety of new trends, and the emergence of exceptionally high standards of culture and craftsmanship. The "silver age" also extended to the theater, music, ballet, painting, and sculpture, and in effect to every form of creative expression. It proved especially beneficial to the visual arts, which had produced little of distinction in the age of arid realism, and it scored perhaps its most resounding successes in the ballet and the theater. In the history of ideas, as well as in literature and art, the period can be divided into two uneven parts: from the 1860s to the end of the century and indeed to the revolutions of 1917, the creed of radicalism, utilitarianism, and materialism first proclaimed by left-wing Westernizers dominated student and other active intellectual circles, finding its best expression in nihilism, different forms of populism, and Marxism; yet with the turn of the century and the "silver age" in culture members of the intellectual elite began to return to idealistic metaphysics and religion. The First World War and later the revolutions struck when Russian intellectual and cultural life was exhibiting more vitality, diversity, and sophistication than ever before.

Education

The death of Nicholas I and the coming of the "great reforms" meant liberalization in education as in other fields. The university statute of 1863 reaffirmed the principle of university autonomy, while Nicholas I's special restrictions on universities were among the first regulations to disappear in the new reign. The zemstvo reform of 1864 opened vast opportunities to establish schools in the countryside. In towns or rural areas, the increasing thirst for knowledge on the part of the Russians augured well for education in a liberal age. However, as already mentioned, official liberalism did not last long, and reaction logically, if unfortunately, showed a particular concern for education. As a result, the growth of education in Russia, while it could not be stopped, found itself hampered and to an extent deformed by government action.

After Dmitrii Tolstoy replaced Alexander Golovnin in 1866 as minister of education, the ministry did its best to control education and to direct it into desirable channels. As in the days of Uvarov, high standards were used in universities and secondary schools to keep the number of students down, hindering especially the academic advancement of students of low social background. In secondary education, the emphasis fell on the so called classical *gymnasia*, which became the only road to universities proper, as distinct from more specialized institutions of higher learning. These gymnasia concentrated on teaching the Latin and Greek languages, to the extent of some 40 percent of the total class time. Largely because of the rigorous demands, less than one-third of those who had entered the gymnasia were graduated. In addition to the natural obstacles that such a system presented to "socially undesirable" elements, ministers of education made direct appeals in their circulars to subordinates to keep "cook's sons" out of the gymnasia, as did one of Dmitrii Tolstoy's successors, Ivan Delianov, in 1887. In general, the government tried to divide education into airtight compartments that students as a rule could not cross. Under Alexander III and Pobedonostsev, Church schools received special attention. Following the statute of 1884 concerning Church-parish schools, an effort was made to entrust elementary education as much as possible to the Church, the number of Church-parish schools increasing from 4,500 in 1882 to 32,000 in 1894. While inferior in quality, these educational institutions were considered "safe." By contrast, advanced education for women, barely begun in Russia, came to be increasingly restricted. And in all schools and at all levels the Ministry of Education emphasized "conduct" and tried to maintain iron discipline.

Yet in spite of all the vicissitudes, education continued to grow in Russia as a result of sustained efforts by the state, the Church, and, especially, the zemstva. Compared to 1856, when official data list only about 8,000 primary schools in the Russian Empire enrolling 450,000 pupils (less than 1 percent of the population, although an estimated 9 percent was school-aged), forty years later in 1896 there were ten times this number of schools enrolling 3.8 million pupils (approximately one-third of all school-age children), and by 1911, 6.6 million children were in Russian schools, which meant nearly half of full enrollment, according to Eklof's calculations. In addition to the exclusive classical gymnasia, *Realschule*, which taught modern languages and science in place of Greek and Latin, provided a secondary education that could lead to admission to technical institutions of higher learning. Other kinds of schools also developed. In addition to the activities of the ministries of education, war, navy, and of the Holy Synod, Witte promoted commercial schools under the jurisdiction of the Ministry of Finance, establishing some 150 of them between 1896 and 1902, and well over 200 altogether. In 1905 these schools were transferred to the Ministry of Trade and Industry. Moreover, after the Revolution of 1905 schools in Russia profited from a more liberal policy as well as from an increasing interest in education on the part of both the government and the public. As mentioned earlier, plans were drawn to institute schooling for all

Russian children by 1922, or, according to a revised estimate following the outbreak of the First World War, by 1925. Educational prospects had never looked brighter in Russia than on the eve of the revolutions of 1917.

The problem, however, remained immense. On the eve of the 1917 revolutions, the majority of Russians remained illiterate. Yet, enormous progress had been made since the end of serfdom. According to data compiled by Rashin, literacy in Russia had increased from only about 6 percent in the 1860s to an estimated 28 percent by 1913. But such aggregate data obscure the significant unevenness of the social geography of literacy in Russia. As revealed by the invaluable 1897 census, literacy rates were higher than average among males, city dwellers (but also peasants living near large cities), workers, youth, and people living in the European parts of the empire. Thus, in place of a simple national aggregate of literacy, it is more telling, for example, that still only 17 percent of peasants in European Russia could read in 1897, while 54 percent of industrial and commercial workers could, or that fully 74 percent of male workers in St. Petersburg were literate in 1897. It is also important to underscore, as recent scholars have, that the impact of literacy on individuals was quite varied. Among the lower classes, for example, literacy could mean no more than a rough skill needed to function better at work or could be an important source of pride and self-esteem and of exposure to new ideas and possibilities.

At the other end of the educational ladder, universities increased in number, although slowly. The so-called Novorossiiskii University—referring to the name of the area, *Novorossiia*, or New Russia—was founded in Odessa in 1864, the University of Tomsk in Siberia in 1888, the University of Saratov in 1910, of Perm in 1915, and of Rostov-on-Don in 1917. That gave Russia a total of twelve universities, all of them belonging to the state. However, in 1917 the empire also possessed more than a hundred specialized institutions of higher learning: pedagogical, technological, agricultural, and other. Gradually it became possible for women to obtain higher education by attending special "courses" set up in university centers, such as the "Guerrier courses," named after a professor of history, Vladimir Guerrier, which began to function in 1872 in Moscow, and the "Bestuzhev courses," founded in 1878 in St. Petersburg and named after another historian, Constantine Bestuzhev-Riumin. The total number of students in Russian institutions of higher learning in 1917 has been variously estimated between 100,000 and 180,000. It should be noted that while the university statute of 1884 proved to be more restrictive than that of 1863 and over a period of time led to the resignation of a number of noted professors, most of the restrictions disappeared in 1905. In general, and especially after 1905, the freedom and variety of intellectual life in imperial Russian universities invite comparison with Western universities.

Science and Scholarship

The Academy of Sciences, the universities, and other institutions of higher learning developed, or rather continued to develop, science and scholarship in Russia. In fact, in the period from the emancipation of the serfs until the revolutions of 1917, Russians made significant contributions in almost every area of knowledge. In mathematics, while no one quite rivaled Lobachevsky, a considerable number of outstanding Russian mathematicians made their appearance, including Pafnutii Chebyshev in St. Petersburg and a remarkable woman, Sophia Kovalevskaia, who taught at the University of Stockholm. Chemistry in Russia achieved new heights in the works of many talented scholars, the most celebrated of them being the great Dmitrii Mendeleev, who lived from 1834 to 1907 and whose periodic table of elements, formulated in 1869, both organized the known elements into a system and made an accurate forecast of later discoveries. Leading Russian physicists included the specialist in magnetism and electricity, Alexander Stoletov, and the brilliant student of the properties of light, Peter Lebedev, as well as such notable pioneer inventors as Paul Iablochkov, who worked before Edison in developing electric light, and Alexander Popov, who invented the radio around 1895, shortly before Marconi. Russian inventors, even more than Russian scholars in general, frequently received less than their due recognition in the world both because of the prevalent ignorance abroad of the Russian language and Russia and because of the backwardness of Russian technology, which usually failed to utilize their inventions.

Advances in the biological sciences rivaled those in the physical. Alexander Kovalevsky produced classic works in zoology and embryology, while his younger brother, Vladimir, the husband of the mathematician, made important contributions to paleontology—and, incidentally, was much appreciated by Darwin. The famous embryologist and bacteriologist Elijah Mechnikov, who did most of his work in the Pasteur Institute in Paris, concentrated on such problems as the function of the white corpuscles, immunity, and the process of aging. Medicine developed well in Russia during the last decades of the empire, both in terms of quality and, after the zemstvo reform, in terms of accessibility to the masses. Following the lead of an outstanding anatomist, surgeon, teacher, and public figure, Nicholas Pirogov, who died in 1881, and others, Russian doctors exhibited a remarkable civic spirit and devotion to their work and their patients.

Russian contributions to physiology were especially striking and important, and they overlapped into psychology. Ivan Sechenov, who taught in several universities for about half a century and died in 1905, did remarkable research on gases in blood, nerve centers, and reflexes and on other related matters. Ivan Pavlov, who lived from 1849 to 1936 and whose epoch-making experiments began in the 1880s, established through his studies of dogs' reactions to food the existence and nature of conditioned reflexes, and, further developing his approach, contributed enormously to both theory and experimental work in physiology and to behavioral psychology.

The social sciences and the humanities also prospered. Russian scholars engaged fruitfully in everything from law to oriental studies and from economics to folklore. In particular, Russian historiography flourished in the last decades of the nineteenth and the first of the twentieth century. Building on the work of Serge Soloviev and other pioneers, Basil Kliuchevsky, Serge Platonov, Matthew Liubavsky, Paul Miliukov, and their colleagues in effect established Russian history as a rich and many-sided field of learning. Other Russians made notable contributions to the histories of other countries and ages, as did the medievalist Paul Vinogradov and the specialist in classical antiquity Michael Rostovtzeff. While Russian historiography profited greatly from the sociological emphasis characteristic of the second half of the nineteenth century, the "silver age" stimulated the history of art, which could claim in Russia such magnificent specialists as Nikodim Kondakov, Alexander Benois, and Igor Grabar, and it led to a revival of philosophy, aesthetics, and literary criticism.

Literature

After the "great reforms" as before them, literature continued to be the chief glory of Russian culture, and it also became a major source of Russian influence on the West, and indeed on the world. That happened in spite of the fact that the intellectual climate in Russia changed and became unpropitious for creative expression. Instead of admiring art, poetry, and genius, as had been common in the first half of the nineteenth century, the influential critics of the generation of the sixties and of the following decades emphasized utility and demanded from the authors a clear and simple social message. Logically developed, civic literature led to Chernyshevsky's novel, *What Is To Be Done?*, a deplorable work artistically, whatever its intellectual and social significance. With better luck, it produced Nicholas Nekrasov's civic poetry, which showed inspiration and an effective use of language. Fortunately for Russian literature, the greatest writers rejected critical advice and proceeded to write in their own manner. That was especially true of the three giants of the age, Ivan Turgenev, Fedor Dostoevsky; and Leo Tolstoy.

Ivan Turgenev lived from 1818 to 1883 and became famous around 1850 with the gradual appearance of his *Sportsman's Sketches*. He responded to the trends of the time and depicted with remarkable sensitivity the intellectual life of Russia, but he failed eventually to satisfy the Left. Six novels, the first of which appeared in 1855 and the last in 1877, described the evolution of Russian educated society and Russia itself as Turgenev, a gentleman of culture, had witnessed it. These novels are, in order of publication, *Rudin, A Gentry Nest, On the Eve,* the celebrated *Fathers and Sons, Smoke,* and *Virgin Soil.* Turgenev depicted Russia from the time of the iron regime of Nicholas I, through the "great reforms," to the return of reaction in the late '60s and the '70s. He concerned himself especially with the idealists of the '40s and the later liberals, nihilists, and populists. Indeed, it was Turgenev's hero, Bazarov, who gave currency to the concept *nihilist* and to the term itself. Although he was a consistent Westernizer and liberal, who was appreciative of the efforts of young radicals to change Russia, Turgenev advocated gradualism, not revolution; in particular he recommended patient work to develop the Russian economy and education. And he refused to be one-sided or dogmatic. In fact, critics debate to this day whether Rudin and Bazarov are essentially sympathetic or unsympathetic characters. Besides, Turgenev's novels were by no means simply *romans à thèse.* The reader remembers not only the author's ideological protagonists, but also his remarkable, strong heroines, the background, the dialogue, and, perhaps above

Fedor Dostoevsky.   (New York Public Library)

all, the consummate artistry. As writer, Turgenev resembled closely his friend Flaubert, not at all Chernyshevsky. In addition to the famous sequence of novels, Turgenev wrote some plays and a considerable number of stories—he has been described as a better story writer than novelist.

Fedor—that is, Theodore—Dostoevsky, who lived from 1821 to 1881, also became well known before the "great reforms." He was already the author of a novel, *Poor Folk,* which was acclaimed by Belinsky when it was published in 1845, and of other writings, when he became involved, as already mentioned, with the Petrashevtsy and was sentenced to death, the sentence being commuted to Siberian exile only at the place of execution. Next the writer spent four years at hard labor and two more as a soldier in Siberia before returning to European Russia in 1856, following a general amnesty proclaimed by the new emperor. Dostoevsky recorded his Siberian experience in a remarkable book, *Notes from the House of the Dead*, which came out in 1861. Upon his return to literary life, the one-time member of the Petrashevtsy became an aggressive and prolific Right-wing journalist, contributing to a certain Slavophile revival, Pan-Slavism, and even outright chauvinism. His targets included the Jews, the Poles, the Germans, Catholicism, socialism, and the entire West. While Dostoevsky's journalism added to the sound and fury of the period, his immortal fame rests on his late novels, four of which belong among the greatest ever written. These were *Crime and Punishment, The Idiot, The Possessed*, and *The Brothers Karamazov,* published in 1866, 1868, 1870–72, and 1879–80 respectively. In fact, Dostoevsky seemed to go from strength to strength and was apparently at the height of his creative powers in working on a sequel to *The Brothers Karamazov* when he died.

Dostoevsky has often been represented as the most Russian of writers and evaluated in terms of Russian messiahship and the mysteries of the Russian soul—an approach to which he himself richly contributed. Yet, a closer study of the great novelist's so-called special Russian traits demonstrates that they are either of secondary importance at best or even entirely imaginary. To the contrary, Dostoevsky could be called the most international or, better, the most human of writers because of his enormous concern with and penetration into the nature of man. The strange Russian author was a master of depth psychology before depth psychology became known. Moreover, he viewed human nature in the dynamic terms of explosive conflict between freedom and necessity, urge and limitations, faith and despair, good and evil. Of Dostoevsky's several priceless gifts the greatest was to fuse into one his protagonists and the ideas—or rather states of man's soul and entire being—that they expressed, as no other writer has ever done. Therefore, where others are prolix, tedious, didactic, or confusing in mixing different levels of discourse, Dostoevsky is gripping, in places almost unbearably so. As another Russian author, Gleb Uspensky, reportedly once remarked, into a small hole in the wall, where the generality of human beings could put perhaps a pair of shoes, Dostoevsky could put the entire world. One of the greatest anti-rationalists of the second half of the nineteenth century, together with Nietzsche and Kirkegaard, Dostoevsky became with them an acknowledged prophet for the twentieth, inspiring existential philosophy, theological revivals, and scholarly attempts to understand the catastrophes of our time—as well as, of course, modern psychological fiction.

It has been said that, if Dostoevsky was not the world's greatest novelist, then Tolstoy certainly was, and that the choice between the two depends on whether the reader prefers depth or breadth. These are quite defensible views, provided one remembers the range of Dostoevsky, and especially his very numerous secondary and tertiary characters who speak their own language and add their own comment to the human tragedy, and provided one realizes that Tolstoy too cuts very deep.

Count Leo Tolstoy lived a long, full, and famous life. Born in 1828 and brought up in a manner characteristic of his aristocratic milieu—magnificently described in *Childhood, Boyhood, and Youth*—he received a cosmopolitan, if dilettante, education; engaged in gay social life; served in the army, first in the Caucasus and later in the siege of Sevastopol; and became a happy husband, the father of a large family, and a progressive landowner much concerned with the welfare of his peasants. In addition to these ordinary activities, however, Tolstoy also developed into one of the greatest writers in world literature and later into an angry teacher of mankind, who condemned civilization, including his own part in it, and called for the abandonment of violence and for a simple, moral life. In fact, he died in 1910 at the age of eighty-two as he fled from his family and estate in yet another attempt to sever his ties with all evil and falsehood and to find truth. It is indeed difficult to determine whether Tolstoy acquired more fame and influence in his own country and all over the world as a writer or as a teacher of nonresistance and unmasker of modern civilization, and whether *Anna Karenina* or *A Confession*—an account of the crisis that split his life in two—carries the greater impact. In Russia at least, Tolstoy's position as the voice of criticism that the government dared not silence, as

Leo Tolstoy.   (New York Public Library)

moral conscience, appeared at times even more extraordinary and precious than his literary creations.

But, whatever can be said against Tolstoy as thinker—and much has been justly said about his extraordinary naïveté, his stubborn and at the same time poorly thought-out rationalism, and his absolute insistence on such items as vegetarianism and painless death as parts of his program of salvation—Tolstoy as writer needs no apologies. While a prolific author, the creator of many superb stories and some powerful plays, Tolstoy, like Dostoevsky, is remembered best for his novels, especially *War and Peace*, published in 1869, and *Anna Karenina*, published in 1876. In these novels, as in much else written by Tolstoy, there exists a boundless vitality, a driving, overpowering sense of life and people. And life finds expression on a sweeping scale. *War and Peace* contains sixty heroes and some two hundred distinct characters, not to mention the unforgettable battle and mob scenes and the general background. The war of 1812 is depicted at almost every level: from Alexander I and Napoleon, through commanders and officers, to simple soldiers, and among civilians from court circles to the common people. *Anna Karenina,* while more restricted in scope, has been praised no less for its construction and its supreme art.

The Russian novel, which in the second half of the nineteenth century won a worldwide reputation because of the writings of Turgenev, Dostoevsky, and Tolstoy, had other outstanding practitioners as well. Ivan Goncharov, who lived from 1812 to 1891, produced at least one great novel, *Oblomov,* published two years before the emancipation of the serfs and representing in a sense a farewell, spoken with mixed feelings, to the departing patriarchal Russia, and a welcome, again with mixed feelings, to the painfully evolving new order. Oblomov himself snored his way to fame as one of the most unforgettable as well as most "superfluous" heroes of Russian literature. Other noteworthy novelists of the period included Nicholas Leskov who developed a highly individual language and style and wrote about the provincial clergy and similar topics associated with the Church and the people, and Gleb Uspensky, a populist and a pessimist, deeply concerned with peasant life as well as with the intelligentsia. An able satirist, Michael Saltykov, who wrote under the pseudonym of N. Shchedrin, fitted well into that critical and realistic age and acquired great popularity. A highly talented dramatist, Alexander Ostrovsky, wrote indefatigably from about 1850 until his death in 1886, creating much of the basic repertoire of the Russian theater and contributing especially to the depiction of merchants, minor officials, and the lower middle class in general.

Toward the end of the nineteenth century and in the early twentieth new writers came to the fore to continue the great tradition of Russian prose. Vladimir Korolenko, a populist and optimist, was the author of charming stories expressing his belief in people's fundamental goodness and in the ultimate victory of truth and justice, even in the face of harsh natural and social conditions. The restless Alexis Peshkov, better known as Maxim Gorky, wrote often of the lives and struggles of outcasts, tramps, and rebels and featured strong and restless plebeian heroes challenging both oppressive authorities and the slavish submissiveness of the masses. Anton Chekhov, who lived from 1860 until 1904, left a lasting imprint on Russian and world literature. A brilliant playwright, he had the good fortune to be writing just as the Moscow Art Theater was rising to its heights. He is even more important as one of the founders and a master craftsman of the modern short story, the literary genre that he usually chose to make his simple, gentle, restrained, and yet wonderfully effective comments on the world.

Poetry remained enormously popular among readers in the years between the "great reforms" and the turn of the century, though a relative lack of originality and innovation and a predominance of realism have led many critics to see these decades as an "unpoetic age." Two trends competed for attention in these years: "art for art's sake" and "civic poetry." Among those inclined toward the first, the best was Athanasius Fet-Shenshin, whose beautiful impressionistic verses, mostly about nature and love, reflected the view, much influenced by the pessimism of Schopenhauer, that reality is ugly and the role of art is to transcend and overcome this world through pure beauty. Utilitarian critics like Chernyshevsky heaped abuse and mockery on Fet, contributing to his silence as a writer during most of the 1860s and 1870s. Likewise, the great lyricist Fedor Tiutchev, perhaps the world's outstanding poet of late love and of nature in its romantic, pantheistic, and chaotic aspects, died in 1873, an iso-

Anton Chekhov.   (New York Public Library)

lated figure. The dominant trend in these years was civic poetry. Realistic, even naturalistic, in portraying the world and optimistic about the possibilities of improving the human condition, the civic poets, encouraged by critics like Chernyshevsky, were determined to use literature to awaken consciences and change the world. With pathos, satire, or sarcasm, using echoes of rough folk speech or soaring moral passion, they described various abuses in Russian life, especially the sufferings of the common people. The leading civic poet was Nekrasov, whose poetic voice could range from poignant realism to eloquent lyricism, often echoing Russian folk songs. His many influential poems were inspired both by the beauty of Russian nature and moral outrage at the poverty and suffering of ordinary Russians.

The "silver age" in Russian literature, which dawned toward the turn of the century, brought new vitality and creativity to Russian culture. Foreshadowed by certain literary critics and poets in the 1890s, the new period has often been dated from the appearance in 1898 of a seminal periodical, *The World of Art,* put out by Serge Diaghilev and Alexander Benois. What followed was a cultural explosion. Almost overnight there sprung up in Russia a rich variety of literary and artistic creeds, circles, and movements. As Mirsky and other specialists have noted, these different and sometimes hostile groups had little in common, except their denial of "civic art" and their high standards of culture and craftsmanship. Form-conscious impressionism and symbolism pushed aside rationalism, positivism, and didactic realism. Aestheticism, mysticism, decadence, sensualism, idealism, and pessimism all intertwined in different combinations. Some critics have found in "silver age" writing a tendency toward pretentiousness, obscurity, or artificiality. But even when short of the best, the works of the "silver age" indicated a new refinement, richness, and maturity in Russian culture.

In literature, the new trends resulted in a great revival of poetry and literary criticism, although some remarkable prose was also produced, for example, by Boris Bugaev, known as Andrei Bely. Among the poets, the symbolist Alexander Blok, who lived from 1880 to 1921 and wrote verses of stunning magic and melody to the mysterious Unknown Lady and on other topics, has been justly considered the greatest of the age and one of the greatest in all Russian literature. But Russia suddenly acquired many brilliant poets; other symbolists, for example, Innokentii Annensky, Bely, Valery Briusov, and Constantine Balmont; "acmeists," such as Nicholas Gumilev and Osip Mandelstam; futurists, such as Velemir Khlebnikov and Vladimir Mayakovsky; or peasant poets, such as Serge Esenin. The poet and novelist Boris Pasternak, who died in 1960, and the poet Anna Akhmatova, who lived until 1966 as probably the last Russian poet of the first rank, also belong fully to the "silver age." In literary criticism, too, the new trends continued to enrich Russian culture after 1917, producing notably an interesting school of formalist critics, until destroyed by Soviet regimentation and "socialist realism."

The "silver age" was a sign not only of Russia's cultural florescence but also, it has been argued, of a troubled cultural spirit of the age. Literary scholars have spoken of a characteristic *fin-de-siècle* sense of uncertainty and disintegration, of deep skepticism about all received truths and certainties, and a pessimistic foreboding (prescient, it turned out), though also hopeful anticipation, of an approaching "end." A major preoccupation was the self—self-discovery, self-development, self-fulfillment. Some writers, such as Gorky, presented the individual human self as a moral ideal upon which society should be constructed and focused their writings on the sufferings and assertions of their characters' inward and social beings. Other writers found meaning for the self, amidst the whirlwind of modern life, in aestheticist (some called it decadent) evocations of love, beauty, and sadness, as in the highly personal and beautifully crafted poetry of Akhmatova and other "acmeists." Still other writers and cultural critics, such as Andreev, Bely, Briusov, Hippius, Merezhkovsky, Rozanov, and Sologub, dwelled on the darker, egoistic, Dionysian side of the awakened modern self. Typically, these writers both admired and dreaded the creative powers of the all-too-human ego and id—the influences of Nietzsche and Freud were widely evident—and explored, in a complex psychological and philosophical frame, sensuality, lust, cruelty, depravity, madness, disease, death, and other drives, passions, and experiences.

The uncertainties and pessimism so characteristic of the silver age nurtured its characteristic aestheticism. Many artists, it was said, felt that the old world was dying, but they were determined at least that it be a beautiful death. By contrast, futurists took a stance of iconoclastic rebellion in the name of new and modern meanings. Writers like Khlebnikov and Mayakovsky loudly and visibly challenged the conventional values of what they called "philistine" cul-

Anna Akhmatova. (Zephyr Press, Brookline, MA)

ture; their most famous manifesto spoke of offering a "slap in the face to public taste." They appeared in public with absurd pictures painted on their faces, peculiarly invented clothing, seashell earrings, and radishes or spoons in their buttonholes. And their works deliberately echoed the noisy confusion and chaos of modern life. Truth and beauty, they insisted, lay not in the creative subjects or vocabularies of past work but in the new noise of factories and the marketplace and in the primitive and transcendent sounds of "transrational" words.

The Arts

In art, as in literature, "realism" dominated the second half of the nineteenth century, only to be enriched and in large part replaced by the varied new currents of the "silver age." In painting the decisive turning to realism can even be precisely dated: in 1863 fourteen young painters, led by Ivan Kramskoy and constituting the entire graduating class of the Academy of Arts, refused to paint their examination assignment, "A Feast in Valhalla." Breaking with the stifling academic tradition, they insisted on painting realistic pictures. Several years later they organized popular circulating exhibitions of their works and came to be known as the "itinerants." With new painters joining the movement and its influence spreading, "critical realism" asserted itself in Russian art just as it had in Russian literary criticism and literature. In accord with the spirit of the age, the "itinerants" and their disciples believed that content was more important than form, that art had to serve the higher purpose of educating the masses and championing their interests, and they depicted such topics as the exploitation of the poor, the drunken clergy, and the brutal police. Basil Vereshchiagin, for example, observed wars at firsthand until he went down with the battleship *Petropavlovsk* when it was sunk by the Japanese. He painted numerous and often huge canvases on the glaring inhumanity of wars, characteristically dedicating his "Apotheosis of War," a pyramid of skulls, "to all great conquerors, present, past, and future." To be sure, painting could not be limited to social protest, and realism naturally extended to portraits, genre scenes, landscapes, historical topics—well handled by Basil Surikov—and other subject matter. Still, some critics maintain, the Russian artists of the period demonstrated earnestness rather than talent, and added more to the polemics of the age than to art. Even the most famous of them, Elijah Repin, who lived from 1844 to 1930, is less likely to be remembered for his contribution to creative art than for his active participation in Russian life and culture and for certain paintings that have become almost inseparable from their subject matter, such as one of the Dnieper cossacks and one of Ivan the Terrible just after he had mortally wounded his son Ivan.

The development of music followed a somewhat different pattern. It, too, responded to the demands of the age, as seen, for example, in Modest Mussorgsky's emphasis on content, realism, and closeness to the masses. Music, however, by its very nature could not be squeezed into the framework of critical realism, and fortunately it attracted much original talent in Russia at the time. The second half of the nineteenth century witnessed a great spread of musical interest and education in the empire, with a conservatory established in St. Petersburg in 1862, headed by the noted composer and magnificent pianist Anton Rubinstein, another one in Moscow in 1866, headed by Anton Rubinstein's younger brother, Nicholas, and still other musical schools in other cities in subsequent years. Moreover, quite a number of outstanding Russian composers came to the fore at that time. The most prominent of them included Peter Tchaikovsky and *dilettante* members of the celebrated "Mighty Bunch," Modest Mussorgsky, Nicholas Rimsky-Korsakov, Alexander Borodin, and Caesar Cui. The "Mighty Bunch," or "The Five"—Milii Balakirev, a professional, trained musician, must be added to the four already mentioned—in effect created the national Russian school of music, utilizing folk songs, melodies, tales, and legends and a romanticized vision of the Russian past to produce such famous operas as Mussorgsky's *Boris Godunov,* Borodin's *Prince Igor,* and Rimsky-Korsakov's *Sadko* and *The Tale of the Town of Kitezh.* It hardly needs to be mentioned that much of the instrumental and vocal music of the "Mighty Bunch" has entered the basic musical repertoire all over the world. The same, of course, holds true of Tchaikovsky, who stood apart from "The Five," developing an elegiac, subjective, and psychological approach of his own. Indeed, few pieces in the world of music are better known than Tchaikovsky's *Sixth Symphony* or his ballets, *Swan Lake* and *The Sleeping Beauty.*

Modest Mussogorsky.   (Sovfoto)

Peter Tchaikovsky.   (New York Public Library)

Vaslav Nijinsky represented a new type of male ballet artist: central to the performance rather than simply assisting ballerinas, openly erotic, sexually ambiguous. (New York Public Library)

The "silver age" brought a renaissance in the fine arts as well as in litera-ture. In music, where Alexander Scriabin initiated the change, it marked the appearance of the genius of Igor Stravinsky and of other brilliant young com-posers. In a sense, the new ballet masterpieces, for example, Stravinsky's *The Firebird, Petrouchka*—which also belongs to Benois—and *Le Sacre du printemps*, combining as they did superb music, choreography, dancing, and décor, expressed best the cultural refinement, craftsmanship, and many-sidedness of the "silver age." The Russian ballet received overwhelming acclaim when Diaghilev brought it to Paris in 1909, starring such choreographers as Michael Fokine and such dancers as Anna Pavlova and Vaslav Nijinsky. From that time on Russian ballet has exercised a fundamental influence on ballet in other countries. On the eve of 1917 Russia could also boast of leading artists in other musical fields, for instance, the bass Theodore Chaliapin, the conductor Serge

Koussevitzky, and the pianist, conductor, and composer Serge Rachmaninov, to mention three of the best-known names. Diaghilev's ballets made such a stunning impression in the West in part because of the superb décor and staging. Benois, Constantine Korovin, and other gifted artists of the "silver age" created a school of stage painting that gave Russia world leadership in that field and added immeasurably to operatic and theatrical productions as well as to the ballet. Still another remarkable development in the "silver age" was the rediscovery of icon painting: both a physical rediscovery, because ancient icons had become dark, been overlaid with metal, or even painted over, and began to be restored to their original condition only around 1900; and an artistic rediscovery, because these icons were newly appreciated, adding to the culture and the creative influences of the period.

The most remarkable achievement in Russian visual arts was the innovative modernism of such artists as Marc Chagall, Basil Kandinsky, and Kazimir Malevich, still renowned throughout the world for their originality and influence. Various trends arose. Some artists took a revivalist turn, evoking a seemingly stable and authentic time of pure national identity before Russia's West-

Exhibition room of "suprematist" paintings by Kazimir Malevich at "0.10: The Last Futurist Painting Exhibition," held in Petrograd in 1915. While most reviewers voiced incomprehension and even scorn in viewing these experiments in abstraction as a new way of seeing, a sympathetic reviewer praised this exhibit as a stand against the "stupidity and vulgarity covering the world." Note the position of the "Black Square" in the traditional icon corner. (Mark Steinberg)

ernization or crafted nostalgic recollections of the elegance of the eighteenth century. Many were attracted to the ideal of beauty for its own sake and to efforts to create "pure painting" that embodied emotion above all. Others sought truth and beauty in other places. Futurist artists, like Michael Larionov, Natalie Goncharova, and Malevich, experimented with images of modern machines in motion, with primitivism in style and subject, with evocations of "Oriental" forms in Russian culture, and with an abstraction of dynamically interacting rays or geometric blocks of primal color.

Theater, like the ballet a combination of arts, also developed splendidly in the "silver age." In addition to the fine imperial theaters, private ones came into prominence. The Moscow Art Theater, directed by Constantine Stanislavsky who emphasized psychological realism, achieved the greatest and most sustained fame and exercised the strongest influence on acting in Russia and abroad. But it is important to realize that it represented only one current in the theatrical life of a period remarkable for its variety, vitality, and experimentation. Russian art as well as Russian literature in the "silver age" formed an inseparable part of the art and literature of the West, profiting hugely, for example, from literary trends in France or from German thought, and in turn contributing in quite original ways to virtually every form of literary and artistic argument and creative expression. In a sense, Russian culture was less directly imitative but also more "Western" than ever on the eve of 1917.

Ideologies

Russian social, political, and philosophical thought also underwent considerable evolution between the emancipation of the serfs and the First World War. As already mentioned, the radicals of the generation of the sixties, Turgenev's "sons," found their spiritual home first in "nihilistic" ideologies, which rejected established political and social authorities in the name of an often vague program of radical change. As their spokesman, the gifted young literary critic Dmitrii Pisarev, 1840–68, said: "What can be broken, should be broken." The new radical spirit reflected both the general materialistic and realistic character of the age and special Russian conditions, such as a reaction to the stifling of intellectual life under Nicholas I, the autocratic and oppressive nature of the regime, the weak development of the middle class or other elements of moderation and compromise, and a gradual democratization of the educated public.

While nihilism emancipated the young Russian radicals from any allegiance to the established order, it was, to repeat a point, more individualistic than social in its spirit of total personal emancipation and lacked much of a positive program, though proclamations produced by radical student groups in the 1860s suggest a vague general commitment to "freedom" embodied in such principles as an end to monarchy, a decentralized society based on communes, cooperative ownership and work in the economy, women's equality, and the rights of nationalities to independence. A more elaborate social creed came with a vengeance in the form of *narodnichestvo*, or populism, which arose in the 1860s and '70s to dominate much of Russian radicalism until the October Revolution. We have already seen its political impact in such events as the celebrated "going to the people" of 1874, the terrorism of the "Peoples' Will," and the activities of the Socialist Revolutionary party. Although in a broad sense Russian populism belonged ideologically to the general European radicalism of the age, it also possessed a distinctively Russian character—for Russia was a peasant country *par excellence*—and numerous Russian prophets. The first prophets were the radical Westernizers Herzen and Bakunin, the former surviving until 1870 and the latter until 1876, who both preached that radical intellectuals should turn to the people and proclaimed the virtues of the peasant commune. Ideologically, populism was defined by devotion to the common people (improving their lives but also inspiring them to revolution), a rejection of capitalism, the belief that Russia had a special historical opportunity to avoid the evils of capitalism thanks to the strength of the peasant commune, and insistence that social revolution was even more essential than political change. Populism also openly reasserted moral argument. Not unlike the generation of Herzen and Belinsky, populists insisted on universal moral truths grounded in human nature, at the heart of which was the natural equality and dignity of all human beings and hence the right to a life of respect and opportunity for personal development. Bakunin's violent anarchism inspired many of the more impatient populists. Anarchism, it might be added, appealed to a variety of Russian intellectuals, including such outstanding figures as Tolstoy and Prince Peter Kropotkin, a noted geographer, geologist, and radical, who lived from 1842 to 1921 and devoted most of his life to the spreading of anarchism. Kropotkin's activities, including a fantastic escape from a prison-hospital, were described in his celebrated *Memoirs of a Revolutionist* written in English for *The Atlantic Monthly* in 1898–99.

Whereas Herzen and Bakunin were émigrés, populist leaders also arose in Russia after 1855. Nicholas Chernyshevsky, whose views and impact were not limited to populism, but who nevertheless exercised a major influence on Russian populists, deserves special attention. Born in 1828, Chernyshevsky actually enjoyed only a few years of public activity as journalist and writer, especially as editor of a leading periodical, *The Contemporary*, before his arrest in 1862. He returned from Siberian exile only in 1883 and died in 1889. It was probably Chernyshevsky more than anyone else who contributed to the spread of utilitarian, positivist, and in part materialist views in Russia. Drawing on Ludwig Feuerbach's materialism and Jeremy Bentham's utilitarianism, Chernyshevsky argued that individual needs and individual happiness must be the basis of all morality, and thus of society, but that this egoism must be tempered with the rational knowledge that true self-interest lay in seeing the greatest benefit among the largest number of people. From this he argued for the necessity of an economy and society based on equality and cooperation. A man of vast erudition, Chernyshevsky concerned himself with aesthetics—developing further Belinsky's ideas on the primacy of life over art—as much as with economics, and wrote on nineteenth-century French history, demonstrating the failure of liberalism, as well as on Russian problems. His extremely popular novel, *What Is To Be Done?*, dealt with the new generation of "critical realists," their ethics and their activities, and sketched both the revolutionary hero and forms of co-operative organization. As to the peasant commune, Chernyshevsky showed more reserve than certain of his contemporaries. Yet he generally believed that it could serve as a direct transition to socialism in Russia, provided socialist revolution first triumphed in Europe. For a time Chernyshevsky collaborated closely in spreading his ideas with an able radical literary critic, Nicholas Dobroliubov, who died in 1861 at the age of twenty-five.

Chernyshevsky's and Dobroliubov's work was continued, with certain differences, by Peter Lavrov and Nicholas Mikhailovsky. Lavrov, 1823–1900, another erudite adherent of positivism, utilitarianism, and populism, emphasized in his *Historical Letters* of 1870, which many young radicals claimed to have read with "hot tears of idealistic enthusiasm," and in other writings the crucial role of "critically thinking individuals" in the revolutionary struggle and the transformation of Russia. Philosophically, he voiced the need for an ethical system that could guide action and argued that the proper center of such a practical philosophy must be the principle of the human person: society must be judged by whether it enhanced or restricted the dignity and development of individuals. Mikhailovsky, a literary critic who lived from 1842 to 1904, employed the "subjective method" in social analysis to stress moral values rather than mere objective description and to champion the peasant commune, which provided for harmonious development of the individual, by contrast with the industrial order, which led to narrow specialization along certain lines and the atrophy of other aspects of personality. The populist defense of the peasant commune became more desperate with the passage of time, because Russia was in fact developing into a capitalist country and because an articulate Marxist school arose to point that out as proof that history was proceeding according to Marxist predictions. Yet the Socialist Revolutionaries of the twentieth century, led by Victor Chernov, although they borrowed much from the Marxists and had to modify their own views, remained essentially faithful to populism, staking the future of Russia on the peasants and on a "socialization of land."

Marxists proved to be strong competitors and opponents of populists. The actual development of Russia seemed to follow the Marxist rather than the populist blueprint. Beginning with the 1890s Marxism made important inroads among Russian intellectuals, gaining adherents both among scholars and in the radical and revolutionary movement. While Marxism will be discussed in a later chapter, it should be kept in mind that Marxism offered its followers an "objective knowledge" of history instead of a mere "subjective method" and a quasi-scientific certainty of victory in lieu of, or rather in addition to, moral earnestness and indignation. Still, Russian Marxists were divided over fundamental questions. The occasion for the split between Bolsheviks and Mensheviks, we have seen, was over how open or disciplined the revolutionary party should be. But there were deeper divisions. The leader of the Mensheviks, Julius Martov, for example, was attracted to Marxism, not only by its "scientific" arguments about the natural progress of history toward socialism, but also by its compelling moral arguments about the justice of ending inequality and suffering. By contrast, the Bolshevik leader Lenin repeatedly voiced his contempt for the political moralizing so common to Russian socialism. Different sensibilities were reflected in different politics. Whereas Martov and the Mensheviks emphasized the value to workers' consciousness of the struggle itself, Lenin and the Bolsheviks emphasized the guidance and leadership workers needed—hence the difference in their visions of the party. And whereas Marxists like Martov viewed the socialist goal of democracy as an inherent value, Marxists like Lenin saw democracy as mainly a means to facilitate the struggle for socialism.

To be sure, not all thinking and articulate Russians were radicals. But the Right, the conservatives and the reactionaries, had very little to offer. The government did little more than repeat the obsolete formula of Official Nationality, and its ablest theoretician, Constantine Pobedonostsev, determinedly refused to come to terms with the modern world. A few reactionary intellectuals not associated with the government, such as the brilliant writer Constantine Leontiev, engaged in violent but fruitless criticism of the trends of the time and placed their hopes—desperate hopes indeed—in freezing the social process, in freezing everything!

Perhaps the new-style violent and demagogic Right had brighter prospects than the conservatives did. Its potential might be suggested by the nationalist rally led by Katkov in 1863, by Pan-Slavism in the late 1870s and at certain other times—although Pan-Slavism, especially when it expanded, was by no means limited to the Right—and by the "Black Hundreds" of the twentieth century. Yet all these movements lacked effective organization, continuity, and cohesion, as well as solid ideology. Pan-Slavism, for example, although it had several prophets, including Dostoevsky, and a painstaking theoretician of the quasi-scientific racist variety, Nicholas Danilevsky, whose magnum opus, *Russia and Europe,* was published in 1869, remained an "attitude of mind and feeling" rather than an "organized policy or even a creed." In other words, in times of Balkan crises many Russians sympathized with the Balkan Slavs, but they forgot them once a crisis passed. As a political factor, Pan-Slavism was more a Western bugaboo than a reality. And, in general, whatever racist and fascist possibilities existed in imperial Russia, they failed to develop beyond an incipient stage. Their flowering required a more modern setting than the one offered by the *ancien régime* of the Romanovs.

It can be argued that liberalism, on the other hand, represented a promising alternative for Russia. Moreover, Karpovich, Fischer, and other scholars, as well as a wealth of sources, have demonstrated that Russian liberalism was by no means a negligible quantity. On the contrary, with its bases in the zemstvo system and the professions, it gained strength steadily and it produced able ideologists and leaders such as Paul Miliukov and Basil Maklakov. Although divided over strategy and tactics—a split manifested most clearly in the post-1905 division between the Cadets and the Octobrists—liberals shared a common set of goals for transforming Russia into a strong and modern polity: the rule of law replacing the arbitrary will of the state; civil rights (freedom of conscience, religion, speech, assembly) for all citizens of the empire; a democratic parliament (Cadets viewed the system established after 1905 as incomplete); strong local self-government; and social reforms to ensure social stability and justice. They also believed strongly in the need for individuals to transform themselves morally into citizens, developing individual initiative, self-reliance, and rational self-improvement. The important position of the Cadets in the first two Dumas, the only Dumas elected by a rather democratic suffrage, emphasizes the liberal potential. But the government never accepted the liberal viewpoint, nor, of course, did the Russian radical and revolutionary movement accept it. The liberals thus had little opportunity to influence state policies or even to challenge them. Whether liberalism could have satisfied Russian needs will remain an arguable question, because Russian liberalism never received its chance in imperial Russia.

The "woman question" was a social issue that engaged almost everyone, from conservatives to socialists. The "emancipation of women" was a central theme in the writings of Chernyshevsky and other radicals in the 1860s and after, though the issue gained particular prominence and urgency during and after the 1905 revolution. Liberal and socialist activists, both men and women, regularly challenged the traditionally subordinate status and role of women in Russian life and targeted the particular humiliations women endured: sexual harassment, domestic violence, prostitution, lack of education, lack of training for employment, lower wages, undeveloped social supports for maternity and child care, and the lack of legal protections or civil rights. Ideologically, the women's movement was as divided as the larger political world. Many activists fought directly to overcome women's inferior status; others, especially socialists, distanced themselves from such feminism, insisting that women should focus on the "larger" cause, since women's position would change only when all people were freed from the old order.

The "silver age" affected Russian thought as well as Russian literature and art. Notably, it marked a return to metaphysics, and often to religion eventually, on the part of a significant sector of Russian intellectuals. Other educated Russians, especially the writers and the artists, tended to become apolitical and asocial, often looking to aesthetics for their highest values. The utilitarianism, positivism, and materialism dominant from the time of the '60s finally had to face a serious challenge.

Philosophy in Russia experienced a revival in the work of Vladimir Soloviev and his followers. Soloviev, a son of the historian Serge Soloviev, lived from 1853 until 1900 and wrote on a variety of difficult philosophical and theological subjects. A study in ethics, *A Justification of the Good*, is generally considered his masterpiece. A trenchant critic of the radical creed of the age, as well as of chauvinism and reaction, Soloviev remained a rather isolated individual during his lifetime, but came to exercise a profound influence on the intellectual elite of the "silver age." In effect almost everything he had stood for, from imaginative and daring theology to a sweeping critique of the radical intelligentsia, suddenly came into prominence in the early twentieth century.

The new critique of the intelligentsia found its most striking expression in a slim volume entitled *Signposts—Vekhi*—which appeared in 1909. *Signposts* contained essays by seven authors, including such prominent converts from Marxism as Peter Struve, Nicholas Berdiaev, and Serge Bulgakov, and constituted an all-out attack on the radical intelligentsia: Russian radicals were accused of an utter disregard for objective truth, religion, and law, and of an extreme application of the maxim that the end justifies the means, with destruction as their only effective passion. Although *Signposts* represented a minority of Russian intellectuals and attracted strong rebuttals, a new cleavage among educated Russians became apparent—a cleavage all the more revealing because the critics of the intelligentsia could by no means be equated with the Right. Eventually Struve, 1870–1944, became a leading thinker and political figure of the moderate conservatives; Berdiaev, 1874–1948, acquired world fame as a personalist philosopher and champion of "creative freedom"; and Bulgakov, 1871–1944, entered the priesthood and developed into the most controversial Orthodox theologian of the twentieth century. Other prominent intellectuals of the "silver age" included the "biological mystic" Basil Rozanov, who was especially concerned with the problem of sex, the brilliant anti-rationalist Leo Shestov—a pseudonym of Leo Schwartzmann—and the metaphysicians Semen Frank—another contributor to *Signposts*—and Nicholas Lossky.

Throughout Russian society in these years we see a remarkable upheaval of spiritual searching and crisis, often called by historians a "religious renaissance." Many educated Russians returned to the Church to revitalize their faith. Many others were drawn to private prayer, mysticism, spiritualism, theosophy, and Eastern religions—a movement known as "God-Seeking." As we have seen, religious associations proliferated among both the educated and the urban poor. Urban movements such as the "Brethren," for example, attracted workers and others with their charismatic preaching, ideas of moral living (to realize the dignity befitting human beings as carriers of the flame of the Holy Spirit), and promises of salvation in this life. Among the peasantry, historians have discovered growing interest in spiritual-ethical literature, an upsurge in pilgrimage and devotions to miracle-working icons, and the proliferation of what the Orthodox establishment branded as "sectarianism." Many artists and writers as well were attracted to the spiritual and the sacred. Thus, many "silver age" poets sought in their writings to penetrate appearances to discover the spiritual essence of things and sometimes voiced apocalyptic visions of a transformed world. Visual artists were also drawn toward a spiritual understanding of the power and function of images, including explicitly religious ones but also abstract forms. Alexander Benois, the leader of the World of Art movement, observed in 1902 that in all the arts there was a widespread feeling that the reigning "materialism" of the age was too "astonishingly simple" to answer questions about life or to express ideals and feelings.

Russian cultural life was not entirely filled with high-minded concerns about politics, society, philosophy, morality, and religion. Modern city life was filled with opportunities, especially for those with some disposable income, for what many intellectuals viewed as quite unenlightened public pleasure: music halls, nightclubs, *cafés chantants,* outdoor "pleasure gardens," cheap theaters, increasing numbers of cinemas, and popular public divertissements like car races or wrestling bouts. Popular reading tastes also seemed far from uplifting. Newspapers, it was said, "pandered to crude instincts" with stories of "scandal" and sensation—though for popular readers this was a fascinating window into the bustling modern world—while widely available popular fiction, it was feared, eroded traditional popular and national values and tastes in favor of preoccupations with adventure, individual daring, exotic locales, and material success. The enormously popular cinema contributed to this changing popular culture with its ethos of spectacle and sensation and its narratives of melodramatic conflict over values in a changing society, materialist consumption, and the often troubled pursuit of pleasure.

Concluding Remarks

The development of Russian culture in the years preceding 1917 suggests certain significant parallels to the political, economic, and social condition of the country. Most striking was the disparity between the few and the many. In the early twentieth century, Russia possessed a rich variety of poetic schools and the best ballet in the world, but the majority of the people remained illiterate. It was even difficult to communicate across the chasm. One is reminded of Chekhov's story, "The Malefactor," in which a peasant brought to court for stealing a bolt from the railroad tracks to weight his fishing tackle fails to see his guilt, explains that enough bolts are left for the train, and in describing his activities constantly refers to "we," meaning the peasants of his village, the people. Again, it can be argued that on the eve of the revolutions Russia exhibited progress and vigorous activity in intellectual as well as in other matters, straining against the confines of the established order. But, contrary to the Soviet view, this intellectual development did not lead ineluctably to Bolshevism. More than that, the cultural climate of the "silver age" indicated that the Russian educated public was finally moving away from the simple materialistic, utilitarian, and activist beliefs professed by Lenin and his devoted followers. It would appear that the Bolsheviks had to succeed soon or not at all. How they did succeed will be told in the next chapter.

Chapter 34

The Revolutions of 1917

The collapse of the Romanov autocracy in March 1917 was one of the most leaderless, spontaneous, anonymous revolutions of all time. While almost every thoughtful observer in Russia in the winter of 1916–17 foresaw the likelihood of the crash of the existing regime no one, even among the revolutionary leaders, realized that the strikes and bread riots which broke out in Petrograd on March 8 would culminate in the mutiny of the garrison and the overthrow of the government four days later.

CHAMBERLIN

The enemies of Bolshevism were numerous, but they were also weak, poorly organized, divided, and apathetic. The strategy of Lenin was calculated to emphasize their divisions, neutralize their opposition, and capitalize on their apathy. In 1902 in *What Is To Be Done?* Lenin had written, "Give us an organization of revolutionaries, and we shall overturn the whole of Russia!" On November 7, 1917, the wish was fulfilled and the deed accomplished.

FAINSOD

As has been indicated in preceding chapters, the constitutional period of Russian imperial history has continued to evoke much controversy, to cite only the contributions by Haimson and other American scholars. Optimistic students of the development of Russia from the Revolution of 1905 to the First World War and the revolutions of 1917 have emphasized that Russia had finally left autocracy behind and was evolving toward liberalism and political freedom. The change in 1907 in the electoral law indicated that the Duma could no longer be abolished. Moreover, the reformed Russian legislature proceeded to play an important part in the affairs of the country and to gain ever-increasing prestige and acceptance at home, among both government officials and the people, as well as abroad. As an Englishman observed, "the atmosphere and instincts of parliamentary life" grew in the empire of the Romanovs. Besides, continue the optimists, Russian society at the time was much more progressive and democratic than the constitutional framework alone would indicate, and was becoming increasingly so every year. Modern education spread rapidly at different levels and was remarkably humanitarian and liberal—as were Russian teachers as a group—not at all likely to serve as a buttress for antiquated ideas or obsolete institutions. Russian universities enjoyed virtually full freedom and a rich creative life. Elsewhere, too, an energetic discussion went on. Even the periodical press, in spite of various restrictions, gave some representation to every point of view, including the Bolshevik. Government prohibitions and penalties could frequently be neutralized by such simple means as a change in the name of a publication or, if necessary, by sending the nominal editor to jail, while important political writers continued their work. To be sure, grave problems remained, in particular, economic backwardness and the poverty of the masses. But, through industrialization on the one hand and Stolypin's land reform on the other, they were on the way to being solved. Above all, Russia needed time and peace.

Pessimistic critics have drawn a different picture of the period. Many of them refused even to call it "constitutional," preferring such terms as *Scheinkonstitutionalismus*—that is, sham constitutionalism—because, both according to the Fundamental Laws and in fact, the executive branch of the government and the ministers in particular were not responsible to the Duma. Limited in power and limited in representativeness by a highly unequal electoral system (especially after the arbitrary electoral change of 1907), the Duma functioned, it is argued, less as an effective channel for the popular redress of grievances than as a constantly frustrating reminder of the autocracy's unwillingness to accept real political reform. Indeed, Nicholas II's hostility to the participation of organized society in Russia's political life seemed to be growing all the more intense in these final years. The power of nonentities, like Goremykin and Sukhomlinov, and the fantastic Rasputin himself, were logical end products of the bankruptcy of the regime. Meanwhile, society appeared to be heading toward crisis. Social discontent, the pessimists argue, was growing not lessening as the economy modernized. They point to ominous signs: the peasants' persistent desire to possess all they land they work as both the practical solution to their poverty and a necessary act of justice, continuing workers' protests against low wages and harsh working conditions and the frequency with which these demands were combined with demands for political change, growing popular support for radical socialists (especially among workers concentrated in St. Petersburg and Moscow), political terrorism both of the Left and the Right, and the widespread influence of the languages of class hostility and democratic freedoms. Assumedly positive developments like urbanization, the growing availability of consumer goods, and widening literacy seemed more likely to generate frustration with the status quo than to lessen social tensions. Even cultural life pointed toward crisis, as artists rejected all tradition as bankrupt and philistine or were drawn toward "decadent" fascination with sex, evil, demons, shadows, and a coming apocalypse. Russia was headed for catastrophe.

The optimists, thus, believe that imperial Russia was ruined by the First World War. The pessimists maintain that the war provided merely the last mighty push to bring the whole rotten structure tumbling down. Certainly it added an enormous burden to the load borne by the Russian people. Human losses were staggering. To cite Golovin's figures, in the course of the war the

Russian army mobilized 15,500,000 men and suffered greater casualties than did the armed forces of any other country involved in the titanic struggle: 1,650,000 killed, 3,850,000 wounded, and 2,410,000 taken prisoner. The destruction of property and other civilian losses and displacement escaped count. The Russian army tried to evacuate the population as it retreated, adding to the confusion and suffering. It became obvious during the frightful ordeal that the imperial government had again failed in its tasks, as in the Crimean War and the Russo-Japanese War, but on a much larger scale. As mentioned earlier, the Russian minister of war and many other high officials and generals failed miserably in the test of war, Russian weapons turned out to be inferior to the enemies', Russian ammunition in short supply. Transportation was generally bogged down and on numerous occasions it broke down altogether. In addition to the army, the urban population suffered as a result of this because it experienced serious difficulties obtaining food and fuel. Inflation ran rampant. Worst of all, the government refused to learn any lessons: instead of liberalizing state policies and relying more on the public, which was eager to help, Nicholas II held fast to his anachronistic political faith in unfettered autocracy. He dismissed appeals by organized civic organizations to be allowed a larger role in the mobilization effort and showed nothing but contempt for demands that he appoint a cabinet of ministers that would enjoy "the confidence of the public." And he ignored all warnings, including blunt reports in the first weeks of 1917, by police agents assigned to keep watch over public opinion, of "a wave of animosity against those in authority in wide circles of the population."

The February Revolution and the Provisional Government

The imperial regime died with hardly a whimper. Popular revolution, which came suddenly, was totally unprepared. In the course of the momentous days of March 8 to 11, 1917 (February 23 to 26, Old Style) riots and demonstrations in the capital—renamed "Petrograd" instead of the German-sounding "St. Petersburg" during the war—occasioned by a shortage of bread and coal assumed a more serious character. On March 8, thousands of women textile workers walked out of their factories—partly in commemoration of International Women's Day but mainly to protest the severe shortages of bread. Already large numbers of men and women were on strike or idled by fuel shortages or lockouts. The numbers of strikers continued to grow, as did the size and vehemence of street demonstrations, at which banners and speeches voiced demands ranging from bread (the most common shout heard from the crowds) to an end to the war to the abolition of autocracy. On March 10 reserve battalions sent to suppress the crowds fraternized with them instead, and there were no other troops in the city. Resolute action, such as promptly bringing in loyal forces from elsewhere, might have saved the imperial government, at least temporarily. Instead, with Nicholas II away at the front, authority simply collapsed and many officials went into hiding. Seemingly with one mind, the population of Petrograd turned to the Duma for leadership.

On March 11 members of the Duma sidestepped an imperial dissolution decree, and the next day they created a Provisional Government, composed of a score of prominent Duma leaders and public figures. Prince George Lvov, formerly chairman of the Union of Zemstva and Towns, assumed the positions of chairman of the Council of Ministers, that is, prime minister, and of minister of the interior. His more important colleagues included the Cadet leader Miliukov as minister of foreign affairs, the Octobrist leader Guchkov as minister of war and of the navy, and Alexander Kerensky, the only socialist in the cabinet—associated with the Socialist Revolutionary party—as minister of justice. The new government closely reflected the composition and views of the Progressive Bloc in the Duma, with the Cadets obtaining the greatest single representation.

Nicholas II bowed to the inevitable and on the fifteenth of March abdicated for himself and his only son, Alexis, in favor of his brother, Michael, who in turn abdicated the next day in favor of the decision of the constituent assembly, or in effect in favor of the Provisional Government pending that decision. Nicholas II, on his side, had appointed Lvov prime minister before renouncing the throne. Thus ended the rule of the Romanovs in Russia.

The Provisional Government was quickly recognized, and hailed, by the United States and other Western democracies. But, in spite of its rapid and general acceptance in Russia and abroad, the new government had to deal from the very beginning with a serious rival: the Petrograd Soviet of Workers' and Soldiers' Deputies, which was modeled on the 1905 Soviet. The new Soviet was formed on the twelfth of March, established itself in the Duma building, and proceeded to assert its authority. True, dominated by moderate socialists until

The first "cabinet of ministers" of the Provisional Government. Prince George Lvov is first on the left. Kerensky is third and Miliukov sixth from the left. By April 1917 crowds in the streets would be calling for the removal of these "bourgeois ministers" (excluding Kerensky). (Russian State Archive of Film and Photographic Documents)

the autumn of 1917, it did not try to wrest power from the "bourgeoisie," for it considered Russia unprepared for a socialist revolution, but it made its weight strongly felt nevertheless. In fact, the Provisional Government had been set up by the Duma in consultation with the Soviet and had to take its unofficial partner into account in all its policies and activities. Moreover, the Soviet acted authoritatively on its own, sometimes in direct contradiction to the efforts of the ministers. Notably, as early as March 14 it issued the famous, or notorious, *Order No. 1* to the troops which proclaimed that military units should be run by elected committees, with officers entitled to command only during tactical operations. Symbolically, soldiers were no longer obliged to salute officers when not on duty (for soldiers were now free citizens in their civic life) nor, even when on duty, to address them with honorific titles like "your Excellency," and officers were forbidden to be "rude" toward soldiers or to address them with the familiar *ty*. Following the Petrograd lead, Soviets began to be formed all over Russia. The first All-Russian Congress of Soviets, which met in the capital on the sixteenth of June, contained representatives from more than 350 local units. The delegates included 285 Socialist Revolutionaries, 245 Mensheviks, and 105 Bolsheviks, as well as some deputies from minor socialist parties. The Congress elected an executive committee which became the supreme Soviet body. Soviets stood much closer to the restless masses than did Lvov and his associates, and thus enjoyed a large and immediate following.

The Provisional Government lasted approximately eight months: from March 12 until November 7, 1917. Its record combined remarkable liberalism with an inability to solve pressing, crucial problems. The new regime promoted democracy and liberty in Russia. All citizens achieved equality before the law. Full freedom of religion, speech, press, assembly, unions, and strikes became a reality. The secret police, flogging, exile to Siberia, and the death penalty were abolished. Town and country administration was revamped to make it more democratic, with zemstvo institutions finally introduced at the level of the volost, that is, the township or canton. In addition to equal rights, ethnic minorities received autonomy, while Poland was declared independent. Labor legislation included the introduction of an eight-hour day for some categories of workers.

However, although the Provisional Government demonstrated what liberalism might have done for Russia, it failed to overcome the quite extraordinary difficulties that beset the country, and those who ruled it, in 1917. The new government continued the war in spite of the fact that support for the war continued to decline among the people and that the army became daily less able to fight on. While convinced that all available land should belong to the peasants, it made no definitive land settlement, leaving that to the constituent assembly and thus itself failing to satisfy the peasantry. It proved unable to check inflation, restore transportation, or increase industrial production. In fact, the Russian economy continued to run rapidly downhill.

A large part of this failure stemmed from the limited authority and power of the new regime. It had little in the way of an effective administrative apparatus, the tsarist police in particular having largely gone into hiding. As already mentioned, it had at all times to contend with the Soviet. While the high command of the army supported the government, enlisted men remained an uncertain quantity; the Petrograd garrison itself was devoted to the Soviet. What is more, the Provisional Government had to promise the Soviet not to remove or disarm that garrison. Kerensky's derisive appellation, "persuader-in-chief," was in part a reflection of his unenviable position.

The government also made mistakes. It refused to recognize the catastrophic condition of the country and misjudged the mood of the people. Of course, many of the government's "mistakes" were understandable given their liberal political values. Thus, as mentioned, it continued the war, believing that the Russians, like the French at the time of the great French Revolution, would fight better than ever because they were finally free men. They also sincerely believed that abandoning the democratic allies France and Great Britain in their struggle against authoritarian Germany would have betrayed their political principles and Russia's best interests as a new democracy. In internal affairs, a moderate and liberal position, generally difficult to maintain in times of upheaval, proved quixotic in a country of desperately poor and largely illiterate peasants who wanted the gentry land above all else. The government's temporary, "provisional," nature constituted a special weakness. Its members were deeply conscious of the fact that they had acquired their high authority by chance and that the Duma itself had been elected by the extremely restricted suffrage of 1907. Believing deeply in the rule of law, they insisted that fundamental questions of Russia's future could only be settled by a fully democratic constituent assembly. Such basic decisions as those involved in the land settlement and in the future status of the national minorities had, therefore, to be left to that assembly. In the suggestive, if controversial, words of a political scientist: "This lack of a representative and responsible parliament helped greatly to distinguish the course of the Russian Revolution from its English, French and American predecessors." Yet, if a constituent assembly meant so much to the members of the Provisional Government, they made perhaps their worst mistake in not calling it together soon enough. While some of the best Russian jurists tried to draw a perfect electoral law, time slipped by. When a constituent assembly finally did meet, it was much too late, for the Bolsheviks had already gained control of Russia.

The Bolshevik victory in 1917 cannot be separated from the person and activity of Lenin. He arrived, together with some of his associates, at the Finland Station in Petrograd on the sixteenth of April, the Germans having let them through from Switzerland in hopes that they would disorganize the Russian war effort. In contrast to the attitude of satisfaction with the course of the revolution and cooperation with the Provisional Government prevalent even in the Soviet, Lenin assumed an extreme and intransigent position in his "April Theses" and other pronouncements. He declared that the bourgeois revolution had already been accomplished in Russia and that history was moving inexorably to the next stage, the socialist stage, which had to begin with the seizure of power by the proletariat and poor peasants. As immediate goals Lenin proclaimed peace, seizure of gentry land by the peasants, control of factories by committees of workers, and "all power to the Soviets." "War to the palaces, peace to the huts!" shouted Bolshevik placards. "Expropriate the expropriators!"

Although Lenin found himself at first an isolated figure unable to win a majority even in his own party, events moved his way. The crushing burden of the war and increasing economic dislocation made the position of the Provisional Government constantly more precarious. In the middle of May, Miliukov and Guchkov were forced to resign because of popular agitation and pressure, and the cabinet was reorganized under Lvov to include five socialists rather than one, with Kerensky taking the ministries of war and the navy. The government declared itself committed to a strictly defensive war and to a peace "without annexations and indemnities." Yet, to drive the enemy out, Kerensky and General Alexis Brusilov started a major offensive on the southwestern front late in June. Initially successful, it soon collapsed because of confusion and lack of discipline. Entire units simply refused to fight. The Germans and Austrians in turn broke through the Russian lines, and the Provisional Government had to face another disaster. The problem of national minorities became ever more pressing as ethnic and national movements mushroomed in the disorganized former empire of the Romanovs. The government continued its increasingly hazardous policy of postponing political decisions until the meeting of a constituent assembly. Nevertheless, four Cadet ministers resigned in July because they believed that too broad a recognition had been accorded to the Ukrainian movement. Serious tensions and crises in the cabinet were also demonstrated by the resignation of the minister of trade and industry, who opposed the efforts of the new Social Democratic minister of labor to have workers participate in the management of industry, and the clash between Lvov and Victor Chernov, the Socialist Revolutionary leader who had become minister of agriculture, over the implementation of the land policy. The crucial land problem became more urgent as peasants began to appropriate the land of the gentry on their own, without waiting for the constituent assembly.

The general crisis and unrest in the country and, in particular, the privations and restlessness in the capital led to the so-called "July days," from the sixteenth to the eighteenth of July 1917, when radical soldiers, sailors, and mobs, together with the Bolsheviks, tried to seize power in Petrograd. Lenin apparently considered the uprising premature, and the Bolsheviks seemed to follow their impatient adherents as much as they led them. Although sizeable and threatening, the rebellion collapsed because the Soviet refused to endorse it, because some military units proved loyal to the Provisional Government, and because the government utilized the German connections of the Bolsheviks to accuse them of treason. Several Bolshevik leaders fled, including Lenin who went to Finland from whence he continued to direct the party; certain others were jailed. But the government did not press its victory and try to eliminate its opponents. On the twentieth of July Prince Lvov resigned and Kerensky took over the position of prime minister; socialists once more gained in the reshuffling of the cabinet.

Ministerial changes helped the regime little. The manifold crisis in the country deepened. In addition to the constant pressure from the Left, the Provisional Government attracted opposition from the Right which objected to its inability to maintain firm control over the army and the people, its lenient treatment of the Bolsheviks, and its increasingly socialist composition. In search of a broader base of understanding and support, the government arranged a State Conference in late August in Moscow, attended by some two thousand former Duma deputies and representatives of various organizations and groups, such as Soviets, unions, and local governments. The Conference produced no tangible results, but underlined the rift between the socialist and the non-socialist approaches to Russian problems. Whereas Kerensky expressed the socialist position and received strong support from socialist deputies, the Constitutional Democrats, army circles, and other "middle-class" groups rallied around the recently appointed commander in chief, General Lavr Kornilov. Of simple cossack origin, Kornilov had no desire to restore the old regime, and he could even be considered a democratic general. But the commander in chief, along with other military men, wanted above all to re-establish discipline in the army and law and order in the country, disapproving especially of the activities of the Soviets.

The "Kornilov affair" remains something of a mystery, although Ukraintsev's testimony and certain other evidence indicate that Kerensky, rather than Kornilov, should be blamed for its peculiar course and its being a fiasco. Apparently the prime minister and the commander in chief had decided that loyal troops should be sent to Petrograd to protect the government. Apparently, too, that "protection" included the destruction of Soviet power in the capital. In any case, when Kornilov dispatched an army corps to execute the plan, Kerensky appealed to the people "to save the revolution" from Kornilov. The break between the prime minister and the general stemmed probably not only from their different views on the exact nature of the strengthened Provisional Government to be established in Russia, and on Kerensky's position in that government, but also from the strange and confusing activities of the man who acted as an intermediary between them.

The revolution was "saved." From the ninth to the fourteenth of September the population of the capital mobilized for defense, while the advancing troops, faced with a railroad strike, encountering general opposition, and short of supplies, became demoralized and bogged down without reaching the destination; their commanding officer committed suicide. Only the Bolsheviks really gained from the episode. Their leaders were let out of jail, and their followers were armed to defend Petrograd. After the Kornilov threat collapsed, they retained the preponderance of military strength in the capital, winning ever more adherents among the increasingly radical masses.

The Provisional Government, on the other hand, came to be bitterly despised by the Right for having betrayed Kornilov—whether the charge was entirely justified is another matter—while many on the Left suspected it of having plotted with him. The cabinet experienced another crisis and was finally able to reconstitute itself—for the third and last time—only on the twenty-fifth of September, with ten socialist and six nonsocialist ministers, Kerensky remaining at the head. It should be added that the Kornilov fiasco, followed by the arrest of Kornilov and several other generals, led to a further deterioration of military discipline, making the position of officers in many units untenable.

Social Revolution

Research on the social history of the revolution has added much to our knowledge of the role workers, soldiers, and peasants played in the coming to power of the Bolsheviks and to our understanding of what these events meant to ordinary Russians. It seems likely that Lenin's arguments would have remained only a footnote to the history of 1917 had not so many people found Bolshevik promises so appealing and had not continuing social discontent and anger undermined Russia's fragile new order. Of course, the erosion of order was in large measure caused by continued economic collapse, especially the abysmal material conditions in the cities and at the front. It seemed to many lower-class Russians, deeply distrustful of existing political and social authorities, that the only solution to this crisis was greater power over their own everyday lives. Thus, factory workers demanded that their elected committees be allowed to supervise production, oversee supplies and fuel, monitor fines and other disciplinary measures, and supervise hiring and firing. As economic conditions worsened and distrust of employers grew, "workers' control" evolved from supervision to demands for complete managerial power by workers. Workers also took revenge on those who had claimed power over their lives in the past, whether simply by being insolent and insubordinate with foremen and employers or through more elaborate rituals in which supervisors or owners were carted out of factories in wheelbarrows. Soldiers and sailors similarly disregarded orders, mocked officers (even beat them), elected new ones (especially when old officers tried to resist the growing demands of soldiers' committees), or simply deserted in increasingly large numbers. Peasants, beginning in the spring, seized and divided up livestock and tools belonging to large landowners, cut wood in private forests, forced independent peasant farmers to return to the communal rules of the village, seized land from both the gentry and richer peasants without waiting for legal sanction, and tried to expel landlords from the countryside by attacking and burning their homes. On the streets of every major town, crowds of workers, soldiers, students, and other townspeople repeatedly took control of public squares, boulevards, and streets for meetings, funeral processions, and demonstrations. Alongside these acts of social defiance was a good deal of drunkenness, hooliganism, robbery, and criminal violence. By the fall of 1917, even many moderate socialists viewed these upheavals with horror as an upwelling of dark popular instincts and destructive class hatred, leading Russia toward a nightmarish abyss of violence and anarchy.

The motivations, goals, and moods of the aroused population were complex and contradictory. Judging by the torrent of words, spoken and written, that accompanied this social revolution, certain ideas seem to have been most pervasive. Freedom pervades the language of almost everyone in the months after the February Revolution, often cast in near religious terms as something "sacred," as enabling the "resurrection" of the Russian people. But freedom

Soldiers at a funeral on Mars Field in Petrograd for those who fell in the February Revolution. Banners read "Eternal and Glorious Memory to the Fallen Comrade Fighters for Freedom," "Long Live the Democratic Republic," and "In Organization Is Strength." Use of symbols such as the rising sun, broken chains, and female personifications of liberty was common. (Russian State Archive of Film and Photographic Documents)

was understood variously: negatively as the end of a long history of subjugation, lack of rights, and repression; positively as one of the fundamental "rights of man"; and quite tangibly as a good that would bring such social benefits as food, land, free education, and an end to the war. Political power also preoccupied people. Side by side with talk of freedom, most Russians also seemed to believe in the need for strong and unified political authority to restore order to the country, especially to the economy. But this must be a political power that would serve the interests of the majority against the minority, of the poor against the rich. Such "democratic" authority, embodied for many in the idea of Soviet power, would, for example, establish a bread monopoly to prevent hunger, distribute land to the poor, introduce workers' control in industry, fix prices to control inflation, expropriate "super-profits," and even suppress opposition to such popular power. As can be seen, social class pervaded popular thinking. Most lower-class Russians distrusted the rich and powerful and tended to blame them for the failures of the revolution since March, even to brand them as "enemies of the people" and "traitors" to Russia and the revolution. Complicating all this, the language of popular revolution was also suffused with moral language and feeling. Talk of "good" and "evil" were common currency in 1917. And ethical notions of honor and dignity, and of the social rights these entailed, were pervasive. The revolution, it was said, was about ending "humiliation and insult" and creating a social and political order defined by the "respect" it gave to ordinary people. Whether this is what the Bolshevik revolution accomplished is another story.

The October Revolution

The Bolsheviks finally captured a majority in the Petrograd Soviet on September 13 and in the Moscow Soviet a week later, although the executive committee elected by the first All-Russian Congress of Soviets continued, of course, to be dominated by moderate socialists. Throughout the country the Bolsheviks were on the rise. From his hideout in Finland, Lenin urged the seizure of power. On October 23 he came incognito to Petrograd and managed to convince the executive committee of the party, with some division of opinion, of the soundness of his view. Lenin apparently considered victory a great gamble, not a scientific certainty, but he correctly estimated that the fortunate circumstances had to be exploited, and he did not want to wait until the meeting of the constituent assembly. His opinions prevailed over the judgment of those of his colleagues who, in more orthodox Marxist fashion, considered Russia insufficiently prepared for a Bolshevik revolution and their party lacking adequate support in the country at large. Leon Trotsky—a pseudonym of Leon Bronstein—who first became prominent in the St. Petersburg Soviet of 1905 and who combined oratorical brilliance and outstanding intellectual qualities with energy and organizational ability, proved to be Lenin's ablest and most active assistant in staging the Bolsheviks' seizure of power.

The revolution succeeded with little opposition. On November 7—October 25, Old Style, hence "the Great October Revolution"—Red troops occupied various strategic points in the capital. In the early night hours of November 8, the Bolshevik-led soldiers of the Petrograd garrison, sailors from Kronstadt, and the workers' Red Guards stormed the Winter Palace, weakly defended by youngsters from military schools and even by a women's battalion, and arrested members of the Provisional Government. Kerensky himself had managed to escape some hours earlier. Soviet government was established in Petrograd and in Russia.

Part
VI

Soviet Russia

Chapter 35

Soviet Russia: An Introduction

The philosophers have only *interpreted* the world in various ways;
the point however is to *change* it.*

—MARX

The conception of a community as an organic growth, which the
statesman can only affect to a limited extent, is in the main modern,
and has been greatly strengthened by the theory of evolution. . . .

It might, however, be maintained that the evolutionary view of
society, though true in the past, is no longer applicable, but must, for
the present and the future, be replaced by a much more mechanistic
view. In Russia and Germany new societies have been created, in
much the same way as the mythical Lycurgus was supposed to have
created the Spartan polity. The ancient law giver was a benevolent
myth; the modern law giver is a terrifying reality.

—RUSSELL

For nearly three-quarters of a century, communist ideology, the Communist
Party, and Communist direction constituted the outstanding characteristics of
Soviet Russia, that is, of the Union of Soviet Socialist Republics. To be sure,
other factors, ranging from the economic backwardness of the country to its
position as a great power in Europe, Asia, and the world, proved to be of major
importance. Still, it would not be an exaggeration to say that, whereas other
elements in the situation exercised very significant influences on Soviet policies, without communism there would have been no Soviet policies at all and
no Soviet Union. Moreover, it is frequently impossible to draw the line
between the communist and the noncommunist aspects of Soviet Russia and
between communist and noncommunist causes of Soviet behavior because the
two modes have influenced and interpenetrated each other and because Soviet
leaders have viewed everything within the framework of their ideology.

---

*Italics in the original.

Marxism

The doctrine of communism represents a variant of Marxism, based on the works of Marx and Engels as developed by Lenin. Working for several decades, beginning in the 1840s, Marx and Engels constructed a huge and comprehensive, although not entirely consistent, philosophical system. The roots of Marxism include eighteenth-century Enlightenment, classical economics, utopian socialism, and German idealistic philosophy—in other words, some of the main traditions of Western thought. Most important, Marx was "the last of the great system-builders, the successor of Hegel, a believer, like him, in a rational formula summing up the evolution of mankind." While an exposition of Marxism would require another book, certain aspects of the doctrine must constantly be kept in mind by a student of Soviet history.

Marxism, especially as it was understood by Soviet ideologists, postulates dialectical materialism as the key to and the essence of reality. While applicable to philosophy, science, and in fact to everything, dialectical materialism exercised its greatest impact on the study—and later manipulation—of human society, on that combination of sociology, history, and economics that represented Marx's own specialty. "Materialism" asserts that only matter exists; in Marxism it also led to a stress on the priority of the economic factor in man's life, social organization, and history.

> In the social production of their means of existence men enter into definite, necessary relations which are independent of their will, productive relationships which correspond to a definite stage of development of their material productive forces. The aggregate of these productive relationships constitutes the economic structure of society, the real basis on which a juridical and political superstructure arises, and to which definite forms of social consciousness correspond. The mode of production of the material means of existence conditions the whole process of social, political and intellectual life. It is not the consciousness of men that determines their existence, but, on the contrary, it is their social existence that determines their consciousness.

The fundamental division in every society is that between the exploiters and the exploited, between the owners of the means of production and those who have to sell their labor to the owners to earn a living. A given political system, religion, and culture all reflect and support the economic set-up, protecting the interests of the exploiters. The base, to repeat, determines the superstructure.

"Dialectical" adds a dynamic quality to materialism, defining the process of the evolution of reality. For the Marxists insist that everything changes all the time. What is more, that change follows the laws of the dialectic and thus presents a rigorously correct and scientifically established pattern. Following Hegel, Marx and Engels postulated a three-step sequence of change: the thesis, the antithesis, and the synthesis. A given condition, the thesis, leads to opposition within itself, the antithesis, and the tension between the two is resolved by a leap to a new condition, the synthesis. The synthesis in turn becomes a thesis producing a new antithesis, and the dialectic continues. The historical dialectic expresses itself in class struggle: "The history of all hitherto existing society is the history of class struggles." As an antithesis grows within a thesis,

V. I. Lenin in 1917   (Gosizdat)

"the material productive forces of a society," always developing, "come into contradiction with the existing productive relationships," and social strife ensues. Eventually revolution leads to a transformation of society, only to become itself the new established order producing a new antithesis. In this manner the Italian towns and the urban classes in general revolted successfully against feudalism to inaugurate the modern, bourgeois period of European history. That period in turn ran its prescribed course, culminating in the full flowering of capitalism. But, again inevitably, the capitalists, the bourgeois, evoked their antithesis, their "grave-diggers," the industrial workers or the proletariat. In the words of Marx foretelling the coming revolution:

> The expropriation is brought about by the operation of the immanent laws of capitalist production, by the centralization of capital. . . . The centralization of the means of production and the socialization of labor reach a point where they prove incompatible with their capitalist husk. This husk bursts asunder. The knell of capitalist private property sounds. The expropriators are expropriated.

Interestingly if illogically, the victorious proletarian revolution would mark the end of all exploitation of man by man and the establishment of a just socialist society. In a sense, humanity would return to prehistory, when, according to Marx and the Marxists, primeval communities knew no social differentiation or antagonism.

Leninism

Lenin's theoretical contribution to Marxism could in no sense rival the contributions of the two originators of the doctrine. Still, he did his best to adapt Marxism to the changing conditions in the world as well as to his own experience with the Second International and to Russian circumstances, and he produced certain important additions to and modifications of the basic teaching. More to the point for students of Soviet history is the fact that these amendments became gospel in the Soviet Union, where the entire ideology was frequently referred to as "Marxism-Leninism."

Among the views developed by Lenin, those on the party, democracy, the revolution, and the dictatorship of the proletariat, together with those on the peasantry and on imperialism, deserve special attention. As already mentioned, it was a disagreement on the nature of the party that in 1903 split the Russian Social Democrats into the Lenin-led Bolsheviks and the Mensheviks. The Mensheviks favored a party open to any who shared its Marxist goals. Lenin insisted on a tightly knit body of dedicated professional revolutionaries, with clear lines of command and a military discipline. Behind these different conceptions of the party lay deeper differences, which would have long-term effects on Soviet politics. One difference concerned the place of workers in the working-class movement. While Mensheviks tended to believe strongly in the consciousness-raising benefits of the experience of struggle itself, Lenin emphasized the need for guidance and leadership by more "conscious" activists. As he famously argued in *What Is To Be Done?* (1902), workers left to themselves would be unable to see beyond the economic struggle and understand that their interests lie in overthrowing the existing social system. A vanguard party was necessary to ensure that socialists did more than "gaze with awe upon the 'posterior' of the Russian proletariat." More generally, Lenin differed from many other Russian Marxists in thinking about democracy. The Mensheviks, and even many Bolsheviks before 1917, were attracted to Marxism precisely for its democratic promise to give all people equal political representation and civil freedom, though they believed this political democracy would need to be supplemented by the democracy of social rights. Lenin, by contrast, was among those who insisted that democracy had no inherent value apart from its usefulness in promoting the cause of the socialist transformation of society. The Bolsheviks, he liked to say, make no "fetish" of democracy. With characteristic determination and believing in the imminent worldwide overthrow of the capitalist system, Lenin decided in 1917 that he and his party could then stage a successful revolution in Russia, although at first virtually no one, even among the Bolsheviks, agreed. After the Bolsheviks did seize power in the October Revolution, Lenin's Bolshevik party, renamed the Communist

Party, drew on these ideas about the party and democracy to shape the new Soviet state.

Lenin's revolutionary optimism stemmed in part from his reconsideration of the role of the peasantry in bringing about the establishment of the new order. Marx, Engels, and Marxists in general have neglected the peasants in their teachings and relegated them, as petty proprietors, to the bourgeois camp. Lenin, however, came to the conclusion that, if properly led by the proletariat and the party, poor peasants could be a revolutionary force: indeed later he proclaimed even the middle peasants to be of some value to the socialist state. The same *April Theses* that urged the transformation of the bourgeois revolution into a socialist one stated that poor peasants were to be part of the new revolutionary wave.

Lenin expanded Marxism in another, even more drastic manner. In his book *Imperialism, the Highest Stage of Capitalism*, written in 1916 and published in the spring of 1917, he tried to bring Marxism up to date to account for such recent developments as intense colonial rivalry, international crises, and finally the First World War. He concluded that in its ultimate form capitalism becomes imperialism, with monopolies and financial capital ruling the world. Cartels replace free competition, and export of capital becomes more important than export of goods. An economic and political partitioning of the world follows in the form of a constant struggle for economic expansion, spheres of influence, colonies, and the like. International alliances and counteralliances arise. The disparity between the development of the productive forces of the participants and their shares of the world is settled among capitalist states by wars. Thus, instead of the original Marxist vision of the victorious socialist revolution as the simple expropriation of a few supercapitalists, Lenin described the dying stage of capitalism as an age of gigantic conflicts, relating it effectively to the twentieth century. Still more important, this externalization, so to speak, of the capitalist crisis brought colonies and underdeveloped areas in general prominently into the picture. The capitalists were opposed not only by their own proletariats, but also by the alien peoples whom they exploited, more or less regardless of the social order and the stage of development of those peoples. Therefore, the proletarians and the colonial peoples were natural allies. Lenin, it is worth noting, paid much more attention to Asia than did Western Marxists. Eventually—in a dialectical *tour de force*—even the fact that the socialist revolution came to Russia, rather than to such industrial giants as Great Britain, Germany, and the United States, could be explained by the theory of the "weakest link," that is, by the argument that in the empire of the Romanovs various forms of capitalist exploitation, both native and colonial or semicolonial, combined to make capitalism particularly paradoxical and unstable, so that the Russian link in the capitalist chain snapped first.

Many critics have pointed out that Lenin's special views, while differing from the ideas of Marx and Engels, found their *raison d'être* both in Russian reality and in the Russian radical tradition. A land of peasants, Russia could not afford to rely for its future on the proletariat alone, and at least the poor peasants, if not the wealthier ones, had to be included to bring theory into some correspondence with the facts. Again, in contrast to, for example, Germany, the socialist parties never acquired in imperial Russia a legal standing or a mass following, remaining essentially a conspiracy of intellectuals and worker activists. If Lenin wanted results, he had to depend on these elites, on a small, dedicated party. Moreover, in doing so he followed the tradition of Chernyshevsky, of Tkachev especially, of the "People's Will," and even, broadly speaking—though he would have denied it vehemently—of such populists as Lavrov and Mikhailovsky, who emphasized the role of the "critically thinking individuals" as the makers of history. Born in 1870, Lenin grew up admiring Chernyshevsky; and his oldest brother, Alexander, was executed in 1887 for his part in a populist plot to assassinate Alexander III. Lenin's later persistent and violent attacks on the populists should not, it has been argued, obscure his basic indebtedness to them.

Yet, although this line of reasoning has some validity and helps to situate the great Bolshevik leader in the history of Russian radicalism—where he certainly belongs as much as in the history of world Marxism—it should not be pursued too far. After all, Lenin dedicated his entire mature life to the theory and practice of Marxism, which he considered to be infallibly true. Besides, while one does not have to subscribe to the official Soviet view that Lenin is the perfect creative Marxist, neither does one have to endorse the view, common among Western Social Democrats, that Lenin and communism betrayed Marxism. In fact, both Lenin's "hard" line, emphasizing the role of the party, revolution, and ruthlessness, and the "soft" approach of Western revisionists can be legitimately deduced from the vast and sometimes inconsistent writings of Marx and Engels.

The Intolerance

Comprehensiveness and ruthless intolerance have been among the most important salient features of Marxism-Leninism. While provoked to an extent by such practical circumstances as the requirements of ruling a state—states, eventually—and the strong and manifold opposition that had to be overcome, these traits nevertheless reside at the heart of the ideology itself. As already explained, Marxism constitutes an all-inclusive view of the world, metaphysical rather than empirical, which omits nothing of importance and possibly—at least so it can be argued in theory—nothing at all. Moreover, its teachings are believed to have the conclusiveness of scientific laws. Appropriately, the Bolshevik and later Communist Party's newspaper was known simply as *Pravda*, or *The Truth*. In other words, to its adherents Marxism-Leninism represents a science, and those who oppose it are regarded by them as absolutely and demonstrably wrong. No matter how sophisticated, these critics ultimately deserve no more consideration than misguided, superstitious peasants who object to inoculation against cholera. More precisely, they are either misguided or class enemies; in the latter case they obviously deserve no favorable consideration at all.

A pseudo-science, Marxism-Leninism also possesses numerous earmarks of a pseudo-religion. Berdiaev and other commentators have emphasized the extent to which it proclaims itself to be the truth, the ultimate and entirely comprehensive total, the first and the last, alpha and omega. It determines in effect the right and the wrong and divides the world into white and black. More specifically, it has been suggested that communism has its doctrine of salvation: its Messiah is the proletariat; its paradise is classless society; its church is the party; and its Scriptures are the writings of Marx, Engels, Lenin and, for many years, Stalin. The dialectic of class struggle will suddenly cease when man attains the just society—when man leaps from the kingdom of necessity into the kingdom of freedom. It is probably this pseudo-religious aspect of Marxism-Leninism, even more than its explicit materialism, that makes its frequently fanatical disciples determined enemies of Christianity and of every other religion—for no human being can serve two gods.

Needless to say, Marxism-Leninism is not a democratic teaching. While its followers remain convinced that it represents the interests of the masses, the correctness of the ideology and the need to carry it out in practice do not depend in the least on popular approval or disapproval. More than that, Marxism-Leninism has been remarkably exclusive. Where most other major beliefs appeal to all human beings, Marx began with the assumption that the exploiting classes can never have a change of heart, but must be overthrown. Struggle and violence—ruthlessness once more—form the very fabric of the Marxist doctrine. Even among the exploited, Lenin insisted, few could fully comprehend their own situation and the course of history. Only the party, only an elite, can really see the full truth.

The Appeal

What makes a communist? The ideology itself has no doubt offered numerous attractions to the intellect and helped many people to understand the world. It does represent one of the most impressive systems in the history of Western thought, and it is related to a number of main intellectual currents of the Western tradition. Its greatest strength lies perhaps in its explanation of human exploitation and misery and in its reasoned promise to end both. Those who fail to see the intellectual attractions communism had on either side of the "iron curtain" should consider carefully the testimony of such writers as Milosz who left the Polish "people's democracy," or of the several brilliant ex-Communists who contributed to the book *The God That Failed*. Yet rational persuasiveness stops far short of accounting entirely for the appeal of communism. Of course, both materialism and the dialectic, which are enormously important assumptions, remain unproved. More specific Marxist doctrines, for instance, the crucial labor theory of value, have been very effectively criticized. In addition, Marxist predictions have often been disproved by time. To cite only two of the more important examples, with the middle class growing rather than declining, a polarization into capitalists and workers has failed to take place in capitalist societies; also, in these societies the standard of living of the workers has been improving rather than deteriorating. Marxism possesses no invincible logic, and no scientific certainty; it does provide an elaborate intellectual rationalization and a splendid intellectual façade for those who subscribe to the teaching for nonintellectual reasons.

Especially significant, therefore, might be the link between Marxism-Leninism on the one hand and alienation and protest on the other. Communism has become the vehicle for almost every kind of criticism of the established order, and it has profited from a wide variety of weaknesses and mistakes of noncommunist societies. Indeed, communists seized power not, as predicted, in the advanced industrial countries of the West, but in Russia and in China where relatively backward economic conditions—very different in degree in the two instances—were combined with misery and great tensions and crises. And in both countries the rising class of intellectuals refused to identify itself with the existing system and led the struggle against it. However, even if we allow much for alienation and protest as factors in the rise of communism, we are faced with the question as to why it is communism, rather than some other teaching, that has attracted so many sensitive or dissatisfied people.

To suggest one answer among many, one might mention the four reasons for the appeal of Marxism emphasized by Isaiah Berlin. These include, to begin with, its comprehensiveness and its claim to be the key to knowing everything in the present, the past, and the future. Moreover, the doctrine itself and the knowledge that it gives are allegedly scientific: many social teachings in the nineteenth century, such as Fourier's peculiar utopian socialism or Comte's positivism, claimed scientific validity, but Marxism managed to identify itself more successfully with science than any other. Comprehensiveness and scientific authority become especially attractive with the abandonment of religion and other secure moorings. In the third place, Marxism, in spite of its deterministic aspect, is an activist and optimistic teaching: history is moving in the right direction, and every true believer can have a useful role in furthering its progress. Finally, Marxism possessed from the start a ready-made audience so to speak, the working class, which was invited to take over the world. Later Lenin tried his best to extend the audience to the poor peasants and to colonial peoples.

To move from Berlin's "semirational" reasons for the appeal of Marxism, Lasswell might serve as a representative guide to the slippery area of the irrational appeal. In the language of social psychology and psychoanalysis, he selected such qualities of Marxism-Leninism as its stress on the transitory nature of the present social order, which leads to a redefinition of expectancies about the future and encourages projection. Marxism condemns the capitalist system in clearly moral terms, accusing it in particular of denying affectionate care and attention to the individual and of giving unfair advantage to some over others. The doctrine gains from its prestigious "scientific" form and from its alleged objective quality as well as from specificity, i.e., in analyzing the unjust capitalist society, Marxists point to "surplus value" and "profits" rather than merely to such general factors as human greed or corruption. The extremely vague Marxist utopia, too, serves valuable purposes: it gives free rein to every individual's choice and his craving for omnipotence, and it protects the Marxist ideal from being tied to unpopular or transitory social phenomena. Doctrines, it should be added, are held no less firmly when they are held irrationally; in fact, it can be argued that they are held more firmly if irrationally.

Concluding Remarks

When Communists seized power in Russia in 1917 they had to face an unforeseen situation: revolution erupted in Russia rather than in the industrial West, and it came to one country only rather than to the entire capitalist world. While Lenin and his associates tried to adjust to these facts, they had also to deal with countless other problems, some of them of utmost urgency. After the first hectic months, and years too, Soviet history continued to be a story of great pressures, crises, and conflicts. Under these difficult, and at times desperate, circumstances it is remarkable not how little but how much Russian Communist leaders adhered to the pursuit of their ideological goals—from Lenin's determination to build socialism on the morrow of the Revolution, to Stalin's fantastic five-year plans, and to Khrushchev's efforts to speed the establishment of a truly communist society. An account of this pursuit belongs to the following chapters.

Chapter 36

War Communism, 1917–21, and the New Economic Policy, 1921–28

You will never be alive again,
Never rise from the snow:
Twenty-eight bayonet,
Five fire wounds.
A bitter new garment
I sewed for my friend.
It does love, does love blood—
The Russian earth.

—AKHMATOVA

Where are the swans? And the swans have left.
And the ravens? And the ravens have remained.

—TSVETAEVA

Of all the Governments which were set up in Russia to combat revolutionary rule, only one, that of the Social Revolutionaries at Samara, had the wisdom to assure the peasants that the counterrevolution did not mean the restoration of the land to the landlords. All the rest, in greater or less degree, made plain their policy of reestablishing or compensating them. It was this, and no transcendent virtue in the Bolsheviks, which decided the issue of the three years' struggle, in despite of British tanks and French munitions and Japanese rifles and bayonets.

—MAYNARD

Although the Bolsheviks seized power easily in Russia in November 1917, they managed to consolidate their new position only after several years of bitter struggle. In addition to waging a major and many-faceted civil war, the Soviet government had to fight Poland and deal with the Allied intervention. The Bolsheviks, in a desperate effort to survive, mobilized the population and resources in the area that they controlled and instituted a drastic regime which came to be known as "War Communism." Communist rule did survive, although at a tremendous price. To revive an utterly exhausted, devastated, and starving country, the so-called "New Economic Policy" replaced War Communism and lasted from 1921 to 1928, until the beginning of Stalin's First Five-Year Plan. The period of the New Economic Policy has been rightly contrasted with that of War Communism as a time of relaxation and compromise: Yet, on the whole the Soviet government showed more continuity than change in its policies and pursued its set goals with intelligence and determination—as a brief treatment of the first decade of Communist rule should indicate.

The New Government. Lenin

The Soviet government was organized two days after the October Revolution, on November 9, 1917, under the name of the Council of People's Commissars. Headed by Lenin as chairman, the Council contained such prominent members of the Bolshevik Party as Trotsky, who became commissar for foreign affairs, Alexis Rykov, who became commissar of the interior, and Joseph Dzhugashvili, better known as Stalin, who assumed charge of national minorities. Lenin thus led the government as well as the party and was recognized as by far the most important figure of the new regime in Russia.

Lenin was born in an intellectual family—his father was a school inspector—in 1870 in a town on the Volga named Simbirsk, later Ulianovsk. Vladimir Ulianov proved to be a brilliant student both in secondary school and at the University of Kazan, where he studied law. He early became a radical—the execution of his eldest brother in 1887 for participating in a plot to assassinate Alexander III has sometimes been considered a turning point for him—and then became a Marxist, suffering imprisonment in 1896 and Siberian exile for the three years following. He participated in the publication of a Social Democratic newspaper, *The Spark,* which was printed abroad beginning in 1900, and in other revolutionary activities, often under the pseudonym of *N. Lenin.* At first awed by the "father of Russian Marxism," Plekhanov, Lenin before long struck out on his own, leading the Bolshevik group in the Social Democratic Party split in 1903. We have already met Lenin as an important Marxist theoretician. But practice meant more than theory for the Bolshevik leader. Most of his writings in fact were polemical, brief, and to the point: they denounced opponents or deviationists in ideology and charted the right way for the faithful. As Lenin remarked when events in 1917 interrupted his work on a treatise, *The State and Revolution:* "It is more pleasant and more useful to live through the experience of a revolution than to write about it."

The October Revolution, masterminded by Lenin, gave him power that he continued to exercise in full until largely incapacitated by a stroke in May 1922. After that he still kept some control until his death on January 21, 1924. Moreover, in contrast to Stalin's later terror, Lenin's leadership of the party did not depend at all on the secret police, but rather on his own personality, ability, and achievement. Perhaps appropriately, whereas Stalin's cult experienced some remarkable reversals of fortune shortly after his demise, that of Lenin kept, if anything, gaining in popularity throughout the communist world until its collapse in the late 1980s.

"A Specter Is Haunting Europe—the Specter of Communism," 1920. *Picturing Lenin in a characteristic pose, the phrase is a quotation from the* Communist Manifesto *of Marx and* Engels. (Victoria Bonnell)

The communist myth of Lenin does not stand far from reality in many respects. For Lenin was a dedicated Bolshevik, who lived and breathed revolution and communism. He combined high intelligence, an ability for acute theoretical thinking, and practical sense to become a great Marxist "realist." The amalgam proved ideal for communist purposes: Lenin never wavered in his Marxist faith; yet he knew how to adapt it, drastically if need be, to circumstances. Other outstanding qualities of the Bolshevik leader included exceptional will power, persistence, courage, and the ability to work extremely hard. Even Lenin's simple tastes and modest, almost ascetic, way of life were transposed easily and appropriately from the actual man to his mythical image. At the same time, devotion to an exclusive doctrine led to narrow vision. Ruthlessness followed from Lenin's conviction that he, and sometimes only he, knew the right answer. In the name of a future utopia, horrible things could be sanctioned in the present. Churchill once commented on Lenin: "His aim to save the world. His method to blow it up." The two objectives go ill together.

At the same time, Lenin and the Bolsheviks came to power without a clear blueprint for ruling the country and building socialism or even a clear strategy for governing. On the one hand, Lenin spoke of the revolution creating a "commune state" by releasing the "energy, initiative and decisiveness" of the people, who could perform "miracles." In a speech in November 1917, for example, he called on "all working people" to "remember that you yourselves are now administering the state" and to "take matters into your own hands below, waiting for no one." At the same time, Lenin never tired of reminding people that "a revolution is the most authoritarian thing imaginable," and after October he spoke often, and quite explicitly, of the need for strict control, ruthless suppression, iron discipline, and even dictatorship. Some historians have argued that Lenin's talk about popular participation was a deceitful fig leaf covering his authoritarian and even tyrannical nature. Others have argued that this contradictory language reflected a contradictory political ideology, which, at least in these early years, combined sincere ideals about popular initiative and creativity with strong convictions about the importance of leadership, discipline, and central control. Whatever Lenin's actual views, much of the first decade of Soviet rule was a history of debates and conflicts over how to balance these two principles.

The First Months

The Second All-Russian Congress of Soviets, which met in Petrograd on the seventh of November, approved the Bolshevik revolution, although moderate socialists walked out of the gathering. In Moscow Soviet authority was established only after a week of fighting, because some military units remained loyal to the Provisional Government. Relying on local Soviets, the Bolsheviks spread their rule to numerous other towns and areas. The first serious challenge to the Bolshevik government occurred in January 1918, when the Constituent Assembly, for which elections had been held in late autumn, finally met. The 707 members who assembled in the capital on January 18 included 370 Socialist Revolutionaries, 40 Left Socialist Revolutionaries who had split from the main party, only 170 Bolsheviks, and 34 Mensheviks, as well as not quite 100 deputies who belonged to minor parties or had no party affiliation. In other words, the Socialist Revolutionaries possessed an absolute majority. Chernov was elected chairman of the Constituent Assembly. It should be remembered that the Assembly had been awaited for months by almost all political groups in Russia as the truly legitimate and definitive authority in the country. Lenin himself had denounced the Provisional Government for failing to summon it promptly. Yet, in the changed circumstances, he acted in his usual decisive manner and had troops disperse the Constituent Assembly on the morning of the nineteenth of January. No major repercussions followed, and Soviet rule appeared more secure than ever. The lack of response to the disbanding of the assembly resulted in part from the fact that it had no organized force behind it, and in part from the fact that on the very morrow of the revolution the Soviet government had declared its intention to make peace and also had in effect granted the peasants gentry land, thus taking steps to satisfy the two main demands of the people. The Bolsheviks even enjoyed the cooperation of the Left Socialist Revolutionaries who received three cabinet positions, including the ministry of agriculture.

But the making of peace proved both difficult and extremely costly, with the very existence of the Soviet state hanging in the balance. The Allies failed to respond to the Soviet bid for peace and in fact ignored the Soviet government, not expecting it to last. Discipline in the Russian army collapsed entirely, with soldiers sometimes massacring their officers. After the conclusion of an armistice with the Germans in December 1917, the front simply disbanded in chaos, most men trying to return home by whatever means they could find. The Germans proved willing to negotiate, but they offered Draconian conditions of peace. Trotsky, who as commissar for foreign affairs represented the Soviet government, felt compelled to turn them down, proclaiming a new policy: "no war, no peace!" The Germans then proceeded to advance, occupying more territory and seizing an enormous amount of military matériel. In Petrograd many Bolshevik leaders as well as the Left Socialist Revolutionaries agreed with Trotsky that German demands could not be accepted. Only Lenin's authority and determination swung the balance in favor of the humiliating peace. By sacrificing much else, Lenin in all probability saved Communist rule in Russia, for the young Soviet government was in no position whatsoever to fight Germany.

The Soviet-German Treaty of Brest-Litovsk was signed on March 3, 1918. To sum up its results in Vernadsky's words:

> The peace conditions were disastrous to Russia. The Ukraine, Poland, Finland, Lithuania, Estonia, and Latvia received their independence. Part of Transcaucasia was ceded to Turkey. Russia lost 26 percent of her total population; 27 percent of her arable land; 32 percent of her average crops; 26 percent of her railway system; 33 percent of her manufacturing industries; 73 percent of her iron industries; 75 percent of her coal fields. Besides that, Russia had to pay a large war indemnity.

Or to put it in different terms, Russia lost over sixty million people and over five thousand factories, mills, distilleries, and refineries. Puppet states dependent on Germany were set up in the separated border areas. Only the ultimate German defeat in the First World War prevented the Brest-Litovsk settlement from being definitive, and in particular made it possible for the Soviet government to reclaim Ukraine.

Since Lenin's firm direction in disbanding the Constituent Assembly and capitulating to the Germans had enabled the Soviet government to survive, the Soviet leader and his associates proceeded rapidly to revamp and even transform Russia politically, socially, and economically, a process that had begun in the first days of Bolshevik power. Many of the earliest acts of the government, it has been argued, reflected a need to secure popular support but also a working out in practice of the emancipatory, even libertarian, side of Bolshevik ideology. Peasants were given complete local control over the use of the land through communes and local Soviets and workers' committees were given the power to supervise their own managers—though these developments were more the results of a social revolution the Bolsheviks could not control than of Bolshevik policy. The existing judicial system was abolished and replaced by elected revolutionary tribunals and people's courts. To democratize local government, Soviets were given extensive powers and workers and soldiers were recruited by the thousands as local officials. National minorities were told they had the right to complete self-determination, a policy decision that was also as much recognition of revolutionary realities as a matter of ideological principle. Many early policies were directed at undermining the position of those who formerly held power and status in Russia. Titles and ranks were abolished. As the state gradually assumed control over the scarce housing and other material aspects of life, those who belonged to the upper and middle classes often lost their property, suffered discrimination, and were considered by the new regime to be suspect by definition. Church property was confiscated and religious instruction in schools terminated. Even time changed. The Gregorian or Western calendar—New Style—was adopted on January 31, 1918. At the same time, much early Soviet policy expressed the Bolsheviks' centralizing and authoritarian approach to transforming Russia, even before the disbanding of the Constituent Assembly. In November 1917, the press was placed under state control and many "bourgeois" and even moderate socialist papers were closed down. To centralize control of the economy, banks and large factories were immediately nationalized, foreign trade was made a state monopoly, and, in December, a committee was formed to develop a national economic plan. Also in December 1917, the government established the Extraordinary Commission to Combat Counterrevolution, Sabotage, and Speculation, the dreaded "Cheka," headed by Felix Dzerzhinsky, which fought against both ordinary hooliganism and looting, which became common after October, and suspected anti-regime activities. From that time on, the political police became a fundamental reality of Soviet life. After the closing of the Constituent Assembly, the government ominously declared the liberal Constitutional Party to be a "party of enemies of the people" and treated even many Mensheviks and Socialist Revolutionaries—except for the Left Socialist Revolutionaries until their break with the Bolsheviks in March 1918—as dangerous opponents of the new order.

War Communism and New Problems

With the summer of 1918, War Communism began to acquire a definite shape. The nationalization of industry, which began shortly after the revolution, was extended by the law of June 28, 1918. To cite Carr's listing, the state appropriated "the mining, metallurgical, textile, electrical, timber, tobacco, resin, glass and pottery, leather and cement industries, all steam-driven mills, local utilities and private railways together with a few minor industries." Eventually private industry disappeared almost entirely. Compulsory labor was introduced. Private trade was gradually suppressed, to be replaced by rationing and by government distribution of food and other necessities of life. On February 19, 1918, the nationalization of land was proclaimed: all land became state property to be used only by those who would cultivate it themselves. The peasants, however, had little interest in supplying food to the government because, with state priorities and the breakdown of the economy, they could not receive much in return. Therefore, under the pressure of the Civil War and of the desperate need to obtain food for the Red Army and the urban population, the authorities finally decreed a food levy, in effect ordering the peasants to turn in their entire produce, except for a minimal amount to be retained for their own sustenance and for sowing. As the peasants resisted, forcible requisitioning and repression became common. Communism, military and militant, swung into full force.

The rigors of War Communism on the home front largely resulted from and paralleled the bitter struggle the Soviet regime was waging with its external enemies. Beginning with the summer of 1918 the country entered a major, many-faceted, and cruel Civil War, when the so-called Whites—who had rallied initially to continue the war against the Germans—rose to challenge the Red control of Russia. Numerous nationalities, situated as a rule in the border areas of the former empire of the Romanovs, proceeded to assert their independence from Soviet authority. A score of foreign states intervened by sending some armed forces into Russia and supporting certain local movements and governments, as well as by blockading Soviet Russia from October 1919 to January 1920. In 1920, Poland fought a war against the Soviet government to win much of western Ukraine and White Russia. It appeared that everyone was trying to strike a blow against the Communist regime.

The Civil War

The counterrevolutionary forces, often called vaguely and somewhat misleadingly the White movement, constituted the greatest menace to Soviet rule, because, in contrast to Poland and various border nationalities, which had aims limited to particular regions, and to the intervening Allied powers, which had no clear aims, the Whites meant to destroy the Reds. The counterrevolutionaries drew their strength from army officers and cossacks, from the "bourgeoisie," including a large number of secondary school students and other educated youth, and from political groups ranging from the far Right to the Socialist Revolutionaries. Such prominent former terrorists as Boris Savinkov fought against the Soviet government, while the crack units of the White Army included a few worker detachments. Most intellectuals joined or sympathized with the White camp.

After the Soviet government came to power, civil servants staged an unsuccessful strike against it. Following their break with the Bolsheviks in March 1918 over excessive authoritarianism and Bolshevik determination to promote class struggle in the villages, the Left Socialist Revolutionaries tried an abortive uprising in Moscow in July. At about the same time and in part in response to the action of the Left SRs, counterrevolutionaries led by the local military commander seized Simbirsk, while Savinkov raised a rebellion in the center of European Russia, capturing and holding for two weeks the town of Iaroslavl on the Volga. These efforts collapsed, however, because of the insufficient strength of the counterrevolutionaries once the Soviet government could concentrate its forces against them. Indeed, it became increasingly clear that the Communist authorities, in particular the Cheka, had a firm grip on the central provinces and ruthlessly suppressed all opponents and suspected opponents. True to their tradition, the Socialist Revolutionaries tried terrorism, assassinating several prominent Bolsheviks, such as the head of the Petrograd Cheka, and seriously wounding Lenin himself in August 1918. Earlier, in July, a Left Socialist Revolutionary had killed the German ambassador, producing a diplomatic crisis. Yet even the terrorist campaign could not shake Soviet control in Moscow—which had again become the capital of the country in March 1918—Petrograd, or central European Russia. And it provoked frightful reprisals, a veritable reign of terror, during which huge numbers of "class enemies" and others suspected by the regime were killed.

The borderlands, on the other hand, offered numerous opportunities to the counterrevolutionaries. The Don, Kuban, and Terek areas in the south and southeast all gave rise to local anti-Bolshevik cossack governments. Moreover, the White Volunteer Army emerged in southern Russia, led first by Alekseev, next by Kornilov, and after Kornilov's death in combat by an equally prominent general, Anthony Denikin. Other centers of opposition to the Communists sprang up in the east. In Samara, on the Volga, Chernov headed a government composed of members of the Constituent Assembly. Both the Ural and the Orenburg cossacks turned against Red Moscow. The All-Russian Directory of five members was established in Omsk, in western Siberia, in September 1918, as a result of a conference attended by anti-Bolshevik political parties and local governments of eastern Russia. Following a military coup the Directory was replaced by another anti-Red government, that of Admiral Alexander Kolchak. A commander of the cossacks of Transbaikalia, Gregory Semenov, ruled a part of eastern Siberia with the support of the Japanese. New governments emerged also in Vladivostok and elsewhere. Russian anti-Bolshevik forces in the east were augmented by some 40,000 members of the so-called Czech Legion composed largely of Czech prisoners of war who wanted to fight on the side of the Entente. These soldiers were being moved to Vladivostok via the Trans-Siberian Railroad when a series of incidents led to their break with Soviet authorities and their support of the White movement. In the north a prominent anti-Soviet center arose in Archangel, where a former populist, Nicholas Chaikovsky, set up a government supported by the intervening British and French. And in the west, where the non-Russian borderlands produced numerous nationalist movements in opposition to the Soviet government, General Nicholas Iudenich established a White base in Estonia to threaten Petrograd.

The Civil War, which broke out in the summer of 1918, first went favorably for the Whites. In late June and early July the troops of the Samara government captured Simbirsk, Kazan, and Ufa. Although the Red Army managed to eliminate that threat, it immediately had to face a greater menace: the forces of Kolchak, supported by the Czechs, and those of Denikin, aided by cossacks. Kolchak's units, advancing from Siberia, took Perm in the Urals and almost reached the Volga. At this time, on the sixteenth of July, Nicholas II, the empress, their son and four daughters, along with a family doctor and three loyal servants, were killed—possibly in compliance with Lenin's secret order—by local Bolsheviks in Ekaterinburg, where they had been confined, when the Czechs and the Whites approached the town. Denikin's army, after some reversals of fortune, resumed the offensive, and its right wing threatened to link with Kolchak's army in the spring of 1919. While Kolchak's forced retreat eliminated this possibility, Denikin proceeded to occupy virtually all of

Ukraine and to advance on Moscow. In the middle of October his troops took
Orel and approached Tula, the last important center south of Moscow. At the
same time Iudenich advanced from Estonia on Petrograd, seizing Gatchina,
only thirty miles from that city, on October 16, and besieging Pulkovo on its
outskirts. As a recent historian of these events has commented: "In the middle

of October it appeared that Petrograd and Moscow might fall simultaneously to the Whites."

But the tide turned. Iudenich's offensive collapsed just short of the former capital. Although the Red Army had had to be created from scratch, it had constantly improved in organization, discipline, and leadership under Commissar of War Trotsky, and it managed finally to turn the tables on both Kolchak and Denikin. The admiral, who had assumed the title of "Supreme Ruler of Russia" and had received recognition from some other White leaders, suffered crushing defeat in late 1919 and was executed by the Bolsheviks on February 7, 1920. The general was driven back to the area of the Sea of Azov and the Crimea by the end of March 1920. At that point the Soviet-Polish war gave respite to the southern White Army and even enabled Denikin's successor General Baron Peter Wrangel to recapture a large section of southern Russia. But with the end of the Polish war in the autumn, the Red Army concentrated again on the southern front. After more bitter fighting, Wrangel, his remaining army, and a considerable number of civilians, altogether about 100,000 people, were evacuated on Allied ships to Constantinople in mid-November. Other and weaker counterrevolutionary strongholds, such as that in Archangel, had already fallen. By the end of 1920 the White movement had been effectively defeated.

Allied Intervention

The great Civil War in Russia was complicated by Allied intervention, by the war between the Soviet government and Poland, and by bids for national independence on the part of a number of peoples of the former empire of the Romanovs who were not Great Russians. The intervention began in 1918 and involved fourteen countries; the Japanese in particular sent a sizeable force into Russia—over 60,000 men. Great Britain dispatched altogether some 40,000 troops, France and Greece two divisions each, and the United States about 10,000 men, while Italy and other countries—except for the peculiar case of the Czechs—sent smaller, and often merely token, forces. The Allies originally wanted to prevent the Germans from seizing war matériel in such ports as Archangel and Murmansk, as well as to observe the situation, while the Japanese wanted to exploit the opportunities presented in the Far East by the collapse of Russian power. Japanese troops occupied the Russian part of the island of Sakhalin and much of Siberia east of Lake Baikal. Detachments of American, British, French, and Italian troops followed the Japanese into Siberia, while other Allied troops landed, as already mentioned, in northern European Russia, as well as in southern ports such as Odessa, occupied by the French, and Batum, occupied by the British. Allied forces assumed a hostile attitude toward the Soviet government, blockaded the Soviet coastline from October 1919 to January 1920, and often helped White movements by providing military supplies—such as some British tanks for Denikin's army—and by their very presence and protection. But they often avoided actual fighting. This fruitless intervention ended in 1920 with the departure of Allied troops, except that the Japanese stayed in the Maritime Provinces of the Russian Far East until 1922 and in the Russian part of Sakhalin until 1925.

The War against Poland

The Soviet-Polish war was fought in 1920 from the end of April until mid-October. The government of newly independent Poland opened hostilities to win western Ukraine and western White Russia, which the Poles considered part of their "historic heritage," although ethnically the areas in question were not Polish. The ancient struggle between the Poles and the Russians resumed its course, with this time the Russians, that is, the Soviet government, in an apparently desperate situation. Actually the war produced more than one reversal of fortune. First, in June and July the Poles overran western Russian areas; next the Red Army, led by Michael Tukhachevsky and others, staged a mighty counteroffensive that reached the very gates of Warsaw; then the Poles, helped by French credits and Allied supplies, defeated the onrushing Reds and gained the upper hand. The Treaty of Riga of March 18, 1921, gave Poland many of the lands it desired, establishing the boundary a considerable distance east of the ethnic line, as well as of the so-called Curzon Line, which approximated the ethnic line and which the Allies had regarded as the just settlement.

National Independence Movements

National independence movements in the former empire of the Romanovs during the years following 1917 defy comprehensive description in a textbook and have to be left to special works, such as Pipes's study. As early as 1917 Finland, Latvia, Lithuania, and White Russia declared their independence. They were followed in 1918 by Estonia, Ukraine, Poland—once German troops were evacuated—the Transcaucasian Federation—to be dissolved into the separate states of Azerbaijan, Armenia, and Georgia—and certain political formations in the east. The Soviet government had proclaimed the right of self-determination of peoples, but it became quickly apparent that it considered independence movements as bourgeois and counter-revolutionary. Those peoples that were successful in asserting their independence, that is, the Finns, the Estonians, the Latvians, and the Lithuanians, as well as the Poles, did so in spite of the Soviet government, which was preoccupied with other urgent matters. Usually they had to suppress their own Communists, sometimes, as in the case of Finland, after a full-fledged civil war. All except Poland and Lithuania became independent states for the first time. In other areas the Red Army and local Communists combined to destroy independence.

Developments in Ukraine turned out to be perhaps the most complicated of all. There the local government, the Rada or central council, and the General Secretariat, proclaimed a republic of the Ukrainian people after the fall of the Provisional Government in Petrograd. Soviet authorities recognized the new republic, but in February 1918 the Red Army overthrew the Rada. Soviet rule, established in the spring of 1918, was in turn overthrown by the advancing German army. The Germans at first accepted the Rada, but before long they sponsored instead a Right-wing government under Paul Skoropadsky. After the Germans left, the Directory of the Rada deposed Skoropadsky in December 1918, only to be driven out in short order by Denikin's White forces. Following Denikin's withdrawal in the autumn of 1919, Soviet troops restored

Soviet authority in Ukraine. Next the Directory of the Rada made an agreement with the Poles, only to be left out at the peace treaty terminating the Soviet-Polish War, which simply divided Ukraine between Soviet Russia and Poland. Ukrainians supported different movements and fought in different armies as well as in countless anarchic peasant bands. Political divisions survived the collapse of the Ukrainian bid for independence and later divided Ukrainian émigrés. Yet it remains an open question to what extent the young Ukrainian nationalism, nurtured especially among Ukrainian intellectuals in Austrian Galicia, had penetrated the peasant masses of Russian Ukraine.

Among the peoples living to the south and southeast of European Russia, many of whom had been joined to the Russian Empire as late as the nineteenth century, numerous independence movements arose and independent states were proclaimed. The new states included the Crimean Tartar republic, the

"The Struggle of the Red Knight against the Dark Force," 1919. Civil War-era images and texts often cast the revolutionary struggle in terms of good and evil. "Dark forces" is also the term used in Russian to speak of devils and other evil spirits. (Gosizdat)

Transcaucasian republics of Georgia, Armenia, and Azerbaijan, the Bashkir, Kirghiz, and Kokand republics, the emirates of Bokhara and Khiva, and others. Time and again local interests clashed and bitter local civil wars developed. In certain instances foreign powers, such as Turkey, Germany, and Great Britain, played important roles. The Menshevik government of Georgia distinguished itself by the relative stability and effectiveness of its rule. But—without going into complicated and varied detail—whether new authorities received much or little popular support, they succumbed eventually to Soviet strength allied with local Communists. The fall of the independent Georgian government in 1921 marked essentially the end of the process, although native partisans in Central Asia, the "Basmachi," were not finally suppressed until 1926.

Reasons for the Red Victory

Few observers believed that the Bolsheviks would survive the ordeal of Civil War, national independence movements, war against Poland, and Allied intervention. Lenin himself, apparently, had serious doubts on that score. The first years of the Soviet regime have justly become a legendary Communist epic, its lustre undimmed even by the titanic events of the Second World War. Yet, a closer look puts the picture into a better focus and helps to explain the Bolshevik victory without recourse to magic in Marxism or superhuman qualities of Red fighters. To begin with, Allied intervention—the emphatic Soviet view to the contrary notwithstanding—represented anything but a determined and coordinated effort to strangle the new Communist regime. Kennan, Ullman, and other scholars have shown how much misunderstanding and confusion went into the Allied policies toward Russia, which never amounted to more than a half-hearted support of White movements. Allied soldiers and sailors, it might be added, saw even less reason for intervening than did their commanders. The French navy mutinied in the Black Sea, while the efficiency of American units was impaired by unrest as well as by a fervent desire to return home. The Labor Party in Great Britain and various groups elsewhere exercised what pressure they could against intervention. Ill-conceived and poorly executed, the Allied intervention produced in the end little or no result. The Poles, by contrast, knew what they wanted and obtained it by means of a successful war. Their goals, however, did not include the destruction of the Soviet regime in Russian territory proper. National independence movements also had aims limited to their localities, and were, besides, usually quite weak. The Soviet government could, therefore, defeat many of them one by one and at the time of its own choosing, repudiating its earlier promises when convenient, as in the cases of Ukraine and the Transcaucasian republics.

The White movement did pose a deadly threat to the Reds. Ultimately there could be no compromise between the two sides. The White armies were many, contained an extremely high proportion of officers, and often fought bravely. The Reds, however, had advantages that in the end proved decisive. The Soviet government controlled the heart of Russia, including both Moscow and Petrograd, most of its population, much of its industry, and the great bulk of military supplies intended for the First World War. The White armies constantly found themselves outnumbered and, in spite of Allied help, more poorly equipped. Also, the Red Army enjoyed the inner lines of communication, while its opponents had to shift around on the periphery. Still more important, the Reds possessed a strict unity of command, whereas the Whites fought, in fact, separate and uncoordinated wars. Politics, as well as geography, contributed to the White disunity. Anti-Bolshevism represented the only generally accepted tenet in the camp, which encompassed everyone from the monarchists to the Socialist Revolutionaries. Few positive programs were proposed or developed. The Whites' inability to come to terms with non-Russian nationalities constituted a particular political weakness. White generals thought naturally in terms of "Russia one and indivisible" and reacted against separatism; or at least, they felt it quite improper to decide on their own such fundamental questions as those of national independence and boundaries. Thus Denikin antagonized the Ukrainians by his measures to suppress the Ukrainian language and schools, and Iudenich weakened his base in Estonia because he would not promise the Estonians independence.

In the last analysis, the attitude of the population probably determined the outcome of the Civil War in Russia. Whereas the upper and middle classes favored the Whites, and the workers, with some notable exceptions, backed the Reds, the peasants, that is, the great majority of the people, assumed a much more cautious and aloof attitude. Many of them came to hate both sides, for White rule, as well as Red rule, often brought mobilization, requisitions, and terror—as cruel as, if less systematic than, that of the Cheka. In many areas anarchic peasant bands attacked both combatants. Indeed, this so-called green resistance proved to be in scope, casualties, and, alas, cruelty quite comparable to the more prominent struggle between the Whites and the Reds, although it was by its very nature local rather than national. Still, on the whole, the peasants apparently preferred the Reds to the Whites. After all, they had obtained the gentry land following the October Revolution, while the Whites were associated in their minds—not entirely unjustly—with some kind of restoration of the old order, a possibility that evoked hatred and fear in the Russian village. *Mutatis mutandis,* one is reminded of the later circumstances of the Communist victory in the civil war in China.

The RSFSR and the USSR

The first Soviet constitution was adopted by the Fifth All-Russian Congress of Soviets and promulgated on July 10, 1918. It created the Russian Soviet Federated Socialist Republic, or the RSFSR. Local Soviets elected delegates to a provincial congress of Soviets, and provincial congresses in turn elected the membership of the All-Russian Congress of Soviets. The latter elected the Executive Committee, which acted in the intervals between congressional sessions, and the Council of People's Commissars. Elections were open rather than secret, and they were organized on a class basis, with the industrial workers especially heavily represented. By contrast, the "non-toiling classes" received no vote. In effect, the Communist Party, particularly its Central Committee and Political Bureau headed by Lenin, from the beginning dominated the government apparatus and ruled the country. Besides, the same leading Communists occupied the top positions in both party and government, with Lenin at the head of both. On December 30, 1922, the Union of Soviet Socialist Republics came into being as a federation of Russia, Ukraine, White Russia, and Transcaucasia. Later in the '20s three Central Asian republics received "Union Republic" status. Compared to the empire of the Romanovs, the new state had lost Finland, Estonia, Latvia, Lithuania, and the Polish territories, all of which had become independent, and had lost western Ukraine and western White Russia to Poland, Bessarabia to Romania, and the Kars-Ardakhan area in Transcaucasia to Turkey. Also, as already mentioned, Japan evacuated all of the Siberian mainland of Russia only in 1922, and the Russian half of the island of Sakhalin in 1925. In spite of these reductions in size, the USSR emerged as an enormous country.

The Crisis

At the end of the Civil War Soviet Russia was exhausted and ruined. The droughts of 1920 and 1921 and the frightful famine during that last year added the final, gruesome chapter to the disaster. In the years following the originally "bloodless" October Revolution epidemics, starvation, fighting, executions, and the general breakdown of the economy and society had taken something like twenty million lives. Another two million had left Russia—with Wrangel, through the Far East, or in numerous other ways—rather than accept Communist rule, the émigrés including a high proportion of educated and skilled people. War Communism might have saved the Soviet government in the course of the Civil War, but it also helped greatly to wreck the national economy. With private industry and trade proscribed and the state unable to perform these functions on a sufficient scale, much of the Russian economy ground to a standstill. It has been estimated that the total output of mines and factories fell in 1921 to 20 percent of the pre–World War level, with many crucial items experiencing an even more drastic decline; for example, cotton fell to 5 percent, iron to 2 percent, of the prewar level. The peasants responded to requisitioning by refusing to till their land. By 1921 cultivated land had shrunk to some 62 percent of the prewar acreage, and the harvest yield was only about 37 percent of normal. The number of horses declined from 35 million in 1916 to 24 million in 1920, and cattle from 58 to 37 million during the same span of time. The exchange rate of an American dollar, which had been two rubles in 1914, rose to 1,200 rubles in 1920.

This unbearable material situation, combined with growing resentment at Communist authoritarianism and brutality, which had intensified in the course of the Civil War, sparked uprisings in the countryside and unrest and strikes in the factories. Already during the Civil War, peasants had occasionally attacked detachments of Communists and workers come to requisition grain. But once no longer faced with the threat of White victory, viewed as the return of the landlords, peasants turned against Bolshevik interference in their economic lives. Grain requisitioning teams were ambushed and other representatives of state authority in the countryside were attacked. In some regions, notably western Siberia, the middle Volga, Tambov province, and Ukraine, massive uprisings broke out starting in late 1920. The goals of these movements varied, and social rebellion often mixed with brigandage, but the basic message was clear: no more grain requisitioning, a restoration of free trade, and the guarantee of complete peasant control of the land they worked. Some peasants also demanded the reconvening of the Constituent Assembly. Although rural unrest was the greatest threat to Communist power, politically more unsettling was the unrest among urban workers that broke out in early 1921. Meetings, demonstrations, and even strikes made clear that discontent was widespread among what was left of the proletariat (the economic devastations of the Civil War era having reduced the number of industrial workers by half). Workers' complaints mainly concerned matters of simple physical survival: larger food rations, distribution of shoes and warm clothing, allowing workers to barter with peasants for food (peasants should be free to sell the produce of their own labor). But economic grievance brought to the surface political discontent. Workers often demanded also the restoration of civil rights, the end of coercive management practices in factories (strict one-man management had been introduced in 1918, effectively ending workers' control), and even the calling of a Constituent Assembly. Finally, in March 1921, the Kronstadt naval base, celebrated by the Communists as one of the sources of the October Revolution, rose in rebellion against Communist rule. It is worth noting that the sailors and other Kronstadt rebels demanded free Soviets an end to one-party rule, freedom of speech and press, the summoning of a Constituent Assembly, and an end not only to forced grain requisitioning but also to all state control of the economy. "Down with the Commissarocracy" was an often heard slogan. Although Red Army units ruthlessly suppressed the uprising, the well-nigh general dissatisfaction with Bolshevik rule could not have been more forcefully expressed. Complicating this crisis still further, Communists who felt that the idealistic purposes of the Revolution were being lost sight of were increasingly outspoken in these months. This was not the first time dissident factions had arisen within the party. In 1918, "Left Communists" opposed the Brest-Litovsk treaty as a betrayal of world revolution and criticized Lenin's proposals to introduce strict labor discipline into industry to revive the economy. In 1919, a similarly short-lived "Military Opposition" opposed Trotsky's plans for a Red Army that would employ traditional discipline and make use of former tsarist officers. But once the Civil War had ended, criticism of party policy became more open and vehement. "Democratic Centralists" criticized growing centralization and bureaucratization and demanded freer discussion within the party and the election of local party officials. The "Workers' Opposition" opposed the imposition of traditional discipline in industry, the use of "bourgeois specialists" in management, and efforts in 1920 to subordinate completely the trade unions to the state.

Against this background of utter devastation and discontent, Lenin, who, besides, had finally to admit that a world revolution was not imminent, proceeded in the spring of 1921 to inaugurate his New Economic Policy (NEP) in place of War Communism. Once more Lenin proved to be the realist who had to overcome considerable doctrinaire opposition to have his views prevail in the party and, therefore, in the entire country.

The New Economic Policy

The New Economic Policy was a compromise, a temporary retreat on the road to socialism, in order to give the country an opportunity to recover. It was, in Lenin's words, a "peasant Brest-Litovsk." The Communist Party, of course, retained full political control; the compromise and relaxation never extended to politics. Indeed, peasant rebellions and the Kronstadt uprising were violently crushed, protesting workers were met with lockouts and mass arrests, and critics within the party were forced into silence with a ban on factions in March 1921. Discipline, Lenin insisted, was essential when an army was retreating. And NEP was that necessary retreat. But this was not a complete retreat. The state kept its exclusive hold on the "commanding heights" of the economy, that is, on finance, on large and medium industry, on modern transportation, on foreign trade, and on all wholesale commerce. Private enterprise, however, was allowed in small industry, which meant plants employing fewer than twenty workers each, and in retail trade. The government's change of policy toward the peasants was perhaps still more important. Instead of requisitioning their produce, as had been done during War Communism, it established a definite tax in kind, particularly in grain, replaced later by a money tax. The peasants could keep and sell on the free market what remained after the payment of the tax, and thus they were given an obvious incentive to produce more. Eventually the authorities even permitted a limited use of hired labor in agriculture and a restricted lease of land. The government also revamped and stabilized the financial system, introducing a new monetary unit, the *chervonets;* and it put into operation new legal codes to help stabilize a shattered society.

The New Economic Policy proved to be a great economic success. After the frightful starvation years of 1921 and 1922—years, incidentally, when many more Russians would have perished, but for the help received from the American Relief Administration headed by Herbert Hoover, from the Quakers, and from certain other groups—the Russian economy revived in a remarkable manner. In 1928 the amount of land under cultivation already slightly exceeded the pre–World War area. Industry on the whole also reached the prewar level. It should be added that during the NEP period, in contrast to the time of War Communism, the government demanded that state industries account for costs and pay for themselves. It was highly characteristic of NEP that 75 percent of retail trade fell into private hands. In general, the so-called Nepmen, the small businessmen allowed to operate by the new policy, increased in number in towns, while the *kulaki*—or kulaks, for the term has entered the English language—gained in the villages. *Kulak,* meaning "fist," came to designate a prosperous peasant, a man who held tightly to his own; the prerevolutionary term, used by Soviet sources, also has connotations of exploitation and greed.

These social results of the New Economic Policy naturally worried the Communists. The Eleventh Party Congress declared as early as 1922 that no further "retreat" could be tolerated. In 1924 and 1925 the government introduced certain measures to restrict the Nepmen, and in 1927 to limit the kulaks.

At the same time, scholars have argued, many Bolsheviks, including Lenin himself, began to view NEP less as a temporary retreat and more as a unique path to socialism in a backward peasant country like Russia. Notions of a decades-long evolution to socialism, based on gradually raising the cultural and economic level of the population and teaching the benefits of socialist cooperation, began to compete with notions of returning to Civil War strategies of forcing the country into socialism. These debates came to be closely linked to personalities and to the struggle for power that gained momentum after Lenin's death in January 1924.

The Struggle for Power after Lenin's Death

Two main points of view competed among the Russian Communists during the twenties. The so-called Left position, best developed by Trotsky, emphasized the need to overcome rapidly Russian backwardness (both in the economy and in the cultural level of the population) through the active leadership of the party and state. These principles produced vigorous criticism of current party policies in both economics and inner-party administration. Rapid industrialization was urgent, the Left argued, if the socialist ideals of Soviet Russia were not to drown in the country's massive petty-bourgeois peasant population. This required aggressive state economic planning and the accumulation of capital for investment by squeezing the peasants and the private sector through high taxes and high industrial prices, but also through wage controls and low investment in consumer goods. At the same time, the Communist "vanguard" leading this effort must be improved by fighting against "bureaucracy" in the party and the state. The Left condemned the widespread practice of appointing local party secretaries, accused the party of nurturing a political culture of "passive obedience" and "careerism," and called for greater freedom of debate and more mass participation in party affairs. Stalin came in for particular criticism, for, as general secretary of the Party, he was in charge of appointments. Such prominent Communist leaders as Gregory Zinoviev—born Radomyslsky—and Leo Kamenev—born Rosenfeld—essentially shared Trotsky's view.

Nicholas Bukharin was the chief opponent of the Left, representing the position of the party majority, including Stalin, until the late 1920s. Bukharin and the Right, as they would be called later when Stalin turned against them, agreed with the Left that Russia's backwardness was the most serious obstacle to building socialism in Russia. But they drew quite different conclusions from this. Bukharin mocked the Left for trying to create a "Genghis Khan plan" that would require such a massive apparatus and such use of coercion that economic growth would be impeded. He agreed that industrialization was essential but insisted that this must be based not on a production model that squeezed the private sector but on a consumption model that used the workings of the market. His objections to the plans of the Left were as much political as economic, however. One must teach the peasants to love socialism, not force them along a socialist path, which would only lead to alienation, resentment, and possibly rebellion. In his words, the road to socialism must be

Nicholas Bukharin around 1917. Unlike many other Bolshevik leaders during the Civil War and after, Bukharin eschewed the style of wearing military dress. In Lenin's letter to the party congress in December 1922 ("Lenin's Testament"), he called Bukharin "the favorite of the whole party." (Stephen Cohen)

"peaceful" and "bloodless," not marked by "the clanging of metal weapons." Stalin, it is clear, never felt entirely comfortable with such arguments, and neither did many of the more militant Communists. But only after defeating the Left did Stalin turn against the "Right Deviation," partly, it is argued, by co-opting the Left's economic program.

As has often been described and analyzed, the struggle for power that followed Lenin's death was decided by Stalin's superior control of the party membership. Acting behind the scenes, Stalin managed to build up a following strong enough to overcome Trotsky's magnificent rhetoric and great prestige, as well as Kamenev's party organization in Moscow and Zinoviev's in Petrograd—named Leningrad after Lenin's death. Stalin intrigued skillfully, first allying himself with Kamenev and Zinoviev against Trotsky, whom they envied and considered their rival for party leadership; then with the Right

Leon Trotsky. In his 1922 "testament," Lenin called Trotsky "personally perhaps the most capable person" in the Central Committee of the party. (New York Public Library)

group against the Left; and eventually, when sufficiently strong, suppressing the Right as well. He kept accusing his opponents of factionalism, of disobeying the established party line and splitting the party. Final victory came at the Fifteenth All-Union Congress of the Communist Party, which on December 27, 1927, condemned all "deviation from the general party line" as interpreted by Stalin. The general secretary's rivals and opponents recanted or were exiled; in any case, they lost their former importance. Trotsky himself was expelled from the Soviet Union in January 1929 and was eventually murdered in exile in Mexico in 1940, almost certainly on Stalin's orders.

Still, although Stalin's rise to supreme authority can well be considered an impressive, if gruesome, study in power politics, its ideological aspect should not be forgotten. Stalin built a following by appealing not only to the careerist aspirations of many Communists but also to widespread desires for the Soviet Union to take a more idealistic path. Two related characteristics of Stalin's

Joseph Stalin. Lenin's view of Stalin in his 1922 letter was that he "has, becoming General Secretary, concentrated boundless power in his hands, and I am not certain he will always be capable of using that power with sufficient caution." (Sovfoto)

political approach attracted allies and admirers. First, he simplified and even sacralized ideology for the masses of ordinary Communists. His popular 1924 book *Foundations of Leninism* reduced Communist ideology to its simplest terms, and after Lenin's death Stalin took the lead in treating Lenin's works as dogma and dissent as heresy. Second, Stalin consistently emphasized optimism, hope, and even faith. When Trotsky, for example, argued (as Lenin had) that, in the long term, the success of socialism in Russia would depend on revolutions bringing socialists to power in more advanced Western countries, Stalin mocked this theory of "permanent revolution" as a theory of "permanent hopelessness," which showed too little "faith" in the Russian proletariat. Offering an alternative theory of "socialism in one country," Stalin argued that Russia did not depend on others to achieve heroic goals. Indeed, he offered an appealingly voluntarist interpretation of Leninism as "neither knowing nor recognizing obstacles." Only Stalin offered a sweeping program and a majestic goal to be achieved by Soviet efforts alone. This heroic spirit would attract many to his side as he launched his economic and social "revolution from above." The same party congress that condemned all deviations from Stalin's line enthusiastically adopted measures that signified the end of the New Economic Policy and the beginning of the First Five-Year Plan.

Chapter 37

The First Three Five-Year Plans, 1928–41

Enough of living by the law
Given by Adam and Eve.
The jade of history we will ride to death.
Left!
Left!
Left!

—MAYAKOVSKY

It [the First Five-Year Plan] asked no less than a complete transformation from backward agricultural individualism to mechanized collectivism, from hothouse subsidized industry to self-sufficient industry on the greatest, most modern scale, from the mentality of feudalism, far behind the Western industrial age, to socialism still ahead of it.

—DURANTY

"When a forest is cut down, splinters fly." Of course, it is unfortunate to be a splinter.

—THE REMARK OF A SOVIET CITIZEN TO NICHOLAS
RIASANOVSKY IN THE SUMMER OF 1958

Stalin's sweeping victory at the Fifteenth All-Union Congress of the Communist Party in December 1927 marked the inauguration of the era of Stalin and his five-year plans. The general secretary was to direct the destinies of the Union of the Soviet Socialist Republics and of world Communism for twenty-five eventful years, becoming in the course of that quarter of a century perhaps the most totalitarian, powerful, and feared dictator of all time.

Stalin

Stalin began his life and career humbly enough. In fact, it has often been mentioned that he was one of the few Bolshevik leaders of more or less proletarian origin. Born a son of a shoemaker in 1879 in the little town of Gori near the Georgian capital of Tiflis—or Tbilisi—Joseph Dzhugashvili attended a Church school in Gori until 1894 and then went to the theological seminary in Tiflis. In 1899, however, he was expelled from the seminary for reasons that are not entirely clear. By that time, apparently, Stalin had become acquainted with some radical writers and in particular with Marx and Lenin. He joined the Social Democratic Party and when it split in 1903 sided firmly with the Bolsheviks. Between 1902 and 1913 Dzhugashvili, or rather Stalin as he came to be known, engaged in a variety of conspiratorial and revolutionary activities, suffering arrest and exile several times. He managed to escape repeatedly from exile, which has suggested police collusion to certain specialists. Stalin's last exile, however, continued from 1913 until the February Revolution. Apparently the Georgian Bolshevik first attracted Lenin's attention when he organized a daring raid to seize funds for the party. Stalin's revolutionary activity developed in such Transcaucasian centers as Tiflis, Batum, and Baku, as well as in St. Petersburg. In contrast to many other Bolshevik leaders, Stalin never lived abroad, leaving the Russian Empire only to attend a few meetings. Because of Stalin's Bolshevik orthodoxy and Georgian origin, the party welcomed him as an expert on the problem of nationalities, a subject to which he devoted some of his early writings.

One of the first prominent Bolsheviks to arrive in Petrograd, Stalin participated in the historic events of 1917, and after the October Revolution he became the first commissar for national minorities. As a member of the Revolutionary Military Council of the Southern Front he played a role in the Civil War, for example, in the defense of Tsaritsyn against the Whites. Incidentally, Tsaritsyn was renamed Stalingrad in 1925 and Volgograd in 1961. It might be noted that in the course of executing his duties he quarreled repeatedly with Trotsky. But Stalin's real bid for power began in 1922 with his appointment as general secretary of the party, a position that gave him broad authority in matters of personnel. The long-time official Soviet view of Stalin as Lenin's anointed successor distorts reality, for, in fact, the ailing Bolshevik leader came to resent the general secretary's rigidity and rudeness and in his so-called testament warned the party leadership against Stalin. But Stalin's rivals failed to heed Lenin's late forebodings, and, before too long, Stalin's party machine rolled over all opponents. The complete personal dictatorship which began in 1928 was to last until the dictator's death in 1953.

Interpreting Stalin and Stalinism has for many years been the subject of sometimes fierce scholarly debate. In part, the heated arguments can be explained by the Cold War (and its lingering influence), which made the interpretation of Soviet history also a matter of ideology and even morality. But serious analytical questions have also been at the heart of the debate: What was the defining character of the Stalinist order, its model of rule? What kept Stalin in power all those years? One answer to this question—long the predominant one outside the Soviet Union and now in post-Soviet Russia—is to view Stalin's regime as "totalitarian." The focus here is on Stalin himself (though scholars have debated whether he was a rational actor or was inspired by unreasonable paranoia, obsession with his own heroic role in history, or even a pathological personality) and on a system of party-state rule in which indoctrination, repression, and terror held all of Soviet political, social, and cultural life in an iron grip and in which social groups and individuals were passive victims. Scholars like Fainsod, Conquest, Ulam, and Tucker have offered excellent, well-documented, and often nuanced examples of this approach. Starting in the 1970s, "revisionist" historians, notably Fitzpatrick, have questioned the one-sidedness of the totalitarian paradigm. Without denying the repressiveness and violence of the regime (though some have deemphasized its extent and centrality), these scholars have argued that the Stalinist system could not and did not rule only through coercion and terror. Reinvestigating the relationship between state and society—facilitated by growing opportunities for research in the Soviet Union—these scholars point to support within the population for many of Stalin's policies and argue that the party and state were often responsive to people's desires and values. The opening of the archives after the end of Communist rule has not resolved these debates, but rather provided evidence of the contradictoriness of the Stalin era: belief in a presumably infallible ideology, a great deal of coercion, force, and terror (sometimes more brutal and systematic than we knew), subtle forms of cultural and psychological control, and support and enthusiasm for Stalin and the Soviet system.

The First Five-Year Plan

The First Five-Year Plan and its successors hit the Soviet Union with tremendous impact. The USSR became a great industrial nation: from being the fifth country in production when the plans began, it was eventually second only to the United States. In agriculture individual peasant cultivation gave way to a new system of collective farming. Indeed 1928 and 1929 have been described as the true revolutionary years in Russia: it was then that the mode of life of the peasants, the bulk of the people, underwent a radical change, whereas until the First Five-Year Plan they continued to live much as they had for centuries. A vast social transformation accompanied the economic, while at the same time the entire Soviet system as we came to know it acquired its definitive form in the difficult decade of the '30s.

Perhaps paradoxically, the five-year plans are not easy to explain. Marxist theory did not specifically provide for them and certainly did not spell out the procedures to be followed. To be sure, the needs of the moment affected the decisions of Soviet leaders. Yet Stalin's and his associates' response to the needs constituted only one alternative line of action, and often not the most obvious. In fact, the leadership rapidly reversed itself on such key subjects as the speed of collectivization.

Certain considerations, however, help to explain the five-year plans. To begin with, although Marxism did not provide for industrialization it insisted on a high level of it. The dictatorship of the proletariat in a land of peasants remained an anomaly. If, contrary to the doctrine, industries and workers were not there in the first place, they had to be created. Marxists in general, and Bolsheviks in particular, thought of socialism entirely in terms of an advanced industrial society. Such authors as Ulam have demonstrated in a rather convincing manner the close and multiple ties between Marxism and industrialization. The collectivization of agriculture, in turn, represented the all-important step from an individual and, therefore, bourgeois system of ownership and production to a collective economy and, therefore, to socialism. As already mentioned, after the October Revolution the Soviet government proceeded to nationalize Russian industry. Lenin showed a special interest in electrification, popularizing the famous slogan: "Electrification plus Soviet power equals communism." In 1921 the State Planning Commission, known as *Gosplan,* was organized to draft an economic plan for the entire country. It studied resources and proposed production figures; eventually it drew up the five-year plans.

Why was the New Economic Policy, which Communists like Bukharin and some later historians have seen as a viable alternative to Stalinism, abandoned? First, NEP raised serious economic problems. While by 1928 Russian industry had regained its pre–World War level, a further rapid advance appeared quite uncertain. With the industrial plant restored and in operation—a relatively easy accomplishment—the Soviet Union needed investment in the producers' goods industries and a new spurt in production. Yet the "socialist sector" of the economy lacked funds, while the "free sector," particularly the peasants, failed to rise to government expectations. The Soviet economy in the 1920s continued to be plagued by pricing problems, beginning with the disparity between the low agricultural prices and the high prices of manufactured consumers' goods, resulting in the unwillingness of peasants to supply grain and other products to the government and the cities—a situation well described as the "scissors crisis." Gerschenkron and other specialists have argued that the Bolsheviks had good reason to fear that a continuation of NEP would stabilize a peasant society at the point where it was interested in obtaining more consumers' goods, but neither willing nor able to support large-scale industrialization. On top of these economic pressures for changing course, there were political pressures. Many rank-and-file Communists, young people, and workers were deeply hostile to the social results of NEP. The persistence of capitalism, the continuation of poverty, the visible social presence of petty capitalists in the city ("Nepmen") and rich peasants in the countryside ("kulaks"), and the unheroic gradualism offered by even those who defended NEP as a path to socialism frustrated and angered many. A character in Gladkov's 1925 novel *Cement* captured these sentiments by comparing the present society to the brutal but heroic Civil War: "I don't know where the nightmare is: in those years of blood, misery, and sacrifice or in this bacchanalia of rich shop windows and drunken cafes! What was the good of mountains of corpses? . . . So that scoundrels and vampires should again enjoy all the good things in life, and get fat by robbery?" Many were ready for this "retreat," as NEP was originally called, to end and longed for a new heroic march forward. Stalin's "revolution from above" seemed to provide just that. Stalin's Five-Year Plan also proved attractive because it promised that the Soviet Union could become a truly socialist country without waiting for world revolution. "Socialism in one country" gripped many imaginations and became the new Bolshevik battle cry.

Once the Plan went into operation, the economic factors involved in its execution acquired great significance, all the more so because the planners set sail in essentially uncharted waters and often could not foresee the results of their actions. In particular, according to Gerschenkron, A. Erlich, and certain other scholars, the fantastically rapid collectivization of agriculture came about as follows: while the Plan had called for a strictly limited collectiviza- tion, set at 14 percent, the unexpectedly strong resistance on the part of the peasants led to an all-out attack on individual farming; moreover, the govern- ment discovered that the collectives, which finally gave it control over the labor and produce of the peasants, enabled it to squeeze from them the neces- sary funds for industrial investment. It has been estimated that the Soviet state paid to the collectives for their grain only a distinctly minor part of the price of that grain charged the consumer; the remaining major part constituted in effect a tax. That tax, plus the turnover or sales tax that the Soviet state charged all consumers, together with the ability of the government to keep the real wages down while productivity went up, produced the formula for financing the con- tinuous industrialization of the Soviet Union.

In addition to ideology and economics, other factors entered into the exe- cution of the five-year plans. Many scholars assign major importance to con- siderations of foreign policy and of internal security and control. Preparation for war, which affected all major aspects of the five-year plans, began in earnest after Hitler came to power in Germany in 1933, and while Japan was further developing its aggressive policies in the Far East. The stress on internal secu- rity and control in the five-year plans is more difficult to document. Yet it might well be argued that police considerations were consistently uppermost in the minds of Stalin and his associates. Collectivization, from that point of view, represented a tremendous extension of Communist control over the popula- tion of the Soviet Union, and it was buttressed by such additional measures— again combining economics and control—as the new crucial role of the Machine Tractor Stations, the MTS, which will be mentioned later.

The First Five-Year Plan lasted from October 1, 1928, to December 31, 1932, that is, four years and three months. The fact that Soviet authorities tried to complete a five-year plan in four years is a significant comment on the enor- mous speed-up typical of the new socialist offensive. Very high targets were set and then revised upward to fantastic levels. As one economic historian has observed, "in the absence of divine intervention it is hard to imagine" how these goals could have been achieved. The intent of these goals, it has therefore been suggested, was more to inspire by their daring than to offer rational tar- gets. The main goal of the Plan was to develop heavy industry, including machine-building, and that emphasis remained characteristic of Soviet indus- trialization from that time on. According to Baykov's calculation, 86 percent of all industrial investment during the First Five-Year Plan went into heavy industry. Whole new branches of industry, such as the chemical, automobile, agricultural machinery, aviation, machine tool, and electrical, were created from slight beginnings or even from scratch. Over fifteen hundred new facto- ries were built. Gigantic industrial complexes, exemplified by Magnitostroi in the Urals and Kuznetsstroi in western Siberia, began to take shape. Entire cities arose in the wilderness. Magnitogorsk, for instance, acquired in a few years a population of a quarter of a million.

"Full Speed Ahead with Shock Tempo: The Five Year Plan in Four Years," 1930.   (Lenizogiz)

The First Five-Year Plan was proclaimed a great success: officially it was fulfilled in industry to the extent of 93.7 percent in four years and three months. Furthermore, heavy industry, concerned with means of production, exceeded its quota, registering 103.4 percent while light or consumers' goods industry produced 84.9 percent of its assigned total. Of course, Soviet production claims included great exaggerations, difficult to estimate because of the limited and often misleading nature of Soviet statistics for the period. To put it very conservatively and without percentages: "The fact remains beyond dispute that quantitatively, during the years covered by the F.Y.P., industrial production did increase and very substantially." Quality, however, was often sacrificed to quantity, and the production results achieved varied greatly from item to item, with remarkable overfulfillments of the plan in some cases and underfulfillments in others. Besides, the great industrial spurt was accompanied by shortages of consumer goods, rationing, and various other privations and hardships which extended to all of the people, who at the same time were forced to work harder than ever before. The whole country underwent a quasi-military mobilization reminiscent of War Communism. Indeed, the language of war was pervasive. Speeches and articles in the press described industry as a battlefield with "fronts," "campaigns," and "breakthroughs," workers were organized into "shock troops," and those who dissented or failed in their tasks were treated as if traitors in wartime. The economic utopianism of the First Five-Year Plan was also reflected in a popular military metaphor, which Stalin especially liked: "there are no fortresses Bolsheviks cannot storm."

The First Five-Year Plan was clearly about more than economics. The "Great Turn," as it was called, was a revolution that sought to transform all aspects of society. Public trials of "bourgeois experts," starting in 1928 with the trial of engineers in the Shakhty coal mines for sabotage and conspiring with imperialists, was the most visible incitement to renewed class struggle. Throughout society, Communists were encouraged to challenge the authority of established experts, especially if they were from "alien" class backgrounds. A storm of purges was unleashed against non-Communist and non-worker engineers, foremen, teachers, journalists, state officials, writers, and others. This "cultural revolution," as it was called, was initiated by the state and party, but it had its enthusiasts throughout Soviet society. Class hatred for "bourgeois" specialists was widespread among working-class Communists. And social purges, as well as special efforts to educate and promote proletarians, created enormous opportunities for upward mobility for workers and Communists. This cultural revolution also brought to the fore radical ideas about transforming society. For example, educators envisioned a system of school communes in which labor and study would be combined. And city planners imagined cities of both hyper-modernity (electrical towns planned by "biogeometrics") and closeness to nature (linear "green cities").

The greatest transformation probably occurred in the countryside. As already mentioned, the collectivization of agriculture, planned originally as a gradual advance, became a flood. Tens of thousands of trusted Communists and proletarians—the celebrated "twenty-five thousand" in one instance, actually twenty-seven thousand—were sent from towns into villages to organize kolkhozes and establish socialism. Local authorities and party organizations, with the police and troops where necessary, forced peasants into collectives. A tremendous resistance developed. About a million of the so-called kulaks, some five million people counting their families, disappeared in the process, often having been sent to concentration camps in far-off Siberia or Central Asia. A frightful famine swept Ukraine. Peasants slaughtered their cattle and horses rather than bring them into a kolkhoz. Thus from 1929 to 1933 in the Soviet Union the number of horses, in millions, declined from 34 to 16.6, of cattle from 68.1 to 38.6, of sheep and goats from 147.2 to 50.6, and of hogs from 20.9 to 12.2. Droughts in 1931 and 1932 added to the horrors of the transition from private to collectivized farming.

Stalin himself applied the brakes to his own policy after the initial fifteen months. In his remarkable article, "Dizzy with Success," published in March 1930, he criticized the collectivizers for excessive enthusiasm and re-emphasized that collectives were to be formed on the voluntary principle, not by force. At the same time he announced certain concessions to collective farmers, in particular their right to retain a small private plot of land and a limited number of domestic animals and poultry. The new stress on the voluntary principle produced striking results: whereas fourteen million peasant households had joined collective farms by March 1930, only five million remained in collectives in May. But before long their number began to increase again when the authorities resorted to less direct pressure, such as a temporary suspension of taxes and priority in obtaining scarce manufactured goods. By the end of the First Five-Year Plan more than fourteen million peasant households had joined the kolkhoz system. According to one count, at that time 68 percent of all cultivated land in the Soviet Union was under kolkhoz agriculture, and 10 percent under sovkhoz agriculture, while only 22 percent remained for independent farmers. The Plan could well be considered overfulfilled.

A sovkhoz is essentially an agricultural factory owned by the state, with peasants providing hired labor. Although sovkhozes, serving as experimental stations, as enormous grain producers in newly developed regions, and in many other crucial assignments, were more important for the Soviet economy than their number would indicate, Communist authorities refrained from establishing them as the basic form of agricultural organization in the country. Instead they relied on the kolkhoz as the norm for the Soviet countryside. A kolkhoz—*kollektivnoe khoziaistvo*, collective economy or farm—was owned by all its members, although it had to deliver the assigned amount of produce to the state and was controlled by the state. Significantly, the produce of a collective farm was generally allocated as follows: first, the part required by the state, both as taxes and as specified deliveries at set prices; next, the seed for sowing and the part to serve as payment to the Machine Tractor Station that aided the kolkhoz; after that, members of the collective received their shares calculated on the basis of the "workdays"—a unit of labor to be distinguished from actual days—that they had put in for the kolkhoz; finally, the remainder went into the indivisible fund of the collective to be used for its social, cultural, and other needs. The members also cultivated their small private plots—and with remarkable intensity and success. The Machine Tractor Stations, finally abolished in 1958, provided indispensable mechanized aid to the collectives, notably at harvest time, helping to coordinate the work of different kolkhozes and acting as another control over them. While it might be noted that the Soviet government found it easier to introduce collective farms in those regions where communal agriculture prevailed than in areas of individual proprietors, such as Ukraine, the kolkhoz bore very little resemblance to the commune. Members of a commune possessed their land in common, but they farmed their assigned lots separately, undisturbed, and in their own traditional way. Organization and regimentation of labor became the very essence of the kolkhoz.

The Second and Third Five-Year Plans

The Second Five-Year Plan, which lasted from 1933 through 1937, and the Third, which began in 1938 and was interrupted by the German invasion in

*"Long Live Our Happy Socialist Motherland. Long Live Our Beloved Great Stalin," 1935.
Stalin and Voroshilov (commissar for defense) stand upon Lenin's Mausoleum on Red Square.
The airplanes flying overhead bear the names of Lenin, Stalin, Gorky, Kalinin, Molotov, and
other Soviet leaders. The planes in the distance spell out "Stalin."*   (Victoria Bonnell)

June 1941, continued on the whole the aims and methods of the initial Plan.
They stressed the development of heavy industry, completed the collectivization of agriculture, and did their best to mobilize the manpower and other
resources of the country to attain the objectives. The Soviet people lived
through eight and a half more years of quasi-wartime exertion. Yet these plans
also differed in certain ways from the first and from each other. The Second
Five-Year Plan, drawn on the basis of acquired knowledge more expertly than
the first, tried to balance production to avoid extreme over- or underfulfill-
ment. It emphasized "mastering the technique," including the making of especially complicated machine tools, precision instruments, and the like. Also, it
allowed a little more for consumers' goods than the first plan did. However, in
the course of the Second Five-Year Plan, and especially during the third, mili-

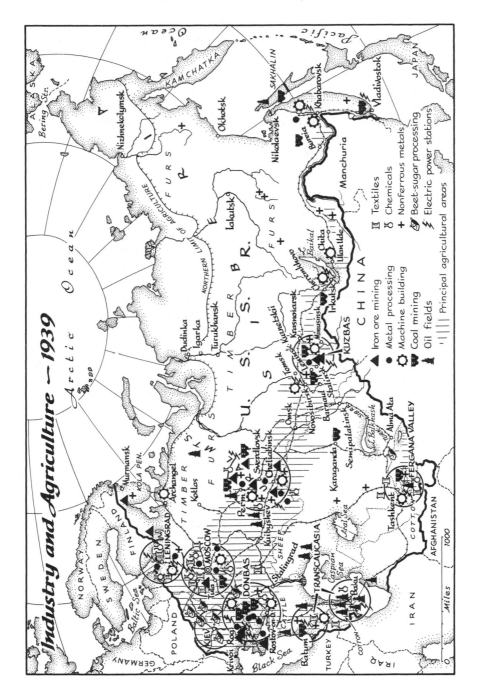

tary considerations became paramount. Military considerations linked to ide-ology had of course always been present in the planning of Soviet leaders. From the beginning of industrialization, Stalin and his associates had insisted that they had to build a powerful socialist state quickly, perhaps in a decade, or be crushed by capitalists. In the 1930s the threat became increasingly real and menacing. Soviet leaders did what they could to arm and equip Red forces, and they accelerated the development of industries inland, east of the Volga, away from the exposed frontiers.

Both the Second Five-Year Plan and the third, as far as it went, were again proclaimed successes, and again the official claims, in spite of their exaggera-tion, had some sound basis in fact. Industry, especially heavy industry, contin-ued to grow. On the basis of official—and doubtful—figures, the Soviet share in world production amounted to 13.7 percent in 1937, compared to 3.7 in 1929 and to 2.6 for the Russian Empire in 1913. In the generation of electrical power, for example, the Soviet Union advanced from the fifteenth place among the countries of the world to the third, and it was second only to the United States in machine building, tractors, trucks, and some other lines of production. Moreover, the Soviet Union made its amazing gains while the rest of the world experienced a terrible depression and mass unemployment.

In agriculture collectivization was virtually completed and, except for the wilderness, the Soviet countryside became a land of kolkhozes and sovkhozes. Slightly less than 250,000 kolkhozes replaced over 25 million individual farms. The famine and other horrors of the First Five-Year Plan did not recur. In fact, agricultural production increased somewhat, and food rationing was abol-ished in 1935. Still, the economic success of Soviet agricultural policy remained much more doubtful than the achievements of Soviet industrialization. Peas-ants regularly failed to meet their production quotas. They showed far greater devotion to their small private plots than to the vast kolkhoz possessions. In other ways, too, they remained particularly unresponsive to the wishes of Communist authorities. A full evaluation of Soviet social engineering should also take account of the costs. As one author summarized the salient human aspects of Soviet agricultural policies during the socialist offensive:

> As a result of collectivization the number of families on the land diminished from 26,000,000 to 21,000,000. This means that 5,000,000 families or approximately 24,000,000 individuals must have left the countryside. Of these the increase in the towns accounts for one half. Twelve millions are not accounted for. A part of them has undoubtedly perished, the other part has found new possibilities in the Far East, in the Arctic, or in Central Asia.

An Evaluation of the Plans

Any overall judgment of the first three five-year plans is of necessity a compli-cated and controversial matter, as the writings of Bergson, Grossman, and other economists clearly indicate. The plans did succeed—and succeed strik-ingly—in developing industry, particularly heavy industry, and in collectiviz-ing agriculture. Skepticism as to the feasibility of the plans, extremely wide-spread outside the Soviet Union, turned to astonishment and sometimes admiration. To repeat, not only did production greatly increase, but entire new industries appeared, while huge virgin territories, including the distant and difficult far north, began to enter the economic life of the country. Red armed forces, by contrast with the tsarist army, obtained a highly developed indus- trial and armaments base, a fact which alone justifies the five-year plans, in the opinion of some critics. Moreover, the entire enormous undertaking was car- ried out almost wholly by internal manpower and financing, except for the very important contribution of several thousand Western specialists in all fields who were invited to help, and some short-term credit extended to the Soviet government by German and other suppliers during the first years of industrialization. Considered by many as Stalin's chimera, the five-year plans proved to be an effective way—if not necessarily the only or the best way—to industrialize a relatively backward country.

Yet the cost was tremendous. Soviet authorities could accomplish their aims only by imposing great hardships on the people and by mobilizing the country in a quasi-military manner for a supreme effort. Piece work became common and wage differentials grew by leaps and bounds. The new emphasis on "socialist competition" culminated in the Stakhanov movement. In 1935 Alexis Stakhanov, a coal miner in the Donets Basin, was reported to have over- fulfilled his daily quota by 1,400 percent in the course of a shift hewing coal. "Stakhanovite" results were soon achieved by other workers in numerous branches of industry. Rewarding the Stakhanovites, whose accomplishments stemmed in different degrees from improved technique, enormous exertion, and cooperation by their fellow workers, the government used their successes to raise general production norms over a period of time. Most workers must have resented this speed-up—some Stakhanovites were actually killed—but they could not reverse it. After the October Revolution, and especially in the '30s, labor unions, to which almost all workers belonged, served as agencies of the state, to promote its policies and rally the workers behind them, rather than as representatives of labor interests and point of view. Hardships of Soviet life included a desperate shortage of consumers' goods, as well as totally inade- quate housing combined with a rigid system of priorities. As a result the black market flourished, and indeed remained an essential part of the Soviet eco- nomic system. Criticisms of the first three five-year plans—in fact, of their suc- cessors as well—have also pointed to top-heavy bureaucracy and excessive red tape, to a relatively low productivity per worker and production per inhabi- tant, to the frequently poor quality of the items produced, and to numerous weaknesses, perhaps outright failure, in agriculture. It can legitimately be asked whether a different regime could have industrialized the country better and with less pain.

For extreme painfulness emerged as a fundamental aspect of the first three five-year plans. While all suffered to some extent, some groups of the popula- tion suffered beyond all measure. One such group, as already mentioned, was the kulaks and their families. Another, overlapping but by no means identical with the kulaks, was the inmates of the forced-labor camps. A history of Soviet forced labor remains to be written in full: it was ignored in Soviet publications as well as by such Soviet sympathizers as Dobb in his interesting and useful studies of the Soviet economy. Scholars who tried to reconstruct reality had to do so on the basis of limited and sometimes controversial evidence. Still, after the information provided by numerous former inmates who left the Soviet Union during the Second World War, the researches of such scholars as D. Dallin and Nicolaevsky, the writings of Solzhenitsyn, and especially the material becoming available after the collapse of the Soviet Union, the basic outlines of the Soviet forced-labor system are reasonably clear. Having begun in the early thirties the system encompassed millions of human beings on the eve of the Second World War, in spite of the extremely high mortality rate in the camps. Forced labor was used especially on huge construction projects, such as the Baltic-White Sea and other canals, and for hard work under primitive conditions in distant areas, as in the case of the lumber and gold industries. The political police—from 1922 to 1934 known as the GPU and the OGPU rather than the Cheka, after 1934 as the NKVD after the People's Commissariat of Internal Affairs, subsequently as MVD and MGB, and after 1954 as KGB— which guarded and administered forced labor, developed veritable concentration-camp empires in the European Russian and Siberian far north, in the Far East, and in certain other areas of the Soviet Union.

The Great Purge

The great purge of the 1930s helped to fill forced-labor camps and formed another major, although perhaps unnecessary, aspect of the five-year plans. It also marked Stalin's extermination of all opposition or suspected opposition and his assumption of complete dictatorial power. Although earlier some engineers and other specialists, including foreigners, had been accused of sabotaging or wrecking the industrialization of the country, the real purge began in December 1934 with the assassination of one of the party leaders who was boss in Leningrad, Serge Kirov, and reached high intensity from 1936 to 1938. The purge eventually became enormous in scope; it was directed primarily against party members, not against the White Guards or other remnants of the old regime as repressive practices had been before.

The assassin of Kirov, proclaimed to be a member of the Left Opposition, was shot, together with about a hundred alleged accomplices. Revelations at the Twenty-second Party Congress strengthened the suspicions of some specialists that Stalin himself was apparently responsible for Kirov's murder. A party purge followed. While uncounted people disappeared, the three great public trials featured sixteen Bolshevik leaders, notably Zinoviev and Kamenev, in 1936, another seventeen in 1937, and twenty-one more, including Bukharin and Rykov, in 1938. The accused were charged variously with espionage, "wrecking," and terrorism on behalf of imperialists, fascists, and Trotsky, and specifically with plotting to murder Stalin, overthrow the Soviet state, restore capitalism, and dismember the USSR with the help of Germany and Japan. Invariably they confessed to the fantastic charges and in all but four cases received the death penalty. Observers and scholars such as Conquest have been trying since to find reasons for the staggering confessions in everything from torture to heroic loyalty to Soviet communism. The purge spread

A 1934 newspaper cartoon depicts an old peasant cart marked "deviationists" carrying Bukharin, Kamenev, and Zinoviev toward a massive tank identified as the Communist Party.
(Mark Steinberg)

and spread, affecting virtually all party organizations and government branches, the army, where Marshal Tukhachevsky and seven other top commanders perished at the same time, and almost every other prominent institution, including the political police itself. Everywhere, party members were expected to denounce enemies of the regime at their places of work. Soon, the movement to expose enemies reached well beyond the party. Even children were encouraged to denounce their parents for criticizing the regime. Those caught up in this widening circle of denunciations would likely be expelled from the party, fired from work, imprisoned, perhaps tortured (starting in the middle of 1937), sent to a labor camp, or perhaps shot. The great purge reached its height when Nicholas Ezhov—hence *Ezhovshchina*—directed the NKVD from late September 1936 until the end of July 1938. Fainsod wrote the best summary of these events:

The period of the Yezhovshchina involved a reign of terror without parallel in Soviet history. Among those arrested, imprisoned, and executed were a substantial proportion of the leading figures in the Party and governmental hierarchy. The Bolshevik Old Guard was destroyed. The roll of Yezhov's victims included not only former oppositionists but many of the most stalwart supporters of Stalin in his protracted struggle with the opposition. No sphere of Soviet life, however lofty, was left untouched. Among the purged Stalinists were three former members of the Politburo . . . and three candidate members. . . . An overwhelming majority of the members and candidates of the Party Central Committee disappeared. The senior officer corps of the armed forces suffered severely. According to one sober account "two of five marshals of the Soviet Union escaped arrest, two of fifteen army commanders, twenty-eight of fifty-eight corps commanders, eighty-five of a hundred ninety-five divisional commanders, and a hundred and ninety-five of four hundred and six regimental commanders." The havoc wrought by the purge among naval commanding personnel was equally great. The removal of Yagoda from the NKVD was accompanied by the arrest of his leading collaborators. . . . The Commissariat of Foreign Affairs and the diplomatic service were hard hit. . . . Almost every commissariat was deeply affected.

The purge swept out in ever-widening circles and resulted in wholesale removals and arrests of leading officials in the union republics, secretaries of the Party, Komsomol, and trade-union apparatus, heads of industrial trusts and enterprises, Comintern functionaries and foreign Communists, and leading writers, scholars, engineers and scientists. The arrest of an important figure was followed by the seizure of the entourage which surrounded him. The apprehension of members of the entourage led to the imprisonment of their friends and acquaintances. The endless chain of involvements and associations threatened to encompass entire strata of Soviet society. Fear of arrest, exhortations to vigilance, and perverted ambition unleashed new floods of denunciations, which generated their own avalanche of cumulative interrogations and detentions. Whole categories of Soviet citizens found themselves singled out for arrest because of their "objective characteristics." Old Bolsheviks, Red Partisans, foreign Communists of German, Austrian, and Polish extraction, Soviet citizens who had been abroad or had relations with foreign countries or foreigners, and "repressed elements" were automatically caught up in the NKVD web of wholesale imprisonment. The arrests mounted into the millions; the testimony of the survivors is unanimous regarding crowded prison cells and teeming forced labor camps. Most of the prisoners were utterly bewildered by the fate which had befallen them. The vast resources of the NKVD were concentrated on one objective—to document the existence of a huge conspiracy to undermine Soviet power. The extraction of real confessions to imaginary crimes became a major industry. Under the zealous and ruthless ministrations of NKVD examiners, millions of innocents were transformed into traitors, terrorists, and enemies of the people.

Orders were even issued to arrest a certain percentage of the entire population. The total number of those taken by the political police has been estimated at at least eight million. Estimates of the number who were shot or who died in the camps range from hundreds of thousands to several million. And the effects of the terror were also felt by the family members and close friends of those arrested. Before the great purge had run its course, Ezhov himself and many of his henchmen fell victim to it after Lavrentii Beria, a Georgian like Stalin, took control of the NKVD.

Stalin's System

The great purge assured Stalin's dictatorial control of the party, the government, and the country. As frequently pointed out, the Old Bolsheviks, members of the party before 1917 and thus not creatures of the general secretary, suffered enormous losses. Virtually all of those who had at any time joined any opposition to Stalin perished. But, as already mentioned, some devoted Stalinists also fell victim to the purge; it was on the whole that group, together with the military men, that was posthumously vindicated by Khrushchev. When the Eighteenth All-Union Party Congress gathered in 1939, Old Bolsheviks composed only about 20 percent of its membership compared to 80 percent at the Seventeenth Congress in 1934. Moreover, except for a few lieutenants of Stalin, such as Viacheslav Molotov, born Skriabin, almost no leaders of any prominence were left. For example, with the exception of Stalin himself and of Trotsky, who was murdered in 1940, Lenin's entire Politburo had been wiped out.

Absolute personal dictatorship set in. While the Politburo remained by far the most important body in the country, because its fourteen or so members and candidate members were the general secretary's immediate assistants, there is much evidence that they, too, implicitly obeyed their master. Other party organizations followed the instructions they received as best they could to the letter. Significantly, no party congress was called between 1939 and 1952. The so-called "democratic centralism" within the party, that is, the practice of discussing and debating issues from the bottom up, but, once the party line had been formed, executing orders as issued from the top down, became a dead letter: even within the Communist Party framework no free discussion could take place in the Soviet Union, and almost every personal opinion became dangerous.

Through the Communist Party apparatus and the several million party members, as well as through the political police, Stalin supervised the government machine and controlled the people of the country. The peculiar relationship between the party and the government in the Soviet Union, in which the party is the leading partner as well as a driving force in carrying out state policies, has been elucidated in such studies as Fainsod's analysis of the Soviet regime in the Smolensk area, based on the Smolensk party archives which had fallen into Western hands, and Armstrong's investigation of the Communist Party in Ukraine. Not in vain did Article 126 of the Soviet Constitution of 1936 declare:

> . . . the most active and most politically conscious citizens in the ranks of the working class and other sections of the working people unite in the Communist Party of the Soviet Union (Bolsheviks), which is the vanguard of the working people in their struggle to strengthen and develop the socialist system and is the leading core of all organizations of the working people, both public and state.

The party, as will be shown in a later chapter, in fact dominated the social and cultural, as well as the political and economic, life in the Soviet Union.

At the same time, recent scholars have argued, Stalin's system could not rely solely on iron-fisted control, repression, and fear. As we have seen, enthusiasm for socialist construction, class hostility to "bourgeois" specialists, and

A 1934 poster depicting a happy peasant family. An award for excellent work hangs on the wall. On the bookshelf are works by Gorky, Lenin, and Stalin and on tractors, agricultural technology, and setting up rural reading rooms. Note the centrality in this poster of electric light and the phonograph. Stalin is quoted: "Any peasant, collective farmer, or individual farmer can now live like a human being, as long as he is willing to work honestly, not loaf, not wander about the country, and not loot the property of the collective farm." (Victoria Bonnell)

personal ambition to rise in the hierarchy at the expense of ideological or social aliens could win the regime allies and supporters. There were also concrete rewards. Especially after the end of the First Five-Year Plan, mobilization for its own sake gave way to a tendency to promise material benefits as well. Stakhanovite workers, for example, were shown being rewarded with new clothes, bicycles, phonographs, radios, china, linen, and pianos and portrayed spending their leisure time not only at party or production meetings but also at parties and dances. Indeed, happiness became a pervasive theme in public life. In 1936, Stalin introduce a new guiding slogan for the day: "Life has become better, life has become more joyous." Movies, popular entertainment, music, art, and literature all held out this promise of a happy life, however allusive it remained for so many and however contradicted by the brutalities of the age. Newspapers were filled not only with stories about enemies and purges but also with advertisements for attractive new hats and shoes and reports of dances and carnivals in the parks. This too was part of Stalin's system.

The Constitution of 1936

The Stalinist Constitution of 1936, which replaced the constitution of 1924 and was officially hailed as marking a great advance in the development of the Union of Soviet Socialist Republics, retained in effect the "dictatorship of the proletariat," exercised by the Communist Party and its leadership, specifically Stalin. At the same time it was meant to reflect the new "socialist" stage achieved in the Soviet Union, based on collective ownership of the means of production and summarized in the formula: "From each according to his ability, to each according to his work." It gave the ballot to all Soviet citizens—for no "exploiters" remained in the country—and made elections equal, direct, and secret. In fact, it emphasized democracy and contained in Chapter X a long list of civil rights as well as obligations. Yet, as has often been demonstrated, the permissiveness of the new constitution never extended beyond the Communist framework. Thus Chapter I affirmed that the basic structure of Soviet society could not be challenged. The civil liberty articles began: "In conformity with the interests of the working people, and in order to strengthen the socialist system . . ."—and could be considered dependent on this condition. The Communist Party, specifically recognized by the Constitution, was the only political group allowed in the Soviet Union. Still more important, the niceties of the Constitution of 1936 mattered little in a country ruled by an absolute dictator, his party, and his police. Ironically, the height of the great purge followed the introduction of the Constitution.

The Union of Soviet Socialist Republics remained a federal state, its component units being increased to eleven: the Russian Soviet Federated Socialist Republic, and ten Soviet Socialist Republics, namely, Ukraine, Belorussia or White Russia, Armenia, Georgia, and Azerbaijan in Transcaucasia, and the Kazakh, Kirghiz, Tajik, Turkmen, and Uzbek republics in Central Asia. While the larger nationalities received their own union republics, smaller ones obtained, in descending order, autonomous republics, autonomous regions, and national areas. Altogether, fifty-one nationalities were granted some form of limited statehood. Yet, like much else in the constitution, this arrangement was largely a sham: while important in terms of cultural autonomy—a subject to be discussed in a later chapter—as well as in terms of administration, in fact it gave no political or economic independence to the local units at all. The Soviet Union was one of the most highly centralized states of modern times.

A bicameral supreme Soviet replaced the congresses of Soviets as the highest legislative body of the land. One chamber, the Union Soviet, represented the entire Soviet people and was to be elected in the proportion of one deputy for every 300,000 inhabitants. The other, the Soviet of Nationalities, represented the component national groups and was to be elected as follows:

twenty-five delegates from each union republic, eleven from each autonomous republic, five from each autonomous region, and one from each national area. The two chambers received equal rights and parallel functions, exercising some of them jointly and some separately. Elected for four years—although with the Second World War intervening the second Supreme Soviet was not elected until 1946—the Supreme Soviet met twice a year, usually for no more than a week at a time. In the interims between sessions a Presidium elected by the Soviet had full authority. Almost always, Supreme Soviets unanimously approved all actions taken by their Presidiums. In the words of one commentator: "The brevity of the sessions, already noted, the size of the body, and the complexity of its agendas are all revealing as to the actual power and place of the Supreme Soviet." Still more revealing was the acquiescence and obsequiousness of the Soviet legislature in its dealings with Soviet rulers.

In the Constitution of 1936 the executive authority continued to be vested in the Council of People's Commissars, which had to be confirmed by the Supreme Soviet. Commissariats were of three kinds: Union—that is, central—Republican, and a combination of the two. Their number exceeded the number of ministries or similar agencies in other countries because many branches of the Soviet economy came to be managed by separate commissariats. In general, heavy industry fell under central jurisdiction, while light industry was directed by Union-Republican commissariats.

The Soviet legal system, while extensive and complicated, served party and state needs both explicitly and implicitly and had only an extremely limited independent role in Soviet society. Besides, the political police generally operated outside even Soviet law. It might be added that the Soviet central government served as the model for the governments of the union republics, although the latter established single-chamber, rather than bicameral, legislatures by omitting a chamber for nationalities.

Stalin's Soviet regime, which took its definitive shape in the thirties, was to undergo before long the awesome test of the Second World War. In a sense it passed the test, although it can well be argued that the war raised more questions about the regime than it settled. But, before turning to the Second World War, it is necessary to summarize Soviet foreign policy from the time of Brest-Litovsk and Allied intervention to the summer of 1941.

Chapter 38

Soviet Foreign Policy, 1921–41, and the Second World War, 1941–45

"Soldiers! isn't Moscow behind us?
Let us then die on the approaches to Moscow,
As our brothers knew how to die!"

—LERMONTOV

Our Government committed no few mistakes; at times our position was desperate, as in 1941–42, when our army was retreating, abandoning our native villages and towns in Ukraine, Byelorussia, Moldavia, the Leningrad Region, the Baltic Region, and the Karelo-Finnish Republic, abandoning them because there was no other alternative. Another people might have said to the government: You have not come up to our expectations. Get out. We shall appoint another government, which will conclude peace with Germany and ensure tranquillity for us. But the Russian people did not do that, for they were confident that the policy their Government was pursuing was correct; and they made sacrifices in order to ensure the defeat of Germany. And this confidence which the Russian people displayed in the Soviet Government proved to be the decisive factor which ensured our historic victory over the enemy of mankind, over fascism.

I thank the Russian people for this confidence!
To the health of the Russian people!

—STALIN

Soviet foreign policy can be considered in several contexts. To begin with, there is Marxist-Leninist ideology. True, Marxism did not provide any explicit guidance for the foreign relations of a Communist state. In fact, it preached a world revolution that would eliminate foreign policy altogether. That Lenin and his associates had to conduct international relations after their advent to power represented, in Marxist terms, one of several major paradoxes of their position. Not surprisingly, they assumed for months and even for a few years the imminence of a revolution that would destroy the entire capitalist world system. The alternative appeared to be their own immediate destruction by the capitalists. When neither happened, the Soviet leadership, in foreign relations as in home affairs, proceeded to adapt ideology to circumstances. Marxism supplied the goal of world revolution, although the time of that revolution could no longer be predicted with exactitude. Marxism, especially as developed by Lenin, with such key concepts as finance capitalism and imperialism, provided also the framework within which the Soviet leadership sought to understand and interpret the world.

However, when Lenin and his associates seized power in Petrograd, they inherited an international position and interests that had nothing in common with Marxism. The Bolsheviks did their best to break the ties with tsarist Russia, repudiating treaties and debts and publishing secret diplomatic documents. Still, they could not entirely divest the country of its past or separate the communist from the noncommunist aspects of their new role in the world. In fact, as the Soviet regime developed and after Soviet Russia explicitly became the center of Communist interest following the inauguration of the First Five-Year Plan, Soviet foreign policy evolved, in the opinion of many observers, in the direction of traditionalism and nationalism, acquiring a pronounced "Russian" character. Or, to make a different emphasis and suggest yet another context for Soviet foreign relations, the USSR can be analyzed simply as a gigantic modern state, and its foreign policy as a product of such considerations of *Realpolitik* as security, rather than considerations of Marxist ideology or of national tradition.

Soviet Foreign Policy in the Twenties

When Trotsky became commissar of war in 1918, his assistant, George Chicherin, replaced him as commissar of foreign affairs. Chicherin was to occupy that position until 1930; because of Chicherin's ill health, however, his eventual successor, Maxim Litvinov, directed the commissariat from 1928. Chicherin was of gentry origin and for many years of Menshevik, rather than Bolshevik, affiliation. In fact, he never entered the narrow circle of Communist leaders. Nevertheless, because of his ability and special qualifications for the post—Chicherin had originally begun his career in the tsarist diplomatic service and was a fine linguist with an excellent knowledge of the international scene—he was entrusted for over a decade with the handling of Soviet foreign policy, although, to be sure, he worked under the close supervision of Lenin, Stalin, and the Politburo. As mentioned previously, positions of real power in the Soviet system have been at the top of the party hierarchy, not in any of the commissariats.

One of Chicherin's main tasks was to obtain recognition for the Soviet Union and to stabilize its position in the world. In spite of transitory successes in Hungary and Bavaria, Communist revolutions had failed outside Soviet borders. On the other hand, with the defeat of the White movement and the end of Allied intervention, the Bolshevik regime appeared to be firmly entrenched in Russia. "Coexistence" became a reality, and both sides sought a suitable modus vivendi. Yet the Soviet Union supported the Third or Communist International—called the Comintern—established in 1919 with Zinoviev as chairman, and it refused to pay tsarist debts or compensate foreigners for their confiscated property, demanding in its turn huge reparations for Allied intervention. In particular the Comintern, composed of Communist parties scattered throughout the world, who were bent on subversion and revolution and were clearly directed from the Soviet Union in Soviet interests, constituted a persistent obstacle to normal diplomatic relations. Most other states, on their side, looked at Soviet Russia with undisguised hostility and suspicion.

The Soviet Union managed to break out of isolation in the spring of 1922. A Soviet delegation attended then for the first time an international economic conference, held in Genoa. Although the conference itself produced no important results, bogging down on the aforementioned issues of debts and reparations, among others, Soviet representatives used the occasion to reach an agreement with Germany. The Treaty of Rapallo of April 16, 1922, supplemented later by a commercial agreement, established economic cooperation between the Soviet Union and Germany and even led to some political and military ties. It lasted until after Hitler's advent to power. While the Treaty of Rapallo produced surprise and indignation in many quarters, its rationale was clear enough and, as in the case of most other Soviet agreements, it had nothing to do with the mutual sympathy or antipathy of the signatories: both Soviet Russia and Germany were outcasts in the post-Versailles world, and they joined hands naturally for mutual advantage.

Early in 1924 Great Britain formally recognized the Soviet Union; it was followed by France, Italy, Austria, Sweden, Norway, Denmark, Greece, Mexico, and China before the end of the year. In 1925 Japan established normal relations with the USSR, evacuating at last the Russian part of the island of Sakhalin, although retaining certain oil, coal, and timber concessions there. The recognition of Soviet Russia by many states marked simply their acceptance of the existence of the Bolshevik regime, accompanied sometimes by hopes of improving trade relations, rather than any real change in their attitude toward the USSR. Lloyd George's remark on trading even with cannibals has often been quoted. Moreover, other countries, including notably the United States and most Slavic states of eastern Europe, continued to ignore the Soviet Union and refuse it recognition. Still, all in all, Chicherin succeeded in bringing Soviet Russia into the diplomatic community of nations.

That the course of Soviet foreign policy could be tortuous and even paradoxical became clear in the case of China. There Stalin chose to support the Kuomintang, the nationalist movement of Sun Yat-sen and Sun's successor Chiang Kai-shek, sending hundreds of military specialists to help the Nationalists and directing the Chinese Communists to follow "united front" tactics. For a time Communist infiltration appeared successful, and Soviet position and prestige stood high in China. But in 1927 as soon as Chiang Kai-shek had assured himself of victory in the struggle for the control of the country, he turned against the Communists, massacring them in Shanghai and evicting Soviet advisers. When the Chinese Communists, on orders from Moscow, retaliated with a rebellion in Canton, they were bloodily crushed. Yet, although defeated in China, the Soviet Union managed to establish control over Outer

Mongolia after several changes of fortune. Also, in the mid-twenties it concluded useful treaties of neutrality and friendship with Turkey, Persia, and Afghanistan. It should be added that the Bolshevik regime renounced the concessions and special rights obtained by the tsarist government in such Asian countries as China and Persia. But it held on to the Chinese Eastern Railway, weathering a conflict over it with the Chinese in 1929.

Soviet Foreign Policy in the Thirties

Chicherin's efforts in the '20s to obtain recognition for his country and to stabilize Soviet diplomatic relations developed into a more ambitious policy in the '30s. Devised apparently by Stalin and the Politburo and executed by Maxim Litvinov, who served as commissar for foreign affairs from 1930 until 1939, the new approach aimed at closer alliances with *status quo* powers in an effort to check the mounting challenges to the postwar order and the growing threat of aggression. It culminated in the Soviet entrance into the League of Nations and Litvinov's emphasis on disarmament and collective security. To appreciate the shift in Soviet tactics, it should be realized that the Bolshevik leadership had for a long time been predicting a great confrontation between the socialist and capitalist worlds and regarded Great Britain and France as their main enemies and the League of Nations as the chief international agency of militant imperialism. Indeed, the Politburo placed its hopes, it would seem, in the expected quarrels among leading capitalist powers, and in particular in a war between Great Britain and the United States! Under the circumstances, the Japanese aggression that began on the Chinese mainland in 1931 and especially the rise of Hitler to power in Germany in January 1933, together with his subsequent policies, came as rude shocks. Anxieties about to the threat posed by Fascism increased during the 1930s and became a major theme in speeches by party leaders, in the press, and, as we have seen, in the purge trials. Thus, in 1934, Soviet diplomacy dramatically changed directions and pursued collective security, which focused on convincing England, France, and the United States to unite with the USSR to contain German expansion. Communist parties all over the world were ordered to support this new "line." Hence the celebrated "popular fronts" of the 1930s and the strange *rapprochement* between the USSR and Western democracies as well as a new cordiality between the USSR and Chiang Kai-shek. Based on dire expediency rather than on understanding or trust and vitiated by mistakes of judgment on all sides, including the preference of the Western powers for appeasement over containment, the *rapprochement* with the West collapsed in a catastrophic manner in 1938 and 1939 to set the stage for the Second World War.

As early as 1929 the Soviet Union used the occasion of the making of the Kellogg-Briand Pact outlawing war to formulate the Litvinov Protocol, applying the pact on a regional basis. Poland, Romania, Latvia, Estonia, Lithuania, Turkey, Persia, and the Free City of Danzig proved willing to sign the Protocol with the USSR. In 1932 the Soviet Union concluded treaties of nonaggression with Poland, Estonia, Latvia, and Finland, as well as with France. In 1933 the United States finally recognized the Soviet Union, obtaining from the Soviets the usual unreliable promise to desist from Communist propaganda in the United States. In the spring of 1934 the nonaggression pacts with Poland and the Baltic states were expanded into ten-year agreements. In the summer of that year the Soviet government signed treaties with Czechoslovakia and Romania—the establishment of diplomatic relations with the latter country marked the long delayed, temporary Soviet reconciliation to the loss of Bessarabia. And in the autumn of 1934 the USSR joined the League of Nations.

The following year witnessed the conclusion of the Soviet-French and the Soviet-Czech alliances. Both called for military aid in case of an unprovoked attack by a European state. The Soviet-Czech treaty, however, added the qualification that the USSR was obliged to help Czechoslovakia only if France, which had concluded a mutual aid treaty with the Czechs, would come to their assistance. France, it is worth noting, failed to respond to Soviet pressure for a precise military convention, while neither Poland nor Romania wanted to allow the passage of the Red Army to help the Czechs in case of need.

Also in 1935 the Third International, which had become somewhat less active as a revolutionary force in the course of the preceding years, at its Seventh Congress proclaimed the new policy of popular fronts: Communist parties, reversing themselves, were to cooperate in their respective countries with other political groups interested in checking Fascist aggression, and they were to support rearmament. In its turn the Soviet government demanded in the League of Nations and elsewhere that severe sanctions be applied to aggressors and that forces of peace be urgently mobilized to stop them. Yet both the League and the great powers individually accomplished little or nothing. Italy completed its conquest of Ethiopia, while Japan developed its aggression on the Asian mainland. In the summer of 1936 a great civil war broke out in Spain, pitting Franco's Fascist rebels and their allies against the democratic and Left-wing republican government. Once more, the Soviet Union proved eager to stop Fascism, while France and Great Britain hesitated, compromised, emphasized nonintervention, and let the Spanish republic go down. Whereas Italian divisions and German airmen and tankmen aided Franco, none but Soviet officers and technicians were sent to assist the Loyalists, while the international Communist movement mobilized its resources to obtain and ship volunteers who fought in the celebrated "international brigades." Although much in the Soviet intervention in Spain remains obscure and controversial, studies by Cattell and others demonstrate both the seriousness of the Soviet effort to defeat Franco and the remarkable way in which the Communists, including the secret police, proceeded to extend their hold on republican Spain and to dispose of their rivals. But, with massive Italian and German backing, the insurgents won the bitter civil war in Spain, hostilities ending in the spring of 1939.

The position and prospects of the Soviet Union became graver and graver in the course of the '30s. In November 1936, Germany and Japan concluded the so-called Anti-Comintern Pact aimed specifically against the USSR. Italy joined the Pact in 1937 and Spain in 1939. In the Far East in 1935 the Soviet Union sold its dominant interest in the Chinese Eastern Railway to the Japanese puppet state of Manchukuo, thus eliminating one major source of conflict.

But relations between Japan and the USSR remained tense, as Japanese expansion and ambitions grew, while the Soviet leaders continued to send supplies to Chiang Kai-shek as well as to direct and support Communist movements in Asia. In fact, in 1938 and again in 1939 Japanese and Soviet troops fought actual battles on the Manchurian and Mongolian borders, the Red Army better than holding its own and hostilities being terminated as abruptly as they had begun. Hitler's Germany represented an even greater menace to the Soviet Union than Japan. The Führer preached the destruction of communism and pointed to the lands east as the natural area of German expansion, its legitimate *Lebensraum*. Again, as in the cases of Japan and Italy, the Western powers failed to check the aggressor. Following the remilitarization of the Rhineland in 1936, Hitler annexed Austria to the Third Reich in March 1938, making a shambles of the Treaty of Versailles.

Soviet Foreign Policy from September 1938 until June 1941

The climax of appeasement came in September 1938 at Munich. Great Britain and France capitulated to Hitler's demand for Germany's annexation of the Sudetenland, a largely ethnically German area of Czechoslovakia; Chamberlain and Daladier flew to Munich and sealed the arrangement with Hitler and Mussolini. The unpreparedness and unwillingness of the Western democracies to fight, rather than any collusion of the West with Hitler against the USSR, motivated the Munich surrender. Still, the extreme Soviet suspicion of the settlement can well be understood, especially since the Soviet government was not invited to participate in it. Although it had expressed its readiness to defend Czechoslovakia, the Soviet Union had been forced to remain a helpless bystander when France failed to come to the aid of the Czechs and Prague had to accept its betrayal by the great powers. Moreover, after Munich the Franco-Russian alliance appeared to mean very little, and the USSR found itself, in spite of all its efforts to promote collective security, in highly dangerous isolation.

His appetite whetted by appeasement, Hitler in the meantime developed further aggressive designs in eastern Europe. In March 1939 he disposed of what remained of Czechoslovakia, establishing the German protectorate of Bohemia and Moravia and another one of Slovakia. This step both destroyed the Munich arrangement and made plain Nazi determination to expand beyond ethnic German boundaries. Next Hitler turned to Poland, demanding the cession of Danzig to Germany and the right of extraterritorial German transit across the Polish "corridor" to East Prussia. The alternative was war.

Poland, however, did not stand alone against Germany in the summer of 1939. France and Great Britain finally saw the folly of appeasement after Germany had seized the remainder of Czechoslovakia. At the end of March they made clear their determination to fight if Poland were attacked. As war clouds gathered, the position of the Soviet Union became all the more significant. In May Molotov replaced Litvinov as commissar for foreign affairs, retaining at the same time his office of Chairman of the Council of People's Commissars, equivalent to prime minister, as well as his membership in the Politburo. Thus for the first time since Trotsky in 1918 a Communist leader of the first rank took charge of Soviet foreign policy. Moreover, in contrast to his predecessor Litvinov, Molotov had not been personally committed to collective security and, therefore, could more easily undertake a fresh start. In retrospect commentators have also noted the fact that Molotov, again in contrast to Litvinov, was not Jewish. After an exchange of notes in the spring of 1939, Great Britain and France began in the summer to negotiate with the USSR concerning the formation of a joint front against aggression. But the Western powers failed to come to terms with the Soviet Union, or even to press the negotiations, sending a weak and low-ranking mission to Moscow. The Soviet government, on its side, remained extremely suspicious of the West, especially after the Munich settlement, and eagerly sought ways of diverting impending hostilities away from its borders. On August 23 a German-Russian agreement of strict neutrality was signed in Moscow—secret talks had begun as early as May—an event which produced surprise and shock in the world. Fortified by the pact, Hitler attacked Poland on the first of September. On the third, Great Britain and France declared war on Germany. The Second World War became a reality.

The Bolsheviks and the Nazis hated each other and considered themselves to be irreconcilable enemies. That no illusions were involved in their agreement is indicated, among many other things, by the fact that Molotov, who signed the treaty for the Soviet Union and thus represented the "pro-German orientation," retained his position and Stalin's favor after Hitler attacked the USSR. Yet both parties to the pact expected to gain major temporary advantages by means of it. Germany would be free to fight Western powers. The Soviet Union would escape war, at least for the time being. Besides, the agreement was accompanied by a secret protocol dividing the spheres of influence and enabling the Soviet Union to expand in eastern Europe, creating a buffer zone.

The Red Army occupied eastern Poland, incorporating its White Russian and Ukrainian areas into the corresponding Soviet republics. Next the Soviet government signed mutual assistance pacts with Estonia, Latvia, and Lithuania, obtaining a lease of Baltic bases. But in July 1940 these states were occupied by Soviet troops, and, following a vote of their beleaguered parliaments, they were incorporated into the USSR as union republics—a procedure that the Western democracies with excellent reasons failed to recognize. Finland was more troublesome: the Finnish government turned down the Soviet demand that they move the Finnish boundary some twenty miles further away from Leningrad, abandoning a Finnish defense line, in exchange for a strip of Karelia; a war between the two countries resulted and lasted from the end of November 1939 until mid-March 1940. In spite of the heroic Finnish defense and the surprising early reverses of the Red Army, the Soviet Union eventually imposed its will on Finland. Finally, in the summer of 1940 the USSR utilized its agreement with Germany to obtain from Romania, by means of an ultimatum, the disputed region of Bessarabia as well as northern Bukovina. The new Moldavian Soviet Socialist Republic was formed from the territory acquired from Romania. In April 1941 the Soviet Union signed a five-year nonaggression treaty with Japan, which had chosen to expand south rather than into Siberia.

But, although the Soviet government did not know it, time was running short for its efforts to strengthen its position on the European and Asian continents. Following his stunning victory in the west in the summer of 1940, Hitler decided to invade the Soviet Union. In December he issued precise instructions for an attack in May 1941. The defeat that Germany suffered in the autumn in the aerial Battle of Britain apparently only helped convince the Nazi dictator that he should strike his next major blow in the east. The schedule, however, could not quite be kept. A change of government in Yugoslavia made the Germans invade Yugoslavia as well as Greece, which had stopped an earlier Italian offensive. While brilliantly successful, the German campaign in the Balkans, together with a certain delay in supplying the German striking force with tanks and other vehicles, postponed by perhaps three weeks the invasion of Soviet Russia. The new date was June 22, and on that day German troops aided by Finnish, Romanian, and other units attacked the USSR along an enormous front from the Baltic to the Black Sea.

The Soviet Union in the Second World War

The blow was indeed staggering. Hitler threw into the offensive some 175 divisions, including numerous armored formations. A huge and powerful air force closely supported the attack. Moreover, perhaps surprisingly, the German blow caught the Red Army off guard. Apparently, although Stalin and the Politburo were preparing for war, they had ignored Western warnings as well as their own intelligence and did not expect such an early, sudden, and powerful offensive. Stalin disappeared from public sight for more than a week—leading to rumors about nervous shock. Only on July 3 did he return, with a grim but confident radio address about the need to fight heroically against what he described as Germany's intent to make "slaves" of the Soviet peoples and destroy its "national culture." The Germans aimed at another *Blitzkrieg*, intending to defeat the Russians within two or three months or in any case before winter. Although it encountered some determined resistance, the German war machine rolled along the entire front, particularly in the north toward Leningrad, in the center toward Moscow, and in the south toward Kiev and Rostov-on-Don. Entire Soviet armies were smashed and taken prisoner at Bialystok, Minsk, and Kiev, which fell in September. The southern wing of the invasion swept across Ukraine. In the north, Finnish troops pushed to the Murmansk railroad, and German troops reached, but could not capture, Leningrad. The city underwent a two-and-a-half-year siege, virtually cut off from the rest of the country; its population was decreased by starvation, disease, and war from four to two and a half million. Yet the city would not surrender, and it blocked further German advance north.

The central front proved decisive. There the Germans aimed their main blow directly at Moscow. But they were delayed in fierce fighting near Smolensk. The summer *Blitzkrieg* became a fall campaign. Hitler increased the number of his and his allies' divisions in Russia to 240 and pushed an all-out effort to capture the Soviet capital. In the middle of October German tanks broke through the Russian lines near Mozhaisk, some sixty miles from Moscow. Stalin and the government left the city for Kuibyshev, formerly Samara, on the Volga.

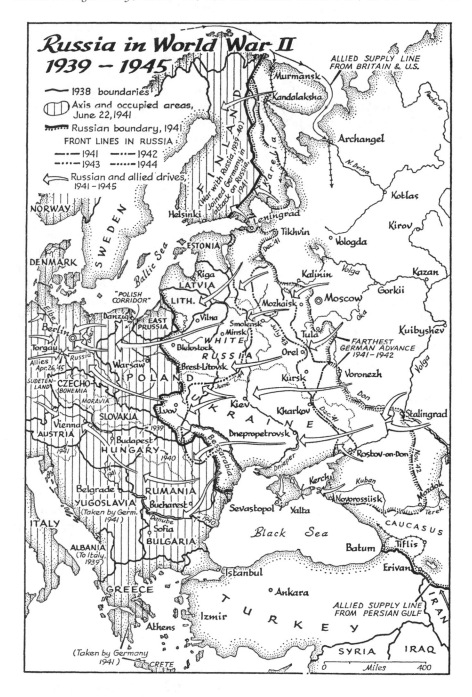

Russia in World War II 1939 – 1945

— 1938 boundaries
Axis and occupied areas, June 22, 1941
Russian boundary, 1941
FRONT LINES IN RUSSIA:
—·— 1941 —··— 1942
—···— 1943 ——···— 1944
Russian and allied drives, 1941–1945

NORWAY
SWEDEN
DENMARK
FINLAND (War with Russia 1939-40) (Joined Germany in attack on Russia, 1941)
Karelia
ALLIED SUPPLY LINE FROM BRITAIN & U.S.
Murmansk
Kandalaksha
Archangel
N. Dvina
Pechora
Kotlas
Kirov
Helsinki
Leningrad
Tikhvin
Vologda
Kazan
Dec. 41
Baltic Sea
ESTONIA
Riga
LATVIA
LITH.
Kalinin
Volga
Gorkii
Mozhaisk
Moscow
"POLISH CORRIDOR"
Danzig
EAST PRUSSIA
Vilna
Smolensk
Minsk
WHITE RUSSIA
Tula
Oka
Kuibyshev
FARTHEST GERMAN ADVANCE 1941-1942
Berlin
Torgau
Elbe
Allies Apr. 26, '45
Russia
Warsaw
Bialostock
Brest-Litovsk
Orel
July
Volga
SUDETEN-LAND
CZECHO-BOHEMIA
MORAVIA
POLAND
UKRAINE
Lvov
Kiev
Kursk
Voronezh
Don
Stalingrad
SLOVAKIA
Vienna
1939
AUSTRIA
1941
Budapest
HUNGARY
1940
Kharkov
Dec. '41
Dnepropetrovsk
Bessarabia
June
Dnieper
Rostov-on-Don
Nov. '42
Belgrade
YUGOSLAVIA (Taken by Germ. 1941)
RUMANIA
Bucharest
Kerch
Kuban
Mozdok
Terek
Sevastopol
Yalta
Novorossiisk
ITALY
Danube
1940
Sofia
BULGARIA
CAUCASUS
Black Sea
Batum
Tiflis
ALBANIA (To Italy, 1939)
Erivan
Istanbul
GREECE
Ankara
ALLIED SUPPLY LINE FROM PERSIAN GULF
Izmir
TURKEY
IRAN
Athens
(Taken by Germany 1941) CRETE
SYRIA
IRAQ
0   Miles   400

Yet, instead of abandoning Moscow as in 1812, its defender, Marshal George Zhukov, had his troops fall slowly back on the capital, reducing the German advance to a crawl. The Germans proceeded to encircle the city on three sides, and they came to within twenty miles of it, but no further. Late in November the Red Army started a counteroffensive against the extremely extended German lines on the southern front, recapturing Rostov-on-Don at the end of the month. In early December it struck on the central front, attacking both north and south of Moscow as well as in the Moscow area itself. The Germans suffered enormous losses and had to retreat. Winter came to play havoc with unprepared German troops and to assist the Russians. On January 20 the Red Army recaptured Mozhaisk, thus eliminating any immediate threat to Moscow. But German troops had to retreat much further west before they could stabilize the front. In fact, its lines overextended, its troops unequipped for cold weather and exhausted, the German army probably came near complete collapse in the winter of 1941/42. Some specialists believe that only Hitler's frantic determination to hold on prevented a catastrophic withdrawal. As it was, the German army gave up about one hundred thousand square miles of Soviet territory, but retained five hundred thousand when fighting finally quieted down.

In retrospect it seems clear that, in spite of its many splendid victories, the great German campaign of 1941 in Russia failed. The Red Army remained very much in the field, and the *Blitzkrieg* turned into a long war on an enormous front. Quite possibly Hitler came close to crushing the Soviet Union in 1941, but he did not come close again. Taking into account Soviet resources and the determination to resist, the Nazis had to win quickly or not at all. German losses in their initial eastern campaign, large in quantity, were still more damaging in quality: the cream of German youth lined the approaches to Moscow.

Furthermore, although the Soviet Union bore the brunt of Nazi armed might from the summer of 1941 until the end of the Second World War in Europe, it certainly did not fight alone. Churchill welcomed Soviet Russia as an ally the day of the German attack—although shortly before he had been ready to wage war against the USSR in defense of Finland. Great Britain and the United States arranged to send sorely needed supplies to the Soviet Union; and after the Japanese strike at Pearl Harbor on December 7, 1941, the United States became a full-fledged combatant. In spite of German submarines and aircraft and the heavy losses they inflicted, British convoys began to reach Murmansk and Archangel in the autumn of 1941, while American aid through Persia started to arrive in large quantity in the spring of 1942. More important, the Axis powers had major enemies to fight in Africa, and eventually in southern and western Europe, as well as in the east.

The second great German offensive in Russia, unleashed in the summer of 1942, was an operation of vast scope and power, even though it was more limited in its sweep and resources than the original attack of 1941: in 1942 the Germans and their allies used about 100 divisions and perhaps a million men in an attack along the southern half of the front, from Voronezh to the Black Sea. Having occupied the Kerch area and captured Sevastopol after a month of bitter fighting, the Germans opened their main offensive early in July. They struck in two directions: east toward the Volga, and south toward the Caucasus.

Blocked on the approaches to Voronezh, the German commander, Marshal Fedor von Bock had his main army of over 300,000 men cross the Don farther south and drive to the Volga. At the end of August the Nazis and their allies reached Stalingrad.

That industrial city of half a million people, strung along the right bank of the Volga, had no fortifications or other defensive advantages. Yet General Basil Chuikov's 62nd Army, supported by artillery massed on the other bank, fought for every house and every foot of ground. Reduced to rubble, the city became only more impassable to the invaders in spite of all their weapons and aircraft. Both sides suffered great losses. Hitler, who had assumed personal command of the German army in December 1941 and possibly saved his troops from catastrophe in the winter of 1941/42, began to make disastrous strategic errors. He kept pounding at Stalingrad for fruitless weeks and even months and, disregarding professional opinion, would not let his troops retreat even when a Soviet counteroffensive began to envelop them. Eventually, at the end of January 1943, Marshal Friedrich Paulus and some 120,000 German and Romanian troops surrendered to the Red Army, their attempt to break through to the Volga thus ending in a complete fiasco. The German offensive southward had captured Rostov-on-Don once more and had swept across the northern Caucasus, the attackers seizing such important points as the port of Novorossiisk and the oil center of Mozdok. But again the extended German lines crumbled under Zhukov's counteroffensive in December. The invaders had to retreat fast into southern Ukraine and the Crimea and were fortunate to extricate themselves at all.

After some further retreats and counterattacks in the winter of 1942/43, the Germans tried one more major offensive in Russia the following summer. They struck early in July in the strategic watershed area of Kursk, Orel, and Voronezh with some forty divisions, half of them armored or motorized, totaling approximately half a million men. But after initial successes and a week or ten days of tremendous fighting of massed armor and artillery the German drive was spent, and the Red Army in its turn opened an offensive. Before very long the Red drive gathered enough momentum to hurl the invaders out of the Soviet Union and eventually to capture Budapest, Vienna, Prague, and Berlin, stopping only with the end of the war. The smashing Soviet victory was made possible by the fact that the German forces had exhausted themselves. Their quality began to decline probably about the end of 1941, while the increasing numbers of satellite troops pressed into service, notably Romanians, could not at all measure up to the German standard. Hitler continued to make mistakes. Time and again, as in the case of Stalingrad, he would not allow his troops to retreat until too late. The Red Army, on the other hand, in spite of its staggering losses, improved in quality and effectiveness. Its battle-tested commanders showed initiative and ability; its weapons and equipment rolled in plentiful supply both from Soviet factories, many of which had been transported eastward and reassembled there, and through Allied aid, while the German forces suffered from all kinds of shortages. As long as they fought on Soviet soil, the Germans had to contend with a large and daring partisan movement in their rear as well as with the Red Army. And they began to experience increasing pressure and defeat on other fronts, as well as from the air, where the Americans and the British mounted a staggering offensive against German cities and industries. The battle of Stalingrad coincided with Montgomery's victory over Rommel in Egypt and Allied landings in Morocco and Algeria. Allied troops invaded Sicily in the summer of 1943 and the Italian mainland that autumn. Finally, on June 6, 1944, the Americans, the British, and the Canadians landed in Normandy to establish the coveted "second front." As the Russians began to invade the Third Reich from the east, the Allies were pushing into it from the west.

The Red Army recovered much of occupied Soviet territory in the autumn of 1943 and in the winter of 1943/44. On April 8, 1944, Marshal Ivan Konev crossed the Pruth into Romania. In the following months Soviet armies advanced rapidly in eastern and central Europe, while other armies continued to wipe out the remaining German pockets on Soviet soil. Romania and Bulgaria quickly changed sides and joined the anti-German coalition. The Red Army was joined by Tito partisans in Yugoslavia and in September 1944 entered Belgrade. After some bitter fighting, Red forces took Budapest in February 1945 and Vienna in mid-April. In the north, Finland had to accept an armistice in September 1944. The great offensive into Germany proper began in the autumn of 1944 when Red forces, after capturing Vilna, penetrated East Prussia. It gained momentum in January 1945 when large armies commanded by Konev in the south, Zhukov in the center, and Marshal Constantine Rokossovsky in the north invaded Germany on a broad front. On April 25, 1945, advanced Russian units met American troops at Torgau, on the Elbe, near Leipzig. On the second of May, Berlin fell to Zhukov's forces after heavy fighting. Hitler had already committed suicide. The Red Army entered Dresden on the eighth of May and Prague on the ninth. On that day, May 9, 1945, fighting ceased: the Third Reich had finally surrendered unconditionally to the Allies, first in Rheims on the seventh of May and then formally in Berlin on the eighth.

Urged by its allies and apparently itself eager to participate, the Soviet Union entered the war against Japan on August 8, 1945, three months after the German surrender. By that time Japan had already in fact been defeated by the United States and other powers. The American dropping of an atomic bomb on Hiroshima on the sixth of August and on Nagasaki on the ninth eliminated the need to invade the Japanese mainland, convincing the Japanese government that further resistance was useless. In spite of subsequent claims of Soviet historians and propagandists, the role of the USSR in the conflict in the Far East and the Pacific was, therefore, fleeting and secondary at best. Yet it enabled the Red forces to occupy Manchuria, the Japanese part of the island of Sakhalin, and the Kurile islands, and to capture many prisoners—all at the price of considerable casualties, for the Japanese did resist. The formal Japanese surrender to the Allies took place on board the U.S. battleship *Missouri* in Tokyo Bay on September 2, 1945. It marked the end of the Second World War.

Wartime Diplomacy

Diplomacy accompanied military operations. In the course of the war the Soviet Union established close contacts with its allies, in particular with Great

Britain and the United States. It accepted the Atlantic Charter formulated by Roosevelt and Churchill in August 1941, which promised freedom, self-determination, and equality of economic opportunity to all countries, and it participated fully in the preparation and the eventual creation of the United Nations Organization. It concluded a twenty-year agreement with Great Britain "for the joint achievement both of victory and of a permanent peace settlement" in June 1942 and later made a treaty with France also.

Of the various high-level conferences of the Allies during the war, the three meetings of the heads of state were the most impressive and important. They took place at Teheran in December 1943, at Yalta in the Crimea in February 1945, and at Potsdam near Berlin in July and August 1945. Stalin, who had assumed the position of prime minister and generalissimo, that is, chief military commander, while remaining the general secretary of the party, represented the Soviet Union on all three occasions. Roosevelt headed the American delegation at Teheran and Yalta, and Truman, after Roosevelt's death, at Potsdam. Churchill and later Attlee spoke for Great Britain. The heads of the three world powers devoted large parts of their conferences to a discussion of such major issues of the Second World War as the establishment of the "second front" and the eventual entry of the Soviet Union into the struggle against Japan. But, especially as victory came nearer, they also made important provisions for the time when peace would be achieved. These included among others: the division of Germany into zones of occupation, with Berlin receiving special status; the acceptance of the incorporation of the Königsberg district of East Prussia into the Soviet Union; the determination of the Polish eastern frontier, which was to follow roughly the Curzon Line, Poland being granted an indefinite compensation in the west; the decision to promote the establishment of democratic governments based on free elections in all restored European countries; and provisions concerning the formation of the United Nations. Considerable, if largely deceptive, harmony was achieved. Roosevelt in particular exuded optimism.

Yet even during the war years important disagreements developed among the Allies. The Soviet Union was bitterly disappointed that the Western powers did not invade France in 1942 or in 1943. In spite of the importance of contacts with the West and the enormous aid received from there, Soviet authorities continued to supervise closely all relations with the outside world and to restrict the movement and activities of foreigners in the Soviet Union. Perhaps more important, early difficulties and disagreements concerning the nature of postwar Europe became apparent. Poland served as a striking case in point. After Germany attacked the Soviet Union, Soviet authorities established relations with the Polish government in exile in London. But the cooperation between the two broke down before long. The Polish army formed in the Soviet Union was transferred to Iran and British auspices, while the Soviet leadership proceeded to rely on a smaller group of Left-Wing Poles who eventually organized the so-called Lublin government in liberated Poland. The historic bitterness between the Poles and the Russians, the problem of the frontier, and other controversial issues were exacerbated by the events of the war years. In April 1943, the German radio announced to the world the massacre by the

Reds of thousands of Polish officers in the Katyn Forest near Smolensk before the capture of that area by German troops. This charge, which led to the break in relations between Moscow and the Polish government in London, has now been confirmed. Again, when the Red Army reached the Vistula in August 1944, it failed to assist a desperate Polish rebellion against the Germans in Warsaw, which was finally crushed in October. In this manner it witnessed the annihilation of the anti-German, but also anti-Soviet, Polish underground. The official assertion that Red troops could not advance because they had exhausted their supplies and needed to rest and regroup had its grounds. But Soviet authorities would not even provide airstrips for Allied planes to help the Poles. Under the circumstances the Yalta decision to recognize the Lublin government expanded by several representatives of the London Poles and to hold free elections and establish a democratic regime in Poland proved unrealistic and amounted in the end to a Western surrender to Soviet wishes. This and other grave problems of postwar eastern Europe are treated in the next chapter.

The Soviet Union in the Second World War: An Evaluation

The Soviet performance in the Second World War presents a fascinating picture of contrasts. Seldom did a country and a regime do both so poorly and so well in the same conflict. Far from purposely enticing the Germans into the interior of the country or executing successfully any other strategic plan, the Red Army suffered catastrophic defeat in the first months of the war. Indeed, the Russians were smashed as badly as the French had been a year earlier, except that they had more territory to retreat to and more men in reserve. Moreover, while the German army was at the time the best in the world, Soviet forces did not at all make the most of their admittedly difficult position. Some top Red commanders, such as the Civil War cavalry hero Marshal Semen Budenny, proved to be as incompetent as the worst tsarist generals. The fighting spirit of Soviet troops varied greatly: certain units fought heroically, while others hastened to surrender. The enormous number of prisoners taken by the Germans testified not only to their great military victory, but also in part to the Soviet unwillingness to fight. Even more significantly, the Soviet population often welcomed the Germans. This was strikingly true in the recently acquired Baltic countries and in large areas of Ukraine and White Russia, but it also occurred in Great Russian regions near Smolensk and elsewhere. After a quarter of a century of Communist rule many inhabitants of the USSR greeted invaders, any invaders, as liberators. In addition to Red partisans there developed anti-Soviet guerrilla movements, which were at the same time anti-German. In Ukraine, nationalist bands continued resisting Red rule even long after the end of the Second World War. To the great surprise of the Western democracies, tens of thousands of Soviet citizens liberated by Allied armies in Europe did all they could not to return to their homeland.

But the Soviet regime survived. In spite of its staggering losses, the Red Army did finally hold the Germans and then gradually push them back until their defeat became a rout. Red infantry, artillery, cavalry, and tanks all repeatedly distinguished themselves in the Second World War. Uncounted soldiers acted with supreme heroism. The names of such commanders as Zhukov and Rokossovsky became synonymous with victory. In addition to the regular army, daring and determined partisans also fought the invader to the death. The government managed under most difficult conditions to organize the supply of the armed forces. It should be stressed that while Soviet military transportation depended heavily on vehicles from Lend-Lease, the Red Army was armed with Soviet weapons. The centralized structure of the Soviet economy enabled it quickly to mobilize resources and adapt production to war needs. The mass evacuation of factories and workers to the east—an impressive organizational feat—was essential in keeping Soviet war industries out of German hands. Although many people died of starvation in Leningrad and elsewhere, government control remained effective and morale did not break on the home front. Eventually the Soviet Union won, at an enormous cost, it is true, a total victory.

"Avenge Us!" 1942.   (Sovetskoe iskusstvo)

Much has been written to explain the initial Soviet collapse and the great subsequent rally. For example, it has been argued that the Germans defeated themselves. Their beastly treatment of the Soviet population—documented in A. Dallin's study and in other works—turned friends into enemies. It has even been claimed that to win the war the Nazis had merely to arm Soviet citizens and let them fight against their own government, but Hitler was extremely reluctant to try that. The Russian Liberation Army of Andrew Vlasov, a Soviet general who had been taken prisoner by the Germans and had proceeded to organize an anti-Communist movement, received no chance to develop and prove itself in combat until it was too late. Others have argued that the mobilization of resources—economic, military, and human—against Nazi aggression was the major reason the Soviet Union prevailed in battle and survived politically. And the human side of this story, commentators have argued, may have been the most important. Official propaganda during the war was filled with true tales of heroism, courage, and sacrifice. One can argue that, as the Nazi onslaught advanced, the Soviet Union became more united than every before. However, what united Soviets behind the war efforts was not class struggle or world revolution but nation, home, and family. The Communist government consciously utilized the prestige of Russian military heroes of the past and the manifold attractions of nationalism. Wartime speeches, journalism, political posters, and literature all emphasized the inhuman brutalities of the enemy and the need to defend the nation (vaguely defined as both Soviet and Russian) and the lives of one's wives and children. The government also took practical measures to strengthen popular support of the war effort, such as making concessions to the practice of religion and giving collective farmers more freedom to market products grown on private plots. And there were implied promises of further changes in political and social relations. The government spoke of a new and better life which would follow the end of the war. The Russians, it has been maintained, proved ready to die for their country, for their families, and for that new life, while they felt only hostility to the Soviet regime.

These and other similar explanations of the Soviet turnabout and of the German defeat appear to contain much truth. Yet, in the last analysis, they might give as one-sided a picture of the Soviet scene as the wholesale admiration of the Communist regime and its virtues popular during and immediately after the war in less critical Western circles. The salient fact remains that in one way or another Stalin and his system prevailed over extreme adversity. Besides, whatever its wartime appeals and promises, the regime did not change at all in essence—as subsequent years were to demonstrate to the again astonished world.

Chapter 39

Stalin's Last Decade, 1945–53

We demand that our comrades, both as leaders in literary affairs and as writers, be guided by the vital force of the Soviet order—its politics. Only thus can our youth be reared, not in a devil-may-care attitude and a spirit of ideological indifference, but in a strong and vigorous revolutionary spirit.

—ZHDANOV

When the immediate passions of the war recede into the background and it becomes possible to view the decade after 1939 in greater perspective, the statesmanship exhibited during World War II by Roosevelt, Churchill, and Stalin will doubtless be more fully understood. What is remarkable is not that the Western democracies and the Soviet Union failed to reach any general agreement as to the postwar organization of Europe, but rather that they were able to maintain their coalition until the end of the war with so few alarms and disagreements. It is now clear that the success of the coalition must be attributed more to the immediacy and gravity of the common danger represented by the military might of Germany and Japan, than to any harmony of opinion among the Allies regarding the political bases of a stable peace. During the long period since the winter of 1917–18, when the Bolsheviks had negotiated a separate peace with the Central Powers, agreement between Russia and the West had been the exception rather than the rule. Close cooperation had been achieved almost as a last resort in the face of an immediate threat to their security, and once the enemy was defeated the differences in political outlook which had been temporarily overlooked inevitably reappeared.

—BLACK AND HELMREICH

T he Second World War brought tremendous human losses and material destruction to the Soviet Union. In addition to the millions of soldiers who died, millions of civilians perished in the shifting battle zone and in German-occupied territory. Of the hundreds of thousands of Soviet citizens who went west, either as Nazi slave labor or of their own will, only a part ever returned to their homeland. The brutality of the invaders defied description. Red Army prisoners starved to death in very large numbers in German camps; whole categories of people, such as Jews, Communists, government officials, and gypsies were exterminated wherever they could be found. Partisan warfare led to horrible reprisals against the population. In contrast to the First World War, most atrocity stories of the Second World War were true. The total number of Soviet military and civilian dead in the dreadful conflict remains quite uncertain. In 1946 the Soviet government set the figure at seven million. A similar total has been reached by a few specialists outside the Soviet Union, such as Mironenko. Most foreign scholars, however, have arrived at much higher figures; for instance, Prokopovich estimates fourteen million and Schuman twenty million. Latest calculations based on some newly available material raised the figure even to twenty-seven million. It is generally believed that the losses were about evenly divided between the military and civilian. To the dead must be added perhaps another twenty million for the children that were not born in the decade of the forties. Population figures announced by the Soviet Union in the spring of 1959 tend to support high rather than low estimates of the Second World War losses. Significantly, the ratio of males to females among the peoples of the USSR in 1959 stood at 45 percent males to 55 percent females.

Material losses were similarly enormous. In addition to the destruction suffered in the fighting, huge areas of the country were devastated—frequently more than once—at the hands of the retreating Red Army or the withdrawing Germans. The Red Army followed the scorched-earth policy, trying to destroy all that could be of military value to the enemy. The Nazis, when they were forced to abandon Soviet territory, attempted to demolish everything, and often did so with remarkable thoroughness. For example, they both flooded and wrecked mines and developed special devices to blow up railroad tracks. Much of the Soviet Union became an utter wasteland. According to official figures—probably somewhat exaggerated as all such Soviet figures tended to be—Soviet material losses in the war included the total or partial destruction of 1,700 towns, 70,000 villages, 6,000,000 buildings, 84,000 schools, 43,000 libraries, 31,000 factories, and 1,300 bridges. Also demolished were 98,000 kolkhozes and 1,876 sovkhozes. The Soviet economy lost 137,000 tractors and 49,000 combine-harvesters, as well as 7,000,000 horses, 17,000,000 head of cattle, 20,000,000 hogs, and 27,000,000 sheep and goats. Soviet authorities estimated the destruction in the USSR at half the total material devastation in Europe during the Second World War. It may have also amounted to two-thirds of the reproducible wealth of occupied Soviet areas and one-quarter of the reproducible wealth of the Soviet Union.

The war affected Soviet Russia in other ways as well. It led to a strong upsurge of patriotism and nationalism, promoted by the Communist government itself which did all it could to mobilize the people for supreme effort and sacrifice. The army acquired new prominence and prestige, whereas from the time of the Civil War it had been kept in the background in the Soviet state. Religion, as already mentioned, profited from a more tolerant attitude on the part of authorities. In addition, a striking religious revival developed in German-occupied territory. While the Soviet government maintained control over the people, in certain respects it relaxed somewhat its iron grip. Many

Soviet citizens apparently felt more free than before the war. In particular, some kolkhozes simply collapsed, the peasants dividing the land and farming it in private. On the whole, because of lessened controls and a great demand for food, many peasants improved their position during the war years. In the German zone of occupation the people immediately disbanded the collectives. The Nazis, however, later in part reintroduced them as useful devices to control peasants and obtain their produce. The war also led to closer and friendlier relations with Western allies and made widespread contacts of the Soviet and the non-Soviet world inevitable. Moreover, millions of Soviet citizens, prisoners of war, deportees, escapees, and victorious Red Army soldiers had their first look at life outside Soviet borders. Other millions, the inhabitants of the Baltic countries, eastern Poland, Bessarabia, and northern Bukovina, brought up under alien systems and in different circumstances, were joined to the Soviet Union.

Another obvious result of the Second World War was the great rise in the Soviet position and importance in the world. The USSR came to dominate eastern Europe, except for Greece, and much of central Europe. Barring the Allied expeditionary forces, it had no military rival on the entire continent. The international Communist movement, which had reached its nadir with the Soviet-German treaty and Hitler's victory in the west, was experiencing a veritable renaissance. After the German attack on the USSR, Communists had played major roles in numerous resistance movements, and they emerged as a great political force in many European countries, including such important Western states as France and Italy. With the total defeat and unconditional surrender of Germany and Japan, the earlier defeat of Italy, and the collapse of France, only exhausted Great Britain and the United States remained as major obstacles to Soviet ambition in the whole wide world.

In a sense, Stalin and the Politburo had their postwar policy cut out for them. They had to rebuild the Soviet Union and to continue the industrial and general economic advance. They had to reimpose a full measure of socialism on the recalcitrant peasant, and to supervise and control closely such non-Marxist sources of inspiration and belief as religion and nationalism. They had to combat the "contamination" that had come to their country from the non-Soviet world, and they had to make all their people, including the inhabitants of the newly acquired territories, into good Soviet citizens. They had to maintain complete control over the army. They had to exploit the new position of the USSR and the new, sweeping opportunities open to the Soviet Union and international communism in the postwar world. Those numerous observers who were surprised by the course of Soviet politics at home and abroad from 1945 until Stalin's death in the spring of 1953 for the most part either had altogether failed to understand the nature of the Soviet system or believed that it had undergone a fundamental change during the Second World War.

Reconstruction and Economic Development

To repair war damage and resume the economic advance, Stalin and the Politburo resorted, characteristically, to a five-year plan, and indeed to a sequence of such plans. The Fourth Five-Year Plan, which lasted from 1946 to 1950 and was proclaimed overfulfilled in four years and three months, was cut out of the same cloth as its predecessors. It stressed heavy industry, which absorbed some 85 percent of the total investment, particularly emphasizing the production of coal, electrical power, iron, steel, timber, cement, agricultural machinery, and trucks. The demobilization of more than ten million men provided the needed additional manpower, for the total number of workers and employees had declined from 31 million in 1940 to 19 million in 1943. The rebuilding of devastated towns and villages, which had begun as soon as the Germans had left, gathered momentum after the inauguration of the Plan. But the Fourth Five-Year Plan aimed at more than restoration: Russian industry, especially heavy industry, was supposed to achieve new heights of production, while labor productivity was to rise 36 percent, based on an increase in the amount of capital per worker of about 50 percent. As usual, every effort was made to force the Soviet people to work hard. A financial reform of December 1947 virtually wiped out wartime savings by requiring Soviet citizens to exchange the money they had for a new currency at the rate of ten to one. Piece work and bonuses received added emphasis. Official retail prices went up, although the concurrent abolition of rationing and of certain other forms of distribution alleviated somewhat the hardships of the consumer. Foreign economists noted a certain improvement in the urban standard of living as well as a redistribution of real income within the urban population, primarily against the poorer groups.

The Fourth Five-Year Plan obtained a great boost from reparations and other payments collected from defeated Germany and its allies. In 1947, for example, three-fourths of Soviet imports came from eastern Europe and the Soviet zone of Germany, that is, from the area dominated by Red military might. The total value of Soviet "political" imports, including reparations, especially favorable trade provisions, and other economic arrangements, as well as resources spent by different countries for the support of Red Army troops stationed in those countries, has been estimated at the extraordinary figure of over twenty billion dollars. Some reparations were made in the form of complete factories that were dismantled, transported to the Soviet Union, and reassembled there.

In the end the Plan could well be considered a success in industry, much like its predecessors, in spite of the frequently inferior quality of products and uneven results, which included large overfulfillments and underfulfillments. While industry was rebuilt and even expanded in Ukraine and other western areas, the Plan marked a further industrial shift east, which grew in relative economic importance compared to the prewar period. By mobilizing resources the Soviet Union managed to maintain during the Fourth and Fifth Five-Year Plans the very high annual industrial growth rate characteristic of the first three plans and estimated by Western economists at some 12 to 14 percent on the average—a figure composed of much higher rates in the late forties and much lower in the early fifties. The Fifth Five-Year Plan lasted from 1951 to 1955 and thus continued beyond Stalin's rule. Similar to all the others in nature and accomplishments, it apparently made great advances in such complex fields as aviation and armament industries and atomic energy. Its completed projects included the Volga-Don canal.

Agriculture, as usual, formed an essential aspect of the plans and, again as usual, proved particularly difficult to manage successfully. The war, to repeat, produced sweeping destruction, a further sharp decline in the already insufficient supply of domestic animals, and at the same time a breakdown of discipline in many kolkhozes, where members proceeded to divide the land and farm it individually or at least to expand their private plots at the expense of the collective. Discipline was soon restored. By September 1, 1947, about fourteen million acres had been taken away from the private holdings of members of collectives as exceeding the permissible norm. Moreover, the Politburo and the government mounted a new offensive aimed at turning the peasants at long last into good socialists. This was to be done by greatly increasing the size of the collectives—thereby decreasing their number—and at the same time increasing the size of working units in a collective, in the interests of further mechanization and division of labor. Nikita Khrushchev, who emerged as one of the leaders in postwar Soviet agriculture, spoke even of grouping peasants in *agrogoroda,* veritable agricultural towns, which would do away once and for all with the diffusion of labor, the isolation, and the backwardness characteristic of the countryside. The agrogoroda proved unrealistic, or at least premature, but authorities did move to consolidate some 250,000 kolkhozes into fewer than 100,000 larger units. In spite of all the efforts—some hostile critics believe largely because of them—peasants failed to satisfy the demands of Soviet leaders, and insufficient agricultural production remained a major weakness of the Soviet economy, as Khrushchev in effect admitted after Stalin's death.

Politics and Administration

The postwar period also brought some political changes. As already mentioned, the Soviet Union acquired five new republics during the time of the Russo-German agreement. They were lost, together with other large territories, when Germany and its allies invaded the USSR and reacquired when the Red Army advanced west. The five Soviet Socialist Republics, the Estonian, Latvian, Lithuanian, Karelo-Finnish, and Moldavian, raised the total number of component units of the USSR to sixteen. In July 1956, however, the Karelo-Finnish SSR was downgraded to its prewar status of an autonomous republic within the RSFSR, reducing the number of union republics to fifteen. The Karelo-Finnish Republic, consisting both of some older Soviet lands and of territory acquired from Finland in 1940 and again in 1944, largely failed as an expression of Finnish culture and nationality; in particular, because the inhabitants had a choice of staying or moving to Finland, virtually no people remained in the area that the Soviet Union annexed from Finland. The downgrading, therefore, seemed logical, although it might have been connected with the desire to Russify that strategic area still more effectively. While the number of union republics increased as a result of the Second World War, the number of autonomous republics was reduced: five of the latter, the Volga-

German Autonomous Republic and four in the Crimea, the northern Caucasus, and adjacent areas were disbanded for sympathizing with or assisting the Germans, their populations being transported to distant regions. In the case of the Volga Germans, the NKVD apparently staged a fake parachute raid, pretending to be a Nazi spearhead in order to uncover the sympathies of the people. Mass deportations also took place in the newly acquired areas that were rapidly and ruthlessly incorporated into the Soviet system. For example, most of the members of the upper and middle classes, including a great many intellectuals, disappeared from the Baltic republics. The concentration-camp empire of Stalin and Beria bulged at the seams.

By contrast, although the Union expanded and rigorous measures were applied to bring all parts of it into conformity with the established order, the Soviet political system itself changed little. Union-wide elections were held in 1946 for the first time since 1937, and again in 1950. The new Supreme Soviets acted, of course, as no more than rubber stamps for Stalin and the government. Republican and other local elections also took place. The minimum age for office holders was raised from eighteen to twenty-three. In 1946 people's commissariats became ministries. More important, their number was reduced in the postwar years and they were more strongly centralized in Moscow. Shortly before his death, Stalin carried out a potentially important change in the top party administration: the Politburo as well as the Organizational Bureau were abolished and replaced by the Presidium to consist of ten Politburo members, the eleventh being dropped, plus another fifteen high Soviet leaders. But Stalin died without calling together the Presidium. After his death its announced membership was reduced to ten, so that as an institution it differed from the Politburo in nothing but name, and even the name was restored after Khrushchev's fall.

The postwar years witnessed also a militant reaffirmation of Communist orthodoxy in ideology and culture. While more will be said about this subject in a later chapter, it might be noted here that scholarship, literature, and the arts all suffered from the imposition of a party strait jacket. Moreover, Andrew Zhdanov, a member of the Politburo and the party boss of Leningrad during the frightful siege, who led the campaign to restore orthodoxy, emerged as Stalin's most prominent lieutenant from 1946 until Zhdanov's sudden death in August 1948. That death—engineered by Stalin in the opinion of some specialists—again left the problem of succession wide open. The aging dictator was surrounded during his last years by a few surviving old leaders, his long-time associates, such as Molotov, Marshal Clement Voroshilov, Lazarus Kaganovich, and Anastasius Mikoyan, as well as by some younger men who had become prominent after the great purge, notably Beria, Khrushchev, and George Malenkov. Malenkov in particular appeared to gain consistently in importance and to loom as Stalin's most likely successor.

Foreign Policy

Stalin's last decade saw extremely important developments in Soviet foreign policy. Crucial events of the postwar years included the expansion of Soviet

ПОД ВОДИТЕЛЬСТВОМ ВЕЛИКОГО СТАЛИНА—ВПЕРЕД К КОММУНИЗМУ!

"Under the Leadership of the Great Stalin—Forward to Communism," 1951. Stalin, the "father of the peoples," stands with representatives of varied Soviet nationalities and before a map showing plans for massive canals and hydroelectric projects. (Victoria Bonnell)

power in eastern Europe, the breakdown of the wartime cooperation between the USSR and its Western allies, and the polarization of the world into the Communist and the anti-Communist blocs, headed by the Soviet Union and the United States respectively. Scholars have much debated the origins of the "cold war." Many have placed the blame chiefly on the Soviet side. That the Soviet Union proved intractable in its dealings with the West, that it did what it could to expand its own bloc, and that it received support from the Communist movement all over the world followed logically from the nature and new opportunities of Soviet communism. A persistent refusal on the part of many circles in the West to face reality testified simply to their wishful thinking or ignorance. Other scholars have pointed to a deep tradition of anticommunism in the West, especially in the United States, and to America's own ambitions for a dominant role in the postwar world. A related argument emphasizes Soviet anxieties about Western, especially American, intentions after the war, specifically fears that the capitalist West (naturally hostile to communism and emerging from the war with America's new atomic power in hand) would take advantage of the Soviet Union's economic debility in the wake of the war. Stalin understood that Russia was not yet ready to survive a major new attack against it. To protect Soviet power against the capitalist West, it is argued, the Soviet Union needed Communist allies on its western borders and to project an image of strength (which required not only showing what the Red Army could do in eastern Europe but also erecting barriers to keep information about real conditions in Russia as hidden as possible). The postwar break between Russia and the West can also be explained by short-term considerations. The

Soviet leaders, too, had prepared little for the postwar period, and in their preparation they had concentrated on such objectives as rendering Germany permanently harmless. The sweeping Soviet expansion in eastern Europe occurred at least in part because of special circumstances: the rapid Western withdrawal of forces and demobilization, the fact that it became apparent that free elections in most eastern European countries would result in anti-Soviet governments, and the pressure of local Communists as well as, possibly, the urging of the more activist group within the Soviet leadership.

The Soviet Union and the Allies cooperated long enough to put into operation their arrangement for dividing and ruling Germany and to bring top Nazi leaders to trial before an international tribunal at Nuremberg in 1946. Also, in February 1947, the victorious powers signed peace treaties with Italy, Romania, Bulgaria, Hungary, and Finland. The Soviet Union confirmed its territorial gains from Romania and Finland, including a lease of the Finnish base of Porkkala, and obtained extensive reparations. Rounding out its acquisitions, the USSR obtained the so-called Carpatho-Ruthenian area from friendly Czechoslovakia in 1945. While most inhabitants of that region spoke Ukrainian, they had not been connected with any Russian state since the days of Kievan Russia.

But on the whole cooperation between the USSR and the Western powers broke down quickly and decisively. No agreement on the international control of atomic energy could be reached, the Soviet Union refusing to participate in the Atomic Energy Commission created by the United Nations in 1946. In the same year a grave crisis developed over the efforts of the Soviet government to obtain significant concessions from Persia, or Iran, and its refusal to follow the example of Great Britain and the United States and withdraw its troops from that country after the end of the war. Although, as a result of Western pressure and the airing of the question in the United Nations, Soviet forces did finally leave Iran, the hostility between former allies became increasingly apparent.

The Communist seizure of power in eastern Europe contributed very heavily to the division of the world into two opposed blocs. While many details of the process varied from country to country, the end result in each case, that is, in Yugoslavia, Albania, Bulgaria, Romania, Hungary, and Poland, was the firm entrenchment of a Communist regime cooperating with and dominated by the Soviet Union. The same happened in eastern Germany. Only Greece and Finland managed to escape the Communist grasp. Liberated Greece fell into the British rather than the Soviet sphere, and its government, supported by Great Britain and the United States, managed to win a bitter civil war from the Communist-led Left. The fact that Finland survived as a free nation remains puzzling. It could be that Moscow first overestimated the strength of Finnish Communists, who did play a prominent part in the government of the country immediately after the war, and then decided not to force the issue in a changing international situation after the Finnish Communists failed to seize power. In particular, the Soviet Union probably wanted to avoid driving Sweden into the camp of Soviet enemies. Similarly—at a greater distance from the USSR—the large and strong Communist and allied parties in France and Italy, very prominent in the first years following the war, were forced out of coalition governments and had to limit themselves to the role of an opposition bent largely on obstruction.

It has frequently been said that communism won in Europe only in countries occupied by the Red Army, and that point deserves to be kept in mind. Yet it does not tell the whole story. Whereas in Poland, for example, native Communists were extremely weak, in Yugoslavia and Albania they had led resistance movements against the Axis powers and had attained dominant positions at the end of the war. Perhaps more important, the Soviet Union preferred to rely in all cases on local party members, while holding the Red Army in readiness as the ultimate argument. Usually, the "reactionary" elements, including monarchs where such were present and the upper classes in general as well as Fascists, would be forced out of political life and a "united front" of "progressive" elements formed to govern the country. Next the Communists destroyed or at least weakened and neutralized their partners in the front to establish in effect, if not always in form, their single-party dictatorship even though the party might be known as the "workers'" or "socialist unity" party rather than simply "Communist." It is worth noting that the eastern European Communists had the most trouble with agrarian parties, just as the Bolsheviks had met their most dangerous rivals in the Socialist Revolutionaries. In Roman Catholic countries, such as Poland and Hungary, they also experienced strong and persistent opposition from the Church. The Communist seizure of power in Czechoslovakia proved particularly disturbing to the non-Communist world, because it occurred as late as 1948 and disposed of a regime headed by President Beneš which had enjoyed popular support and maintained friendly relations with the Soviet Union. The new Communist governments in eastern Europe proclaimed themselves to be "popular democracies." They followed the Soviet lead in introducing economic plans, industrializing, collectivizing agriculture—sometimes gradually, however—and establishing minute regulation of all phases of life, including culture. As in the USSR, the political police played a key role in social transformation and control. An "iron curtain" came to separate the Communist world from the non-Communist.

Churchill, at the time out of office, in a speech in Fulton, Missouri, in March 1946, stressed the danger to the democratic world of the Communist expansion. He was one of the first Western statesmen to point out this danger. When another year of negotiations with the USSR produced no results, President Truman appealed to Congress for funds to provide military and economic aid to the neighbors of the USSR—Greece and Turkey—the independence of which was threatened directly or indirectly by the Communist state; this policy came to be known as the Truman Doctrine. In June 1947 the Marshall Plan was introduced to help rebuild the economies of European countries devastated by war. Because the Soviet Union and its satellites would not participate, the plan became a powerful bond for the Western bloc. Next, in 1949, twelve Western countries, the United States, Great Britain, Canada, France, Belgium, the Netherlands, Luxembourg, Norway, Denmark, Iceland, Italy, and Portugal signed the Atlantic Defense Pact of mutual aid against aggression. A permanent North Atlantic Treaty Organization and armed force were subsequently created, under General Eisenhower's command. Also in 1949, the U.S. Congress passed a broad Mutual Defense Assistance Program to aid American allies all over the world. With these agreements and with numerous bases girding the USSR, the United States and other countries organized to meet the perceived Soviet threat.

The Communist bloc also organized. In 1947 the Communist Information Bureau, known as Cominform, replaced the Communist International which had been disbanded in 1943. Bringing together the Communist parties of the USSR, eastern Europe, France, and Italy, the Cominform aimed at better coordination of Communist efforts in Europe. Zhdanov, who represented the Soviet party, set the unmistakably militant tone of the organization. But Communist cooperation was dealt a major blow by the break between Yugoslavia and the USSR, backed by its satellites, in the summer of 1948. Tito chose to defy Stalin because he wanted to retain full effective control of his own country and resented the role assigned to Yugoslavia in the economic plans and other plans of the Soviet bloc. He succeeded in his bold undertaking because he had a strong organization and support at home in contrast to other eastern European Communist leaders, many of whom were simply Soviet puppets, and because the Soviet Union did not dare invade Yugoslavia, apparently from fear of the probable international complications. Tito's unprecedented defection created the new phenomenon of "national" communism, independent of the Soviet bloc. It led to major purges of potential heretics in other eastern European Communist parties, which took the lives of some of the most important Communists of eastern Europe and resembled in many respects the great Soviet purge of the thirties.

The Western world confronted the Soviet in many places and on many issues. Continuous confrontation in the United Nations resulted in little more than Soviet Russia's constant use of its veto power in the Security Council. Thus, of the eighty vetoes cast there in the decade from 1945 to 1955, seventy-seven belonged to the Soviet Union. The two sides also faced each other in Germany. Because of the new enmity of the wartime allies, the Allied Control Council in Germany failed to function almost from the beginning, and no agreement could be reached concerning the unification of Germany or the peace treaty with that country. Finally, the Federal Republic of Germany with its government in Bonn was established in the Western-occupied zones in May 1949, while the German Democratic Republic was created in the Soviet-held area in October of the same year. The first naturally sided with the West and eventually joined NATO. The second formed an integral part of the Soviet bloc. Cold war in Germany reached its height in the summer of 1948 when Soviet authorities stopped the overland supply of the American, British, and French sectors of Berlin. Since that city, located 110 miles within the Soviet zone, was under the jurisdiction of the four powers, three of them Western, it, or rather West Berlin, remained a highly provocative and disturbing "window of freedom" in rapidly Communized eastern Germany and eastern Europe. But Soviet hopes to force the Western powers to abandon their part of the city failed: a mammoth airlift was maintained for months by American and British planes to keep West Berlin supplied until the Soviet Union discontinued its blockade.

Postwar events in Asia were as important as the developments in Europe. Communists made bids to seize power in such different areas as Indonesia, Malaya, and Burma. They succeeded in China. The great Chinese civil war ended in 1949 with Chiang Kai-shek's evacuation to Formosa—or Taiwan—and the proclamation of the Communist Chinese People's Republic, with Mao Zedong at its head, on the mainland. While the Soviet Union took no direct part in the Chinese war and at first apparently even tried to restrain Mao, it helped Chinese Communists with supplies and backed fully Mao's new regime. And indeed Communist victory in a country of great size inhabited by some half a billion people meant an enormous accretion of strength to the Soviet bloc, although it also created serious problems: China could not be expected to occupy the role of a satellite, such as Bulgaria or Czechoslovakia, and the Communist world acquired in effect a second center of leadership. By an agreement concluded in 1950, the USSR ceded to Communist China its railroad possessions in Manchuria, although briefly retaining a naval base at Port Arthur.

In Korea cold war turned to actual hostilities. There, as in Germany, no agreement could be reached by the victorious powers, and eventually two governments were formed, one in American-occupied southern Korea and the other in the Soviet north, the thirty-eighth parallel dividing the two. At the end of June 1950, North Korea attacked South Korea. In the ensuing years of fighting, which resulted in the two sides occupying approximately the same positions when the military action stopped as they had in the beginning, U.S. forces and some contingents from other countries came to the assistance of South Korea in execution of a mandate of the United Nations, whereas tens and even hundreds of thousands of Chinese "volunteers" intervened on the North Korean side. The Soviet army itself did not participate in the war, although the North Koreans and the Chinese used Soviet-made aircraft and weapons, and although Soviet advisers, as well as Soviet pilots and other technicians, were in North Korea. Although the front became stabilized in the summer of 1951, no armistice could be concluded until the summer of 1953, after Stalin's death.

The End of Stalin

Stalin's final years were also marked by an intensified "cult of personality," as Khrushchev would brand it. Statues and pictures of the "great leader" proliferated, songs and poems were written in his honor, public ceremonies honored him, his every pronouncement was treated as sacred truth, and his eulogists vied with one another to find greater superlatives with which to describe this "greatest genius of humankind" who brought nothing but joy to every decent Soviet person and struck terror in the hearts of all the enemies of socialist happiness. At the same time, Stalin grew increasingly distrustful of all around him. Stalin's final months, especially, had a certain weird quality to them. It could be that the madness that kept peering through the method during his entire rule asserted itself with new vigor. With international tension high, dark clouds gathered at home. In January 1953, nine doctors were accused of having assassinated a number of Soviet leaders, including Zhdanov, and of planning to murder others. Seven of the arrested doctors were Jewish, and anti-Semitism, visibly on the rise in the postwar years (including anti-Jewish purges in some institutions), especially after the establishment of the State of Israel in 1948, was clearly evident in reporting about the "doctor's plot." But Jews were only one of the targets. Beria's police were charged with insufficient vigilance. The press whipped up a campaign against traitors. Everything pointed to another great purge. Then on March 4 it was announced that Stalin had suffered a stroke on the first of the month, and on the morning of the sixth the news came that he had died the previous night. Some of the dictator's entourage especially close to him disappeared at the same time.

Chapter 40

The Soviet Union after Stalin, 1953–85

One of the fundamental principles of party leadership is collectivity in deciding all important problems of party work. It is impossible to provide genuine leadership if inner party democracy is violated in the party organization, if genuine collective leadership and widely developed criticism and self-criticism are lacking. Collectiveness and the collegium principle represent a very great force in party leadership. . . .

—SLEPOV

As long as we confine ourselves, in substance, to denouncing the personal faults of Stalin as the cause of everything we remain within the realm of the "personality cult." First, all that was good was attributed to the superhuman, positive qualities of one man: now all that is evil is attributed to his equally exceptional and even astonishing faults. In the one case, as well as in the other, we are outside the criterion of judgment intrinsic in Marxism. The true problems are evaded, which are why and how Soviet society could reach and did reach certain forms alien to the democratic way and to the legality which it had set for itself, even to the point of degeneration. . . .

—TOGLIATTI

It is difficult to exaggerate the historical significance of the Sino-Soviet conflict. It has influenced every facet of international life, not to speak of the Soviet block itself. No analysis of the relationship between Washington and Moscow, of the problem of nuclear proliferation, or the orientation of Indian nationalism, of the thrust of revolutionary movements in the Third World would be complete without taking into account the impact of the increasingly bitter dispute between the two onetime seemingly close allies. For the international Communist movement, it has been a tragic disaster, comparable in some respects to the split in Christianity several centuries ago. The Communist and Christian experience both showed that in theologically or ideologically oriented movements disagreements even only about means and immediate tactical concerns can escalate into basic organizational and doctrinal, indeed, even into national conflicts, fundamentally destructive of the movement's unity.

—BRZEZINSKI

Stalin's stroke—if its official date is to be believed—was followed by three days of silence from the Kremlin and, in all probability, by hard bargaining among top Soviet leaders. When the dictator's demise was announced, the new leadership proclaimed itself ready to govern the country, emphasizing the solidarity of its members as well as its unity with the people. The shrill tone and the constant repetition of both assertions must have covered many suspicions and fears. Malenkov emerged clearly in the chief role, for he became presumably both the senior party secretary, which had been Stalin's most important office, and prime minister. Beria and Molotov stood next to Malenkov, forming a triumvirate of successors to the dictator. The three, in that order, were the key living figures during the burial of Stalin in the Lenin Mausoleum in Red Square on the ninth of March, making appropriate speeches on the occasion.

The Rise, Rule, and Fall of Nikita Khrushchev

As early as the middle of March, however, it was announced that Malenkov had resigned as the party secretary, although he remained prime minister and continued to be treated as the top personage in the Soviet Union. The new Presidium of the party was reduced to ten members. Later it was announced that Khrushchev had been promoted to the position of first party secretary, the title used instead of that of general secretary associated with Stalin. In the summer of 1953, Beria was arrested and then executed in secret, with a number of his followers, on charges of treason and conspiracy; or, as Khrushchev related to

Stalin's funeral. From right: Khrushchev, Beria, Chou En-Lai, Malenkov, Voroshilov, Kaganovich, Bulganin, Molotov. (Sovfoto)

some visitors, Beria was killed at the Presidium meeting at which he had expected to assume full power. In any case, it would seem that in the race to dispose of one another Beria had narrowly lost out. Beria's fall marked a certain weakening in the power of the political police. In February 1955, Malenkov resigned as prime minister, saying that he was guilty of mistakes made in the management of Soviet agriculture and of having incorrectly emphasized the production of consumer goods at the expense of heavy industry. Nicholas Bulganin, a prominent Communist leader who had been a member of the Politburo since 1948, replaced Malenkov as head of the government. Bulganin and Khrushchev, the chief of the government and the chief of the party, then occupied the center of the Soviet stage and also held the limelight in international affairs, suggesting to some observers the existence of something resembling a diarchy in the USSR. Marshal Zhukov, a great hero of the Second World War who had been reduced by Stalin to provincial commands and had returned to prominence after Stalin's death, took over Bulganin's former office of minister of defense. Zhukov's rise marked the first appearance of an essentially military, rather than party, figure in high governing circles in Soviet Russia.

The struggle in the Kremlin continued. Probably its most astounding event was Khrushchev's speech to a closed session of the Twentieth Party Congress in February 1956, in which the new first secretary denounced his predecessor, Stalin, as a cruel, irrational, and bloodthirsty tyrant, who had destroyed many innocent with the guilty in his great purge of the party and the army in the thirties and at other times. In fact, Stalin and the "cult of personality" he had fostered were blamed also for military unpreparedness and defeats in the Second World War as well as for other Soviet mistakes and weaknesses. At the same time, paradoxically, Khrushchev presented Stalin's colossal aberrations as mere deviations of an essentially correct policy, entirely rectified by the collective leadership that replaced the despot. Khrushchev's explosive speech remains difficult to explain: after all, it was certain to produce an enormous shock among Communists and do great damage to the Communist cause—to say the least, the transition from years of endless adulation of Stalin to Khrushchev's revelations was bound to be breathtaking; besides, Khrushchev could not help but implicate himself and his associates, at least indirectly, in Stalin's crimes and errors. The answer to the riddle of the speech lies probably in the exigencies of the struggle for power among Soviet leaders. Khrushchev's sensational denunciation of Stalin struck apparently at some "old Stalinists," his main competitors. Besides, it would seem that Khrushchev tried both to put the blame for many of the worst aspects of the Soviet past on Stalin, implying that these evils could not happen again, and to set the correct line of policy for the future.

The conflict at the top reached its culmination in the spring and early summer of 1957, after the Hungarian rebellion of the preceding autumn and certain other events at home and abroad had raised grave questions concerning the orientation and activities of the new Soviet administration and indeed concerning the stability of the whole Soviet system. Defeated in the Presidium of the party, Khrushchev took his case to its entire Central Committee, successfully reversing the unfavorable decision and obtaining the ouster from the Presidium and other positions of power of the "anti-party group" of Malenkov, Molotov, Kaganovich, and Dmitrii Shepilov, a recent addition to the Soviet front ranks. While Khrushchev's enemies were dropped from the Presidium, its membership was increased to fifteen, giving the general secretary further opportunities to bring his supporters into that extremely important body. Marshal Zhukov, who, it would seem, had provided valuable assistance to Khrushchev in the latter's bid for power, again fell into disgrace several months later. Finally in March 1958, Bulganin, who had been disloyal to Khrushchev the preceding year, resigned as head of the government. Khrushchev himself replaced Bulganin, thus combining the supreme effective authority of the party and of the state. Clearly that self-made man of peasant background and limited education no longer had any equals within the collective leadership or elsewhere in the USSR.

The remarkable Twenty-second Party Congress held in the second half of October 1961 confirmed on the whole Khrushchev's dominant position. As expected, it gave ready approval to the new leader's twenty-year program of "building communism" and denounced his enemies at home and abroad. Another old leader, Voroshilov, was linked to the "anti-party group." In a much more unexpected development, however, Khrushchev and the Congress returned to the grizzly issue of Stalinism, detailing and documenting many of its atrocities. The removal of Stalin's body from the mausoleum in Red Square, the renaming of the cities named after Stalin, with Stalingrad becoming Volgograd, and the publicity given for the first time to certain aspects of the great purge must have had a powerful impact on many Soviet minds.

Yet, although Khrushchev managed to assert his will at the Twenty-second Party Congress and even evict Stalin from the mausoleum, it can be seen in retrospect that by 1961 his fortunes were on the decline. In fact, 1958 probably marked Khrushchev's zenith. The year followed the new leader's decisive victory over the "anti-Party group," and the sensational Soviet inauguration of the space age the preceding autumn. It was blessed with a bounteous harvest. In spite of serious problems, industrial production continued to grow at a high rate. The ebullient Khrushchev could readily believe that all roads led to a communism that was bound to bury capitalism in the not-too-distant future.

Disillusionments followed in rapid succession. Economic development went sour; Khrushchev's exhortations, and his economic, administrative, and party reorganizations, together with his hectic campaigns to remedy particular deficiencies—all to be discussed later in this chapter—were increasingly ineffective in resolving the crisis. In his last years and months in office Khrushchev saw the rate of industrial growth decline sharply while he had to resort to an unprecedented purchase of Canadian wheat to forestall hunger at home. De-Stalinization or, more broadly, a certain "liberalization" of Soviet life seemed to produce as many problems as it resolved. It led in effect to soul-searching and instability rather than to any outburst of creative communist energy. The world situation—also to be discussed later—deteriorated even more sharply from the Soviet point of view. In 1960 the conflict with China,

Nikita Khrushchev. (Sovfoto)

which dated back at least to Khrushchev's original de-Stalinization of 1956, burst into the open, and from about 1963 the break between the former allies seemed irreparable. In the relations with the West, Khrushchev's aggressive enthusiasm, spurred by the successes of Soviet space technology, received repeated checks in Germany and finally suffered a smashing defeat in October 1962 in the crucial confrontation with the United States over the Soviet missiles in Cuba. Khrushchev's survival of the catastrophe of his apparently largely personal foreign policy might be considered a tribute to Soviet totalitarianism. Yet totalitarianism too was deteriorating in the Soviet Union. Observers noted that although the Twenty-second Party Congress confirmed and extended Khrushchev's victory over the "anti-party group" these enemies of the leader were not even expelled from the party. New fissures and problems appeared in the ensuing months and years. It would seem that during this time Khrushchev made the mistake of acting in an increasingly autocratic and arbitrary manner even though his power was not nearly as great as Stalin's had been.

On October 15, 1964, it was announced in Moscow that Nikita Sergeevich Khrushchev had been "released" from both his party and his government positions, because of "advanced age and deterioration of his health."

Brezhnev and Kosygin

The ten years or so of Khrushchev's rule of the Soviet Union have often been described as a transitional period, but they also marked a culmination. When Khrushchev assumed power in the Kremlin he became both the head of the USSR and the leader of an essentially united, ever-victorious, and ever-expanding world communism. He could still believe in the identity of interests of the state and the movement. Indeed he delighted in counting the years, twenty or fifteen, at the end of which the Soviet Union would enter full communism, and additional years, perhaps to the time of "our grandchildren," which would establish communism all over the globe. Khrushchev's own rags-to-riches story was about to be repeated on a universal scale. By the time the enthusiastic leader "retired," communism was hopelessly split between the antagonistic centers of Moscow and Peking, while the Cuban confrontation and defeat spelled out to the Soviet leaders in an unforgettable manner the realities of the atomic age, of which Marx and Engels and even Lenin had had no inkling. At home de-Stalinization kept releasing new furies, and the economic situation called for emergency measures to improve productivity, distribution, and services rather than for blueprints of a communist utopia. All these, and many other problems, fell upon the shoulders of Khrushchev's successors, and in particular on Leonid Brezhnev, who obtained the top position in the party, and Alexis Kosygin, who as prime minister became the effective head of the government.

The new leaders had the usual record of party and government service, and their views could not be easily distinguished from those of Khrushchev. In fact, Khrushchev apparently had thought of Brezhnev as his eventual successor. The Chinese and certain others who expected Soviet policy to be transformed by the fall of Khrushchev were quickly disappointed. Instead of challenging Khrushchev on fundamentals, the new leadership assailed his personal performance and style of work, accusing him of "subjectivism," authoritarianism, ignorance, "hare-brained schemes," and "mad improvisations." Khrushchev's sweeping reorganizational reforms were repealed, some promptly and some after a period of time. It was a certain businesslike, low-key quality of the new administration that presented a striking contrast to the flamboyancy and bombast of the deposed leader. The overturn of October 1964 could also be considered a reassertion of collective leadership, eliminating as it did the latest cult of personality.

Although the fall of Khrushchev strengthened the forces opposed to de-Stalinization, they proved unable to gain the upper hand. Instead the leadership resorted to compromise which found its characteristic expression in the mammoth Twenty-third Party Congress held in the spring of 1966. There were 4,942 delegates and additional representatives of 86 foreign communist parties and sympathizing organizations—the number announced was 86, but there were actually somewhat fewer. The Congress avoided mention of such crucial issues as China, Stalin, or, for that matter, Khrushchev. With the Vietnam war in full swing, it adopted doctrinaire, anti-imperialistic planks in foreign policy and expounded a hard line in matters of ideology and culture. On the other hand, it upheld a certain economic "liberalization" and took a more realistic view of the economic and social development and potentialities of the Soviet Union than had been customary under Khrushchev. In the words of critical commentators, the Soviet authorities opted for economic development without its consequences. It was by the decision of the Twenty-third Congress that the Presidium became again, as in the days of Stalin, the Politburo, and the first secretary of the party became again the general secretary.

Brezhnev was also the central figure and delivered the main address at the Twenty-fourth Party Congress in March and April 1971, the Twenty-fifth Party Congress in late February 1976, and the Twenty-sixth Party Congress in February and March 1981. His authority grew with the years, and one could speak even of a cult of Brezhnev, especially after the general secretary of the party also became, in 1976, a Marshal of the Soviet Union and his autobiographical writings were given tremendous prominence. Yet he continued, apparently, to work closely with other leaders of the Politburo; besides, Brezhnev, born in 1906, was becoming increasingly an old and sick man. His name and efforts came to be associated with the policy of détente, which the Soviet propaganda machine preferred to call "irreversible," with the great strengthening of the Soviet military might vis-à-vis the United States, and also with economic policies emphasizing such crucial sectors as agriculture and energy.

At the heart of domestic politics during the Brezhnev years, and key to the regime's stability, it has been argued, was a generous policy of catering to the

Soviet leaders at Kremlin Meeting of the Supreme Soviet Celebrating the Fiftieth Anniversary of the Bolshevik Revolution, November 4, 1967. From left: Brezhnev, Kosygin, Podgorny, Suslov. (World Wide Photos)

interests of elites combined with a growing welfare state for the population at large. In 1965, the Brezhnev leadership took as its motto the phrase "trust in cadres." In practice, this meant, for example, that greater job security than ever before was assured—no longer would they be threatened by either Stalin's purges or Khrushchev's attacks on "bureaucracy." The most visible sign of this policy was the dramatic aging of the leadership. Material interests were also taken into account. Institutional interests were respected by providing their departments with good budgets. Most important, personal interests and desires were catered to with extensive privileges in such areas as consumer goods, housing, medical care, and travel abroad. The effect, scholars have argued, was to create a loyal managerial class, one of the keys to the stability of the system. At the same time, the Soviet welfare state grew, partly as a means to ensure popular toleration of this increasingly hierarchical society. Individuals were offered opportunities for upward mobility—even the opportunity to join the privileged elite—through hard work and political loyalty. But efforts were also made to ensure broader benefits. Political scientists have spoken of an implicit "social contract" between the government and the population. Repression remained (for publicly criticizing policies, for spending unauthorized time with foreigners, for damaging or stealing socialist property, for illegal buying and selling) but it was not random or inexplicable. Most important, material promises were made and partly fulfilled: free medical care to all citizens (though quality was often low), the complete lack of unemployment, guaranteed pensions at retirement, more housing so that families could live in their own apartments, subsidized prices for essential food products, and a growing consumer economy. Indeed, living standards measurably rose, and some commentators began to write of a Soviet version of consumer attitudes and a consumer society. This is not to say that Soviet citizens did not notice or resent the growing privileges of the elite. Anecdotes, a widespread form of subtle everyday critique of the systems, often spoke of this inequality. In one, Brezhnev's uneducated mother, at the sight of her son's splendid collection of motor cars, voiced concern: "That is fine, my dear son, but what if the Bolsheviks return?" As the Soviet economic situation became more difficult in the late 1970s and early 1980s, this system of rewards and welfare became more difficult to sustain. Yet, the Brezhnev government attempted essentially palliatives rather than fundamental reform: "the decision has been made 'to settle for short-run solutions to long-term problems.'" Certain observers concluded that, although Brezhnev did not have complete control of the Soviet Union, he had full veto power of any reforms and that, therefore, no real change could be expected as long as he remained at the helm.

When Brezhnev died, finally, on November 10, 1982, at the age of seventy-five, he had outlived such near-peers as Kosygin, by about two years, and the chief party ideologist, Michael Suslov, by less than a year; Nicholas Podgorny had been ousted from the leadership in 1977; Brezhnev's long-time lieutenant, Andrew Kirilenko, slightly older than his patron, lost his Politburo position in 1982, whether for political or medical reasons. Yet the remaining leaders still belonged to the same well-established group and were of comparable age and, as far as one could tell, orientation. Nicholas Tikhonov, who replaced Kosygin

Brezhnev on a skimobile, probably near his country house. Among the many material benefits of power he enjoyed, Brezhnev had a particular fondness for motor vehicles of all sorts. In particular, he had a large collection of luxury and imported cars. (V. Musaelyan)

as prime minister, was born, like Brezhnev, in 1906; Constantine Chernenko, probably closest to Brezhnev at the time of the latter's death, was only five years younger; Dmitrii Ustinov, the man in charge of what may be described as the Soviet military-industrial complex, was born in 1908. That the General Secretaryship of the party went to Iurii Vladimirovich Andropov, sixty-eight, was not unexpected, although some observers were surprised by the rapidity and smoothness of the transition. Credited with uncommon intelligence and general ability, as well as a certain sophistication, Andropov became well-known as the head of the KGB, the political police, for the fifteen years before he switched in May 1982 to work in the party secretariat. He had also been a prominent Politburo member from 1973. Andropov's earlier service included the position of ambassador to Hungary in 1954–57, when he became linked, apparently, both to the brutal suppression of the Hungarian revolt and to the institution of a liberal economic policy in Hungary in its wake. A sharp critic of the stagnation and corruption under Brezhnev and, apparently, a determined reformer of sorts, Andropov addressed himself immediately to purging the administrative apparatus and to strengthening labor discipline by such spectacular measures as police searches in public places for absentee workers. But his activity was cut short by kidney failure, and he died after only about a year and three months in office. Andropov was replaced by Chernenko, Brezhnev's intended heir and already a sick man, who lived for barely another year. Then, on March 11, 1985, Mikhail Sergeevich Gorbachev, Andropov's fifty-four-year-old protégé, was elected by the Politburo to the general secretaryship of the party.

Economic Development

When Stalin died, the Fifth Five-Year Plan was in full swing. It was duly completed in 1955, yielding the usual result of accomplishment in industry—checkered, to be sure, with huge overfulfillments and underfulfillments—based on great exertion and privation. The Sixth Five-Year Plan, scheduled to run from 1956 to 1960, promptly succeeded the fifth. Its period was truncated in 1958, however, and a Seven-Year Plan to last from 1959 through 1965 was proclaimed instead. The official explanation for the change, which stressed the discovery of vast new natural resources that altered Soviet economic prospects, was not convincing. Apparently, the Sixth Five-Year Plan had fallen considerably behind its assigned norms of production and the Soviet leadership decided to try a fresh start.

Another change in Soviet economic life occurred in 1957, when Khrushchev, in a move aimed at a geographic dispersion, or deconcentration—although not organizational decentralization—of authority, transferred the direction of a good proportion of industry from the ministries in Moscow to regional Economic Councils. Reflecting the constant Soviet search for the most effective and efficient economic organization, this reform was nevertheless considered by many observers as primarily political in motivation: it removed from Moscow large economic managerial staffs which, it would seem, had supported Malenkov in the struggle for power within the Kremlin. Another aim might have been to give the local party bosses more authority in economic matters.

The industrial goals of the Seven-Year Plan were pronounced reallistic by such Western economists as Campbell and Jasny. While concentrating as usual on heavy industry, with special attention paid to, for example, further electrification and development of the chemical industry, the plan called for a rate of industrial growth approximately 20 percent slower than that achieved during the Fifth Five-Year Plan. In this sense it was also less ambitious than the abortive Sixth Five-Year Plan. In evaluating the Seven-Year Plan, Campbell made the following comparison between the Soviet and the U.S. economies:

> If it is assumed that industry in the United States will continue to expand at the rate of about 4 percent that has characterized the postwar period, and that the rate of growth planned by the Russians for their industry is actually achieved, their industrial output will rise from about 45 percent of ours at the beginning of the seven-year period to about 61 percent at the end. In other words they will still be a long way behind us (and even further behind in terms of *per capita* output, it may be added), though they will certainly have made a remarkable gain on us.

In fact, Campbell's prediction proved to be generally intelligent, although impossible to evaluate definitively with any degree of precision—incidentally, such comparisons give vastly different results depending on whether they are made in rubles or in dollars. After Khrushchev too, it might be added, the Soviet economy continued to gain in relative output on the American economy, helped by such developments as the recession in the United States and the Western world in general in the 1970s and 1980s.

Although concentrating on capital goods, the Seven-Year Plan allowed somewhat more for the everyday needs of the people than had generally been true of previous Soviet industrialization. Especially interesting was the ambitious housing and general building program of the plan, which aimed to increase the total Soviet building investment by 83 percent. Even when executed not in its entirety and with buildings of inferior quality, this aspect of the Seven-Year Plan constituted a major contribution to the improvement of the Soviet standard of living. Superior quality and unflagging attention were devoted, by contrast, to such advanced technical fields as atomic energy, rockets, missiles, and space travel. From the launching of the first artificial earth satellite, Sputnik I, in October 1957, the USSR achieved a remarkable series of pioneer successes in rockets and space travel.

Important developments took place in Soviet agriculture during the Khrushchev years. Indeed, frantic efforts to raise agricultural production constituted, together with certain concessions to the consumer, the salient new features of Soviet economic policy. The magnitude of the Soviet farm problem can be seen from the fact that, by contrast with industrial achievements, the gross output of agriculture in 1952 was only some 6 percent above 1928. In 1954 Khrushchev set into full operation his sweeping "virgin lands" project: huge areas of arid lands in Asian Russia, eventually totaling some seventy million acres, were to be brought under cultivation. The undertaking, supported by great exertion as well as by a mighty propaganda effort, gave remarkably mixed results from year to year, depending in large part on weather conditions, but did not live up to expectations. The new first secretary also started a huge corn-planting program. He further decided to boost drastically the production of such foods as meat, milk, and butter. These items came to rival electric power and steel in Soviet propaganda and to serve as significant gauges in "surpassing America."

Yet the condition of Soviet agriculture remained bad. Official claims and promises, especially the latter, differed sharply from reality. Indeed, the mass planting of corn, often in unsuitable conditions, and even the huge gamble on the virgin lands, which are difficult to cultivate, might have been unwise. To increase production Soviet authorities resorted to the old method of further socialization. Between 1953 and 1957 the number of sovkhozes increased from 4,857 to 6,000, while the number of kolkhozes declined at the same time from 91,000 to 78,900, reducing the kolkhoz share of land under cultivation from 84 to 72 percent. By 1961 the number of collective farms had fallen to 44,000—and by the end of the decade they were to be reduced further, through amalgamation, and absorptions by the sovkhozes, to under 35,000; by 1974, there was in the Soviet Union slightly more land under sovkhoz than under kolkhoz cultivation, with only some 30,000 collective farms still in operation. As late as September 1958, Khrushchev, other leaders, and the propaganda machine still spoke of the more truly socialist nature, as well as of the technical superiority, of the sovkhoz system of agriculture over that of the kolkhoz. Yet, apparently because of the strength of peasant resistance, especially of the passive kind, the first secretary stopped the attack on kolkhozes in early 1959 at the Twenty-first Party Congress.

The official policy toward the collective farms continued to be ambivalent. There is a consensus among experts that the income of the members of the kolkhozes, extremely low at the time of Stalin's death, increased markedly in subsequent years. The set prices paid by the state for compulsory deliveries of collective farm produce were raised to more realistic levels in 1956 and immediately afterward, enlarging the income of individual kolkhoz members by as much as 75 percent, according to Marchenko's calculations. The collectives themselves also gained in strength. In 1958, in an abrupt reversal of previous policy, the government enacted measures to disband the Machine Tractor Stations, enabling the kolkhozes to obtain in ownership all the agricultural equipment which they needed. And, as already mentioned, early in 1959 attacks on the collectives ceased and they were again recognized as the proper form of agricultural organization at the given stage of development of the Soviet economy and society.

But, on the other hand, state and party pressure on the kolkhozes continued and in certain respects even gained momentum. The years witnessed a great stress on increasing the "indivisible fund" of a collective—that is, that part of its revenue which belongs to the entire kolkhoz and is not parceled out among individual members—and on using this fund for such "socially valuable" undertakings as building schools and roads in the locality. The purchase of MTS machinery by the collectives in itself necessitated heavy expenditure. Also, Khrushchev and other leaders returned to the theme that the private plots of the members of a kolkhoz are meant merely to augment a family's food supply rather than to produce for the market and that they should become entirely unnecessary with further successes of socialist agriculture.

Moreover, the Seven-Year Plan goals of increasing agricultural production by 70 percent and raising labor productivity in the kolkhozes by 100 percent and in the sovkhozes by 60 to 65 percent proved to be impossible to attain. Perhaps they had been predicated on a further drastic socialization of Soviet agriculture, and in particular the elimination or near elimination of the twenty million small private plots of the members of the collectives, which the leadership did not dare carry out.

Again, in the opinion of Bergson and other Western observers, the agricultural goals adopted by the Twenty-second Party Congress as part of the program of creating a "material basis" for communism by 1980 seemed fantastically optimistic and quite unreal—an estimate that did not apply to nearly the same extent to the industrial goals. Khrushchev's frantic efforts after the Congress to bolster farm production—this time demanding the abolition of the grass rotation system in favor of planting feed crops such as sugar beets, corn, peas, and beans—served to emphasize further the crisis of Soviet agriculture. It is also probably in connection with the economic, especially the agricultural, crisis that Khrushchev enacted, in 1962, his strangest reorganizational measure: the across-the-board division of the hitherto monolithic Communist Party into two party hierarchies, one to deal with industry and the other with agriculture.

Khrushchev's enthusiasm and ambition in the economic and other fields found characteristic expression in his insistence on the early building of communism, which was to replace socialism as the culminating phase in the evolution of Soviet society. The Twenty-second Party Congress, in October 1961, paid much attention to this issue, proclaiming that the preconditions for communism should be established in the USSR by 1980. Although the concept of communism remained fundamentally vague and lacked substantiating detail, Feldmesser and other Western scholars have been able to draw a generally convincing picture of the projected Soviet utopia.

Communism would be based on an economy of abundance which would satisfy all the needs of the population. These needs, however, were to be defined by the authorities. In the words of Khrushchev, "Of course, when we speak of satisfying people's needs, we have in mind not whims or claims to luxuries, but the healthy needs of a culturally developed person." Presumably, the authorities could also determine that some people had more needs than others. Nevertheless, the main thrust of communism would be toward equality. Income differentials would be drastically reduced. More than that, communism would finally eliminate the distinction between town and country, industrial and agricultural work, mental and manual labor, and thus the differences in the styles of life. Members of the new society would be "broad-profile workers," that is, persons trained in two or three related skills who would, in addition, engage without pay in one or more other socially useful occupations in their leisure hours.

The collective would obviously dominate. Even some of the abundant consumer goods would be available in the form of "appliance pools" of refrigerators, washing machines, or vacuum cleaners. Apparently, Khrushchev objected to the last to private automobile ownership and projected instead public car pools. On a still broader scale, life would become increasingly socialized. Free public health services and transportation would be followed, for example, by free public meals which would virtually eliminate kitchen drudgery for women. The Academician Stanislav Strumilin and others constructed models of communal cities of the future, with parents allowed a daily visit to their children, who would live separately under the care of a professional staff. Indeed communism would seem to imply a great diminution in the role of the family, if not its abolition. By contrast, the role of the school would expand, and so would the roles of labor brigades, comrades' courts, and other public organizations. Lenin's, or Khrushchev's, authoritarian Marxist system would in no sense be diluted, or even diversified, in communism, but only strengthened and more effectively "socialized," so to speak, and internalized. In the end, only mentally deranged persons would seriously object to it.

According to a bitter Chinese remark, largely applicable in the economic as in other fields, the fall of Khrushchev resulted simply in Khrushchevism without Khrushchev. Yet, as already indicated, it brought at least a striking change in the manner of execution and in tone, if not in fundamental policy. The new leaders abolished Khrushchev's reorganizational reforms, such as the division of the party in two and the creation of the sovnarkhozy, and discontinued some of his pet projects. They stopped the discussion of the imminent building of communism and the propaganda concerning the early surpassing of the United States in the production of consumer goods. Instead they revealed grave economic shortcomings and failures of the past administration and took a more realistic view of the potentialities of the Soviet economy.

It was in the middle and late 1960s especially that fundamental measures were enacted to bolster Soviet agriculture. Collective farmers finally received a guaranteed wage, which made their position comparable to that of the sovkhoz workers, whereas earlier they had the last claim in the distribution of gain, frequently rendering their very existence marginal, a point emphasized by Lewin and other scholars. Also, pensions and social services were extended to the kolkhoz members. Over a period of years the state greatly increased the amount of resources devoted to agriculture so that investment in agriculture came to constitute over a third in the allocation of the total national investment. Another 4½ percent of the national income was assigned to subsidize retail food prices to consumers, to keep these prices down in spite of heavy production costs. Still other large sums went into agricultural research. If one adds to these huge expenses some five billion dollars spent by the Soviet Union in 1975–76 alone to buy grain abroad, more money to buy meat and butter, as well as similar huge purchases later, one can get an idea of the enormous effort mounted by the Soviet leadership to develop the agricultural sector and to supply the Soviet public with increasing amounts of food at more or less stable prices. Indeed it has been said that instead of being the most depressed social group in their country the Soviet peasants became the most pampered. But that only made the generally miserable condition of Soviet agriculture all the more striking.

The new Five-Year Plan, 1966–70—eventually designated as the Eighth—presented by Kosygin to the Twenty-third Party Congress in the spring of 1966, reset a number of Khrushchev's economic goals from 1965 to 1970. The economy was to strive for a 49–52 percent increase in the output of heavy industry and a 43–46 percent increase in consumer goods, with the annual growth rate of 8.5 percent and 7.7 percent respectively—a very high figure for consumer goods in relation to heavy industry, although in line with Khrushchev's thought on the matter on the eve of his fall. Subsequently the Soviet government signed contracts with Italian and French companies to help develop the automobile industry in the Soviet Union.

The Eighth Five-Year Plan was followed by the Ninth, 1971–75, then the Tenth was promoted as the "Five-Year Plan of Quality," the "Basic Directions" for which came out in mid-December 1975, some two months before the Twenty-fifth Party Congress. Yet rather than recapturing the earlier drive the new Plans seemed to testify to a slowdown of the Soviet economy, accentuated by the disastrous crop failures of 1972 and especially of 1975, which necessitated massive purchase of grain abroad—supplied, particularly by the United States in 1972, on terms remarkably advantageous, to be sure, to the Soviet Union. To quote an expert evaluation of the economic position of the USSR at the time of the Twenty-fifth Party Congress:

> Soviet economic growth slowed down significantly during the Ninth FYP period (1971–75), and the Plan's ambitious targets were generally—sometimes widely—missed, affected as the USSR has been by declining reserves of labor and other

retardational forces and under the blows of two major crop failures. Particularly hard hit was agricultural production, and consumer goods output and consumption levels rose much less than planned. Civilian equipment production and capital formation also fell short of expectations. Nonetheless, Soviet heavy industries expanded at high rates, and (presumably) military production did well too. The recession in the West made Soviet industrial performance look particularly good.

The just-announced Tenth FYP (1976–80) provides for further retardation in growth throughout the economy. The advance in consumption levels is expected to slow down even further, as are fixed investment and capital formation. Labor productivity will also rise more slowly. Despite the relative moderation of the Plan's goals, they may still turn out to be rather ambitious in relation to resources. No liberalizing reforms seem to be in the wings; rather, there is strong emphasis on centralism in planning and management, with considerable hope placed on mergers of enterprises into rather large units and on computerization. Yet withal the industrial basis of Soviet power—including military might—will certainly continue to grow at a pace that would be creditable for any advanced industrial power.

Since the fall of Khrushchev and in general since the death of Stalin, the standard of living of the urban, and especially of the poverty-stricken rural, population apparently continued to improve. During the 1960s and 1970s, wages and salaries steadily increased (and there was little inflation), food supplies improved, the amount and variety of consumer goods grew, and new housing continued to be built. Additional needs could often be satisfied in the growing "second economy" (the "black market" or "unofficial economy"), where one could purchase foreign products, illegally (i.e., privately) manufactured goods, scarce Soviet goods purchased legally and then resold, goods obtained illegally (for example, by truck drivers or by store managers), and services. As the economy began to falter in the 1970s and early 1980s, however, these improvements slowed. At the same time, the Soviet Union was bearing very heavy military expenditures, exemplified by the deployment of antimissile ballistic systems and by the tremendous growth of the Soviet navy. Economic activities in the USSR spread out, and the economic map of the country underwent constant change. Illustrations of this change include the rise of Novosibirsk as a great scientific and technological center in Siberia, the Bratsk Dam, the Baikal-Amur mainline railway, the new problem of the industrial pollution of Lake Baikal, and the shift in the center of oil production since the Second World War from its long-time location in the Caucasus to new fields between the Volga and the Urals, and also to oil and natural gas fields beyond the Urals.

The new leadership also resorted to economic reform, described generally as an economic "liberalization" and associated with the name of a Kharkov economist, Evsei Liberman. Faced with an economic slow-down, characterized by a drop in the growth rate of the gross national product and by a marked decline in the return from investment and in the growth of productivity of labor as well as by a great loss accruing from an underutilization of capital and labor resources, the government decided to shift the emphasis and the incentives from the sheer volume of production, where they had been from the inauguration of the First Five-Year Plan, to sales and profits. Under the new system managerial bonuses were to depend not on the output as such, but on sales and profits, the latter factor finally giving serious recognition to the element of cost in Soviet production. In January 1966 forty-three enterprises from seventeen industries, with a total of 300,000 workers, were switched to the new system. Others followed in subsequent months and years. Some economic reform was realized in industry, transportation, and retail trade, and it spread to the sovkhozes and to the construction sector. Yet, ambivalent and probably insufficient to begin with, it was emasculated in the process of implementation, with the result that there proved to be very little difference between the new system and the old system before 1965. More prominent was the new emphasis on material incentives, provisions of more and more differentiated rewards. However, although widely applied, these incentives did not lead to an important improvement in performance.

Indeed, the Tenth Five-Year Plan, 1976–80, and the Eleventh which succeeded it, although on the whole less ambitious than their predecessors, witnessed repeated inability of the Soviet economy to meet set goals, a decline in the increase of labor productivity, and other signs of stagnation. Some specialists considered 1979, the first of the unprecedented four successive years of bad grain harvests, a disastrous turning point. Then and in the years immediately following, seemingly everything, from transportation bottlenecks and difficulty in maintaining the supply of energy to ever-increasing alcoholism and inflation, combined to retard Soviet economic development and to emphasize the seriousness of Soviet economic problems. Other observers wrote more generally of the first successful period of the Brezhnev regime, when the growth of Soviet military and industrial might went hand in hand with a sharp rise in living standards, and of the last stagnant and disappointing years with their ubiquitous shortages of food and consumer goods. At the time of Brezhnev's death perhaps the best evaluation of his eighteen-year stewardship of the Soviet economy, from 1964 to 1982, went as follows (accompanied by a telling comparison with the United States). On the one hand, there was

> Steady growth of aggregate output over the eighteen-year period, averaging 3.8 percent per year, with industrial output growing at an average annual rate of 4.9 percent.

> Steady increase in living standards of the Soviet population, with per capita consumption rising at an average annual rate of 2.7 percent.

> Significant growth in Soviet military power in absolute terms—achieved through a steady increase in real Soviet defense expenditures averaging 4 to 5 percent per year—as well as in relative terms vis-à-vis the United States.

> Reduction of the gap in aggregate and per capita output (GNP) between the Soviet Union and the United States. Whereas in 1965 Soviet GNP was only about 46 percent that of the United States (38 percent on a per capita basis), by 1982 it was 55 percent (47 percent on a per capita basis).

> Reduction of the gap in productivity between the Soviet Union and the United States. While in 1965 the productivity of an average Soviet worker was only 30 percent that in the United States, by 1982 it was 41 percent.

Increase in the output of major industrial commodities to the point where, at the beginning of the 1980s, the physical output of many key commodities in the Soviet Union equaled or exceeded that of the United States.

On the other hand, there also was

Steady deceleration in the growth of the Soviet economy. The average annual growth of GNP declined from the peak of 5.2 percent during 1966–70 to 3.7 percent during 1971–75, to 2.7 percent during 1976–80, and to an estimated 2.0 percent during 1981–82.

Steady deceleration in the growth of living standards, with the average annual growth of per capita consumption declining from a peak of 4.3 percent during 1966–70 to 2.6 percent during 1971–75, to 1.7 percent during 1976–80, and to an estimated 1.2 percent during 1981–82.

Failure to achieve satisfactory growth in Soviet agriculture. Over the eighteen-year period the average growth rate of GNP originating in agriculture amounted to only 1.7 percent.

Lack of growth of agricultural productivity both in absolute terms and in relative terms vis-à-vis the United States. While in 1965 the productivity of an average Soviet farm worker was only 14 percent that in the United States (in the Soviet Union one worker supplied six persons; in the United States one worker supplied forty-three persons), by 1981 it actually declined to a mere 12 percent (in the Soviet Union one worker supplied eight people; in the United States the corresponding figure was sixty-five).

Although a significant effect of *long-term* weather cycles on grain output in the Soviet Union cannot be ruled out, the most significant failure of the Brezhnev era appears to be grain harvests, which after 1972 repeatedly fell far short of expectations and needs. There were six of these poor harvests over the eleven years: 1972, 1975, 1979, 1980, 1981, and 1982. Whereas the Soviets appeared to be closing the gap in aggregate output with respect to the United States through the mid-1970s, the dramatic slowdown that has taken place in the Soviet Union since 1976 has resulted in some widening of the output gap. The Brezhnev reign was characterized by the highest priority being given to the growth of investment and defense spending except during the period 1964–70. As a result, the per capita consumption of an average Soviet citizen today is still not much more than one-third that in the United States—in fact, over the eighteen-year period under Brezhnev's rule the relative gap remained almost constant.

But while the facts and the statistics seemed reasonably reliable, explanations of them differed. Possibly the most important issue was to what extent Soviet economic difficulties were of a temporary and relatively remediable character and to what extent they were intrinsic to the system.

"The Thaw"

Khrushchev's "secret speech" to the Twentieth Party Congress in 1956 (read at party meetings throughout the country and soon known to many outside the party) was the most dramatic gesture in the process of de-Stalinization of Soviet life—though it was also, as noted, part of the struggle for power within the party leadership. One thing was clear to Stalin's successors: they could not rule as he had—if only because they lacked his charisma (and perhaps his ruthlessness) but also because the Soviet people were expecting so much more. For the system to survive, it needed to be more responsive to the needs and wishes of the population. This was especially evident, as we have seen, in economic policies, which paid much more attention than in the past to raising the material standard of living. The renunciation of terror was another essential step away from the past. Stalin's death and especially Beria's fall in the summer of 1953 resulted in a considerable diminution in the role and power of the political police. Immediate steps were taken to assure the population, and especially the party, that terror would no longer be part of the Soviet system of rule. The "doctors' plot" was declared to be a fabrication. New regulations and supervisory structures limited the autonomy of the political police. Immediate work began on a new legal code, promulgated in 1958, which offered citizens more legal protections. And of course, Khrushchev's 1956 speech openly castigated the state's security apparatus for mistakes and crimes, leading to the posthumous vindication ("rehabilitation" in the language of the time) of some of its most prominent victims. Living victims benefited as well. Thousands, perhaps millions, of political prisoners were released from the notorious "Gulag" of forced labor camps. Still, dissent was not tolerated. It seems that Soviet citizens gradually lost the immediate and all-pervasive dread of the political police which they had acquired under Stalin. But, although milder, the Soviet Union remained a police state.

As we shall see in a later chapter, Stalin's death was also followed by some relaxation of party control in the field of culture. Khrushchev's denunciation of the late dictator in itself suggested the need of thorough reevaluation of a great many former assumptions and assertions. It also created much confusion. For a number of months in 1956 some Soviet writers exercised remarkable freedom in their approach to Soviet reality and their criticism of it. But, after the Polish crisis and the Hungarian uprising in the autumn of that year, severe restrictions reappeared. After 1956 and until the proclamation of *glasnost*, in the "quiet" years between Stalin and Gorbachev, actual Soviet culture, although not as much hampered and badgered as in the worst days of Stalin and Zhdanov, on the whole faithfully reflected party control and official ideology. Khrushchev's fall made little difference in this respect. In fact, it can be argued that his successors generally assumed a harder line against dissent, as illustrated by the arrest, trial, and sentencing of Andrei Siniavsky and Julius Daniel in 1965–66 and numerous other instances of cultural suppression.

The amount of covert opposition and bitterness that this control and the Soviet system in general created can only be surmised. Yet it should be noted that uprisings against Communist regimes took place not only in East Germany, Poland, Czechoslovakia, and Hungary, but also in the USSR itself: notably in the

Vorkuta forced-labor camps in the north of European Russia in 1953; in Tbilisi—or Tiflis—the capital of Georgia, in 1956; in Temir-Tau in Kazakhstan among young Russian construction workers, most of them members of the Union of Communist Youth—or Komsomol—in 1959; and in Novocherkassk in 1962. Sporadic riots, strikes, and student demonstrations against the government also occurred in the Soviet Union in later years, as in Dneprodzherzhinsk in 1973.

Short of physical violence, the thawing of Soviet society and the emerging opposition views gave rise to the blossoming of a striking and varied *samizdat,* that is, self-published, illegally produced, reproduced, and distributed literature, and to the appearance of dissenting intellectuals and even groups of intellectuals on the fringes of official cultural life. Numerous dissident groups and trends emerged in these years: religious study-prayer groups (Orthodox, Protestant, Jewish, Buddhist, and others), non-conformist artists displaying their works in private apartments, dissident poets and songwriters, feminists, liberals, socialists, and anarchists. Harassed and suppressed in many ways, including on occasion incarceration in dreadful mental hospitals, the opposition nevertheless kept delivering its message, or rather messages, ranging from a kind of conservative nationalism and neo-Slavophilism to former hydrogen-bomb physicist, the late Andrei Sakharov's, progressive, generally Westernizer, views and the late Andrei Amalrik's personal, catastrophic, almost Chaadaev-like vision, to the dissident Marxism of Roy Medvedev. And it produced the phenomenon of Alexander Solzhenitsyn. Whatever one thinks of that writer in terms of literary stature, ideological acumen, or scholarly precision, most of his works, especially the *Gulag* volumes, are likely to be linked as indissolubly to the Russia of Stalin as Pushkin's *Eugene Onegin* and Turgenev's *Gentry Nest* have been linked to the Russia of the landed gentry—probably unto the ages of ages. Isolated, weak, armed only with a belief in individual moral regeneration, so prominent in Solzhenitsyn, the intellectual opposition remained a highly troublesome element in Soviet society and a forerunner of glasnost.

Jewish self-affirmation, protest, and massive migration to Israel (about 235,000 emigrants up to 1985, some 10 percent of the total Jewish population of the USSR, with many more applying)—together with the permitted emigration of some non-Jews—represented another development to disturb the post-Stalin Soviet scene, a development closely linked to the intellectual opposition, although also quite distinct. One suspects that the decision to let numerous dissatisfied Soviet citizens leave, while solving the immediate problem of dealing with those people as well as responding in a conciliatory way to world public opinion, potentially raised more questions for the Soviet system than it settled. It is apparently among many Soviet Jews that the alienation from the established order was especially thoroughgoing, as in the anecdotal story of the Moscow Jew who was accused of receiving a letter from a brother in Tel Aviv, although he had claimed that he had no relatives abroad. He explained: "You don't understand: my brother is at home; I am abroad."

The post-Stalin relaxation of restrictions appeared especially striking in an area that spans domestic and foreign policies: foreign travel and international contacts in general. Modifying the former Draconian regulations, which had made a virtually impenetrable "iron curtain" between the Soviet people and the outside world, Soviet authorities began to welcome tourists, including Americans, and allow increasing numbers of their citizens to travel abroad. Always strong on organization, they proceeded to arrange numerous "cultural exchanges," ranging from advanced study in many fields of learning to motion pictures and books for children. Soviet scientists, scholars, athletes, dancers, and musicians, not to mention the astronauts, drew deserved attention in many countries of the world. At the same time Soviet citizens welcomed distinguished visitors from the West and vigorously applauded their performances. In 1976, following the Helsinki agreements of the preceding year, foreign travel and cultural exchange gained further strength, supplying the USSR with more international contacts than had been the case at any time since the discontinuation of NEP. Bit by bit, the Soviet Union was becoming better acquainted with the West and the world.

Foreign Relations

Soviet foreign policy after Stalin's death also continued to follow the established pattern in many respects as the USSR and the Communist bloc faced the United States and its allies. No conclusive agreements on such decisive issues as control of atomic weapons, general disarmament, or Germany were reached between the two sides. Crises in widely scattered areas appeared in rapid succession. The Soviet Union made a special effort to profit by the emancipation of former Asian and African colonies from Western rule. Yet the post-Stalin policy, especially as developed by Khrushchev, also had its more conciliatory side. The new party secretary elevated the fact of coexistence of the two worlds into a dogma and asserted that all problems would be solved without war. The apparent contradiction of the two approaches probably stemmed from a real inconsistency in Khrushchev's thinking rather than from tactical considerations. It reflected further the dilemma faced by aggressive communism in an age of hydrogen warfare. Brezhnev was to pursue the substance, if not the flamboyant style, of his predecessor's foreign policy, engaging in an enormous arms race and pushing hard Soviet influence and interests in Europe, Asia, the Near East, Africa, and elsewhere, while emphasizing at the same time détente with the United States and the march of history toward peaceful evolution and international cooperation.

Stalin's death and Malenkov's assumption of the leading role in the Soviet Union marked some lessening of international tensions as well as some relaxation at home. The new prime minister asserted that all disputed questions in foreign relations could be settled peacefully, singling out the United States as a country with which an understanding could be reached. In the summer of 1953 an armistice was finally agreed upon in Korea. In the spring of 1954 an international conference ended the war in Indo-China by partitioning it between the Communist Vietminh in the north and the independent state of Vietnam in the south. Although the Soviet Union had not participated directly in the Indo-Chinese conflict, that local war had threatened to become a wider conflagration, and its termination enhanced the chances of world peace. In January 1954, the Council of Foreign Ministers of the four powers, inoperative for a long time, met in Berlin to discuss the German and Austrian treaties, but without result. The Soviet Union joined the United Nations Educational, Scientific, and Cultural Organization, or UNESCO, and the International Labor Organization, or ILO, that April. Malenkov spoke of a further improvement of international relations and of a summit meeting.

That a policy of even moderate relaxation had its dangers for the Soviet bloc became, however, quickly apparent. In early June 1953, demonstrations and strikes erupted in Czechoslovakia, assuming a dangerous form in Pilsen— or Plzeň—where rioters seized the city hall and demanded free elections. In the middle of the month East Berlin and other centers in East Germany rose in a rebellion spearheaded by workers who proclaimed a general strike. Soviet troops re-established order after some bitter fighting. Beria's fall that summer might have been affected by these developments, for the police chief had stressed relaxation and legality since the death of Stalin. Malenkov's resignation from the premiership in February 1955 ended the role of that former favorite of Stalin on the world scene.

Bulganin, who replaced Malenkov as head of the government, became the most prominent Soviet figure in international affairs, although he usually traveled in the company of and acted jointly with the party chief, Khrushchev. Molotov, in the meantime, continued in charge of the foreign office. "B. and K." diplomacy, as it came to be known, included much showy journeying on goodwill missions in both Europe and Asia. The Soviet Union paid special court to India and other neutralist countries, which had formerly been condemned as lackeys of imperialism. At the same time the two Soviet leaders claimed to be ready to settle the points at issue with the United States and the West. And, indeed, in May 1955 the great powers managed to come to an agreement and conclude a peace treaty with Austria, which included the permanent neutralization of that state as well as certain Austrian payments and deliveries to the USSR in recompense for the Soviet return of German property in Austria to the Austrian government. The height of the détente was reached at the summit conference in Geneva in July 1955. While no concrete problems were solved at that meeting, the discussion took place in a remarkably cordial atmosphere, with both Bulganin and Eisenhower insisting that their countries would never engage in aggressive action. The following month Soviet authorities announced a reduction of their armed forces by 640,000 men. In September the USSR returned the Porkkala base to Finland and concluded a treaty of friendship with the Finns for twenty years. Yet in the autumn of 1955, as soon as the ministers of foreign affairs tried to apply the attitude of accommodation and understanding expressed by their chiefs to the settlement of specific issues, a deadlock resulted, with Molotov not budging an inch from the previous Soviet positions and demands. The "spirit of Geneva" proved to be an enticing dream rather than a reality.

Since the *rapprochement* between the USSR and the West failed to last, the polarization of the world continued. Following the Communist victory in northern Indo-China, the Manila pact of September 1954 created the Southeast Asia Treaty Organization, or SEATO. Great Britain, France, Pakistan, and Thailand joined the four countries already allied, the United States, Australia, New Zealand, and the Philippines, to establish a new barrier to Communist expansion in Asia. In Europe, West Germany rose steadily in importance as an American ally and a member of the Western coalition. The Soviet Union in its turn concluded the so-called Warsaw Treaty with its satellites in May 1955 to unify the Communist military command in Europe.

The year 1956 was a memorable one in Soviet foreign policy. Khrushchev's February speech denouncing Stalin further shook the discipline in the Communist world. On the other hand, the improvement in Soviet-Yugoslav relations, which had begun with Bulganin's and Khrushchev's visit to Belgrade in 1955, received a boost, the break between the two states now being blamed on Stalin himself as well as on Beria. In April 1956 the Cominform was dissolved, and in June Shepilov replaced Molotov as foreign minister. The ferment in the Soviet satellite empire finally led to explosions in Poland and in Hungary. In late June 1956, workers in Poznan clashed with the police and scores of people were killed. Polish intellectuals and even many Polish Communists clamored for a relaxation of controls and a generally milder regime. On October 19, Wladyslaw Gomulka, who had been imprisoned as a Titoist and had been reinstated in August, became the party secretary. That same day Khrushchev and other Soviet leaders flew to Warsaw to settle the crisis. In spite of extreme tension, an understanding was reached: the USSR accepted Gomulka and a liberalization of the Communist system in Poland and agreed to withdraw Soviet troops from that country.

Events in Hungary took a graver turn. There, under the influence of the happenings in Poland, a full-scale revolution took place in late October, during which the political police were massacred. The army sided on the whole with the revolutionaries. The overturn was spearheaded by young people, especially students and workers. The new government of a revisionist Communist, Imre Nagy, constituted a political coalition rather than single-party rule and withdrew Hungary from the Warsaw Treaty. But on November 4, after only a few days of freedom, Soviet troops began storming Budapest and crushed the revolution. The imprudent attack on Egypt staged at that time by Great Britain, France, and Israel over the issue of the Suez Canal helped the Soviet move by diverting the attention of the world, splitting the Western camp, and engaging some of its forces. While crushing the Hungarians, the USSR championed the cause of Egypt and threatened its assailants. But the moral shock of the Hungarian intervention proved hard to live down: it led to the greatest popular condemnation of the Communist cause and the most widespread desertions from Communist Party ranks in the free world since the Second World War. There were strikes, demonstrations, and protests even in the Soviet Union.

As already suggested, Khrushchev might have been lucky to survive these grave perturbations in the Communist world. Yet he did defeat and dismiss Malenkov, Molotov, and Kaganovich, together with Shepilov who sided with them, in the spring and summer of 1957. After Bulganin's fall in March 1958, the first secretary, now also prime minister, became the undisputed chief of Soviet foreign policy, while Andrei Gromyko headed the foreign office. Khrushchev's behavior on the international scene showed a certain pattern. He remained essentially intransigent, pushing every advantage he had, be it troubles in newly independent states, such as the Congo, or Soviet achievements in armaments and space technology. Nevertheless, he talked incessantly in favor of coexistence and summit conferences to settle outstanding issues. Also, he paid friendly visits to many countries, including the United States in 1959. The summit conference in the summer of 1960 was never held, for two weeks before it was scheduled to begin Khrushchev announced that an American U-2 spy plane had been brought down deep in Soviet territory. But in 1961 Khrushchev met the new American president, John F. Kennedy, in Vienna. In the summer of 1962 both aspects of Soviet foreign policy stood in bold relief: fanned by the USSR, a new Berlin crisis continued to threaten world peace; yet, on the other hand, Khrushchev emphasized more than ever coexistence abroad and peaceful progress at home, having made that his signal theoretical contribution to the program that was enunciated at the Twenty-second Party Congress. To be sure, as officially defined in the Soviet Union, co-existence meant economic, political, and ideological competition with the capitalist world until the final fall of capitalism. But that fall, Soviet authorities came to assert, would occur without a world war.

However, in the autumn of that same year, Khrushchev overreached himself and brought the world to the brink of a thermonuclear war. The confrontation between the United States and the USSR in October 1962 over the Soviet missiles in Cuba, which resulted in a stunning Soviet defeat, can be explained, at least in part, by the Soviet leader's enthusiasm and his conviction that the United States and capitalism in general were on the decline and would retreat when hard pressed. The outcome, no doubt, strengthened the argument for peaceful coexistence and emphasized caution and consultation in foreign policy, symbolized by the celebrated "hot line" between Washington and Moscow. The Soviet Union proceeded to measure carefully its reactions and its involvement even in such complicated and entangling crises as the Israeli-Arab wars of 1967 and 1973 and the Vietnam War. In the latter conflict, the Soviet Union denounced of course "American imperialism" and provided extremely valuable matériel to North Vietnam, but it avoided escalation. Yet, following the complete victory of communism in Indo-China in 1975 and the shattering impact of the catastrophic American policy in Vietnam on the American public, the Soviet Union might have felt that it had a freer hand on the international stage, in Angola or elsewhere.

With the Soviet Union as well as the United States acquiring a second-strike capability, that is, the ability to retaliate and inflict "an unacceptable damage" on the enemy after absorbing a nuclear blow, a true balance of terror settled on the world. Ever-improving technology made virtually all established strategic concepts obsolete. Numerous bases and indeed whole sections of the globe lost their importance in terms of the possible ultimate showdown between the two nuclear giants.

From the mid-seventies it was authoritatively estimated in the West—and apparently realistically in contrast to earlier alarms about alleged "missile gaps" and the like—that the USSR had caught up with the United States in overall nuclear military strength, and indeed had perhaps moved slightly ahead. Even the Soviet navy, insignificant compared with its American rival at the end of the Second World War, had risen to be, according to many indices, the strongest fleet in the world, although still behind the Americans in aircraft carriers and perhaps in such intangibles as naval tradition and the expertise and spirit of its personnel. Yet the enormous economic burden, terror, and inconclusiveness of the arms race did not lead to a full negotiated settlement. Important results were achieved, to be sure. Following the earlier banning of nuclear tests in the atmosphere, the nuclear non-proliferation agreement was signed by the two superpowers and other states in early 1968. Other agreements were reached concerning outer space, where 1975 witnessed the celebrated joint effort of the Russians and the Americans. The crucial issue of military limitations itself was tackled in numerous negotiations, including the so-called SALT II talks and President Ford's discussions with Brezhnev in Vladivostok in 1974. Still, in spite of a considerable measure of agreement, the SALT II talks remained inconclusive, primarily because of the problems of the Backfire bombers on the Soviet side and of the cruise missile on the American. Moreover, as Edward Teller and other scientists have pointed out, the difficulty in the negotiations resided not only in the entire complex of aims, attitudes, and policies of the two superpowers, but also in the very nature of scientific and technological advance, which rapidly makes pre-arranged schemes of limitation obsolete.

The very closely related but even larger issue of détente between the Soviet Union and the United States also sailed to an uncertain future. With explicit "cold war" a thing of the past, détente scored a resounding success at the Helsinki conference in the summer of 1975, where the United States and other Western countries accepted in effect the communist redrawing of the map of central and eastern Europe following the Second World War in exchange for unsubstantiated promises of greater contacts between the two worlds and a greater degree of freedom in those contacts. But a comprehensive economic agreement between the USSR and the United States failed over the questions of the most favored nation clause, credits, and the American concern with the fate of Soviet Jews. Furthermore, before long détente was again swamped by new international developments, to be detailed later in this chapter.

Ironically, while Soviet-American relations improved and became more stable after the Cuban confrontation, and while the Soviet leaders found welcome in Gaullist France and other capitalist countries, their standing in the communist world deteriorated. The conflict with China broke out into the open around 1960 and widened and deepened thereafter. After the abrupt withdrawal of Soviet personnel from China in August of that year and the discontinuance of assistance, relations between the two countries quickly became those of extreme antagonism. To the sound of violent mutual denunciations the two states and parties competed with each other for the leadership of world communism, the Chinese usually championing the revolutionary position against Soviet "revisionism." Moreover, China became an atomic power and formulated large claims on Soviet Asian territory. Observers noted that international crises such as the war in Vietnam only intensified the hostility between the two great communist states. Although China remained far behind the USSR in industrial and technological development and although it was fully preoccupied with a "cultural revolution," its aftermath, and other internal problems, it was still viewed as posing a major threat to the Soviet Union in the future, if not in the immediate present.

Problems in eastern Europe proved to be more pressing. The twelve years which followed the suppression of the Hungarian revolution witnessed Soviet attempts to adjust to changing times, to allow for a communist pluralism with a considerable measure of institutional and eventually even ideological diversity. In Brzezinski's phrase, satellites were to become junior allies. Even Tito usually received a kind of fraternal recognition, and he spoke with authority. Yet tensions persisted and indeed increased, both between the different east European countries and the Soviet Union and within those countries as most of them proceeded with de-Stalinization, economic liberalization, and other important changes. The break with China led in 1961 to the unexpected departure of Albania into "the Chinese camp." Romania under its new leader, Nicholas Ceausescu, showed a remarkable, even stunning, independence from the Soviet Union, although it remained barely within the communist bloc and continued a hard-line policy at home. Poland, belying the promise of 1956, had its progress toward freedom arrested, and concentrated its energy on trying to contain, by petty and persistent persecution, the Catholic church, liberal intellectuals and students, and other forces favoring change.

The developments in Czechoslovakia led to a catastrophe. That highly Western country with a democratic tradition remained long under a form of Stalinism practiced by Antonin Novotny and his clique. But when in the early months of 1968 Novotny was finally deposed, the new party leadership, of Alexander Dubček and others, championed an extremely liberal course which included the abolition of censorship. The sweeping liberal victory in Czechoslovakia which was to be confirmed and extended at a forthcoming party congress led to consternation in the governing circles of the Soviet Union, East Germany, Poland, Bulgaria, and possibly Hungary. Exchanges of opinion and an unprecedented face-to-face discussion between the members of the Politburos of the Soviet Union and of Czechoslovakia seemed momentarily to resolve the conflict. Then on the twentieth of August, Soviet troops, assisted by the troops of the four allies, invaded Czechoslovakia and quickly occupied the country. There was very little bloodshed, because the Czechoslovak armed forces had been instructed not to resist. Soviet intervention was probably caused, in no certain order of priority, by fear for the Warsaw Pact which the Czechs wanted to modify although not abandon, by the hatred of Czech liberalization with its critique of the USSR, by the concern lest liberalism at home be too much encouraged, and by the need to respond to the pleas of the Soviet allies, especially East Germany, who saw the developments in Czechoslovakia as an immediate threat to their own regimes. The repercussions of the intervention lasted long after the summer of 1968.

In Poland, the 1970 replacement of Gomulka by Gierek as party secretary was followed by the introduction of an ambitious scheme to modernize and expand Polish industry and trade with the aid of Western capital and technology. By 1976, it was evident that Gierek's loudly hailed economic "acceleration" had begun to fail. Continuing world economic crisis and mismanagement and corruption at all levels of party and government apparatus, as well as the ever-increasing cost of participating in the Soviet-directed Council of Mutual Economic Assistance (COMECON) and the Warsaw Pact, all contributed to Poland's difficulties. In 1976, workers' protests and strikes over drastic increases in food prices were followed by the rapid formation and activation of dissident organizations and clandestine printing establishments. The Catholic Church, its traditional prestige fortified by the election of the Archbishop of Cracow, Cardinal Karol Wojtyla, to the papal throne (Pope John Paul II), also spoke out strongly against many of the Communist government's policies. The Gierek regime was unable to suppress the opposition effectively, in part at least, it would seem, because of its heavy dependence on continuing Western loans, required to keep the economy solvent, and the consequent need to avoid drastic action which could lead to the cutting off of Western funds.

The summer of 1980, with continuing labor unrest and economic near-collapse, led to the change of party leadership and to a formal agreement between the Polish government and the great majority of Polish workers, now mostly represented by independent "Solidarity" trade unions and led by a charismatic veteran of the struggle for workers' rights in Poland, electrician Lech Walesa. The agreement, accepted by the workers as a foundation for a dialogue with the government, appears to have been a tactical maneuver of the Communist authorities. No regular contacts with the Solidarity leadership and the Catholic hierarchy aimed at creating a constructive and meaningful national consensus were initiated by the government. By exploiting its monopoly over the mass media and over the distribution of increasingly scarce food supplies and consumer goods, the government attempted to undermine the position of the opposition while at the same time strongly seconding Moscow's accusations that Solidarity was attempting to subvert the political structure and international position of People's Poland. The rise to prominence of General Wojciech Jaruzelski, who progressively combined the posts of Minister of Defense, Premier, and First Secretary of the Party, coincided with a gradual militarization of the administration of important branches of government and industry.

All this was done in preparation for the military coup which was executed in close cooperation with the Soviet authorities on December 13, 1981. Active resistance against the overwhelming forces of the regime was quite limited, and, from a military standpoint, the operation was carried out rather effectively. Nevertheless, the "success" of General Jaruzelski's junta was very dubious. Although thousands of Solidarity activists, including Lech Walesa, and other dissidents were arrested and placed in internment camps, some leaders of the movement escaped arrest and an underground opposition began to form. Western economic sanctions and continuing passive resistance to the regime in the factories, offices, schools, and universities were making the task of running the country extremely difficult for the Jaruzelski regime. By the end of 1982, there appeared to be two clear choices before the military government of Poland: either to continue with the martial law administration, further alienating the population and risking a total economic collapse of the country, or to end martial law and attempt to open the few remaining channels of contact with the great majority of the Polish population in an effort to reduce tensions and improve the performance of the economy. The choice was not an easy one for the Polish Communist authorities—and their Soviet sponsors.

The Soviet invasion of Afghanistan in late December 1979 produced a strong impression in the world. The impression was exacerbated by the fact that, although the so-called Afghan rebels could not match the Red Army in open fighting, they could not be entirely destroyed either. More than five years after the original invasion, when Gorbachev came to power, the Soviet Union was still employing perhaps 100,000 of its troops in the Muslim country, and it was not clear how much of that country, outside the main cities, was under Soviet control. Critics pointed out that the Afghan invasion represented the first direct Soviet use of military force outside "its own" east European empire since the Second World War. The massive intervention was also interpreted as the first step in a bid for the oil of the Middle East and a general takeover of that region. It can well be argued, on the other hand, that the decisive Soviet move was essentially defensive: communism had actually come to Afghanistan some two years earlier in a peculiar internal struggle which pitted two communist factions against each other as well as against other groups; the Soviet choice in late 1979 was that between intervention and witnessing a neighboring communist state, which it had already welcomed and supported as part of the communist world, go down to popular opposition. But, defensive or not, the Soviet step was certainly a grave and disturbing one.

As of 1985, tension between the Soviet Union and the United States, the East and the West, was not confined to the crucial problems of Afghanistan and Poland. Rather, the two sides opposed each other all over the world, from Central America to southern Africa, Lebanon, and Cambodia. To be sure, western European countries, in spite of strong United States objections and even sanctions against particular companies, continued to support the building of a natural-gas pipeline from western Siberia to western Europe. But they were also apparently prepared to proceed with the installation of United States middle-range missiles to counteract the already established Soviet ones, an installation most especially opposed for years by Brezhnev. The virtually all-important Soviet-American disarmament negotiations remained deadlocked. SALT II was not ratified by the United States Senate, and its future chances appeared slim, especially after the departure of Carter from the Presidency. In fact, numerous critics accused the tougher anti-Soviet tone of the Reagan administration as largely precluding adjustment and agreement. Yet the administration itself and others claimed that it was precisely this firmer approach, and especially the concurrent building up of the United States nuclear and military might, that would force the USSR to negotiate effectively for disarmament.

Chapter 41

Soviet Society and Culture

The Soviet Union is a contradictory society halfway between capitalism and socialism, in which: (a) the productive forces are still far from adequate to give the state property a socialist character; (b) the tendency toward primitive accumulation created by want breaks out through innumerable pores of the planned economy; (c) norms of distribution preserving a bourgeois character lie at the basis of a new differentiation of society; (d) the economic growth, while slowly bettering the situation of the toilers, promotes a swift formation of privileged strata; (e) exploiting the social antagonisms, a bureaucracy has converted itself into an uncontrolled caste alien to socialism; (f) the social revolution, betrayed by the ruling party, still exists in property relations and in the consciousness of the toiling masses; (g) a further development of the accumulating contradictions can as well lead to socialism as back to capitalism; (h) on the road to capitalism the counterrevolution would have to break the resistance of the workers; (i) on the road to socialism the workers would have to overthrow the bureaucracy. In the last analysis, the question will be decided by a struggle of living social forces, both on the national and the world arena.

—TROTSKY

The party leadership of literature must be thoroughly purged of all philistine influences. Party members active in literature must not only be the teachers of ideas which will muster the energy of the proletariat in all countries for the last battle for its freedom; the party leadership must, in all its conduct, show a morally authoritative force. This force must imbue literary workers first and foremost with a consciousness of their collective responsibility for all that happens in their midst. Soviet literature, with all its diversity of talents, and the steadily growing number of new and gifted writers, should be organized as an integral collective body, as a potent instrument of socialist culture.

—GORKY

The Bolsheviks' seizure of power in Russia in November 1917 meant a social as well as a political revolution. The decades that followed "Great October" witnessed a transformation of Russian society into Soviet society. They also saw the emergence and development of an unmistakably Soviet style of culture. In spite of its enormous size, huge population, and tremendous variety of ethnic and cultural strains, the USSR became a remarkably homogeneous land, for it reflected throughout its length and breadth—"from Kronstadt and to Vladivostok," to quote a Soviet song—some seventy-five years of Communist engineering, social and cultural as well as political and economic. At the same time, these were years of imagination and experimentation, of sudden shifts in social and cultural policy, of widespread enthusiasm for the new, and of much disorientation, disappointment, and discontent. Indeed, it is precisely in social and cultural life that we begin to see signs of the disintegration of the Communist order that would contribute to its collapse in 1991.

The Communist Party of the Soviet Union

The Communist Party played in fact, as well as in theory, the leading role in Soviet society. Its membership, estimated at the surprisingly low figure of less than twenty-five thousand in 1917, passed the half million mark in 1921 and the million mark in the late twenties. The number of Soviet Communists continued to rise, in spite of repeated purges which included the frightful great purge of the thirties, and reached the total of almost four million full members and candidates when Germany invaded the USSR. While many Communists perished in the war, numerous new members were admitted into the party, especially from frontline units. Postwar recruitment drives further augmented party membership to seven to nine million in the immediate postwar years, as much as thirteen million in 1967, 16,380,000 in 1978, and almost 20 million in the 1980s.

These figures, of course, by no means tell the entire story of Communist penetration into Soviet life. As already emphasized, the party, in the Leninist view which served to differentiate the Bolsheviks from the Mensheviks, comprised a fully conscious and dedicated elite, exclusive by definition, but also educating and guiding other organizations and, indeed, the broad masses. In addition to the party proper, there existed huge youth organizations: Little Octobrists for young children, Pioneers for those aged from nine to fifteen, and the Union of Communist Youth, or Komsomol, with members in the fourteen to twenty-six age range. The first two organizations, and eventually even the Komsomol, acted as party agencies for the general education of the younger Soviet generations, opening their doors wide to members. The party also worked with and directed uncounted institutions and groups: professional, social, cultural, athletic, and others. In fact, from the official standpoint, Soviet society had only one ideology and only one outlook, the Communist; citizens and groups of citizens differed solely in the degree to which they incarnated it.

That sweeping assumption, it might be added, expresses especially well the monolithic and totalitarian aspirations of the Soviet system.

The party demanded the entire man or woman. Lenin's example illustrated the ideal of absolute and constant dedication to party purposes. The word *partiinost*, translated sometimes as "party-mindedness," summarized the essential quality of a Communist's life and work. While the early emphasis on austerity was greatly relaxed after the thirties, especially in the upper circles, the requirements of implicit obedience and hard work generally remained. In particular, party members were expected throughout their lives both to continue their own education in Marxism-Leninism and to utilize their knowledge in all their activities, carrying out party directives to the letter and influencing those with whom they come in contact. While exacting, the "party ticket" opened many doors. It constituted in effect the greatest single mark of status, importance, and, above all, of being an "insider" in the Soviet Union. Although, to be sure, many Soviet Communists were people of no special significance, virtually all prominent figures in the country were members of the party. After the Second World War special efforts were made to assure that such fields as university teaching and scientific research were largely in the hands of Communists. Conversely, it became much easier for outstanding people to join the party.

The social composition of the Communist Party of the Soviet Union indicated fluctuation. Ostensibly the true party of the proletariat, prior to 1917 it had a largely bourgeois leadership and no mass following of any kind. The workers as a group, however, did support it in November 1917 and during the hard years that followed the Bolshevik seizure of power. The party naturally welcomed them, while at the same time displaying extreme suspiciousness toward those of "hostile" class origin. With the stabilization of the Soviet system and the inauguration of the five-year plans, "Soviet intellectuals," in particular technical and administrative personnel of all sorts, became prominent. On the eve of the Second World War the party was described as composed of 50 percent of workers, 20 percent of peasants, and 30 percent of Soviet intellectuals, with the last group on the increase. That increase continued after the war, as social origin became less significant with time and the authorities tried to bring all prominent people into the party. It might be noted that, in relation to their numbers, peasants were poorly represented, indicating the difficulty the Communists experienced in permeating the countryside. The proportion of women increased up to about one-quarter of the membership of the party.

The Communist Party of the Soviet Union was very thoroughly organized. Starting with primary units, or cells, which were established where three or more Communists could be found, that is, in factories, collective farms, schools, military units, and so forth, the structure rose from level to level to culminate in periodic party congresses, which constituted important events in Soviet history, and in the permanently active Central Committee, Secretariat, and Politburo. At every step, from an individual factory or collective farm to the ministries and other superior governing agencies, Communists were supposed to provide supervision and inspiration, making it their business to see that no undesirable trends developed and that production goals were overfulfilled. At higher government levels, as already indicated, the entire personnel consisted of Communists, a fact which nevertheless did not eliminate party vigilance and control. In general, rotation between full-time government positions and party administrative positions was common. It should be noted that the guiding role of the party asserted itself with increased force after Stalin's death, for—as L. Schapiro and other close students of Soviet communism have indicated—the late general secretary's dictatorial power had grown to such enormous proportions that it had put even the party into the shade.

The Destruction of the Old Society

Whereas the October Revolution catapulted the Communist Party to power, it led to the destruction of entire social classes. The Revolution was in many ways inspired by a hatred of the old dominant classes, which led to widespread assaults on their property and position and sometimes on their persons. The result was a rapid and sweeping leveling of traditional Russian society. The landowning gentry, for centuries the top social group in Russia, disappeared rapidly in 1917 and 1918 as peasants seized their land and often demolished their homes. The upper bourgeoisie, financial, industrial, and commercial, was similarly eliminated when workers seized control of many businesses and then when the Bolsheviks nationalized finance, industry, and trade. The middle and especially the lower bourgeoisie, to be sure, staged a remarkable comeback during the years of the New Economic Policy. Their final destruction, however, came with the implementation of the five-year plans. If the gentry occupied the stage in Russia too long, the bourgeoisie was cut down before it came into its own. The clergy, the monks and nuns, and other people associated with the Church constituted yet another group to suffer harsh persecution, although in their case it stopped short of complete annihilation. The great majority of the intellectuals, too, found themselves in opposition to the new regime. Many of them emigrated. Many others perished in the frightful years of civil war and famine. In fact, although some of its members remained, the intelligentsia as a cohesive, articulate, and independent group was no more.

The Peasants

While traditional Marxism envisioned socialism coming to an urbanized and industrialized society, the Soviet Union was for most of its history a land of peasants. In 1926, 82 percent of the population lived in rural areas. Only in the mid-1960s did the number of city dwellers finally exceed the number living in the countryside. Even in the final years of the Soviet Union, the rural population still numbered almost a third of the total. Not surprisingly, the peasants bore the brunt of the privations and sacrifices imposed by the Soviet "builders of socialism." The total population of the USSR was officially given in the spring of 1959 as only 208,826,000—and as 262,400,000 according to the census of 1979—a low figure which testifies to two demographic catastrophes: the one associated with the First Five-Year Plan, more especially the collectivization of agriculture, and the other resulting from the Second World War. In both cases peasants—and peasants as soldiers—suffered the most, dying by the millions.

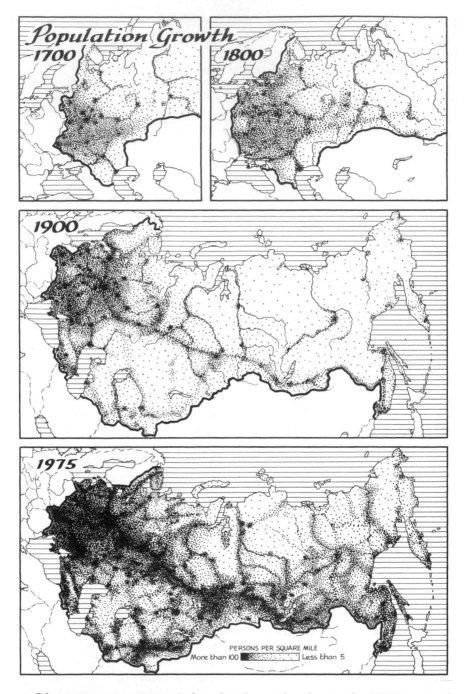

Of course, peasants carried such a heavy burden in the USSR not only because of their vast numbers, but also because of the policies pursued by the government. The Communist view of peasants was always ambivalent. On the one hand, Bolsheviks believed themselves to be acting in the name of "the people," that is, of the workers and the peasants. On the other hand, as Marxists, they viewed peasants (with the possible exception of semi-proletarianized "poor peasants") as petit bourgeois property owners who would support the building of communism only after they were fully proletarianized by leaving the countryside or once agriculture had been transformed along collective industrial lines. Initial policies reflected this ambivalence. Lenin's original endorsement of the peasant seizure of land, though understood by Lenin to be a necessary but temporary "compromise" with peasant desires, had great appeal in the countryside. Influenced by the Bolshevik land policy and by revolutionary soldiers returning home—a point effectively emphasized by Radkey—the rural masses proved reasonably well inclined toward the new regime and on the whole apparently preferred it to the Whites during the great Civil War. But War Communism antagonized many of them. Besides, the Bolsheviks tried to split the peasants, inciting the poor against the better-off. During NEP, the official policy was one of *smychka,* of the "bond" uniting the proletariat (and the ruling party of the proletariat) with the peasants. But already, we see efforts to promote proletarianization. Rural soviets, staffed by urban Communists along with some poor peasants, competed with the traditional power of the peasant commune. Cooperatives and collective farms were organized. Communists tried to organize the poorer peasants against the richer kulaks, though this required greatly exaggerating the actual extent of social differentiation in the villages. And efforts were made to transform peasant manners and beliefs. But many Communists found this gentle approach to peasants distasteful and dangerous and called for a more aggressive policy toward the traditional peasantry.

The First Five-Year Plan resulted in such an all-out offensive against the peasantry, often framed in the language of class war and proletarianization. Five million kulaks and members of their families disappeared. Countless peasants, recalcitrant or relatively prosperous or simply unlucky, populated forced-labor camps. Other uncounted peasants starved to death. Scenes of horror in once bounteous Ukraine defied description. But, as we know, the peasants, in spite of their resistance, were finally pushed and pulled into collectives. The typical member of a kolkhoz was a new phenomenon in Russian history. The novelty resided not in his wretched poverty, not even in the extremely heavy exactions imposed upon him, but in the minute state organization and control of his work and life. While peasants profited from certain Soviet policies, notably the spread of education, and while some of them rose to higher stations in society, on the whole the condition of the rural masses, the bulk of the Soviet people, remained miserable and at times desperate. Largely supporting the five-year plans by their labor, as already explained, Soviet peasants received very little in return. After Stalin's death, Khrushchev and other leaders admitted the grave condition of the Soviet countryside, while writers presented some unforgettable pictures of it during the relative freedom of expression that prevailed for several months in 1956. Subsequent years, to be sure, witnessed an improvement. Yet rural Russia remained poor. Moreover, the party and the government continued their social engineering, as clearly indicated in such postwar measures and projects as the increase in the size of the collective farms, the abortive agrogoroda, the temporary emphasis on the

This 1925 poster, by the noted Russian painter Boris Kustodiev, is titled "Leningrad Society for the Smychka (Bond) between City and Country." An urban worker and a peasant and his son are shown in stereotypical dress. Note the differences. The worker is handing the boy a pamphlet of writings by Lenin, who is also quoted at the bottom of the poster: "Establishing connections between city and country is one of the fundamental tasks of the working class holding power." (Gosizdat)

sovkhoz form of agriculture, and the periodic campaigns against the private plots of kolkhoz members. Indeed—logically, from their point of view—Communists were not likely to relax until peasants disappeared as a separate group, having been integrated into a completely socialized, mechanized, and urbanized economy. No wonder that the coming of *perestroika* made peasant landownership a central issue and one very difficult to handle.

The Workers

Industrial workers in many ways profited most from the Bolshevik revolution. That revolution was made in their name, and they gave the new regime its greatest social support. Because of this, perhaps a million and a half workers and their children rose to new importance. They became party functionaries, Red Army officers, and even organizers of collective farms. Many received rapid training to be graduated as technologists. Persons of a proletarian background enjoyed priorities in institutions of higher learning and elsewhere. The upward social mobility of workers was all the more remarkable because their total number was not very large, and it contrasted sharply with the relatively static nature of tsarist society. Many prominent people throughout Soviet life owed their positions to that rise.

But, of course, while many workers went up the social ladder, new men and women entered the factories. After the inauguration of the five-year plans the influx turned into a deluge. Peasants of yesterday became workers of today. Russia finally acquired vast crowds of proletarians characteristic of the industrial revolution. Whether the condition of the workers in the Soviet Union improved compared to tsarist times remains an open question. That it continued to be miserable cannot be reasonably doubted. Soviet workers profited from increased educational and cultural opportunities, and the expanding welfare state, but their pitiful real wages probably remained below the prerevolutionary level as late as the early fifties. After all, the huge industrialization was made possible by keeping industrial wages down as well as by squeezing the peasants. In addition, workers suffered from the totally inadequate and deteriorating urban housing, and, together with other Soviet citizens, they had to contribute their efforts and their scarce time to various "voluntary" projects, to their own and others' political education, and to other prescribed activities. In the workplace, the revolutionary ideals of "workers' control" were quickly set aside as the needs of increasing production took precedence. The power of management over the everyday lives of workers was matched by trade unions made to serve the interests of the state more than the needs of individual workers. In contrast to tsarist days, workers could not strike or otherwise express their discontent. Perhaps a reflection of these conditions, alcoholism, indiscipline, and poor work habits persisted—and evidently increased in the late Soviet years—signs, much talked about, that many Soviet workers remained far from the model of conscious proletarians. The material condition of the Soviet proletariat did improve, however, after the death of Stalin. Still, it remained quite poor as the Soviet system came to its end.

The "New Class"

Whereas the initial impact of the Bolshevik revolution, coupled with famine and other catastrophes, did much to level Russian society, smashing the rigid class structure of imperial Russia and even destroying entire classes, before long social differentiation began to grow again. In particular, the five-year plans produced a tremendous expansion of administrative and technical personnel, which, together with the already existing party and government bureaucracies, became, broadly speaking, the leading class in the country. One author estimated that the Soviet economy employed 1,700,000 bookkeepers alone! Scientists, writers, artists, professors, and other intellectuals, purged and integrated into the new system, became prominent members of the privileged group. Army and naval officers and their families provided additional members. Altogether, the privileged, distinguished primarily by their education and non-manual occupations, came to compose about 15 percent of the total population. Relatively speaking—paradoxically, if you will—they enjoyed greater advantages compared to the masses than their counterparts in Western capitalist societies. It is also of interest that material differences within the educated class and within the worker and peasant classes, who were often paid according to some form of the piece rate, were very marked in Soviet Russia. Paid vacations and other rewards supplied by the regime were distributed in a similarly uneven manner. In fact, wages and salaries tended to show a greater differentiation in the USSR than in the West, although, of course, Soviet citizens could not accumulate fortunes based on profits, rent, or interest.

"Cultural Revolution" and the "Great Retreat"

As the new Soviet elite advanced to the fore, Soviet society lost many of its revolutionary traits and began to acquire in certain respects a strikingly conservative character. The transformation occurred essentially during the thirties, but on the whole it continued and developed further during the Second World War and in the postwar years. While state laws and regulations were crucial in this process, they reflected, as well as contributed to, basic social and economic changes.

Soviet history began with radical experiments to transform society. Experiments such as the "Orchestra without a Conductor" or house communes and attacks on "bourgeois specialists" were meant to nurture a spirit of collectivism and egalitarianism. Iconoclasm and imagination were encouraged in the arts and literature, as will be discussed later. Perhaps most important, as part of an effort to liberate individuals, a sustained effort was made to undermine the family. Marriage was no longer a sacrament, but a simple legal agreement between two people, easily broken. A divorce could be obtained merely at the request of one of the partners—a postcard was enough. Children were optional and abortions were legal and quite common. Some Bolshevik leaders even spoke of "free love." Efforts were made to establish collective kitchens and day care centers.

In the 1930s, all that changed. Artistic and literary expression, as will be seen, was made more uniform and conventional than ever before. The discourse of egalitarianism was overturned: attacks on engineers and other professionals were halted, Stalin explicitly repudiated wage equality as "silly chatter" and "fashionable leftism," and inequality and privilege were allowed to grow. Discipline was reinforced in the army and other institutions. Ranks, titles, decorations, and other distinctions, whether bureaucratic, military, or academic, were restored and acquired vast importance. Traditional uniforms blossomed everywhere, reminding observers of tsarist Russia. Generalissimo Stalin toasting his marshals at a gargantuan Kremlin reception presented a far different picture from Lenin in his worn-out coat haranguing workers in squares and factory yards. In schools, the experiments of the 1920s were halted and classroom discipline reinstated along with uniforms, formal lecturing, learning by rote, standardized textbooks, and homework. The content of education also shifted. While instruction in Marxism-Leninism and party history remained obligatory, traditional academic subjects were reemphasized. And glorification of the party and its leaders was joined by a new emphasis on patriotism and Russian national tradition. In family policy, greater ceremony was restored to marriage, divorce became difficult and expensive, homosexuality was made a criminal offense, and abortion was outlawed. Especially after the losses of the Second World War, particular emphasis was placed on having many children. Mothers with five or six living offspring received the Motherhood Medal, those with seven or eight were awarded a decoration known as Motherhood Glory, while those with ten achieved the status of Heroine Mother. Financial grants to large families helped further the implementation of the new policy. Throughout these years, the press extolled family life and the role of women as mothers as mainstays of the socialist order.

In the post-Stalin years, especially, other signs of social and cultural "retreat" were noticed, though these were less the result of official policy than of gradual changes in everyday life and mentalities, which often ran against the grain of party policy. Most often mentioned at the time was the widespread retreat into private life. Soviet sociologists, around the 1970s, began documenting what one researcher called a "drift toward domesticity." Opinion surveys showed that Soviet citizens valued family above work, social recognition, or participation in organizations. Making "cozy" private spaces for oneself and one's family became of prime importance. No less value was placed on friendship. Scholars have argued that family and friends in the late Soviet years became "private institutions" that offered bases of loyalty and cultural value that functioned as alternatives, and even as subtle opposition, to the official order. These same years also saw the growth of wider alternative networks of affinity and values, especially among the young: devotees of various trends in Western rock music, sports fan gangs known as *fanaty,* counter-cultural identities such as "hippies" or "punks" (the English words were used), and, among the intelligentsia, private cultural circles where new poetry or prose was read, art displayed, and ideas discussed. It was precisely in these expanding semi-private spaces where the dissident movement developed from the late 1960s into the 1980s. Drinking, of course, was pervasive throughout this bourgeoning private and unofficial civic life. That so much of this was at odds with official ideology led sociologists and party officials to worry about the "lack of Soviet consciousness" among the youth in the 1970s and led Gorbachev in the mid-1980s to speak of a "spiritual crisis" in the Soviet Union in which much of the population had become alienated from the established order in their values, judgments, tastes, and beliefs.

Women and Feminism

Women constituted half, at times considerably more than half, the population of the Soviet Union, and they certainly contributed their share to its history. In a very real sense they carried half, or more, of the burden of that history on

Young women and soldiers on a Moscow street in the 1980s. The freedom to visibly dissent from established tastes was a sign both of greater personal freedom in Russia after Stalin's death and of growing alienation from the system. (I. Moukhin)

their shoulders. The communist program included liberating women from oppression, discrimination, and drudgery as part of the liberation of humankind. The first decade or more after the October Revolution was full of promise for Soviet feminists, as well as of new departures in the position and activities of Soviet women, perhaps most notably and permanently so among the Islamic peoples of the country. But, for the Soviet leaders, feminist ideals were always ancillary to the fundamental Marxist vision of class struggle and the building of socialism. And they were crushed, together with other autonomous views, once the USSR was set in the firm Stalinist mold. There was some relaxation but no basic change in the situation after the death of the crucial dictator.

Lapidus and other scholars have done much to present and interpret the position of Soviet women in both its positive and its negative aspects. The former include, notably, the great increase in education, to where women came to be proportionately better represented as students in Soviet institutions of higher learning than men. Concurrently women rose remarkably in the professions, so that, for example, the great majority of the doctors of medicine in the late Soviet years were women. Yet, as it has been repeatedly pointed out, few women reached the top rungs of their profession, medicine included, and they were strikingly absent at the highest levels of both party and government. Moreover, Soviet women both held full-time jobs and performed the great bulk of the work at home, a task made all the more difficult by the hard conditions of life in the Soviet Union. It might be added that feminism in the Western sense was at best in its incipient stage in the USSR. Nor were all its emphases— as a student of Soviet society will readily understand—particularly relevant to the Soviet scene.

The Nationalities

Its multinational composition was a major problem for the Soviet Union as it had been for the Russian Empire. While in 1917 Great Russians formed about half of the population of the country, and Ukrainians and White Russians, or Belorussians, approximately another quarter, the remaining quarter consisted of a staggering variety of ethnic and linguistic groups. The Caucasus alone contains a fantastically complicated mixture of peoples. More than a hundred and fifty languages and dialects were spoken in the Soviet Union. Soviet nationalities ranged from ancient civilized peoples, such as the Armenians and the Georgians, to primitive Siberian tribes. They included Lutherans and Catholics as well as Orthodox, and Muslims and Buddhists together with shamanists. Moreover, many of these peoples showed nationalist tendencies in the years of revolution and civil war, which corresponded only too well to the generally nationalist atmosphere of the twentieth century.

Soviet authorities developed several basic policies in dealing with national groups, which were often quite contradictory. On the one hand, the Soviet state promoted education (including the creation of local intelligentsias), created opportunities for individuals from local nationalities to hold positions of local influence (such that the Soviet Union has even been described as an "affirmative action empire"), and allowed the languages and cultures of local peoples to be preserved. At the same time, the Soviet authorities allowed no independence in ideological, political, economic, or social matters, discouraged and sometimes punished religious practice (often closely tied to national identities), settled large numbers of ethnic Russians in the national republics and autonomous regions, and discriminated against minority nationalities in the recognized national republics (such as the Abkhaz in Georgia). Even cultural traditions were restricted by the stipulation that they be "national in form and socialist in content." All histories had to be interpreted in the simple terms of class struggle and the progressive march of secular civilization. Above all, the centralized unity of the USSR was an absolute principle and the single Communist Party of the Soviet Union was an important foundation and guarantee of that unity.

But this dual approach to nationalities proved difficult to maintain in practice. Cultural autonomy could easily become cultural nationalism, and that in turn would lead to separatism. Always suspicious, the Soviet leadership kept uncovering "bourgeois nationalists" in union republics and lesser subdivisions of the USSR. In the crucially important case of Ukraine, for example, the party apparatus itself suffered several sweeping purges because of its "deviations." Moreover, after a controlled measure of Great Russian patriotism and nationalism became respectable in the Soviet Union, Stalin and the Politburo began to stress the Russian language and the historical role of the Great Russian people as binding cement of their multinational state. This trend continued during the Second World War and in the postwar years. Eastern peoples of the USSR were made to use the Cyrillic in place of the Latin alphabet for their native tongues, while the Russian language received emphasis in all Soviet schools. Histories had to be rewritten again to demonstrate that the incorporation of minority nationalities into the Russian state was a positive good rather than merely the lesser evil as compared to other alternatives. Basically contrary to Marxism, the new interpretation was fitted into Marxist dress by such means as stress on the progressive nature of the Russian proletariat and the advanced character of the Russian revolutionary movement, which benefited all the peoples fortunate enough to be associated with Russians. But Stalin, and some other Soviet leaders as well, went further, giving violent expression to some of the worst kinds of prejudices. Notably the quite un-Marxist vice of anti-Semitism found fertile soil in the Soviet Union. Yiddish intellectuals were among the groups virtually wiped out by the purges. Jews were generally excluded from the Soviet diplomatic service. Stalin's and Zhdanov's fierce attack on "cosmopolitanism" after the Second World War seemed particularly difficult to reconcile with the international character of Marxism or with the legacy of Lenin. The Jewish emigration from the USSR had more than one sound reason behind it.

Education

Education played an extremely important role in the development of the Soviet Union. Educational advances were a most important part of state planning and made the striking Soviet economic and technological progress possible. As already indicated, education also stood at the heart of the evolution of Soviet society.

Somewhat less than half of the Russian people were literate at the time of the Bolshevik revolution. Furthermore, the years of civil war, famine, epidemics, and general disorganization that followed the establishment of the Soviet regime resulted in a decline of literacy and in a general lowering of the educational level in the country. Beginning in 1922, however, the authorities began to implement a large-scale educational program, aiming not only at establishing schools for all children, but also at eliminating illiteracy among adults. By the end of the Second Five-Year Plan, that is, by 1938, a network of four-year elementary schools covered the USSR, while more advanced seven-year schools had been organized for urban children. The total elimination of illiteracy proved more difficult, although the government created more than 19,000 "centers for liquidating illiteracy" by 1925 and persevered in its efforts. The census of 1926 registered 51 percent of Soviet citizens, aged ten and above, as literate; that of 1939 81.1 percent. Projecting the increase, 85 percent of the Soviet people must have been literate at the time of the German invasion, and almost all at the end of the Communist regime.

The four-year and the seven-year schools became basic to the Soviet system. But ten-year schools also appeared in quantity. This type of school, for

"Literacy Is the Path to Communism," 1920. Note the mythic imagery with which the power of literacy was imagined. The book being held by the rider reads "proletarians of all countries, unite." (Gosizdat)

boys and girls from seven to seventeen, provides more class hours in its ten years than does the American educational system in twelve. Although in 1940 tuition was introduced in the last three years of the ten-year school, as well as in the institutions of higher learning—and repealed and restored since—an extremely widespread system of scholarships and stipends was used at all times to make advanced education available to those with ability.

After initial experimentation with some progressive education and certain quite radical methods of teaching the young and combining school and life, Soviet education returned to entirely traditional, disciplinarian, and academic practices. The emphasis centered on memorization and recitation, with a tremendous amount of homework. It has been estimated that, if Soviet schoolchildren were to do all their assignments conscientiously and to the full, they would be reading 280 printed pages a day! Soviet schools were especially strong in mathematics and science, that is, in physics, chemistry, biology, and astronomy, as well as in geography and drafting. But they also stressed language, literature, foreign languages, and history, together with certain other academic subjects. For instance, six years of a foreign language were taught in a ten-year school. There were no electives. Before he lost power Khrushchev emphasized the need to bring schools closer to life and to combine education in the upper grades with some apprenticeship work in factories and farms. But educational reforms along these lines proved to be abortive. Many students, however, were forced to spend at least two years "in production," that is, in factory or agricultural work, before proceeding from secondary to higher education. The Soviet Union also had special schools for children with musical and artistic gifts, military schools, foreign language schools, and the like. In addition, many boarding schools for the general education of Soviet children were established. They numbered 2,000, with 500,000 pupils, in the autumn of 1961, and were described as the "new school of Communist society" at the Twenty-second Party Congress. Probably because of their great expense and the generally more modest tone of subsequent leadership, they lost their prominence.

Beyond secondary schools, there stood technical and other special schools, as well as full-fledged institutions of higher learning. The number of these higher schools was constantly growing. While Soviet authorities developed the old university system, they placed much more emphasis in higher education on institutes that concentrated on a particular field, such as technology, agriculture, medicine, pedagogy, or economics. Study in the institutes ranged from four to six years; a university course usually took five years. Applicants to universities and institutes had to take competitive entrance examinations, and it has been estimated that frequently as many as two out of three qualified candidates had to be rejected because of lack of space. The older Soviet students, as well as the schoolchildren, were required to attend all their classes, were in general subject to strict discipline, and followed a rigidly prescribed course of study.

The educational effort of the party and the government extended beyond schools to libraries, museums, clubs, the theater, the cinema, radio, television, and even circuses. All of these, of course, were owned by the state, were constantly augmented, and were closely coordinated to serve the same purposes. More peculiarly Soviet was the practice of constant oral propaganda in squares and at street corners, with more than two million propagandists sponsored by the party. Bereday has written authoritatively on the spread of education in the Soviet Union, and has compared this spread with the situation in the United States:

> ... [In 1958] there were in the Soviet Union approximately 110,000 elementary four-year schools, 60,000 seven-year schools, and 25,000 ten-year schools, a total of nearly 200,000 regular schools of general education. There are, in addition, some 7,000 auxiliary special and part-time schools, 3,750 technikums and professional schools, 730 institutes of higher education, and 39 universities. The countryside is dotted by 150,000 libraries, 850 museums, 500 theaters, 2,700 Pioneer palaces, 500 stations for young technicians and naturalists, 240,000 movie theaters, and 70 circuses. A task force of 1,625,000 teachers and other personnel mans this extensive

enterprise. . . . Population and school-attendance figures substantiate the ambitions of the Soviet educational plan to reach all the people. The figures now available estimate the situation as follows: 2,500 out of each 10,000 people were in some type of school in 1955–1956; 814 of these were in grades five to ten of the general secondary school, 100 were in professional secondary schools, and 93 were in institutions of higher learning. These figures, which account for one-fourth of the total population, expand as we single out for consideration only the present younger generation. Approximately 10 percent of the appropriate age group attend institutions of higher education, the second largest proportion in the world after the United States, with 33 percent of its youth in colleges. About 30 percent of the appropriate age group complete secondary education, a close second after the United States, with 45 percent. At the age of fourteen 80 percent of the age group are still in school, in the United States some 90 percent.

Education on the job and by correspondence was also extremely widespread in the USSR. Moreover, a further expansion and diffusion of education constituted an essential part of the later five-year plans, although the rate of educational advance slowed down compared to the earlier period, while comparison with the United States was affected by the great expansion of American higher education in the 1960s.

Soviet education, and indeed Soviet culture in general, greatly profited from the prerevolutionary legacy. The high standards, the serious academic character, and even the discipline of Soviet schools dated from tsarist days. The main Communist contribution was the dissemination of education at all levels and on a vast scale, although it should be remembered that imperial Russia was, on the whole, moving in the same direction and that given a little more time it would have established universal schooling. Many observers noted that Soviet students studied with remarkable diligence and determination. That probably stemmed both from the old tradition, which held education in high esteem, and from contemporary conditions of life: education provided for Soviet citizens the only generally available escape from the poverty and drabness of the kolkhoz and the factory. If generous subsidization and energetic promotion constituted the main Soviet virtues in education, the all-pervasive emphasis on Marxism was the chief vice. While a detailed criticism of the Soviet school system must be left to DeWitt, Lilge, Kline, and other specialists, it is important to realize that Soviet Marxism distorted whatever it touched and that, therefore, the quality of Soviet education and culture frequently deteriorated in direct proportion to its proximity to doctrine. For this reason Soviet mathematics, in schools or universities, is vastly preferable to Soviet history, and Soviet chemistry to Soviet philosophy.

Soviet Culture

Soviet science, scholarship, literature, and arts did not stand outside the currents of Soviet history. The political drive to transform the country and its people, the traumas of civil war and world war, the dramatic shifts in policy, the idealism, and the repression were all reflected in Soviet culture. There was one constant, though: growing party control. Already in the first years after the October Revolution, Bolshevik cultural leaders were insisting that science, literature, and the arts must to be "proletarian." While this often meant that priority was given to individuals of working-class backgrounds, "proletarian" was mainly understood in ideological terms as reflecting a properly understood Marxist point of view. In later years, the notion of *partiinost* (party-mindedness) served the same function. At the same time, the development of culture was valued as an essential part of socialist development. Thus, by the Stalin years, Soviet science, scholarship, literature, and the arts were well-funded, thoroughly organized, and closely tied to the policies of the party and the state. All Soviet intellectuals were in effect employed by the state. Even when their income depended primarily on royalties, their books could not be published nor their music played without official authorization. The quality of Soviet creative work varied enormously over time and by field. The experimentalism of the first years after the Revolution and of the early 1920s, the radicalism of the First Five-Year Plan, the conservative rigidities of the 1930s, the "thaw" of the late 1950s and early 1960s, and the growth of underground dissent in the Brezhnev years, all created different opportunities and constraints for creative thought. And different fields were more or less subject to the demands of doctrine. Thus it was easier to do excellent work in science or to compose original music than to write the best possible history or literature. Still, in almost all fields, fruitful as well as barren, the influence of the party and its ideology left its mark.

Science and Scholarship

For a variety of reasons, science was a privileged area of Soviet culture. It was obviously and immediately useful and, indeed, indispensable if the USSR were to become the military, technological, and economic leader of the world. It was fully endorsed by Marxism, which prided itself on its own allegedly scientific character. In fact, some writers have commented on an almost religious admiration of science and technology in the Soviet Union, an expression in part of the old revolutionary titanism and determination to transform the world. Yet science, while subject to the dialectic, lies on the whole outside Marxist doctrines, which concentrate on human society, and thus constituted a "safer" field in the Soviet Union than, for example, sociology or literature. Not that it escaped the party and the ideology altogether. Communist interference with science included such important instances as Soviet difficulties in accepting Einstein's "petty bourgeois" theories, as well as Trofim Lysenko's virtual destruction of Soviet biology, particularly genetics, together with the elimination of a number of leading Soviet biologists, notably Nicholas Vavilov. Lysenko, an agricultural expert and a dangerous quack and fanatic, claimed to have disproved the basic laws of heredity and obtained party support for his claims: Lysenko's theories gave Marxist environmentalism a new dimension and made a Communist transformation of the world seem more feasible than ever—the only trouble was that Lysenko's theories were false. But Einstein's views had to be accepted, at least for practical purposes; and even Soviet biology staged a comeback, although it took many years and several turns of fortune finally to dispose of Lysenko's authority. Moreover, thousands of scientists, in contrast, for example, to writers, could continue working in their fields more or less undisturbed. And science especially profited from the large-scale financing and organization of effort provided by the state.

The Sputniks, the shot at the moon, the photographing of the far side of the moon, and Soviet astronauts' orbiting of the earth, together with atomic and hydrogen explosions, have emphasized the achievements of Soviet applied science, and in particular Soviet rockets, missiles, and atomic and space technology.* In these fields, as in others, the Soviet Union profited from the prerevolutionary legacy, especially from the continuing work of such scholars as the pioneer in space travel Constantine Tsiolkovsky, 1857–1935. The contributions of espionage and of German scientists brought to the USSR after the Second World War are more difficult to assess. The state, of course, financed and promoted to the full all the extremely expensive technological programs referred to above. It also organized, in connection with the five-year plans, a great search for new natural resources, vast geographic expeditions, and other, similar projects. The work of Soviet scientists in the far north acquired special prominence. The Academy of Sciences continued to direct Soviet science as well as other branches of Soviet scholarship.

While Soviet applied science has received perhaps too much praise in the press of the world, the overall excellence of Soviet science has on the whole not yet been sufficiently appreciated. With theoretical physicists like Leo Landau, experimental physicists like Abraham Joffe and Peter Kapitza, chemists like Nicholas Semenov, mathematicians like Ivan Vinogradov, astronomers like Victor Ambartsumian, geochemists like Vladimir Vernadsky, and botanists like Vladimir Komarov—to select only a very few out of many names—the Soviet Union had outstanding scientific talent, while the scope of its scientific effort exceeded that of all other countries except the United States.

Soviet social sciences and humanities did not compare with the sciences. The dead hand of Soviet Marxism stifled virtually all growth in such fields as philosophy and sociology, although the 1920s, the "thaw" years, and, to a lesser extent, the later Brezhnev years, were more open to work that made gestures toward official ideology but was not entirely constrained by it. Official ideology itself, especially after the 1920s and before the brief Gorbachev era,

---

*Soviet "firsts" in space include: first earth satellite, Sputnik I, launched October 4, 1957; first satellite with animal aboard, Sputnik II, November 3, 1957; first moon rocket, Lunik I, January 2, 1959; first photographs of hidden side of moon, October 18, 1959; first retrieval of animal from orbit, August 20, 1960; first launching from orbit, Venus probe, February 12, 1961; first man in space, Lieut. Col. Iurii A. Gagarin, April 12, 1961; first double launching with humans, Major Andrian Nikolaev, August 11, 1961, Lieut Col. Pavel Popovich, August 12, 1962; first woman in space, Valentina Tereshkova, June 16, 1963; first triple-manned launching, Col. Vladimir Komarov, space commander, Konstantin Feoktistov, scientist, Dr. Boris Egorov, physiologist, October 12, 1964; first man to walk in cosmic space, Lieut. Col. Aleksei A. Leonov from Voskhod II (flight commander, Col. Pavel Beliaev) March 19, 1965; first flight around the moon and return of an automatic space craft, Zond 5, September 15–22, 1968; establishment of first orbital experimental station during flight of Soyuz 4 and Soyuz 5 spaceships, January 1969; first self-propelled automatic laboratory on the surface of the moon, Lunokhod-1, November 17, 1970; first manned research station, Salyut, in circumterrestrial orbit, June 7, 1971; first soft landing on the surface of Mars and transmission of video signal to Earth by Mars-3 probe, December 2, 1971; first soft landing on the sunward surface of Venus by Venera-8 probe and transmission to Earth of atmospheric and surface measurements for 50 minutes, July 22, 1972. The Soviet Union also announced the first loss of a man in actual space flight, Col. Vladimir Komarov, Soyuz 1, April 24, 1967.

proved to be remarkably barren, with the result that even Marxist thought in the USSR was crude and undeveloped compared to certain Western and satellite varieties.

In history, until the early and middle thirties Mikhail Pokrovsky's negativistic school held sway. A convinced Marxist, Pokrovsky took an extremely critical and bitter view of the Russian past, in effect declaring it of no importance. With the Soviet consolidation and turn to cultural conservatism in the thirties, Pokrovsky and his school were denounced, and the authorities began to promote intense work in the field of history and in such related disciplines as archaeology. In particular, Soviet historians turned to collecting and editing sources. Some valuable work was also done in social and economic history, with at least one Soviet historian, Boris Grekov, originally a prerevolutionary specialist, making contributions of the first rank. Yet in general, in spite of the change in the thirties and a certain further liberalization following Stalin's death, Soviet historiography suffered enormously from the party strait jacket, most especially in such fields as intellectual history and international relations.

Linguistic studies followed a somewhat different pattern. There Nicholas Marr, 1864–1934, an outstanding scholar of Caucasian languages who apparently fell prisoner to some weird theories of his own invention, played the same sad role that Trofim Lysenko had played in biology. Endorsed by the party, Marr's strange views almost destroyed philology and linguistics in the Soviet Union, denying as they did the established families of languages in favor of a ubiquitous and multiform evolution of four basic sounds. The new doctrine seemed Marxist because it related, or at least could relate, different families of languages to different stages of the material development of a people, but its implications proved so confusing and even dangerous that Stalin himself turned against the Marr school in 1950, much to the relief and benefit of Soviet scholarship.

Most areas of Soviet scholarship, however, profited much more by Stalin's death than by his dicta. From the spring of 1953, Soviet scholars enjoyed more contact with the outside world and somewhat greater freedom in their own work. In particular, they no longer had to praise Stalin at every turn, prove that most things were invented first by Russians, or deny Western influences in Russia—as they had had to do in the worst days of Zhdanov. Entire disciplines or sub-disciplines, such as cybernetics and certain kinds of economic analysis, were eventually permitted and even promoted. Yet, while some of the excesses of Stalinism were gone, compulsory Marxism-Leninism and *partiinost* remained. Soviet assertions that their scholars were free retained a hollow— and indeed tragic—ring. Glasnost, to be sure, represented a real breakthrough into honest scholarship, but it could not immediately eliminate all institutional, psychological, and material obstacles to it.

Literature and the Arts

Like other educated Russians, writers and artists responded to the Communist revolution differently. A large number felt like outsiders in the new Russia. Socially, most were from the despised upper classes. Politically, most had been vaguely liberal or quite apolitical. And as artists, many felt aesthetically alienated from the new proletarian standards for culture. As a result, many fled Soviet Russia, frequently enriching European and American culture. But many artists and writers remained. The least political tried to ignore the new order—to create art outside official channels, to write or paint for art's sake alone, and for oneself and one's friends. Other writers and artists sought to be part of the revolution, as they understood it, to produce "revolutionary" art and literature. It helped that in the early years the Soviet government tolerated a variety of artistic currents and positively encouraged avant-garde artists. Many received paid government positions as cultural officials. More commonly, writers and artists benefited from a state that provided subsidies, studio space, and publishing and exhibition opportunities. This attachment to the cause of the party and the state, however, and this dependence on official aid, would soon prove to be increasingly constraining.

Literature in the early Soviet years continued in certain ways the trends of the "silver age," in spite of the heavy losses of the revolutionary and civil war years and the large-scale emigration of intellectuals. Symbolists like Blok and Bely and acmeists like Mandelshtam and Akhmatova continued publishing excellent poetry and developing their work in new directions. Futurists like Mayakovsky crafted modernist odes to the revolution. And many brilliant new writers emerged, often elaborating on prerevolutionary traditions. Important authors whose first major works appeared after 1917 (though some had begun publishing just before the revolution) included Isaac Babel, Mikhail Bulgakov, Iurii Olesha, Boris Pasternak, Boris Pilnyak, Andrei Platonov, Evgeny Zamiatin, and Mikhail Zoshchenko. Formalist criticism rose and flourished, as did the highly original work of the literary critic and language theorist Mikhail Bakhtin. Non-Communist writers created numerous groups and movements, tolerated by the party as "fellow travelers," a term coined to denote non-proletarian or non-revolutionary writers who were willing to accept Soviet power and work constructively within the socialist order. At the same time, organizations of "left" or "proletarian" authors competed for influence and state support. Starting in 1918 and continuing through the 1920s, the Proletcult established studios to promote literary and artistic creativity among workers. Proletcult leaders insisted on creating a pure, class art. In practice, however, workers in the studios often studied with such non-proletarian writers as Bely and Briusov, and many worker writers developed quite distinctive and heterodox voices (to the great dismay of Proletcult leaders). Among professional "proletarian" writers, conflicts over literary style and content (for example, was lyricism and inwardness tolerable?) and over party policy produced a whole series of proletarian writers organizations, beginning in 1920 with the All-Union Association of Proletarian Writers (VAPP) and ending during the First Five-Year Plan with the militant Russian Association of Proletarian Writers (RAPP), which often viciously condemned the existence of all approaches but their own. Until the late 1920s, in part due to the influence of Anatoly Lunacharsky, the Commissar of Enlightenment until 1929, diverse approaches were tolerated. Even RAPP's demands for proletarian hegemony were largely ignored.

Signs of trouble were already looming in the late 1920s. The voices of orthodox Marxist critics of deviant literary trends were become more shrill and influential. A number of suicides could be read as marks of disillusionment or even protest. The celebrated "peasant" poet Sergei Esenin hanged himself in 1925, writing that "there's nothing new in dying/But living is no newer," and the leftist Mayakovsky took his own life in 1930, observing in a last poem that he had been made to "step on the throat of my own song." But the greater change came in 1932, when all literary groupings were abolished, along with all independent publishing houses and journals, replaced by a single Union of Soviet Writers. In 1934, at the first All-Union Congress of Soviet Writers, party leaders proclaimed that there was only one correct approach in literature: "socialist realism." In effect, Soviet literature now literally became an organ of the government and writers employees of the state. Members of the Writers' Union enjoyed secure incomes and potential privileges but were required to write according to official standards. And when writings did not conform, or when standards changed, authors had to be ready to rewrite the offending texts. Many writers—including Akhmatova, Mandelshtam, Pasternak, Olesha, Babel, and Bulgakov—withdrew into public literary silence.

Socialist realism was officially defined in 1934 as "the truthful, historically concrete depiction of reality in its revolutionary development," with the caveat that "the truthfulness and historical concreteness of the artistic depiction of reality must be combined with the task of ideologically remolding and edu-cating the working people in the spirit of socialism." Other doctrinal notions were soon added. Literature, it was said, must by guided by *partiinost* (accord with the policies of the party), *ideinost* (being inspired by lofty ideas and prin-ciples), and *narodnost* (being comprehensible to ordinary people—the *narod*—and serving their needs). Sufficiently vague in theory, socialist realism often meant in practice that Stalin and his associates dictated proper literary form and content. Indeed, writers were urged to study Stalin's works for inspiration. The result was a flood of novels, stories, poems, and plays, as well as movies (a genre much valued by the party for its propaganda value), idealizing Soviet life, portraying the Russian past in a patriotic light, glorifying individual hero-ism (in the revolution, in production, in history), and highlighting the high ide-alism of the new Soviet man and woman. The socialist realist hero was always a paragon of both moral and physical beauty, with no fundamental inner con-flicts and no psychological ambiguities. Instead of the grim world around them, authors were urged to see things as they should appear and will appear in the future. Pessimism was banned.

Not surprisingly, in terms of artistic quality the results of "socialist realism" have been appalling. After Gorky's death in 1936—a death arranged by Stalin, according to some specialists—no writer of comparable stature rose in Soviet letters. A few gifted men, such as Alexis N. Tolstoy, 1883–1945, the author of popular historical and contemporary novels, and Michael Sholokhov, 1905–1984, who wrote the novels *The Quiet Don* and *Virgin Soil Upturned*, describing Don cossacks in civil war and collectivization, managed to produce good works more or less in line with the requirements of the regime, although they too had to revise their writings from edition to edition to meet changing party demands. Other talented writers, for instance, Iurii Olesha, failed on the whole to adjust to "socialist realism." Soviet poetry, especially hampered by the injunction to be simple and easy to understand, as well as socialist and realist, proved to be inferior even to Soviet prose. The government no doubt contributed more to the enjoyment of its readers by publishing on a large scale the Russian classics and world classics in translation.

In the post-Stalin years, the Writers' Union continued to insist on the socialist realist principles of *partinost, ideinost,* and *narodnost,* though greater flexibility was allowed. Forbidden themes such as Stalin's purges and labor camps were briefly allowed. And greater objectivity was accepted in writing about everyday Soviet life. Literary critics openly admitted that much socialist realist literature was emotionally shallow and false. Still, strong limits remained in place. For example, when Pasternak was offered the Nobel prize in 1958 for his novel, *Doctor Zhivago* (completed in 1955), which was rejected for publication in the Soviet Union but was published abroad to great acclaim, he was forbidden to travel abroad to accept the prize and was excoriated in the Soviet press for the novel's ideologically incorrect perspective on the Soviet past. The post-Khrushchev years saw increasing demands to depict Soviet achievements, but also increasing variety and even subtle deviance. Many writers avoided heroic topics to focus on the complexities of everyday human relationships. The "village prose" school of writers offered readers more realistic portraits of the hardships of rural life that emphasized traditional values such as closeness to nature, simplicity, and moral decency. We see a similar emphasis on individual experience and feelings in the songs of popular bards like Vladimir Vysotsky and Bulat Okudzhava. While classic socialist realism continued to be produced, studies of readers' tastes make it clear that most Soviet readers preferred books about individuals, feelings, and relationships to accounts of heroic labor or revolutionary devotion. Works about the war, crime and detection, and espionage were especially popular. The limits of tolerance were regularly reasserted, however. For example, Alexander Solzhenitsyn, whose story about the forced labor camps, *One Day in the Life of Ivan Denisovich* (published in 1962 with Khrushchev's direct approval), one of the hallmarks of the literature of the "thaw," was forbidden after 1965 to publish anything. All of his later works were published abroad and smuggled back into the Soviet Union. In 1969, he was expelled from the Writers' Union and in 1973 he was expelled from the USSR. The poet Joseph Brodsky, whose works, publishable only in the West or in *samizdat,* are pervaded by sadness and nostalgia derived from contemplating the human condition, was sentenced to five years' hard labor in 1964 (released after a year in the face of protests by Russian authors and the world) and forced to leave the Soviet Union in 1972. Many writers similarly found themselves forbidden to publish or even on trial for sedition. In fact, much of the best Russian literature in the Soviet era had been written abroad. Some of the outstanding expatriate authors of the "first wave" of emigration were the novelist, story writer, and poet Ivan Bunin and the highly original prose writer with a unique style, Alexis Remizov, who both died in Paris, in 1953 and 1957, respectively. Some émigré Russian writers, notably the novelist Vladimir Nabokov and later the poet Brodsky, wrote influential works in English or other languages. In recent years, especially since the fall of communism, émigré literature had been reclaimed as an essential part of the whole of Russian literature.

The Soviet record in the arts paralleled that in literature. Again, the first postrevolutionary decade was linked closely to the silver age and to contemporary trends in the West. Most of the artists who embraced the Revolution viewed it as essentially about freedom and possibility, often expressed artistically in art fully freed from the conventions ("bourgeois conventions") of representational art. Many artists insisted that revolutionary art had to be useful to the revolution as well. "Art into Life!" became a popular slogan. Artists designed monuments and festival decorations for public squares, clothing, books, and other objects, using the most modern designs. As a rule, whatever the style adopted—and in the first Soviet decade diverse styles thrived, ranging from Kazimir Malevich's transcendental abstractions to Marc Chagall's nostalgic and magical portraits to Vladimir Tatlin's fantastic constructions to traditional paintings of revolutionary leaders and events—imagination thrived. The same applied to architecture in these early years, in which revolutionary visions of flying cities and towering iron skyscrapers with revolving glass interiors (which could not be built) coexisted with modernist functionalism (which did produce a number of lasting buildings). However, once "socialist realism" established its hold on Soviet culture, arts in the Soviet Union acquired a most conservative and indeed antiquated character. Impressive in quantity and interesting to analyze as evidence of an ideology, Stalin-era realistic painting and sculpture are essentially worthless in quality, being in general poor imitations of a bygone style. Paintings of happy peasants and workers, and of Stalin and other heroic and virtuous leaders, all painted in sunny colors, predominated. Soviet architecture also traveled the sad road from inspired and novel creations in the earlier period of Communist rule to heavily ornamented apartment and office buildings, grand boulevards and squares suitable for parades that replaced old neighborhoods and churches, the traditionalist mosaics and chandeliers of the Moscow metro, and the famously tasteless and contrived Moscow skyscrapers of Stalin's declining years. Music was somewhat more fortunate, both because of its greater distance from Marxist and "realistic" injunctions—which nevertheless did not prevent the party from attacking "formalism" and modernism in music and from tyrannizing in that field—and, perhaps, because of the accident of talent. In any case, the one-time figure of the "silver age" and émigré Serge Prokofiev, 1891–1953, the creator of such well-known pieces as the *Classical Symphony* and *Peter and the Wolf*, and Dmitrii Shostakovich, 1906–75, together with a few other composers, managed to produce works of lasting value in spite of ideological obstacles.

Short on creativity and development, certain Soviet arts were long on execution and performance. Again, the high standards were continuations from tsarist days, aided by increased state subsidies and by the fact that schooling and culture spread to more people. Soviet musicians performed brilliantly on many instruments, both at international competitions in the thirties, and again in later years when the best among them, such as the violinist David Oistrakh and the pianists Sviatoslav Richter and Emil Gilels, were allowed to tour the

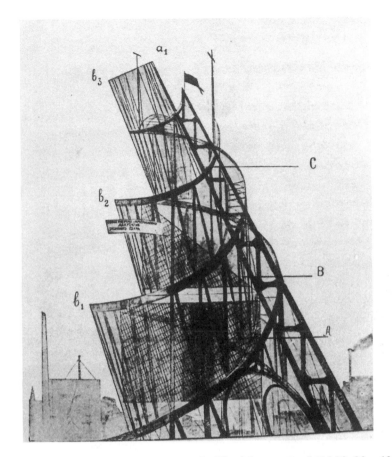

Vladimir Tatlin's design for a Monument to the Third International, 1919–20. Although never built, Tatlin's utopian design for a headquarters for the Communist International was a massive symbol of revolutionary modernism. Envisioned as the tallest man-made structure in the world, its spiral iron structure was to contain interior halls made of glass, each above the other and rotating in harmony with nature: a bottom cube revolving on its axis once a year, a cone making a full circle monthly, and a top cylinder making one revolution each day. The building was to provide meeting space, offices, and a communications center. (Punin, Pamiatnik III Internatsionala)

world. The ballet, while in a sense stagnant—the clock having stopped for most purposes in 1917—continued to dance beautifully and was apparently backed by more funds and a better system of schools and selection than in any other country. Nonetheless, the rigid traditionalism of Russian ballet (along with the many other restrictions in Soviet life) led some of its best dancers to defect to the West, notably Rudolf Nureyev in 1961 and Mikhail Baryshnikov in 1974. The Moscow Art Theater remained one of the most remarkable centers of acting anywhere, although unfortunately its school of acting had for a long time a monopoly in the Soviet Union, all other approaches to acting and the theater having been proscribed. Good acting also characterized many Soviet films. In fact the Soviet cinema continued to be creative longer than other

Moscow State University. Built after the war on the Lenin hills, the university was one of a series of towers in Moscow built in a style sometimes called "Stalinist gothic." Classical columns, large exterior ornaments, grand entryways, and marble interiors decorated with chandeliers in the main public spaces were characteristic of these buildings, which were meant to convey the grandeur and power of socialism. (World Wide Photos)

Soviet arts—in part probably because it had no nineteenth-century tradition in the image of which it could be conveniently frozen. Soviet film directors included at least one great figure, Serge Eisenstein, 1898–1948, as well as other men of outstanding ability. More popular, however, were Grigory Alexandrov's happy musical comedy films of the 1930s.

With the coming of the "thaw" after Stalin's death, and the development of a dissident movement, alternative artistic approaches again surfaced, sometimes tolerated but often criticized and forbidden public display—as in 1962, when Khrushchev visited an exhibit of modern art in Moscow only to mock it with crude humor, and especially in 1974 when bulldozers were sent to destroy an informal exhibit in a park outside Moscow. Unofficial art differed from the dictates of party ideology in almost every respect: it might be melancholy and even pessimistic in mood (with dark colors predominant), hint at religious belief or suggest existential doubt, favor abstraction or symbolism over representational realism, or be subtly ironic. In theater, as well, innovation and iconoclasm thrived, though less on the main official stages than in smaller theaters such as Yury Liubimov's Taganka in Moscow and the many informal "studio-theaters." Although effectively marginalized, these non-conformist artistic currents were among the many signs of growing alienation, especially among the educated, from official ideology.

Religion

Religion in the Soviet Union constituted an anomaly, a threat, and a challenge from the Communist point of view. Bolshevik efforts to "modernize" Russia necessarily meant, as they saw it, replacing the superstition, mysticism, and fictions of religion with a scientific worldview. Initially, this campaign was directed mainly against the Orthodox Church as an institution. Immediately after coming to power, the Bolsheviks disestablished the Orthodox Church, which had been closely linked to the imperial regime, ended financial support for the Church, confiscated vast amounts of property, and transferred control of thousands of parish schools to the state. During the Civil War, revolutionaries frequently arrested and sometimes summarily executed priests and monks, confiscated or destroyed sacramental objects, and closed many churches and monasteries. Once victorious in the Civil War, the government moved even more vigorously, if less violently, against the Church. The government ordered the seizure of all Church valuables, temporarily imprisoned Patriarch Tikhon (elected by a Church council in 1918 to resume the patriarchal form of ecclesiastical organization that had been discontinued by Peter the Great), tried to break up the Church from within by assisting a modernist "Renovationist" or "Living Church" group within it, and began to assault popular religious belief directly through a "militant atheist" movement. After Tikhon's death in 1925, the government prevented any new patriarch being elected and Church leadership fell to provisional appointees. Although atheism indeed grew in the Soviet Union, this anti-religious movement was far from successful. Attacks on the Church often inspired resistance and solidarity with Church and clergy and local efforts to ensure that religion thrived even without state support. Also, the disestablishment of the Orthodox Church enabled "sectarian" Christian faiths to thrive as well as other religions. More generally, in the turmoil and uncertainties of these revolutionary years, faith and spirituality flourished as a source of meaning and hope. During the radical upheavals of the First Five-Year Plan and during the bloody terror of the late 1930s, persecution of religion was particularly intense. However, the assumption that severely restricting religious institutions and promoting rationalist thought would lead religion to disappear proved vain. According to an official report based on the unpublished census of 1936, 55 percent of Soviet citizens still identified themselves as religious—while many others presumably concealed their belief.

That stubborn fact in conjunction with the general social stabilization of the thirties made Stalin and the Politburo assume a more tolerant attitude toward religion. The war and the patriotic behavior of the Church in the war added to its acceptance and standing. In 1943 the Church was permitted to elect a patriarch, the statesmanlike Metropolitan Sergius obtaining that position. After his death in 1945, Sergius was succeeded by Alexis, who continued as "Patriarch of Moscow and All Russia" for a quarter of a century. In 1971, following Alexis's death, Pimen was elected patriarch, followed in 1990 by Alexis

The seventeenth-century Simeon Stolpnik church on Moscow's Kalinin Prospect in front of a Soviet housing project. Huge numbers of churches in Russia were shut down and often demolished. Some churches continued to function, but most of the church buildings that survived, such as this one, were put to secular uses as factories, warehouses, and museums or simply stood empty, their ritual objects removed and their walls whitewashed, but "protected by the state" as monuments of architecture. (Sovfoto)

II. The ecclesiastical authorities were also allowed to establish a few theological schools, required to prepare students for the priesthood, and to open a limited number of new churches. The activities of the League of the Militant Godless and anti-religious propaganda in general were curtailed. In return the patriarchal Church declared complete loyalty to the regime, and supported, for example, its international peace campaigns and its attempts to influence the Balkan Orthodox. More unfortunately, the two cooperated in bringing the two or three million Uniates of former eastern Poland into Orthodoxy. The Church in the USSR, however, remained restricted to strictly religious, rather than more general social and educational, functions—even the constitution proclaimed merely the freedom of religious confession, as against the freedom of anti-religious propaganda—and, while temporarily tolerated within limits, it remained a designated enemy of Marxist ideology and Communist society. In fact, Khrushchev especially, as well as his successors, increased the pressures against religion even when "liberalizing" other aspects of Soviet life. It should be added that other Soviet Christians, such as Baptists, and other religious groups, such as Jews and the numerous Muslims, shared their histories with the Orthodox. They, too, led a constricted and precarious existence within a fundamentally hostile system, profiting from relaxations when they occurred. Even before Gorbachev's policy of glasnost and the collapse of Communist rule enabled a new renaissance of religion in Russia, its revival in the growing unofficial space in everyday social and cultural life was another visible sign of the weakening hold of the Communist regime over people's lives. The 1970s and 1980s, in particular, saw a proliferation of religious prayer and study groups (Orthodox, Protestant, Jewish, and others), the rediscovery among young people of their family's religious traditions, and growing attendance at religious services. In this sense too, as Gorbachev worried aloud when he came to power in 1985, Communist rule in the Soviet Union was facing a "spiritual crisis."

Chapter 42

The Gorbachev Years, 1985–91, and the Collapse of the Soviet Union

We want a type of socialism that has been cleansed of the encrusted layers and perversions of past eras but retains everything that is best from the founders of socialist teaching.... We see socialism as a system of high culture and morality...a society in which the life of working people is saturated with material and spiritual fulfillment, rejecting consumerism, lack of spirituality, and cultural primitiveness.

—GORBACHEV (1988)

The most perilous moment for a bad government is when it seeks to mend its ways. Only consummate statecraft can enable a king to save his throne when, after a long spell of oppressive rule, he sets to improving the lot of his subjects.

—DE TOCQUEVILLE

The river of time in its flow
Carries away all the works of human beings . . .
—DERZHAVIN

In the years leading to the collapse of the Soviet Union and Communist rule in 1991, no scholars predicted its imminent demise. Many Russians themselves in the 1980s were predicting that the Communist regime would last at least as long as the 300-year reign of the Romanov dynasty. As the preceding chapters have described, the system was pervaded by problems, both structural and in people's attitudes. But there was nothing inevitable about the outcome of this situation. As most Russians who lived through these years readily acknowledged, though variously with blame or appreciation, Mikhail Gorbachev was a primary cause of that historic collapse. To be sure, the Soviet leader was not in control of his country and its citizens, and, indeed, he had been repeatedly obtaining results opposite to those intended—after all, Nicholas II also made important contributions to the revolutions of 1917. And as many of our best specialists tell us, it is dangerous to personalize major historical issues, and another Gorbachev or still other lines of development would have produced similar results. But as long as history is an account of what happened and is happening rather than of the logical alternatives, the period of glasnost and perestroika will remain linked to its extraordinary protagonist, a contradictory man of intelligence, optimism, insatiable energy, intensity, and self-confidence, but a man also noted for his prudence and even conservatism, his glibness, and his remarkable political agility and adroitness in the face of the unexpected and often unwanted results of his own reforms. He was an obvious transitory figure who long refused to transit.

Gorbachev and Reform

Exactly what Gorbachev and his original associates, such as Eduard Shevard-nadze and Alexander Yakovlev, had in mind when they began reforming the Soviet Union may never become clear, even to them. Suppositions and explanations of their intent abound, but the overwhelming factors in what transpired appear to have been a sincere desire to address the Soviet Union's deepening problems, a persistent effort to balance transformation with traditional values and political stability, a gap between plans and real accomplishments, the dizzying power of contradictory forces unchained by even slight reform, and continual improvisation in the face of the unexpected. The unfolding events in the USSR and eastern Europe stunned everyone, especially those who had any regard for the communist system, and that includes by definition the entire Soviet leadership. There may well be, however, one quite major exception to this almost total disjunction between purpose and accomplishment. Gorbachev, Shevardnadze especially, and other prominent Soviet figures insisted that one of the pillars of their new thinking was the absolute realization of the inadmissibility of nuclear war in human affairs and, therefore, of the necessity for at least a minimum of international cooperation, in particular between the Soviet Union and the United States. With all qualifications, it can be argued that Soviet foreign policy came to reflect that realization. If so, the gain to the world was incalculable, although the realization itself is elementary and its roots even in the Soviet Union largely preceded Gorbachev. Otherwise, one hardly needs reminding that in his book *Perestroika*—published in English as well as in Russian in October 1987 and a good way to become acquainted with its author—and even later Gorbachev emphasized the supreme importance of Lenin and the Communist Party in the Soviet Union, rejected privatization and political pluralism in communist states, and praised Soviet solutions to social and nationality problems. And it should be remembered that the Warsaw Pact was renewed and extended for twenty years on April 26, 1985; it was abolished following the complete collapse of communism in eastern Europe on February 25, 1991. The river of time does carry away the works of human beings.

At the foundation of Gorbachev's reform lay the recognition that the Soviet Union was facing a crisis. Slowing rates of economic growth combined with growing disillusionment and pessimism. When Mikhail Gorbachev was named general secretary, his mandate was to address this crisis, first by admitting it publicly. The government and the party spoke openly about economic problems: the slowing of economic growth, the negative effects on the standard of living, the dismal condition of agriculture, the poor quality of manufactured products, the failure to keep up with world developments in science and technology (including computing), and the huge proportion of the gross national product devoured by military needs (more than twice the percentage in the United States). Recognition of deepening "stagnation"—the term widely used to speak of the 1970s and early 1980s—was matched by recognition of the cultural and ideological crisis of these years. Gorbachev and other party leaders acknowledged the widespread withdrawal from public life, the spread of alcoholism and drug addiction, the growth of crime, "weakened respect for work," pessimism, and cynicism. In a word, Gorbachev pronounced, the Soviet Union was facing a "spiritual crisis" (*dukhovnyi krizis*) along with an economic one, and it needed structural and spiritual reconstruction (perestroika).

Gorbachev's actions—which had such profound consequences for history—were also shaped by a fairly well developed set of ideological beliefs, evident in his many speeches as he rose through the ranks as Komsomol activist, party chief in the Stavropol region near the Caucasus, young new recruit to the Politburo, and then general secretary. Most important, Gorbachev believed strongly in the ideals of Leninist socialism, so much so that he found it difficult to accept the widespread cynicism he found throughout much of Soviet life, including in the party, not to mention the very tangible decline of Soviet society. Often echoing Lenin's statements during the first Soviet years (the Lenin Gorbachev most admired), Gorbachev argued that the country could be revitalized through a combination of "democratization" and an improved vanguard. Democratization was key to revitalizing the economy and people's faith in the socialist system. Thus, Gorbachev constantly appealed to citizens to become more involved in public life and to take more initiative. At the same time, he also believed, following Lenin as well as a longer Russian political tradition, that strong central authority was essential in times of change. For both democracy and strong power to be effective, however, certain qualities were necessary. Strong power is of no use, he insisted, if leaders are not of the highest quality, are not a true vanguard. Thus, even before he came to power, he fought to improve the behavior of local leaders, to eradicate what he called bureaucratic boorishness, self-satisfaction, red-tapeism (*volokita*), inertia, careerism, and incompetence. In turn, for socialist democracy, in all of its potential dynamism, to work, ordinary people must also rid themselves of the sins of passivity, irresponsibility, indiscipline, drunkenness, acquisitiveness, materialism, and cultural vulgarity (*poshlost*).

For Gorbachev, these were practical ideas. If economic stagnation was to be overcome, citizens and leaders alike would have to play a more active, committed, and responsible role in the country's development. Democracy, Gorbachev liked to say, "must not be understood abstractly" but as "an instrument for the development of the economy" (1985). But there were also deeper moral notions at work in Gorbachev's thinking about democracy and reform. His language, as can be seen, was full of disgust for undisciplined and irresponsible behavior. Personally, we know, Gorbachev was exceptionally hard working and refused to drink hard liquor. More complexly, Gorbachev's moralism was ideological. When speaking of socialism he often spoke of its essential "humanism," its commitment to seeking the fullest development of the "human person" (*lichnost*), its defense and promotion of "universal human values." These were clichés in Soviet ideology, though the emphasis on universal as opposed to class values was not entirely orthodox. More to the point, every indication is that Gorbachev took these clichés quite seriously and sought to make them real.

The first two or three years of the Gorbachev regime, inaugurated on March 11, 1985, displayed a fairly "traditional" cast. The new party secretary, then the youngest man in the Politburo, had to concentrate on strengthening his position, and, indeed, over a period of time he effected a major turnover of ruling and high administrative personnel. Thus on July 1, 1985, Shevardnadze became a member of the Politburo, and on the following day he was appointed foreign minister, replacing Andrei Gromyko, who was moved to a more ceremonial high office. Other new men entered the Politburo, while Victor Grishin, Gorbachev's original rival for the position of party secretary, retired. These reorganizations of leadership notwithstanding, Gorbachev continued in the coming years to face opposition in the Central Committee and the Politburo: from "puritans" such as Yegor Ligachev, whose interest in reform was limited to ending the corruption of the Brezhnev era, to "technocrats" like Prime Minister Nikolai Ryzhkov, who sought only more scientific expertise and rational procedures in Soviet administrative and economic life, to radicals like Boris Yeltsin who were increasingly disillusioned with Gorbachev's hesitations (which were partly a function of a desire to avoid a split in the ruling party).

In fact, while Gorbachev's early talk about the need for reform was relatively bold, actual policy was cautious and relatively traditional. Some have suggested he was biding his time until his power base was strong enough. Others argue he was responding to his growing knowledge of the depth of the problems and the failure of his earliest measures. In any case, from March 1985 to the fall of 1986, his policies were quite similar to the proposals and exhortations of earlier Soviet reformers. The draft plan, as presented by Gorbachev in October 1985, called for doubling the national income in fifteen years, with special emphasis on the modernization of equipment and an increase in labor productivity. This was to be realized by an economic policy of "acceleration," which involved a major campaign against alcoholism, a struggle against absenteeism, increased pressure on managers to economize on materials and balance their books, and an anti-corruption campaign. As the months passed, Gorbachev began to talk of more radical change. At the Twenty-Seventh Party Congress in February 1986, he first used the phrase "radical reform," and in July he spoke of perestroika as a "real revolution." But this radicalism remained mainly rhetorical. The policies of glasnost, in these early months, were closely linked to economic acceleration. Allowing greater freedom of criticism in print and speech, though an important policy shift, was treated not as an end in itself but as a way to expose incompetent and corrupt managers or bureaucrats and to begin mobilizing society to participate in developing the economy. Similarly, in foreign policy, Gorbachev combined talk of improving relations with the Western powers, developing more respectful relations with other Communist countries, and acknowledging that the war in Afghanistan was a disaster (an "oozing sore," he called it in 1986) with continued criticism of "U.S. imperialism."

Unfortunately, almost none of Gorbachev's initial effects made any difference. The economy would not respond to mere exhortations. Indeed, the government's own economic, especially financial, policies led to budget deficits and inflation and thus made matters worse. Even the anti-alcohol campaign proved to be a disaster, its only incontrovertible result a great increase in the illegal production of spirits, to the extent that sugar disappeared from stores in parts of the USSR. Before long under the new administration and its vacillating and confusing direction, the economy began to lose what cohesion it had had under Brezhnev without gaining anything to replace it. The war in Afghanistan continued to take its toll. On April 28, 1986, a nuclear reactor exploded in Chernobyl; the resulting medical and environmental catastrophe threw a glaring light on multiple Soviet deficiencies, from those in engineering to those in the news media. Indeed, that tragic episode, treated at first in the firm tradition of Stalinist secrecy, eventually became both an opening into a more radical glasnost and a strong argument in its favor.

In 1986 and 1987, Gorbachev's policies became more radical—though opposition to his reforms within the party leadership also began to grow as did pressures from Communists like Boris Yeltsin who wanted reform to go faster and farther. The meaning of glasnost expanded. In late 1986, Gorbachev made it clear that censorship would be relaxed and journals would be given much greater freedom to criticize and offer solutions to problems. Reform-minded

Leaders of the communist world in Moscow, 1986. From left: Kadar of Hungary, Ceausescu of Romania, Honecker of East Germany, Gorbachev of the Soviet Union, Chinh of Vietnam, Jaruzelski of Poland, Castro of Cuba, Zhivkov of Bulgaria, Husak of Czechoslovakia, Tsedenbal of Mongolia.   (World Wide Photos)

editors were put at the helm of leading publications and journals began discussing political and social problems, past and present, as never before. Newly daring and previously banned works of literature and history were published. Movies with critical social perspectives were shown. Political prisoners were released—especially after the definition of anti-Soviet propaganda was greatly narrowed in a 1987 law—and dissident exiles like Andrei Sakharov (forced to live in isolation in the city of Gorky) were allowed to return home and be active in politics. Gorbachev and his allies also openly encouraged Soviet citizens to form voluntary civic associations, called "informals." In the economy, in 1987, directors of enterprises were given greater autonomy in setting prices, wages, and output targets, thus beginning a turn away from centralized planning. Laws on "individual labor activity" (1986) and cooperatives (1988) resulted in the emergence of the first private businesses since the 1920s, usually small service enterprises like cafes, but also distribution companies and even a few private banks. These new entrepreneurs, many of whom would make great fortunes after 1991, were mainly individuals already having access to material and political resources, which meant primarily officials of the state and the party. "Joint-ventures" with foreign firms were also authorized. Gorbachev insisted that these changes were consistent with "the socialist choice" the Soviet Union had made and would adhere to, though this was to be a middle ground between the failed system of planned Communist economics and the exploitative economics of capitalism. These measures also created opportunities for corrupt officials and organized crime to extort money from this emerging, but still fragile, private sector.

Political reform followed an even bolder course beginning with the dramatic Nineteenth Party Conference in June 1988. The entire meeting was televised—an unprecedented level of openness and publicity for the party. Speeches detailed the worsening economic conditions in the country, the problems in education and health care, the past lies about achievements, and some of the crimes of the past. Divisions in the party also became clear, as conservatives castigated the press for excessive criticism and radicals like Yeltsin attacked the continuing privileges of the old party elite who, he said, were to blame for many of the country's problems. The most dramatic moment came when Gorbachev announced his plan to create a new national parliamentary body, the Congress of People's Deputies, to be chosen in part through multi-candidate elections, which would be the "supreme body of power." The old Supreme Soviet would be made into a smaller, full-time legislative body elected by the Congress. This was the beginning of a process, it seemed, of shifting power away from the often distrustful and divided party and toward a reformed state. This shift continued during the next couple of years, though not all of it was controlled. The elections to the new Congress in March 1989 saw unprecedented public mobilization and many official party candidates defeated, including by mavericks like Yeltsin. In 1990, to link his own power more to the reformed state than to the troublesome party, Gorbachev created the new post of president of the USSR, to which the Congress of People's Deputies elected him in March 1990. At the same time, Article 6 of the Constitution, which made the Communist Party the "leading and guiding force" throughout Soviet society and all Soviet organizations, was repealed at Gorbachev's suggestion, but also in response to great public pressure. Gorbachev was even, by 1989, distancing himself from one of the hallmarks of Leninist ideology: the Communist monopoly on truth. "We no longer think that we are the best and that we are always right, and that those who disagree with us are our enemies."

This was not entirely a revolution from above nor an entirely coherent one. Gorbachev continually hesitated before more radical steps. Trying to maintain a centrist position, he vacillated between allying himself with party radicals and conservatives, eventually alienating both. In any case, the party was less and less in control of society. Reform was spinning out of Gorbachev's control, often forcing him to leap forward to keep up with the changes or leading him onto the defensive. The party's humiliation in the 1989 elections was a dramatic sign of this loss of control. The rise of nationalist and secessionist movements in the various republics, to be discussed later, was another. Finally, the public sphere of the press and even the streets became an arena of civic political activity such as had not been seen in Russia since the first years after the 1917 Revolution. Intellectuals, journalists, and literary writers were publishing increasingly bold works in which no issue or argument seemed taboo. Mass demonstrations in favor of greater reform were organized, especially in Moscow, often by "informal" democratic organizations such as the Democratic Union, the Moscow Popular Front, Memorial (formed to document past Communist crimes), and Democratic Russia (a national electoral bloc that

"We shall look at things realistically" declares this typical glasnost poster from 1987, which shows rose-colored glasses having been removed.   (Sovetskii khudozhnik)

would win many seats in the new parliament), but also by neo-communist organizations such as the Russian United Workers' Front. In 1989, thousands of coal miners struck, first demanding improved living conditions but soon escalating their demands to a new constitution and a ban on Communist Party activity in the workplace. Most dangerously, these years saw the revival of numerous nationalisms, suppressed but still alive in the Marxist superstate. The new time of troubles, like the original one at the end of the sixteenth century and the beginning of the seventeenth, was to have its national phase.

The Rise of Nationalisms and the Breakup of the Soviet Union

Because of the number, richness, variety, and specificity of ensuing developments, it is impossible to present in a brief general account an adequate summary of the rise of nationalism, or rather nationalisms, in the Soviet Union after centralized control was removed or even merely weakened. All fifteen constituent republics were radically affected. Moreover, many ethnic subdivisions within these republics and still other ethnic minorities also entered the fray. In line with the nature of nationalism, the relations of the participants were usually antagonistic, sometimes to the point of physical combat. It was illustrative of the many-sided struggle that Tskhinvali, the main town of the South Ossetian Autonomous Region within the Georgian Soviet Socialist Republic, came to be held one-third by the local Ossetian militia, one-third by Georgian nationalist forces, and one-third by the Soviet army. This treatment of the issue of nationalism in the Soviet Union is limited to mentioning a few highlights and suggesting certain emerging patterns.

Once Gorbachev loosened the bonds on public expression, it became clear that Soviet policies had not eradicated national identities and aspirations. At the same time, demands for greater autonomy were also often about local power and independence from the stifling Soviet state. Nationalism was not simply a revival of the past, a return of the repressed. For many Soviet citizens, alienated from the Soviet system and even from Gorbachev's idealistic promises to make Soviet socialism work, nationalism offered an alternative faith, and an alternative path to prosperity and freedom. Four types of national or ethnic upheaval arose in these last years of the Soviet Union: resistance by self-conscious national groups such as Lithuanians, Ukrainians, or Georgians to continued rule by the Soviet Russian imperial center; protests by ethnic minorities against the dominant nationalities in the union republics, as in the case of Armenians living in the Nagorno-Karabakh region of Azerbaijan; the rise of Russian nationalism or at least of a movement favoring Russian secession from the USSR; and the problem of diasporas living outside their ethnic homelands or lacking a territory of their own, including large numbers of Russians living outside the Russian republic who were facing national movements that excluded them.

In many respects, the three Baltic republics—Estonia, Latvia, and Lithuania—led the way. Independent states between the two world wars (and in the case of Lithuania, of course, in the much longer, richer, and more complex historical past), forced to join the Soviet Union only about fifty years ago, and possessed of their own languages and, on the whole, of a skilled and well-educated citizenry, the three republics, once self-expression became possible, made no doubt of their desire for independence. It was in Estonia that the first large-scale non-communist political coalition, the People's Front, received recognition, in June 1988, and it was Estonia that proclaimed on November 17, 1988, the right to reject Soviet laws when they infringed on its autonomy. On January 18, 1989, Estonian became the official language of the republic; legislation was enacted in an even more rigorous form a week later for the Lithuanian language in Lithuania, and still later, after mass demonstrations, for the Latvian language in Latvia. In May 1989, the Lithuanian legislature adopted a resolution seeking independence, and on August 22, 1989, it declared null and void the Soviet occupation and annexation of Lithuania in 1940. In early December 1989, Lithuania became the first republic to abolish the Communist Party's guaranteed monopoly of power, while later that month the Communist Party in Lithuania voted to break away from Moscow, thus becoming the first local and independent Communist Party in the USSR, and to endorse political separation. On March 11, 1990, Lithuania, led by its president, Vytautas Landsbergis, proclaimed full independence. Events in Estonia and Latvia followed a similar course. It is worth noting that whereas Lithuanians constituted at least three-quarters of the total population of their republic, Latvians and Estonians composed only a little more than half of theirs, and that all three new states tended toward rather exclusive policies that mandated a single official language and, for citizenship, a residential or familial connection with the pre-Soviet period to eliminate Russian newcomers. Yet in spite of the resulting built-in opposition, which claimed discrimination, in February 1991, 91 percent of the voters in Lithuania approved independence; in March, referendums in Estonia and Latvia gave independence a three to one majority—clearly, not only the Balts, but also many Russians and people of still other ethnic backgrounds wanted above all to escape the Soviet system.

Gorbachev drastically underestimated the power of nationalism in the Baltic area, as well as elsewhere, and at first tried to ignore or dismiss the demands for recognition and independence. Once the crisis became obvious, he attempted persuasion, political maneuvering with the many elements involved, including different kinds of communists, and coercion, although never to the extent of mass military repression. Thus on January 11, 1990, he went to Vilnius, the capital of Lithuania, hoping to convince both leaders and milling crowds to check the nationalist course of development, but his trip was in vain. More successful was the oil blockade, a great reduction in the supply of oil to Lithuania, which began in mid-April 1990 and forced the republic to suspend, although not repeal, its declaration of independence on May 16. More violent coercion consisted of such incidents as army intervention in Vilnius, resulting in the death of fourteen people, and the assault by Black Berets on a Latvian government ministry building in Riga, both in January 1991—aborted coups d'état in the opinion of some—as well as repeated attacks on border posts and customs personnel of the nationalist republics, the signs of their new independence. The perpetrators included special army forces, such as the Black Berets, and perhaps some paramilitary groups, as in the case of seven

Lithuanian customs and police officers killed on July 31, 1991. Officially, all these violent acts were labeled local incidents or transgressions; Gorbachev, in particular, denied any complicity. In fact, he emphasized that he objected to the manner of procedure of the Baltic republics, not to their goal of independence, which could be legitimately obtained in time, although personally he retained the hope that they would decide to remain in the new Soviet Union.

While nationalisms developed in a parallel and even cooperative way in the Baltic area, they were from the start on a collision course in Transcaucasia. Of the three Soviet republics beyond the great Caucasian mountain range—Armenia, Georgia, and Azerbaijan—the first two represent two of the oldest yet entirely distinct peoples and cultures of the world. With their histories antedating Christianity by far, the Georgians and the Armenians also built Christian states and cultures centuries before the vaunted conversion of the Rus in A.D. 988. The Georgians are Orthodox; the Armenians are Eastern Christians but not Orthodox. Becoming part of the Russian Empire when it finally reached them in the early nineteenth century may have been important, even essential, for their survival in the face of hostile Muslim Turks and Persians, now Iranians. (Very few Armenians who remained in Turkey survived.) Yet if the Baltic republics kept referring to 1940 as the crucial year when Soviet power crushed their independence, the Georgians focused on 1918, when, following the Russian revolutions of 1917, they created an independent Menshevik-led state, only to be overcome after three years by the Red Army. Azerbaijan, not a distinct historical entity, represented the Turkic element so prominent in the past and present life of the area; its inhabitants are historically Muslim and are closely related to other Turkic speakers in the USSR from the Volga to the Chinese border, especially in four of the five Soviet Central Asian republics, as well as to Turks abroad.

The Georgian revolution had its central event, a Georgian "Bloody Sunday." On April 9, 1989, the particularly brutal suppression of a nationalist demonstration in Tbilisi led to the death of 20 participants and the injury of more than 200. Although authorities in Moscow blamed local officials and started an investigation, communist control could not in effect be restored. The local party, which, as in Lithuania, tried to play an independent role, lost the crucial ensuing election, and Georgia emerged with a noncommunist government headed by Zviad Gamsakhurdia. On April 1, 1991, Georgians responded to the question of whether they agreed "that the state independence of Georgia should be restored on the basis of the independence act of May 26, 1918," with a turnout, according to official sources, of 90.53 percent of the 3.4 million Georgian voters and the affirmative reply of 98.93 percent of them. Whatever their exact political future, Georgians, like the Baltic peoples, definitely wanted to live outside the Soviet Union. In the summer of 1991, there even existed widespread interest in restoring the ancient Georgian monarchy, although in a modern constitutional form, in the person of Georgii II Bagration, presently living in Spain but invited by President Gamsakhurdia and the parliament to visit Georgia. Yet in Georgia, too, nationalism brought no easy solutions. In particular, while asserting their own rights, Georgians did their best to limit and control those of the constituent minority groups in their state—the

Adzharians, the Abkhazians, and perhaps especially the Ossetians—sometimes to the point of fighting on a considerable scale.

But the most extensive fighting in Transcaucasia, and indeed in the entire Soviet Union, took place between the Armenians and the Azerbaijanis and their respective republics. The historical hostility of the two peoples came to center on Nagorno-Karabakh, an Armenian-populated area within the republic of Azerbaijan. The Armenians claimed it for themselves on grounds of nationality and of alleged mistreatment of its inhabitants. The Azerbaijanis refused to give up what they considered part of their national homeland. Demonstrations and violence broke out on both sides, notably in Sumgait where anti-Armenian crowds rioted for two days. Azerbaijan blockaded railroads carrying vital supplies into Armenia and Armenia deported Azeris. Especially traumatic were assaults in Baku, the capital of Azerbaijan, on Armenians and some Russians in January 1990 which resulted in at least twenty-five deaths. On January 20, the Soviet army intervened against the Azerbaijani rioters, who were also seeking independence. The central government was blamed both for intervening and for intervening late and was even accused by both sides of inflaming hostility among nationalities for its own nefarious purposes. The Armenian-Azerbaijani border was transformed into front lines, with the opponents remarkably well provided with weapons and matériel stolen or otherwise obtained from the Soviet army. Although active fighting gradually abated, the situation remained volatile. Masses of people migrated between the two republics and even to Moscow and other distant points. Some Armenians were brutally moved by the Soviet army into the Armenian republic from their native villages in Azerbaijan.

Slower to develop popular nationalist movements were the five "Muslim" republics of the USSR located in Central Asia: the Turkic Kazakh, Kirghiz, Turkmen, and Uzbek republics and the Iranian Tajik republic. Deeply affected by the political and nationalist turmoil, affirming in the train of other republics their "rights" and their "sovereignty," and in constant conflict with central authorities, their minorities, and at times one another, they proved among the less self-assertive major components of the former Soviet Union. The party and the administration were relatively successful in maintaining their positions in Soviet Central Asia. The explanation for that success may well lie in the comparative underdevelopment of the area, with its extreme reliance on a single crop (cotton), its poverty, its population explosion, and especially its dependence on huge government subsidies vital to the economy and even to the existence of its peoples. Kazakhstan, by far the largest republic of the five, represents a special case: it is little more than half Kazakh, the southern half, while the north is predominantly Russian and therefore claimed even by such Russian nationalists as Solzhenitsyn who are eager to separate Russians from alien peoples.

Whereas all the republics discussed thus far can be considered peripheral from the standpoint of Russian geography as well as Russian history and, typically, entered that history relatively recently, this judgment in no sense applies to Ukraine, as readers of this book or of any other book treating Russian history in the large must know. Correspondingly, the historic future of Ukraine will be of immense importance to that of Russia proper. The nationalist tide brought to power in Kiev, after elections, a coalition government led by rather nationalistically minded Ukrainian communists and joined by a noncommunist nationalist movement known as Rukh. In contrast to more exclusive Baltic nationalists, Ukrainian politicians appealed to all the inhabitants of the republic. As to its relation to Soviet and, later, Russian governments, Ukraine gave some indication of willingness to participate in certain kinds of associations but always with reservations and conflicting problems. The problems included Ukrainian sovereignty over the Crimea, the management and disposal of atomic weapons, and the division and control of the armed forces, in particular of the Black Sea fleet. The eastern and the smaller western parts of Ukraine are sharply different from each other. It is especially in the latter, Soviet only since 1939 or 1945, that the many-sided religious revival included the restoration, at times a militant restoration, of the formerly prohibited Uniate Church, a Catholic jurisdiction, while anticommunism and anti-Russian nationalism rode high.

Adjacent and closely related to Ukrainians, as well as involved in the general course of Russian history from its very inception, Belorussians have been slow in developing a nationalism of their own, perhaps a generation or two behind the Ukrainians. Also, the party proved to be stronger in the Belorussian republic than in some others. Still, the new nationalist wave had its effect. Thus in late July 1990, Belorussia issued a resounding declaration of its "sovereignty."

The Moldavian Soviet Socialist Republic, bordering Ukraine on the southwest, exemplifies well some of the conundrums and miseries of contemporary nationalisms in the Soviet Union. In a sense a contrived nationalism to begin with—for the Moldavian language is really Romanian and Moldavians are part of the Romanian people, the postulation and promotion of differences between the two being a deliberate Soviet policy—it has nevertheless gripped the titular ethnic group, to the detriment of numerous minorities, such as the Turkic-speaking Gagauz people, the Ukrainians, and the Russians. In August and September 1989, large demonstrations and counterdemonstrations erupted over the introduction of Moldavian as the only official language of the republic. Tensions exploded sporadically into fighting and led to Soviet army intervention, along the lines of its peacekeeping efforts in Transcaucasia. Moldavian authorities announced their break with the Soviet Union and their refusal to take part in any new federal or other arrangements.

Gorbachev and his government received no support from the Russian republic, the gigantic RSFSR, as they were trying to control the non-Russian nationalities of the Soviet Union. To the contrary, before long the leaders of the Russian government began to treat the "center"—Soviet authorities in Moscow—as standing in the way of Russia's progress, insisted on Russian "autonomy" and even "sovereignty," supported other republics doing the same, and initiated a "war of laws," in which new Russian laws countermanded Soviet laws on Russian territory. To be sure, Russians enjoyed certain advantages within the Soviet Union, such as the privileged position of their language and a greater acceptance of their cultural and historical past, albeit in a Marxist-Leninist interpretation, but they remained poor, even poorer than the inhabitants of a number of other republics, and, all in all, they bore their full share of the deprivation, suffering, and oppression characteristic of the Soviet system. They were even denied such "local" institutions, granted to other republics, as their own branch of the Communist Party and their own academy of sciences, apparently, at least in part, because of the fear that these organizations might become too powerful and compete with the central Soviet ones.

The Russian republic acquired a remarkable, idiosyncratic leader in the person of Boris Yeltsin, whom Gorbachev had brought to leadership positions in Moscow in 1985 from provincial Sverdlovsk (now Yekaterinburg), where Yeltsin had been party boss. Gorbachev saw in him a fellow reformer but soon found him to be a most difficult ally, bridling at authority and demanding a faster pace of change. Gorbachev would also find in Yeltsin a man completely unlike him in his extravagant manner (including heavy drinking) and populist leadership style (riding buses and subways as Moscow party chief, personally raiding stores in search of hidden goods, and forcing officials to face the public in open discussions of problems). In October 1987, Yeltsin delivered a harsh speech before the Central Committee criticizing the slow pace of reform, the obstructionism of the central party apparatus and especially the Politburo, and Gorbachev's complacent and hesitant leadership. He asked to resign from the Politburo. In turn, he was denounced by Gorbachev and the Politburo and dismissed as head of the Moscow party organization. This only fueled Yeltsin's ambitions and popularity. In 1989, he won a landslide victory to the new Con-

Patriarch Alexis II of the Russian Orthodox Church blessing Yeltsin, the first freely elected president of the Russian Soviet Federated Socialist Republic. (World Wide Photos)

gress of People's Deputies from the city of Moscow, the largest electoral district in the Soviet Union, though the party leaders had openly backed another candidate and regularly smeared Yeltsin in the press. In the Congress, the meetings of which were televised, he continued to speak out boldly against privilege and corruption and for a faster pace of economic and political reform. He began to focus his efforts on the emerging Russian rather than Soviet political arena, however. In March 1990, he won election to the newly created parliament of the Russian republic and was elected head of its Supreme Soviet. He then convinced the Russian parliament to hold a referendum that approved creating a new post of president directly elected by the citizens of the Russian republic, an election Yeltsin won on June 12, 1991, a stunning display of democratic procedure and popular support which neither Gorbachev nor any other leader in the central government could claim. Elections had already brought other liberals to office in the Russian republic, especially in its great cities, with Anatolii Sobchak becoming mayor of Leningrad and Gavriil Popov, of Moscow. It is worth noting that Yeltsin resigned from the Communist Party on July 12, 1990, and Sobchak and Popov on the following day. Liberalism was combined with nationalism and a religious revival as historic towns, places, and streets regained their old names, the white-blue-red flag and double-headed eagle of the tsarist state were restored, and religious services, including public religious services, multiplied. The day Yeltsin was elected president, the Leningrad voters also decided that their city should again become St. Petersburg. At the same time, Russian leaders made it clear that their vision of Russian statehood was based not on ethnic Russian nationalism—though this was on the rise in the Russian population and associated with a number of right-wing nationalist groups—but on a concept of Russia as a multinational federation. Immense problems, of course, continued; indeed, the entire dazzling change acquired a certain operatic quality, while the basic processes of economic and social life were grinding down. The mere administration of the RSFSR became a near impossibility, with everyone from the Tartars on the Volga to the Yakuts in eastern Siberia and the nomadic tribes of the far north laying claim to their historic rights, their diamonds, or their reindeer. The excruciating interplay between Gorbachev and Yeltsin, with its repeated reversals of positions, ranging from close collaboration to determined attempts by each to drive the other out of politics, came to occupy center stage on the Soviet scene.

Eastern Europe and the World

Just when everything was beginning to become unglued at home, Gorbachev and the Soviet Union lost eastern Europe, which, in turn, contributed mightily to a further ungluing. In retrospect, there appear to be two main explanations for the stunning events of the miraculous year of 1989: the enormous extent of the opposition—indeed, hatred—of the peoples of the satellite states to their communist system and regimes, and Gorbachev's decision against any Soviet army intervention in defense of his communist allies. It was the extent to which communism was bankrupt and despised in eastern Europe that most outside observers failed to take into account. As to Gorbachev's decision, this was a matter of both political principle and reasoned pragmatism. The Soviet leader apparently initially naively believed that there should be perestroika in the satellite countries, as well as in the Soviet Union, and that restructuring would only strengthen the system. But once the system unraveled, and at a terrifying speed, he concluded that nothing could be done to save the old order. As he thundered against Soviet hardliners who accused him of betrayal, only tanks could block change in eastern Europe, which would have violated Gorbachev's often stated opposition to foreign military intervention in the internal politics of sovereign nations; in any case, he understood that tanks could not be used forever.

Thus 1989 witnessed the collapse of communism in Poland, Czechoslovakia, Hungary, Romania, Bulgaria, and, of course, East Germany, which was to disappear entirely through absorption into the Federal Republic of Germany. Masses of refugees crossing newly opened frontiers, the once-formidable Berlin Wall acquiring souvenir status as it was disassembled piece by piece, the corpses of Ceausescu and his wife, executed immediately after the overturn in Romania, and so many other episodes and details will be enshrined in history books and human memory for ages to come. While each national case had its own peculiarities, such as the tremendous importance of West Germany for what happened in and to East Germany or the unique role of Solidarity and the Catholic Church in Poland, there were also common characteristics. Above all, communist regimes proved unable to survive intellectual and political freedom—glasnost, if you will—and, especially, free elections, beginning with the election in Poland on June 5, 1989. Even in the controversial cases of Romania and Bulgaria—perhaps especially relevant for the Russian future—where much of the establishment survived the fall of communism, the issues were the continuation of privilege and the brakes that old personnel might put on the democratic development of these countries, not the fear of a return to the days of Ceausescu and Zhivkov.

Although very hard hit, Gorbachev reacted to the events rapidly and imaginatively. Instead of mounting any kind of rear-guard action, especially on the central issue of the unification of Germany, Gorbachev fully accepted the unification, earning German gratitude—in particular, that of Chancellor Helmut Kohl—as well as advantageous financial provisions for the withdrawal and relocation at home of Soviet troops and some other German aid. Moreover, the solution of the German problem and the Soviet abandonment of troublesome eastern Europe meshed well with Gorbachev's policy of peace and international cooperation.

Gorbachev's foreign policy, crafted together with his foreign minister Eduard Shevardnadze, shifted in a more liberal direction after 1987. Doctrinally, he began to argue that Soviet world power in the future would be based not mainly on military might but on cooperating with other world powers in developing solutions to international problems and respecting national sovereignties. The ruling principles of his "new thinking" were multilateralism, cooperation, non-intervention, and, as he often repeated, a recognition of "common human values." In 1989, Soviet army troops finally left Afghanistan, although the Soviet Union continued to provide massive military aid to the government forces in the seemingly endless civil war. Extremely complex and long-drawn-out negotiations with the United States resulted, at the end of July 1991, in an agreement to reduce certain kinds of armaments. Commentators noted at the time that the new spirit of cooperation was even more significant than the particular provisions of the treaty. Although some disagreements and tensions remained, for example, in connection with the Japanese determination to regain some small islands in the Kurile chain seized by the Soviet Union toward the end of the Second World War or the American pressure to have the USSR dump Castro and Cuba altogether, Gorbachev and his country were rapidly becoming respected supporters of world order. They played that role successfully in 1990 in the crisis and war following the Iraqi occupation of Kuwait, although the Soviet Union did not intervene militarily, and in 1991 in the aftermath of that war when international attention shifted to the continuous Arab-Israeli conflict. It should be added that in October 1990, Gorbachev was awarded the Nobel Peace Prize. Gorbachev's foreign policy could thus be considered a catastrophe, a great success, or both, depending largely on the point of view. In any case, at this point, Gorbachev was certainly more popular outside Russia than within it.

The Final Crisis

At home, the situation was becoming catastrophic. The optimism and confidence of the early Gorbachev years were gone. Gorbachev had hoped and believed that glasnost would unleash popular enthusiasm for his efforts at reform, which would, as he put it in 1987, "multiply the good and combat the bad" and help cure the "spiritual crisis" in the country. Instead, that crisis seemed only to deepen. The flood of open discussion about the evils of the past seemed to produce not new optimism about reform but derision for all the ideals of the socialist project. The fact that the present was filled with high idealism and greater opportunities to make one's voice heard but only decline in everyday material life seemed part of the same long and tragic story of Soviet history. In both the press and in everyday conversation, glasnost produced not optimism and commitment to the good cause but growing anger about both past and present, cynicism (especially about the rhetoric and promises of leaders), and what observers in those years called a pervasive discourse of lament, disintegration, and "the dead end."

Russians had good reasons to despair. The economy kept deteriorating. By 1990, gross domestic product and industrial growth rates were declining while retail prices were on the rise. In 1991, industrial decline and inflation were beginning to spin out of control. Shortages of consumer goods were more severe than in recent memory, producing long lines at stores, and there was even fear of famine. In the spring of 1990, miners in the Ural region, Siberia, and Ukraine went on strike again, first over intolerable material conditions but soon denouncing Gorbachev and the Soviet government, while expressing support for Yeltsin and the new Russian government. Meanwhile crime, prostitution, and other social problems were on the rise. A growing budget deficit and intensive printing of new money (one of the few things not in short supply) only made matters worse. Many attempts to solve problems, such as the decree of January 23, 1991, withdrawing 50- and 100-ruble notes from circulation and compelling the exchange of these notes under highly restrictive conditions, turned into disasters. Very poorly managed, that decree failed to check inflation or limit crime, while it hit hard the average working citizens and pensioners. In fact, proliferating decrees and directives only led to utter confusion. With the new self-assertion of the union republics and of lesser jurisdictions, it was not at all clear who owned or managed what. The same piece of property or sphere of economic activity could be claimed by the central government, a union republic, a regional administration, or a municipality. Reforming measures by all kinds of authorities were at best partial, haphazard, and difficult, if not impossible, to implement. Major general economic reform, while repeatedly promised, kept being postponed.

Natural and man-made catastrophes together with their aftermaths, whether in the case of the earthquake in Armenia in December 1988, which killed some 25,000 people and left another 500,000 homeless, or in that of the train collision and gas explosion near Asha in the Urals in June 1989, with 190 persons listed as dead, 270 as missing, and 720 as hospitalized, served to underline the manifold deficiencies, including the incompetence, of the Soviet system. Ecological issues loomed ever larger as the nature and extent of the ecological damage in the country became better known. Perhaps even more damaging to the government and system were repeated discoveries of mass graves: some 102,000 bodies found near Minsk in Belorussia in October 1988; between 200,000 and 300,000 burials outside Kiev which a special commission determined in March 1989 to contain victims of Stalin, not of the Nazis; about 300,000 more bodies in mass graves near Cheliabinsk and Sverdlovsk in the Urals, uncovered on October 2, 1989; and still others. Glasnost not only provided information about all these matters and contributed to the rehabilitation of many communists executed in the purges of the 1930s as well as of Russian cultural figures abroad, such as the distinguished musician Mstislav Rostropovich and the brilliant satirist Vladimir Voinovich, but also led to a great diversity of opinion and variety of criticism. Gorbachev and his policies were attacked from the right, from the left, and from every direction.

Meanwhile, Gorbachev's formal power was growing. That Gorbachev was leader of both the party and the state was nothing new for Soviet leaders; the novelty of the latest arrangement consisted in the fact that the state position could now be used against the party. Gorbachev had prepared his state base of power well, succeeding Gromyko to the title of president in October 1988, obtaining election to that office by the 2,250-member Congress of People's Deputies on April 25, 1989, and being elected by the Congress to the newly enhanced post of President of the USSR in 1990. As the sway of the Politburo and the party declined, close advisory bodies to the president, such as the eighteen-member Presidential Council, which lasted from March to December 1990, and then the eight-member Security Council of the USSR, which succeeded it, acquired greater significance. The latter was composed mainly of the more important ministers of state. Gorbachev was granted greater powers to appoint ministers, conduct international negotiations, and control executive organs. He was given special authority to deal with economic problems and strengthen "law and order" in the country, including by executive decree. In the summer of 1991, speculation was rife that Gorbachev might abandon the party altogether and stake everything on the state administration and reform. Actually, he turned in the opposite direction, winning once more sufficient party support and apparently determined to carry it with him on his wayward way.

It is not easy to evaluate or even simply present Gorbachev's policy. Often it seems impossible to distinguish his own projects, plans, and aims from the political and other tactical concessions and compromises he had to make, and even from extraneous elements imposed on him by other political forces in the Soviet Union. The net result was a tortuous course most notable for its meandering between reform and restraint. To mention only some of his last turnings, in October 1990 Gorbachev endorsed the so-called Shatalin plan, associated with the economist Stanislav Shatalin and meant to establish within five hundred days a market economy in the USSR. But soon, feeling pressure from conservatives, Gorbachev retreated, moderating the plan by borrowing from less radical market-reform proposals, and soon gutting it of all its key measures, while relying ever more strongly on the old administrative system and his own powers to manage the economy. Gorbachev was also seen to be retreating from radical reform and to be making common cause with party conservatives. In December 1990, he purged from his government many liberals and centrists, placing conservatives in some of the most powerful government positions, and granted new powers to the police and the army acting as police. Many democrats became convinced that cooperation with Gorbachev was no longer possible. It was at just this time that Shevardnadze, one of Gorbachev's closest allies, resigned as foreign minister in protest and warning. Yet spring and summer brought another turning, with Gorbachev more enthusiastic than ever in the cause of economic and general reform, although still without specifics or a timetable. In July 1991, Gorbachev proposed that the Communist Party, which had already lost its legal claim to a monopoly on power, drop Marxism-Leninism as its official ideology and transform itself into a party committed to a market economy and multi-party politics. This revolutionary new party program was to be considered at the Twenty-Ninth Party Congress scheduled for November.

It may be most appropriate to end this brief discussion of perestroika where it began, that is, with the economic crisis, and for that to turn to Gregory Grossman's compelling presentation of the nature and the problem of the Soviet economic collapse in his testimony to congressional committees on June 25, 1991.*

> One can hardly recall an instance in modern history in which—major war or its effects apart—the economic condition of an important country plunged so deep so fast as has that of the Soviet Union in the last few years. Less than a decade ago,

---

*Slightly abridged statement of Gregory Grossman (Berkeley) submitted at the Joint Hearing of the Subcommittee on Europe and the Middle East of the Committee on Foreign Affairs of the U.S. House of Representatives and of the Joint Economic Committee of the U.S. Congress.

serious Western observers could still seriously consider whether the global economic competition would eventually be "won" by the East, with all that implied for the world's future. Today, equally serious people equally seriously advocate Marshall-like assistance from the West in the hundreds of billions of dollars lest the Soviet economy (and polity and society) fall even deeper into destitution and disorder, with all *that* would imply for the world's future.

Although the present economic condition is indeed catastrophic, it has not been quite as unexpected as one might have assumed from appearances alone. In fact, the underlying forces of rot and ruin have been at work for decades, albeit concealed by the secretiveness of the dictatorial regime and the silence of an intimidated population (but for a relatively few dissidents). Among such long-term, corrosive trends one might mention the huge diversion of national resources to military and imperial ends; heedlessly wasteful depletion of natural and human reserves for economic growth and progress, combined with lags in civilian technological advance and improvement in quality; inability to feed the population without massive imports; enormous physical degradation and contamination of the environment with major effects on human health; growing sclerosis of the centralized system of economic planning and governance, aggravated by rigid price-wage controls and monetary mismanagement; steady growth of a large underground economy intimately linked with widespread official corruption and (with time) major organized crime; deterioration of work incentives and work morale, not to say initiative, enterprise (except in the underground), and sense of responsibility. And consequent steady retardation of economic growth, and actual decline.

One could extend this dismal list of the underlying economic factors (not to mention the political, social, and ethnic ones) that have been propelling the Soviet economy for decades towards its historic moment of deep crisis. That moment arrived under Gorbachev, not because Gorbachev is the most skilled economic reformer the USSR could have sooner or later produced—very likely he is not—but because it is difficult to imagine another communist leader, and it would have to be one, who could have more quickly and thoroughly discredited the shams of the past.

But Gorbachev has not yet destroyed, if indeed he intends to fully destroy, either the old ways of running the economy or the social groups that have traditionally run it, namely, the Party apparat (himself being its titular head) and the state's nomenklatura, or the idea of socialism itself. Which is one reason why the economy is currently in such deep trouble. . . .

Now, in mid-1991, important developments are moving at once on several planes and in contradictory ways. First and foremost, the economy's downward slide has accelerated markedly. Above, I used the word "catastrophic" in this regard; it is not overdrawn. For the first four months of this year GNP fell by over 9 percent in relation to the corresponding period the year before (but see the remarks regarding Soviet statistics immediately below). The record for the whole year may well be substantially worse, as is generally believed likely by well-informed Soviet economists with whom I met in Moscow and in the West during the past 30 days. Hence, I find myself in broad agreement with the "grim" conclusions in the paper entitled "Beyond Perestroyka: The Soviet Economy in Crisis" (16 May 1991, presented by the CIA and the DIA to the Joint Economic Committee of the U.S. Congress). To wit:

> There is no doubt that 1991 will be a worse year for the Soviet economy than 1990, and it is likely to be radically worse. . . . [If the standoff between the center and the

republics continues], real gross national product likely would decline 10 to 15 percent and the annual inflation rate could easily exceed 100 percent. (p. iv)

The last may have already happened, largely by virtue of the sharp and mostly administrative increases in official retail prices on 2 April 1991. (It seems that the producers and ministries "ran away" with the prices and raised them significantly above permitted levels.) The monetary "compensation" for the April retail price increase that is being paid to the public, differentiated by social groups, offsets perhaps about half of the actual price rise. Further price increases can be expected before the end of this year.

In the event that the standoff between the center and the republics moderates, the results for 1991 could be less "grim"—but hardly very much less.

This said, in truth it is extremely difficult to establish with any numerical exactness just what is currently happening in the Soviet economy. Although, under its current leadership, the official statistical establishment is trying to improve the quality and comparability of its data, as well as increase the volume of statistical publication, its efforts are thwarted by the fractious realities of the moment. Great ranges of multiple prices for individual goods in a given place and time; physical shortages of goods; wide use of barter (for lack of faith in money); corruption, ubiquitous black markets, evasion of taxes and of administrative regulations; the fragmentation of the country into scores if not hundreds of what amounts to semi-independent principalities (due to erosion of central control), each with its own rationing norms, administrative rules, trade barriers, price controls, etc.—combine to make the statistician's lot not a happy one in the USSR. And yet, the broad trends in production and consumption are probably what we think they are; in other words, close to catastrophic.

No less important is the picture in regard to the distribution of personal income and wealth. Here, our data are even more opaque; yet it is difficult to escape the impression that 1991 has hit a new high (or low) in terms of the differentiation of personal income and wealth. The losers are that large portion of the population whose livelihood depends chiefly on official sources of income (wages, salaries, pensions, etc.), which have generally fallen in real terms this year; and/or whose *informal* incomes have risen less than inflation; and/or those with few lucrative personal connections. But many others have gained considerably riding the crest of the many new opportunities both for profitable production and commerce and for quick arbitrage and black-market dealing—by dint of growing shortages and soaring prices, substantial liberalization of private business activity in various new legal forms, and the chaos itself.

Thanks to such rising private opportunities in the midst of general confusion and chaos in the economy, the Soviet Union may today present some of the best prospects for quick personal enrichment. Nor need one keep one's wealth in rubles; there are innumerable ways of various degrees of legality or illegality for transferring private money abroad.

But note that until money and prices are stabilized, the federal issue is resolved, and the legal underpinnings of private business are further secured, private money will continue to shun long-term, illiquid investment and to seek the quick and easy deals. We must not be misled by stories of successful new Soviet entrepreneurs. Few of them are long-term investors.

Needless to say, large personal gain frequently derives from *de jure* or *de facto* "spontaneous appropriation" at the state's expense. And since those closest to the state's assets, the traditional elite (including the old management), obviously have the best possibilities of appropriating it, the phenomenon of the "propriation of the nomenklatura" has acquired if not mass dimensions then at least mass attention (as in Eastern Europe) with definite political implications.

There may be nothing wrong with the propriation of the nomenklatura or the use of "dirty money" to buy the state's assets—and indeed this may be the quickest road to privatization—but is this the kind of privatization we have in mind when we list the conditions for Western assistance, such as marketization and privatization of the economy and democratization of the polity? Do we want to see a market economy of sorts run by cartels of the same old communist bosses and the same lords of corruption and organized crime in a new guise?

This situation of economic, social, and political crisis and uncertainty was the setting for the final drama, which brought down the whole Soviet system. But it was the specific question of preserving the Soviet Union that provoked this last act. Following a referendum in March 1991 that showed majority support for keeping the Soviet Union together but on new terms in which the "sovereignty" of each republic is guaranteed—though Lithuania, Latvia, Estonia, Armenia, Georgia, and Moldavia refused to participate in the voting—Gorbachev set out to write a new Union Treaty. On July 11, the Congress of People's Deputies approved a plan to create a Union of Soviet Sovereign States in which a great deal of economic and administrative authority devolved to the constituent states. Communist conservatives were determined not to allow this weakening of the Soviet Union, though this was only the final straw in their growing dismay with Gorbachev's reforms. On August 19, one day before the treaty was to be signed, a State Committee for the State of Emergency (GKChP), composed of leading officials Gorbachev had himself appointed in trying to make peace with the conservatives, arrested Gorbachev at his vacation house (though they told the country he was ill and incapacitated and had voluntarily relinquished power to them), placed tanks and soldiers in the center of Moscow, and vowed to protect the Soviet Union against "political adventurers" who were destroying it. The coup collapsed within three days in the face of mass demonstrations in the streets, resistance by republic governments (including Yeltsin's daring speech from the top of a tank in front of the Moscow parliament building), the refusal of key military and police units to obey the orders of the coup leaders, and poor planning and organization.

In the wake of the coup, Gorbachev returned to his post, but little remained of his power. The dissolution of the USSR gathered great momentum. Lithuania, Latvia, and Estonia declared immediate independence, which received international and even Soviet recognition. Most other republics, including Ukraine, also proclaimed independence. Meanwhile, Yeltsin's Russian government proceeded to take over the offices of the union government and outlaw the Communist Party of the Soviet Union, seizing its property. On December 9, the leaders of the Russian, Ukrainian, and Belorussian republics met to declare the USSR abolished and replaced by a loose association of states to be called the Commonwealth of Independent States. Within the next couple of weeks, the remaining republics declared their independence as well. On December 25, 1991, Gorbachev went on television to announce his resignation

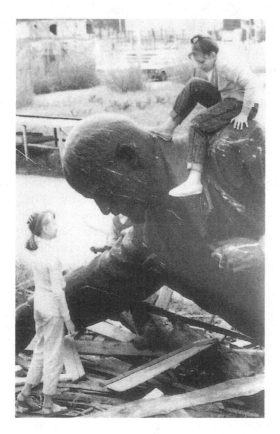

Children playing on toppled statue of Lenin in Lithuania following the failed Kremlin coup, August 1991.

as president of a country that, in reality, no longer existed. A triumphant Boris Yeltsin stood out as the central figure in a new and highly unsettled situation.

Concluding Remarks

The disappearance of the Soviet Union proved to be at least as unexpected and sudden as its appearance, and as controversial. Bitterly hated as well as enthusiastically admired during three-quarters of a century of its existence, the USSR seemed to receive a universal recognition of its might and its durability after the victory over Germany in the Second World War and its attaining the position of one of only two superpowers in the world. Worshipful communists and related elements aside, numerous more judicious observers interpreted Soviet history in terms of continuity and stabilization bringing it closer to Western nations whether after the inauguration of NEP, the cultural "great retreat" of the 1930s, the gigantic war itself and the victory over Germany and Japan, the death of Stalin, or the ascendancy of Khrushchev. Although none of these varied developments proved to be a decisive turning point, it was within that framework that many in the West welcomed perestroika and glasnost: The Soviet Union would join democratic states as a major partner, perhaps even with much to offer. Very few expected total unraveling and collapse.

There were plenty of signs that the Soviet system was failing, however. Gorbachev admitted as much himself when he spoke of a "spiritual crisis" in Soviet society. Widespread pessimism and cynicism, disillusionment with the promises of Marxist rhetoric, social problems such as alcoholism and crime, the widespread retreat into private life, and the rise of cultural values and tastes at odds with socialist norms, together with the stagnating economy, were among many signs that the Soviet Union was a mammoth power with clay feet. Gorbachev's reforms were premised on the optimistic faith that the Soviet people could be inspired again by the humanistic ideals of socialism and that the system itself needed only to be improved not scrapped. Or as Yeltsin argued after Gorbachev's fall, "He thought he could unite the impossible: communism with the market, ownership by the people with private ownership, a multi-party system with the Communist Party of the Soviet Union." One can admire Gorbachev for his idealism and recognize him as one in a long line of Communist visionaries. But his dream appears to have been an impossible one.

Economists had been warning that this system was flawed for a long time. As early as the first years of the Soviet regime, certain economists pointed to the basic flaws of the Soviet economic system, and that initial critique was continued by such specialists as János Kornai who worked within the system in Hungary and Gregory Grossman and Vladimir Treml, who studied the second, unofficial, Soviet economy from the vantage point of American universities. Indeed it became a commonplace to claim that whereas the Soviet Union did well in terms of a traditional industrialization based on coal and iron, it could not keep up with the West in cybernetics, computers, and in general the new communication technology. And modern technology made isolation always more difficult, and Soviet citizens better acquainted with the rest of the world. The arms race continued to cost the Soviet Union twice the percentage of its much smaller productive capacity than in the case of the United States. Grossman pointed out repeatedly that only a massive export of oil and natural gas kept the Soviet economy for fifteen years, 1970–85, from sliding downhill rather than being merely in a kind of cul-de-sac. Behind the strange course of the Soviet economy, as of Soviet policies in general, was the utopian Marxist vision perhaps analyzed best in Andrzej Walicki's brilliant *Marxism and the Leap to the Kingdom of Freedom: The Rise and Fall of the Communist Utopia.*

The mistakes were many. Possibly the worst was the inability through the prism of ideology to see reality. Nationalism was misjudged until it destroyed the Soviet Union. Indeed Gorbachev apparently believed that he could go to Vilnius and persuade the Lithuanians not to secede. But the understanding of Russia itself was not much better, and Russian interests and Russian nationalism played a major role in the abolition of the USSR. As to Gorbachev's contribution, it was extremely important from any point of view, although it was not what Gorbachev had planned. It was most impressive for those who believe in the great power of totalitarianism and the inability of a fragmented society to challenge it successfully. If so, a totalitarian system can unravel only from the top down. In the Soviet Union it did. In any case, there glasnost and other measures meant to strengthen the system led to a complete collapse. To cite, as a counter-point to Derzhavin's, Heraclites' even more famous statement: "τά πάντα ῥεῖ" ("Everything flows").

Part
VII

Russian Federation

Russia after Communism: Yeltsin, 1991–99, and Putin, 2000–

Much has been written about my visit to the United States both in the United States themselves and in our country. . . . I shall appear banal, for sure, but still I was most impressed precisely by the simple people, by Americans who exude a remarkable optimism, a faith in themselves and their country. Although, of course, there were also other shocks, for instance, from a supermarket. When I saw all those shelves with hundreds, with thousands of little cans, little boxes, and so on, and so forth, I was for the first time struck with an all-embracing pain for us, for our country. To bring the richest nation to such destitution. It is terrifying.

—YELTSIN (1990)

Our democracy is like a sickly child. But the main choice has already been made. We have determined to go the whole way, climbing up the ladder to civilization.

—YELTSIN (SEPTEMBER 1991)

Revolution is usually followed by counter-revolution, reforms by counter-reforms, and then by the search for those guilty of revolutionary misdeeds and by punishment. . . . Russia's historical experience is rich in such examples. But I think it is time to say firmly that this cycle has ended. There will be no revolution or counter-revolution. Firm and economically supported state stability is a good thing for Russia and its people and it is long overdue that we learn to live according to this normal human logic.

—PUTIN (MARCH 2001)

Russia's history after the collapse of the Soviet Union and Communist rule has most often been viewed as an era of "transition." But toward what? From the perspective of the United States and western Europe, the idea of transition usually has been assumed to mean market capitalism and liberal democracy, and many Russians have hoped for the same. But the question remains and the passage of time is still too brief to be able confidently to define the political, social, and cultural shape of Russia after communism. The pervasiveness of "posts" in speaking of Russia since 1991—postcommunist, postsocialist, post-Soviet, post-totalitarian—reminds us of the uncertainty of the present and the weight of the past. Scholars in both Russia and the West have offered varying definitions of the recent history of Russia that also suggest the ambiguity of the transition: "unfinished revolution," "illiberal democracy," or "managed democracy" in speaking of the political transition from Communist authoritarianism, and "crony capitalism," "oligarchical corporatism," "industrial feudalism," or "bureaucratic capitalism" in characterizing the economic transition from Communist control and planning. Beyond political and economic structures, many other questions have remained unsettled and often preoccupying in these years, none of them new in Russian history: the meaning of Russia as a nation (the "Russian idea"), the place of national minorities in Russia's multinational state, Russia's cultural relation to the West, and the moral values that should guide everyday public and private life. As will be seen, Russians themselves have remained uncertain about where they are as a country and often even where they want to go, though most have spoken of a desire for Russia to become a "normal" society. At the center of this history of change and uncertainty have stood Russia's first two elected presidents, Boris Yeltsin and Vladimir Putin. Still, though these two former Communists both valued state power and individual leaders as makers of history, neither were ever completely in control of the situation around them—they experienced daily what Karl Marx long ago observed: "Men make their own history, but they do not make it just as they please, under conditions of their own choosing."

Yeltsin's Presidency

Boris Nikolaevich Yeltsin, a construction engineer by profession and a party administrator by occupation, rose by dint of hard and diligent work to the top ranks of the party. Like Gorbachev, he evidently believed in the system and was skilled at making it work. But then, he fell out with both Gorbachev and the party over the slowness of reform. Yeltsin's career, as well as his pronouncements and his writings (especially the two autobiographical books he produced with his friend the young journalist Valentin Yumashev), depict an extremely high-strung individual, a courageous fighter, and a very poor loser, on occasion volatile and unpredictable. Those who have worked with Yeltsin have described him as energetic, impulsive, temperamental, easy to offend, a risk-taker, relatively uncorrupt, and always preferring to be in charge—he was long a local party "boss," whether in Sverdlovsk from the mid-1970s or in Moscow in the late 1980s. Frequent and at times very serious illnesses and heavy drinking further complicate evaluations of his actions and aims. Still, it is worth remembering that Yeltsin surged past Gorbachev as a radical, i.e., favoring the breakup of the Soviet Union and a major reform of Russia. Even more a Soviet and a party product than Gorbachev, for he came from a still poorer, indeed semi-starving, background, and had no cultural baggage except that provided by the Soviet system, Yeltsin broke with that system more

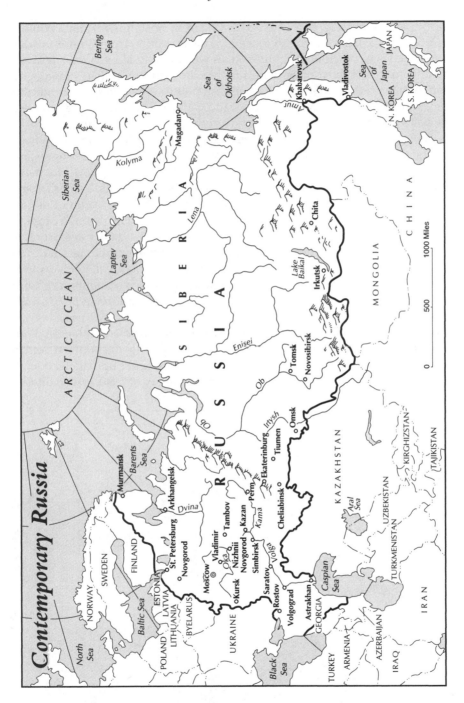

sharply and decisively. No adjusted Leninism or nostalgia for him. Whether
the two men represent successive stages of the transition from Communism to
a new Russia, or whether their differences were merely idiosyncratic and personal, is for future historians to decide. Needless to say, Yeltsin's ideological
reorientation did not change his career-long political manner of an authoritarian Communist boss. Notably, as one studies his battle with his legislatures,
one has to recognize that time and again both sides acted illegally.

Yeltsin came to power with a program for changing Russia in which negative goals were much clearer than positive aims. He was strongly anti-
corruption, anti-privilege, anti-Communist, and anti-Gorbachev. His heroic
defiance of the 1991 coup, standing on a tank in front of the Russian parliament,
was a symbolic moment cementing his popularity as a figure leading Russians
in their effort to break with the bankrupt Soviet system. His positive program
was less clear. There is no doubt that Yeltsin sincerely desired to transform Russia into a capitalist, or at least market-oriented, and democratic state. The first
probably meant to him above all a great abundance of material goods, as in an
American supermarket. The second signified especially an abolition of Communist control and restrictions with real popular participation in political life,
freedom of speech, and freedom of the press. He wished to see Russia become
a "normal" and "civilized" nation, respected in the world and integrated into
the global capitalist economy. Yeltsin was also something of a populist, and he
owed his initial rise to the very top to popular appeal and popular election.

Yeltsin's years in power, from 1991 to the final day of 1999, can be divided

*Russian President Boris Yeltsin climbs on a tank in August 1991 to call on the army and cit-
izens to defy the coup.*   (Associated Press)

into several key periods: August 1991 to October 1993 (sometimes referred to as the "first Russian republic"), which began with radical reform from above and ended with growing polarization and open conflict; October 1993 to August 1998, a period marked by Yeltsin's growing power but also by deepening problems, even crisis, in the course of reform; and August 1998 to December 1999, which saw retreat from reform and growing emphasis on social stability and Yeltsin's own personal power and security. His own administrative style complicated all this. Yeltsin put economic change at the top of his agenda, but since he had little understanding of economics, he repeatedly put his confidence in such economic reformers as Anatoly Chubais, Yegor Gaidar, or Sergei Kiriyenko. Only this confidence did not last long. The enormous difficulties of the reform process and the opposition of the increasingly powerful interests that did not want economic reform, or at least that particular kind of economic reform, made the President retreat repeatedly and try something else. In this tortuous process, Yeltsin, like Gorbachev before him, was vilified from all sides, and time and again buried politically if not physically by foe and even friend. Once the most acclaimed politician in Russia, Yeltsin's support in opinion polls would drop to as low as 2 or even 1 percent. Yet Yeltsin refused to die either physically, in spite of a very dangerous bypass operation and constant illness, or even politically, but actively reemerged, greatly assisted by the extremely strong position of the President in the Russian constitution, often to fire leading figures in the government and change its course somewhat. George Breslauer and other specialists have commented trenchantly on this idiosyncratic ruling style. The Russian President's ability to survive and even to remain, at least in a sense, on top of Russian politics, continuously baffled many observers, and it even led some of them to despair. Survivability, however, exacted a heavy price. Most commentators came to interpret Yeltsin's behavior simply in terms of his determination to hold on to his position rather than as a pursuit of any economic or political principles.

The year 1992 began with a radical economic program of "shock therapy," developed by Gaidar, Chubais, and other young Russian economists brought into the government, and influenced by Western economic advisors. Gaidar joined Yeltsin's government as deputy prime minister for economic reform on November 7, 1991, first deputy prime minister on March 2, 1992, and acting prime minister on June 15, 1992, to be replaced by Prime Minister Viktor Chernomyrdin on December 14, 1992. Gaidar returned to the government as first deputy prime minister in charge of the economy in September 1993 only to be dismissed again in January 1994. Chubais became minister for privatization and chairman of the State Committee for the Management of State Property (GKI). He was to serve in several important capacities later and, like other of Yeltsin's assistants, would fall in and out of the President's favor. But privatization—however one judges it—remains Gaidar's main contribution to the transformation of Russia. Shock therapy was intended to "cure" the Russian economy of its attachments to central state planning and Russian citizens of their passivity as economic individuals and to create the foundation of a self-sustaining market system by quickly ending price controls, cutting subsidies to industry and agriculture (which would also help balance the budget), and privatizing industry, finance, commerce, agriculture, and real estate. It has been argued that like Stalin's economic revolution from above, shock therapy was as much a political and cultural as an economic program—as much, or more, about destroying the communist economy as about building the foundations for an effective capitalist one. In any case, Yeltsin was attracted to this breakthrough strategy and to promises of rapid success. He repeatedly assured the population—evidently sincerely—that the pain from shock therapy would last no more than six months to a year. The chief economist of the World Bank would later observe that Yeltsin's reforms were inspired by a nearly mystical faith in the market, which underplayed the role of the state in economic transition and ignored the need first to create institutional frameworks for effective markets.

In practice, the course of reform was uneven, protracted, and created much suffering—though some economists argued that it was the incompleteness of reform that was the main source of problems, while others proposed a still more gradual course to allow social institutions and attitudes to adapt. In any case, faced with opposition in parliament by communists and nationalists (though Yeltsin sometimes got around them by ruling by decree), the powerful interests of vested elites (especially industrial managers and officials), and public discontent and even unrest in the face of the suffering caused by the reforms and the still declining economy, Yeltsin often modified the radical proposals for reform he was given. The pace of change was slowed, plans to cut subsidies to some industries were lessened or scrapped, and most agricultural property remained nationalized. Still, economic reform was dramatic. Price controls were lifted on almost all goods as were many subsidies for industry. Most important, privatization moved forward rapidly. Starting in 1992, state firms were turned into joint-stock companies and citizens were given vouchers to help buy shares, though it was mainly insider managers and workers of firms who purchased these shares. In practice, directors continued to control most enterprises, ownership began to accumulate in a smaller number of hands as shares were re-sold, and organized criminal "mafias" gained growing influence in the economy. A second round of privatization, which started in July 1994, has been described by political scientist George Breslauer as "one of the largest and most blatant cases of plutocratic favoritism imaginable." Huge industries were sold by the government to influential wealthy individuals at a fraction of their value—most often through "loans" by banks and individuals to the government, which were not paid back. Again, the logic was more political than economic: to speed up the transition to capitalism and create a potentially loyal and supportive class of wealthy property owners.

The results of these reforms were contradictory. On the one hand, private enterprise spread rapidly in Russia, ranging from the activities of leading international companies to those of the uncounted and often miserably poor local entrepreneurs. Commercial banks and stock exchanges were established and foreign investment grew. Gradually, Moscow and to a lesser extent St. Petersburg and other cities acquired a great variety of consumer goods of every kind, mostly imported, impossible even to imagine in Soviet times. In fact, luxury items, such as Mercedes cars, became particularly prominent. Concurrently

Russians obtained the unrestricted right to travel abroad, and colonies of rich Russians appeared in the French and the Italian Rivieras, in Switzerland, and on Greek islands. At the same time, however, terrible inflation in the first years of reform (at least 300 percent in the month of January 1992 alone, though declining to 800 percent annually in 1993 and then to only 22 percent in 1996) quickly wiped out the savings of millions, devalued salaries, and made the pensions of the elderly worthless. Citizens complained that reform was all shock and no therapy. GDP dropped a staggering 43 percent from 1991 to the end of 1997 (when the economy finally began again to grow). Investment fell 92 percent between 1989 and 1997. Agriculture was in shambles, with the old structure in disarray and no effective substitute in place. Some critics argued that Russia had devolved from a "command economy" to economic "anarchy." As Russian manufacturing declined, imports grew, though the majority of the population could not afford them. In fact, in cities like Moscow, whole streets were lined with people selling off personal goods. Homelessness and unemployment rose. Not surprisingly, the Russian capital and other cities often saw mass anti-government demonstrations, some of them leading to violent clashes with police. These marches and rallies were usually organized by the new Communist Party of the Russian Federation, various neo-communist groups such as Working Russia, and nationalist organizations; cooperation between communists and nationalists, as in the National Salvation Front organized in 1992, was derisively called the "Red-Brown" alliance. Strikes became more frequent. Indeed, it was common in 1992 and the years following to hear Russians talk of impending catastrophe, an anti-reform coup d'etat, and possibly civil war.

The government itself seemed to become a victim of its own policies. The declining economy hurt tax revenues; in any case, the disorder in the country meant that taxes were often left uncollected or deliberately unpaid. The government kept borrowing money to stay afloat and sought large foreign loans. Short of funds, the government fell months behind in paying wages and salaries, and this lack of payments and lack of money spread throughout the economy. Pensioners were among the obvious sufferers. The situation was made worse by the fact that the Soviet Union had never had a strong social security system, especially if we exclude the social services of the very enterprises that were collapsing. Because of a drastic shortage of funds, such state institutions as the prison system and the armed forces themselves reached a desparate state. Prisoners' conditions, political persecution and punishment aside, declined compared to the Soviet period. Soldiers and officers were "advised" by their superiors to fish, hunt, farm, and gather mushrooms in order to survive until the federal government accumulated enough cash to pay military wage arrears. At times uniformed servicemen begged in the streets. As usual, the situation was more complicated than a very brief summary can indicate. Thus the penury of the army resulted partly because the high command and certain other elements were blocking its effective reduction in size. Similarly other, and sometimes the same, interests kept hanging on to the heavy and largely obsolete defense industry. And it proved very difficult to close mines, even when they operated at a loss or became superfluous. Entrenched administrators on top had a common cause with workers who were losing their jobs, often with nothing to replace them. Yet with all the variations and qualifications, the financial catastrophe loomed ever larger.

The central Russian government found it very difficult or impossible to control and sometimes simply to influence the component parts of the huge Russian state even after the fourteen non-Russian republics had separated themselves. Eventually eighty-nine distinct autonomous units, these component parts claimed often far-reaching rights and privileges, stopping in the case of Tatarstan just short of full sovereignty, although so far only Chechnia has fought a major war for independence. As regional interests and electoral democracy gained ground, local officials had all the less reason to obey Moscow. Most of the directives from the center were simply ignored. Corruption and crime grew rapidly, to the point that Russia was listed as the third most corrupt country on the face of the earth by an organization issuing such statistics. Exploiting privatization or exporting oil, gas, metals, and other valuable materials abroad, often with the aid of special permissions or even illegally, as well as profiting in other ways from the unhinged economy, some people quickly became enormously rich. Often compared to the robber barons of the early stage of capitalism in other countries, the Russian barons unfortunately proved to be different in that they took their enormous fortunes abroad rather than use them to develop the economy of their native land. In fact, very much more capital left Russia than came in the form of loans, aid, and investments put together.

Political life in these first years of Yeltsin's leadership (1991–96) was also increasingly marked by crisis. Indeed, economic problems greatly exacerbated Yeltsin's efforts to create a working democratic political order, while political conflict often made effective economic reform difficult. The Russian Congress of People's Deputies and its Supreme Soviet, the legislature, still had a majority communist presence and its members, even many non-communists, were increasingly opposed to Yeltsin's radical reforms of the economy, troubled by the deepening social disorder, and offended by Yeltsin's authoritarian style of rule. They were also fully aware of public suffering and discontent. The legislators, therefore, had some reason to believe that in a showdown with Yeltsin they would be supported by the army and the people. A very mixed group or, perhaps better, combination of groups, their leaders included the Vice President, Alexander Rutskoi, whom Yeltsin had hastily appointed to that position probably because of his military record and impressive appearance, and the leader of the legislature Ruslan Khasbulatov. By the end of 1992, under pressure, Yeltsin had to let Gaidar go, and the more generally acceptable Viktor Chernomyrdin became prime minister. The Congress succeeded in limiting Yeltsin's power to rule by decree and passed a number of laws limiting the President's power, though legislators failed in their efforts to impeach him or to limit drastically his powers by law, although on one occasion by a very narrow margin. All sides recognized that the legislature was determined to shift the balance of power away from the President and was making progress. Yeltsin responded by holding a popular referendum in April 1993—though he had to threaten the legislature to approve this—on support for his authority and a number of other key issues (although not on that of private property). The results were gratifying for Yeltsin: 59 percent affirming their "trust" in the President, 53 percent supporting the social and economic policies of the government, 49.5 percent favoring an early election for President, but 67.2 percent favoring an early election for parliament.

Yeltsin—convinced of the need for strong central authority and of his own personal role as guarantor of Russia's progress away from communism and satisfied that the 1993 referendum had given him a new popular mandate— was determined to increase his power and freedom to act at the expense of the legislature. His advisors drafted a constitution that enhanced presidential power over the courts, the bureaucracy, and the legislature. The legislature, meanwhile, drafted its own constitution limiting the power of the President. Yeltsin decided to rid himself of this obstacle. On September 21, he dissolved the Congress of People's Deputies and announced that elections would be held in December to ratify a new constitution and to elect representatives to a new bicameral parliament, leaving him to rule by decree in the meantime. He also cut off communication lines from the parliament's "White House" headquarters to hinder his opponents' ability to organize resistance. The parliament fought back: they barricaded themselves in the building (some accounts suggest they did this before Yeltsin's announcement, on rumors of his impending coup, forcing his hand), declared Yeltsin unfit to govern for having violated the constitution, swore in Rutskoi as the new Russian President, and handed out arms to civilians willing to guard the parliament. Supplies of armaments and a great variety of rebellious individuals and groups flocked toward the White House, where Rutskoi and others tried to organize them into an effective military force. Witnesses remember the standard of the Romanov family flying next to the red flag of communism; the cossacks and even the neo-Nazis were also prominent. Mediation under the auspices of the Patriarch failed, because the rebels were in an upbeat mood at that point in time and would not seriously consider a compromise settlement. To be sure, Yeltsin can be blamed for setting off the entire collision by his coup against the legislature and for acting, to put it mildly, in an unconstitutional manner. But it was the legislature that first brought violence into play. Already on the twenty-fourth of September a woman was killed when an extremist military leader in the parliament staged an attack on a military communications office. More important, on the third of October, having gained more followers and some crowd support, Rutskoi and Khasbulatov endorsed attacks on the Ostankino television center and the headquarters of the mayor of the city, i.e., tactics of a classical military rebellion and takeover. It was on the fourth that troops, with tanks, finally arrived to bombard the White House rebels into submission and to arrest them. More than a hundred people were killed, many of them bystanders; the building itself presented a picture of utter devastation. Russians had not seen such use of military force in politics, or this level of bloodshed on the streets, since the Civil War. The violence further deepened the political divisions in the country and alienated even many democrats from Yeltsin.

The parliamentary catastrophe of 1993 was followed in 1994 by a still greater disaster, the Chechen war. One of the 89 units of the new Russian Federation, the Chechens constituted less than 1 percent of its population and were located on a far Caucasian periphery, important perhaps only for oil and gas transport. An Islamic people, the Chechens had fought under Shamil against the imposition of Russian rule in the mid-nineteenth century and resisted Soviet power after 1917. Stalin considered them disloyal in the Second World War and had them transported, under atrocious conditions, to Central Asia, from which they were allowed to return to their native land only after the supreme dictator's death. At the time of the 1991 coup, as the Soviet Union was collapsing as states declared their independence, a general in the Soviet air force, Dzhokar Dudayev, was elected leader of Chechnia by a council of elders and declared independence. He was then elected President of the Chechen republic, though in quite uncertain elections. Dudayev regularly defied Moscow's authority and allowed his country to become a base for much criminal activity in Russia. Several covert attempts by Russian agents to overthrow Dudayev failed. Yeltsin decided to invade (he called it a "peacemaking mission"), though the new parliament, the State Duma, and even many military leaders opposed military intervention. On December 11, 1994, forty thousand troops were sent to Chechnia. No doubt, Yeltsin grossly underestimated the military preparedness and the fighting quality of the Chechens, as did Minister of Defense Pavel Grachev, who promised a very quick and easy victory. Also, the President did not want to antagonize Russian nationalists and wished to assure himself and all others that a component unit could not simply leave the Russian Federation at will. Pride and stubbornness certainly entered the picture on both sides. When the initial military effort failed, the Chechen capital city of Grozny and the land of Chechnia became a battlefield, often compared to Vietnam, or, to keep the analogy closer, to Afghanistan.

Perhaps not so unexpectedly to those who followed the evolution of Russia in the Gorbachev and Yeltsin years, but to the great surprise of the world, the Russian army proved to be in an appalling condition and totally unprepared for a war with the Chechens. Tank assaults on Grozny without the necessary infantry support and even without maps of the city led to the isolation and annihilation of the attackers. Massive bombardment eventually reduced much of the city to rubble, but probably killed mostly its peaceful ethnic Russian inhabitants, for the Chechen urbanites were much quicker to take to the hills. As to the Chechen fighters, they proved remarkably elusive, usually escaping with ease and striking suddenly from all sides. Some forty thousand people perished in Grozny. To be sure, the Russian army did capture, or recapture, the city, but only to abandon it again. And the total Russian military casualties in Chechnia were estimated as exceeding those of the Soviet army in Afghanistan. The unavoidable death and destruction of war were underlined by particular acts of deliberate cruelty, such as the massacre of civilians in the village of Samashki by the special forces of the ministry of the interior on the sixth through the eighth of April 1995. In general, there was much cruelty on both sides, but it was the Russians who were the aggressors. About a year after the assassinations in Samashki they even succeeded in killing by a rocket from a Russian aircraft, which had homed in on a satellite telephone in Chechen headquarters, President Dudayev. Yet the bitter war, although deadlocked, continued. It was only several months later, in August 1996, that Aleksandr Lebed, representing Russia, and Aslan Maskhadov, a more moderate Chechen leader, signed a peace pact. Victorious, the Chechens had in effect gained their independence and retained all their land for themselves, although the formulation of their exact relationship to Russia was left for the future.

One great fear of Yeltsin and his government, associated with the Chechen war, did not materialize: The inability to suppress the Chechens did not lead, in a domino effect, to other nationalities or parts of the country separating themselves from Moscow. But in other major respects the war was indeed a disaster. The utterly miserable performance of the Russian army was a shame and a scandal for patriotic Russians, and even Russians in general, and it was blamed directly on Yeltsin, Grachev, and their assistants. Perhaps an even more significant divide came to separate the president from the liberals who could not pardon him the stubborn pursuit of the Chechen war and its cruelty. In the Duma, only nationalists and communists supported the war. Indeed, most of the population was against this disastrous war: a national poll in January 1995 showed 71 percent opposed. The war also damaged Yeltsin's already declining popularity. By January 1995, fully 80 percent of the population expressed disapproval of Yeltsin as President. The much respected Sergei Kovalev's resignation from his position as head of the President's human rights commission was more than an individual gesture. Yeltsin's humanitarian and progressive mystique was no more. Abroad, too, the Chechen war produced a most painful impression, even if no state rushed to recognize the new Chechen government.

Yeltsin's bloody victory over the parliament in October 1993 did not establish either cooperation or a stable balance between the executive and the legislative branches of the Russian government. Yeltsin seemed to have become even more convinced that his own personal role was essential to keep Russia on the path to civilization and that all opposition to him represented the threat of a return to communism. The successful referendum on the new constitution of December 12, 1993, further strengthened the President's powerful position. In full charge of the executive, he could appoint and dismiss ministers and even pass measures by executive decree, when legislative approval was not available. Yeltsin's constitution gave the central government greater power over the regions. It also made it virtually impossible to impeach the President or amend the constitution. Specialists have described the constitution as "super-presidentialist." Yet ultimately he needed the agreement of the two-house legislature—the Upper House, the Federation Council, representing the federal units of the state, and the Lower House, the State Duma, representing the people at large—to enact a budget and a full legislative program. The parliament could also reject the proposed prime minister, although a third rejection would lead to the dissolution of the legislature and new elections, a threat that was to be effective in obtaining approval.

The victory of Yeltsin's constitution in the December 1993 election was undermined by the startling outcome of the simultaneous elections to the new Duma. Yeltsin had expected liberal parties loyal to his reforms, like Gaidar's Russia's Choice (widely treated as "the President's party) or Grigory Yavlinsky's Yabloko (the Russian word for "apple," constructed of the first letters in the names of the party's original founders), to win a majority of seats. Instead, the largest unified bloc of seats went to a variety of nationalist and communist parties, increasingly allied in their opposition to radical market reforms and to Yeltsin personally. The largest share of the vote (23 percent) was won by Vladimir Zhirinovsky's paradoxically named Liberal Democratic Party of Russia (LDPR). The closely allied Communist Party of the Russian Federation (KPRF, led by Gennady Zyuganov) and the Agrarian Party won 12 percent and 8 percent respectively. Many smaller nationalist and communist deputies were also elected, though many deputies, elected directly rather than from party lists in the complicated procedures Yeltsin set up, declared themselves independents. The two largest centrist parties, the Democratic Party of Russia and Women of Russia, won about 15 percent of the votes. Meanwhile, Russia's Choice and Yabloko won only 23 percent of the vote. Many explanations have been offered for the failure of the reformists to win a majority. As has been repeatedly noted, neither Gorbachev nor Yeltsin made a determined effort to establish and lead a strong political party. They had little appreciation of party politics and preferred to think of themselves as national leaders on a presumably higher plane. Moreover, through the years Russian liberals and moderates could not create an effective united party, but stayed divided into quarreling factions. The most prominent liberal politician, the able economist Grigory Yavlinsky, has been frequently criticized for his vanity and exclusiveness, but it may be unfair to single him out in that connection. The main reason for the poor showing of the liberals, however, was likely the unpopularity of the policies introduced under the banner of liberalism. By contrast, communists and nationalists sought to capitalize on widespread discontent in Russia over the results of postcommunist reform, though it should be noted that about half of all eligible voters refrained from voting at all. The new Duma remained hostile to Yeltsin throughout his tenure in office. Symbolically, one of the Duma's first acts was a declaration of amnesty for Yeltsin's opponents in the conflict of October 1993 as well as for those who attempted the coup in August 1991. The December 1995 Duma elections brought more bad news. Reformers, organized around the moderate new party Our Home Is Russia, associated with Prime Minister Chernomyrdin, and with Yavlinsky's more liberal Yabloko, ended up with even fewer seats than before while communists and nationalists gained additional seats—together winning nearly 54 percent of the vote. The biggest losers were the moderate centrists. The country was ever more deeply divided. Not surprisingly, the new Duma was more oppositional than the previous.

Two political figures who would remain key players in Russian national politics for a number of years to come became especially prominent as a result of the 1993 elections: Zhirinovsky and Zyuganov. Zhirinovsky became politically prominent rather suddenly in 1991, when he came in third in the first Russian presidential election won by Yeltsin. Much of Zhirinovsky's support was a protest vote for a man who challenged the government, the establishment, and even the world in a most extreme and vulgar manner, including physical assault on his opponents in the Duma, who promised everything to all, and who never hesitated to lie or to deny well-known facts. Yet beyond that amazing behavior—similar in some important ways to that of Zhirinovsky's friend, the French Right-wing leader Jean-Marie Le Pen—many observers seemed to detect a fundamental fanaticism in Zhirinovsky's proposals, which included restoring the nineteenth-century Russian Empire, Russian expansion to the Indian ocean, taking back Alaska from the United States, and such solutions for establishing peace in the world as another major war, which would destroy Turkey and the Turks and ensure the legitimate Russian expansion to the south. Zhirinovsky certainly made his contribution to the frequently drawn analogy between Yeltsin's Russia and the Weimar Republic in Germany. At the same time, Zhirinovsky was not opposed to market economics and accepted the new political structures Yeltsin had established, especially the strong presidential system. Still, it was his persona as audacious and charismatic nationalist rebel, as well his party's superb grassroots organizing, that attracted voters to his party, though he gradually lost popularity to more serious opposition politicians like Zyuganov. Unlike such virulent communists as Viktor Anpilov, Zyuganov also accepted the necessity of a market economy and the new political principles—he insisted that communists may come to power only through the ballot box. In fact, he admitted that Soviet communism failed because of its impossible attempt to maintain a monopoly on political and economic power. He also combined traditional communist concern for the material suffering of ordinary citizens with nationalist ideology. He often spoke of fighting to protect Russia's "spiritual heritage" against the degrading effects of postcommunist change in Russia. He even avoided speaking of socialism or communism, preferring instead to talk of "the Russian tradition of community and collectivism." Meanwhile, Yeltsin himself backed away from liberalism—leading some liberals, such as Gaidar, to quit his administration. In 1994–95, Yeltsin began to talk less about structural transformation (notwithstanding the new round of privatization about to take place) than about "normalization" and "stability" as what Russia needed most, adding (as he wrote in his 1994 memoir) that "the only guarantor of calm is the president himself." In policy, he began to pay more attention to social programs, improving the legal system, and fighting crime. He also began making more use of nationalist discourse, talking of Russia's cultural and religious rebirth and of the Motherland; at the same time, in 1995, he cracked down on nationalist movements by banning all "fascist" organizations and activities.

As the June 1996 presidential elections approached, Yeltsin's chances of political survival looked minimal. After five years of his rule most of the Russian people were in dire and still worsening economic straits, with no end to their tribulations in sight. As already stated, agriculture was in shambles, industrial output kept declining, the government went on borrowing money, but did not even provide wages or social security payments to its millions of employees and retirees who had to survive somehow for weeks, months, and sometimes years on their own. The war in Chechnia continued. Enormous corruption and organized crime held sway in the country. The polls indicated that popular approval and support of Yeltsin had fallen to several percentage points. Yeltsin's main challenger, the communist leader Zyuganov, while deficient in charisma and even in simple personal appeal, had a huge nationwide party behind him and aimed to mobilize all discontent, including the nationalist variety. There was widespread anxiety among Russia democrats and in the West that Zyuganov might win this election, bringing the communists back to power.

Yeltsin, who always relished a fight, was determined to do battle, despite his own deteriorating health. To be sure, he had certain advantages in the election, and he utilized them to the full and even beyond the legally proper and permissible. Notably the government had a virtual monopoly on television and used this opportunity to display communists' oppression and atrocities during their seventy-five years of rule, to denigrate Yeltsin's opponents, and to portray the campaign as a fundamental struggle to prevent the return of communism. Repeatedly, Yeltsin depicted himself as the candidate of peace, order, stability, and progress—not radical reform—and depicted Zyuganov as totalitarian restorationist. The entire administrative and bureaucratic apparatus was urged to do everything possible to turn out the right vote. The fabulously wealthy "oligarchs," such as Boris Berezovsky and Vladimir Gusinsky, naturally feared the return to power of communists and agreed to end their rivalries and support Yeltsin's campaign with their influence and millions of dollars. The press was also heavily in favor of the incumbent President, though the stance of the media was complex. The Russian press was generally pluralistic and free, though the oligarchs controlled a great deal of it (often at a loss, but they saw this is the best means to influence public opinion and the public). Many journalists themselves, however, were highly professional and had been quite critical of the government. However, the fear of Zyuganov and the communists made it rally solidly behind Yeltsin, including some publications that switched from sharp criticism to support, only to return to criticism after the election. The communists had their advantages, too. They represented the only huge, well-organized, and territorially comprehensive political party in Russia, while Yeltsin in effect had no party of his own. Candidates could have their representatives at the polling places, but only the communists provided them everywhere.

The first round of voting, on June 16, gave Yeltsin 35 percent of the vote, Zyuganov 32 percent, Aleksandr Lebed (a charismatic retired general credited with preventing civil war in Moldova, who campaigned as a moderate national patriot) 15 percent, Yavlinsky 7 percent, Zhirinovsky 6 percent, and so on down the line, with Gorbachev getting one-half of 1 percent. Because no one obtained a majority of votes, the two leading candidates had to compete in a second round. Two days after the first round, Lebed joined Yeltsin's government as National Security Advisor (he would later become a regional governor before dying in a helicopter crash in 2002), effectively transferring most of his voters to Yeltsin. Ultimately, however, it appears to have been public distaste for the communists, however reformed Zyuganov appeared to have been, that ensured Yeltsin's victory. In the final election, on July 3, Yeltsin gained 53.8 percent of the vote against Zyuganov's 40.3 percent. Sixty-nine percent of the electorate voted. The support for Zyuganov was impressive. However, the communists had great difficulty expanding their electorate in the second round after they had gathered the faithful and the susceptible protesters in the first. Later analyses indicated that the party relied very heavily for support on the elderly and the retired, and had little acceptance among the young.

Yeltsin's electoral victory in June and July 1996 was followed by other events propitious for the President and his government. Late in August the Chechen war came to an end. On the fifth of November Yeltsin underwent quintuple bypass heart surgery. In spite of many fears, the surgery proved to be successful and eventually enabled the President to return to his work with a renewed vigor. The year 1997 witnessed a stabilization of the ruble in Russia, and a great increase in capitalist activity, international and national, in the country. Many participants and observers believed that the country had finally turned the corner. On September 19 it was even announced that because of a bumper crop Russia would be able to export grain for the first time in fifty years.

Encouraged by these and certain other developments, but continuously beset by mounting indebtedness, the increasing poverty, even penury, of the people, widespread problems of crime and corruption, the inability of the government to collect most of the taxes and of industry to increase production, Yeltsin turned to one more burst of economic reform. In his State of the Federation speech of March 1997, Yeltsin warned that "the people's patience is at a breaking point." He blamed high officials and promised to bring into the government "competent and energetic people." However, he spoke of "reform" not as further structural transformation but, as he had begun to do since 1995, as improving tax collection, raising pensions, fighting corruption, enhancing social services, and strengthening the armed forces. He fired a number of ministers and deputy ministers close to Chernomyrdin and brought Chubais back to government along with Boris Nemtsov, the reformist young governor of the Nizhnii Novgorod region. Both were determined to weaken the political influence of the oligarchs as a class (though some individual oligarchs remained influential). By the end of 1997, Chernomyrdin, seen by many as the protector of the oligarchs, convinced Yeltsin to dismiss Chubais and Nemtsov. In Yeltsin's State of the Federation speech in February 1998, however, he repeated his concerns about widespread social problems in the country, warning again that if the government failed to solve these problems "we shall have a different government." Again he fired ministers, including, this time, the prime minister, Chernomyrdin, who had the remarkable distinction of having lasted in that position for several years. Chernomyrdin, an old-timer, and manager of the enormous natural gas monopoly in Soviet days, with a certain relaxed manner and numerous connections in important circles, was told by the President that younger and more energetic reformers were needed, while he, Chernomyrdin, should prepare for the presidential election in the year 2000. The new leader was a relatively little-known economist Sergei Kiriyenko, who after a long battle was finally endorsed by the Duma and became prime minister in March 1998.

The Kiriyenko government developed an anti-crisis austerity plan of reduced government expenditures and increased tax collections (though the Duma rejected increasing personal taxes) and effectively convinced the International Monetary Fund to release part of its multi-billion-dollar rescue package of loans. The situation was dire: indebtedness was growing, wage payments to state workers were often unpaid, hard currency and gold reserves were being depleted, investment was minimal, capital continued to flee the country, and the Russian stock market was plummeting as was the value of the ruble. The problems were not entirely internal to Russia. For one thing, Russia became embroiled in the world financial crisis, which began in Asia but was spreading to other continents. Another devastating factor outside Russian control was the plunge in the price of natural gas and oil, which constituted over 50 percent in value of Russian exports. But, probably more important, Russia was paying for a failure to restructure effectively its economy and operating a kind of a pyramid scheme where only ever-new international loans kept the economic machinery going. On August 17, 1998, "Black Monday," the government defaulted on billions of dollars of short-term, high-interest treasury bills that the government had issued to meet its expenses and devalued the ruble by 50 percent. The stock market collapsed, many of Russia's largest banks failed, small businesses were wiped out, and real wages fell severely. Most of the foreigners working in the country left faster than they had come in and the International Monetary Fund refused further loans. Kiriyenko was dismissed. Yeltsin again proposed Chernomyrdin as prime minister, but this time he could not push him through the Duma, because of the obvious long-term connection between the candidate and the system that had failed so disastrously.

Yeltsin was clearly losing influence. His feeble health was also becoming more and more visible. Under pressure from the Duma, he nominated as prime minister Evgeny Primakov, the foreign minister, who was perceived as politically neutral and a pragmatist but who also had an important past in the Communist Party and the police establishment. Yeltsin's prestige sank lower than ever, and it was expected that he would be promptly forced to resign or at least become unmistakably a mere figurehead. But Yeltsin was not ready to give up. His State of the Federation speech in April 1999 was often feebly presented, disjointed, and defensive, but his message was clear enough: Russia needed order, stability, and security, in both economic and political life; he warned against communists and nationalists whose goals were "revenge" and the return of "directives and plans in the economy, censorship in media, and another round of the Cold War and refusal to integrate into the global economy." A month later, he fired Primakov (viewed, it has been argued, as too popular and too independent) and appointed Sergei Stepashin, the former head of the interior ministry, as prime minister. And he implicitly warned the Duma that if they rejected Stepashin—who represented the security services, after all—he might use force against the Duma. In the words of a leading political scientist, Yeltsin was again "ready to rumble." The Duma accepted Stepashin, who worked hard to stabilize the economy and win more Western economic aid, not without some success. A few months later, however, amidst new violence in Chechnia, Yeltsin announced that he was replacing Stepashin with another veteran of the security services, the relatively unknown former KGB officer from St. Petersburg, forty-six-year-old Vladimir Putin, whom Yeltsin effusively described as representing the new generation of leaders for Russia's future. Together they faced a new crisis in Chechnia. Armed militants invaded neighboring Dagestan, perhaps, some Chechen leaders suggested, to set up an independent Islamic republic uniting Chechnia and Dagestan. That summer, bombs destroyed two apartment buildings in Moscow and two in southern Russia, killing more than 300 people. Chechen terrorists were blamed and in September 1999, a massive Russian invasion opened the second Chechen war. The still shadowy Putin showed his style by declaring "we will wipe them out in their outhouses" and authorizing extreme force.

Initial successes in this war, along with improvements in the economy, helped the government achieve a rare victory in the Duma elections in December 1999. A new pro-government party, Unity—whose platform was limited to supporting the government and ensuring Russia's "territorial integrity and national greatness"—benefited from massive financial and media support from the oligarchs and won 23.8 percent of the party-list vote. With the support of individual deputies and other reformist parties, the government found itself with a likely working majority in the Duma for the first time. Also for the first time, the communist and nationalist opposition was in a minority, though still a strong one. Putin's approval ratings in polls soared to 50 percent, while Yeltsin, increasingly incoherent in his public statements and seemingly more preoccupied with his own power and personal security than with the politics of the country, was left with a mere 1.7 percent approval. Even Yeltsin now recognized that the time had come for him to step aside. In his New Year's address on December 31, 1999, Yeltsin announced his resignation as President, effective immediately. Putin was named acting President. He immediately showed his gratitude: he guaranteed Yeltsin and his family a lifetime of immunity from legal prosecution and a generous pension. In the presidential elections held in March 2000, Putin won 53 percent of the votes in the first round, twice as many votes as his only serious opponent, the communist Zyuganov. It seemed to many that a new age of stability—the goal Yeltsin had been talking of for the last few years—was now truly underway. Huge social and economic problems remained, though these were easing. Most important, politics was evidently outgrowing its years of tumult and uncertainty. Or, at least, it has been argued, that was what most Russians were voting for.

Putin

Vladimir Vladimirovich Putin was born in Leningrad in October 1952, so neither the war nor Stalin were part of his immediate experience. He believed completely in the system. From the time of his youth, according to his own account, he dreamed of working in Soviet intelligence. Advised that good training for such work was law, he entered law school at Leningrad State University and was accepted into the KGB after graduation. He was posted to East Germany, in Dresden, though was never a major spy. Perhaps the most dramatic moment in his career in foreign intelligence came when he helped the East German secret police, the Stasi, burn files as the Berlin Wall came down. Putin returned home to work briefly at Leningrad State University in the office watching foreigners. In 1990, when the liberal reformer Anatoly Sobchak (one of Putin's former law professors) was elected mayor, Putin became his assistant for international affairs, building a reputation as an excellent administrator. When Sobchak led the resistance in Leningrad to the 1991 coup, Putin resigned from the KGB and sided with the mayor. In 1995, at Sobchak's request, Putin organized and led the St. Petersburg branch of the moderate reformist party Our Home Is Russia in preparation for the Duma elections. When Sobchak lost the mayoral election in 1996, Putin also resigned. Putin's loyalty and his reputation as a man who could get things done impressed Yeltsin, who brought him to Moscow that same year to work in his administration. In 1999, Yeltsin named Putin his new prime minister and then acting President.

What do we know of Putin's thinking? The U.S. ambassador to Russia at the time of Putin's appointment and election has described him as intelligent, well-informed, pragmatic, and logical, never emotional, but also "difficult to read as an individual." Most observers have said the same. Even when Putin was overwhelmingly elected President in March 2000, beyond standing for stability, he remained a political mystery to most. Time will reveal more about the man and his thinking, and later historians will benefit from greater perspective on his rule. Still, his first term in office cleared away much of that initial mystery—by the beginning of 2004 most observers were predicting that Putin would easily win a second term in the March 2004 elections, and a number of politicians were proposing that the constitution be revised to allow the President more than two terms and to extend the term of office to seven years. Putin has always claimed to be non-ideological, opposed to the establishment of any

Vladimir Putin speaking with American journalists, 2001. (Associated Press)

official state dogma. To be sure, he grew up believing in the Soviet system, but he came to understand its failures, especially the failure of absolute ideology as a nation's guide. Many have described him as a pragmatist, though many specialists see Putin as inspired by at least one "ism": "statism," the belief that a strong state is the necessary means for Russia's progress and part of the definition of that progress. Many would add that Putin is in his own way also a "nationalist," committed to Russia's strength in the world and at home. These values have shaped his view of the Soviet past, which differ considerably from that of Yeltsin and many radical reformers. In speeches, to much sympathetic applause, he has often said that "anyone who does not regret the collapse of the Soviet Union has no heart, but anyone who wants it restored has no brain." He acknowledges that there were "very harsh, dark periods" in the Soviet past, but he insists this is Russia's heritage, part of people's experiences and memories, and contains many moments to be proud of. While it was Yeltsin who brought back the imperial flag and crowned double-headed eagle as Russia's national symbols, Putin restored as the Russian national anthem the Soviet hymn (a melody by Glinka had been used during the 1990s), with new words by the original author, and gave the red star back to the army. But for all his patriotic, even nationalist, language, what Putin seems most to want—which he likely shares with much of the population—is not a return to the past but a restoration of Russia's strength, which requires engagement with the larger world rather than isolation or defiance. Putin regularly insists that Russians are Europeans and that Russia is part of the West. And he talks of Russia's modernization in what he understands to be Western terms. He speaks of the need for the "rule of law," and even of the protection of individual rights, though his initial frequent use of the phrase "dictatorship of the law" made many uneasy. And he insists on the need to "combine the principles of a market economy and democracy with Russian realities."

We see these values reflected in the party that Putin endorsed for the 2003 parliamentary elections, which ultimately won the largest number of seats in the Duma. The United Russia Party was established in 2001 by a merger of the pro-government Unity Party and Moscow Mayor Yury Luzhkov's Fatherland-All-Russia Party. Led by the interior minister, Boris Gryzlov, and the minister for emergencies and civil defense, Sergei Shoigu, along with the powerful mayor of Moscow, it is been widely described as a "party of power." Certainly, its success was helped by copious favorable coverage in the largely state-controlled media (a process to be discussed later). But it was the party's message—or what some specialists have called its carefully crafted "non-message"—that was key to its success with voters. Few specific programs were proposed and candidates refused to be drawn into televised debates over issues. Instead the party conveyed a upbeat and patriotic message of a country moving "together with the president" along a path toward increasingly stability and prosperity, inspired by the vague but compelling idea of "Russia united and strong." Advertisements and speeches regularly reminded voters that the economy was improving, political stability restored, and Russia's stature in the world growing. Images used in the campaign conveyed this message as strongly as words: figures from Russian and Soviet history, happy families, gleaming new buildings, beautiful rural scenes. Pride in country, a desire for respect in the world, prosperity, a "decent life" for every person, stability, honesty, and happiness—these were the themes that inspired so many voters.

Many have criticized Putin for a weak commitment to democracy. Government officials themselves have used terms like "managed democracy" to suggest their approach. Observers have worried about the dominant role in the government and in the leadership of United Russia of the so-called *siloviki*—the power elites, or individuals with past or present associations with the intelligence services, the ministry of the interior, the military, and other agencies of armed state power—whom Putin has often promoted in his government and relied on for advice. Many critics have also noted Putin's indifference to human rights abuses in Chechnia and the growing harassment of human rights activists, environmentalists, religious groups, and others. Above all, perhaps, Putin's relations with the parliament, with the so-called oligarchs, and with the media have been seen as key signs of his weak attachment to democracy.

Putin's relations with the State Duma and the upper house of parliament, the Federation Council, have been cooperative, though he has gradually increased his own power in relationship to the parliament. After the December 1999 election, the strong presence in the Duma of the pro-government Unity Party, which held the most important chairmanships of committees in the Duma, helped. But Unity did not hold an outright majority, so Putin's supporters had to regularly cobble together coalitions with other factions, including the communists, through persistent parliamentary bargaining and compromise. The result was a growing list of legislative successes (evidence of Putin's effectiveness, though also of his commitment to continued economic and social reform): a Land Code allowing private ownership of land, a new Labor Code giving employers more authority over workers, comprehensive tax reform, expansion of the jury system and the rights of defense lawyers in trials, and laws lowering the regulatory burden for businesses. A number of new laws were seen as further concentrating power at the center: purely regional political parties were prohibited; regional governors could be dismissed by the President; a state of emergency could by declared by the President during crises; and elected local representatives in the upper house of parliament were to be replaced by appointed legislators. In the 2003 Duma elections, the pro-government United Russia Party won 37 percent of the party-list total; combined with support from individuals and smaller parties, the party commanded a decisive majority in the Duma and was able to take control of almost all Duma committees. By contrast, the Communist Party and Zhirinovsky's nationalist Liberal Democrats each won around 12 percent of the vote, while a newly formed union of thirty nationalist parties, calling itself Motherland, won 9 percent. The two main liberal democratic parties, Yabloko and the Union of Right Forces, failed to pass the minimum threshold for party-list representation at all (though they won a handful of individual seats). The leaders of Yabloko, the Union of Right Forces, the Communist Party, and others complained of irregularities and falsifications, but to no effect. More than any time since 1991, the Duma became less a critical and competing center of power within the state than a rubber stamp for the President.

In elections and speeches, Putin has often promised to fight against corruption, to free Russia from the power of the "oligarchs" who, in his words, have dangerously "merged power with capital." The government launched a series of targeted investigations, raids of business offices, arrests, and legal actions against some of the most politically influential moguls. While the Putin government insisted in each case that it was simply enforcing laws against tax evasion, fraud, and embezzlement, many observers believed the goal was more to rid the government of political competition (and criticism) and thus increase its own power. Vladimir Gusinsky's independent television network often criticized the government's war in Chechnia and the undemocratic practices of the government; he was arrested in 2000. Boris Berezovsky, once a close ally of Yeltsin and Putin, became a regular critic of Putin and tried to organize his own political movement and to fund anti-government human rights groups; to avoid arrest, he fled the country. Mikhail Khodorkovsky, head of the huge Yukos oil company and, some say, one of the richest men in the world, used his money to support civic organizations and liberal opposition parties (including, perhaps, Yabloko and the Union of Right Forces) and actively lobbied for business interests in the Duma; he was arrested and jailed in 2003. These three most famous targets of investigation all criticized Putin for excessive fondness for centralized state power and too little respect for democratic civil society; all seemed to have political ambitions for themselves as extensions of their huge business interests. It remains quite plausible—and polls showed this is what most Russians thought—that these men were crooks. No one became rich honestly in the postcommunist 1990s, it was widely said. But the main reason these particular oligarchs were targeted, critics maintained, was that they challenged Putin's political power. Indeed, Putin publicly made it clear to other oligarchs, and to the foreign investors who were often partners in their firms, that their fortunes and property were safe as long as they paid their taxes and kept out of national politics (their local political power, at least for the moment, was also left alone). This promise was in stark contrast with the communists who continued to talk of renationalizing property to undo the unquestionably corrupt privatizations of the 1990s. If anything, Putin's years have been economically good for the oligarchs. During 2000–3, the richest few began buying up still wider swaths of the economy, consolidating ownership in more industries than in the 1990s, when their wealth was concentrated in natural resources, banking, and the media.

The story of Putin's relations with the non-government media is closely tied to these questions of political power, democracy, and corruption. In 1993, Vladimir Gusinsky established the first private television network in Russia, NTV (Independent Television). Its independent news shows, political talk shows, and satirical puppet show, *Kukly*, were enormously popular and influential; in particular, NTV was valued (and reviled) for revealing the suffering on both sides in the war in Chechnia. Gusinsky also published his own widely read newspaper and weekly magazine, both admired for their critical independence of the government, and he funded an influential radio station. Other financial tycoons established media outlets or took control of state-owned media—Berezovsky acquired control of the state television network ORT and founded his own smaller channel. Most of Russia's national newspapers fell under the control of a small circle of banks or energy companies. After Putin's victory in the March 2000 presidential elections, he announced a new press policy. He believed in the principle of a free press, he insisted, but this should not allow the media to become "a means of mass disinformation and tools of struggle against the state." He also insisted that state-owned media must dominate the market in order to ensure that the population had "objective" information. Already in 2000, Putin began openly attacking his critics in the media, accusing them of harming Russia and even of treason. In May 2000, Gusinsky's headquarters were raided by masked police and he was pressured to sign away control of his media empire, Media-MOST, to the oil and gas industry cartel, Gazprom, which was close to Putin, in return for his freedom. Attempts to make NTV journalists change their style or force them out led to mass demonstrations in Moscow. But by 2001 Gazprom and the government prevailed—though most of the public agreed with the government's claim that this was about corruption not media control. A similar conflict broke out over Berezovsky's TV-6, to which many NTV reporters had fled; in 2002, the station was forced off the air, soon to be restored by pro-Kremlin insiders who openly spoke of "self-censorship" as the key to survival, a strategy shared by many journalists. Comparisons to Soviet television are now common, especially now that all networks are in the hands of the state or of state corporations and news broadcasts are filled with lengthy and uncritical reports on the leader.

Putin's popularity, notwithstanding his enhanced political power and his attacks on oligarchs and critics (or perhaps even because of it), has depended in very large part on the progress of the economy. The evidence is impressive. The performance of the Russian economy in 2000 was the best since Yeltsin's radical reforms began in 1992 and growth has continued, if at more modest levels, in the years following. By the end of 2000, GDP had grown 8–10 percent over the previous year, inflation had declined to about 20 percent a year, and reserves of gold and hard currency had grown. During the first three years of Putin's presidency, incomes rose (especially in Moscow where much of this growth remained concentrated, though growth began to spread to other parts of Russia); foreign loans were being paid off, decreasing Russia's debt burden from 146 percent of GDP in 1998 to 41 percent in 2002; investment in manufacturing grew and Russian-made consumer products became more common; capital flight to offshore banks and other foreign havens slowed; and wages were paid more regularly and in cash, replacing widespread payment in kind in the early reform years.

This economic progress was fueled in large part by two windfalls: the increase in world oil prices, which doubled between 1998 and 2003, and the devaluation of the ruble after the crisis of 1998, which, by making imports more expensive, stimulated domestic production and export. But these are temporary conditions. Some economists believe the Putin government has not made good use of these opportunities to push forward the reforms that will be needed to ensure continued economic development. Many structural problems remain behind the encouraging macroeconomic indicators. Manufacturing is still concentrated in large firms rather than in the small and medium-sized firms that have been so critical to growth in eastern Europe. Too much of the recovery is centered in Moscow, such that the economic gap between the capital and the rest of the country has grown as the economy has improved. The banking system is poorly developed. The tax code is not conducive to investment. New laws to adjudicate disputes are far from effective. Inflation is still too high, and wages, for most of the population, remain too low to allow much spending beyond necessities. Low productivity in agriculture, which is still overwhelmingly under the control of the state or of the former collective farms, and profound rural poverty hold back the economy in many ways, though harvests have for the first time been increasing. And Russia remains poorly integrated into the global economy. Putin and his allies have recognized these problems and tried to address some of them: they cut taxes to a flat rate of 13 percent and reduced a number of business taxes; the government officially announced that no review of past privatization would be undertaken (a fear raised by the attacks on oligarchs); and they put a bill before the Duma to dismantle collective farms in favor of private agriculture. More systematic reform plans have been drafted and widely discussed. Perhaps the greatest problem remaining is growing economic inequality—in fact a double inequality of both class and region—which contains all sorts of hazards for both economic progress and political stability. Polls in 2004 record that most Russians still define Russia's economic situation as "bad." On the other hand, fewer think so than in the Yeltsin years.

Chechnia has remained a serious problem. As mentioned, the second Chechen war began in September 1999. By March 2000, after a two-month siege, the capital Grozny was taken and largely destroyed. At this point, though Putin could declare a measure of victory, the war reverted to insurgency. As Chechnia's new leader Moscow chose Akhmad Kadyrov, a former mufti who had fought against Russia in the first Chechen war. Kadyrov could not bring order to the country or end the insurgency, though his personal power grew with Moscow's help and the help of his own militia, which often terrorized his opponents. Since coming to power, and especially since the terrorist attack on the United States on September 11, 2001, Putin has repeatedly argued that the Chechen war is not a response to an independence movement but to illegitimate terrorists and bandits, a necessary fight again "religious extremists and international terrorists." Western specialists and Russian critics have tended to see the Chechen turn to terrorism, and the internationalization and Islamicization of the conflict, which few deny, as a result of this unsettled war rather than its cause. Whatever the reasons, the lingering Chechen conflict has been a source of great suffering. Mines, laid across the country by both sides, continued to maim and kill. International organizations repeatedly condemned the Russian government and military and security forces in Chechnia for human rights violations, including beatings, abductions, torture, summary executions of civilians and prisoners, and looting Chechen homes—all charges Russian commanders denied. Rebel ambushes continued to kill or maim Russian servicemen. Many Chechens have "disappeared" after being picked up by federal security forces or their local Chechen representatives. Young people, growing up in these conditions, have been seen as particularly prone to join

terrorist groups. Terrorism has certainly been on the rise. Car bombings, suicide bombings, and kidnappings against Russians increased in Chechnia. And
a series of terror attacks struck Moscow. In 2000 and 2001, bombs exploded in
a pedestrian tunnel and a subway station, killing eight people and injuring
twenty. In October 2002, at a Moscow theater, a large group of armed young
Chechen men and women took hostage an entire audience watching a popular
musical. After three days, when the Chechen fighters had said they would
begin killing the hostages, special forces troops pumped knock-out gas into the
theater and stormed the auditorium. All of the Chechens were killed by entering forces and more than a hundred of the hostages died, mostly due to the
effects of the gas. In July 2003, two female suicide bombers killed seventeen
people at a rock concert in Moscow. In December, a women blew herself up in
front of the National Hotel near the Kremlin, killing five. In February 2004, at
least forty people were killed and more than a hundred injured in an apparent
suicide bombing inside a crowded subway car. The October 2003 election of
Kadyrov as Chechen president, widely criticized for irregularities, did little to
stop the violence. And the rebuilding of a normal life in the Chechen republic
remained slow and uncertain. In late 2003 Grozny, the capital, could still be
described as a "city of violence, fear, and despair." Indeed, in May 2004, Kadyrov himself was killed in a bomb attack.

The condition of the military was another lingering problem. The end of
communism was devastating to the Russian army. The Russian defense budget
decreased steadily from 1994 until 2000. As a result, according to official
reports, weapons and equipment were in short supply, the strategic missile
system was growing obsolete and ill-repaired, and most of the navy's ships
were in need of modernization and often simple maintenance (dramatized for
the world when internal explosions led to the loss of the nuclear submarine
Kursk and its entire crew in the Arctic circle in August 2000). No less, serious
problems plagued the army's human resources. Pay and prestige of officers
was so low that recruitment was difficult. Avoidance of the draft, which
remained universal, was endemic and many of those who did join were physically or socially unfit. Hazing of soldiers by senior enlisted men was pervasive, reaching extremes of theft, beatings, rape, and even murder. Suicide was
pervasive among both officers and men. Rates of desertion, by individuals and
whole units, were growing. Alcoholism, drugs, and AIDS were growing problems. Food was sometimes in short supply and often of low quality. And effective training exercises became increasingly difficult due to the lack of funds.
Finally, many officers were guilty of selling off valuable military assets for their
own personal benefit, though sometimes for the good of their hungry and ill-
equipped troops. Although there was much talk of "military reform" under
Yeltsin, little was done. Putin was fully aware of these problems and increased
the military budget significantly. Plans gradually to create a professional rather
than conscript army were announced. And he made systematic modernization
of the armed forces a top priority. Specialists have described this as the first
serious effort to address the military's problems since the collapse of the Soviet
Union, but they remain wary. Like so much else Putin has undertaken, military
reform will be a lengthy and difficult process. Given Putin's—and most

Russians'—view that a revitalized military is central to Russia's becoming a strong and respected country, reform will remain both practically and symbolically important.

Foreign Policy

It was Gorbachev and his associates, not Yeltsin and his government, who made the historic decision to let eastern Europe go and who ended the cold war. They also made a major contribution to the breakup of the Soviet Union itself, although in that development Yeltsin too played a prominent part. The net result was a transformation of international relations and, indeed, of the political map. Most important, the dread of an impending mutual atomic annihilation disappeared. Much as one can rightly worry about the possibility of an atomic war, for example, between Pakistan and India, or about the use of atomic weapons by small nations seeking to have a more powerful place in their region and the world or even a private group, these dangers do not begin to compare to the Armageddon threatened by the intense, decades-long confrontation of the two superpowers. International relations still contained plenty of tensions over conflicting perceptions and interests, but they lost their apocalyptic character and became more a matter of common sense and adjustment. Yeltsin and Russian foreign ministers, in particular Aleksandr Kozyrev, continued the orientation and the work of Gorbachev and Shevardnadze.

Taking into account the immensity of the change, the breakup of the Soviet Union, which resulted in the sudden appearance of fifteen independent states in Europe and Asia where there had previously been one, occurred amazingly peacefully, in particular as far as Russia was concerned, though Russia insisted that the former Soviet space was properly within its own special sphere of interest and influence and referred to it as the special "near abroad." To be sure, the bloody and tragic Chechen war must be kept in mind, although, strictly speaking, it represented a struggle within the Russian Federation itself rather than between that Federation and other newly created republics. Otherwise, the Russian army played a secondary role in the bitter fighting between Armenia and Azerbaijan, which came to center on Nagorno-Karabakh, in purportedly supporting or even promoting the rebellion of the Abkhazians against Georgia, in guarding the southern border of Tajikistan, and in still other instances of crisis and war. Characteristically, Russian interventions were marginal both geographically and in their importance for the evolution of Russia proper.

More central were Russian relations with Ukraine and Belarus, connected with Russia by centuries of history and by very numerous cultural and personalities, and, perhaps to a lesser extent, Russian relations with the Baltic states to the west and northern Kazakhstan to the east, which, while not "Russian" in the same sense as Ukraine and Belarus, or even Slavic, contained a very large percentage of Russians in their populations. In fact, some thirty million ethnic Russians found themselves outside the Russian Federation—a new diaspora—perhaps twenty million in Ukraine and ten million in other new republics, where sometimes, as in such small countries as Estonia and Latvia, they formed a third or more of the population. Russian-Ukranian relations have been most significant and problematic. Whereas much of eastern Ukraine is ethnically Russian and Russians constitute the largest ethnicity also in the Crimea, transferred to Ukraine by Soviet authorities as recently as 1954, western Ukraine is not only solidly Ukrainian, but also, in part, ardently nationalist, and, again in part, even different in religion, professing Uniate Catholicism rather than Orthodoxy. Under the circumstances, and pressed hard by their respective nationalists, the two governments did well to settle their mutual affairs peacefully, as reflected in the treaty of friendship of May 30–31, 1997, signed by Yeltsin and Leonid Kuchma, confirming the boundary between the two countries and agreeing that Russia lease from Ukraine for twenty years the great Crimean naval base of Sevastopol (so prominent in the Crimean War of 1853–56). The Russian need for peace followed readily from everything discussed previously; as to Ukraine, it was probably worse off economically than Russia, on which it depended for fuel and other imports and to which it was heavily in debt.

White Russia, or Belarus, has been very different from Ukraine. Behind Ukraine in developing a sense of identity or nationalism of any kind (the Lithuanian-Russian state is one of its main historical assets), Belarus has also exhibited little or no hostility toward Russia, a feeling that has been one of the inspirations of Ukrainian nationalism. Poor, its economy unreformed, and dependent on Russia for fuel and other needs, Belarus seemed to be in many ways an ideal junior partner for its giant neighbor. And indeed Belarus and Russia signed on April 2, 1997, a Treaty of Union. Although Yeltsin presented that treaty as a major success, it was not clear what it meant or where it would lead. In fact, economists in particular asked, what could Russia gain from Belarus? In addition, the crude, dictatorial head of Belarus, Aleksandr Lukashenko, kept arousing opposition at home and even in the world (as when he was forcing foreign diplomatic representatives to vacate their domiciles in Minsk), and, albeit in his own way pro-Russian, was regarded with much suspicion by the Russians.

In the cases of the Baltic countries, Kazakhstan and most other successor states, the Russian government was not concerned with their historical past or their ethnic and cultural closeness to the Russians, but only with how these obviously foreign entities treated their ethnically Russian subjects. Yet tensions were raised by the possibility that a change in the Russians' approach might lead to their claiming on ethnic grounds territories all the way from a strip along the Estonian border to the entire northern Kazakhstan. Nor was the issue of "the treatment" of Russians in the succession republics an easy one. It pivoted on requirements for citizenship and especially on how quickly and how well Russian inhabitants must learn the official language of their republic to qualify for citizenship, although sometimes when the candidates for citizenship or their families moved into the area also mattered. And the languages in question range from difficult to very difficult. Still, some adjustments and compromises were made, and the attitude of the Russian government on this entire issue deserves to be considered on the whole reasonable, unless one is to assume that it has no right at all to be concerned with the fate of Russians outside Russia.

The Soviet government and the Red Army also gave up eastern Europe, including East Germany, and in fact evacuated it, in general, in a remarkably precipitous and total way. During the years that followed, the countries in that area underwent different experiences, some of them like and others unlike those of Russia, ranging from the absorption of East Germany into a larger Germany, and Václav Havel's liberal regime in Czechoslovakia to strong residual communism and neo-communism in such states as Romania, Bulgaria, and even to some extent Poland. Yet throughout eastern Europe the period preceding the collapse of 1989 was regarded as that of Russian, as well as communist, oppression, and, once the oppression ended, the inhabitants of the area were at best indifferent to the Russians and their fate. In fact, as debates about the expansion of NATO and other evidence indicated, East European countries could be considered as much enemies as friends of Russia.

A greater sympathy awaited new Russia in central and western Europe and in the United States. Yeltsin favored a strongly pro-Western foreign policy, too pro-Western his communist and nationalist opponents would say. He unilaterally destroyed many ballistic missiles, negotiated further reductions, cut subsidies to Cuba and Afghanistan, supported U.S. policies toward Iraq, and maintained excellent personal relations with Western leaders, such as Chancellor Kohl and President Clinton, whom he liked to refer to as "my friend Helmut" and "my friend Bill." But tensions were growing. In return for Russia's cooperative relations with the Western powers, Yeltsin expected respect for Russia's "national interests and national pride" (as he said in his 1994 State of the Federation address) and financial aid. On both counts, Yeltsin would be increasingly disappointed, making political criticisms at home of Yeltsin's subservience before the West increasingly effective. As a result, tensions in Russian relations with the Western powers, especially the United States, began to grow.

In the pursuit of loans and aid from Western states, the World Bank, and the International Monetary Fund, Yeltsin found himself as early as 1992 reminding Western leaders, who made strong demands about the domestic economic policies that would be required before Russia would be given aid, that Russian is a great power in the midst of a great transition away from communism, not a "charity case," and that "we should not be forced onto our knees" for loans. When Yeltsin and Clinton met in Moscow in 1994, Yeltsin complained of many deficiencies in U.S. policy toward Russia, including tangible material support. In fact, billions would be loaned to Russia in the 1990s, mainly through the IMF and the World Bank (though this also added to Russia's debt burden), but frustration remained. There is no doubt that Clinton and other West European leaders and states, including Germany, strongly supported Yeltsin and his limping program of democracy and modernization. Yet no Marshall Plan was established for Russia, and Russians felt deceived in their expectations of a much larger sponsorship.

Another major source of tension was the plan to enlarge NATO into eastern Europe. Judged, with some reason, to be anti-Russian as well as unnecessary, the move produced a strong negative reaction in Russia. In March 1997, the Duma voted 300–1 against expansion, a rare example of political unanimity in Russia. Compromises were offered to help Russians accept the growth of this former anti-Soviet military alliance closer to Russian borders—which, in any case, they knew they could not prevent—including membership in a vague "Partnership for Peace" with the Western powers and a slowed pace of enlargement. But none of this made it easy to see any benefits to Russia when the official invitation was issued by NATO on July 8, 1997, to Poland, the Czech Republic (Slovakia had seceded from Czechoslovakia), and Hungary to join the alliance by 1999. (The three countries became members of NATO on March 19, 1999). N.A.T.O.'s enlargement bolstered the arguments of Yeltsin's anti-Western critics, who insisted the West wanted a weakened and isolated Russia.

The conflict in the former Yugoslavia further damaged Russian–NATO, and especially Russian–U.S., relations. From the first, the Yeltsin government insisted on its special relationship with the Serbs (for practical as well as for sentimental reasons: Serbs were Slavic and Orthodox and, before the Bolshevik revolution, Russia had considered itself a protector of the Serbs). When the United States bombed the Bosnian Serbs in 1994, though without UN sanction, for failing to respect UN warnings, the Russians were furious, including at what was seen as the hypocritical unilateralism of the world's one remaining superpower, which seemingly did not have to follow the rules it set for others. Russian troops were soon invited to serve beside NATO forces under UN command, however, and Russia was able to broker a cease-fire that prevented further U.S. air strikes. But relations remained tense. By the end of 1994, Yeltsin was warning that a "cold peace" was replacing the Cold War, and his foreign minister, Kozyrev, was soon to declare that "the honeymoon is over." By January 1996, after an hour-long telephone conversation with Clinton, Yeltsin proclaimed a "second honeymoon" in Russian–U.S. relations, but this too would cool as NATO expansion plans moved forward, foreign aid remained inadequate and often delayed, the United States revived plans to develop a missile defense system, and the conflict in the former Yugoslavia deepened. Russia too helped sour the relationship by selling military goods and nuclear technology to "rogue" states like Iran and coming to an agreement with China in 1996 to coordinate foreign policy and resist "unipolarity" in the world (a code word for American hegemony).

The Kosovo tragedy was a milestone. As what was left of Yugoslavia continued to disintegrate—a problem the Russians could well sympathize with—the Serbian-Yugoslav leader Slobodan Milosevic sought to prevent the largely Muslim Albanian province of Kosovo from seceding. Arguing that violent atrocities and "ethnic cleansing" made intervention necessary, NATO, led by the United States (again without UN sanction), bombed Serbia in March 1999. Both the public and the government in Russia were outraged. Many argued that the United States was the main "rogue" state in the world, determined to intervene whenever and wherever it wished. The liberals who had put their trust in the West were probably even more upset than the nationalists, the conservatives, and the communists. A notable exception were the people of Islamic background inhabiting the Russian federation, such as the Tartars, who came out strongly in support of the victimized Muslim Albanians of Kosovo. The Russian government denounced the aggression and pointedly refused to attend as a guest the celebration by NATO of its fiftieth anniversary. Still,

Yeltsin and his government maintained essential ties with the West. Moreover, continuous aerial bombardment as well as quite possibly Russian efforts at negotiation made Milosevic finally give in to NATO, and peace was established in Kosovo in the second half of June. Russia went on to participate—not without new tensions—in the occupation and the restoration of the devastated area. On the whole its international position improved because of its role in the Kosovo tragedy, with, in particular, promises of more Western financial help. Russia disagreed with the United States and other Western countries on many issues. This, however, no longer represented the dreaded confrontation of the communist and the free worlds. Indeed, in numerous matters, whether related to Bosnia or to Iraq, France, for example, often stood closer to Russia than to the United States.

When Putin came to power he inherited relatively good relations with other countries, but he also faced growing condescension for postcommunist Russia. It had become common to hear Western commentators dismiss Russia as a political has-been on the world stage with a basket-case economy, a chaotic and corrupt political order, and a deteriorating military. For Putin, as for most Russians citizens and politicians, it was essential to restore Russia's place in the world as a respected and influential power. Two interrelated principles seem to have guided Putin in his emerging foreign policy. One is patriotism—a nationalism built less on cultural and ethnic identification than on the idea of a people's unifying loyalty to their state and their determination that it be respected in the world. The other is realpolitik. Putin has understood, perhaps better than many of his foreign policy advisors, that Russia is still weak economically and politically, that the military is in shambles, that the Commonwealth of Independent States is little more than a fig leaf of cooperation between the former Soviet states hiding considerable distrust and lack of support for Russia, and that, for better or worse, the United States remains the only superpower. Putin has been determined to assert Russia's global role, while remaining quite aware that this must be done in a world in which "when the Russian bear growls" few any longer worry.

The "near abroad" has remained a major concern. Although nationalists, communists, and even, most recently, leading members of the pro-government United Russia Party have publicly talked of someday reuniting the lost parts of the Russian Empire and the Soviet Union, Putin's policy has been decidedly pragmatic, though always focused on Russia's own national interests. Putin has largely ignored the Commonwealth of Independent States, recognizing it to be little more than a pretense of cooperation, and focused on direct relations with the former Soviet states. In 2001, Russia united with Kazakhstan, Kyrgyzstan, Tajikistan, and China to build cooperative economic and security ties, including basing Russian troops in Kyrgyzstan. The entry of the U.S. military into Central Asia after the September 11, 2001, attacks complicated this effort, though this could be seen as pointing toward either a new site of cooperation between Russia and the United States or a source of renewed "great game" competition. In other cases as well, efforts have been made to nurture cooperative and beneficial relationships. Trading and financial relations with Ukraine were improved (though Ukraine's increasing inclinations toward the West and

NATO have created tensions). Efforts to create a unified economic zone uniting Russia and Belarus, perhaps even with a common currency, have continued. Although Russia and Georgia had been arguing constantly over allegations of Russian attacks on Chechen fighters across the border with Georgia and over the continued presence of Russian troops on former Soviet bases, when Georgia invited U.S. military advisors in 2002 to help them battle Chechen fighters holed up on the Georgian side of the border, Putin declared it "no tragedy," even though his foreign minister had condemned it.

The exceptionally powerful position of the United States in the world has shaped most of Russia's foreign policy in recent years. An official foreign policy concept paper in June 2000 highlighted Putin's emerging approach: given limited resources Russia must concentrate on areas where Russia has vital interests but must insist on these interests; while NATO expansion is undesirable, Russian cooperation in both security and economic partnerships is more important; and, for the longer term, the present unipolar economic and political domination by the United States must be replaced by a "multipolar world." Putin continued negotiating reductions of strategic weapons (persuading the Duma to ratify the START 2 treaty in April 2000), showed willingness to compromise on U.S. plans to modify the anti-ballistic missile (ABM) treaty so that it could begin testing its national missile defense system (NMD) in return for deep mutual cuts in strategic weapons, and signed other agreements. Still, tensions persisted. Conflicts over the NMD continued and there was little personal rapport between presidents Clinton and Putin. When George W. Bush was elected U.S. president in November, relations further chilled. Bush advisors like Condoleezza Rice, a former Soviet specialist, argued openly that Russia's weakness made cooperation unnecessary and unwise: its economic problems were its own to solve, sharing security information was dangerous due to the risks of leaks, and Russia remained "a threat to the West." In particular, U.S. officials accused the Russians of violating the nuclear non-proliferation regime. In February 2001, in an echo of Cold War relations, the United States arrested an FBI agent said to have been spying for Russia and ejected fifty Russian diplomats, leading Russia to expel fifty American diplomats.

Russia was also actively challenging U.S. unipolar power in the world and its own post-Soviet isolation. Putin was building strong relations with Britain's Tony Blair (who eased Russian concerns about NATO expansion by creating a special joint council of the nineteen member states plus Russia) and especially Germany's Gerhard Schroeder, who shared Russian anxieties about the United States. In the Middle East, Russia directly intervened in peace negotiations despite being formally excluded by the United States (though Russia had been a cosponsor of the 1993 Oslo accords). Russia rebuilt relations with Iran, even resuming arms sales, and actively urged that sanctions be lifted against Iraq (though also pressuring Iraq to allow UN weapon inspectors) with the hope for oil exploration contracts and weapon sales to Iraq once sanctions were lifted. Putin visited Castro in Havana to pledge continued economic relations and joined the Cuban President in deploring U.S. efforts to dominate Latin America and the world. He traveled to North Korea, where he believed that he convinced the Koreans to give up their nuclear weapons program (they denied any pledge), and to Vietnam and South Korea to improve business opportunities for Russian companies. He met with the leaders of India, to restore Russian relations in direct competition with U.S. efforts in South Asia, and with the leaders of China to pledge economic and security cooperation and, again, to criticize U.S. aspirations for hegemony. Russian relations with the United States appeared to be on a downhill slope.

However, Putin's pragmatism led him to resist the temptation—and to resist much of the advice of his own foreign policy and military establishment—to continue too far along this path. After all, Russia's goal was a seat at the table of world politics, not the stance of outsider and spoiler. And the realities of U.S. power could not be ignored. The personal chemistry between Bush and Putin helped. After their first meeting in the summer of 2001, Bush famously observed, "I was able to get a sense of his soul." Several months later, after their meeting at the presidential ranch in Texas, Bush would add, "the more I get to see his heart and soul, the more I know we can work together in a positive way." Discussions on allowing a U.S. missile defense system, to which Bush was strongly committed, revived (though Russia still hoped to convince the United States not to scuttle the treaty altogether), and Bush promised to support Russia's entry into the World Trade Organization, a Putin priority. Most important (even prophetic), they found strong common interest in fighting what they viewed as the threat of Islamic fundamentalism. Bush's comments after their meetings showed that he did understand Putin in some ways: "I found a man who realizes his future lies with the West. . . . On the other hand, he doesn't want to be diminished by America."

Then came September 11, 2001. Putin was the first world leader to call President Bush with sympathy and shared outrage against what Putin called "barbarous terrorist acts aimed against wholly innocent people." Obviously, the Chechen conflict was in Putin's mind, for he had already been linking it to Islamic fundamentalism and international terrorism and was now likely to find more sympathy for Russia's brutal fight there. More subtly, many Russians saw September 11 as bursting the illusion of a unipolar world and likely to lead the United States into more cooperative engagement with other nations in the common struggle for security and peace. By offering Russian "solidarity" with America in the fight against world terrorism, Russia was again inviting itself to the table. Putin offered to share intelligence and (though against much internal government resistance) to support U.S. plans to go after Al Qaeda and the Taliban in Afghanistan, including by tacitly accepting U.S. troops on former Soviet bases in Central Asia. When, in December 2001, the U.S. Secretary of State informed Moscow that they were pulling out of the ABM treaty, the Russian response was muted. During the following months, Russia actively cooperated with the United States in a number of areas: as a full member of the newly expanded Group of Eight (G8) industrialized nations; as coauthor with the United States, the United Nations, and the European Union (the "Quartet") of a roadmap for peace between Israel and the Palestinians; in negotiating world energy policies and technological exchanges; in measures to stem the proliferation of "weapons of mass destruction"; and in cooperating in the "war on terrorism." Relations again began to deteriorate, however. Many

Russian political leaders were troubled by Putin's policies and he could not entirely ignore their growing unease over the United States tearing up the ABM treaty, stationing troops in Central Asia and Georgia, and openly speaking of forcible "regime change" in Iraq, along with continued movement toward incorporating East European nations and the former Soviet Baltic states into NATO and the European Union. Above all, Putin's critics complained, what had all these concessions gained for Russia? When a U.S.-led coalition invaded Iraq, without UN sanction, in March 2003, Russia joined France and Germany in condemning the war. Pressure from political elites, the coming Duma elections in December, and intelligence forecasts that indicated that this war would be a quagmire for U.S. troops and would inflame passions in the Arab world, as well as the possibility of standing side by side with France and Germany, shaped this decision. But this defiance failed to derail U.S.–Russian relations. In fact, some specialists have seen this conflict as marking a still higher stage in improving these relations: "Moscow dared to disagree and Washington grudgingly accepted its right to do so." In any case, Putin quickly showed again his pragmatic desire to cooperate, supporting a UN resolution making the United States and Great Britain responsible for Iraq after the war, thus legitimizing the occupation, offering assistance in the reconstruction, and even refraining from a public fight over Russian companies' drilling rights in Iraq. Other sources of tension remained. U.S. officials regularly criticized the Russian government for arrests of business moguls and attacks on the independent media and publicly voiced dismay over the lack of a stable system of competing political parties and a still rudimentary "civil society." In turn, Russian officials reminded U.S. leaders of the problems created by American troop presence in the near abroad and eastern Europe and of the global dangers of American unilateralism. Nonetheless, both continued to insist that the relationship between Russia and the United States was now founded on "friendship" and "trust." For Russian leaders like Putin, this was a friendship based on both pragmatism and idealism. As one Russian foreign policy advisor put it, "Many in the Russian leadership resent the United States, but they have decided it is better to adapt to American power." In any case, although the United States may often do "stupid" and harmful things in the world, it is "the only steamship we can hitch ourselves to and go in the direction of modernity."

Chapter 44

Society and Culture since 1991

When the collective farm was here you could get a sled or roofing or any kind of nail you wanted. Now everything is coming apart. That's all. Little by little it's all coming apart. That's my story. Nothing good about it.

—V. BYKOV, SEVENTY-SIX-YEAR-OLD RESIDENT OF THE VILLAGE OF ISUPOVA, 2004

Where are you racing, troika? Where does your path lie?
The coachman's drunk again on vodka. . . .
As the saints foretold, everything is hanging by a thread.
I look at it all with ancient Russian sorrow and longing.

—BORIS GREBENSHCHIKOV, 1996

I was told to come here, but I can't see a thing in all this damned fog.

—VIKTOR PELEVIN, *THE LIFE OF INSECTS*, 1996

Uncertainty may be the defining experience of social and cultural life since the end of Communist rule in 1991. Yeltsin's early promises of a quick transition to a prosperous market democracy, and widespread hope for what freedom would bring, were replaced less by simple disillusionment and anger than by a more subtle disorientation. Polls during these years repeatedly showed that citizens were troubled less by material suffering (this was not new, after all) than by the pervasive instability (*nestabil'nost*), disintegration, and uncertainty about the future. Scholars have defined these years in historically negative terms as the "unmaking of Soviet life." We have seen that the aim of dismantling past economic, social, and political structures was precisely what inspired much radical reform. In everyday practice, this historical destruction entailed a great deal of everyday havoc, disorder, loss, and confusion. This could be an exhilarating experience and could offer new opportunities and hope, but it was more likely to be frightening and depressing. For many, it could be both at once. This chapter surveys this contradictory social experience, but it also considers how people have tried to make sense of the world around them, to figure out where Russia is heading, how they fit in, and what they believe.

Poverty and Wealth

One of the most visible effects of the unmaking of communism has been the intense restratification of Russian society. Socialist leveling—though always more ideological ideal than real social fact—was wholly thrown out in favor of relentless acquisition of property and wealth by private entrepreneurs, new freedom for individuals to struggle and compete, and rapidly growing social inequality. Many Russians found this change personally and morally offensive. The privatization of the economy was widely stigmatized as prikhvatizatsion (changing the normal, if new, word *privatizatsiia* into the mocking neologism *prikhvatizatsiia*, adding the meanings of snatching or grabbing) and Russians began to speak with contempt (though also derisive humor) of the *nouveau riche* "New Russians," a class defined not only by their recent and rapid acquisition of wealth but also by their presumed dishonesty, selfish greed, links with corrupt political privilege and underground crime, showy consumerism, and low cultural level. Other terms used, by Russians and in the Western press, to describe the new Russian rich reflected the same mixture of social analysis and moral judgment: robber barons, crony capitalists, kleptocrats. A more generous interpretation of the rise of this new economic elite, favored by liberal social scientists, sees them, like other historical bourgeoisies, contributing to the development of market democracy in Russia, especially given the presumably natural tendency of educated, urbanized, propertied groups to support individual initiative, economic and political freedom, and citizen participation in public life. Other analysts have noted the many obstacles entrepreneurship has faced in postcommunist Russia, hindering and distorting normal business in many ways: the Soviet legacy in which private entrepreneurship was a criminal activity; the inadequacy of institutional, legal, and fiscal conditions; the strong place of corruption, crime, and even violence in the creation and conduct of Russian business (to be discussed more later), and widespread negative or ambivalent attitudes in the Russian public toward private business. What is certain is that a powerful new class emerged virtually overnight into Russian life, though, as we have seen in the previous chapter, it did not emerge out of the blue. Most of the leading capitalists of the 1990s already had access to resources and power, though they were also individuals with personal drive and motivation—viewed by some as vision and others as greed. According to specialists, five of the seven powerful financial-industrial groups in the mid-1990s, headed by businessmen known as "oligarchs" for their fabulous wealth and closeness to political power, had been established with the direct political and financial support of Soviet-era officials and institutions. Mikhail Khodorkovsky (widely believed to be one of the richest men in the world at the start of the new century) had been an official in the Communist Youth League, the Komsomol. Vladimir Vinogradov had been an economist at a government bank and a Komsomol official. Boris Berezovsky had been an information management specialist in the Academy of Sciences working as a consultant for the largest Soviet automobile manufacturer. Looking beyond this super-elite, studies have found that the majority of entrepreneurs of the mid-1990s had been managers or enterprise directors, typically members of the Communist Party, and often well-educated, though some entrepreneurs, such as Vladimir Gusinsky, enjoyed good educations (typically humanistic rather than technical) but felt themselves to be outsiders to the system—Gusinsky, for example, was a minor theater director and a cab driver before beginning his rise to wealth by helping to establish a Soviet-American joint venture.

Notwithstanding all the attention paid the oligarchs, who indeed managed to concentrate exceptional wealth in their hands, Russia's new entrepreneurial class was diverse. Most of the "New Russians" were not oligarchs, though they had much in common with them. They were young and rich and made their fortunes not in manufacturing—a more respectable area of the economy in public opinion, though a stagnant one—but in finance, commerce, services, and crime. Most had some connection to criminal organizations, if only in needing to pay for protection-patronage "roofs" for their businesses. Much attention has been paid to the "New Russians" not only because of their wealth but also because they were most demonstrative in standing for a new economic ethos. Their Mercedes and Land Cruisers, their expensive Western

Demonstrator at the "People's Veche *(Assembly)" in Moscow in 1992. Poster reads "The Goal of Perestroika in the USSR: To Each Their Own? Prikhvatizatsiia" (Privatization as Grabbing). The drawing shows enterprise directors and bureaucrats taking control of factories while ordinary citizens are given only "vouchers." In the background, demonstrators carry red flags.* (Mark Steinberg)

clothing, their styling salons and gyms, their brick villas (*kottedzhi*) decked out with imported furnishings and Jacuzzis inspired by Western magazines, and their women (the "New Russian" was always said to be male—the role of a woman, whether as wife or the ubiquitous mistress, was to be possessed, cared for, and to ornament the man's life), as well as their occupations and wealth, all marked them as profoundly different from the old Soviet elite. This was only the visible tip of the capitalist-entrepreneurial iceberg, however. Various groups of new business operators, both men and very often women, emerged after 1991, including top managers of privatized firms, officials who became business directors, founders of new medium and small businesses, and leaders of "mafia" protection rackets. Despite conditions far from conducive to rational capitalism, tens of thousands of entrepreneurs have been conducting business throughout the country. The 1998 financial collapse drove many out of business; even some oligarchs suffered severe losses, though the greatest impact was felt by the many smaller companies who lost all of their bank deposits. One-third of small businesses were reported to have had to close. On the other hand, the devalued ruble created new possibilities for domestic production, leading to a rise in small and medium businesses engaged in domestic manufacturing as well as services and trade. Indeed, by 1999, small businesses were proliferating, though they remained concentrated in Moscow, St. Petersburg, and other large cities. Many problems have persisted, though sociologists and economists have tended to argue that the challenges facing business people in the new Russia are less public attitudes (the often described "traditional" moral disdain for wealth not earned through direct labor) than the legacy of the structural conditions in which Russia's new capitalism arose: the massive transfer of state and public assets into private hands, which created, in the words of the sociologist Victoria Bonnell, a "mode of acquisitiveness" that was less the rationalist model of modern capitalism described by Max Weber—though that model is precisely the "civilized" state of business and society that many entrepreneurs long for—than a system based on "personalistic ties, political influence, crime, corruption, and violent entrepreneurship." And yet, individuals have been ready to take part in this uncertain system. Indeed, not only entrepreneurs have embraced capitalist behaviors and value, but also growing numbers of consultants, stockbrokers, commodity traders, and employees in all sorts of businesses. More broadly, a growing number of salary- and wage-earning Russians have begun to identify themselves as "middle class," by virtue of their education, professional skills and occupations, limited but still increased ability to buy consumer goods, both domestic and imported, and, one may suggest, acceptance of the new economic order.

The growth of wealth in Russia has been inseparable from the persistence and growth of poverty. The bare facts are sobering. Throughout this period, average real wages declined, variously affected by extreme inflation, direct pay cuts, reduced working hours, temporary layoffs, wages paid in kind rather than in cash (widespread in the early 1990s), and delayed payments; throughout the 1990s, huge numbers of workers, perhaps the majority, did not receive their wages on time, sometimes waiting months for a paycheck. Economists

In the early years of free trade after 1991, small sales booths like this one in Moscow in 1994 proliferated. As here, alcohol, cigarettes, and snack food, almost all of it imported, were particularly common items. Also note the German advertisement, the plastic shopping bags (one decorated with an American flag), and the bra. (Mark Steinberg)

agree that most enterprises preferred wage reductions to unemployment—fearing social disorder but also reflecting the notion that firms should care for their workers, a heritage of Soviet paternalism—thus limiting this scourge. Still, official unemployment data, which most specialists agree have been too conservative, record steadily rising joblessness, from about 5 percent in 1992 to 13 percent in 1999, though the number of unemployed has since begun slowly to decline as the economy has started to grow (the government reported a rate of 9 percent joblessness at the start of 2004). These structural degradations strongly affected standards of living, already low in Soviet times. The everyday diet for the majority of the population declined throughout the 1990s. Per capita consumption of meat and dairy products fell, such that the overall caloric intake reached a level well below the minimum established by the World Health Organization. And all of this, at least in the major cities, occurred while shops filled with imported luxury foods and expensive new restaurants proliferated. Conditions have been even worse, of course, for those who could not work. Scholars have spoken of a growing class of "dispossessed," including the jobless, the disabled, refugees from post-Soviet successor states, economic migrants, and people living in cities without proper residence permits. Desperate rural poverty produced a mass migration out of the countryside, leaving tens of thousands of villages home to no more than a handful of usually elderly residents; by 2004, 13,000 villages stood officially empty. The

A small grocery store and currency exchange in Moscow in 1999. A picture of Pushkin is in the window. Such mixing of commerce, Russian national cultural pride, and foreign advertising have been common. (Mark Steinberg)

declining value of government pensions relative to the cost of living pushed the huge class of the elderly into poverty. Homelessness—including the "dispossessed" as well as abandoned, orphaned, and runaway children who formed gangs of waifs in many urban areas—became endemic in larger cities. That many Russians were not surviving the transition was often literally true. Mortality rates were on the increase. Compared to 1985, when life expectancy for Soviet men had reached sixty-five years, by the end of the 1990s men were likely to live on average to only fifty-nine years (women's life expectancy declined more modestly from seventy-four to seventy years). A contributing factor, of course, was the increasing abuse of alcohol and tobacco. Rising mortality (a growth of 30 percent from 1990 to 2000, giving Russia the highest rate of any major nation) combined with a falling birthrate—many families, given the insecurities of the age have been having few children or foregoing them altogether—resulted in a declining Russian population. As the new century began, Russia's population was falling by about a million people a year. In addition, many Russians, including some of the ablest, were emigrating.

Surprisingly, perhaps, this deepening stratification of Russian society has not so far led to open social polarization or mass protest—apart from a series of sometimes violent demonstrations led by communists and nationalists in the early 1990s. To be sure, opinion polls have shown a great deal of contempt for the immoral and illegal means by which the new rich have aggrandized themselves and for their corrupt links to political power. And the success of both communists and nationalists in elections throughout the 1990s reflected what has been called a "politics of resentment" that combined relatively abstract feelings of political loss over the demise of the Soviet Union with very tangible and personal feelings of material suffering. But acceptance of the new social conditions—shaped, many have argued, by disillusionment with socialism, such that no plausible alternatives seem to exist—and a focus on survival rather than on the struggle for change, has been the most visible response to hardship. Strikes have been rare. Trade unions have not enjoyed a revival. And polls of workers show hope that more and more ordinary Russians will be able to take advantage of the greater availability of goods and the new possibilities for upward mobility. But most of all, individuals and families have focused their energies on finding ways to survive. People have taken multiple jobs, supplemented impossibly low pensions and disability payments by finding menial jobs, cultivated garden plots for food, obtained help from relatives when possible, and sold goods they no longer needed or found to resell in markets and street corners. In the early 1990s, especially, the sight of long rows of individuals selling handfuls of goods in the street became common—as did simple begging. Women, in particular, both as individuals and as key figures in the family economy, have been in the forefront of these strategies of survival. Ordinary Russians have not been passive in the face of the economic hardships of postsocialism, but they also seem to have been more patient with the "transition" than many expected.

Decay, Disintegration, and Disorder

Decay and disintegration have pervaded public perceptions of social life since the end of communism. Quite literally, the conditions of buildings and roads could be seen to suffer after 1991—with the exception of many places in Moscow, where the concentration of new wealth has led to intensive reconstruction and modernization, and to a lesser extent in St. Petersburg, especially as streets, facades, and palaces were refurbished for the 300th-anniversary celebrations in 2003. Newspapers and government commissions have regularly reported, and citizens been able to easily witness, decaying and malfunctioning machinery, collapsing buildings (old ones due to disrepair and new ones due to faulty construction), accidents and explosions caused by the age and ill-repair of equipment of all sorts, gas and oil pipeline ruptures, fires, electricity failures, toxic spills, airplane crashes, and other signs that Russia was becoming "a perpetual calamity zone." Lenin had declared that communism equaled Soviet power plus the electrification of the whole country; now newspapers reported an epidemic of looting of electric wires and equipment to sell as metal scrap, resulting not only in power interruptions but also in many electrocutions. The tragic sinking in August 2000 of the nuclear submarine *Kursk*, which resulted in the death of its entire crew, shortly followed by a devastating fire in the Ostankino television tower in Moscow, both symbols of Soviet technological prowess (the tower had been erected to celebrate the fiftieth anniversary of the Bolshevik Revolution), seemed symbolic. As one Russian scholar put it, "The dark television screens seemed to say that Russia was entering an age of catastrophes." Human bodies, as mortality statistics showed, were also suffering. Each year a large percentage of military recruits were found to be physically unfit; the head of the draft, General Galkin, declared the health condition of recruits in the late 1990s to be "catastrophic." The health care system staggered under the pressures of low salaries for doctors and health care workers, shortages of medicines and other supplies, and backward and decaying technologies. Limited privatization benefited only a tiny minority. Combined with other social problems, the result has been a steady rise in infectious diseases as well as of heart attacks, strokes, and cancer. Tuberculosis has reached epidemic proportions. Rates of hepatitis, syphilis, and AIDS have been skyrocketing, and there have been severe outbreaks of diphtheria, encephalitis, typhoid fever, malaria, polio, pneumonia, and influenza. The prison system in particular has been described as an "epidemiological pump," though specialists agree that widespread poverty, stress, alcoholism, smoking, overcrowding, unprotected sex (especially with prostitutes), and intravenous drug use are major contributors. Mortality from disease has been higher than in most developed countries.

For many Russians, what seemed to be postcommunist Russia's moral decay was as troubling as its physical breakdown. Epidemics of drug use, prostitution, alcoholism, and sexually transmitted diseases seemed emblematic of moral decline. Studies of youth particularly emphasized the degraded lives of so many. Young people—Russia's future, it is always said—faced new opportunities and choices and have, on average, adapted better to the new economic conditions than their elders (and females, on average, have adapted better than males). Many Russians complain, however, that money is the only thing that matters to this new generation, said to be cynical about every other value. Also, huge numbers of young Russians have remained anchorless, alienated, and vulnerable, uncertain about their futures while still in school, and finding material success elusive after entering the workforce. Drug use, prostitution, and AIDS have been most widespread among teenagers and youths—and the fact that these problems were relatively "unknown" in Soviet times, which is to say that they were not officially reported, is as much a part of the perception of their meaning as that these problems have increased. As will be discussed later, popular culture among the young—music, clothing styles, and leisure activities (summarized by some youths as limited to "buying beer, sitting with friends, and listening to music")—has been seen as another sign that Russian society has been heading in the wrong direction. Indeed, polls throughout the 1990s find that many Russians (still 37 percent in early 2004) view the whole course of postcommunist economic, social, and cultural development in Russia as leading to a "dead end."

The spread of crime after 1991 has represented for many the surest sign of Russia's social and moral fall and the inability of the state to maintain needed order and normalcy, notwithstanding Yeltsin's and especially Putin's declarations of war on crime. Organized crime—the "mafia"—has loomed larger in the imagination of both foreigners and Russians than in reality; a 1997 poll found that more Russians believed organized crime ran the country than those who felt the government was in charge. Nonetheless, crime has remained a real problem, taking a variety of forms. With the collapse of the Soviet economy and the rise of private enterprise, "protection rackets" proliferated. At its most simple, a protection racket involved extorting regularly paid dues in return for a "roof" (*krysha*) of protection against other gangs, street bandits, police, and politicians (all of whom competed in offering "roofs"). At their best, these rackets offered real protection and even the enforcement of contracts and property rights between businesses and individuals at a time when state and legal structures remained weak. At their worse, rackets engaged in unambiguous extortion: pay us or we will make you pay, even with your lives. Often, they were a mixture of both. Criminal groups, often styled as "mafias," also became involved in smuggling, the drug trade, counterfeiting, and organized prostitution, but they also invested in banks, casinos, and other businesses. Indeed, specialists have described a large criminal "shadow economy." This criminal economy has often been entwined with the legal economy, including illegal and sometimes violent means in the pursuit of legal economic activities, illegal privatizations left uncontested by law, criminals involved in entirely legal activities, and ordinary citizens engaged in illegal activities without connections to mobs. Even worse are what have been called "social black holes" where state authority, legal order, and a functioning civil society have been replaced by lawlessness, invisible social networks that rule a locality through predation and violence, and the breakdown of confidence and social norms in favor of an ethos of individual survival by any means. Emerging social black holes have been described in the north Caucasus and the Russian North and Far East. Perhaps the most spectacularly disturbing criminal activity has been contract assassinations. Politicians (such as the noted liberal reformer Galina Starovoitova in St. Petersburg in 1998), bankers, businessmen, and journalists have been gunned down, often on the streets in broad daylight, and many have had their lives threatened for challenging local authorities, for overly zealous investigations of criminals, for violating agreements with racketeers, for refusing to agree to extortionist protection or patronage demands, or for reasons unknown. Of course, most of the victims have been fellow criminals. Contract killings became especially common in some provincial towns, such as the automobile manufacturing center Togliatti, where the power of organized crime was especially strong. While true gangsters are said to adhere to certain criminal cultural conventions—a recognized thieves' "law"—the problem of thugs who lack any moral or rational restraint has made even the criminal underworld a dangerous and uncertain order. Less brutal, but no less troubling to Russians, have been widespread reports and rumors of corruption, ranging from local police officers to Kremlin officials. Bribery of public officials has ranged from payments to expedite matters that were otherwise quite legal to payments made to secure an exception to some rule or law to outright purchase of the ongoing support of an official. Amounts have ranged from petty bribes to million-dollar kickbacks for government contracts. In one characteristic case—which also underscores the government's regular efforts to combat corruption—the Ministry of Interior sent a vodka truck on a route through southern Russia in 1995. Of the twenty-four traffic police inspection (GAI) points encountered, bribes were demanded to allow the truck to continue at twenty-two of these. Complicating all of this are ambiguous definitions of what is "crime" and what is simply necessary "reciprocity," especially in a context in which laws and legal norms are still evolving.

Beliefs and Ideologies

How Russians have understood and interpreted the realities around them has been as important in modern Russian history as the facts themselves. Perceptions, desires, and ideals have shaped responses to social and economic conditions. Since 1991, Russians have been struggling to decide what they believe about such crucial questions as the meanings of freedom and democracy, the cultural values and ethics that should guide everyday life, and the very nature of the Russian nation. A useful source has been regular public opinion polls, especially by such professional and independent organizations as the All-Russian Center for the Study of Public Opinion (VTsIOM). Polls have shown much uncertainty about Russia's "transition." At the end of the 1990s, the vast majority of Russians continued to believe that dismantling the Soviet Union was a mistake and to view a "democratized" version of the Soviet system as the preferred political form for Russia (only 9 percent spoke of desiring "Western-type democracy"); indeed, as disappointment with the results of reform grew, the view that "it would have been better had the country remained as it was before 1985" also increased from a minority viewpoint in 1994 to majority opinion by 1999. As late as 2003, fully 42 percent of the population opined that had they lived in 1917, they would have sided with the Bolsheviks—though 16 percent said they would have left the country and 10 percent would have done battle against the revolution. Most Russians professed to value a "strong leader" and a "strong state" over "democratic institutions." Half the population, according to a 2000 survey, insisted that order is more important than personal freedom. And most believe that Russia's course in history cannot be the same as other countries, because Russia is "distinguished by a unique way of life and spiritual culture." In particular, polls find most Russians dismayed with Russia's humiliation as a world power, the perceived moral breakdown in society, and the invasion of the country by Western popular culture.

In general, pollsters maintain that, at the start of the twenty-first century, "Russians' support for civil liberties is weak, especially when they are asked concrete questions rather than abstract ones." Still, "democracy" as a principle is overwhelmingly endorsed as the best possible system even when its problems are admitted, and specific questions make it clear that democratic public opinion is specific and strong. In polls taken in recent years (1996–2003), most Russians—though not all it bears remembering—agreed that the life and rights of the individual are more important than any other value (and that this is a "universal" truth), that laws should apply equally to everyone, that property rights are inviolable, that freedom of thought and expression is as necessary to Russians as to people in the West, and that citizens should elect their leaders in a free and competitive environment. Even in the name of restoring "Russia's great power potential" or restoring "order," most Russians rejected curtailing freedom of speech and the press and democratic elections. Better to "know the truth," it was agreed, even when the media is filled with frightening "problems and scandals," than return to a time when the media focused only on "good things." No less important, opinion studies show deep skepticism about the utopian promise that the state or leaders can create a perfect society. Of course, democratic ideas have been much stronger among the young than the old— half of men and women over the age of sixty-nine in 1999 voiced a preference for the old Soviet system, compared to only 10 percent of those under thirty. Not surprisingly, one's degree of success in the new order similarly correlated with support for democracy, though some support for democracy could be found even among those who felt that they had not yet benefited from the end of communism. In fact, at the end of the 1990s, the overwhelming majority of Russians (70 percent) believed they had lost more than they had gained from the changes of that decade. As specialists have observed about all this data, Russians have "assimilated democratic values" faster than the elite have established completely democratic institutions or ensured that democracy has made most people's lives tangibly better. To be sure, since 1991, discontent and the sense of loss have remained widespread. Disillusionment—the awareness that there are no better alternatives than the difficult present—may be the dominant sentiment. This worries both public officials and specialists. As Lilia Shevtsova, a leading Russian political scientist, has observed, "hopelessness breeds frustration, despair, and violence. How strong can a government be that is built on the disenchantment of the population? . . . Who can guarantee that at some moment the desire for violent revenge will not overtake those who feel they have been betrayed? Russia has a long and tragic history of attempts to find justice." Observers have noted pervasive skepticism, fatalism, and passivity in public opinion—also reflected in declining participation in elections. "We just have to bear up," one Russian specialist summarized the most common opinion. Many polls suggest that enduring has continued to mean, for most Russians, also staying on the path of Westernized democracy. But specialists on Russian public opinion warn that attitudes have remained volatile since 1991 and "ambivalence" is the most characteristic feature of public views on such critical issues as democracy, markets, and Westernizing reform. This may be, as scholars have termed it, an "unstable stability."

Nationalists and communists have thrived in Russian civic life since 1991 partly because their rhetoric has echoed widespread anxieties, discontents, and ideals. Important differences continued to separate the communists of the Left from the nationalists of the Right: communists were more likely to speak of social justice for the common person while nationalists of the harm alien ideas and ethnicities have brought to the Russian people. But both took the stance, often in alliance, of offering a "national-patriotic" and "spiritual" opposition to liberal democratic reform, which is seen to have resulted in a loss of national and moral strength. A variety of militant nationalist groups formed during the crisis years of the early 1990s, often taking to the streets of Moscow and other cities in demonstrations and regularly clashing with police, leading many to speak of a Weimar-like situation: newspapers of "national and spiritual opposition" like Alexander Prokhorov's *Den* (Day, renamed *Zavtra*, Tomorrow, in 1993); anti-Semitic and anti-Western organizations like Pamyat (Memory),

Communists demonstrate on Red Square in Moscow in 1992.   (P. Gorshkov)

which had formed in 1987; numerous small-scale publishers of scurrilously anti-Semitic and anti-government pamphlets and newspapers (easily found for sale on the street corners of major cities); neo-Stalinist groups like Viktor Anpilov's Working Russia; movements openly laying claim to the prerevolutionary legacy of the "Black-Hundred" Union of the Russian People; monarchists who looked to a restoration of the empire and the Romanovs; neo-fascists like Russian National Unity with their uniformed storm troopers and use of a slightly modified swastika as their symbol; the writer Eduard Limonov's somewhat bizarre (even postmodern, it has been said) "left-fascist" National Bolshevik Party; "statist" and "national-patriotic" groupings of parliamentary deputies; gatherings such as the "People's *Veche*" (a term invoking a medieval Russian political tradition) of 1992; the nationalist Union of Officers; a revived cossack movement; and the National Salvation Front, which united nationalists and communists. Socially, these movements attracted a mixture of unskilled workers, pensioners, and military men, though many activists were intellectuals attracted by the idea of restoring a "Russian idea" to public life. At the same time, there has been a strong cultural and emotional, rather than simply socioeconomic, dimension to what has attracted many Russians, especially urban youths, to Nazi paraphernalia, violent attacks on non-Russians, skinhead dress and association, and tough racist and right-wing talk about "yids" and "democrashit" (*dermokratiia*), or to fashionable leftist groups like the Ho Chi Minh Club in Moscow. These were youths lost in time, seeking, as Svetlana Boym described them, to "restore the dreams of someone else's youth," to "mimic the fantasies of others." Many of these trends persisted on the margins of Russian life into the new century. By the mid-1990s, however, two main groups dominated the movement of "patriotic" opposition in Russia in terms of national organization and electoral success: the re-legalized Communist Party of the Russian Federation, led by Gennady Zyuganov, and Vladimir Zhirinovsky's Liberal Democratic Party.

Ideologically, the radical critique of postcommunism has focused on two interrelated themes of concern: Russia's crisis of national strength and its moral ("spiritual") crisis. Nationalists and neo-communists alike have echoed and encouraged widespread feelings that Russia has been humiliated in the world. Russia's loss of political space (the Soviet Union, which was largely coextensive with the Russian Empire), the decline of Russia's military might, and the weakness of the economy were seen as resulting in the loss of status as a great power. Symbolic of the loss of sovereignty and dignity was the flood of foreign goods pouring into Russia in the early 1990s—Fords and Mercedes, Barbie dolls, food, even vodka, not to mention the ubiquitous use of dollars— along with foreign popular culture, including popular music, imported television and movies, McDonald's, and MTV. Russia's weakness was also seen to result from its moral disintegration. Pornography and prostitution, garish gambling parlors in city centers, a new economy marked more by trade than productive work, conspicuous consumption by rich "New Russians" and their imitators, sexual explicitness in films and television, a decadent youth culture, and pervading materialism were all seen as bleeding Russia of its sources of spiritual and hence national strength. A leaflet left to explain a 1998 bombing in the food court of a new expensive shopping mall in Moscow near the Kremlin declared an "urban guerilla war" against consumerism, targeting hamburgers and Russians who consume them as a particularly odious symbol.

Radicals have blamed various enemies for Russia's moral fall. "Democrats," in particular, have been castigated as traitors who "stabbed the Fatherland in the back" in alliance with foreign powers who conspired to weaken a once mighty nation. The most extreme denounced the government as nothing less than a foreign "occupation," though even Zyuganov spoke of a Western conspiracy to destroy the Soviet Union. Indeed, communists have tended to attack capitalism less in class terms as the exploitation of the proletariat than in national terms as the exploitation of peripheral nations like Russia by the "new world order." The mass media have been regularly condemned for "Russophobia." Reformers have been accused of "subservience to the West" and even of "economic genocide." In all cases, the language of nationalism has been deeply emotional. At its most positive, this has been a language of love for the Russian motherland, its nature and history, its people, and its "spiritual heritage"—a rhetoric also adopted by Yeltsin, Putin, and their supporters. The unique "Russian idea," it has been said, is characterized by collectivism (*sobornost'*), a statist ideal that links the interests of the individual to the strength of the state, and a "spiritual" commitment to truth, goodness, and justice. But nationalist and communist movements have also often expressed great resentment, anger, and hatred. Democracy, capitalism, cosmopolitanism, and bourgeois culture have been castigated for the harm they bring individuals and the nation. The most extreme voices have spoken of Russia's "spiritual occupation" by an alien Western culture and called for uniting the "simple people" in "holy struggle" against the "parasites" and "Judases." The language has sometimes been extremely anti-Western and anti-Semitic: "a foreign 'for sale' sign has been affixed to the body of our country with patented, American-made nails," wrote one influential writer; others have blamed Jews for all of Russia's problems (noting, in particular, the Jewish ancestry of a number of the oligarchs) and branded the government a "Yidocracy."

More socially minded movements, mainly on the communist Left, have added the suffering of the common people to this critique and advocated a reborn nation characterized by egalitarianism, social justice, and care for the unprotected poor. Indeed, the popular success of Zhirinovsky and Zyuganov has been as much due to their readiness to voice people's social grievances as to their emotional nationalism. The two themes have been interconnected, of course. Communists and nationalists alike, scholars have argued, have effectively tapped into a "politics of *ressentiment*," which has been central to nationalist ideologies in many parts of the world in recent times. It is a harsh reality that the end of communism has resulted in much suffering, alienation, and perceived humiliation. Nationalists and communists have offered both explanations and promises of redemption or revenge.

The government has not let this develop without opposition and competition, however. In the wake of the October 1993 battle over parliament, Yeltsin banned the most extreme groups. And government leaders themselves, as noted in the preceding chapter, especially Putin, have often adopted the rhetoric of nation and social welfare. Putin's restoration of the Soviet national anthem (with new words) and the army's red star have been part of a larger campaign to appropriate nationalism for the state. In addition, Putin's government has joined the struggle to impose cultural order on Russia's disordered freedom and to stem the perceived tide of cultural decadence. During 2003 and 2004, for example, government officials proposed such cultural "reforms" as restoring to mandated school history books a view of the past uncorrupted by "pseudo-liberalism," placing and even restoring statues commemorating Russia's imperial and Soviet past, requiring the study of "Russian Orthodox Culture" in all schools, legislating fines and even jail time for swearing in public, banning beer advertising on television during prime time (vodka advertising was earlier banned), forbidding the celebration of the newly imported Halloween as "morally damaging," and even ordering police, as a way to "improve morals," to fine people for kissing in public places—to be sure, many of these proposals have been met with public criticism and even scorn.

Religion

The patriarchal Russian Orthodox Church benefited enormously from the fall of communism and has continued to grow and prosper. Of course, all religions and all denominations had reason to celebrate the end of communism, which intended to exterminate them. Newly available sources underline Lenin's personal hatred for and desire to destroy Orthodox priests and other proponents of the Church, quite in accord with the official ideology and attitude to be perpetuated by his successors. Religion as such was the main enemy, and it is impossible to decide whether the massacres of Russian priests or the killing of Buddhist lamas in Outer Mongolia, formally not even part of the Soviet Union, was more horrible. But because of its importance, size, and geographic extent, Russian Orthodoxy was the greatest sufferer, with uncounted martyrs, many of them formally canonized since 1991, including the last tsar and his family. Orthodoxy survived, as outlined in preceding chapters, because of the unexpectedly strong support of the faithful, because when total destruction failed, the government instituted a certain compromise accepted by the patriarchal Church, because of the mobilization of the nation during the Second World War, and other special circumstances. With the fall of communism the Church suddenly emerged from what has been described as the greatest religious persecution in human history to a central and privileged position. In the years since, the Church has been openly favored by Yeltsin and Putin and by almost all political parties; even Zyuganov and his communists have proclaimed religion to be part of Russia's essential heritage and declared the party open to believers. The Church's membership includes perhaps one-third of the Russian people, although many of them do not regularly attend services. What is more, repeated polls in the 1990s indicated that the population had a higher regard for and more confidence in the Church than in any other institution in the country, be it the government, the armed forces, or the political parties. For its part, the Church has been seeking a larger role in the country's civil and moral life. The Patriarch has been close to the government and has actively spoken out on public issues. In 2000, the Church hierarchs adopted a social doctrine condemning abortion, homosexuality, euthanasia, and genetic engineering, warning against the new capitalist ethos of selfish materialism, and endorsing ecumenical engagement (though this was opposed by the Church's right wing and even the majority made it clear that they were offended by efforts by other religions to convert Orthodox Russians), support for the military (though acknowledging that war is an evil), and the concept of private property.

Many problems remain for the Russian Orthodox Church. One of the most severe stems from the persecution and aggressive de-Christianization of the Soviet period. The Church is short of everything, and the large-scale construction and restoration of church buildings represents only a portion of the most visible part of its needs. At times the Church seems to operate as a striving missionary establishment rather than one that celebrated a thousand years of existence in 1988. Another complex problem is that of ecclesiastical jurisdiction in newly independent states, such as Ukraine and the Baltic republics. The Church is also divided ideologically. There exists a strong and extreme right wing, characterized among its other qualities by anti-Westernism, anti-Semitism, and isolationism, and headed until his death in 1995 by the second-ranking hierarch of the Church, the Metropolitan of St. Petersburg John (Ioann). Patriarch Alexis II managed to contain Metropolitan John and his followers and to continue a rather moderate and flexible policy, but the tension between the two points of view has by no means been resolved. At the other end of the spectrum, dissident priests and laypeople have organized movements within the Church—

A woman crosses herself in a former church in 1991. Many church buildings, which had been turned into storage buildings or factories during Soviet times, were reclaimed by the Church, re-sanctified, and restored.　(M. Rogozin)

though some clerical leaders have been defrocked—favoring a new, more relevant, liturgy in the vernacular, greater lay participation in services, regular Bible study, ecumenicalism, and an active social mission.

The Church's relations with the state have also been complicated. Although the government has treated the Church very favorably, the state has remained secular, while the Church, though formally recognizing the law stipulating separation of Church and state, has sought a greater role in education and in general to have Orthodoxy recognized more formally and fully as the religion of Russia. Taking one step in this direction, in September 1997 the parliament passed and President Yeltsin signed what was described as a religious protection bill, which declared Orthodoxy, Islam, Judaism, and Buddhism as the established religions of Russia—since these were the only religions officially recognized in 1982—and requiring complicated registration procedures for other religious groups to operate in the country, especially where they had not been previously entrenched. Although the bill was internationally denounced as an infraction of the freedom of religion, its defenders insisted that this move was necessary to prevent well-funded and organized movements from unfairly filling a vacuum created by decades of Soviet oppression of native religions. Many Orthodox churches posted at their entrances a long list of "false faiths," ranging from Catholicism to Krishna Consciousness, against which Orthodox believers were to guard themselves. In practice, Catholics and some main-stream Protestant groups have been tacitly recognized and non-traditional denominations have persisted, though they face regular obstacles from a state and Church seeking to create order and control in Russia's chaotic religious life. No less, heightened anxieties about the role in Russia of Jews, Muslims, and other non-Orthodox have reflected the intensified search to define Russianness. Putin, among other leaders, has increasingly insisted that Russianness is linked to Orthodoxy. "Of course, by law the Church in Russia is separate from the state," Putin declared in January 2004 while on a Christmas tour of ancient monasteries and churches, "but in our souls as well as in our history, we are together. So it is and shall be forever."

Many Russians have been turning to religion and spirituality since com-munism began to collapse, though often along divergent paths of belief and practice, much reminiscent of (and sometimes explicitly a revival of) trends during Russia's prerevolutionary religious renaissance. Influential poets, writ-ers, artists, and even rock musicians have made religion, sometimes tied to ideas of nation, central to their work, though references to pre-Christian Slavic elements, vague mysticism, and illusions to Christ, Mary, saints, and the Church have often been ambiguously intertwined. Intellectuals have written much about a unique Russian spirituality that is central to the "Russian idea" and the "Russian soul," prerevolutionary themes again being evoked. Many prerevolutionary and émigré religious authors, such as Vladimir Soloviev and Nicholas Berdiaev, have been widely republished and reread. And most nationalist movements have linked their notions of the nation to Orthodox faith and have defined Russia's salvation as fundamentally "spiritual." Still, many who have rediscovered Christian faith find themselves uncomfortable with the Church as an institution. Other religions have also enjoyed a revival. Among Buddhists, Muslims, and Jews various new organizations, religious and communal festivals, study groups, and temples and synagogues have developed. Meanwhile, evangelical Christians, Mormons, Hare Krishnas, the Unification Church, Scientology, Jehovah's Witnesses, and other religious groups have been increasingly active in Russia in search of converts, to the great dismay of the established Church and many Russians. But the "threat" to the Church has not been limited to foreign imports. These years have also seen a proliferation of original new domestic "cults." New religious movements like the Great White Brotherhood of Maria Devi Khristos, which has been described as a "New Age goulash of chakras, karma, Kabbalah, and music the-ory" combined with belief in the incarnation of Christ and Mary in one person, as well as the popularity of astrology, mysticism, ESP, and spiritualism, have been variously seen as evidence of Russia's spiritual degeneration and crisis

Christ the Savior cathedral in Moscow being rebuilt in 1997. To commemorate the Russian victory over Napoleon, Alexander I ordered the construction of a great cathedral in Moscow, dedicated to Christ the Savior. Consecrated by Alexander III in 1883, it was destroyed on Stalin's orders in 1931, in order to build in its place a massive Palace of Soviets. Due to unstable ground, the Palace could not be built; believers saw divine intervention in this failure. A public swimming pool was built instead. With the support of the government of the city of Moscow, the cathedral was reconstructed according to the original plans as a symbol of defeated communism and resurrected faith. The completed cathedral was consecrated in 2000, though many believers expressed discomfort that so much money was spent on this project while material suffering in the country remained so great. (Mark Steinberg)

and signs of new postcommunist freedom and creativity. For most Russians, however, spirituality is a simpler and more personal matter. If anything, religion is becoming normalized in Russia along European lines. Recent data suggest that Church attendance has been declining since the revival of the early 1990s, though professed belief in God has continued to grow.

Literature, the Arts, and Popular Culture

The immediate impact of the collapse of communism was as sweeping in culture as in politics, economics, and foreign policy. Marxism-Leninism disappeared from sight—whatever its underground residue—both as a massive presence in schools and other academic institutions and as the universal guiding doctrine; even the new Communist Party, as we have seen, distanced itself from this one-time sacred canon. Teachers of the official ideology turned to more traditional philosophy or history, or switched professions. Instead Russia became immediately open to every conceivable idea and doctrine, with Russian intellectuals reveling in the latest Western views and teachings, but also in the accomplishments of their own prerevolutionary "silver age." Unfortunately, the new intellectual richness coincided with a diminishing support from the state and general economic decline and even disaster. Ballet, opera, classical music, painting, theater, film, and literature, along with institutions of science and scholarship, all found themselves foundering financially, forced to function in a suddenly market-oriented society. Musicians and dancers, and some painters, were in a better situation than most artists, for their work, needing no translation, was more easily marketed to tourists and taken on the road. Overall, however, postcommunist freedom from state tutelage was a mixed blessing for the arts, as it was for education and the sciences. Another phenomenon of these early postcommunist years was the return of dissenters and other émigrés for a visit, a few performances, or more permanently. Many will never forget Vladimir Horowitz playing the piano in the very hall in St. Petersburg where he began his professional career, or Alexander Solzhenitsyn coming back to his native land in the summer of 1994 to denounce at close range the new Russia, as he had so effectively denounced its Soviet predecessor—though the fact that few Russians have paid much attention to Solzhenitsyn since his initial grand return is also part of the story. In a deeper sense, the "myth of return" is a characteristic of much postcommunist culture: nostalgic return to the "Russia we have lost" (also the title of a popular documentary film in the early 1990s), return to "Western civilization," or return to suppressed or forgotten values. It is too early to discuss with any finality or precision the shape and characteristics of postcommunist Russian culture. We can, however, usefully pause over certain important developments and trends.

In literature, the virtually unbridled freedom along with the social and political uncertainties and turmoil after 1991 combined to offer readers a wide range of genres and tendencies. Huge quantities of translated foreign works appeared, ranging from pornography to detective novels to literary classics. Readers could now find long-forbidden émigré fiction, such as the works of Bunin, Nabokov, and Solzhenitsyn, or previously restricted Soviet writers, such as Babel, Bulgakov, Olesha, and Pasternak—sometimes called "returned literature." The dominance of the commercial market in publishing, however, has been the chief fact since 1992—and the source of much dismay by intellectuals, who have complained that the public seems to prefer trashy literature and pornography to serious writing and that poets and writers have quickly been losing their status as figures of inspiration. Literary scholars have agreed, speaking of "the wholesale displacement of the cult of high culture." As late as 1992, the typical Moscow book stand or book table, which were to be found everywhere on city streets and in the corners of stores, might have displayed the works of "silver age" poets like Anna Akhmatova alongside translations of Western detectives like Raymond Chandler or Agatha Christie, émigré authors like Solzhenitsyn, alternative writers like Venedikt Erofeev, works on astrology and the occult, the Bhagavad Gita, and the Bible. By 1993, many of these booths and tables had vanished and those that remained were largely devoid of works of serious literature. This was, a critic has observed, "the symbolic banishment of high literature from the tables of commerce." Pornography has been particularly pervasive. Naked bodies have adorned the covers of numerous magazines (so pervasively that the public, it is said, grew bored with the sight and some of these magazines failed), movies have regularly featured graphic sex, pornographic videos and web-sites have proliferated, "erotic festivals" have become common, and pornographic as well as more serious erotic literature can be found everywhere. The most popular genre, however, has been crime fiction, or *detektivy*. Lurid images and bad writing characterize most *detektivy*: "Take a look at any bookstand," a reviewer commented with disgust in 1996, "and you'll be dazzled by the distorted physiognomies and black muzzles of pistols aimed right at the forehead of the potential reader." But some crime fiction has attracted the admiration even of serious readers, such as Aleksandra Marinina's work, with her tough, independent, and highly intelligent female detective or Boris Akunin's nostalgic novels set in the nineteenth century, when, in the words of advertisements, "literature was great, faith in progress was unlimited, and crimes were committed and investigated with grace and refinement." Belles lettres have not entirely been displaced, however, though commercial success has been elusive for many of the best writers. The work of Liudmila Petrushevskaia, Viktor Erofeev, Tatiana Tolstaia, Vladimir Sorokin, Viktor Pelevin, and others offer clear evidence of the vitality and originality of Russian writing.

Literature has tended to reflect and ponder the flux and uncertainties of life after communism. In the view of Viktor Erofeev, who has made his mark as a literary critic as well as a fiction writer, much postcommunist prose (continuing trends begun in the late communist years) has abandoned the humanism and hope that inspired both Soviet and dissident authors in favor of a more uncertain outlook that rejects any causes or universal truths. Suffering is recognized, but not valued as ennobling. Hope is viewed as illusion. Faith in reason is repudiated. The everyday is valued over idealistic heroism. Moralism is replaced by postmodern doubt and irony. Every value is called into question. The mood alternates between despair and indifference. And there is a certain smell in this literature, Erofeev suggests: no longer the "perfume of wild flowers and hay," which pervaded older Russian and Soviet literature, but the "stench" of "death, sex, old-age, bad food, everyday life." Other critics have similarly noted the centrality in the new literature of chaos, betrayal, physical need, sexuality, social degeneration (crime, prostitution, violence, crass materialism), moral transgression (or the absence of moral boundaries altogether), the deconstruction of subjectivity, an iconoclastic tendency to shock, skepticism, personal failure (though also, more optimistically, survival, but rarely personal fulfillment), and existential despair. Liudmila Petrushevskaia (b. 1938), for example, has been described as "an existentialist who conceives of human life as an unrelievedly punitive condition," which "charts the daily psychic monstrosities of a spiritual wasteland populated by victims and victimizers bound by an endless chain of universal suffering and abuse." Viktor Pelevin (b. 1962), who has been both critically acclaimed and relatively successful commercially, writes ironic, surreal, and often quite funny works filled with uncertainties, shadows, ambiguous metaphors, the fantastic, and the absurd. His work explores the unleashed imagination and universal questions about human existence, but also, it has been said, the "dark chaos of New Russia." His stories and novels are about the myth of individual freedom, unrealized love and longing, the ubiquity of money and materialism, mindless conformity (with television and the obsession with imitating and consuming Western things central to this theme), and the unending and unsatisfied search for existential and metaphysical meaning.

In visual culture, television, imported movies, new realistic statues (replacing disgraced and fallen Soviet monuments, though some old monuments remain and some are even being restored), and rebuilt churches and old buildings (or new buildings in both imperial and Soviet styles) have been more noticeable than innovative painting, photography, and sculpture. Indeed, television may well be the most important of the postcommunist arts. Every critical event and trend—the 1991 coup, the 1993 battle over parliament, wealth and poverty, crime, cultural debates—have been made visible through television. Political satires like *Kukly* (*Puppets*), sex talk shows like *Pro eto* (*About That*), game shows in which materialist consumption is idealized, music television, extremely popular crime dramas set in postcommunist Russia, discussions with philosophers and writers, and historical documentaries and debates about the past have put Russian television at the center of how Russians think about the experience of postcommunism. Perhaps more than any other medium, Russian television, in the words of one scholar, "has been largely responsible for the production of the new post-Soviet culture." No wonder that television also became a battleground for control and that growing control over its content by the state, and self-censorship in the face of this control, has become the subject of much criticism and concern.

The more traditional forms of art—especially painting—have also thrived, even if audiences remain small and art buyers mostly foreigners. In many ways, Russian art after communism has become fully a part of world art. As in other countries, contemporary work has been variously abstract and philosophical, performative (an *aktsionizm* in which the reactions of viewers are part of the work), symbolic, magical, pop-artistic, nostalgic kitsch, primitivist, technological, and sensual. Some artists have been preoccupied with texture and form, but almost all have been concerned with meaning, even if meaning remains obscure and uncertain, including to the artist. Philosophically, however, Russian painting of the late 1990s has emphasized many of the same themes we see in postcommunist literature. Spirituality—as a search for spiritual feeling if not certain meaning or faith—has been pervasive (as in the often abstract and semi-abstract work of the St. Petersburg painter Viacheslav Mikhailov). Memory and nostalgia—though much of it tinged with a knowing irony that the past can never be restored—has been no less ubiquitous (notably in the influential work of émigré Moscow conceptual artists like Ilya Kabakov and the collaborative duo Vitaly Komar and Alexander Melamid, or of the late Timur Novikov's New Academy of Fine Arts in St. Peterburg, which played with classical-imperial reminiscences). Many other themes have been noted in recent art, such as a desire magically to transcend the everyday (Nikolai Sazhin, for example), expressions of artistic inwardness, playful and ironic reworkings of images from the Soviet past (Larisa Zvezdochetova), urban dreams and phantoms (the theme of the St. Petersburg "master class" exhibition of 1997), the heroism of the individual artist, and catastrophe and cataclysm (Mikhailov). In almost all of this work, we see what the Russian art historian Aleksei Kurbanovsky has called a characteristically Russian "logocentrism" in which intellectual and verbal associations—implied words and ideas—pervade the visual. In Moscow, this has taken a more conceptualist turn, working intellectually with language and images, and in St. Petersburg a more painterly and semi-abstract form, though rich in religious, literary, and historical illusions. Still, postcommunist art has rarely been about art for art's sake, but rather most often about art that seeks to make viewers think and feel about the world around them.

In the first years after the collapse of the communist system, the film industry, which for all its many artistic and ideological restrictions had produced some excellent films, notably by such talented directors as Andrei Tarkovsky, Andrei Konchalovsky, and Nikita Mikhalkov, languished for lack of funds. In 1990, 300 feature films were made; by 1995, the number had sunk to only 46. The Russian film market was flooded with foreign films, very often the worst of them. In the years since, the Russian film industry has continued to struggle to survive in the face of low funding, rising costs, and the problems of distribution and declining attendance. The problem of attendance is due not simply to the fact that foreign, mainly American, films continue to dominate the repertoire on Russian movie screens; no less, television and video have undermined theater attendance altogether, though some excellent films have been produced for television. As with literature, the decline of art films has been decried as further evidence that Russian culture has been debased, that high art and culture have been dethroned by mere entertainment. Still, a number of talented Russian directors, often creating films as internationally funded joint productions, have been able to appeal at least to a select Russian and international audience—and some films, such as Aleksei Balabanov's *Brother* (*Brat*, 1996), with its themes of organized crime, violence, murder, and youthful alienation from the new Russia, have been relatively successful with mass audiences. Directors such as Balabanov, Pavel Lungin, Kira Muratova, and Aleksandr Sokurov have created an impressive body of artistic Russian films. In genre, new Russian films are enormously diverse, including urban crime dramas (very popular and perhaps the dominant form in the early 1990s), historical-costume dramas, romantic melodramas, and (often dark) comedies. Stylistically, these films range from the fantastic to the romantic, to objective realism, to the harshly naturalistic, to the abstract and symbolic. But almost all of these

Viacheslav Mikhailov, "Metaphysical Icon," 1994. A leading St. Petersburg artist, Mikhailov's works are filled with spiritual and philosophical reflections on both beauty and suffering. In this painting, part of a series called "The Russian Home," one sees both a simple domestic reference to a window and echoes of Kazimir Malevich's famous black square (see page 431), which also echoed the icon as an opening to a spiritual sphere. Here the color of the square is red, long a sacred color. (Mark Steinberg)

films contain ideas and arguments about the present (or about the past as helping to define the present). As director and studio head Sergei Livnev explained in 1996, our purpose is "not the introduction of innovations in film language," but engagement in a discussion with Russian audiences, through film, of "those questions that mutually concern us." The themes to be found in postcommunist films are not unlike those in other arts, and they echo many contemporary intellectual concerns: time and memory (including reflections on both the imperial and Soviet pasts), nostalgia for what has been "lost," the meanings of Russianness (or of other ethnic and national identities), spirituality and morality (and materialism and decadence), community and individuality, the role of men and women, generational differences, love and its absence, sex, crime, death (including suicide), and survival. The ever-present search for meanings and ideals, the often intense posing of questions "that mutually concern us," has remained largely unresolved, however. Indeed, critics have complained that too much of Russia's new cinema has offered audiences bleak and depressing portraits of Russian life rather than needed comfort and hope. Audiences and conservative critics have complained of a pervading cynicism and coldness in much postcommunist film. On the other hand, such "dark" films (*chernukha*), with their depressing images of everyday life (such as Pavel Lungin's *Taxi Blues* or Balabanov's *Brother*), which predominated in the late glasnost and early postcommunist years, have gradually been replaced since the late 1990s by more lyrical and positive films—not to mention by television, which has tended to accept the present without angst or nostalgia, and even to enjoy it. Some critics have suggested that Russian film and culture has begun its post-postcommunist stage. Overall, though, what one critic has written about the work of Aleksandr Sokurov applies to most Russian films after 1991: rather than offering mere entertainment or distraction, these films have reflected upon and even heightened what the "silver age" poet Osip Mandelshtam called "the noise of time."

As during the late communist years, young people and their culture have often been seen as a bellwether of Russia's cultural direction. Rampant consumerism, cultural imitativeness, loss of ideological and moral bearing, and enormous uncertainties about the future, as well as the flourishing of new opportunities, have afflicted teenagers and young adults with particular force. Journalists, public officials, and scholars have described new and much less restrictive attitudes among young people about such questions as premarital sex, gender roles, homosexuality, and drug use. Trends in rock and popular music has often been viewed as evidence of a decadent youth culture. Overwhelmingly, the popular music heard on Russian radio, available for purchase on tapes and CDs, and visible on Russian MTV and its equivalents has been Western, especially American. Two styles have been particularly popular among youths in recent years: techno-trance (described as "give me a space to forget about the rest of the world") and hard rock ("I am pained and angry and don't really know why"). Dancing—free-formed, ungendered, and very physical—has been essential to all popular music. A number of Russian bands have adapted popular music styles, including by giving greater weight to lyrics than most recent Western music. The popularity of groups like Alisa or Kino, whose songs often evoked a despondent gloom and alienation, seem to suggest a disturbed and dark youth culture, as do songs like Agata Kristi's "Opium," with its dark romanticization of drugs and explicit decadence. The brief sensation during the early Putin years of the invented "lesbian" duo Tatu—a group deliberately manufactured by a self-made producer seeking to make a profit by marketing a certain edgy adolescent sexuality—was seen as no less emblematic of a debased culture. Plenty of other signs of this culture could be found, such as a St. Petersburg club named Decadence or an all-night dance party (a "rave") on an abandoned military base near St. Petersburg. The pervasive mixtures of irony and pleasure in postcommunist popular culture have suggested to many a society losing its way. Complicating all this, spirituality has also been pervasive in contemporary Russian rock, ranging from Boris Greben-shchikov's folk-rock explorations (in his *Russian Album* of 1991 and after) of ancient saints, Christ's passion, pre-Christian Slavic spiritual traditions, and "ancient Russian sorrow" (*drevnerusskaia toska*) to Alisa's hard rock images of "the blood on the Cross" that leads toward "love." To be sure, for most young people, the literary side of rock music has been less important—if noticed at all—than the danceable rhythms and compelling tunes of the music itself. Consuming music, like consuming fashionable clothing styles, has been about pleasure and fun above all. Indeed, much recent music has eschewed complex lyrics or dark melodic styles in favor of upbeat tunes and light lyrics.

Notwithstanding the anxieties popular youth culture have provoked for many Russians, one can see a great deal of ordinariness and normalcy. Studies suggest that most young Russians share the same concerns and values as other Russians: they think about Russia's character as a nation (including the place of ethnic difference and religious belief); they are troubled by the spread of poverty on the one hand and the selfishness and greed of the new rich on the other; they find the spread of crime and corruption disturbing; they are distrustful of the promises of politicians and the passions of political movements of both the Left and the Right (though they tend to be more politically liberal than older generations); they are increasingly ambivalent about mere imitation and borrowing of Western culture; they want Russia to be a "normal" and stable society; and they are concerned first and foremost with making decent lives for themselves. According to the research of anthropologists and sociologists who have worked with young Russians, the pursuit of normalcy is what most defines the lives of youth. They have responded to Russia's jolting transition by being, in the words of one specialist, "neither inspired nor defeated, not happy or sad, encouraged or frustrated, creative or rebellious." They have simply been getting on with the task of making a life for themselves. They have dreamed not of the "bright future" of communism nor the similar promises of what capitalism would bring, but simply "to live well, to live at ease."

This desire for "normalcy" is pervasive, polls and other research show. What most Russians want for themselves and for their country is nothing more nor less than a "normal life" (*normal'naia zhizn'*). When asked, most define normalcy similarly: economic stability and security, public safety, an effective government respected in the world, freedom, and a moral and just society in which both social needs and individual rights are protected. In many ways, Russia remains far from "normal." A large minority, polls show, continue to doubt that Russia will ever attain this goal. Still, most of the population believe this is possible. That so many young people believe that it is reasonable to hope "to live well, to live at ease" may be one of the most encouraging developments in the still brief history of Russia after communism.

Appendix

RUSSIAN RULERS
TABLE 1

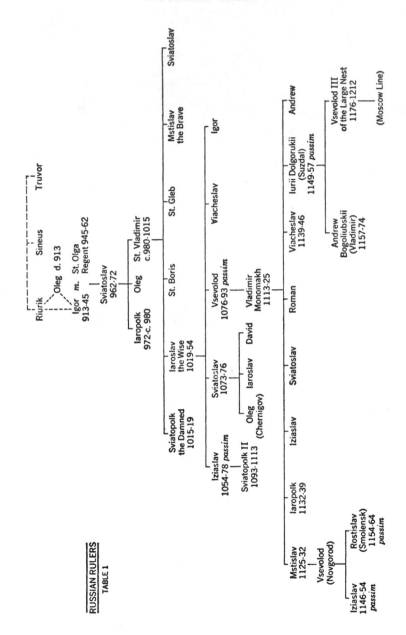

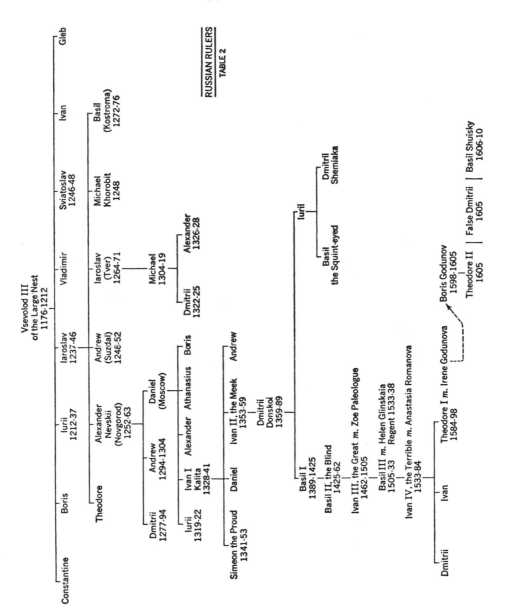

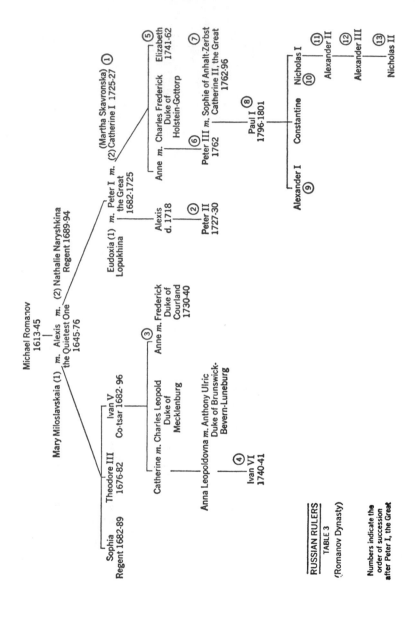

RUSSIAN RULERS
TABLE 3
(Romanov Dynasty)

Numbers indicate the
order of succession
after Peter I, the Great

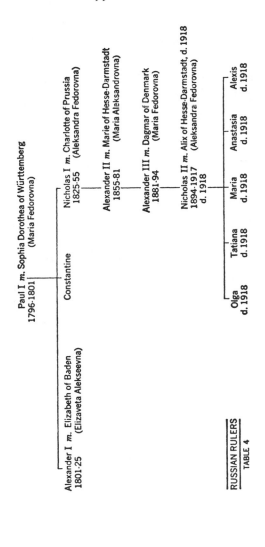

Paul I *m.* Sophia Dorothea of Württemberg
1796-1801
(Maria Fedorovna)

Alexander I *m.* Elizabeth of Baden
1801-25   (Elizaveta Alekseevna)

Constantine

Nicholas I *m.* Charlotte of Prussia
1825-55   (Aleksandra Fedorovna)

Alexander II *m.* Marie of Hesse-Darmstadt
1855-81   (Maria Aleksandrovna)

Alexander III *m.* Dagmar of Denmark
1881-94   (Maria Fedorovna)

Nicholas II *m.* Alix of Hesse-Darmstadt, d. 1918
1894-1917   (Aleksandra Fedorovna)
d. 1918

Olga   Tatiana   Maria   Anastasia   Alexis
d. 1918   d. 1918   d. 1918   d. 1918   d. 1918

RUSSIAN RULERS
TABLE 4

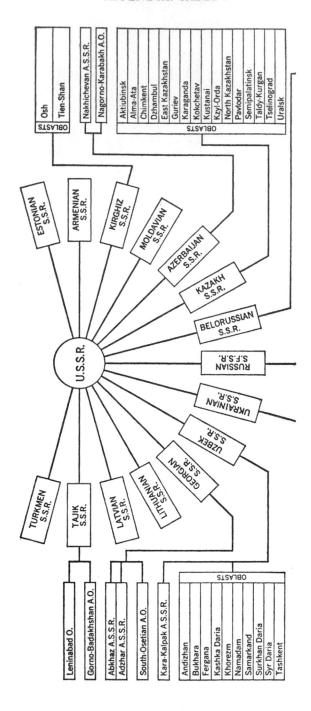

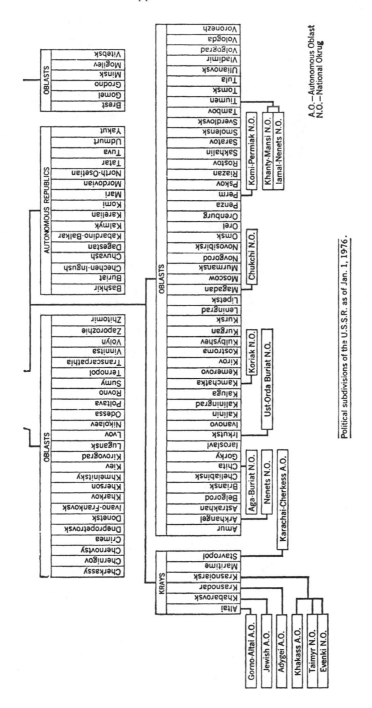

A.O.—Autonomous Oblast
N.O.—National Okrug

Political subdivisions of the U.S.S.R. as of Jan. 1, 1976.

Bibliography

Armstrong, John A. (1922–) American political scientist. Works include *The Politics of Totalitarianism: The Communist Party of the Soviet Union from 1934 to the Present; The Soviet Bureaucratic Elite: A Case Study of the Ukrainian Apparatus; Ukrainian Nationalism, 1939–1945; The European Administrative Elite; Ideology, Politics and Government in the Soviet Union; Nations before Nationalism.*

Ascher, Abraham (1928–) American historian. Works include *Pavel Axelrod and the Development of Menshevism; The Revolution of 1905; P. A. Stolypin: The Search for Stability in Late Imperial Russia.*

Baumgarten, Nicolas Pierre Serge von (1887–1939) Russian historian. Works include "Aux origines de la Russie," *Orientalia Christiana Analecta* 119 (1939); "Chronologie ecclésiastique des terres russes du Xe au XIIIe siècle," *Orientalia Christiana* (January 1930); "Généalogies des branches régnantes des Rurikides russes du XIIIe au XVIe siècle," *Orientalia Christiana* (June 1934); "Généalogies et mariages occidentaux des Rurikides russes du Xe au XIIIe siècle," *Orientalia Christiana* (May 1927).

Bayer, Gottlieb Siegfried (1694–1738) German historian who worked in Russia under Empress Anne. Works include *De Russorum prima expeditione Constantinopolitana; De Varagis; Geographia Russiae . . . ex Constantino Porphyrogenneta; Geographia Russiae ex Scriptoribus Septentrionalibus; Origines Russicae.*

Baykov, Alexander (1899–) Russian-British economist. Works include *The Development of the Soviet Economic System: An Essay on the Experience of Planning in the USSR; Soviet Foreign Trade.*

Berdiaev, Nikolai Aleksandrovich (1878–1948) Russian cultural philosopher. Works include *Istoki i smysl russkogo kommunizma (The Origin of Russian Communism); The Russian Revolution: Two Essays on its Implications in Religion and Psychology; Russkaia ideia: Osnovnye problemy russkoi mysli XIX veka i nachala XX veka (The Russian Idea).*

Bereday, George Z. F. (1920–) American specialist on Soviet education. Works include *The Changing Soviet School: The Comparative Education Society Field Study in the U.S.S.R.* (ed. with William W. Brickman and Gerald H. Read); *The Politics of Soviet Education* (ed. with Jaan Pennar); "Education: Organization and Values since 1917," in *Transformation of Russian Society* (ed. C. E. Black).

Bergson, Abram (1914–2003) American economist. Works include *The Real National Income of Soviet Russia since 1928; The Structure of Soviet Wages: A Study in Socialist Economics; Soviet Economic Growth: Conditions and Perspectives* (ed.).

Berlin, Sir Isaiah (1909–1997) British intellectual historian. Works include *The Hedgehog and the Fox, An Essay on Tolstoy's View of History; Karl Marx: His Life and Environment;* "Russia and 1848," *Slavonic and East European Review* (April 1948); "The Marvelous Decade," *Encounter* (June, November, December 1955; May 1956); "The Silence in Russian Culture," *Foreign Affairs* (October 1957); "Tolstoy and Enlightenment," *Encounter* (February 1961); *Russian Thinkers.*

Black, Cyril E. (1915–1989) American historian. Works include *Twentieth-Century Europe: A History* (with E. C. Helmreich); *Rewriting Russian History: Soviet Interpretations of*

Russia's Past (ed.); *The Transformation of Russian Society: Aspects of Social Change since 1861* (ed.); *The Modernization of Japan and Russia* (with others); "The Nature of Imperial Russian Society," *Slavic Review* (December 1961); *Understanding Soviet Politics: The Perspective of Russian History.*

Blum, Jerome (1913–1993) American historian. Works include *Lord and Peasant in Russia from the Ninth to the Nineteenth Century;* "The Rise of Serfdom in Eastern Europe," *American Historical Review* (July 1957); "Russian Agriculture in the Last 150 Years of Serfdom," *Agricultural History* (January 1960).

Bogoslovsky, Mikhail Mikhailovich (1867–1929) Russian historian. Works include *Oblastnaia reforma Petra Velikogo, provintsiia 1719–1727 gg.; Petr I, materialy dlia biografii* (5 vols.).

Boltin, Ivan Nikitich (1735–1792) Russian historian. Works include *Kriticheskie primechaniia gen.-maiora Boltina na pervyi-vtoroi tom istorii kniazia Shcherbatova* (2 vols.); *Otvet gen.-maiora Boltina na pismo Kn. Shcherbatova; Primechaniia na istoriiu gospodina Leklerka* (2 vols.).

Bonnell, Victoria E. (1942–) American sociologist. Works include *Roots of Rebellion: Workers' Politics and Organizations in St. Petersburg and Moscow, 1900–1914; Iconography of Power: Soviet Political Posters under Lenin and Stalin.*

Boym, Svetlana (1959–) Russian-American cultural historian and literary scholar. Works include *Common Places: Mythologies of Everyday Life in Russia; The Future of Nostalgia.*

Breslauer, George (1946–) American political scientist. Works include *Khrushchev and Brezhnev as Leaders: Building Authority in Soviet Politics; Gorbachev and Yeltsin as Leaders.*

Briusov, Valerii Iakovlevich (1873–1924) Russian poet, writer, and literary scholar. Works include "Mednyi Vsadnik," in *Biblioteka velikikh pisatelei pod redaktsiei S. A. Vengerova: Pushkin* (vol. 3).

Brumberg, Abraham (1926–) American specialist on communism and editor of *Problems of Communism.* Works include "Apropos of Quotation Mongering," *New Republic* (August 29, 1960); *Chronicle of a Revolution: A Western-Soviet Inquiry into Perestroika* (ed.).

Brzezinski, Zbigniew K. (1928–) American political scientist. Works include *The Soviet Bloc: Unity and Conflict; The Permanent Purge; Ideology and Power in Soviet Politics; Alternative to Partition: For a Broader Conception of America's Role in Europe; The Grand Failure: The Birth and Death of Communism in the Twentieth Century; Russia and the Commonwealth of Independent States: Documents, Data, and Analysis.*

Campbell, Robert W. (1926–) American economist. Works include *Soviet Economic Power: Its Organization, Growth, and Challenge.*

Carr, Edward H. (1892–1982) British historian. Works include *A History of Soviet Russia: The Bolshevik Revolution, 1917–1922* (vols. 1–3), *The Interregnum, 1923–1924* (vol. 4), *Socialism in One Country, 1924–1926* (vols. 5–7), *Foundations of a Planned Economy, 1926–1929* (vol. 8, in two parts; with R. W. Davies, vol. 9); *Michael Bakunin; The Romantic Exiles: A Nineteenth-Century Portrait Gallery; The Soviet Impact on the Western World; The October Revolution: Before and After.*

Cattell, David T. (1923–) American political scientist. Works include *Communism and the Spanish Civil War; Soviet Diplomacy and the Spanish Civil War.*

Chamberlin, William Henry (1897–1969) American journalist and specialist on the Soviet Union. Works include *The Russian Revolution, 1917–1921* (2 vols.); *Russia's Iron Age.*

Charques, Richard Denis (1899–) British writer, literary scholar, and historian. Works include *A Short History of Russia; The Twilight of Imperial Russia.*

Cherepnin, Lev Vladimirovich (1905–1977) Soviet historian. Works include *Obrazovanie russkogo tsentralizovannogo gosudarstva: Ocherki sotsialno-ekonomicheskoi i politicheskoi istorii Rusi; Osnovnye etapy razvitiia feodalizma v Rossii; Russkaia istoriografiia do XIX veka: Kurs lektsii; Russkie feodalnye arkhivy XIV-XV vekov; Knigi moskovskikh prikazov v fondakh TsGADA: opis, 1495–1718 gg.; Novgorodskie berestianye gramoty kak istoricheskii istochnik, Krestianskie voiny v Rossii semnadstatogo-vosemnadtsatogo vekov: problemy, poiski, resheniia. Sbornik statei* (ed.); *Feodalnaia Rossiia vo vsemirno-istoricheskom protsesse; Puti razvitiia feodalizma* (with A. P. Novoseltsev and V. T. Pashuto); *Zemskie sobory russkogo gosudarstva v XVI–XVII vv; Otechestvennye istoriki XVIII–XX vv.*

Chizhevsky (Chyzhevskyi), Dmitrii (1894–1977) Ukrainian-German specialist in Russian and Slavic literature and thought. Works include *Gegel v Rossii* (Ger. *Hegel in Russland*); *Geschichte der altrussischen Literatur im 11., 12., und 13. Jahrhundert, Kiever Epoche; Hegel bei den Slaven* (ed.); *Das heilige Russland: Russische Geistesgeschichte 1, 10–17. Jahrhundert; History of Russian Literature from the Eleventh Century to the End of the Baroque; Russische Literaturgeschichte des 19. Jahrhunderts* (2 vols.); *Outline of Comparative Slavic Literatures.*

Conquest, Robert (1917–) British specialist in the Soviet Union. Works include *The Great Terror: Stalin's Purge of the Thirties; The Great Terror: A Reassessment; The Harvest of Sorrow; Agricultural Workers in the USSR* (ed.); *Industrial Workers in the USSR* (ed.); *The Nation Killers: The Soviet Deportation of Nationalities; V. I. Lenin; Stalin and the Kirov Murder; Stalin: Breaker of Nations.*

Cross, Samuel H. (1891–1946) American specialist in Slavic languages, literatures, and cultures. Works include *Medieval Russian Churches* (ed. Kenneth J. Conant); *The Russian Primary Chronicle, Laurentian Text* (trans. and ed. with O. P. Sherbowitz-Wetzor); "The Lay of the Host of Igor" (trans.), in *La Geste du Prince Igor* (ed. Henri Grégoire, Roman Jakobson, and Marc Szeftel).

Crossman, R. H. S. (1907–1974) British intellectual and politician. Works include *The God that Failed: Six Essays on Communism* (ed.).

Dallin, Alexander (1921–2000) American political scientist. Works include *German Rule in Russia, 1941–1945: A Study of Occupation Policies; The Soviet Union and Disarmament, an Appraisal of Soviet Attitudes and Intentions; The Soviet Union at the United Nations; The Black Box.*

Dallin, David J. (1889–1962) Russian-American historian. Works include *The Changing World of Soviet Russia; Forced Labor in the Soviet Union* (with B. I. Nicolaevsky); *The New Soviet Empire; Russian and the Far East; Soviet Foreign Policy after Stalin.*

Deutscher, Isaac (1907–1967) Polish-British historian. Works include *The Prophet Armed: Trotsky, 1879–1921; The Prophet Unarmed: Trotsky, 1921–1929; The Prophet Outcast: Trotsky, 1929–1940; Stalin: A Political Biography; The Unfinished Revolution, 1917–1967.*

Dewitt, Nicholas (1923–) American specialist in Soviet education and economics. Works include *Education and Professional Employment in the U.S.S.R.; Soviet Professional Manpower: Its Training and Supply.*

Diakonov, Mikhail Aleksandrovich (1856–1919) Russian historian. Works include *Izbranie Mikhaila Fedorovicha na tsarstvo; Ocherki obshchestvennogo i gosudarstvennogo stroia drevnei Rusi* (Ger. *Skizzen zur Gesellschaft und Staatsordnung des alten Russlands*); *Vlast moskovskikh gosudarei: Ocherki po istorii politicheskikh idei drevnei Rusi do kontsa XVI veka.*

Dobb, Maurice Herbert (1900–1976) British economist. Works include *Soviet Economic Development since 1917.*

Druzhinin, Nikolai Mikhailovich (1886–1986) Soviet historian. Works include *Gosudarstvennye krestiane i reforma P. D. Kiseleva* (2 vols.); *Krestianskoe dvizhenie v 1861 godu posle otmeny krepostnogo prava; Russkaia derevnia na pereloma, 1861–1880 gg.*

Dunlop, Douglas Morton (1909–1987) British historian. Works include *The History of the Jewish Khazars*.

Duranty, Walter (1884–1957) American journalist. Works include *Duranty Reports Russia; I Write as I Please; Stalin & Co.: The Politburo, the Men Who Run Russia*.

Dvornik, Francis (1893–1975) Czech-American historian. Works include *The Slavs in European History and Civilization;* "Byzantine Influences in Russia," *Geographical Magazine* (1947); "The Kiev State and Its Relations with Western Europe," *Transactions of the Royal Historical Society* (1947); "Byzantine Political Ideas in Kievan Russia," *Dumbarton Oaks Papers* (1956).

Eklof, Ben (1946–) American historian. Works include *Russian Peasant Schools: Officialdom, Village Culture, and Popular Pedagogy, 1864–1914; Soviet Briefing: Gorbachev and the Reform Period*.

Erlich, Alexander (1912–1985) American economic historian. Works include *The Soviet Industrialization Debate, 1924–1928*.

Fainsod, Merle (1907–1972) American political scientist. Works include *How Russia Is Ruled; Smolensk under Soviet Rule*.

Fay, Sidney B. (1876–1967) American historian of Europe. Works include *The Origins of the World War* (2 vols.).

Fedotov, Georgii Petrovich (1886–1951) Russian-American historian of religion and culture. Works include *The Russian Religious Mind: Kievan Christianity, the Tenth to the Thirteenth Centuries* (vol. 1), *The Middle Ages, the Thirteenth to the Fifteenth Centuries* (vol. 2); *Sviatye Drevnei Rusi (X-XVII st.); A Treasury of Russian Spirituality*.

Feldmesser, Robert A. (1925–) American sociologist. Works include "Stratification and Communism," in *Prospects for Soviet Society* (ed. A. Kassof).

Feshbach, Murray (1929–) American demographer. Works include *Rising Infant Mortality in the U.S.S.R. in the 1970s* (with Christopher Davis); *A Compendium of Soviet Health Statistics; Ecocide in the USSR: Health and Nature under Siege* (with Alfred Friendly, Jr.); *Ecological Disaster: Cleaning Up the Hidden Legacy of the Soviet Regime*.

Fischer, George (1923–) American historian and political scientist. Works include *Russian Liberalism, from Gentry to Intelligenntsia; Soviet Opposition to Stalin: A Case Study in World War II*.

Fitzpatrick, Sheila (1941–) Australian-American historian. Works include *The Commissariat of Enlightenment; Education and Social Mobility in the Soviet Union, 1921–34; Cultural Revolution in Russia, 1928–1931; The Russian Revolution; Everyday Stalinism: Ordinary Life in Extraordinary Times; The Cultural Front: Power and Culture in Revolutionary Russia*.

Florinsky, Michael T. (1894–1981) Russian-American economist and historian. Works include *The End of the Russian Empire; Russia: A History and Interpretation* (2 vols.).

Florovsky, George Vasilevich (1893–1979) Russian-American Orthodox theologian and intellectual historian. Works include *Puti russkogo bogosloviia (Ways of Russian Theology,* part 1); "O patriotizme pravednom i grekhovnom," in the Eurasian book *Na putiakh;* "The Problem of Old Russian Culture," *Slavic Review* (March 1962).

Freeze, Gregory (1945–) American historian. Works include *Description of the Clergy in Rural Russia: The Memoir of a Nineteenth Century Parish Priest* (ed. and trans.); *The Parish Clergy in Nineteenth Century Russia: Crisis, Reform, Counter-reform; The Russian Levites: Parish Clergy in the Eighteenth Century; From Supplication to Revolution: A Documentary Social History of Imperial Russia*.

Gerschenkron, Alexander (1904–1978) Russian-American economist. Works include *Economic Backwardness in Historical Perspective;* "Agrarian Policies and Industrialization, Russia 1861–1917," in *Cambridge Economic History of Europe* (vol. 6, pt. 2);

Continuity in History and Other Essays; Europe in the Russian Mirror: Four Lectures in Economic Theory.

Gide, André (1869–1951) French writer. Works include *Retour de l'U.R.S.S. (Back from the USSR); Retouches à "Retour de l'U.R.S.S." Afterthoughts, A Sequel to "Back from the USSR").*

Goldsmith, Raymond W. (1904–1988) American economist. Works include "The Economic Growth of Tsarist Russia 1860–1913," *Economic Development and Cultural Exchange* (April 1961).

Golikov, Ivan Ivanovich (1735–1801) Russian historian who collected source material on Peter the Great. Works include *Deianiia Petra Velikogo, mudrogo preobrazitelia Rossii: Sobrannye iz dostovernykh istochnikov i raspolozhennye po godam* (12 vols.); *Dopolnenie* (18 vols.).

Golovin, Nikolai Nikolaevich (1875–1944) Russian general and author. Works include *Rossiiskaia kontrrevoliutsiia v 1917–1918 gg.* (5 vols.), *The Russian Army in the World War.*

Golubinsky, Evgenii Evsigneevich (1834–1912) Russian Church historian. Works include *Istoriia russkoi tserkvi* (2 vols.).

Gooch, George Peabody (1873–1968) British historian of Europe. Works include *Catherine the Great and Other Studies.*

Grabar, Igor Emmanuilovich (1871–1960) Russian-Soviet specialist in art and art history. Works include *Istoriia russkogo iskusstva* (6 vols.).

Grekov, Boris Dmitrievich (1882–1953) Soviet historian. Works include *Feodalnye otnosheniia v kievskom gosudarstve; Kievskaia Rus (Kiev Rus); Krestiane na Rusi s drevneishikh vremen do XVII veka* (Ger. *Die Bauern in der Rus von den altesten Zeiten biz zum 17. Jahrhundert* [2 vols.]); *Zolotaia Orda i ee padenie* (with A. Iu Iakubovskii) (Fr. *La Horde d'or*).

Grossman, Gregory (1921–) American economist. Works include *Value and Plan: Economic Calculation and Organization in Eastern Europe* (ed.); "National Income," in *Soviet Economic Growth* (ed. A. Bergson); "A Note on the Fulfillment of the Fifth Five-Year Plan in Industry," *Soviet Studies* (April 1957); "The Structure and Organization of the Soviet Economy," *Slavic Review* (June 1962); "Thirty Years of Soviet Industrialization," *Soviet Survey* (October–December 1958); "Notes for a Theory of the Command Economy," *Soviet Studies* (October 1963); "The Soviet Economy and the Waning of the Cold War," in *Beyond the Cold War* (ed. R. Goldwin); "Innovation and Information in the Soviet Economy," *The American Economic Review* (May 1966); "Economic Reforms: A Balance Sheet," *Problems of Communism* (November–December 1966); "Gold and the Sword: Money in the Soviet Command Economy," in *Industrialization in Two Systems: Essays in Honor of Alexander Gerschenkron* (ed. H. Rosovsky); "The Solidary Society: A Philosophical Issue in Communist Economic Reforms," in *Essays in Socialism and Planning in Honor of Carl Landauer;* "The Economy at Middle Age," *Problems of Communism* (March–April 1976); "Economics of Virtuous Haste: A View of Soviet Industrialization and Institutions," in *Marxism, Central Planning, and the Soviet Economy: Economic Essays in Honor of Alexander Erlich* (ed. Padma Desai); "A Note on Soviet Inflation," in U.S. Congress, Joint Economic Committee, *Soviet Economy in the 1980s, Problems and Prospects, Part I: Selected Papers;* "The Party as Manager and Entrepreneur," in *Entrepreneurship in Imperial Russia and the Soviet Union* (ed. Gregory Guroff and Fred V. Carstensen); "The Second Economy: Boon or Bane for the Reform of the First Economy?" in *Economic Reforms in the Socialist World* (ed. Stanislaw Gomulka, Yong-Chool Ha, and Cae-One Kim); "Subverted Sovereignty-Historic Role of the Soviet Underground," in *The Tunnel at the End of the Light-Privatization, Business Networks, and Economic Transformation in Russia* (eds. Stephen S. Cohen, Andrew Schwartz, and John Zysman).

Grunwald, Constantine de ( ) Russian-French historian. Works include *Allexandre Ier: Le tsar mystique; La Russie de Pierre le Grand (Peter the Great); Trois siècles de diplomatie russe; La Vie de Nicolas Ier (Tsar Nicholas I)*.

Haimson, Leopold (1927–) American historian. Works include "The Problem of Social Stability in Urban Russia, 1905–1917," *Slavic Review* (December 1964–March 1965); *The Russian Marxists and the Origins of Bolshevism; The Politics of Rural Russia, 1905–1914* (ed.).

Halecki, Oscar (1891–1973) Polish-American historian. Works include *Borderlands of Western Civilization: A History of East Central Europe; From Florence to Brest (1459–1596); A History of Poland; The Limits and Divisions of European History; Cambridge History of Poland* (ed. with W. F. Reddaway, J. H. Penson, and R. Dyboski [2 vols.]); "Imperialism in Slavic and East European History," *American Slavic and East European Review* (February 1952).

Hellie, Richard (1937–) American historian. Works include *Enserfment and Military Change in Muscovy;* "Recent Soviet Historiography on Medieval and Early Modern Russian Slavery," *Russian Review* (January 1976); *Slavery in Russia; The Muscovite Law Code (Ulozhenie) of 1649. Part I: Text and Translation* (ed. and trans.).

Hook, Sidney (1902–1989) American political philosopher. Works include *From Hegel to Marx; The Hero in History: A Study in Limitation and Possibility; Towards an Understanding of Karl Marx*.

Hrushevsky (Grushevsky), Mikhail Sergeevich (1866–1934) Ukrainian historian. Works include *Istoriia Ukrajiny-Rusy* (10 vols.) (Eng. trans. of a different, much briefer study, *A History of the Ukraine*).

Ignatovich, Inna Ivanovna (1879–1967) Russian-Soviet historian. Works include *Borba krestian za osvobozhdenie; Pomeshchichi krestiane nakanune osvobozhdeniia;* "Krestianskie volneniia pervoi chetverti XIX veka," *Voprosy istorii* (1950).

Inkeles, Alex (1920–) American sociologist. Works include "Models and Issues in the Analysis of Soviet Society," *Survey* (July 1966); *How the Soviet System Works* (with R. Bauer and C. Kluckhohn); *The Soviet Citizen* (with R. Bauer); *Public Opinion in the Soviet Union*.

Itenberg, Boris Samuilovich (1921–) Soviet historian. Works include *Dvizhenie revoliutsionnogo narodnichestva; Pervyi Internatsional i revoliutsionnaia Rossiia; Iuzhnorossiiskii soiuz rabochikh: vozniknovenie i deiatelnost; P. L. Lavrov v russkom revoliutsionnom dvizhenii*.

Jakobson, Roman (1896–1982) Russian-American philologist and historian of literature. Works include *Remarques sur l'évolution phonologique du russe comparée à celle des autres langues slaves; Russian Epic Studies* (with E. J. Simmons); *Slovo o Polku Igoreve v perevodakh kontsa vosemnadtsatogo veka; La Geste du Prince Igor* (ed. with Henri Grégoire and Marc Szeftel).

Jasny, Naum (1883–1967) Russian-American economist. Works include *The Socialized Agriculture of the U.S.S.R.: Plans and Performance; Soviet Industrialization, 1928–1952; The Soviet 1956 Statistical Handbook: A Commentary;* "The Soviet Seven-Year Plan: Is It Realistic?" *Bulletin of the Institute for the Study of the USSR* (May 1959); "The Soviet Statistical Yearbooks, 1955–1960," *Slavic Review* (March 1962).

Jelavich, Charles (1922–) American historian of Eastern Europe. Works include *Tsarist Russia and Balkan Nationalism, 1879–1886*.

Johnson, Robert E. (1943–) American historian. *Peasant and Proletarian: The Working Class of Moscow at the End of the Nineteenth Century*.

Karamzin, Nikolai Mikhailovich (1766–1826) Russian writer and historian. Works include *Istoriia Gosudarstva Rossiiskogo* (12 vols.); *Karamzin's Memoir on Ancient and Modern Russia: The Russian Text* (ed. R. E. Pipes) (*Karamzin's Memoir on Ancient and Modern Russia: A Translation and Analysis,* ed. R. E. Pipes).

Karpovich, Michael (1888–1959) Russian-American historian. Works include *Economic History of Europe since 1750* (with Witt Bowden and Abbott P. Usher); *Imperial Russia, 1801–1917;* Russian sections of *An Encyclopedia of World History* (ed. W. L. Langer); "A Forerunner of Lenin: P. N. Tkachev," *Review of Politics* (1944); "Two Types of Russian Liberalism: Maklakov and Miliukov," in *Continuity and Change in Russian and Soviet Thought* (ed. E. J. Simmons); "Vladimir Soloviev on Nationalism," *Review of Politics* (1946).

Keep, J. L. H. (1926–) British historian. Works include "The Decline of the Zemsky Sobor," *Slavonic and East European Review* (December 1957); "The Regime of Filaret," *Slavonic and East European Review* (June 1960); *The Russian Revolution: A Study in Mass Mobilization; Soldiers of the Tsar: Army and Society in Russia, 1462–1874.*

Kennan, George F. (1904–) American diplomat and historian. Works include *Soviet-American Relations, 1917–1920: Russia Leaves the War* (vol. 1), *The Decision to Intervene* (vol. 2); *Soviet Foreign Policy, 1917–1941;* "Russia and the Versailles Conference," *American Scholar* (Winter 1960–61); "Soviet Historiography and America's Role in the Intervention," *American Historical Review* (January 1960); *The Decline of Bismarck's European Order: Franco-Russian Relations, 1875–1890.*

Kerner, Robert J. (1887–1956) American historian. Works include *Northeastern Asia: A Selected Bibliography; Slavic Europe: A Selected Bibliography; The Urge to the Sea: The Course of Russian History.*

Khodsky, Leonid Vladimirovich (1854–1918) Russian economist. Works include *Osnovy gosudarstvennogo khoziaistva; Politicheskaia ekonomiia v sviazi s finansami; Pozemelnyi kredit v Rossii i otnoshenie ego k krestianskomu zemlevladeniiu.*

Khromov, Pavel Alekseevich (1907–) Soviet economic historian. Works include *Ekonomicheskoe razvitie Rossii v XIX–XX vekakh; Ocherki ekonomiki feodalizma v Rossii; Ocherki ekonomiki Rossii perioda monopolisticheskogo kapitalizma; Ocherki ekonomiki tekstilnoi promyshlennosti SSSR; Ocherki ekonomiki dokapitalisticheskoi Rossii.*

Kirchner, Walther (1905–) German-American historian. Works include *The History of Russia; Eine Reise durch Sibirien im achtzehnten Jahrhundert: Die Fahrt des schweizer Doktors Jakob Fries; The Rise of the Baltic Question.*

Kizevetter, Aleksandr Aleksandrovich (1866–1933) Russian historian. Works include *Gorodovoe polozhenie Ekateriny II: Istoricheskie ocherki; Istoricheskie otkliki; Na rubezhe dvukh stoletii: Vospominaniia 1881–1914; Posadskaia obshchina v Rossii v XVIII st.;* chapters in *Histoire de Russie* (ed. P. N. Miliukov, C. Seignobos, and L. Eisenmann [3 vols.]); "Vnutrenniaia politika v tsarstvovanie Nikolaia Pavlovicha," in *Istoriia Rossii v XIX veke* (vol. 1).

Kline, George L. (1921–) American specialist in Russian philosophy and culture. Works include *Soviet Education* (ed.); *Spinoza in Russian Philosophy* (ed.); "Recent Soviet Philosophy," *Annals of the American Academy of Political and Social Science* (January 1956); "Russia's Lagging School System," *New Leader* (March 16, 1959); "Philosophy, Ideology, and Policy in the Soviet Union," *Review of Politics* (April 1964); "Economic Crime and Punishment," *Survey* (October 1965).

Kliuchevsky (Klyuchevsky), Vasilii Osipovich (1841–1911) Russian historian. Works include *Boiarskaia duma drevnei Rusi; Istoriia soslovii v Rossii; Kurs russkoi istorii* (5 vols.) (*A History of Russia*); *Opyty i issledovaniia* (3 vols.).

Kornai, Janos (1928–) Hungarian economist. Works include *The Socialist System: the*

Political Economy of Communism; Contradictions and Dilemmas: Studies on the Socialist Economy and Society; Highway and Byways: Studies on Reform and Post-Communist Transition; Struggle and Hope: Essays on Stabilization and Reform in a Post-Socialist Economy; Vision and Reality, Market and State: Contradictions and Dilemmas Revisited.

Konovalov, Sergei (1899–1982) Russian-British historian, former editor and frequent contributor to the *Oxford Slavonic Papers.*

Kostomarov, Nikolai Ivanovich (1817–1888) Ukrainian historian. Works include *Deiateli russkoi tserkvi v starinu; Deux nationalités russes; Istoricheskie monografii i issledovaniia; O znachenii Velikogo Novgoroda; Russkaia istoriia v zhizneopisaniiakh ee glavneishikh deiatelei* (3 vols.).

Kovalchenko, Ivan Dmitrievich (1923–1995) Soviet historian. Works include *Russkoe krepostnoe krestianstvo v pervoi polovine XIX veka.*

Kovalevsky, Maksim Maksimovich (1851–1916) Russian sociologist, political scientist, and historian. Works include *Istoriia nashego vremeni; Modern Customs and Ancient Laws of Russia; Ocherk proiskhozhdeniia i razvitiia semi i sobstvennosti; Le Régime économique de la Russie; Russian Political Institutions; La Russie sociale.*

Kucherov, Samuel (1892–1972) Russian-American specialist in legal history and Soviet affairs. Works include *Courts, Lawyers, and Trials under the Last Three Tsars; The Organs of Soviet Administration of Justice: Their History and Operation.*

Langer, William L. (1896–1977) American historian of Europe. Works include *The Diplomacy of Imperialism, 1890–1902* (2 vols.); *European Alliances and Alignments, 1870–1890; The Franco-Russian Alliance, 1890–1894; An Encyclopedia of World History* (ed.).

Lantzeff, George V. (1892–1955) Russian-American historian. Works include *Siberia in the Seventeenth Century: A Study in Colonial Administration; Eastward to Empire* (with R. A. Pierce).

Lapidus, Gail Warshofsky (1939–) American political scientist. Works include *Women in Soviet Society: Equality, Development, and Social Change; Women in Russia* (ed. with Dorothy Atkinson and Alexander Dallin); *From Union to Commonwealth: Nationalism and Separatism in the Soviet Republics* (ed. with Victor Zaslavsky with Philip Goldman); *The New Russia: Troubled Transformation* (ed.); *The Soviet System: From Crisis to Collapse* (ed. with Alexander Dallin).

Lasswell, Harold D. (1902–1978) American sociologist and psychologist. Works include *World Politics and Personal Insecurity.*

Lednicki, Waclaw (1891–1967) Polish-American specialist in Slavic and European literature. Works include *Pushkin's Bronze Horseman: The Story of a Masterpiece; Russia, Poland and the West: Essays in Literary and Cultural History; Russian-Polish Relations: Their Historical, Cultural and Political Background.*

Lemke, Mikhail Konstantinovich (1872–1923) Russian historian. Works include *Epokha tsenzurnykh reform, 1859–1865; Politicheskie protsesy; Nikolaevskie zhandarmy i literatura.*

Leontovich (Leontovitsch), Victor (1922–1960) German historian. Works include *Geschichte des Liberalismus in Russland (A History of Liberalism in Russia).*

Lewin, Moshe (1921–) British historian. Works include *Russian Peasants and Soviet Power: A Study of Collectivization* (trans.); 'Soviet Policies of Agricultural Procurements before the War,' in *Essays in Honor of E. H. Carr* (ed. Ch. Abramsky); *Lenin's Last Struggle* (trans. A. M. Sheridan Smith); *The Gorbachev Phenomenon: A Historical Interpretation.*

Liashchenko, Petr Ivanovich (1876–1955) Russian-Soviet economic historian. Works include *Istoriia narodnogo khoziaistva SSSR (History of the National Economy of Russia to the 1917 Revolution); Krestianskoe delo i poreformennaia zemleustroitelnaia politika;*

Ocherki agrarnoi evoliutsii Rossii; Russkoe zernovoe khoziaistvo v sisteme mirovogo khozi-
aistva; Sotsialnaia ekonomiia selskogo khoziaistva (2 vols.).

Lilge, Frederic (1911–) German-American specialist in Soviet education. Works include
Anton Semyonovitch Makarenko: An Analysis of His Educational Ideas in the Context of
Soviet Society; "Impressions of Soviet Education," *International Review of Education*
(1959); "The Soviet School Today," *Survey* (July 1963); "Lenin and the Politics of
Education," *Slavic Review* (June 1968).

Liubavsky, Matvei Kuzmich (1860–1937) Russian historian. Works include *Lektsii po*
drevnei russkoi istorii do konsta shestnadtsatogo veka; Obrazovanie osnovnoi gosu-
darstvennoi territorii velikorusskoi narodnosti; Ocherk istorii Litovsko-Russkogo gosu-
darstva.

Lord, Robert Howard (1885–1954) American historian of European diplomacy. Works
include *The Second Partition of Poland: A Study in Diplomatic History;* "The Third Partition of Poland," *Slavonic and East European Review* (1925).

Madariaga, Isabel de (1919–) British historian. Works include *Britain, Russia, and the*
Armed Neutrality of 1780; Russia in the Age of Catherine the Great.

Makovsky, D. P. (1899–1970) Soviet historian. Works include *Razvitie tovarnodenezhnykh*
otnoshenii v selskom khoziastve russkogo gosudarstva v XVI veke.

Malia, Martin E. (1924–) American historian. Works include *Alexander Herzen and the*
Birth of Russian Socialism, 1812–1855; "Schiller and the Early Russian Left," in *Har-*
vard Slavic Studies (vol. 4); "What Is the Intelligentsia?" in *The Russian Intelligentsia*
(ed. R. Pipes); *Comprendre la Révolution russe; The Soviet Tragedy; A History of Social-*
ism in Russia, 1917–1941; Russia under Western Eyes: From the Bronze Horseman to the
Lenin Mausoleum; The Soviet Tragedy: A History of Socialism in Russia, 1917–1991.

Malozemoff, Andrew Alexander (1910–1954) American historian. Works include *Rus-*
sian Far Eastern Policy, 1881–1904, with Special Emphasis on the Causes of the Russo-
Japanese War.

Marchenko (Martschenko), Vasilii Pavlovich (1900–) Soviet-Canadian economist.
Works include *Osnovnye cherty khoziaistva poslestalinskoi epokhi,* in *Issledovaniia i*
materialy of the Institute for the Study of the USSR.

Markov, Vladimir (1920–) American specialist on Russian language and literature.
Works include "Unnoticed Aspect of Pasternak's Translations," *Slavic Review*
(October 1961).

Mathewson, Rufus W., Jr. (1918–1978) American specialist in Russian literature. Works
include *The Positive Hero in Russian Literature;* "The Hero and Society: The Literary
Definition, 1855–1865, 1934–1939," in *Continuity and Change in Russian and Soviet*
Thought (ed. E. J. Simmons); "The Soviet Hero as the Literary Heritage," *American*
Slavic and East European Review (December 1953).

Maynard, Sir John Herbert (1865–1943) British historian. Works include *Russia in Flux:*
Before October (abridged as *Russia in Flux*); *The Russian Peasant and Other Studies.*

Mazon, André (1881–1967) French specialist in Russian language and literature. Works
include *Le Slovo d'Igor.*

Menshutkin, Boris Nikolaevich (1874–1938) Russian-Soviet historian of science. Works
include *Mikhail Vasilevich Lomonosov (Russia's Lomonosov: Chemist, Courtier, Physi-*
cist, Poet).

Merezhkovsky, Dmitri Sergeevich (1865–1941) Russian writer and critic. Works include
Gogol i chort, issledovanie.

Meyendorff, John (1926–1992) Russian-American theologian and historian. Works
include *The Byzantine Legacy in the Orthodox Church; Byzantium and the Rise of Rus-*
sia: A Study of Byzantino-Russia Relations in the Fourteenth Century.

Miakotin, Venedikt Aleksandrovich (1867–1937) Russian historian. Works include

Ocherki sotsialnoi istorii Ukrainy v XVII–XVIII vv. (3 vols. in 1); *Protopop Avvakum, ego zhizn i deiatelnost: Biograficheskii ocherk; chapters in Histoire de Russie* (ed. P. N. Miliukov, C. Seignobos, and L. Eisenmann [3 vols.]).

Miliukov, Pavel Nikolaevich (1859–1943) Russian historian and statesman. Works include *Glavnye techeniia russkoi istoricheskoi mysli* (Eng. summary "The Chief Currents of Russian Historical Thought," in *The American Historical Association Annual Report for 1904); Gosudarstvennoe khoziaistvo Rossii v pervoi chetverti XVIII stoletiia i reforma Petra Velikogo; Histoire de Russie* (with C. Seignobos, L. Eisenmann, and others [3 vols.]); *Iz istorii russkoi intelligentsii (Fr. Le Mouvement intellectuel russe); Ocherki po istorii russkoi kultury* (4 vols.) (abridged Eng. trans. *Outlines of Russian Culture;* abridged Fr. trans. *Essais sur l'histoire de la civilisation russe); Russia and Its Crisis; Spornye voprosy finansovoi istorii moskovskogo gosudarstva.*

Milosz, Czeslaw (1911–) Polish-American poet, writer, and specialist in Slavic literature. Works include *The Captive Mind.*

Mironenko, Iurii Pavlovich (1909–) Soviet-German specialist on the Soviet Union. Works include "K voprosu o dinamike naseleniia Sovetskogo Soiuza s 1939 po 1956 god," *Vestnik Instituta po Izucheniiu SSSR* (1956).

Mirsky (Sviatopolk-Mirsky), Dmitrii Petrovich (1890–1938) Russian-British historian of Russian literature. Works include *Contemporary Russian Literature, 1881–1925; A History of Russian Literature from Its Beginnings to 1900* (ed. Francis J. Whitfield); *A History of Russian Literature from the Earliest Times to the Death of Dostoevsky; Russia: A Social History.*

Mosely, Philip Edward (1905–1972) American historian and political scientist. Works include *The Kremlin and World Politics; Russian Diplomacy and the Opening of the Eastern Question in 1838 and 1839; Russia since Stalin* (ed.).

Muratov, Pavel Pavlovich (1881–1950). Russian-French art historian. Works include *L'Ancienne Peinture russe; Les Icones russes.*

Nabokov, Vladimir V. (1899–1977) Russian-American writer. Works include *Nikolai Gogol.*

Nicolaevsky, Boris I. (1889–1966) Russian-American specialist in the Russian revolutionary movement and the U.S.S.R. Works include *Azeff, the Russian Judas; Forced Labor in the Soviet Union* (with D. J. Dallin).

Nolde, Boris E. (1876–1948) Russian-French historian and legal scholar. Works include *L'Alliance franco-russe: Les Origines du système diplomatique d'avant guerre; L'Ancien Régime et la révolution russe; La Formation de l'empire russe* (2 vols.); *Ocherki russkogo gosudarstvennogo prava; Russia in the Economic War; Vneshniaia politika.*

Nosov, Nikolai Evgenievich (1925–) Soviet historian. Works include *Ocherki po istorii mestnogo upravleniia russkogo gosudarstva pervoi poloviny XVI veka.*

Obnorsky, Sergei Petrovich (1888–1962) Soviet philologist and historian of literature. Works include *Khrestomatiia po istorii russkogo iazyka; Kultura russkogo iazyka; Ocherki po istorii russkogo literaturnogo iazyka starshego perioda.*

Obolensky, Dimitrii (1918–2001) British historian. Works include "Russia's Byzantine Heritage," in *Oxford Slavonic Papers* (vol. 1); "Byzantium, Kiev and Moscow: A Study in Ecclesiastical Relations," *Dumbarton Oaks Papers (1957); The Byzantine Commonwealth.*

Oganovsky, Nikolai Petrovich (1874–) Russian economist. Works include *Narodnoe khoziaistvo SSSR v sviazi s mirovym; Selskoe khoziaistvo Rossii v dvadtsatom veke.*

Okun, Semen Bentsionovich (1908–1972) Soviet historian. Works include *Ocherki istorii SSSR: Konets XVIII-pervaia chetvert XIX veka; Ocherki istorii SSSR: Vtoraia chetvert XIX veka; Rossiisko-Amerikanskaia Kompaniia (The Russian-American Company).*

Pares, Sir Bernard (1867–1949) British historian. Works include *The Fall of the Russian Monarchy; A History of Russia; My Russian Memoirs; Russia.*

Pavlov-Silvansky, Nikolai Pavlovich (1869–1908) Russian historian. Works include *Feodalizm v drevnei Rusi; Feodalizm v udelnoi Rusi; Gosudarevy sluzhilye liudi: Proiskhozdenie russkogo dvorianstva; Ocherki po russkoi istorii XVIII–XIX vv.*

Pavlovsky, Georgii Alekseevich (1887–) Russian-British agrarian historian. Works include *Agricultural Russia on the Eve of the Revolution.*

Pipes, Richard E. (1923–) American historian. Works include *The Formation of the Soviet Union: Communism and Nationalism, 1917–1923; Karamzin's Memoir on Ancient and Modern Russia: A Translation and Analysis; Social Democracy and the St. Petersburg Labor Movement, 1885–1897;* "Karamzin's Conception of the Monarchy," in *Harvard Slavic Studies* (vol. 4); "The Russian Military Colonies," *Journal of Modern History* (1950); *The Russian Intelligentsia* (ed.); *Revolutionary Russia* (ed.); *Struve: Liberal on the Left, 1870–1905; Russia under the Old Regime; Struve: Liberal on the Right, 1905–1944; U.S.-Soviet Relations in the Era of Détente; Russia Observed: Collected Essays on Russian and Soviet History; The Russian Revolution; The Unknown Lenin: From the Secret Archive* (ed.); *A Concise History of the Russian Revolution; Russia under the Bolshevik Regime.*

Platonov, Sergei Feodorovich (1860–1933) Russian historian. Works include *Boris Godunov* (Fr. *Boris Godounov, tsar de Russie, 1598–1605*); *Lektsii po russkoi istorii* (Fr. *Histoire de Russie*); *Moskva i zapad v XVI–XVII vekakh* (Moscow and the West); *Ocherki po istorii smuty v moskovskom gosudarstve XVI–XVII vv; Petr Velikii, lichnost i deiatelnost; Smutnoe vremia: Sotsialnyi krizis smutnogo vremeni* (Time of Troubles: A Historical Study of the Internal Crisis and Social Struggle in 16th and 17th Century Muscovy); "Ivan Groznyi v russkoi istoriografii," in *Russkoe proshloe* (vol. 1).

Pogodin, Mikhail Petrovich (1800–1875) Russian historian and right-wing intellectual. Works include *Issledovaniia, zamechaniia i lektsii o russkoi istorii* (7 vols.).

Pokrovsky, Mikhail Nikolaevich (1868–1932) Russian-Soviet historian. Works include *Dekabristy: Sbornik statei; Diplomatiia i voiny tsarskoi Rossii v XIX stoletii; Istoricheskaia nauka i borba klassov* (2 vols.); *Ocherk istorii russkoi kultury; Russkaia istoricheskaia literatura v klassovom osveshchenii* (2 vols.) (ed.); *Russkaia istoriia s drevneishikh vremen* (5 vols.) (abridged Eng. trans. *History of Russia from the Earliest Times to the Rise of Commercial Capitalism* [2 vols.]; *Russkaia istoriia v samom szhatom ocherke* (2 vols.) (*Brief History of Russia* [2 vols.]).

Poliansky, Fedor Iakovlevich (1907–) Soviet historian. Works include *Ekonomicheskii stroi manufaktury v Rossii XVIII veka; Istoriia narodnogo khoziaistva SSSR; Pervonachalnoe nakoplenie kapitala v Rossii; Remeslo v Rossii XVIII veka.*

Polievktov, Mikhail Aleksandrovich (1872–1946) Russian historian. Works include *Baltiiskii vopros v russkoi politike; Nikolai I: Biografiia i obzor tsarstvovaniia.*

Presniakov, Aleksandr Evgenievich (1870–1929) Russian historian. Works include *Kniazhoe pravo v drevnei Rusi, ocherki po istorii X–XII stoletiia; Lektsii po russkoi istorii: Kievskaia Rus; Moskovskoe tsarstvo; Obrazovanie velikorusskogo gosudarstva, ocherki po istorii XII–XV stoletti* (Eng. trans. without notes, *The Formation of the Great Russian State*).

Priselkov, Mikhail Dmitrievich (1881–1941) Russian-Soviet historian. Works include *Ocherki po tserkovno-politicheskoi istorii kievskoi Rusi X–XII vv.*

Prokopovich, Sergei Nikolaevich (1871–1955) Russian-American economic historian. Works include *Krestianskoe khoziaistvo; Narodnoe khoziaistvo SSSR* (Fr. *Histoire économique de l'URSS*).

Puryear, Vernon J. (1901–1970) American historian of European diplomacy. Works include *England, Russia, and the Straits Question, 1844–1856; International Economics and Diplomacy in the Near East: A Study of British Commercial Policy in the Levant, 1834–1853; Napolean and the Dardanelles.*

Radkey, Oliver Henry (1909–) American historian. Works include *The Agrarian Foes of Bolshevism: The Promise and Default of the Russian Socialist Revolutionaries; The Sickle under the Hammer: The Russian Socialist Revolutionaries in the Early Months of Soviet Rule; The Elections to the Russian Constituent Assembly of 1917;* "Chernov and Agrarian Socialism before 1918," in *Continuity and Change in Russian and Soviet Thought* (ed. E. J. Simmons); *The Unknown Civil War in Soviet Russia: A Study of the Green Movement in the Tambov Region, 1920–1921.*

Raeff, Marc (1923–) American historian. Works include *Michael Speransky: Statesman of Imperial Russia; Siberia and the Reform of 1822; Origins of the Russian Intelligentsia: The Eighteenth-Century Nobility; Imperial Russia, 1682–1825: The Coming of Age of Modern Russia; Russia Abroad: A Cultural History of the Russian Emigration, 1919–1939; Political Ideas and Institutions in Imperial Russia.*

Rashin, Adolf Grigorevich. Soviet statistical and demographic historian. Works include *Formirovanie promyshlennogo proletariata v Rossii; Naselenie Rossii za 100 let: 1811–1913 gg.*

Rieber, Alfred J. (1931–) American historian. Works include *The Politics of Autocracy: Letters of Alexander II to Prince A. T. Bariatinsky, 1857–1864* (ed.); *Merchants and Entrepreneurs in Imperial Russia.*

Robinson, Geroid Tanquary (1892–1971) American historian. Works include *Rural Russia under the Old Regime.*

Rogger, Hans (1923–2003) American historian. Works include *National Consciousness in Eighteenth-Century Russia;* "Russian Ministers and the Jewish Question, 1881–1917," *California Slavic Studies* (1975); *Jewish Policies and Right-Wing Politics in Imperial Russia.*

Rostovtzeff, Mikhail I. (1870–1952) Russian-American historian of the ancient world. Works include *Iranians and Greeks in South Russia;* "South Russia in the Prehistoric and Classical Period," *American Historical Review* (January 1921).

Rozhkov, Nikolai Aleksandrovich (1868–1927) Russian-Soviet historian. Works include *Agrarnyi vopros v Rossii i ego reshenie v programmakh razlichnykh partii; Gorod i derevnia v russkoi istorii; Obzor russkoi istorii s sotsiologicheskoi tochki zreniia; Russkaia istoriia* (12 vols.); "Ekonomicheskoe razvitie Rossii v pervoi polovine XIX veka," and "Finansovaia reforma Kankrina," in *Istoriia Rossii v XIX veke* (vol. 1).

Russell, Bertrand, Earl (1872–1970) British philosopher. Works include *Bolshevism: Practice and Theory; A History of Western Philosophy.*

Rybakov, Boris Aleksandrovich (1908–) Soviet historian. Works include *Istoriia kultury drevnei Rusi; Obrazovanie drevnerusskogo gosudarstva; Remeslo drevnei Rusi;* "Predposylki obrazovaniia drevnerusskogo gosudarstva," in *Ocherki istorii SSSR III–IX vv; Gerodotova Skifiia.*

Ryndziunsky, Pavel Grigorievich (1909–) Soviet historian. Works include *Gorodskoe grazhdanstvo doreformennoi Rossii; Utverzhdenie kapitalizma v Rossii, 1850–1880 g.*

Sakharov, Andrei Nikolaevich (1921–) Soviet and Russian historian. Works include *Aleksandr Pervyi; Stepan Razin; Chelovek na trone; Diplomatiia drevnei Rusi; Diplomatiia Sviatoslava; Voina i diplomatiia: 1939–1945 gg.; Russkaia derevnia XVII v.; po materialam patriarshego khoziaistva.*

Savelev (Saveliev) Pavel Stepanovich (1814–1859) Russian numismatist and historian. Works include *Mukhammedanskaia numizmatika v otnoshenii k russkoi istorii.*

Schapiro, Leonard (1908–1983) British historian and political scientist. Works include *The Communist Party of the Soviet Union; The Origins of the Communist Autocracy: Political Opposition in the Soviet State, First Phase, 1917–1922; Rationalism and Nation-*

alism in Russian Nineteenth-Century Political Thought; 1917: The Russian Revolutions and the Origins of Modern Communism; Russian Studies.

Schiemann, Theodor (1847–1921) German historian. Works include *Geschichte Russlands unter Kaiser Nikolaus I* (4 vols.).

Schilder (Shilder), Nikolai Karlovich (1842–1902) Russian historian. Works include *Imperator Aleksandr Pervyi, ego zhizn i tsarstvovanie* (4 vols.); *Imperator Nikolai Pervyi, ego zhizn i tsarstvovanie* (2 vols.).

Schlözer, August Ludwig von (1735–1809) German historian who worked in Russia. Works include *Nestor: Russische Annalen in ihrer slavonischen Grundsprache verglichen, übersetzt und erklärt von A. L. Schlözer; Tableaux de l'histoire de Russie; Probe russischer Annalen.*

Schuman, Frederick L. (1904–1981) American political scientist. Works include *Russia since 1917: Four Decades of Soviet Politics; Soviet Politics at Home and Abroad.*

Semevsky, Vasilii Ivanovich (1848–1916) Russian historian. Works include *Krestiane v tsarstvovanie imperatritsy Ekateriny II; Krestianskii vopros v Rossii v XVIII i pervoi polovine XIX veka* (2 vols.); *Obshchestvennye dvizheniia v Rossii v pervuiu polovinu XIX veka* (with V. I. Bogucharsky and P. E. Shchegolev); *Politicheskie i obshchestvennye idei dekabristov.*

Seton-Watson, Hugh (1916–1984) British historian. Works include *The Decline of Imperial Russia, 1855–1914; The East European Revolutions; Eastern Europe between the Wars, 1918–1941; From Lenin to Khrushchev; The Russian Empire, 1801–1917.*

Shakhmatov, Aleksei Aleksandrovich (1864–1920) Russian specialist in Slavic languages and literature. Works include *Drevneishiia sudby russkogo plemeni; Razyskaniia o drevneishikh russkikh letopisnykh svodakh; Povest vremennykh let: Vvodnaia chast, Tekst, Primechaniia; "Povest vremennykh let" i ee istochniki.*

Shchapov, Afanasii Prokofevich (1830–1876) Russian historian. Works include *Russkii raskol staroobriadstva, rassmatrivaemyi v sviazi s vnutrennim sostoianiem russkoi tserkvi i grazhdanstvennosti v XVII veke i pervoi polovine XVIII; Sotsialno-pedagogicheskie usloviia umstvennogo razvitiia russkogo naroda.*

Shcherbatov, Mikhail Mikhailovich (1733–1790) Russian historian. Works include *Istoriia Rossiiskaia ot drevneishikh vremen* (7 vols.); *Kratkaia povest o byvshikh v Rossii samozvantsakh; O povrezhdenii nravov v Rossii.*

Shevtsova, Lilia Fedorovna (1951–) Russian political scientist. Works include *Yeltsin's Russia: Myths and Reality; Putin's Russia.*

Simmons, Ernest Joseph (1903–1972) American historian and specialist in Russian literature. Works include *Continuity and Change in Russian and Soviet Thought* (ed.); *Dostoevsky: The Making of a Novelist; Leo Tolstoy; An Outline of Modern Russian Literature; Pushkin; Through the Glass of Soviet Literature; Views of Russian Society* (ed.).

Slepov, Lazar Andreevich (1905–) Soviet journalist. Works include "Collectivity Is the Highest Principle of Party Leadership," *Pravda,* reprinted in *A Documentary History of Communism* (ed. R. V. Daniels).

Solovev (Soloviev), Sergei Mikhailovich (1820–1879) Russian historian. Works include *Istoriia otnoshenii mezhdu russkimi kniaziami Riurikova doma; Istoriia Rossii s drevneishikh vremen* (29 vols.) (certain volumes in Eng.).

Soloveytchik (Soloveichik), George M. de (1902–1982) Russian-British author. Works include *Potemkin: Soldier, Statesman, Lover, and Consort of Catherine of Russia.*

Sorokin, Pitirim A. (1889–1968) Russian-American sociologist. Works include *Russia and the United States; Sovremennoe sostoianie Rossii.*

Steinberg, Isaac Nachman (1888–1957) Russian political figure and intellectual. Works include *Ot fevralia po oktiabr 1917 g. (In the Workshop of the Revolution).*

Stender-Petersen, Adolph (1893–1963) Danish philologist and historian of literature.

Works include *Geschichte der russischen Literatur; Slavisch-germanische Lehnwortkunder: Eine Studie über die ältesten germanischen Lehnwörter im Slavischen in sprach- und kulturgeschichtlicher Beleuchtung;* "Die Varägersage als Quelle der altrussischen Chronik," *Acta Jutlandica 6, no. 1; Varangica.*

Stepun, Fedor Avgustovich (1884–1965) Russian-German intellectual historian. Works include "Die deutsche Romantik und die Geschichtsphilosophie der Slavophilen," *Logos* (1927); "Nemetskii romantism i russkoe slavianofilstvo," *Russkaia Mysl* (March 1910).

Stokes, Antony Derek (1927–) British historian. Works include "The Status of the Russian Church, 988–1037," *Slavonic and East European Review* (June 1959); "Tmutarakan," *Slavonic and East European Review* (June 1960).

Struve, Gleb (1898–1985) Russian-American specialist in Russian literature. Works include *Russkaia literatura v izgnanii; Russian Literature Under Lenin and Stalin, 1917–1953.*

Sumner, Benedict Humphrey (1893–1951) British historian. Works include *Peter the Great and the Emergence of Russia; Peter the Great and the Ottoman Empire; Russia and the Balkans, 1870–1880; A Short History of Russia.*

Tarle, Evgenii Viktorovich (1874–1955) Russian-Soviet historian. Works include *Evropa v epokhu imperializma, 1871–1918 gg.; Kontinentalnaia blokada; Krymskaia voina* (2 vols.) *Nashestvie Napoleona na Rossiiu v 1812 godu (Napoleon's Invasion of Russia in 1812); Ocherki i kharakteristiki iz istorii evropeiskago obshchestvennago dvizheniia v XIX veke; Severnaia voina i shvedskoe nashestvie na Rossiiu.* Concerning the revising of Tarle's study of Napoleon's invasion of Russia mentioned in the text, see Ann K. Erickson, "E. V. Tarle, the Career of a Historian under the Soviet Regime," *American Slavic and East European Review* 14 (April 1960): 202–16.

Tatishchev, Vasilii Nikitich (1686–1750) Russian historian. Works include *Istoriia Rossiiskaia s samykh drevneishikh vremen* (7 vols.).

Temperley, Harold W. V. (1879–1939) British diplomatic historian. Works include *England and the Near East, the Crimea; The Foreign Policy of Canning.*

Thomsen, Vilhem Ludvig Peter (1842–1927) Danish philologist. Works include *The Relations between Ancient Russia and Scandinavia and the Origins of the Russian State.*

Tikhomirov, Mikhail Nikolaevich (1893–1965) Soviet historian. Works include *Drevnerusskie goroda (The Towns of Ancient Rus); Issledovanie o russkoi pravde: Proiskhozhdenie tekstov; Istochnikovedenie istorii SSSR* (with S. A. Nikitin); *Krestianskie i gorodskie vosstaniia na Rusi XI–XII vv.; Ocherki istorii istoricheskoi nauki v SSSR* (ed. with others [2 vols.]); "Soslovnopredstavitelnye uchrezhdeniia (zemskie sobory) v Rossii XVI veka," *Voprosy istorii* (1958).

Timasheff, Nikolai S. (1886–1970) Russian-American sociologist. Works include *The Great Retreat: The Growth and Decline of Communism in Russia; Religion in Soviet Russia, 1917–1942.*

Treadgold, Donald W. (1922–1994) American historian. Works include *The Great Siberian Migration: Government and Peasant in Resettlement from Emancipation to the First World War; Lenin and His Rivals: The Struggle for Russia's Future; Twentieth-Century Russia;* "Was Stolypin in Favor of the Kulaks?" *American Slavic and East European Review* (February 1955); *The West in Russia and China: Religion and Secular Thought in Modern Times: Russia, 1472–1917* (vol. 1).

Treml, Vladimir G. (1929–) Russian-American economist. Works include *The Development of the Soviet Economy: Plan and Performance* (ed.); *Soviet Economic Statistics* (ed. with John P. Hardt); *Studies in Soviet Input-Output Analysis* (ed.); *Input-Output Analysis and the Soviet Economy: An Annotated Bibliography; Alcohol in the USSR: A*

Statistical Study; Study of Employee Theft of Materials from Places of Employment (ed. with Gregory Grossman).

Trotsky, Leon (Lev Davidovich Bronstein) (1879–1940) Russian revolutionary figure, Soviet leader, and historian. Works available in many languages include in English *The History of the Russian Revolution* (3 vols.); *My Life; The Permanent Revolution; The Revolution Betrayed: What Is the Soviet Union and Where Is It Going?; Stalin: An Appraisal of the Man and His Influence.*

Tucker, Robert C. (1918–) American political scientist. Works include *Stalin as Revolutionary, 1879–1929: A Study in History and Personality; Philosophy and Myth in Karl Marx; The Soviet Political Mind; The Marxian Revolutionary Idea; The Great Purge Trial* (ed. with S. F. Cohen); *Stalin in Power: The Revolution from Above, 1928–1941.*

Ukraintsev, N. Russian military jurist. Works include "Delo Kornilova," *Novoe russkoe slovo* (August 12, October 21, and October 28, 1956) ("A Document in the Kornilov Affair," *Soviet Studies* [October 1973]).

Ulam, Adam Bruno (1922–2000) American political scientist. Works include *The Unfinished Revolution: An Essay on the Sources of Influence of Marxism and Communism; The New Face of Soviet Totalitarianism; The Bolsheviks; Stalin: The Man and His Era; Expansion and Coexistence: The History of Soviet Foreign Policy, 1917–1967; In the Name of the People; Russia's Failed Revolutions: From the Decembrists to the Dissidents.*

Ullman, Richard H. (1933–) American historian. Works include *Anglo-Soviet Relations, 1917–1921: Intervention and the War* (vol. 1), *Britain and the Russian Civil War, November 1918–February 1920* (vol. 2), *Anglo-Soviet Accord* (vol. 3).

Ustrialov, Nikolai Vasilevich (1890–1937) Russian legal scholar. Works include *Na novom etape; Pod znakom revoliutsii;* "Patriotica," *Smena Vekh* (July 1921).

Vasilev (Vasiliev), Aleksandr Aleksandrovich (1867–1953) Russian-American historian of Byzantium. Works include *The Goths in the Crimea; the Russian Attack on Constantinople in 860.*

Venturi, Franco (1914–) Italian historian. Works include *Il moto decabrista e i fratelli Poggio; Il populismo russo* (2 vols.) (*Roots of Revolution: A History of the Populist and Socialist Movements in Nineteenth-Century Russia*).

Vernadsky, George (1887–1973) Russian-American historian. Works include *A History of Russia* (1 vol.); *A History of Russia: Ancient* (vol. 1), *Kievan Russia* (vol. 2), *The Mongols and Russia* (vol. 3), *Russia at the Dawn of the Modern Age* (vol. 4), *The Tsardom of Moscow, 1547–1682* (vol. 5, 2 books); *The Origins of Russia;* "The Death of the Tsarevich Dmitry: A Reconsideration of the Case," in *Oxford Slavonic Papers* (vol. 5).

Vladimirsky-Budanov, Mikhail Flegontovich (1838–1916) Russian legal historian. Works include *Gosudarstvo i narodnoe obrazovanie v Rossii s XVII veka do uchrezhdeniia ministerstv; Gosudarstvo i narodnoe obrazovanie v Rossii XVIII veka; Obzor istorii russkogo prava.*

Von Laue, T. H. (1916–) American historian. Works include *Sergei Witte and the Industrialization of Russia; Why Lenin? Why Stalin?; The Global City.*

Voyce, Arthur (1889–) American art historian. Works include *The Moscow Kremlin: Its History, Architecture, and Art Treasures; Russian Architecture: Trends in Nationalism and Modernism; The Art and Architecture of Medieval Russia.*

Walicki, Andrzej (1930–) Polish-American historian. Works include *The Controversy over Capitalism: Studies in the Social Philosophy of the Russian Populists; A History of Russian Thought from the Enlightenment to Marxism; Legal Philosophies of Russian Liberalism; The Slavophile Controversy; History of a Conservative Utopia in Nineteenth-Century Russian Thought; Russian Social Thought: An Introduction to the Intellectual History of Nineteenth-Century Russia; Russia, Poland, and Universal Regeneration: Stud-*

ies on Russian and Polish Thought of the Romantic Epoch; Marxism and the Leap to the Kingdom of Freedom: The Rise and Fall of the Communist Utopia.

Walsh, Warren B. (1909–1979) American historian. Works include *Russia and the Soviet Union; Readings in Russian History* (ed.); "Political Parties in the Russian Dumas," *Journal of Modern History* (June 1950).

Webb, Sidney (1859–1947) and Beatrice (1858–1943) Lord and Lady Passfield. British writers and Fabian socialists. Works include *Soviet Communism: A New Civilisation?; The Truth about Soviet Russia.*

Weidle, Wladimir (1895–1979) Russian-French historian of art and culture. Works include *La Russie absente et presente (Russia Absent and Present)*; "Some Common Traits in Early Russian and Western Art," in *Oxford Slavonic Papers* (vol. 4).

Wipper (Vipper), Robert Iurevich (1859–1954) Russian-Soviet historian. Works include *Ivan Groznyi (Ivan Grozny).*

Wortman, Richard (1938–) American historian. Works include *Crisis of Russian Populism; Development of a Russian Legal Consciousness; Scenarios of Power: Myth and Ceremony in the Russian Monarchy.*

Zaionchkovsky, Petr Andreevich (1904–1983) Soviet historian. Works include *Otmena krepostnogo prava a Rossii (The Abolition of Serfdom in Russia); Provedenie v zhizn krestianskoi reformy 1861 g.; Voennye reformy 1860–1870 godov v Rossii; Krizis samoderzhaviia na rubezhe 1870–1880 godov (The Russian Autocracy in Crisis, 1878–1882); Rossiiskoe samoderzhavie v kontse XIX stoletiia (The Russian Autocracy under Alexander III); Samoderzhavie i russkaia armiia na rubezhe XIX–XX stoletii, 1881–1903.*

Zelnik, Reginald E. (1936–2004) American historian. Works include *Labor and Society in Tsarist Russia: The Factory Workers of St. Petersburg, 1855–1870; A Radical Worker in Tsarist Russia: The Autobiography of Semen Ivanovich Kanatchikov* (ed. and trans.); "Russian Bebels," in *Russian Review* (July and October 1976); "'To the Unaccustomed Eye': Religion and Irreligion in the Experience of St. Petersburg Workers in the 1870s," in *Russian History* (1989); *Law and Disorder on the Narova River: The Kreenholm Strike of 1872.*

Zenkovsky, Serge A. (1907–1990) Russian-American historian. Works include *Pan-Turkism and Islam in Russia;* "The Ideological World of the Denisov Brothers," in *Harvard Slavic Studies* (vol. 3); "The Russian Church Schism: Its Background and Repercussions," *Russian Review* (October 1957); *Russkoe staroobriadchestvo: dukhovnye dvizheniia semnadtsatgogo veka.*

Zimin, Aleksandr Aleksandrovich (1920–1980) Soviet historian. Works include *I.S. Peresvetov i ego sovremenniki, ocherki po istorii russkoi obshchestvenno-politicheskoi mysli serediny XVI veka; Reformy Ivana Groznogo, ocherki sotsialno-ekonomicheskoi i politicheskoi istorii Rossii serediny XVI veka; Oprichnina Ivana Groznogo; Rossiia na poroge novogo vremeni: ocherki politicheskoi istorii Rossii pervoi treti XVI veka; Kholopy na Rusi (s drevneishikh vremen do kontsa XV veka);* "Pripiska k Pskovskomu Apostolu 1307 Goda i 'Slovo o polku Igoreve,'" *Russkaia Literatura* (1966); "Spornye voprosy tekstologii 'Zadonshchiny,'" *Russkaia Literatura* (1967).

A Select List of Readings in English on Russian History

From Earliest Times to 2004

A. Bibliography and Historiography

American Bibliography of Slavic [previously Russian] and East European Studies (ABSEES). Bloomington, Ind., and Urbana-Champaign, Ill., since 1957 (now on-line).

Brumfield, W. A History of Russian Architecture. New York, 1993.

Fisher, H. H., ed. American Research on Russia. Bloomington, Ind., 1959.

Horak, S. M. Russia, the USSR, and Eastern Europe: A Bibliographic Guide to English-Language Publications. Littleton, Colo. (1964–74—1979; 1975–80—1982; 1981–85—1987).

Horecky, P., ed. Basic Russian Publications: A Selected and Annotated Bibliography on Russia and the Soviet Union. Chicago and London, 1962.

Horecky, P., ed. Russia and the Soviet Union: A Bibliographic Guide to Western-Language Publications. Chicago and London, 1965.

Kaiser, D. H., ed. "Rus', Russia, and the Russian Empire." Section 34 of the American Historical Association's Guide to Historical Literature. 3rd ed. New York, 1995.

Konn, T., ed. Soviet Studies Guide. London, 1992.

Maichel, K. Guide to Russian Reference Books. Stanford, 1962.

Mazour, A. G. Modern Russian Historiography. Princeton, N.J., 1958.

Orlovsky, D. T., ed. "Soviet Union." Section 35 of the American Historical Association's Guide to Historical Literature. 3rd ed. New York, 1995.

Pierce, R. A. Soviet Central Asia. A Bibliography: Part I: 1558–1866. Part 2: 1867–1917. Part 3: 1917–1966. Berkeley, 1966.

Pushkarev, S. G. A Source Book for Russian History from Early Times to 1917. Edited by A. Ferguson et al. 3 vols. New Haven, Conn., 1972.

Pushkarev, S. G., comp. Dictionary of Russian Historical Terms from the Eleventh Century to 1917. Edited by G. Vernadsky and R. Fisher, Jr., New Haven, Conn., 1970.

Sanders, T., ed. Historiography of Imperial Russia: The Profession and Writing of History in a Multinational State. Armonk, N.Y., 1999.

Shapiro, D. A Selected Bibliography of Works in English on Russian History, 1801–1917. New York and London, 1962.

Sullivan, H. F. and R. Burger. Russia and the Former Soviet Union: A Bibliographic Guide to English Language Publications, 1986–1991. Englewood, Colo., 1994.

Szeftel, M. Russia before 1917, in Bibliographical Introduction to Legal History and Ethnology. Edited by J. Glissen. Brussels, 1966.

B. Encyclopedias

Brown, A., et al., eds. The Cambridge Encyclopedia of Russia and the Soviet Union. Cambridge, 1982.

Florinsky, M. T., ed. *McGraw-Hill Encyclopedia of Russia and the Soviet Union*. New York, 1961.

Kubijovyč, V., et al., eds. *Ukraine: A Concise Encyclopedia*. Vol. 1. Toronto, 1963.

Utechin, S. V. *Everyman's Concise Encyclopedia of Russia*. New York, 1961.

Wieczynski, J. L., ed. *The Modern Encyclopedia of Russian and Soviet History*. 54 vols. Gulf Breeze, Fla., 1976. Continued by *The Supplement to the Modern Encyclopedia of Russian, Soviet, and Eurasian History*. Gulf Breeze, Fla., 1995–.

C. Geography and Demography

Chew, A. F. *An Atlas of Russian History: Eleven Centuries of Changing Borders*. New Haven, Conn., 1970.

Gilbert, M. *Atlas of Russian History*. New York, 1993.

Hooson, D. J. *The Soviet Union: People and Regions*. Belmont, Calif., 1966.

Jorré, G. *The Soviet Union: The Land and Its People*. Translated by E. D. Laborde. London, 1950. 3rd ed., 1967.

Kaiser, R.J. *The Geography of Nationalism in Russia and the USSR*. Princeton, N.J., 1994.

Milner-Gulland, R. R., and N. Dejevsky. *Cultural Atlas of Russia and the Soviet Union*. New York, 1989.

D. Nationalities

Allen, W. E. D. *A History of the Georgian People*. New York, 1971.

Allworth, E. A. *The Modern Uzbeks from the Fourteenth Century to the Present: A Cultural History*. Stanford, 1990.

Aronson, I. M. *Troubled Waters: The Origins of the 1881 Anti-Jewish Progroms in Russia*. Pittsburgh, 1990.

Baron, S. W. *The Russian Jew under Tsars and Soviet*. New York, 1964.

Becker, S. *Russia's Protectorates in Central Asia: Bukhara and Khiva, 1865–1924*. Cambridge, Mass., 1968.

Brower, D. and E. Lazzerini, eds. *Russia's Orient: Imperial Borderlands and Peoples, 1700–1917*. Bloomington, Ind., 1997.

Chase, T. *The Story of Lithuania*. New York, 1946.

Chirovsky, N. L. *Old Ukraine: Its Socio-Economic History Prior to 1781*. Madison, N.J., 1963.

Dmytryshyn, B. *Moscow and the Ukraine, 1918–1953*. New York, 1956.

Doroshenko, D. *History of the Ukraine*. Edmonton, Alberta, 1941.

Dubnow, S. M. *History of the Jews in Russia and Poland*. 3 vols. Philadelphia, 1916.

d'Encausse, H. C. *Islam and the Russian Empire: Reform and Revolution in Central Asia*. Berkeley, 1988.

Geraci, R. *Window on the East: National and Imperial Identities in Late Tsarist Russia*. Ithaca, N.Y., 2001.

Greenberg, L. S. *The Jews in Russia*, 2 vols. New Haven, Conn., 1944, 1951.

Grousset, R. *The Empire of the Steppes: A History of Central Asia*. Translated by N. Walford. New Brunswick, N.J., 1970.

Hosking, G. and R. Service, eds. *Russian Nationalism, Past and Present*. New York, 1997.

Halecki, O. *A History of Poland*. New York, 1943.

Hrushevskyi, M. *A History of the Ukraine*. New Haven, Conn., 1941.

Khalid, A. *Politics of Muslim Cultural Reform: Jadidism in Central Asia*. Berkeley, 2000.

Kubijovyč, V., et al., eds. *Ukraine: A Concise Encyclopedia*. Vol. 1. Toronto, 1963.

Lang, D. M. *A Modern History of Georgia*. London, 1962.

Lewis, R. A., R. H. Rowland, and R. S. Clem, eds. *Nationality and Population Change in Russia and the USSR: An Evaluation of Census Data, 1870–1970.* New York, 1976.

Nathans, B. *Beyond the Pale: The Jewish Encounter with Late Imperial Russia.* Berkeley, 2002.

Nelbandian, L. *The Armenian Revolutionary Movement.* Berkeley, 1967.

Olcott, M. B. *The Kazakhs.* 2d ed. Stanford, 1995.

Pierce, R. A. *Russian Central Asia, 1867–1917: A Study in Colonial Rule.* Berkeley, 1960.

Potichnyj, P. J., and H. Aster, eds. *Ukrainian-Jewish Relations in Historical Perspective.* Edmonton, Alberta, 1988.

Raun, T. U. *Estonia and the Estonians.* Stanford, 1987.

Rorlich, A-A. *The Volga Tatars: A Profile in National Resilience.* Stanford, 1986.

Senn, A. E. *The Emergence of Modern Lithuania.* New York, 1959.

Senn, A. E. *Lithuania Awakening.* Berkeley, 1990.

Slezkine, Y. *Arctic Mirrors: Russia and the Small Peoples of the North.* Ithaca, N.Y., 1994.

Suny, R. G. *The Making of the Georgian Nation.* Bloomington, Ind., 1988.

Suny, R. G., ed. *Transcaucasia: Nationalism and Social Change. Essays in the History of Armenia, Azerbaijan, and Georgia.* Ann Arbor, Mich., 1983.

Swietochowski, T. *Russian Azerbaijan, 1905–1920: The Shaping of National Destiny in a Muslim Community.* Cambridge, 1985.

Thaden, E. C., ed. *Russification in the Baltic Provinces and Finland.* Princeton, N.J., 1981.

Vakar, N. *Belorussia: The Making of a Nation.* Cambridge, Mass., 1956.

Weeks, T. *Nation and State in Late Imperial Russia: Nationalism and Russification on the Western Frontier, 1863–1914.* DeKalb, Ill., 1996.

Wheeler, G. *The Modern History of Soviet Central Asia.* London, 1964.

Zenkovsky, S. A. *Pan-Turkism and Islam in Russia.* Cambridge, Mass., 1960.

E. General Histories

Auty, R., and D. Obolensky, eds. *An Introduction to Russian History.* Vol. 1, *Companion to Russian Studies.* Cambridge, 1976.

Charques, R. *A Short History of Russia.* London, 1959.

Clarkson, J. *A History of Russia.* New York, 1961.

Evtuhov, C., D. Goldfrank, L. Hughes, and R. Stites. *A History of Russia: Peoples, Legends, Events, Forces.* Boston, 2004.

Florinsky, M. T. *Russia: A History and an Interpretation.* 2 vols. New York, 1953.

Freeze, G. L., ed. *Russia: A History.* New York, 1997. Rev. ed. 2002.

Harcave, S. *Russia: A History.* Chicago, 1956.

Hosking, G. *Russia and Russians: A History.* Cambridge, Mass., 2001.

Klyuchevsky (Kliuchevsky), V. O. *Course of Russian History.* Translated by C. J. Hogarth. 5 vols. New York, 1911–31.

Miliukov, P., C. Seignobos, L. Eisenmann, et al. *History of Russia.* Translated by C. L. Markmann. 3 vols. New York, 1968.

Pares, B. *A History of Russia.* London, 1926.

Pipes, R. E. *Russia Under the Old Regime.* New York, 1974.

Pokrovsky, M. N. *Brief History of Russia.* 2 vols. London, 1933.

Sumner, B. H. *Survey of Russian History.* London, 1944.

Vernadsky, G. *A History of Russia.* New Haven, Conn., 1929. 5th rev. ed., 1961.

Vernadsky, G., and M. Karpovich. *A History of Russia.* Vol. 1, *Ancient Russia.* Vol. 2, *Kievan Russia.* Vol. 3, *The Mongols and Russia.* Vol. 4, *Russia at the Dawn of the Modern Age.* Vol. 5, *Tsardom of Moscow, 1547–1682.* 2 books. New Haven, Conn., 1943, 1948, 1953, 1959, 1968.

F. Specialized Histories and Interpretative Essays

Avrich, P. *Russian Rebels, 1600–1800.* New York, 1972.

Billington, J. *The Icon and the Axe: An Interpretative History of Russian Culture.* New York, 1966.

Black, C., et al. *The Modernization of Japan and Russia.* New York, 1975.

Blum, J. *Lord and Peasant in Russia from the Ninth to the Nineteenth Century.* Princeton, N.J., 1961.

Brumfield, W. *A History of Russian Architecture.* New York, 1993.

Bulgakov, S. N. *The Orthodox Church.* New York and London, 1935.

Cherniavsky, M. *Tsar and People: Studies in Russian Myths.* New Haven, Conn., 1961.

Chyzhevskyi, D. *History of Russian Literature from the Eleventh Century to the End of the Baroque.* New York and The Hague, 1960.

Fennell, J., and A. Stokes. *Early Russian Literature.* Berkeley, 1974.

Gasiorowska, X. *The Image of Peter the Great in Russian Fiction.* Madison, Wis., 1979.

Gerschenkron, A. *Continuity in History and Other Essays.* Cambridge, Mass., 1968.

Gerschenkron, A. *Europe in the Russian Mirror: Four Lectures in Economic History.* Cambridge, Mass., 1970.

Grey, I. *The Romanovs. The Rise and Fall of a Dynasty.* Garden City, N.Y., 1970.

Hans, N. *History of Russian Educational Policy, 1701–1917.* London, 1931.

Hans, N. *The Russian Tradition in Education.* London, 1963.

Haxthausen, A. von. *The Russian Empire, Its People, Institutions, and Resources.* Translated by R. Farie. New York, 1970.

Hingley, R. *The Russian Secret Police: Muscovite, Imperial Russian and Soviet Political Security Operations, 1565–1970.* New York, 1970.

Hosking, G. *Russia: People and Empire, 1552–1917.* Cambridge, Mass., 1997.

Hunczak, T., ed. *Russian Imperialism from Ivan the Great to the Revolution.* New Brunswick, N.J., 1974.

Iswolsky, H. *Christ in Russia: The History, Tradition and Life of the Russian Church.* Milwaukee, 1960.

Kappeler, A. *The Russian Empire: Ethnicity and Nationalism.* Harlow, Eng., 2001.

Kerner, R. J. *The Urge to the Sea: The Course of Russian History.* New York, 1971.

Kochan, L., and J. Keep. *The Making of Modern Russia: Fom Kiev Rus' to the Collapse of the Soviet Union.* 3rd ed. London, 1997.

Lantzeff, G. V., and R. A. Pierce. *Eastward to Empire.* Montreal and London, 1973.

Lewin, M. *Russia—USSR—Russia: The Drive and Drift of a Superstate.* New York, 1995.

Leonard, R. *A History of Russian Music.* London, 1956.

Liashchenko, P. I. *A History of the National Economy of Russia to the 1917 Revolution.* Translated from Russian. New York, 1949.

Lincoln, W. B. *The Romanovs: Autocrats of All the Russias.* New York, 1981.

Lincoln, W. B. *Between Heaven and Hell: The Story of a Thousand Years of Artistic Life in Russia.* New York, 1998.

Lincoln, W. B. *The Conquest of a Continent: Siberia and the Russians.* New York, 1994.

Longworth, P. *The Cossacks: Five Centuries of Turbulent Life on the Russian Steppes.* New York, 1970.

Lossky, N. O. *History of Russian Philosophy.* New York, 1951.

Masaryk, T. G. *The Spirit of Russia.* Translated from German. 3 vols. New York, 1955–67.

Miliukov, P. N. *Outlines of Russian Culture.* Edited by M. Karpovich. Translated and abridged from Russian. 4 vols. Philadelphia, 1942–75.

Miliukov, P. N. *Russia and Its Crisis.* Chicago, 1905.

Mirsky, D. S. *A History of Russian Literature.* New York, 1927.

Mirsky, D. S. *Russia: A Social History.* London, 1931.

Obolensky, D. *The Byzantine Commonwealth*. New York, 1971.

Pokrovsky, M. N. *Russia in World History: Selected Essays*. Edited by R. Szporluk. Translated by R. Szporluk and M. Szporluk. Ann Arbor, Mich., 1970.

Ragsdale, H. *The Russian Tragedy: The Burden of History*. Armonk, N.Y., 1996.

Rice, T. T. *Russian Art*. London, 1949.

Schmemann, A. *The Historical Road of Eastern Orthodoxy*. New York, 1963.

Soloviev, A. V. *Holy Russia: The History of a Religious-Social Idea*. New York, 1959.

Stephan, J. J. *Sakhalin. A History*. New York, 1971.

Stokes, A. D. (with John Fennell). *Early Russian Literature*. Berkeley, 1974.

Thaden, E. C. *Russia since 1801: The Making of a New Society*. New York, 1971.

Treadgold, D. W. *The West in Russia and China: Religion and Secular Thought in Modern Times*. Vol. 1, *Russia, 1472–1917*. Cambridge, Mass., 1973.

Utechin, S. V. *Russian Political Thought: A Concise History*. New York and London, 1964.

Volin, L. *A Century of Russian Agriculture: From Alexander II to Khrushchev*. Cambridge, Mass., 1970.

Vucinich, A. S. *Science in Russian Culture: A History to 1860*. Stanford, 1963.

Vucinich, A. S. *Science in Russian Culture (1861–1917)*. Stanford, 1970.

Weidle, V. *Russia Absent and Present*. New York, 1952.

Wren, M. C. *The Western Impact upon Tsarist Russia*. Chicago, 1971.

Zenkovsky, V. V. *A History of Russian Philosophy*. 2 vols. New York, 1953.

G. Collected Essays

Atkinson, D., A. Dallin, and G. W. Lapidus, eds. *Women in Russia*. Stanford, 1977.

Cherniavsky, M., ed. *The Structure of Russian History*. New York, 1970.

Clements, B., B. Engel, and C. Worobec, eds. *Russia's Women: Accommodation, Resistance, Transformation*. Berkeley, 1991.

Curtiss, J. S., ed. *Essays in Russian and Soviet History in Honor of G. T. Robinson*. Leiden, 1963.

Edmondson, L., ed., *Women and Society in Russia and the Soviet Union*. Cambridge, 1992.

Ferguson, A. D., and A. Levin, eds. *Essays in Russian History: A Collection Dedicated to George Vernadsky*. Hamden, Conn., 1964.

McLean, H., M. Malia, and G. Fischer, eds. *Russian Thought and Politics*. Harvard Slavic Studies, vol. 4. Cambridge, Mass., 1957.

Mendelsohn, E., and M. S. Shatz, eds. *Imperial Russia, 1700–1917: Essays in Honor of Marc Raeff*. DeKalb, Ill., 1988.

Oberlander, E., et al., eds. *Russia Enters the Twentieth Century, 1894–1917*. Translated by G. Onn. New York, 1971.

Oliva, L. Jay, ed. *Russia and the West from Peter to Khrushchev*. Boston, 1965.

Pipes, R., ed. *Revolutionary Russia*. Cambridge, Mass., 1968.

Pipes, R., ed. *The Russian Intelligentsia*. New York, 1961.

Rabinowitch, A., J. Rabinowitch, and L. Kristof, eds. *Revolution and Politics in Russia: Essays in Memory of B. I. Nicolaevsky*. Bloomington, Ind., 1972.

Treadgold, D. W., ed. *Soviet and Chinese Communism: Similarities and Differences*. Seattle, 1967.

Vucinich, W. S., ed. *The Peasant in Nineteenth Century Russia*. Stanford, 1968.

Vucinich, W. S., ed. *Russia and Asia: Essays on the Influence of Russia on the Asian Peoples*. Stanford, 1972.

H. Readings, Anthologies

Harcave, S., ed. *Readings in Russian History*. 2 vols. New York, 1962.

Kaiser, D. and G. Marker, eds. *Reinterpreting Russian History: Readings, 860–1860s.* New York, 1994.

Kollman, N., ed. *Major Problems in Early Modern Russian History.* New York, 1992.

Page, S. W., ed. *Russia in Revolution: Selected Readings in Russian Domestic History since 1855.* Princeton, N.J., 1965.

Raeff, M., ed. *Russian Intellectual History: An Anthology.* New York, 1966.

Riha, T., ed. *Readings in Russian Civilization.* 3 vols. Chicago, 1964.

Schmemann, A., ed. *Ultimate Questions: An Anthology of Modern Russian Religious Thought.* New York, 1965.

Vernadsky, G., R. Fisher, A. Ferguson, A. Lossky, and S. Pushkarev, eds. *A Source Book for Russian History from Early Times to 1917,* 3 vols. New Haven, Conn., 1972.

Pre-Petrine Russia (to 1682)

A. Source Materials

Avvakum. *The Life of the Archpriest Avvakum by Himself.* Translated by V. Nabokov. New York, 1960.

Baron, S. H., ed. and trans. *The Travels of Olearius in Seventeenth-Century Russia.* Stanford, 1967.

Berry, L. E., and R. O. Crummey, eds. *Rude and Barbarous Kingdom: Russia in the Accounts of Sixteenth-Century English Voyagers.* Madison, Wisc., 1968.

Cross, S. H., and O. P. Sherbovitz-Wetzor, trans. and eds. *The Russian Primary Chronicle, Laurentian Text.* Cambridge, Mass., 1953.

Dewey, H. W. "The White Lake Chapter: A Medieval Russian Administrative Statute." *Speculum* 32 (1957).

Dmytryshyn, B., ed. *Medieval Russia: A Source Book, 900–1700.* New York, 1967.

Esper, T., ed. and trans. *Heinrich von Staden: The Land and Government of Muscovy: A Sixteenth-Century Account.* Stanford, 1967.

Fedotov, G. P. *A Treasury of Russian Spirituality.* New York, 1948.

Fennell, J., ed. and trans. *The Correspondence between Prince A. M. Kurbsky and Tsar Ivan IV of Russia, 1564–1579, with Russian Text.* New York, 1955.

Fletcher, G. *Of the Russe Commonwealth, 1591.* Facsimile ed. Introduction by R. Pipes. Cambridge, Mass., 1966.

Heppell, M., trans. and ed. *The Paterik of the Kievan Caves Monastery.* Cambridge, Mass., 1989.

Hollingsworth, P., trans. and ed. *The Hagiography of Kievan Rus.* Cambridge, Mass., 1992.

Howes, R. C., ed. and trans. *The Testaments of the Grand Princes of Moscow.* Ithaca, N.Y., 1967.

Michell, R., and N. Forbes, trans. *The Chronicle of Novgorod, 1016–1471.* In *Royal Historical Society Publications,* Camden 3rd ser., vol. 25. London, 1914.

Palmer, W. *The Patriarch and the Tsar.* 6 vols. London, 1871–76.

Pouncy, C., ed. *Domostroi: The Rules for Russian Households in the Time of Ivan the Terrible.* Ithaca, N.Y., 1994.

Vernadsky, G., trans. *Medieval Russian Laws.* In *Records of Civilization,* no. 41, edited by A. P. Evans. New York, 1947.

Zenkovsky, S. A. *Medieval Russian Epics, Chronicles and Tales.* New York, 1963.

B. Specialized Studies

Anderson, M. S. *Britain's Discovery of Russia, 1553–1815.* London, 1958.

Baron, S. H. *Muscovite Russia.* London, 1980.

Baron, S. H., and N. S. Kollmann, eds. *Religion and Culture in Early Modern Russia and Ukraine.* DeKalb, Ill., 1997.

Bushkovitch, P. *Religion and Society in Russia: The Sixteenth and Seventeenth Centuries.* New York, 1992.

Cherniavsky, M. "Old Believers and the New Religion." *Slavic Review* 25 (March 1966).

Cherniavsky, M. *Tsar and People: Studies in Russian Myths.* New Haven, Conn., 1961.

Chyzhevskyi, D. *History of Russian Literature from the Eleventh Century to the End of the Baroque.* New York and The Hague, 1960.

Conybeare, F. C. *Russian Dissenters.* Cambridge, Mass., 1921.

Crummey, R. O. *Aristocrats and Servitors: The Boyar Elite in Russia, 1613–1689.* Princeton, N.J., 1983.

Crummey, R. O. *The Formation of Muscovy, 1304–1613.* London and New York, 1987.

Dewey, H. W. "The 1497 Sudebnik: Muscovite Russia's First National Law Code." *American Slavic and East European Review* 29 (1951).

Dukes, P. *The Making of Russian Absolutism, 1613–1801.* London and New York, 1990.

Dunlop, D. M. *The History of the Jewish Khazars.* Princeton, N.J., 1954.

Dunning, C. S. L. *Russia's First Civil War: The Time of Troubles and the Founding of the Romanov Dynasty.* University Park, Pa., 2001.

Dvornik, F. *The Slavs, Their Early History and Civilization.* Boston, 1956.

Fedotov, G. *The Russian Religious Mind.* Vol. 1, *Kievan Christianity: The Tenth to the Thirteenth Centuries.* Vol. 2, *The Middle Ages: The Thirteenth to the Fifteenth Centuries.* Edited by J. Meyendorff. Cambridge, Mass., 1946, 1966.

Fennell, J. *The Crisis of Medieval Russia, 1200–1304.* London and New York, 1983.

Fennell, J. *The Emergence of Moscow, 1304–1359.* Berkeley, 1968.

Fennell, J. *A History of the Russian Church to 1448.* London, 1995.

Fennell, J. *Ivan the Great of Moscow,* London, 1961.

Flier, M. S. and D. Rowland, eds. *Medieval Russian Culture,* Berkeley, 1994.

Florovsky, G. "The Problem of Old Russian Culture." *Slavic Review* 21 (March 1962).

Franklin, S. *Writing, Society, and Culture in Early Rus, c. 950–1300.* Cambridge, 2002.

Franklin, S. and J. Shepard. *The Emergence of Rus, 750–1200.* London, 1996.

Fuhrmann, J. T. *The Origins of Capitalism in Russia: Industry and Progress in the Sixteenth and Seventeenth Centuries.* Chicago, 1972.

Graham, S. *Boris Godunov.* London, 1933.

Grekov, B. *Kiev Rus.* Translated from Russian. Moscow, 1959.

Grey, I. *Ivan III and the Unification of Russia.* New York, 1964.

Halperin, C. *Russia and the Golden Horde: The Mongol Impact on Russian History.* Bloomington, Ind., 1985.

Hammer, D. P. "Russia and the Roman Law." *American Slavic and East European Review* 16 (1957).

Hellie, R. *Enserfment and Military Change in Muscovy.* Chicago, 1971.

Hellie, R. *Slavery in Russia, 1450–1725.* Chicago, 1982.

Hughes, L. *Sophia, Regent of Russia, 1657–1704.* New Haven, Conn., 1990.

Kaiser, D. H. *The Growth of the Law in Medieval Russia.* Princeton, N.J., 1980.

Keenan, E. "Muscovite Political Folkways." *Russian Review* 45, no. 2 (1986). Discussions in *Russian Review* 46, no. 2 (1987).

Keep, J. "The Decline of the Zemsky Sobor." *Slavonic and East European Review* 36 (1957).

Keep, J. "The Regime of Filaret." *Slavonic and East European Review* 38 (1960).

Kivelson, V. A. *Autocracy in the Provinces: The Muscovite Gentry and Political Culture in the Seventeenth Century.* Stanford, 1996.

Kliuchevsky, V. O. *A Course in Russian History: The Seventeenth Century* (translation of Vol. 3 of the 1957 Soviet edition of his *Collected Works*). Translated by N. Duddington. Introduction by A. Rieber. Chicago, 1968.

Kliuchevsky, V. O. *Peter the Great*. New York, 1959 (part of Vol. 4 of his *Course of Russian History*).

Kliuchevsky, V. O. *The Rise of the Romanovs*. Edited and translated by L. Archibald. New York, 1970.

Kliuchevsky, V. O. "St. Sergius: The Importance of His Life and Work." *Russian Review* (London) 2 (1913).

Kollmann, N. S. *By Honor Bound. State and Society in Early Modern Russia*. Ithaca, N.Y., 1999.

Kollmann, N. S. *Kinship and Politics: The Making of the Muscovite Political System, 1345–1547*. Stanford, 1987.

Kondakov, N. P. *The Russian Icon*. Translated from Russian. Oxford, 1927.

Lantzeff, G. *Siberia in the Seventeenth Century: A Study of Colonial Administration*. Berkeley, 1943.

Leatherbarrow, W. J., and D. C. Offord, eds. *A Documentary History of Russian Thought: From the Enlightenment to Marxism*. Ann Arbor, Mich., 1987.

Levin, E. *Sex and Society in the World of the Orthodox Slavs, 900–1700*. Ithaca, N.Y., 1989.

Martin, J. *Medieval Russia, 980–1584*. Cambridge, 1995.

Medlin, W. K. *Moscow and East Rome: A Political Study of the Relation of Church and State in Muscovite Russia*. New York and Geneva, 1952.

Medlin, W. K., and C. G. Patrinelis. *Renaissance Influences and Religious Reforms in Russia: Western and Post-Byzantine Impacts on Culture and Education (16th–17th Centuries)*. Geneva, 1971.

Michels, G. B. *At War with the Church: Religious Dissent in Seventeenth Century Muscovy*. Stanford, 1999.

Norretranders, B. *The Shaping of Tsardom under Ivan Grozny*. Copenhagen, 1964.

Nowak, F. *Medieval Slavdom and the Rise of Russia*. New York, 1970.

Obolensky, D. *The Byzantine Commonwealth: Eastern Europe, 500–1453*. London, 1971.

O'Brien, C. B. *Muscovy and the Ukraine: From the Pereiaslavl Agreement to the Truce of Andrusovo*. Berkeley, 1963.

Ostrowski, D. *Muscovy and the Mongols: Cross-Cultural Influences on the Steppe Frontier, 1304–1589*. Cambridge, 1998.

Paszkiewicz, H. *The Making of the Russian Nation*. London, 1963.

Paszkiewicz, H. *The Origin of Russia*. London, 1954.

Payne, R., and N. Romanoff. *Ivan the Terrible*. New York, 1975.

Pelenski, J. *Russia and Kazan: Conquest and Imperial Ideology (1438–1560's)*. The Hague and Paris, 1974.

Platonov, S. F. *Moscow and the West*. Edited and translated by J. Wieczynski. Hattiesburg, Miss., 1972.

Platonov, S. F. *The Time of Troubles: A Historical Study of the Internal Crisis and Social Struggle in Sixteenth- and Seventeenth-Century Muscovy*. Translated by J. Alexander. Lawrence, Kans., 1970.

Pokrovsky, M. N. *History of Russia from the Earliest Times to the Rise of Commercial Capitalism*. Translated and edited by J. D. Clarkson and M. R. Griffiths. New York, 1931.

Prawdin, M. *The Mongol Empire: Its Rise and Legacy*. Translated by E. Paul and C. Paul. New York and London, 1940. 2nd ed., 1967.

Presniakov, A. E. *The Formation of the Great Russian State: A Study of Russian History in the Thirteenth to Fifteenth Centuries*. Translated by A. E. Moorhouse. Chicago, 1970.

Raeff, M. "An Early Theorist of Absolutism: Joseph of Volokolamsk." *American Slavic and East European Review* 8 (1949).

Riasanovsky, N. V. "The Norman Theory of the Origin of the Russian State." *Russian Review* (Autumn 1947).

Ševčenko, I. "Byzantine Cultural Influences." In *Rewriting Russian History,* edited by C. Black. Princeton, N.J. 1962.

Ševčenko, I. "A Neglected Byzantine Source of Muscovite Ideology." *Harvard Slavic Studies* 2 (1945).

Soloviev, A. V. *Holy Russia: The History of a Religious-Social Idea.* New York, 1959.

Spinka, M. "Patriarch Nikon and the Subjection of the Russian Church to the State." *Church History* 10 (1941).

Stremoukhoff, D. "Moscow, the Third Rome: Sources of the Doctrine." *Speculum* (1953).

Szeftel, M. *Russian Institutions and Culture up to Peter the Great.* London, 1975.

Thomsen, V. *Relations Between Ancient Russia and Scandinavia and the Origins of the Russian State.* Oxford, 1877.

Thyret, I. *Between God and the Tsar: Religious Symbolism and the Royal Women of Muscovite Russia.* DeKalb, Ill., 2001.

Tikhomirov, M. N. *The Towns of Ancient Rus.* Translated from Russian. Moscow, 1959.

Vasiliev, A. A. *The Goths in the Crimea.* Cambridge, Mass., 1936.

Vernadsky, G. *Ancient Russia.* New Haven, Conn., 1943.

Vernadsky, G. *Bohdan, Hetman of Ukraine.* New Haven, Conn., 1941.

Vernadsky, G. *Kievan Russia.* New Haven, Conn., 1948.

Vernadsky, G. *The Mongols and Russia.* New Haven, Conn., 1953.

Vernadsky, G. *The Origins of Russia.* Oxford, 1959.

Vernadsky, G. *Russia at the Dawn of the Modern Age.* New Haven, Conn., 1959.

Vernadsky, G. *The Tsardom of Moscow, 1547–1682.* New Haven, Conn., 1959.

Voyce, A. *The Art and Architecture of Medieval Russia.* Norman, Okla., 1967.

Voyce, A. *Moscow and the Roots of Russian Culture.* Norman, Okla., 1964.

Voyce, A. *The Moscow Kremlin.* Berkeley, 1954.

Wolff, R. L. "The Three Romes: The Migration of an Ideology and the Making of an Autocrat." *Daedalus* (Spring 1959).

Zernov, N. *St. Sergius, Builder of Russia.* London, 1938.

Zernov, N. "Vladimir and the Origin of the Russian Church." *Slavonic and East European Review* 28 (1949–50).

Imperial Russia, 1682–1917

A. Source Materials

Annenkov, P. *The Extraordinary Decade: Literary Memoirs by P. V. Annenkov.* Edited by A. P. Mendel. Ann Arbor, Mich., 1968.

Bakunin, M. *Selected Writings.* Edited by A. Lehning. New York, 1974.

Barratt, G. R. V. *Voices in Exile: The Decembrist Memoirs.* Montreal and London, 1974.

Bisha, R., J. Gheith, C. Holden, and W. Wagner, eds. *Russian Women, 1698–1917: Experience and Expression: An Anthology of Sources.* Bloomington, Ind., 2002.

Bing, E. J., ed. *The Letters of Tsar Nicholas and Empress Marie.* London, 1937.

Bock, M. P. von. *Reminiscences of My Father, Peter A. Stolypin.* Edited and translated by M. Patoski. Metuchen, N.J., 1970.

Buchanan, G. *My Mission to Russia.* 2 vols. Boston, 1923.

Catherine the Great. *The Memoirs of Catherine the Great.* Edited by D. Maroger. Translated by M. Budberg. New York, 1961.

Chaadaev, P. *The Major Works of Peter Chaadaev.* Translated and with commentary by R. T. McNally. Notre Dame, Ind., 1969.

Chernyshevsky, N. G. *Selected Philosophical Essays.*

Chernyshevsky, N. G. *What Is to Be Done?* Translated by M. Katz and annotated by W. Wagner. Ithaca, N.Y., 1989.

Dostoevsky, F. M. *The Diary of a Writer*. Translated by R. Brasol. New York, 1954.

Engel, B. A. and C. Rosenthal, *Five Sisters: Women Against the Tsar*. New York, 1975.

Freeze, G. L. *From Supplication to Revolution: A Documentary Social History of Imperial Russia*. New York, 1988.

Geldern, J. von and L. McReynolds, eds. *Entertaining Tsarist Russia, 1779–1917*. Bloomington, Ind., 1998.

Giers, N. K. *The Education of a Russian Statesman: The Memoirs of N. K. Giers*. Edited by C. Jelavich and B. Jelavich. Berkeley, 1962.

Golder, F. A., ed. *Documents of Russian History, 1914–1917*. New York and London, 1927.

Gurko, V. I. *Features and Figures of the Past. Government and Opinion in the Reign of Nicholas II*. Stanford, 1939.

Herzen, A. I. *My Past and Thoughts*. Translated by C. Garnett. 6 vols. New York, 1924–28; abridged edition by D. Macdonald, 1973.

Izvolsky, A. P. *Recollections of a Foreign Minister*. Garden City, N.Y., 1921.

Karamzin, N. M. *Letters of a Russian Traveler, 1789–1790: An Account of a Young Russian Gentleman's Tour through Germany, Switzerland, France and England*. Translated by F. Jonas. Edited by E. Simmons. New York, 1957.

Karamzin, N. M. *Memoir on Ancient and Modern Russia*. Translated and analysis by R. Pipes. Edited by R. Pipes. Cambridge, Mass., 1959.

Kokovtsov, V. N. *Out of My Past*. Edited by H. H. Fisher. Stanford, 1935.

Kravchinsky, S. M. (Stepniak) *Underground Russia: Revolutionary Profiles and Sketches from Life*. Preface by P. L. Lavrov. New York, 1883.

Kropotkin, P. A. *Memoirs of a Revolutionist*. New York, 1899.

Kropotkin, P. A. *Modern Science and Anarchism*. London, 1913.

Kropotkin, P. A. *The State: Its Part in History*. London, 1898, 1943.

Lavrov, P. *Historical Letters*. Edited and translated by J. P. Scanlan. Berkeley, 1967.

Maklakov, V. A. *Memoirs of V. A. Maklakov: The First State Duma: Contemporary Reminiscences*. Edited by M. Belkin. Bloomington, Ind., 1964.

Maximoff, G. P., ed. *The Political Philosophy of Bakunin: Scientific Anarchism*. Chicago, 1953.

Miliukov, P. *Political Memoirs, 1905–1917*. Edited by A. P. Mendel. Ann Arbor, Mich., 1967.

Paleologue, G. *An Ambassador's Memoirs*. 3 vols. London, 1925.

Pares, B. "Conversations with Mr. Stolypin." *Russian Review* (London) 2 (1913).

Pares, B. *My Russian Memoirs*. London, 1931.

Pares, B., ed. *Letters of the Tsaritsa to the Tsar, 1914–1916*. London, 1923.

Pobedonostsev, K. P. *Reflections of a Russian Statesman*. London, 1898.

Radishchev, A. N. *A Journey from St. Petersburg to Moscow*. Edited with an introduction and notes by R. P. Thaler. Cambridge, Mass., 1958.

Raeff, M., ed., *The Decembrist Movement*. Englewood Cliffs, N.J., 1966.

Raeff, M., ed. *Plans for Political Reform in Russia, 1730–1905*. Englewood Cliffs, N.J., 1966.

Read, H., ed. *Kropotkin: Selections from His Writings*. London, 1942.

Reddaway, W. F., ed. *Documents of Catherine the Great*. Cambridge, 1931.

Rieber, A. *The Politics of Autocracy: Letters of Alexander II to Prince A. I. Bariatinskii, 1857–1864*. Paris, 1966.

Rosen, R. R. *Forty Years of Diplomacy*. 2 vols. New York, 1922.

Rozanov, V. V. *Fallen Leaves*. Translated by S. S. Koletiansky. London, 1920.

Rozanov, V. V. *Selected Works*. Edited by G. Ivask. New York, 1956.

Sazonov, S. D. *Fateful Years, 1909–1916*. New York, 1928.

Signposts. See *Vekhi*.

Soloviev, V. S. *Lectures on Godmanhood.* Poughkeepsie, N.Y., 1944. London, 1948.

Soloviev, V. S. *Russia and the Universal Church.* Translated by H. Rees. London, 1948.

Soloviev, V. S. *A Soloviev Anthology.* Edited by S. L. Frank. London, 1950.

Soloviev, V. S. *War, Progress and the End of History.* Translated by A. Bakstry. London, 1915.

Tikhomiroff, L. *Russia: Political and Social.* Translated by E. Aveling. 2 vols. London, 1888.

Tolstoy, L. *Works.* Translated by L. Maude and A. Maude. 21 vols. London and New York, 1928–37.

Vekhi: Landmarks: A Collection of Articles about the Russian Intelligentsia [Moscow, 1909]. Translated and edited by M. Shatz and J. Zimmerman. Armonk, N.Y., 1994.

Wallace, D. M. *Russia.* New York, 1880.

Watrous, S. D., ed. *John Ledyard's Journey through Russia and Siberia, 1787–1788: The Journal and Selected Letters.* Madison, Wis., 1966.

Witte, S. *The Memoirs of Count Witte.* Edited by A. Yarmolinsky. Garden City, N.Y., 1921.

B. General Studies

Benois, A. *The Russian School of Painting.* London, 1916.

Bird, A. *A History of Russian Painting.* Boston, 1987.

Burbank, J. and D. L. Ransel, eds. *Imperial Russia: New Histories for the Empire.* Bloomington, Ind., 1998.

Dmytryshyn, B., ed. *Modernization of Russia under Peter I and Catherine II.* New York and Toronto, 1974.

Florinsky, M. T. *The End of the Russian Empire.* New Haven, Conn., 1931.

Harcave, S. *Years of the Golden Cockerel: The Last Romanov Tsars, 1814–1917.* New York, 1968.

Ivanits, L. J. *Russian Folk Belief.* Armonk, N.Y., 1989.

Karpovich, M. *Imperial Russia, 1801–1917.* New York, 1932.

Kornilov, A. *Modern Russian History from the Age of Catherine the Great to the End of the Nineteenth Century.* Translated by A. Kaun. Bibliography by J. Curtiss. 2 vols. New York, 1970.

Lincoln, W. B. *In War's Dark Shadow: The Russians before the Great War.* New York, 1983.

Maynard, J. *Russia in Flux.* New York, 1948.

Miliukov, P. *Russia and Its Crisis.* Chicago, 1905; New York, 1962.

Mirsky, D. S. *History of Russian Literature.* New York, 1927.

Pares, B. *The Fall of the Russian Monarchy: A Study of the Evidence.* New York, 1939.

Pares, B. *Russia: Between Reform and Revolution.* Edited by F. B. Randall. New York, 1962.

Pavlovsky, G. *Agricultural Russia on the Eve of the Revolution.* London, 1930.

Pushkarev, S. *The Emergence of Modern Russia.* Translated from Russian. New York, 1963.

Raeff, M. *Imperial Russia, 1682–1825: The Coming of Age of Modern Russia.* New York, 1971.

Robinson, G. T. *Rural Russia under the Old Regime: A History of the Landlord-Peasant World and a Prologue to the Peasant Revolution of 1917.* New York, 1932.

Rogger, H. *Russia in the Age of Modernization and Revolution, 1881–1917.* London, 1983.

Seton-Watson, H. *The Russian Empire, 1801–1917.* Oxford, 1967.

Treadgold, D. W. *Twentieth Century Russia.* Chicago, 1959.

Vucinich, A. S. *Science in Russian Culture: A History to 1860.* Stanford, 1963.

Vucinich, A. S. *Science in Russian Culture (1861–1917).* Stanford, 1970.

Vucinich, W. S., ed. *The Peasant in Nineteenth Century Russia.* Stanford, 1968.

Wallace, D. M. *Russia on the Eve of War and Revolution.* New York, 1961.

Westwood, J. N. *Endurance and Endeavour: Russian History, 1812–1980.* 3rd ed. The Short Oxford History of the Modern World. Oxford, 1987.

C. Specialized Studies: Government, Institutions, Society, and Culture

Alexander, J. *Emperor of the Cossacks: Pugachev and the Frontier Jacquerie of 1773–1775.* Lawrence, Kans., 1973.

Alexander, J. T. *Catherine the Great: Life and Legend.* New York, 1989.

Anderson, B. *Internal Migration during Modernization in Late Nineteenth Century Russia.* Princeton, N.J., 1980.

Anisimov, E. V. *The Reforms of Peter the Great: Progress through Coercion in Russia.* Armonk, N.Y., 1993.

Ascher, A. *P. A. Stolypin: The Search for Stability in Late Imperial Russia.* Stanford, 2001.

Ascher, A. *The Revolution of 1905.* 2 vols. Stanford, 1988, 1992.

Becker, S. *Nobility and Privilege in Late Imperial Russia.* DeKalb, Ill., 1985.

Black, C., ed. *Aspects of Social Change since 1861: The Transformation of Russian Society.* Cambridge, Mass., 1960.

Bonnell, V. *Roots of Rebellion: Workers' Politics and Organizations in St. Petersburg and Moscow, 1900–1914.* Berkeley, 1983.

Blum, J. *Lord and Peasant in Russia from the Ninth to the Nineteenth Century.* Princeton, N.J., 1961.

Bradley, J. *Muzhik and Muscovite: Urbanization in Late Imperial Russia.* Berkeley, 1985.

Brooks, J. *When Russia Learned to Read: Literacy and Popular Literature, 1861–1917.* Princeton, N.J., 1985.

Clausewitz, Carl von. *The Campaign of 1812 in Russia.* London, 1843.

Clowes, E., S. Kassow, and J. West, eds. *Between Tsar and People: Educated Society and the Quest for Public Identity in Late Imperial Russia.* Princeton, N.J., 1991.

Crisp, O., and L. Edmonson, eds. *Civil Rights in Imperial Russia.* New York, 1989.

Crummey, R. O. *The Old Believers and the World of the Anti-Christ; The Vyg Community and the Russian State, 1864–1855.* Madison, Wisc., 1970.

Curtiss, J. S. *Church and State in Russia, 1900–1917.* New York, 1940.

Curtiss, J. S. *The Russian Army under Nicholas I, 1825–1855.* Durham, N.C., 1965.

Dukes, P. *Catherine the Great and the Russian Nobility: A Study Based on the Materials of the Legislative Commission of 1767.* Cambridge, 1968.

Edelman, R. *Gentry Politics on the Eve of the Russian Revolution: The Nationalist Party, 1907–1917.* New Brunswick, N.J., 1980.

Edelman, R. *Proletarian Peasants: The Revolution of 1905 in Russia's Southwest.* Ithaca, N.Y., 1987.

Eklof, B. *Russian Peasant Schools: Officialdom, Village Culture, and Popular Pedagogy, 1864–1914.* Berkeley, 1986.

Eklof, B. and S. Frank, eds. *The World of the Russian Peasant: Post-emancipation Culture and Society.* Boston, 1990.

Eklof, B., J. Bushnell, and L. Zakharova, eds. *Russia's Great Reforms, 1855–1881.* Bloomington, Ind., 1994.

Emmons, T. *The Russian Landed Gentry and the Peasant Emancipation of 1861.* Cambridge, 1967.

Emmons, T., ed. *Emancipation of the Russian Serfs.* New York, 1970.

Emmons, T. and W. Vucinich, eds. *The Zemstvo in Russia: An Experiment in Local Self-Government.* Cambridge, 1982.

Engel, B. A. *Between the Fields and the City: Women, Work, and Family in Russia, 1861–1914.* Cambridge, 1994.

Engelstein, L. *The Keys to Happiness: Sex and the Search for Modernity in Fin-de-Siècle Russia.* Ithaca, N.Y., 1992.

Field, D. *The End of Serfdom: Nobility and Bureaucracy in Russia, 1855–1861.* Cambridge, Mass., 1976.

Frank, S. P. *Crime, Cultural Conflict, and Justice in Rural Russia, 1856–1914.* Berkeley, 1999.

Frank, S. P. and M. D. Steinberg, eds., *Cultures in Flux: Lower-Class Values, Practices, and Resistance in Late Imperial Russia.* Princeton, N.J., 1994.

Freeze, G. *The Parish Clergy in Nineteenth Century Russia: Crisis, Reform, Counter-Reform.* Princeton, N.J., 1983.

Freeze, G. *The Russian Levites: The Parish Clergy in the Eighteenth Century.* Cambridge, Mass., 1977.

Frierson, C. *Peasant Icons: Representations of Rural People in Late Nineteenth Century Russia.* New York, 1993.

Glickman, R. L. *Russian Factory Women: Workplace and Society, 1880–1914.* Berkeley, 1984.

Golovin, N. N. *The Russian Army in the World War.* New Haven, Conn., 1931.

Gooch, G. P. *Catherine the Great and Other Studies.* London, 1954.

Gronsky, P., and N. Astrov. *The War and the Russian Government.* New Haven, Conn., 1929.

Haimson, L. H. "The Problem of Social Stability in Urban Russia, 1905–1917." *Slavic Review* (December 1964 and March 1965).

Haimson, L. H., ed. *The Politics of Rural Russia, 1905–1914.* Bloomington, Ind., 1979.

Hamm, M. F. *The City in Russian History.* Lexington, Ky., 1976.

Hartley, J. M. *Alexander I.* New York, 1994.

Hoch, S. *Serfdom and Social Control in Russia.* Chicago, 1986.

Hosking, G. *The Russian Constitutional Experiment: Government and Duma, 1907–1914.* Cambridge, 1973.

Hughes, L. *Russia in the Age of Peter the Great.* New Haven, Conn., 1998.

Hutchinson, J. F. *Politics and Public Health in Revolutionary Russia, 1890–1918.* Baltimore, 1990.

Jones, R. E. *The Emancipation of the Russian Nobility, 1762–85.* Princeton, N.J., 1973.

Kassow, S. D. *Students, Professors, and the State in Tsarist Russia.* Berkeley, 1989.

Keep, J. *Soldiers of the Tsar: Army and Society in Russia, 1462–1874.* Oxford, 1985.

Kelly, C. and D. Shepherd, eds. *Constructing Russian Culture in the Age of Revolution: 1881–1940.* Oxford, 1998.

Kennan, G. *Siberia and the Exile System.* 2 vols. New York, 1891.

Kliuchevsky, V. O. *Peter the Great.* New York, 1959.

Kolchin, P. *Unfree Labor: American Slavery and Russian Serfdom.* Cambridge, Mass., 1987.

Kovalevsky, M. M. *Russian Political Institutions.* Chicago, 1902.

Kucherov, S. *Courts, Lawyers and Trials under the Last Three Tsars.* New York, 1953.

LeDonne, J. P. *Absolutism and Ruling Class: The Formation of the Russian Political Order, 1700–1825.* New York, 1991.

LeDonne, J. P. *Ruling Russia: Politics and Administration in the Age of Absolutism, 1762–1796.* Princeton, N.J., 1984.

Levin, A. *The Second Duma: A Study of the Social-Democratic Party and the Russian Constitutional Experiment.* New Haven, Conn., 1940.

Lieven, D. C. B. *Nicholas II: Twilight of the Empire.* New York, 1994.

Lincoln, W. B. *The Great Reforms: Autocracy, Bureaucracy, and the Politics of Change in Imperial Russia.* DeKalb, Ill., 1990.

Lincoln, W. B. *In the Vanguard of Reform: Russia's Enlightened Bureaucrats, 1825–1861.* DeKalb, Ill., 1986.

Lincoln, W. B. *Nicholas I: Emperor and Autocrat of All the Russias.* Bloomington, Ind., 1978.

Lincoln, W. B. *The Romanovs: Autocrats of All the Russias.* New York, 1981.

MacDaniel, T. *Autocracy, Capitalism, and Revolution in Russia.* Berkeley, 1988.

MacKenzie, D. *The Lion of Tashkent: The Career of General M. G. Cherniaev.* Athens, Ga., 1974.

Madariaga, I. de. *Russia in the Age of Catherine the Great.* New Haven, Conn., 1981.

Manning, R. *The Crisis of the Old Order in Russia: Gentry and Government.* Princeton, N.J., 1982.

Martin, A. *Romantics, Reformers, Reactionaries: Russian Conservative Thought and Politics in the Reign of Alexander I.* DeKalb, Ill., 1997.

Massie, R. K. *Nicholas and Alexandra.* New York, 1967.

McClelland, J. C. *Autocrats and Academics: Education, Culture, and Society in Tsarist Russia.* Chicago and London, 1979.

McGrew, R. E. *Russia and the Cholera, 1823–1832.* Madison, Wis., 1965.

Mehlinger, H. D. and J. M. Thompson. *Count Witte and the Tsarist Government in the 1905 Revolution.* Bloomington, Ind., 1972.

Miller, F. *Dimitrii Miliutin and the Reform Era in Russia.* Nashville, Tenn., 1968.

Mironov, B., with Ben Eklof. *The Social History of Imperial Russia, 1700–1917.* 2 vols. Boulder, Colo., 2000.

Monas, S. *The Third Section: Police and Society under Nicholas I.* Cambridge, Mass., 1961.

Neuberger, J. *Hooliganism: Crime, Culture, and Power in St. Petersburg, 1900–1914.* Berkeley, 1993.

Nichols, R. L. and T. G. Stavrou, eds. *Russian Orthodoxy under the Old Regime.* Minneapolis, 1978.

O'Brien, C. B. *Russia under Two Tsars, 1682–1689.* Berkeley, 1952.

Orlovsky, D. T. *The Limits of Reform: The Ministry of Internal Affairs in Imperial Russia, 1802–1881.* Cambridge, Mass., 1981.

Paleologue, G. M. *The Enigmatic Tsar: The Life of Alexander I of Russia.* London, 1938.

Papmehl, K. A. *Freedom of Expression in Eighteenth Century Russia.* The Hague, 1971.

Pearson, T. S. *Russian Officialdom in Crisis: Autocracy and Local Self-Government, 1861–1900.* Cambridge, 1989.

Pintner, W. M., and D. K. Rowney, eds. *Russian Officialdom: The Bureaucratization of Russian Society from the Seventeenth to the Twentieth Century.* Chapel Hill, N.C., 1980.

Pipes, R., ed. *Revolutionary Russia.* Cambridge, Mass., 1968.

Raeff, M. *Michael Speransky: Statesman of Imperial Russia.* The Hague, 1957.

Raeff, M. *Siberia and the Reforms of 1822.* Seattle, 1956.

Raeff, M. *The Well-Ordered Police State: Social and Institutional Change through Law in the Germanies and Russia, 1600–1800.* New Haven, Conn., 1983.

Raeff, M., ed. *Peter the Great: Reformer or Revolutionary?* Boston, 1963.

Ransel, D. L. *Mothers of Misery: Child Abandonment in Russia.* Princeton, N.J., 1988.

Ransel, D. L. *The Politics of Catherinean Russia: The Panin Party.* New Haven, Conn., 1975.

Rheinelander, A. *Prince Michael Vorontsov: Viceroy to the Tsar.* Montreal, 1990.

Rodzianko, M. V. *Reign of Rasputin: An Empire's Collapse.* New York, 1927.

Rogger, H. *National Consciousness in 18th Century Russia.* Cambridge, Mass., 1960.

Rogger, H. "Russian Ministers and the Jewish Question 1881–1917." *California Slavic Studies* 8 (1975).

Roosevelt, P. R. *Life on the Russian Country Estate: A Social and Cultural History.* New Haven, Conn., 1995.

Ruud, C. A. *Fighting Words: Imperial Censorship and the Russian Press, 1804–1906.* Toronto, 1982.

Sablinsky, W. *The Road to Bloody Sunday: Father Gapon and the St. Petersburg Massacre of 1905.* Princeton, N.J., 1976.

Schneiderman, J. *Sergei Zubatov and Revolutionary Marxism: The Struggle for the Working Class in Tsarist Russia.* Ithaca, N.Y., 1976.

Schwarz, S. M. *The Russian Revolution of 1905: The Workers' Movement and the Formation of Bolshevism and Menshevism.* Chicago and London, 1967.

Seregny, S. *Russian Teachers and Peasant Revolution: The Politics of Education in 1905.* Bloomington, Ind., 1989.

Shevzov, V. *Russian Orthodoxy on the Eve of Revolution.* New York, 2003.

Sinel, A. *The Classroom and the Chancellery: State Education Reform in Russia under Count Dimitrii Tolstoy.* Cambridge, Mass., 1973.

Soloveytchik, G. *Potemkin: Soldier, Statesman, Lover and Consort of Catherine of Russia.* New York, 1947.

Starr, S. F. *Decentralization and Self-Government in Russia, 1830–1870.* Princeton, N.J., 1972.

Steinberg, M. D. *Proletarian Imagination: Self, Modernity, and the Sacred in Russia, 1910–1925.* Ithaca, N.Y., 2002.

Sumner, B. H. *Peter the Great and the Emergence of Russia.* New York, 1962.

Surh, G. D. *1905 in St. Petersburg: Labor, Society, and Revolution.* Stanford, 1989.

Treadgold, D. W. *The Great Siberian Migration: Government and Peasant in Resettlement from Emancipation to the First World War.* Princeton, N.J., 1957.

Troyat, H. *Catherine the Great.* Translated by J. Pinkham. New York, 1980.

Verner, A. *The Crisis of Russian Autocracy: Nicholas II and the 1905 Revolution.* Princeton, N.J., 1990.

Wade, R. A., and S. J. Seregny, eds. *Politics and Society in Provincial Russia: Saratov, 1590–1917.* Columbus, Ohio, 1989.

Wagner, W. *Marriage, Property, and Law in Late Imperial Russia.* New York, 1994.

Walkin, J. *The Rise of Democracy in Pre-Revolutionary Russia: Political and Social Institutions under the Last Three Tsars.* New York, 1962.

Wildman, A. *The Making of a Workers' Revolution: Russian Social Democracy, 1891–1903.* Chicago, 1967.

Wirtschafter, E. K. *From Serf to Russian Soldier.* Princeton, N.J., 1990.

Wirtschafter, E. K. *Social Identity in Imperial Russia.* DeKalb, Ill., 1997.

Wirtschafter, E. K. *Structures of Society: Imperial Russia's "People of Various Ranks."* DeKalb, Ill., 1994.

Worobec, C. *Peasant Russia: Family and Community in the Post-Emancipation Period.* 1991.

Wortman, R. *Scenarios of Power: Myth and Ceremony in Russian Monarchy.* 2 vols. Princeton, N.J., 1995, 2000.

Wortman, R. S. *The Development of a Russian Legal Consciousness.* Chicago and London, 1976.

Yaney, G. *Systematization of Russian Government: Social Evolution in the Domestic Administration of Imperial Russia, 1711–1905.* Urbana, Ill., 1973.

Zaionchkovskii, P. A. *The Abolition of Serfdom in Russia.* Gulf Breeze, Fla., 1978.

Zaionchkovskii, P. A. *The Russian Autocracy in Crisis, 1878–1882.* Gulf Breeze, Fla., 1979.

Zaionchkovskii, P. A. *The Russian Autocracy under Alexander III.* Gulf Breeze, Fla., 1976.

Zaitsev, P. *Taras Shevchenko: A Life.* Edited, abridged, and translated with an introduction by G. S. N. Luckyj. Toronto, 1988.

Zelnik, R. E. *Labor and Society in Tsarist Russia: The Factory Workers of St. Petersburg, 1855–1870.* Stanford, 1971.

Zelnik, R. *Law and Disorder on the Narova River: The Kreenholm Strike of 1872.* Berkeley, 1995.

D. Specialized Studies: Foreign Affairs

Barker, A. J. *The War Against Russia, 1854–1856.* New York, 1971.

Bromley, J. S., ed. *The Rise of Great Britain and Russia, 1688–1715/25.* Vol. 6 of *The New Cambridge Modern History.* Cambridge, Mass., 1970.

Curtiss, J. S. *Russia's Crimean War.* Durham, N.C., 1979.

Dallin, D. J. *The Rise of Russia in Asia*. New Haven, Conn., 1949.

Donnelly, A. S. *The Russian Conquest of Bashkiria: A Case Study in Imperialism, 1552–1740*. New Haven, Conn., 1968.

Fay, S. B. *The Origins of the World War*. 2 vols. New York, 1928.

Fisher, A. W. *The Russian Annexation of the Crimea, 1772–1783*. Cambridge, 1970.

Golder, F. A. *Russian Expansion on the Pacific, 1641–1850*. Cleveland, 1914.

Goldfrank, D. *The Origins of the Crimean War*. New York, 1994.

Jelavich, B. *A Century of Russian Foreign Policy, 1814–1914*. New York, 1964.

Jelavich, B. *Russia and Greece During the Regency of King Otton, 1832–1835*. Thessalonika, 1962.

Jelavich, B. *Russia and the Greek Revolution of 1843*. Munich, 1966.

Jelavich, B. *Russia and the Rumanian National Cause, 1858–1859*. Bloomington, Ind., 1959.

Jelavich, B., and C. Jelavich. *Russia in the East, 1876–1880*. Leiden, 1959.

Jelavich, C. *Tsarist Russia and Balkan Nationalism: Russian Influence in the Internal Affairs of Bulgaria and Serbia, 1879–1886*. Berkeley, 1958.

Kaplan, H. H. *The First Partition of Poland*. New York, 1962.

Kennan, G. F. *The Decline of Bismarck's European Order: Franco-Russian Relations, 1875–1890*. Princeton, N.J., 1979.

Langer, W. L. *The Diplomacy of Imperialism, 1890–1902*. 2 vols. New York, 1935.

Langer, W. L. *The European Alliances and Alignments, 1871–1890*. New York, 1950.

Langer, W. L. *The Franco-Russian Alliance, 1890–1894*. Cambridge, Mass., 1929.

Lederer, I., ed. *Russian Foreign Policy: Essays in Historical Perspective*. New Haven, Conn., 1962.

LeDonne, J. P. *The Russian Empire and the World, 1700–1917: The Geopolitics of Expansion and Containment*. New York, 1997.

Lensen, G. A. *The Russian Push toward Japan: Russo-Japanese Relations, 1697–1875*. Princeton, N.J., 1959.

Lobanov-Rostovsky, A. *Russia and Asia*. Ann Arbor, Mich., 1951.

Lobanov-Rostovsky, A. *Russia and Europe, 1789–1825*. Durham, N.C., 1947.

Lobanov-Rostovsky, A. *Russia and Europe, 1825–1878*. Ann Arbor, Mich., 1954.

Lord, R. H. *The Second Partition of Poland*. Cambridge, Mass., 1915.

Madariaga, I. de. *Britain, Russia, and the Armed Neutrality of 1780: Sir James Harris's Mission to St. Petersburg During the American Revolution*. New Haven, Conn., 1962.

Malozemoff, A. *Russian Far Eastern Policy, 1881–1904*. Berkeley, 1958.

Montesquiou-Fezensac, R. *The Russian Campaign, 1812*. Translated by L. Kennett. Athens, Ga., 1970.

Mosely, P. *Russian Diplomacy and the Opening of the Eastern Question in 1838 and 1839*. Cambridge, Mass., 1934.

Mosse, W. E. *The European Powers and the German Question, 1848–1871*. Cambridge, 1958.

Okun, S. B. *The Russian-American Company*. Translated from Russian. Cambridge, Mass., 1951.

Pierce, R. A. *Russian Central Asia, 1867–1917: A Study in Colonial Rule*. Berkeley, 1960.

Pierce, R. A. *Russia's Hawaiian Adventure, 1815–1817*. Berkeley, 1965.

Puryear, V. J. *England, Russia and the Straits Question, 1844–1856*. Berkeley, 1931.

Ragsdale, H. *Détente in the Napoleonic Era: Bonaparte and the Russians*. Lawrence, Kans., 1980.

Romanov, B. *Russia in Manchuria, 1892–1906*. Translated by S. Jones. Ann Arbor, Mich., 1952.

Saul, N. E. *Concord and Conflict: The United States and Russia, 1867–1914*. Lawrence, Kan., 1996.

Smith, C. J. *The Russian Struggle for Power, 1914–1917: A Study of Russian Foreign Policy During the First World War*. New York, 1956.

Sumner, B. H. *Peter the Great and the Ottoman Empire.* Oxford, 1949.

Sumner, B. H. *Russia and the Balkans, 1870–1880.* Oxford, 1937.

Sumner, B. H. *Tsardom and Imperialism in the Far East and Middle East, 1880–1914.* London, 1940.

Tarle, E. V. *Napoleon's Invasion of Russia, 1812.* Translated from Russian first edition. New York, 1942.

Taylor, A. J. P. *The Struggle for Mastery in Europe, 1848–1918.* Berkeley, 1931.

Thaden, E. C. *Russia and the Balkan Alliance of 1912.* University Park, Pa., 1965.

Thomson, G. S. *Catherine the Great and the Expansion of Russia.* London, 1947.

Warner, D., and P. Warner. *The Tide at Sunrise: A History of the Russo-Japanese War, 1904–1905.* New York, 1974.

White, J. A. *The Diplomacy of the Russo-Japanese War.* Princeton, N.J., 1964.

F. Specialized Studies: Economic Development

Ames, E. "A Century of Russian Railway Construction, 1837–1936." *American Slavic and East European Review* 6 (1947).

Blackwell, W. L. *The Beginnings of Russian Industrialization, 1800–1860.* Princeton, N.J., 1968.

Gerschenkron, A. "Agrarian Policies and Industrialization, Russia 1861–1917." In *The Cambridge Economic History.* Vol. 6, part 2. Cambridge, 1966.

Gerschenkron, A. "The Early Phases of Industrialization in Russia." In *The Economics of Take-Off into Sustained Growth,* edited by W. Rostow. London, 1963.

Gerschenkron, A. *Economic Backwardness in Historical Perspective.* Cambridge, Mass., 1962.

Kahan, A. *The Plow, the Hammer, and the Knout: An Economic History of Eighteenth-Century Russia.* Chicago, 1985.

Lih, L. *Bread and Authority in Russia, 1914–1921.* Berkeley, 1990.

Marks, S. G. *Road to Power: The Trans-Siberian Railroad and the Colonization of Asian Russia, 1850–1917.* Ithaca, N.Y., 1991.

McKay, J. P. *Pioneers for Profit: Foreign Entrepreneurship and Russian Industrialization, 1885–1913.* Chicago, 1970.

Owen, T. *Capitalism and Politics in Russia: A Social History of the Moscow Merchants, 1855–1905.* Cambridge, 1981.

Pintner, W. W. *Russian Economic Policy under Nicholas I.* Ithaca, N.Y., 1967.

Portal, R. "The Industrialization of Russia." In *The Cambridge Economic History.* Vol. 6, part 2. Cambridge, 1966.

Rieber, A. J. *Merchants and Entrepreneurs in Imperial Russia.* Chapel Hill, N.C., 1982.

Rozman, G. *Urban Networks in Russia, 1750–1800, and Premodern Periodization.* Princeton, N.J., 1976.

Smith, R. E. F., and D. Christian. *Bread and Salt: A Social and Economic History of Food and Drink in Russia.* New York, 1981.

Tugan-Baranovsky, M. I. *The Russian Factory in the 19th Century.* Translated by A. Levin, C. Levin, and G. Grossman. Homewood, Ill., 1970.

Von Laue, T. H. "Russian Labor between Field and Factory, 1892–1903." *California Slavic Studies* 3 (1964).

Von Laue, T. H. *Sergei Witte and the Industrialization of Russia.* New York, 1963.

F. Specialized Studies: Intellectual History and the Intelligentsia

Ambler, E. *Russian Journalism and Politics 1861–1881: The Career of Aleksei S. Suvorin.* Detroit, 1972.

Andrew, J. *Women in Russian Literature, 1780–1863.* New York, 1988.

Avrich, P. *The Russian Anarchists*. Princeton, N.J., 1967.

Baron, S. H. *Plekhanov: The Father of Russian Marxism*. Stanford, 1963.

Berdiaev, N. *Constantin Leontieff*. Translated by H. Iswolsky. Paris, 1937.

Berdiaev, N. *The Russian Idea*. Translated by R. French. London, 1947.

Berlin, I. *Russian Thinkers*. Edited by H. Hardy and A. Kelly. New York, 1978.

Billington, J. *Mikhailovsky and Russian Populism*. New York, 1958.

Bowman, H. *Vissarion Belinskii, 1811–1848: A Study in the Origins of Social Criticism in Russia*. Cambridge, Mass., 1954.

Broido, E. *Memoirs of a Revolutionary*. Edited and translated by V. Broido. New York, 1967.

Brower, D. R. *Training the Nihilists: Education and Radicalism in Tsarist Russia*. Ithaca, N.Y., 1975.

Brown, E. J. *Stankevich and His Moscow Circle, 1830–1840*. Stanford, 1966.

Byrnes, R. F. *Pobedonostsev: His Life and Thought*. Bloomington, Ind., 1968.

Byrnes, R. F. *V. O. Kliuchevskii, Historian of Russia*. Bloomington, Ind., 1995.

Carr, E. H. *Michael Bakunin*, New York, 1961.

Carr, E. H. *The Romantic Exiles: A Nineteenth Century Portrait Gallery*. London, 1933.

Chmielewski, E. *Tribune of the Slavophiles: Konstantin Aksakov*. University of Florida Monograph. Social Sciences, no. 12. Gainesville, Fla., 1961.

Christoff, P. K. *An Introduction to Nineteenth-Century Russian Slavophilism: A Study in Ideas*. Vol. 1, *A. S. Xomjakov*. The Hague, 1961.

Christoff, P. K. *An Introduction to Nineteenth-Century Russian Slavophilism: A Study in Ideas*. Vol. 2, *I. V. Kireevskij*. The Hague, 1972.

Christoff, P. K. *An Introduction to Nineteenth-Century Russian Slavophilism*. Vol. 3, *K. S. Aksakov: A Study in Ideas*. Princeton, N.J., 1982.

Christoff, P. K. *An Introduction to Nineteenth-Century Russian Slavophilism*. Vol. 4, *Iu. F. Samarin*. Boulder, Colo., 1991.

Christoff, P. K. *Third Heart: Some Intellectual-Ideological Currents in Russia, 1800–1830*. The Hague, 1970.

Clark, K. *Petersburg: Crucible of Revolution*. Cambridge, Mass., 1986.

Engel, B. *Mothers and Daughters: Women of the Intelligentsia in 19th Century Russia*. Cambridge, 1983.

Evtuhov, C. *The Cross and the Sickle: Sergei Bulgakov and the Fate of Russian Religious Philosophy*. Ithaca, N.Y., 1997.

Fadner, F. *Seventy Years of Pan-Slavism: Karazin to Danilevskii, 1800–1870*. Washington, D.C., 1962.

Field, D. *Rebels in the Name of the Tsar*. Boston, 1976.

Fischer, G. *Russian Liberalism, from Gentry to Intelligentsia*. Cambridge, Mass., 1958.

Frank, J. *Dostoevsky: The Mantle of the Prophet, 1871–1881*. Princeton, N.J., 2002.

Frank, J. *Dostoevsky: The Miraculous Years, 1865–1871*. Princeton, N.J., 1995.

Frank, J. *Dostoevsky: The Seeds of Revolt, 1821–1849*. Princeton, N.J., 1976.

Frank, J. *Dostoevsky: The Stir of Liberation, 1860–1865*. Princeton, N.J., 1986.

Frank, J. *Dostoevsky: The Years of Ordeal, 1850–1859*. Princeton, N.J., 1983.

Galai, S. *The Liberation Movement in Russia, 1900–1905*. Cambridge, 1973.

Gerstein, L. *Nikolai Strakhov*. Cambridge, Mass., 1971.

Getzler, I. *Martov: A Political Biography of a Russian Social Democrat*. New York, 1967.

Haimson, L. H. *The Russian Marxists and the Origins of Bolshevism*. Cambridge, Mass., 1955.

Hardy, D. *Land and Freedom: The Origins of Russian Terrorism, 1876–1879*. Westport, Conn. 1987.

Hare, R. *Portraits of Russian Personalities between Reform and Revolution*. New York, 1959.

Karpovich, M. "P. L. Lavrov and Russian Socialism." *California Slavic Studies* 2 (1963).

Katz, M. *Mikhail N. Katkov: A Political Biography, 1818–1887*. The Hague, 1966.

Keep, J. L. H. *The Rise of Social Democracy in Russia*. Oxford, 1963.

Kelly, A. *Toward Another Shore: Russian Thinkers between Necessity and Chance*. New Haven, Conn., 1998.

Kindersley, R. *The First Russian Revisionists: A Study of Legal Marxism in Russia*. Oxford, 1962.

Kline, G. *Religious and Anti-Religious Thought in Russia*. Chicago, 1968.

Kohn, H. *Pan Slavism: Its History and Ideology*. Notre Dame, Ind., 1953; New York, 1960.

Lampert, E. *Sons against Fathers: Studies in Russian Radicalism and Revolution*. London, 1965.

Lampert, E. *Studies in Rebellion*. London, 1957.

Lang, D. M. *The First Russian Radical: Alexander Radishchev, 1749–1802*. New York, 1960.

Lednicki, W. *Russia, Poland and the West: Essays in Literary and Cultural History*. London and New York, 1954.

Leslie, R. F. *Reform and Insurrection in Russian Poland, 1856–1865*. London, 1963.

Lukashevich, S. *Ivan Aksakov, 1823–1866: A Study in Russian Thought and Politics*. Cambridge, Mass., 1965.

Lukashevich, S. *Konstantin Leontev, 1831–1891: A Study in Russian "Heroic Vitalism."* New York, 1967.

Lukashevich, S. *N. F. Fedorov (1828–1903): A Study in Roman Eupsychian and Utopian Thought*. Newark, N.J., 1977.

Malia, M. *Alexander Herzen and the Birth of Russian Socialism, 1812–1855*. Cambridge, Mass., 1961.

Malia, M. "What Is the Intelligentsia?" In *The Russian Intelligentsia*, edited by R. Pipes. New York, 1961.

Mazour, A. *The First Russian Revolution, 1825: The Decembrist Movement*. Stanford, 1937.

Mazour, A. G. *Women in Exile: Wives of the Decembrists*. Tallahassee, Fla., 1975.

McNally, R. T. *Chaadaev and His Friends: An Intellectual History of Peter Chaadaev and His Russian Contemporaries*. Tallahassee, Fla., 1971.

Mendel, A. P. *Dilemmas of Progress in Tsarist Russia: Legal Marxism and Legal Populism*. Cambridge, Mass., 1961.

Mendel, A. P. *Michael Bakunin: Roots of Apocalypse*. New York, 1981.

Mochulsky, K. *Dostoevsky: His Life and Work*. Translated by M. Minihan. Princeton, N.J., 1967.

Mohrenschildt, D. von. *Russia in the Intellectual Life of 18th Century France*. New York, 1936.

Paperno, I. *Chernyshevsky and the Age of Russian Realism*. Stanford, 1988.

Petrovich, M. B. *The Emergence of Russian Pan-Slavism, 1856–1870*. New York, 1956.

Pipes, R. *Social Democracy and the St. Petersburg Labor Movement, 1885–1897*. Cambridge, Mass., 1963.

Pipes, R. *Struve: Liberal on the Left, 1870–1905*. Cambridge, Mass., 1970.

Pipes, R. *Struve: Liberal on the Right, 1905–1944*. Cambridge, Mass., 1980.

Pipes, R., ed. *The Russian Intelligentsia*. New York, 1961.

Plamenatz, J. *German Marxism and Russian Communism*. London, 1954.

Pollard, A. "The Russian Intelligentsia: The Mind of Russia." *California Slavic Studies* 3 (1964).

Pomper, P. *Peter Lavrov and the Russian Revolutionary Movement*. Chicago, 1972.

Pomper, P. *The Russian Revolutionary Intelligentsia*. Arlington Heights, Ill., 1970.

Putnam, G. F. *Russian Alternatives to Marxism: Christian Socialism and Idealistic Liberalism in Twentieth-Century Russia*. Knoxville, Tenn., 1977.

Raeff, M. *Origins of the Russian Intelligentsia: The Eighteenth Century Nobility*. New York, 1966.

Randall, F. *N. G. Chernyshevskii*. New York, 1967.

Rawson, D. C. *Russian Rightists and the Revolution of 1905*. New York, 1995.

Read, C. *Religion, Revolution and the Russian Intelligentsia, 1900–1912*. Totowa, N.J., 1979.

Riasanovsky, N. V. *The Image of Peter the Great in Russian History and Thought*. New York, 1985.

Riasanovsky, N. V. *Nicholas I and Official Nationality in Russia, 1825–1855*. Berkeley, 1959.

Riasanovsky, N. V. *A Parting of Ways: Government and the Educated Public in Russia, 1801–1855*. Oxford, 1976.

Riasanovsky, N. V. *Russia and the West in the Teachings of the Slavophiles*. Cambridge, Mass., 1952.

Rogger, H. *National Consciousness in 18th Century Russia*. Cambridge, Mass., 1960.

Rosenthal, B. G., ed. *Nietzsche in Russia*. Princeton, N.J., 1986.

Schapiro, L. *Rationalism and Nationalism in Russian Nineteenth Century Political Thought*. New Haven, Conn., 1967.

Serge, V. *Memoirs of a Revolutionary, 1901–1941*. Translated by P. Sedgwick. London, 1963.

Service, R. *Lenin: a Political Life*. Vols. 1–2. Bloomington, Ind., 1985, 1991.

Stites, R. *The Women's Liberation Movement in Russia: Feminism, Nihilism, and Bolshevism, 1860–1930*. Princeton, N.J., 1978.

Thaden, E. C. *Conservative Nationalism in 19th Century Russia*. Seattle, 1964.

Treadgold, D. W. *Lenin and His Rivals: The Struggle for Russia's Future, 1898–1906*. New York, 1955.

Trotsky, L. *1905*. Translated by A. Bostock. New York, 1971.

Ulam, A. B. *The Bolsheviks*. New York, 1965.

Venturi, F. *Roots of Revolution: A History of the Populist and Socialist Movements in Nineteenth Century Russia*. Translated by F. Haskell. New York, 1960.

Vucinich, A. *Social Thought in Tsarist Russia: The Quest for a General Science of Society 1861–1917*. Chicago and London, 1976.

Walicki, A. *The Controversy Over Capitalism*. Oxford, 1969.

Walicki, A. *A History of Russian Thought from the Enlightenment to Marxism*. Stanford, 1979.

Walicki, A. "Personality and Society in the Ideology of Russian Slavophiles: A Study in the Sociology of Knowledge." *California Slavic Studies* 2 (1963).

Walicki, A. *The Slavophile Controversy. History of a Conservative Utopia in Nineteenth Century Russian Thought*. Translated by H. Andrews-Rusiecka. Oxford, 1975.

Weeks, A. L. *The First Bolshevik: A Political Biography of Peter Tkachev*. New York, 1968.

Wilson, E. *To the Finland Station*. New York, 1940.

Woehrlin, W. F. *Chernyshevsky: The Man and the Journalist*. Cambridge, Mass., 1971.

Wolfe, B. E. *Three Who Made a Revolution: A Biographical History*. New York, 1948.

Yarmolinsky, A. *Road to Revolution: A Century of Russian Radicalism*. London, 1957.

Zenkovsky, V. V. *Russian Thinkers and Europe*. Translated from Russian. Ann Arbor, Mich., 1953.

Zetlin, M. *The Decembrists*. Translated by G. Panin. New York, 1958.

Soviet Russia, 1917–1991

A. Revolution and Civil War

1. General Studies, Including Works by Participants

Acton, E., V. Iu. Cherniaev, and W. G. Rosenberg, eds. *Critical Companion to the Russian Revolution*. Bloomington, Ind., 1997.

Carr, E. H. *A History of Soviet Russia.* Vols. 1–3, *The Bolshevik Revolution, 1917–1923.* Vol. 4, *The Interregnum, 1923–1924.* Vols. 5–7, *Socialism in One Country, 1924–1926.* Vols. 8–9, *Foundations of a Planned Economy, 1926–1929* (Vol. 8 with R. W. Davies). New York, 1951–53, 1954, 1958, 1971–72.

Chamberlin, W. N. *The Russian Revolution, 1917–1921.* 2 vols. New York, 1935.

Chernov, V. *The Great Russian Revolution.* New Haven, Conn., 1936.

Curtiss, J. S. *The Russian Revolutions of 1917.* Princeton, N.J., 1957.

Denikin, A. I. *The Russian Turmoil.* London, 1922.

Figes, O. *A People's Tragedy: The Russian Revolution, 1891–1924.* New York, 1997.

Fitzpatrick, S. *The Russian Revolution.* New York, 1994.

Footman, D. *Civil War in Russia.* New York, 1961.

Footman, D. *The Russian Revolution.* New York, 1962.

Gorky, M. *Untimely Thoughts: Essays on Revolution, Culture, and the Bolsheviks, 1917–1918.* Translated by H. Ermolaev. Introduction by M. Steinberg. New Haven, Conn., 1995.

Katkov, G. *Russia, 1917: The February Revolution.* New York, 1967.

Kerensky, A. *The Catastrophe: Kerensky's Own Story of the Russian Revolution.* New York, 1927.

Kerensky, A. *The Crucifixion of Liberty.* New York, 1934.

Kerensky, A. *Russia and History's Turning Point.* London, 1965.

Liebman, M. *The Russian Revolution.* Translated by A. Pomperans. New York, 1970.

Lincoln, W. B. *Passage Through Armageddon: The Russians in War and Revolution, 1914–1918.* New York, 1986.

Mawdsley, E. *The Russian Civil War.* Boston, 1987.

Steinberg, M. D. *Voices of Revolution, 1917.* New Haven, Conn., 2001.

Sukhanov, N. N. *The Russian Revolution of 1917.* New York, 1955.

Trotsky, L. *The History of the Russian Revolution,* 3 vols. New York, 1932–57.

Tucker, R. C., ed. *The Lenin Anthology.* New York, 1975.

Von Mohrenschildt, D., ed. *The Russian Revolution of 1917: Contemporary Accounts.* New York, 1971.

Woytinsky, W. S. *Stormy Passage. A Personal History through Two Russian Revolutions to Democracy and Freedom: 1905–1960.* New York, 1961.

2. READINGS ON SPECIAL TOPICS

Adams, A. E. *Bolsheviks in the Ukraine: The Second Campaign.* New Haven, Conn., 1963.

Adams, A. E., ed. *The Russian Revolution and Bolshevik Victory: Why and How?* Boston, 1960.

Anweiler, O. *The Soviets: The Russian Workers, Peasants, and Soldiers Councils, 1905–1921.* Translated by R. Hein. New York, 1974.

Avrich, P. *Kronstadt 1921.* Princeton, N.J., 1970.

Browder, R., and F. Kerensky, eds. *The Russian Provisional Government, 1917.* 3 vols. Stanford, 1961.

Bunyan, J., ed. *Intervention, Civil War and Communism in Russia, April-December, 1918: Documents.* Baltimore, 1936.

Bunyan, J., and H. H. Fisher, eds. *The Bolshevik Revolution, 1917–1918: Documents.* Stanford, 1934.

Burdzhalov, E. N. *Russia's Second Revolution: The February Uprising in Petrograd.* Translated and edited by D. J. Raleigh. Bloomington, Ind., 1987.

Carr, E. H. *The October Revolution: Before and After.* New York, 1969.

Dan, Th. *The Origins of Bolshevism.* London, 1964.

Daniels, R. V. *Red October. The Bolshevik Revolution of 1917.* London, 1968.

Deutscher, I., ed. *The Age of Permanent Revolution: A Trotsky Anthology.* New York, 1964.

Farnsworth, B. *Alexandra Kollontai: Socialism, Feminism, and the Bolshevik Revolution.* Stanford, 1980.

Ferro, M. *The Russian Revolution of February 1917*. Translated by J. L. Richards. Engle-wood Cliffs, N.J., 1972.

Figes, O. *Peasant Russia, Civil War: The Volga Countryside in Revolution, 1917–1921*. Oxford, 1989.

Figes, O. and B. Kolonitskii. *Interpreting the Russian Revolution: The Language and Symbols of 1917*. New Haven, Conn., 1999.

Fischer, Louis. *The Life of Lenin*. New York, 1964.

Galili, Z. *The Menshevik Leaders in the Russian Revolution: Social Realities and Political Struggles*. Princeton, N.J., 1989.

Gankin, O. H., and H. H. Fisher, eds. *The Bolsheviks and the World War: Documents*. Stanford, 1940.

Getzler, I. *Kronstadt, 1917–1921: Fate of a Soviet Democracy*. Cambridge, 1983.

Haimson, L. H., ed. *The Mensheviks: From the Revolution of 1917 to the Second World War*. Chicago, 1974.

Hasegawa, T. *The February Revolution: Petrograd, 1917*. Seattle, 1981.

Holquist, P. *Making War, Forging Revolution: Russia's Continuum of Crisis, 1914–1921*. Cambridge, Mass., 2002.

Hunczak, T., ed. *The Ukraine, 1917–1921: A Study in Revolution*. Cambridge, Mass., 1977.

Keep, J. *The Russian Revolution: A Study in Mass Mobilization*. New York, 1976.

Kennan, G. F. *Soviet-American Relations, 1917–1920*. Vol. 1, *Russia Leaves the War*. Vol. 2, *The Decision to Intervene*. Princeton, N.J., 1956, 1958.

Koenker, D. *Moscow Workers and the 1917 Revolution*. Princeton, N.J., 1981.

Koenker, D. P. and W. G. Rosenberg. *Strikes and Revolution in Russia, 1917*. Princeton, N.J., 1989.

Koenker, D. P., W. G. Rosenberg, and R. G. Suny, eds. *Party, State, and Society in the Russian Civil War*. Bloomington, Ind., 1989.

Laqueur, W. *The Fate of the Revolution: Interpretations of Soviet History*. New York, 1967.

Lehovich, D. V. *White Against Red: The Life of General Anton Denikin*. New York, 1974.

Lenin, V. I. *Collected Works*. New York, 1927–42.

Lenin, V. I. *Imperialism: The Highest Stage of Capitalism*. New York, 1927.

Lenin, V. I. *The State and Revolution*. New York, 1927.

Lenin, V. I. *What Is to Be Done?* Moscow, 1947.

Lewin, M. *Lenin's Last Struggle*. New York, 1968.

Luckett, R. *The White Generals: An Account of the White Movement and the Russian Civil War*. New York, 1987.

Mally, L. *Culture of the Future: The Proletkult Movement in Revolutionary Russia*. Berkeley, 1990.

McAuley, M. *Bread and Justice: State and Society in Petrograd, 1917–1922*. Oxford, 1991.

Mawdsley, E. *The Russian Civil War*. Boston, 1987.

Medvedev, R. A. *The October Revolution*. Translated by G. Saunders. Foreword by H. G. Salisbury. New York, 1979.

Melgunov, S. P. *The Bolshevik Seizure of Power*. Edited by S. G. Pushkarev and B. S. Pushkarev. Translated by J. Beaver. Santa Barbara, Calif., 1972.

Payne, R. *The Life and Death of Lenin*. New York, 1964.

Pipes, R. *The Formation of the Soviet Union: Communism and Nationalism, 1917–1923*. Cambridge, Mass., 1954.

Pipes, R., ed. *Revolutionary Russia: A Symposium*. 2nd ed. rev. Cambridge, Mass., 1968.

Possony, S. T. *Lenin: The Compulsive Revolutionary*. Chicago, 1964.

Rabinowitch, A. *The Bolsheviks Come to Power: The Revolution of 1917 in Petrograd*. New York, 1976.

Rabinowitch, A. *Prelude to Revolution: The Petrograd Bolsheviks and the July 1917 Uprising*. Bloomington, Ind., 1968.

Radkey, O. H. *The Agrarian Foes of Bolshevism: Promise and Default of the Russian Socialist Revolutionaries, February to October, 1917.* New York, 1958.

Radkey, O. H. *The Election to the Russian Constituent Assembly of 1917.* Cambridge, Mass., 1950.

Radkey, O. H. *The Sickle under the Hammer: The Russian Socialist Revolutionaries in the Early Months of Soviet Rule.* New York, 1963.

Raleigh, D. J. *Revolution on the Volga: 1917 in Saratov.* Ithaca, N.Y., 1986.

Raskolnikov. F. F. *Kronstadt and Petrograd in 1917.* Translated and annotated by B. Pearce. London, 1982.

Reed, J. *Ten Days That Shook the World.* New York, 1960.

Reshetar, J. S. *The Ukrainian Revolution, 1917–1920.* Princeton, N.J., 1952.

Rosenberg, A. *A History of Bolshevism.* Garden City, N.Y., 1967.

Rosenberg, W. G. *A. I. Denikin and the Anti-Bolshevik Movement in South Russia.* Amherst, Mass., 1961.

Rosenberg, W. G. *Liberals in the Russian Revolution: The Constitutional Democratic Party, 1917–1921.* Princeton, N.J., 1974.

Rosmer, A. *Moscow under Lenin.* Translated by I. Birchall. New York, 1972.

Serge, V. *Year One of the Russian Revolution.* Translated by P. Sedgwick. New York, 1972.

Shapiro, L. *The Origins of the Communist Autocracy: Political Opposition in the Soviet State: First Phase, 1917–1922.* Cambridge, Mass., 1955.

Smith, E. E. *The Young Stalin.* New York, 1967.

Smith, S. A. *Red Petrograd: Revolution in the Factories.* Cambridge, 1983.

Stewart, G. *The White Armies of Russia.* New York, 1933.

Stites, R. *Revolutionary Dreams: Utopian Vision and Experimental Life in the Russian Revolution.* New York, 1989.

Suny, R. G. *The Baku Commune, 1917–1918: Class and Nationality in the Russian Revolution.* Princeton, N.J., 1972.

Tirado, I. A. *Young Guard! The Communist Youth League, Petrograd 1917–1920.* New York, 1988.

Ukraintsev, N. "A Document in the Kornilov Affair." *Soviet Studies* (October 1973).

Varnock, E., and H. H. Fisher. *The Testimony of Kolchak and Other Siberian Materials and Documents.* Stanford, 1935.

Wade, R. *The Russian Revolution, 1917.* Cambridge, 2000.

Wheeler-Bennett, J. W. *The Forgotten Peace: Brest-Litovsk.* New York, 1939.

Wildman, A. K. *The End of the Russian Imperial Army.* 2 vols. Princeton, N.J., 1980, 1987.

B. Soviet Period: General

Abramovitch, R. *The Soviet Revolution, 1917–1939.* New York, 1962.

Alliluyeva, S. *Twenty Letters to a Friend.* New York, 1967.

Amalrik, A. *Involuntary Journey to Siberia.* New York, 1970.

Amalrik, A. *Notes of a Revolutionary.* Translated by G. Daniels. New York, 1982.

Amalrik, A. *Will the Soviet Union Survive until 1984?* New York, 1970.

Benet, S., ed. and trans. *The Village of Viriatino: An Ethnographic Study of a Russian Village from before the Revolution to the Present.* Garden City, N.Y., 1970.

Berdiaev, N. *The Origins of Russian Communism.* London, 1948.

Berdiaev, N. *The Russian Revolution: Two Essays on Its Implications in Religion and Psychology.* London, 1931.

Bialer, S. *Stalin's Successors: Leadership, Stability, and Change in the Soviet Union.* Cambridge, 1980.

Breslauer, G. W. *Khrushchev and Brezhnev as Leaders: Building Authority in Soviet Politics.* London, 1982.

Chalidze, V. *To Defend These Rights: Human Rights and the Soviet Union.* Translated by G. Daniels. New York, 1974.

Cohen, S. F. *Bukharin and the Bolshevik Revolution.* New York, 1973.

Cohen, S. *Rethinking the Soviet Experience: Politics and History since 1917.* New York, 1985.

Conquest, R. *Stalin and the Kirov Murder.* New York, 1989.

Crossman, R., ed. *The God That Failed.* London, 1950.

Daniels, R. V. *A Documentary History of Communism.* New York, 1960.

Daniels, R. V. *Russia: The Roots of Confrontation.* Cambridge, Mass., 1985.

Daniels, R. V., ed. *The Stalin Revolution: Fulfillment or Betrayal of Communism?* Boston, 1965.

Davies, S. *Popular Opinion in Stalin's Russia: Terror, Propaganda and Dissent, 1934–1941.* New York, 1997.

Deutscher, I. *The Prophet Armed: Trotsky, 1879–1921.* New York, 1954.

Deutscher, I. *The Prophet Outcast: Trotsky, 1929–1940.* New York, 1963.

Deutscher, I. *The Prophet Unarmed: Trotsky, 1921–1929.* New York, 1959.

Deutscher, I. *Stalin: A Political Biography.* New York, 1949. 2nd ed., 1966.

Dmytryshyn, B. *USSR: A Concise History.* New York, 1971.

Dornberg, J. *Brezhnev: The Masks of Power.* New York, 1974.

Dunn, S., and E. Dunn. *The Peasants of Central Russia.* New York, 1967.

Farnsworth, B. *Alexandra Kollontai: Socialism, Feminism, and the Bolshevik Revolution.* Stanford, 1980.

Feshbach, M., with A. Friendly, Jr. *Ecocide in the USSR: Health and Nature under Siege.* New York, 1992.

Fischer, G. *Soviet Opposition to Stalin: A Case Study in World War II.* Westport, Conn., 1970.

Fitzpatrick, S., A. Rabinowitch, and R. Stites, eds. *Russia in the Era of NEP.* Bloomington, Ind., 1991.

Friedrich, C. J., and Z. K. Brzezinski. *Totalitarian Dictatorship and Autocracy.* Cambridge, Mass., 1956.

Galanskov, I., et al. *The Trial of the Four: A Collection of Materials on the Case of Galanskov, Ginzberg, Dobrovolsky and Lashkova, 1967–68.* Edited by P. Reddaway. Translated by J. Saprets, H. Sternberg, and D. Weissbort. New York, 1972.

Geiger, H. K. *The Family in Soviet Russia.* Cambridge, Mass., 1968.

Gerstenmaier, C. *The Voices of the Silent.* Translated by S. Hecker. New York, 1972.

Hahn, W. G. *Postwar Soviet Politics: The Fall of Zhdanov and the Defeat of Moderation, 1946–53.* Ithaca, N.Y., 1982.

Harding, N. *Leninism.* Durham, N.C., 1996.

Heller, M., with A. Nekrich. *Utopia in Power: The History of the Soviet Union from 1917 to the Present.* New York, 1986.

Hendel, S., and R. Braham, eds. *The USSR after 50 Years: Promise and Reality.* New York, 1967.

Hindus, M. *Red Bread: Collectivization in a Russian Village.* Foreword by R. G. Suny. Bloomington, Ind., 1988.

Hosking, G. *The First Socialist Society: A History of the Soviet Union from Within.* Cambridge, Mass., 1985.

Khrushchev, N. S. *Khrushchev Remembers.* Vol. 1, edited and translated by S. Talbott. Introduction and Commentary by E. Crankshaw. Vol. 2. *The Last Testament.* Edited and translated by S. Talbott. Foreword by E. Crankshaw. Introduction by J. L. Schecter. Boston and Toronto, 1970, 1974.

Knight, A. *Beria: Stalin's First Lieutenant.* Princeton, N.J., 1996.

Lapidus, G. W. *Women in Soviet Society: Equality, Development, and Social Change.* Berkeley, 1978.

Lapidus, G. W., ed. *Women, Work and Family in the Soviet Union.* Armonk, N.Y., 1982.

Mandelshtam, N. *Hope Abandoned.* Translated by M. Hayward. New York, 1974.

Mandelshtam, N. *Hope Against Hope.* Translated by M. Hayward. New York, 1970.

Marcuse, H. *Soviet Marxism.* New York, 1958.

McNeal, R. *Stalin: Man and Ruler.* New York, 1988.

McNeal, R. H. *The Bolshevik Tradition: Lenin, Stalin, Khrushchev.* Englewood Cliffs, N.J., 1963.

McNeal, R. H., ed. *Lenin, Stalin, Khrushchev: Voices of Bolshevism.* Englewood Cliffs, N.J., 1963.

Medvedev, R. *Let History Judge. The Origins and Consequences of Stalinism.* Edited by D. Joravsky and G. Haupt. Translated by C. Taylor. New York, 1971.

Medvedev, R. *On Socialist Democracy.* Edited and translated by E. de Kadt. New York, 1975.

Medvedev, Zh. A., and R. A. Medvedev. *A Question of Madness.* New York, 1971.

Meyer, A. *Communism.* New York, 1960.

Meyer, A. *Leninism.* Cambridge, Mass., 1957.

Meyer, A. *Marxism.* Cambridge, Mass., 1954.

Nettl, J. P. *The Soviet Achievement.* London, 1967.

On Trial: The Case of Sinyavsky (Tertz) and Daniel (Arzhak). Documents edited by L. Labedz and M. Hayward. Russian text translated by M. Harari and M. Hayward. French texts translated by M. Villiers. London, 1967.

Pankratova, A. M., ed. *A History of the USSR.* Compiled by K. V. Bazilevich et al. 3 vols. New York, 1970.

Rabinowitch, A., and J. Rabinowitch, eds. *Revolution and Politics in Russia. Essays in Memory of B. I. Nicolaevsky.* Bloomington, Ind., 1972.

Ratushinskaya, I. *In the Beginning.* Translated by A. Kojevnikov. New York, 1991.

Rauch, B. von. *A History of Soviet Russia.* New York, 1957.

Reddaway, P., ed. and trans.*Uncensored Russia: Protest and Dissent in the Soviet Union.* The unofficial Moscow journal *A Chronicle of Current Events.* London, 1972.

Reve, K. van het, ed. *Dear Comrade: Pavel Litvinov and the Voices of Soviet Citizens in Dissent.* New York, 1969.

Rieber, A. J., and R. C. Nelson. *A Study of the USSR and Communism: An Historical Approach.* Chicago, 1962.

Rostow, W. W. *The Dynamics of Soviet Society.* New York, 1963.

Rothberg, A. *The Heirs of Stalin: Dissidence and the Soviet Regime, 1953–1970.* Ithaca, N.Y., 1972.

Ruder, C. A. *Making History for Stalin: The Story of the Belomor Canal.* Gainesville, Fla., 1998.

Schlesinger, R. *Changing Attitudes in Soviet Russia: The Family.* London, 1949.

Service, R. *Lenin: a Political Life.* Vol. 3. Bloomington, Ind., 1995.

Shatz, M. S. *Soviet Dissent in Historical Perspective.* Cambridge, 1981.

Shentalinskii, V. *Arrested Voices: Resurrecting the Disappeared Writers of the Soviet Regime.* New York, 1996.

Siegelbaum, L. H. *The Soviet State and Society between Revolutions, 1918–1929.* Cambridge, 1992.

Souvarine, B. *Stalin, A Critical Survey of Bolshevism.* New York, 1939.

Suny, R. G. *The Soviet Experiment: Russia, the USSR, and the Successor States.* New York, 1998.

Treadgold, D. W. *Twentieth-Century Russia.* Chicago, 1959. 6th ed., 1987.

Trotsky, L. *The Revolution Betrayed.* New York, 1937.

Trotsky, L. *Stalin: An Appraisal of the Man and His Influence.* New York, 1941.

Tucker, R. C. *Stalin as Revolutionary, 1879–1929: A Study in History and Personality.* New York, 1973.

Tucker, R. C. *Stalin in Power: The Revolution from Above, 1929–1941.* New York, 1990.

Ulam, A. B. *Stalin: The Man and His Era.* New York, 1973.

Von Laue, T. H. *The Global City.* Philadelphia and New York, 1969.

Von Laue, T. H. *Why Lenin? Why Stalin?* Philadelphia and New York, 1964.

Webb, S., and B. Webb. *Soviet Communism. A New Civilization?* 2 vols. New York, 1936.

Werth, A. *Russia: The Post-War Years.* New York, 1972.

Westwood, J. N. *Endurance and Endeavour: Russian History, 1812–1980.* 3rd ed. The Short Oxford History of the Modern World. Oxford, 1987.

C. Ideology, Government, Administration, and Law

Armstrong, J. A. *The Politics of Totalitarianism: The Communist Party of the Soviet Union.* New York, 1961.

Armstrong, J. A. *The Soviet Bureaucratic Elite: A Case Study of the Ukrainian Apparatus.* New York, 1961.

Avtorkhanov, A. *Stalin and the Soviet Communist Party.* Munich, 1959.

Azrael, J. R. *Managerial Power and Soviet Politics.* Cambridge, Mass., 1966.

Barghoorn, F. C. *Soviet Russian Nationalism.* New York, 1956.

Barron, J. *KGB: The Secret Work of Soviet Agents.* New York, 1974.

Berman, H. J. *Justice in Russia.* Cambridge, Mass., 1950. Rev. ed., 1963.

Berman, H. J., and M. Kerner. *Soviet Military Law and Administration.* Cambridge, Mass., 1955.

Berman, H. J., and P. B. Maggs. *Disarmament Inspection under Soviet Law.* Dobbs Ferry, N.Y., 1967.

Berman, H. J., and J. W. Spindler, trans. *Soviet Criminal Law and Procedure: The RSFSR Code.* Introduction and analysis by H. J. Berman. Cambridge, Mass., 1965.

Brzezinski, Z. K. *The Permanent Purge.* Cambridge, Mass., 1956.

Conquest, R. *The Great Terror: A Reassessment.* New York, 1990.

Conquest, R. *The Great Terror: Stalin's Purge of the Thirties.* New York, 1971.

Dallin, A., and T. B. Larson, eds. *Soviet Politics since Khrushchev.* Englewood Cliffs, N.J., 1968.

Daniels, R. V. *The Conscience of the Revolution: Communist Opposition in Soviet Russia.* Cambridge, Mass., 1960.

Deacon, R. *A History of the Russian Secret Service.* New York, 1972.

Dinerstein, H. S., and L. Goure. *Communism and the Russian Peasant.* Glencoe, Ill., 1955.

Dinerstein, H. S., and L. Goure. *War and the Soviet Union.* New York, 1962.

Erickson, J. *The Soviet High Command: A Military-Political History, 1918–1941.* New York, 1962.

Fainsod, M. *How Russia Is Ruled.* Cambridge, Mass., 1953.

Fainsod, M. *Smolensk under Soviet Rule.* Cambridge, Mass., 1958.

Fischer, G. *Soviet Opposition to Stalin.* Cambridge, Mass., 1952.

Getty, J. A. and R. Manning, eds. *Stalinist Terror: New Perspectives.* Cambridge, 1993.

Graham, L. R. *The Soviet Academy of Sciences and the Communist Party, 1927–1932.* Princeton, N.J., 1967.

Gsovsky, V. *Soviet Civil Law.* 2 vols. Ann Arbor, Mich., 1948, 1949.

Gsovsky, V., and K. Grybowski. *Government, Law and Courts in the Soviet Union and Eastern Europe.* New York, 1959.

Hahn, W. G. *Postwar Soviet Politics: The Fall of Zhdanov and the Defeat of Moderation, 1946–1953.* Ithaca, N.Y., 1982.

Hammer, D. P. *USSR: The Politics of Oligarchy.* Hinsdale, Ill., 1974.

Harcave, S. *The Structure and Functioning of the Lower Party Organizations in the Soviet Union.* University, Ala., 1954.

Harvey, M. L., L. Goure, and V. Prokofieff. *Science and Technology as an Instrument of Soviet Policy.* Washington, D.C., 1972.

Hazard, J. N. *The Soviet System of Government.* Chicago, 1957.

Hendel, S., ed. *The Soviet Crucible: Soviet Government in Theory and Practice.* Princeton, N.J., 1960.

Inkeles, A., and R. A. Bauer. *The Soviet Citizen.* Cambridge, Mass., 1959.

Inkeles, A., R. Bauer, and C. Kluckhohn. *How the Soviet System Works.* Cambridge, Mass., 1956.

Karcz, J., ed. *Soviet and East European Agriculture.* Berkeley, 1967.

Kassof, A., ed. *Prospects for Soviet Society.* New York, 1968.

Kotkin, S. *Magnetic Mountain: Stalinism as a Civilization.* Berkeley, 1995.

Kucherov, S. *The Organs of Soviet Administration of Justice: Their History and Operation.* London, 1970.

Leites, N., and E. Bernaut. *Ritual of Liquidation: The Case of the Moscow Trials.* Glencoe, Ill., 1954.

Leonard, W. *The Kremlin since Stalin.* New York, 1962.

Levytsky, B. *The Uses of Terror. The Soviet Secret Police, 1917–1970.* Translated by H. Piehler. New York, 1972.

Malia, M. E. *The Soviet Tragedy: A History of Socialism in Russia, 1917–1991.* New York, 1994.

Matthews, M. *Class and Society in Soviet Russia.* New York, 1972.

Matthews, M., ed. *Soviet Government: A Selection of Official Documents on Internal Policies.* New York, 1974.

Meissner, B. *The Communist Party of the Soviet Union: Party Leadership.* New York, 1956.

Moore, B. *Soviet Politics: The Dilemma of Power.* Cambridge, Mass., 1950.

Odom, W. E. *The Soviet Volunteers: Modernization and Bureaucracy in a Public Mass Organization.* Princeton, N.J., 1973.

Pipes, R. *Russia under the Bolshevik Regime.* New York, 1994.

Reshetar, J. S. *A Concise History of the Communist Party of the Soviet Union.* New York, 1960.

Rigby, T. H. *Communist Party Membership in the USSR, 1917–1967.* Princeton, N.J., 1968.

Schapiro, L. B. *The Communist Party of the Soviet Union.* New York, 1971.

Schlesinger, R. *Soviet Legal Theory.* London, 1945.

Schuman, F. *Government in the Soviet Union.* New York, 1961.

Scott, D. J. R. *Russian Political Institutions.* New York, 1958.

Solomon, P. H., Jr. *Soviet Criminal Justice under Stalin.* Cambridge, 1996.

Sorenson, R. *The Life and Death of Soviet Trade Unionism.* New York, 1969.

Swearer, H. R., and M. Rush. *The Politics of Succession in the USSR: Materials on Khrushchev's Rise to Leadership.* Boston, 1964.

Towster, J. *Political Power in the USSR, 1917–1947.* New York, 1948.

Tucker, R. C. *The Soviet Political Mind.* New York, 1963.

Tucker, R. C., ed. *Stalinism: Essays in Historical Interpretation.* New York, 1977.

Ulam, A. *The New Face of Soviet Totalitarianism.* Cambridge, Mass., 1963.

Ulam, A. *The Unfinished Revolution: An Essay on the Sources of Influence of Marxism and Communism.* New York, 1960.

Vyshinsky, A. *The Law of the Soviet State.* New York, 1948.

Walicki, A. *Marxism and the Leap to the Kingdom of Freedom: The Rise and Fall of the Communist Utopia.* Stanford, 1995.

Weinberg, E. A. *The Development of Sociology in the Soviet Union.* Boston, 1974.

Wolin, S., and R. Slusser, eds. *The Soviet Secret Police.* New York, 1957.

D. Economic Development

Ball, A. M. *Russia's Last Capitalists: The Nepmen, 1921–1929.* Berkeley, 1987.

Baykov, A. *The Development of the Soviet Economic System.* Cambridge, 1947.

Bergson, A. *The Economics of Soviet Planning.* New Haven, Conn., 1964.

Bergson, A. *Planning and Productivity under Soviet Socialism.* New York, 1968.

Bergson, A. *Real National Income of Soviet Russia since 1928.* Cambridge, Mass., 1961.

Bergson, A. *Soviet Economic Growth.* Evanston, Ill., 1953.

Bergson, A. *The Structure of Soviet Wages.* Cambridge, Mass., 1944.

Bergson, A., and S. Kuznets, eds. *Economic Trends in the Soviet Union.* Cambridge, Mass., 1963.

Campbell, R. *Soviet Economic Power: Its Organization, Growth and Challenge.* Boston, 1960.

Dallin, D. J., and B. I. Nicolaevsky. *Forced Labor in Soviet Russia.* New Haven, Conn., 1947.

Davies, R. W. *The Industrialization of Soviet Russia.* 2 vols. Cambridge, Mass., 1980.

Davies, R. W. *The Socialist Offensive: The Collectivization of Soviet Agriculture, 1929–30,* Cambridge, Mass., 1980.

Deutscher, I. *Soviet Trade Unions.* London, 1950.

De Witt, N. *Education and Professional Employment in the USSR.* Washington, D.C., 1961.

Dobb, M. *Soviet Economic Development Since the 1917 Revolution.* London, 1948.

Erlich, A. *The Soviet Industrialization Debate, 1924–28.* Cambridge, Mass., 1960.

Grossman, G. "Subverted Sovereignty: Historic Role of the Soviet Underground." *The Tunnel at the End of the Light: Privatization, Business Networks, and Economic Transformation in Russia,* edited by Stephen S. Cohen, Andrew Schwartz, and John Zysman. Berkeley, 1998.

Gregory, P. R., and R. C. Stuart. *Soviet Economic Structure and Performance.* New York, 1974.

Grossman, G. "The Economy at Middle Age." *Problems of Communism* (March–April 1976).

Grossman, G. "The Solitary Society: A Philosophical Issue in Communist Economic Reforms." In *Essays in Socialism and Planning in Honor of Carl Landauer,* edited by G. Grossman. Englewood Cliffs, N.J., 1970.

Grossman, G., ed. *Money and Plan: Financial Aspects of East European Economic Reforms.* Berkeley, 1968.

Holzman, F. *Soviet Taxation.* Cambridge, Mass., 1955.

Holzman, F., ed. *Readings on the Soviet Economy.* Chicago, 1962.

Jasny, N. *The Socialized Agriculture of the USSR.* Stanford, 1949.

Jasny, N. *Soviet Economy during the Plan Era.* Stanford, 1951.

Jasny, N. *Soviet Industrialization, 1928–1932.* Chicago, 1961.

Laird, R. D., ed. *Soviet Agricultural and Peasant Affairs.* Lawrence, Kans., 1963.

Lewin, M. *Russian Peasants and Soviet Power: A Study of Collectivization.* Translated by I. Nove. Evanston, Ill., 1968.

Lewin, M. "Soviet Policies of Agricultural Procurements before the War." In *Essays in Honor of E. H. Carr,* edited by Ch. Abramsky, and B. I. Williams. Hamden, Conn., 1974.

Moskoff, W. *The Bread of Affliction: The Food Supply in the USSR during World War II.* Cambridge, 1990.

Nove, A. *An Economic History of the USSR.* London, 1969.

Pryde, P. R. *Conservation in the Soviet Union.* Cambridge, 1972.

Quigley, J. *The Soviet Foreign Trade Monopoly: Institutions and Laws.* Columbus, Ohio, 1974.

Schwartz, H. *Russia's Soviet Economy.* 2nd ed. New York, 1954.

Schwartz, H. *The Soviet Economy since Stalin*. Philadelphia, 1965.

Schwarz, S. *Labor in the Soviet Union*. New York, 1952.

E. Foreign Affairs

Adams, A. E. *Readings in Soviet Foreign Policy: Theory and Practice*. Boston, 1961.

Barber, J. and M. Harrison. *The Soviet Home Front 1941–1945: A Social and Economic History of the USSR in World War II*. London, 1991.

Barghoorn, F. C. *The Soviet Cultural Offensive: The Role of Cultural Diplomacy in Soviet Foreign Policy*. Princeton, N.J., 1960.

Barghoorn, F. C. *Soviet Foreign Propaganda*. Princeton, N.J., 1964.

Beloff, M. *The Foreign Policy of Soviet Russia, 1929–1941*. 2 vols. New York, 1947, 1949.

Beloff, M. *Soviet Foreign Policy in the Far East, 1944–1951*. London, 1953.

Bishop, D. G., ed. *Soviet Foreign Relations: Documents and Readings*. Syracuse, N.Y., 1952.

Brandt, C. *Stalin's Failure in China, 1924–1927*. Cambridge, Mass., 1958.

Brzezinski, Z. K. *The Soviet Bloc: Unity and Conflict*. Cambridge, Mass., 1960. Rev. ed., 1967.

Carell, P. *Scorched Earth: The Russian-German War, 1943–1944*. Translated by E. Osers. Boston, 1970.

Carr, E. H. *The Soviet Impact on the Western World*. London, 1946

Carr, E. H. *Twilight of the Comintern, 1930–1935*. New York, 1982.

Cattell, D. T. *Communism and the Spanish Civil War*. Berkeley, 1955.

Chew, A. F. *The White Death: The Epic of the Soviet-Finnish Winter War*. East Lansing, Mich., 1971.

Dallin, A. *German Rule in Russia, 1941–1945: A Study of Occupation Policies*. New York, 1957.

Dallin, D. J. *Soviet Russia and the Far East*. New Haven, Conn., 1948.

Dallin, D. J. *Soviet Russia's Foreign Policy, 1939–1942*. New Haven, Conn., 1942.

Degras, J. *The Communist International, 1919–1943*. New York, 1956.

Degras, J. *Soviet Documents on Foreign Policy, 1917–1941*. 3 vols. New York, 1951–53.

Degras, J., ed. *Calendar of Soviet Documents on Foreign Policy, 1917–1941*. London, 1948.

Erickson, J. *The Road to Stalingrad: Stalin's War with Germany*. New York, 1975.

Eudin, X., and H. H. Fisher. *Soviet Russia and the West, 1920–1927*. Stanford, 1957.

Eudin, X., and R. C. North, eds. *Soviet Russia and the East, 1920–1927*. Stanford, 1957.

Farnsworth, B. *William C. Bullitt and the Soviet Union*. Bloomington, Ind., 1967.

Fischer, L. *The Soviets in World Affairs, 1917–1929*. Princeton, N.J., 1951.

Fischer, R. *Stalin and German Communism*. Cambridge, Mass., 1948.

Floyd, D. *Mao against Khrushchev: A Short History of the Sino-Soviet Conflict*. New York, 1963.

Gaddis, J. L. *We Now Know: Rethinking Cold War History*. New York, 1997.

Garthoff, R. L. *Soviet Strategy in the Nuclear Age*. New York, 1962.

Gleason, A. *Totalitarianism: The Inner History of the Cold War*. New York, 1995.

Gorodetsky, G. *Grand Illusion: Stalin and the German Invasion of Russia*, New Haven, Conn., 1999.

Griffith, W. E. *Communism in Europe: Continuity, Change and the Sino-Soviet Dispute*. Cambridge, Mass., 1966.

Gruber, H. *International Communism in the Era of Lenin: A Documentary History*. Greenwich, Conn., 1967.

Harvey, D. L., and L. C. Ciccoritti. *U.S.-Soviet Cooperation in Space*. Washington, D.C., 1974.

Holloway, D. *Stalin and the Bomb: The Soviet Union and Atomic Energy, 1939–1956*. New Haven, Conn., 1994.

Jamgotch, N., Jr. *Soviet-East European Dialogue: International Relations of a New Type.* Stanford, 1968.

Kapur, H. *Soviet Russia and Asia, 1917–1927: A Study of Soviet Policy towards Turkey, Iran and Afghanistan.* London, 1966; New York. 1967.

Kennan, G. F. *Russia and the West under Lenin and Stalin.* Boston, 1961.

Kennan, G. F. *Soviet Foreign Policy, 1917–1941.* Princeton, N.J., 1960.

Laqueur, W. Z. *The Soviet Union and the Middle East.* New York, 1959.

Laserson, M. M., ed. *The Development of Soviet Foreign Policy in Europe, 1917–1942: A Selection of Documents.* International Conciliation, no. 386 (January 1943).

Leach, B. A. *German Strategy Against Russia, 1939–1941.* Oxford, 1973.

Mackintosh, J. *Strategy and Tactics of Soviet Foreign Policy.* New York, 1962.

Maisky, I. *Memoirs of a Soviet Ambassador: The War 1939–1943.* New York, 1968.

Menon, R. *Soviet Power and the Third World.* New Haven, Connecticut, and London, 1986.

Moore, H. L. *Soviet Far Eastern Policy, 1931–1945.* Princeton, N.J., 1945.

Mosely, P. E. *The Kremlin and World Politics.* New York, 1961.

Mosely, P. E. *Russia after Stalin.* New York, 1955.

Mosely, P. E., ed. *The Soviet Union, 1922–1962: A Foreign Affairs Reader.* New York and London, 1963.

Nation, R. *Black Earth, Red Star: A History of Soviet Security Policy.* Ithaca, N.Y., 1992.

Nekrich, A. M. *Pariahs, Partners, Predators: German-Soviet Relations, 1922–1941.* Edited and translated by Gregory L. Freeze; with a foreword by Adam B. Ulam. New York, 1997.

North, R. C. *Moscow and Chinese Communists.* 2nd ed. Stanford, 1962.

O'Connor, T. *Diplomacy and Revolution: G. V. Chicherin and Soviet Foreign Affairs, 1918–1930.* Ames, Ia., 1988.

Pethybridge, R., ed. *The Development of the Communist Bloc.* Boston, 1965.

Ro'i, Y. *From Encroachment to Involvement: A Documentary Study of Soviet Policy in the Middle East, 1945–1973.* New York, 1974.

Rubinstein, A. Z. *Soviet Foreign Policy Since World War II: Imperial and Global.* Cambridge, Mass., 1981.

Rubinstein, A. Z., ed. *The Foreign Policy of the Soviet Union.* New York, 1960.

Rubinstein, A. Z., ed. *Soviet and Chinese Influence in the Third World.* New York, 1975.

Seaton, A. *The Battle for Moscow, 1941–1942.* New York, 1971.

Seaton, A. *The Russo-German War, 1941–45.* New York, 1971.

Seton-Watson, H. *The East European Revolution.* 3rd ed. New York, 1956.

Seton-Watson, H. *From Lenin to Khrushchev: The History of World Communism.* New York, 1951.

Shotwell, J. T., and M. M. Laserson. *Poland and Russia, 1919–1945.* New York, 1945.

Shulman, M. D. *Beyond the Cold War.* New Haven, Conn., 1966.

Shulman, M. D. *Stalin's Foreign Policy Reappraised.* Cambridge, Mass., 1963.

Sontag, R. J., and J. S. Beddie, eds. *Nazi-Soviet Relations, 1939–1941: Documents from the Archives of the German Foreign Office.* Washington, D.C., 1948.

Swearingen, A. R., and P. Langer, *Red Flag in Japan.* Cambridge, Mass., 1952.

Ulam, A. B. *Expansion and Coexistence: A History of Soviet Foreign Policy, 1917–1967.* New York, 1968.

Ulam, A. B. *Titoism and the Cominform.* Cambridge, Mass., 1952.

Ullman, R. H. *Anglo-Soviet Relations, 1917–21.* Vol. 1, *Intervention and the War.* Vol. 2, *Britain and the Russian Civil War, November 1918–February 1920.* Vol. 3, *Anglo-Soviet Accord.* Princeton, N.J., 1961, 1968, 1973.

Villmow, J. R. *The Soviet Union and Eastern Europe.* Englewood Cliffs, N.J., 1965.

Warth, R. *Soviet Russia in World Politics.* New York, 1963.

Weinberg, G. *Germany and the Soviet Union, 1939–1941.* Leiden, 1954.

Weiner, A. *Making Sense of War: The Second World War and the Fate of the Bolshevik Revolution.* Princeton, N.J., 2001.

Werth, A. *Russia at War, 1941–1945.* New York, 1964.

Zinner, Paul E. *Communist Strategy and Tactics in Czechoslovakia, 1918–1948.* New York, 1963.

F. Nationalities

Armstrong, J. A. *Ukrainian Nationalism, 1939–1945.* New York, 1955.

Browne, M., ed. *Ferment in the Ukraine: Documents by V. Chornovil, I. Kandyba, L. Lukyanenko, V. Moroz and Others.* New York, 1971.

Carrere d'Encausse, H. *Decline of an Empire: Soviet Socialist Republics in Revolt.* New York, 1980.

Carrere d'Encausse, H. *The Great Challenge: Nationalities and the Bolshevik State, 1917–1930.* New York, 1992.

Carve, Sir O. *Soviet Empire: The Turks of Central Asia and Stalinism.* London, 1967.

Comrie, B. *The Languages of the Soviet Union.* Cambridge, 1981.

Conquest, R. *The Nation Killers: The Soviet Deportation of Nationalities.* London, 1970.

Dmytryshyn, B. *Moscow and the Ukraine, 1918–1952: A Study of Russian Bolshevik Nationality Policy.* New York, 1956.

Dunlop, J. B. *The Faces of Contemporary Russian Nationalism.* Princeton, N.J., 1983.

Dunn, S. P. *Cultural Processes in the Baltic Area under Soviet Rule.* Berkeley, 1967.

Fedyshyn, O. S. *Germany's Drive to the East and the Ukrainian Revolution, 1917–1918.* New Brunswick, N.J., 1971.

Gitelman, Z. Y. *Jewish Nationality and Soviet Politics: The Jewish Sections of the CPSU, 1917–1930.* Princeton, N.J., 1972.

Goldhagen, E., ed. *Ethnic Minorities in the Soviet Union.* New York, 1967.

Hovannisian, R. G. *The Republic of Armenia.* Vol. 1, *The First Year, 1918–1919.* Berkeley, 1971.

Israel, G. *The Jews in Russia.* Translated by S. L. Chernoff. New York, 1975.

Katz, Z., R. Rogers, and F. Harned, eds. *Handbook of Major Soviet Nationalities.* New York and London, 1975.

Kazemzadeh, F. *The Struggle for Transcaucasia, 1917–1921.* New York, 1961.

Kirchner, W. *The Rise of the Baltic Question.* Westport, Conn., 1970.

Kolarz, W. *Russia and Her Colonies.* New York, 1953.

Kolasky, J. *Education in the Soviet Ukraine.* Toronto, 1968.

Kolasky, J. *Two Years in Soviet Ukraine: A Canadian's Personal Account of Russian Oppression and the Growing Opposition.* Toronto, 1970.

Levin, N. *The Jews in the Soviet Union Since 1917: Paradox of Survival.* 2 vols. New York and London, 1990.

Lubachko, I. S. *Belorussia under Soviet Rule, 1917–1957.* Lexington, Ky., 1972.

Martin, T. *The Affirmative Action Empire: Nations and Nationalism in the Soviet Union, 1923–1939.* Ithaca, N.Y., 2001.

Massell, G. J. *The Surrogate Proletariat: Moslem Women and Revolutionary Strategies in Soviet Central Asia, 1919–1929.* Princeton, N.J., 1974.

Nahaylo, B., and V. Swoboda. *Soviet Disunion: A History of the Nationalities Problem in the USSR.* New York, 1991.

Nove, A., and J. A. Newth. *The Soviet Middle East.* London, 1967.

Peters, V. *Nestor Makhno: The Life of an Anarchist.* Winnipeg, 1970.

Ro'i, Y. and A. Beker. *Jewish Culture and Identity in the Soviet Union.* New York, 1991.

Rumer, B. Z. *Soviet Central Asia: "A Tragic Experiment."* Boston, 1989.

Schwarz, S. *The Jews in the Soviet Union*. Syracuse, N.Y., 1951.

Sullivant, R. S. *Soviet Politics and the Ukraine, 1917–1957*. New York, 1962.

Tarulis, A. N. *Soviet Policy toward the Baltic States, 1918–1940*. Notre Dame, Ind., 1959.

von Rauch, G. *The Baltic States: The Years of Independence: Estonia, Latvia, Lithuania, 1917–1940*. Translated by G. Onn. Berkeley, 1974.

G. Society, Culture, Education, Religion

Bailes, K. E. *Technology and Society under Lenin and Stalin: Origins of the Soviet Technical Intelligentsia, 1917–1941*. Princeton, N.J., 1978.

Bereday, G., and J. Pennar, eds. *The Politics of Soviet Education*. New York, 1960.

Bonnell, V. *Iconography of Power: Soviet Political Posters under Lenin and Stalin*. Berkeley, 1997.

Bowlt, J. E., ed. and trans. *Russian Art of the Avant-garde: Theory and Criticism, 1902–1934*. New York, 1988.

Boym, S. *Common Places: Mythologies of Everyday Life in Russia*. Cambridge, Mass., 1994.

Brown, E. J. *The Proletarian Episode in Soviet Literature, 1929–1932*. New York, 1953.

Brown, E. J. *Russian Literature since the Revolution*. New York, 1963, 1982.

Churchward, L. G. *The Soviet Intelligentsia: An Essay on the Social Structure and Roles of Soviet Intellectuals during the 1960's*. London and Boston, 1973.

Clark, K. *Petersburg: Crucible of Cultural Revolution*. Cambridge, Mass., 1995.

Clark, K. *The Soviet Novel: History as Ritual*. Chicago, 1981.

Clements, B. E. *Bolshevik Women*. Cambridge, 1997.

Curtiss, J. S. *The Russian Church and the Soviet State, 1917–1950*. Boston, 1953.

Danilov, V. P. *Rural Russia under the New Regime*. Translated by O. Figes. Bloomington, Ind., 1988.

Dunham, V. S. *In Stalin's Time: Middle-Class Values in Soviet Fiction*. New York, 1976.

Dunlop, J. B., R. Haugh, and A. Klimoff, eds. *Aleksandr Solzhenitsyn: Critical Essays and Documentary Materials*. Belmont, Mass., 1973.

Edmondson, L., ed. *Women and Society in Russia and the Soviet Union*. Cambridge, 1992.

Ehrenburg, I. *Memoirs: 1921–1941*. Translated by T. Shebunina. New York, 1963.

Ellis, J. *The Russian Orthodox Church: A Contemporary History*. Bloomington, Ind., 1986.

Enteen, G. M. *The Soviet Scholar-Bureaucrat: M. N. Pokrovskii and the Society of Marxist Historians*. University Park, Pa., 1978.

Evtushenko, E. *A Precocious Autobiography*. New York, 1963.

Fitzpatrick, S. *The Cultural Front: Power and Culture in Revolutionary Russia*. Ithaca, N.Y., 1992.

Fitzpatrick, S. *Education and Social Mobility in the Soviet Union, 1921–1934*. Cambridge, 1979.

Fitzpatrick, S. *Everyday Stalinism: Ordinary Life in Extraordinary Times: Soviet Russia in the 1930s*. New York, 1999.

Fitzpatrick, S. *Stalin's Peasants: Resistance and Survival in the Russian Village after Collectivization*. New York, 1994.

Fitzpatrick, S., ed. *Cultural Revolution in Russia, 1928–1931*. Bloomington, Ind., 1978.

Fletcher, W. C. *A Study in Survival: The Church in Russia, 1927–1943*. New York, 1965.

Geldern, J. von and R. Stites. *Mass Culture in Soviet Russia*. Bloomington, Ind., 1995.

Gleason, A., P. Kenez, and R. Stites, eds. *Bolshevik Culture: Experiment and Order in the Russian Revolution*. Bloomington, Ind., 1985.

Goldman, W. Z. *Women, the State, and Revolution: Soviet Family Policy and Social Life, 1917–1936*. Cambridge, 1993.

Gorsuch, A. *Youth in Revolutionary Russia: Enthusiasts, Bohemians, Delinquents*. Bloomington, Ind., 2000.

Graham, L. *Science and Philosophy in the Soviet Union.* New York, 1972.

Groys, B. *The Total Art of Stalinism: Avant-garde, Aesthetic Dictatorship, and Beyond.* Translated by Charles Rougle. Princeton, N.J., 1992.

Hansson, C., and K. Linden. *Moscow Women: Thirteen Interviews by Carola Hansson and Karin Linden.* Translated by G. Bothmer, G. Blechler, and L. Blechler. Introduction by G. W. Lapidus. New York, 1983.

Hayward, M., and W. C. Fletcher, eds. *Religion and the Soviet State: A Dilemma of Power.* New York, 1969.

Heller, M. *Cogs in the Soviet Wheel: The Formation of Soviet Man.* New York, 1988.

Hosking, G. *Beyond Socialist Realism: Soviet Fiction Since "Ivan Denisovich."* New York, 1980.

Jacoby, S. *Inside Soviet Schools.* New York, 1974.

Johnson, P. *Khrushchev and the Arts: The Politics of Soviet Culture, 1962–1964.* Cambridge, Mass., 1965.

Josephson, P. R. *New Atlantis Revisited: Akademgorodok, the Siberian City of Science.* Princeton, N.J., 1997.

Keep, J., ed. *Contemporary History in the Soviet Mirror.* New York, 1964.

Kenez, P. *The Birth of the Soviet Propaganda State: Soviet Methods of Mass Mobilization, 1917–1930.* Cambridge, 1985.

Kenez, P. *Cinema and Soviet Society, 1917–1953.* Cambridge, 1992.

Kozlov, V. *Mass Uprisings in the USSR: Protest and Rebellion in the Post-Stalin Years.* Armonk, N.Y., 2002.

Lewin, M. *Russian Peasants and Soviet Power: A Study of Collectivization.* New York, 1968.

Lewin, M. *The Making of the Soviet System: Essays in the Social History of Interwar Russia.* London, 1985.

Lowe, D. *Russian Writing Since 1953: A Critical Survey.* Cambridge, 1987.

Luckyj, G. *Literary Politics in the Soviet Ukraine, 1917–1934.* New York, 1955.

McLean, H., and W. N. Vickery. *The Year of Protest, 1956: An Anthology of Soviet Literary Materials.* New York, 1961.

Medvedev, Zh. A. *The Rise and Fall of T. D. Lysenko.* Translated by I. M. Lerner. New York, 1969.

Mihailov, M. *Moscow Summer.* Translated from Serbo-Croatian. New York, 1965.

Pospielovsky, D. *The Russian Church Under the Soviet Regime, 1917–1982.* 2 vols. Crestwood, N.Y., 1984.

Rosenberg, W. G., ed. *Bolshevik Visions: First Phase of the Cultural Revolution in Soviet Russia.* Ann Arbor, Mich., 1984.

Sakharov, A. D. *Progress, Coexistence and Intellectual Freedom.* Translated and introduction by H. Salisbury. New York, 1968.

Shlapentokh, V. *Public and Private Life of the Soviet People: Changing Values in Post-Stalin Russia.* New York, 1989.

Siegelbaum, L. H. and Ronald Grigor Suny, ed. *Making Workers Soviet: Power, Class, and Identity.* Ithaca, N.Y., 1994.

Siegelbaum, L. H. *Stakhanovism and the Politics of Productivity in the USSR, 1935–1941.* Cambridge, 1988.

Simon, G. *Church, State and Opposition in the USSR.* Translated by K. Matett. Berkeley, 1974.

Slonim, M. *Soviet Russian Literature: Writers and Problems.* New York, 1964.

Solzhenitsyn, A. *The Cancer Ward.* Translated by R. Frank. New York, 1968.

Solzhenitsyn, A. *The First Circle.* Translated by M. Guydon. London, 1968.

Solzhenitsyn, A. *The Gulag Archipelago.* 3 vols. Vols. 1 and 2 translated by T. Whitney; vol. 3 translated by H. Willetts. New York, 1974–1978.

Starr, S. F. *Red and Hot: The Fate of Jazz in the Soviet Union, 1917–1980*. New York, 1994.

Steinberg, M. D. *Proletarian Imagination: Self, Modernity, and the Sacred in Russia, 1910–1925*. Ithaca, N.Y., 2002.

Stites, R. *Russian Popular Culture: Entertainment and Society since 1900*. Cambridge, 1992.

Stroyen, W. *Communist Russia and the Russian Orthodox Church, 1943–1962*. Washington, D.C., 1967.

Struve, G. *Russian Literature under Lenin and Stalin, 1917–1953*. Norman, Okla., 1971.

Struve, N. *Christians in Contemporary Russia*. Translated by L. Sheppard and A. Manson. New York, 1967.

Swayze, H. *Political Control of Literature in the USSR, 1946–1959*. Cambridge, Mass., 1962.

Timasheff, N. *The Great Retreat*. New York, 1946.

Timasheff, N. *Religion in Soviet Russia*. New York, 1942.

Viola, L. *Peasant Rebels under Stalin: Collectivization and the Culture of Peasant Resistance*. New York, 1996.

Vucinich, A. *Empire of Knowledge: The Academy of Sciences of the USSR, 1917–1970*. Berkeley, 1984.

Tumarkin, N. *Lenin Lives!: The Lenin Cult in Soviet Russia*. Cambridge, Mass., 1983.

Weiner, D. *A Little Corner of Freedom: Russian Nature Protection from Stalin to Gorbachev*. Berkeley, 1999.

Weiner, D. R. *Models of Nature: Ecology, Conservation, and Cultural Revolution in Soviet Russia*. Bloomington, Ind., 1988.

Wood, E. *The Baba and the Comrade: Gender and Politics in Revolutionary Russia*. Bloomington, Ind., 1997.

H. Gorbachev and the Collapse of the Soviet Union

Breslauer, G. W. *Gorbachev and Yeltsin as Leaders*. Cambridge, 2002.

Brown, A. *The Gorbachev Factor*. Oxford; New York, 1996.

Carrere d'Encausse, H. *The End of the Soviet Empire: The Triumph of the Nations*. New York, 1993.

Castells, M., with E. Kiselyova. *The Collapse of Soviet Communism: A View from the Information Society*. Berkeley, 1995.

Dunlop, J. *The Rise of Russia and the Fall of the Soviet Union*. Princeton, N.J., 1995.

Fowkes, B. *The Disintegration of the Soviet Union: A Study in the Rise and Triumph of Nationalism*. New York, 1997.

Goldman, M. *What Went Wrong with Perestroika*. New York, 1992.

Hough, J. F. *Democratization and Revolution in the U.S.S.R., 1985–1991*, Washington, D.C., 1997.

Kaiser, R. G. *Why Gorbachev Happened: His Triumphs and His Failure*. New York, 1991.

Kotkin, S. *Armageddon Averted: The Soviet Collapse, 1970–2000*. New York, 2001.

Kotkin, S. *Steeltown, USSR: Soviet Society in the Gorbachev Era*. Berkeley, 1991.

Kotz, D. M., with F. Weir. *Revolution from Above: The Demise of the Soviet System*. New York, 1997.

Lewin, M. *The Gorbachev Phenomenon: A Historical Interpretation*. Berkeley: University of California Press, 1991.

Lieven, A. *The Baltic Revolution: Estonia, Latvia, Lithuania, and the Path to Democracy*. New Haven, Conn., 1993.

Remnick, D. *Lenin's Tomb: The Last Days of the Soviet Empire*. New York, 1993.

Ries, N. *Russian Talk: Culture and Conversation during Perestroika*. Ithaca, N.Y., 1997.

Strayer, R. W. *Why Did the Soviet Union Collapse?: Understanding Historical Change*. Armonk, N.Y., 1998.

Suny, R. G. *The Revenge of the Past: Nationalism, Revolution, and the Collapse of the Soviet Union*. Stanford, 1993.

Walicki, A. *Marxism and the Leap to the Kingdom of Freedom: The Rise and Fall of the Communist Utopia*. Stanford, 1995.

White, S. *Gorbachev and After*. 3rd ed. Cambridge, 1992.

Russian Federation, 1991–

Barker, A. M., ed. *Consuming Russia: Popular Culture, Sex, and Society since Gorbachev*. Durham, N.C., 1999.

Bonnell, V. E. and G. W. Breslauer. *Russia in the New Century: Stability or Disorder*. Boulder, Colo., 2001.

Brown, A., ed. *Contemporary Russian Politics: A Reader*. Oxford, 2001.

Ellis, J. *The Russian Orthodox Church: Triumphalism and Defensiveness*. New York, 1996.

Feshbach. M. *Ecological Disaster: Cleaning Up the Hidden Legacy of the Soviet Regime*. New York, 1995.

Gessen, M. *Dead Again: The Russian Intelligentsia after Communism*. New York, 1997.

Goldman, M. *Lost Opportunity: Why Economic Reforms in Russia Have Not Worked*. New York, 1994.

Handelman, S. *Comrade Criminal: Russia's New Mafiya*. New Haven, Conn., 1995.

Herspring, D. R., ed. *Putin's Russia: Past Imperfect, Future Uncertain*. New York, 2003.

Humphrey, C. *The Unmaking of Soviet Life: Everyday Economies after Socialism*. Ithaca, N.Y., 2002.

Kampfner, J. *Inside Yeltsin's Russia: Corruption, Conflict, Capitalism*. London, 1994.

Khazanov. A. M. *After the USSR: Ethnicity, Nationalism, and Politics in the Commonwealth of Independent States*. Madison, Wisc., 1995.

Knight, A. *Spies without Cloaks: The KGB's Successors*. Princeton, N.J., 1998.

Lieven, A. *Chechnya: Tombstone of Russian Power*. New Haven, Conn., 1998.

McFaul, M. *Russia's Unfinished Revolution: Political Change from Gorbachev to Putin*. Ithaca, N.Y., 2001.

Mikheyev, D. *Russia Transformed*. Indianapolis, 1996.

Remnick, D. *Resurrection: The Struggle for a New Russia*. New York, 1997.

Shevtsova, L. *Putin's Russia*. Washington, D.C., 2003.

Shevtsova, L. *Yeltsin's Russia: Myths and Reality*. Washington, D.C., 1999.

Volkov, V. *Violent Entrepreneurs: The Role of Force in the Making of Russian Capitalism*. Ithaca, N.Y., 2002.

Woodruff, D. *Money Unmade: Barter and the Fate of Russian Capitalism*. Ithaca, N.Y., 1999.

Index

Abaza, Alexander, 363
Aberdeen, Lord, 313
Abkhaz and Abkhazians, 360, 567, 594, 633
Abortion, 564, 565, 655
Abo (Turku): Treaty of, 233; university of, 325
Abraham of Smolensk, 117
Academy of Arts, 277, 340, 427
Academy of Sciences: Imperial, 219, 228, 277, 382, 418; Soviet, 267, 573, 642
Acceleration policy, 587
Acmeists, 426, 575
Adashev, Alexis, 133, 137–38
Admiralty building, 340
Admiralty schools, 266
Adrianople, 29; Treaty of, 308
Adriatic Sea, 66
Adzharians, 594
Aegean Sea, 360
Aehrenthal, Count Alois von, 391
Aestheticism, 425
Afghanistan, 618; Imperial Russia and, 372, 390; trade with, 400; Soviet relations with, 504, 554, 588, 598–99; Russian Federation and, 635; Islamic terrorist groups in, 639
Africa, 510, 548, 555
Agapius, Saint, 80
Age of Reason, 213, 237, 264, 272, 297, 334, 336
Agnosticism, 337
Agrarian Party, 620
Agriculture: quality of land, 5, 8, 257; in Kievan Russia, 41–42, 43–44, 61; in Muscovite Russia, 102, 169–71, 180; in appanage Russia, 105–6; in Imperial Russia, 257–58, 261, 317–19, 397, 401(map), 404; in Soviet Russia, 491(map), 521, 539–40, 545, 586; in Russian Federation, 615, 631, *see also* Collective farms; Sovkhozes
Agrogoroda, 521, 561
Ahmad, Khan, 95, 98
AIDS, 632, 648
Aigun, Treaty of, 361
Akhmatova, Anna, 426, 427(figure), 460, 575, 576, 660
Aksakov, Constantine, 39, 336, 337
Aksakov, Ivan, 336, 350
Aksakov, Serge, 324, 333
Alans, 13–14, 29
Alaska, 4, 8, 288, 327, 621; discovery of, 276; sale of, 360
Albania: Soviet domination in, 524; Communism in, 525; sides with China, 553
Albanians, in Kosovo, 636
Alcoholism, 409, 544, 563, 586, 587, 588, 606, 646, 648
Aleksandrov (town), 138
Alekseev, Michael, 392, 467
Alesha Popovich, 52
Alevisio, 118, 120
Alexander I, Emperor, 212, 214, 246, 253, 255, 261, 271, 279–300, 302, 304, 306, 321, 322, 329, 330, 333, 334, 339, 358, 382, 423; architecture supported by, 276, 340; character and activities of, 280–82; background of, 281; death of, 282, 299; reforms of, 282–87, 324–25; second half of reign, 296–98; Nicholas I compared with, 301, 303; literature during reign of, 323; science during reign of, 327; Karamzin's *Memoir* and, 328
Alexander II, Emperor, 328, 338, 341–61, 378; Crimean War and, 316; background of, 341–42; assassination of, 342, 357; reforms of, 342–53, 362; assassination attempts on, 351, 353, 356; difficulties faced by, 351–53
Alexander III, Emperor, 351, 362–67, 370, 372, 378, 397, 417; background of, 363; assassination plot against, 456, 461
Alexander Nevskii (film), 75
Alexander Nevskii, Prince, 76, 85, 102; reign of, 74–75; canonization of, 112; literature inspired by, 117
Alexander of Battenberg, 371
Alexander of Tver (brother of Dmitrii), 91
Alexandra, Empress, 368, 395
Alexandria, Patriarch of, 184, 185
Alexandrov, Gregory, 580
Alexis, Saint and Metropolitan, 91–92, 104, 112
Alexis, Tsarevich (son of Nicholas II), 442
Alexis, Tsarevich (son of Peter I), 220
Alexis I, Patriarch, 581
Alexis II, Patriarch, 581–82, 596(figure), 655
Alexis or Aleksei, Tsar (Quietest One), 163(figure), 171, 174, 175, 182, 183, 221, 306; Western influences and, 164, 193, 194, 216; reign of, 164–68; theater established by, 188; succession after, 197–98
Algeria, 512
Alipii, Saint, 56
Alisa (music group), 664, 665
Alliance of the Three Emperors, 371
Allied Control Council, 526
All-Russian Center for the Study of Public Opinion (VTsIOM), 650

All-Russian Congress of Soviets: First, 443, 449; Second, 463; Fifth, 473, *see also* Communist Party Congress
All-Russian Directory, 467
All-Russian Union for Women's Equality, 412
All-Union Association of Proletarian Writers (VAPP), 575
All-Union Congress of Soviet Writers, 576
Alphabet: Cyrillic, 50–51, 568; Glagolithic, 51; civil Russian, 266
Altai mountains, 4, 5
Altranstädt, Treaty of, 206
Alvensleben, Count Constantine, 357
Amalrik, Andrei, 547
Amastris, 24
Ambartsumian, Victor, 573
Ambrosius (monk), 122
American Relief Administration, 476
Amu Daria river, 4
Amur river, 4, 361
Amur river basin, 178
Anarchism, 338, 339, 433
Anastasia (wife of Ivan IV), 133, 137, 139, 158
Anatolia, 310
Andersen, Hans Christian, 228
Andrew (son of Alexander Nevskii), 85
Andrew, King of Hungary, 83
Andrew, Saint, 100, 115
Andrew or Andrei Bogoliubskii, Prince of Rostov and Suzdal, 27, 36, 85, 87
Andrew the Little (brother of Ivan III), 96
Andropov, Iurii Vladimirovich, 537
Andrusovo, Treaty of ("the Ruin"), 167
Anglo-Russian Entente, 390
Angola, 551
Anhalt-Zerbst, 230, 235
Anna Karenina (Tolstoy), 423
Anne (daughter of Peter I), 224, 229
Anne (sister of Alexander I), 290
Anne (wife of St. Vladimir), 32
Anne, Empress, 224, 227, 232, 246, 250; reign of, 225–26; cadet school founded by, 230–31, 267
Annensky, Innokentii, 426
Anpilov, Viktor, 621, 652
Antarctic continent, 328
Antes (designation of Slavs), 18, 19, 22, 42
Anthony the Great, Saint, 49
Anti-ballistic missile (AMB) systems, 543
Anti-ballistic missile (AMB) treaty, 638, 639, 640
Anti-Comintern Pact, 505
Antioch, Patriarch of, 184, 185
Anti-Semitism, 651–52, 655, *see also* Jews
Apology of a Madman (Chaadaev), 335
Appanage Russia, 59–129; map, 60(figure); northeast, 82, 85–87; southwest, 82–85, 87; termination of era, 95–96; economy of, 105–6; society and institutions in, 108–10; religion in, 111–16; culture of, 111–22
Appeasement policy, 504, 506
Appliance pools, 541

Apraksin, Theodore, 202
"April Theses," 444, 455
Arabic numerals, introduction of, 266
Arabs, 15, 23–24
Arakcheev, Alexis, 296–97
Aral Sea, 4
Archangel (province), 320
Archangel or Arkhangelsk (port), 136, 141, 193, 194, 257; dockyard established in, 202; trade and, 260; Civil War and, 467, 469; World War II and, 510
Archbishoprics, 50, 112, 180
Architecture: in Kievan Russia, 53–56; of Novgorod, 79; of Pskov, 81; in appanage Russia, 112, 117–20; in Muscovite Russia, 189–90; in Imperial Russia, 276–77, 340; in Soviet Russia, 579
Arctic Ocean, 4, 5, 135
Armenia, 308, 472; Mongol conquest of, 65; Russification in, 366; split from Transcaucasian Federation, 470; Soviet rule in, 499; nationalistic movements in, 593, 594; earthquake in, 600; Union Treaty rejected by, 604; Russian Federation and, 633
Armenian Church, 370
Armenians, 43, 567, 591, 593, 594
Armstrong, John A., 497
Army: in Time of Troubles, 156; of Imperial Russia, 211–12, 217, 234, 305, 350–51; Provisional Government and, 444; of Soviet Russia, 495; of Russian Federation, 632, *see also* Red Army
Arsenii of Rostov, Metropolitan, 239
Arteli, 258
Art for art's sake movement, 424
Arts: of Kievan Russia, 56; of appanage Russia, 117–22; of Muscovite Russia, 189–91; of Imperial Russia, 276–78, 324, 339–40, 427–32; of Soviet Russia, 547, 578–81; of postcommunist Russia, 659, 661–64
Asha, train collision in, 600
Asher, A., 386
Asia: Russian expansion in, 360–61; Soviet Russia and, 455, 527, 548; financial crisis in, 624, *see also* Central Asia
Asia Minor, 12, 37
Assemblées, 219, 222
Assembly of Russian Factory Workers, 380
Astrakhan, 67, 95; Muscovite Russia and, 134, 135, 139, 146, 152, 161, 162, 165, 177, 178; Imperial Russia and, 206, 221; trade in, 261
Astronomy, 327
Atheism, 337, 581
Atlantic Charter, 513
Atlantic Defense Pact, 525
Atomic bomb, in World War II, 512
Atomic Energy Commission, 524
Atomic weapons, 524, 534, 548, 551–52, 595, 633, 638–39
Attlee, Clement, 513
Auerstädt, battle of, 287
Augustus, sovereign of Rome, 115

Augustus II, ruler of Saxony and Poland, 204–5, 206, 233
Augustus III, King of Poland, 233
Austerlitz, 287
Australia, 550
Austria: Imperial Russia and, 208, 220, 232–33, 245, 247, 248, 250–51, 254, 287, 311–12; Peter I and, 208, 220; War of the Austrian Succession and, 233; Seven Years' War and, 234; Catherine II and, 245, 247, 248, 250–51; partition of Poland and, 248, 250–51; Galicia acquired by, 250, 471; Paul I and, 254; education system in, 269; Alexander I and, 287; Napoleonic Wars and, 290, 292; at Congress of Vienna, 293; in Quadruple Alliance, 294; Italian revolution and, 296; Nicholas I and, 311–12; Straits Convention and, 313; Crimean War and, 314, 316, 357; Polish rebellion and, 352, 353, 357; World War I and, 445; Soviet Russia and, 503, 549; German annexation of, 506, *see also* Austria-Hungary
Austria-Hungary: Imperial Russia and, 358–60, 371, 372, 390; Turkish war with, 358–60; Congress of Berlin and, 371, 372; in Triple Alliance, 372, 390; Serbian conflict with, 390; World War I and, 391–92
Autocracy, 110; Ivan III and, 99; Ivan IV and, 131, 141; Basil Shuisky and, 151; in Time of Troubles, 159, 160; Michael Romanov and, 161; in Muscovite Russia, 174–76, 187; Peter I and, 213; Anne and, 225; Catherine II and, 240, 243; Alexander I and, 282, 283, 284, 286; Nicholas I and, 301, 303, 304, 306, 307; in Official Nationality doctrine, 302, 303, 362; Slavophiles on, 337; Alexander II and, 351; Alexander III and, 363; Nicholas II and, 367, 369, 382, 383, 441
Automobile industry, 542
Avars, 15, 18
Avvakum or Habakkuk, Archpriest, 183, 185; quoted, 181–82; autobiography of, 187
Azeff, Evno, 388
Azerbaijan, 472, 499; split from Transcaucasian Federation, 470; nationalistic movements in, 591, 593, 594; Russian Federation and, 633
Azov, 175, 203, 205; cossack seizure of, 162; Great Northern War and, 207; Treaty of Belgrade and, 233; Treaty of Kurchuk Kainrji and, 246
Azov Sea, 14, 15, 30, 33, 469

Babar (founder of Mogul empire), 100
Babel, Isaac, 575, 576, 659
Baer, Charles Ernst, 327
Baghdad, Caliphate of, 37
Bagration, Georgii II, 593
Bagration, Prince Peter, 290, 291
Baikal-Amur mainline railway, 543
Baikal Lake, 4, 375, 469, 543
Bakhtin, Mikhail, 575

Baku, 399, 483, 594
Baku oil field strike, 410
Bakunin, Michael, 337, 354; philosophy and activities of, 338–39; populism and, 355, 433
Balabanov, Aleksei, 662, 664
Balakirev, Milii, 428
Balaklava, battle of, 316
Balkans, 186, 371, 390; Khazars in, 15; Kievan Russia and, 26, 29–30; Mongols in, 65; First Turkish War and, 246; French interest in, 290; Nicholas I and, 308; Crimean War and, 314, 315; redrawing of map, 357, 360; Turkish invasions of, 357, 358–60; map of, 359(figure); Izvolsky's policy in, 391
Balkan Slavs, 95
Ballet, 277, 340, 428, 430–31, 579
Ballistic missiles, 635
Balmont, Constantine, 426
Baltic region and ports, 15, 30, 76; role in Russian history, 4, 8; Teutonic Knights and, 75; Lithuanian sway in, 123, 125; Muscovite Russia and, 135, 139, 140; Imperial Russia and, 204, 208, 212, 233, 243, 257, 261; Thirty Years' War and, 205; Great Northern War and, 206, 207, 208, 257; Russian acquisition of, 208; First Turkish War and, 246; trade and, 261, 320–21; serfs emancipated in, 296; Crimean War and, 315; industry in, 319; World War I and, 392; canals and, 494; World War II and, 508
Baltic republics: nonaggression pact with Soviets, 505; in Soviet Union, 514, 519; independence movements in, 591–93; Russian Federation and, 633, 634, 640, 655
Banks, 402, 631; Gentry, 231; State Lending, 262; State, 351; State Gentry Land, 364, 397; Peasant Land, 367, 389, 406; Russo-Chinese, 400; Russo-Persian, 400; in Soviet Russia, 465; private, 589; commercial, 614; failure of, 624
Banquet campaign, 379
Baptism of Russia, 32, 48, 52
Baptist Church, 583
Barclay de Tolly, Prince Michael, 290, 291
Bariatinsky, Prince Alexander, 361
Barma (architect), 190
Baroque architectural style, 190, 276
Barshchina or corvée, 171, 257, 274; defined, 109; increase in, 261–62, 318
Baryshnikov, Mikhail, 579
Bashkir republic, 472
Bashkirs, 206, 221, 241
Basil, Archbishop, 80
Basil I, Grand Prince of Moscow, 93–94
Basil II, Emperor of Byzantium, 32
Basil II, the Blind, Grand Prince of Moscow, 94–95, 96, 98, 102, 103
Basil III, Grand Prince, 62, 95, 102, 115, 131, 154, 190; Lithuania and, 100, 123; reign of, 100–101; views on government, 187
Basil of Kostroma, Grand Prince, 85
Basil the Squint-eyed, 94

Basmanov, Theodore, 149, 150, 151
Bathory, Stephen, 166
Battle Organization, 379, 388
Batu, Khan, 66, 67, 68
Batum, 360, 469, 483
Baumgarten, Nicolas Pierre Serge von, 34
Bavaria, 502
Bayer, Gottlieb S., 21
Baykov, Alexander, 486
Bay of Shesme, 246
Bayonets, 212
Bazhenov, Basil, 277
Beccaria, 240
Bekovich-Cherkassky, Prince Alexander, 210
Belarus, 633, 634, 638, *see also* White Russia or
    Belorussia
Belgium: revolution against Dutch, 309; capi-
    talism in, 322; World War I and, 392;
    Atlantic Defense Pact and, 525
Belgrade, 512, 550; Treaty of, 233
Beliaev, Pavel, 573n
Belingshausen, Thaddeus, 328
Belinsky, Vissarion, 328, 333, 337, 338, 354,
    421
Belorussia, *see* White Russia
Belsky family, 133
Bely, Andrei, 426, 575
Benckendorff, Count Alexander, 305
Beneš, Eduard, 525
Benois, Alexander, 420, 425, 430, 431, 437
Bentham, Jeremy, 433
Berdiaev, Nicholas, 436, 437, 456, 657
Bereday, George Z. F., 570–71
Berezina river, 291
Berezovsky, Boris, 622, 629–30, 642–43
Bergson, Abram, 492, 540
Beria, Lavrentii, 522, 528, 546, 549, 550; great
    purge and, 496; execution of, 530–31
Bering, Vitus, 201
Bering Sea, 315
Bering Strait, 178
Berlin, 234, 511, 512, 513, 526, *see also* East
    Berlin; West Berlin
Berlin, Isaiah, 458
Berlin-Baghdad railway, 391
Berlin crisis, 551
Berlin Wall, tearing down of, 598, 625
Bertinian Annals, 23
Bespopovtsy, 185
Bessarabia, 246, 288, 316; Lithuanian
    suzerainty accepted by, 126; ceded to
    Turkey, 359, 360; ceded to Romania, 474,
    505; ceded to Soviet Union, 507, 519
Bestuzhev-Riumin, Count Alexis, 228, 232,
    233
Bestuzhev-Riumin, Constantine ("Bestuzhev
    courses"), 418
Betsky, Ivan, 269
Bialystok, 508
Bible Society, 297
Bibliography, 192
Bichurin, Father Iakinf, 328

Birchbark documents, 80
Biren or Biron, Ernst-Johann, 223, 226
Birger (Swedish commander), 75
Bironovshchina or Bironism, 226
Birthrate, 646
Bismarck, Prince Otto von, 353, 358; Polish
    rebellion and, 357; Congress of Berlin and,
    360; wire to St. Petersburg, 371–72
Björkö, Treaty of, 390
Black, Cyril E., 517
Black Hundreds, 381–82, 435, 652
Black market, 493, 543
Black Monday, 624
Black Partition or Total Land Repartition, 356
Black Sea, 33, 37, 95, 257, 318, 381, 595; role in
    Russian history, 4, 5, 8; in ancient Russia,
    10, 13, 14, 15, 16; trade and, 39, 261, 317,
    320–21; Turkey's claim on, 106, 233, 246,
    247; Lithuanian sway in, 125; Russian fleet
    in, 247, 322; Treaty of Bucharest and, 288;
    Crimean War and, 314, 315; neutralization
    of, 316; Treaty of Paris, 358; World War
    I and, 392; French naval mutiny in, 472;
    World War II and, 508, 510
Black soil, 5, 257
Blackstone, Sir William, 243
Blair, Tony, 638
Blitzkrieg, 508, 510
Blok, Alexander, 10, 416, 426, 575
Bloody Sunday, 380
Blum, Jerome, 321, 343
Bobrikov, Nicholas, 370
Bock, Fedor von, 511
Bogatyri, 38, 51–52
Bogoslovsky, Mikhail M., 221
Bohemia, 34, 506
Bokhara, 361, 472
Bolotnikov, Ivan, 152, 153, 159, 160, 241
Bolsheviks, 440, 443, 557, 558, 561, 650; split
    from Social Democrats, 379, 454; growing
    popularity of, 410; split from Mensheviks,
    434–35; reasons for 1917 victory, 444–45;
    447; Provisional Government and, 444–46;
    attempt to seize power, 445; October Revo-
    lution and, 449; renamed Communist
    Party, 454–55; consolidation of power, 460;
    Constituent Assembly and, 463; first
    months in power, 463–65; assassinations of,
    466; Stalin's relationship with, 483; in great
    purge, 495–96, 497; foreign relations and,
    502–4, *see also* Civil War; Communist Party;
    Red Army; War Communism
Boltin, Ivan, 276
Bonn, 526
Bonnell, Victoria, 644
Books, publication of, 268
Books about Poverty and Wealth (Pososhkov),
    276
Boretsky, Martha, 96
Boris (Bulgarian ruler), 29
Boris, Saint, 33, 49, 120
Boris Godunov (Musorgsky), 143, 331, 428

Borodin, Alexander, 428
Borodino, battle of, 291
Bosnia: Austrian annexation of, 358, 359, 360, 391; ethnic conflicts, 636–37
Bosporan kingdom, 14
Bosporus, 310, 313
Botkin, Basil, 337
Bourbon dynasty, 293
Bourgeoisie, 378; the Duma and, 385; Provisional Government and, 443; Marxism and Leninism on, 452, 455; in Soviet Russia, 465, 466, 558, 559, *see also* Middle class
Bourgeois nationalists, 567
Bourgeois specialists, 475, 488, 497, 564
Boyar duma: in Kievan Russia, 45, 46; development of, 46; in appanage Russia, 110; in Muscovite Russia, 110, 131, 161, 174–75; in Time of Troubles, 151, 154, 155; in Imperial Russia, 198, 202, 213
Boyars, 44, 107, 108, 173–74; of Novgorod, 78, 145; of Galicia and Volynia, 84–85; Ivan III and, 96, 97; Basil III and, 100; Lithuania and, 125; Ivan IV and, 133, 137, 138, 139, 141, 142; in Time of Troubles, 145, 154, 158, 160; False Dmitrii I and, 147–48, 150; in zemskii sobor, 157
Boym, Svetlana, 652
Bozh (prince of Antes), 19
Bratsk Dam, 543
Breslauer, George, 613, 614
Brest-Litovsk, Treaty of, 464, 475, 500
Brethren movement, 411, 437
Brezhnev, Leonid, 534–37, 544, 545, 573, 587, 588; foreign relations under, 548, 552, 555; culture under, 572
Bribery of public officials, 649–50
Brigadier, The (Fonvizin), 272
Britain, Battle of, 508
Briullov, Karl, 340
Briusov, Valery, 331, 426, 575
Brodsky, Joseph, 578
Bronze Horseman, The (Pushkin), 331
Brother (film), 662, 664
Brotherhood of Cyril and Methodius, 310
Brothers Karamazov, The (Dostoevsky), 421
Bruce, James, 202
Brusilov, Alexis, 445
Brzezinski, Zbigniew K., 529, 553
Bucharest, Treaty of, 288
Budapest, 511, 512, 550
Buddhism, 365, 567, 656, 657
Buddhist lamas, murder of, 655
Budenny, Semen, 514
Bugaev, Boris, *see* Bely, Andrei
Bug river, 4, 11, 12, 233
Bukhara, 70
Bukharin, Nicholas, 477–78, 485, 495
Bukovina, 507, 519
Bulavin, Conrad, 206, 215, 221, 241
Bulgakov, Mikhail, 575, 576, 659
Bulgakov, Serge, 436, 437
Bulganin, Nicholas, 531, 532, 549, 550

Bulgaria, 527, 553; Khazars in, 15; Kievan Russia and, 29, 30; religion in, 51; Mongols in, 67; Turkish conflicts with, 358, 359–60, 391; division of, 360; unification denied to, 371; World War I and, 392; World War II and, 512; post-World War II treaty, 524; Communism's collapse in, 598; Communism's resurgence in, 635
Bulgars, 17, 32, 35; Khazars and, 15, 16; Sviatoslav's attack on, 29; trade and, 43; Mongols and, 65, 66; Moscow conquest of, 92, 94
Bunge, Nicholas, 367, 408
Bunin, Ivan, 578, 659
Burckhardt, Jacob, 72
Bureaucracy: in Muscovite Russia, 177; in Imperial Russia, 218, 254, 286, 303, 365, 369, 397; in Soviet Russia, 477, 493
Bush, George W., 638, 639
Buslaev, Basil, 80
Butashevich-Petrashevsky, Michael, 339, 350
Buturlin, Basil, 166
Bykov, V., 641
Byliny, 51–52, 80, 116, 188
Byron, Lord, 280
Byzantium, 23, 25, 26, 34, 37, 41, 46, 49, 50, 51, 57, 70, 76; early cultures in, 10, 14, 15; Russian invasions of, 27–28, 29–30; Vladimir (Saint) and, 30–33; trade with, 42–43; architecture influenced by, 54, 56, 118; Mongols and, 68; Roman of Volynia and, 83; Russian Church independence from, 95, 112; Ivan III and, 98–99

Cadets, *see* Constitutional Democratic party
Calendars: East Slavic, 42; changes made by Peter I, 204, 219, 222; Gregorian, 465
California, Russians in, 8, 288
Calvinism, 186
Cambodia, 555
Campbell, Robert W., 538
Canada, 4; Russian immigration to, 370; World War II and, 512; Atlantic Defense Pact and, 525; wheat sales to Soviet Russia, 532
Canals, 218–19, 260, 320, 494, 521, 550
Capital (Marx), 409
Capitalism: in Imperial Russia, 260, 318, 319, 322, 346–47, 351, 378, 398, 400, 409; populist rejection of, 433; Marxism and Leninism on, 453, 454, 455, 458; Soviet Russia and, 485, 501–2, 589; in Russian Federation, 613–16, 623, 642–44, 653
Capital punishment, 46, 78, 227, 240, 337, 443, 495
Captain's Daughter, A (Pushkin), 241, 331
Carpathian mountains, 4, 17, 66, 82
Carpatho-Ruthenian area of Czechoslovakia, 524
Carr, Edward H., 465
Carter, Jimmy, 555
Casimir IV, of Lithuania and Poland, 97, 98, 126

Caspian Sea, 4, 29, 165, 210, 308
Castlereagh, Viscount, 293, 296
Castro, Fidel, 599, 638
Catherine (daughter of Ivan V), 224, 226
Catherine I, Empress (wife of Peter I), 220, 224
Catherine II, the Great, 223, 232, 233, 234, 235–53, 254, 261, 262, 266, 271, 273, 274, 282, 314, 321, 324, 348; background of, 230, 235; character of, 237; first years of reign, 239–41; reforms of, 239–41, 243–45; foreign policy of, 245–52, 257; evaluations of, 252–53; Western influences and, 253, 264–65; state debt and, 263; education under, 268–69; literary efforts of, 272, 278; architecture supported by, 276, 340; Alexander's relationship with, 281
Catholic Church, see Roman Catholic Church
Cattell, David T., 505
Caucasus, 4, 344, 543; early cultures in, 12, 14; trade with, 43; Mongols in, 65; Russian expansion in, 288, 357, 360–61; Treaty of Adrianople and, 308; partition of Poland and, 310; Crimean War and, 315; poetry inspired by, 332; Turkish-Austrian conflict and, 359, 360; pacification of, 360–61; exiles in, 370; the Duma and, 385; World War I and, 392; World War II and, 510, 511; post-World War II fate of, 522; nationalities represented in, 567; social black holes in, 649; see also Chechnia
Ceausescu, Nicholas, 553, 598
Cells (Communist Party), 558
Cement (Gladkov), 485
Censorship: under Nicholas I, 305, 307; in Poland, 310; in Imperial Russia, 324, 411; of Slavophiles, 337; under Alexander II, 351; in Soviet Russia, 588–89; in Russian Federation, 630
Censuses: Mongol, 66, 69; in Muscovite Russia, 172; in Imperial Russia, 217, 244, 397, 402, 404, 418; in Soviet Russia, 559, 581
Central Asia, 4, 594; deserts of, 5; early cultures in, 10, 12, 15; Mongols in, 65; Peter I and, 210; trade with, 261, 321; expeditions to, 328; Russian expansion in, 357, 360, 361, 372; the Duma and, 385; Soviet republics in, 499; United States entry into, 637; Russian Federation and, 639, 640
Central Committee of the Communist Party, 473, 531–32, 558, 587
Centralization, 110; under Ivan III, 95–100; in Time of Troubles, 159; in Muscovite Russia, 171, 177, 182; under Peter I, 213–14; of education, 325; in Soviet Russia, 465, 499, 515, 522; in Russian Federation, 629, see also Gathering of Russia
Chaadaev, Peter, 335, 340
Chagall, Marc, 431, 579
Chaikovsky, Nicholas, 467
Chaliapin, Theodore, 430
Châlons, battle of, 15

Chamberlain, Neville, 506
Chamberlin, William H., 439
Chancellery language, 187
Chancellor, Richard, 135
Chandler, Raymond, 660
Chang-chun, 376
"Charge of the Light Brigade" (Tennyson), 316
Charlemagne, Emperor, 15
Charles I, King of England, 193
Charles II, King of England, 182, 193
Charles VI, Emperor of Austria, 220
Charles XII, King of Sweden, 205–9, 215, 229, 291
Charles Frederick, Duke of Holstein-Gottorp, 229
Charques, Richard D., 279
Charter of 1785, 263
Charter to the Nobility (1785), 243–44
Chebyshev, Pafnutti, 419
Chechnia: wars with, 360, 616, 617–19, 621, 623, 624–25, 633, 638, 639; history of, 617; human rights abuses in, 628, 631; media criticism of policy in, 629; terrorism in, 631–32
Checkerboard system, 232
Cheka, 465, 466, 473, 495
Chekhov, Anton, 416, 424, 425(figure), 438
Cheliabinsk, 600
Cherepnin, Lev V., 96
Cherkassky, Prince Vladimir, 345, 352
Chernenko, Constantine, 537
Cherniaev, Michael, 358
Chernigov, 33, 35, 87; trade with, 39; Mongols in, 66; Ivan III and, 98; Olgerd and, 125; False Dmitrii I in, 149
Chernigov-Seversk, 98, 100
Chernobyl nuclear disaster, 588
Chernomyrdin, Viktor, 613, 616, 620, 623, 624
Chernov, Victor, 379, 434, 445, 463, 467
Chernukha, 664
Chernyshevsky, Nicholas, 353, 354, 355, 421, 424, 425, 436, 456; work of, 420; ideas and activities of, 433–34
Chersonesus, 14, 32
Chervonets, 476
Chiang Kai-shek, 503, 504, 506, 527
Chicherin, George, 502, 503, 504
Childhood, Boyhood, and Youth (Tolstoy), 423
Children: labor laws and, 367, 408; official policy on, 564, 565; runaway, 646
Chiliarch, see Tysiatski or chiliarch
China, 41, 458, 505–6, 534; river boundary between Russia and, 4; Mongols in, 65, 66, 70; Muscovite Russia and, 178; Peter I and, 210; trade with, 261, 321, 400; Bichurin's work on, 328; Russian expansion in, 361; war with Great Britain and France, 361; Japanese conflicts with, 374, 504; Trans-Siberian railroad in, 374; Tibet and, 390; civil war in, 473, 527; Soviet Union recognized by, 503; Communist, 503–4, 527;

Soviet conflicts with, 529, 532–33, 552–53; Russian Federation and, 636, 637, 639

Chin empire, 65

Chinese Eastern Railway, 504, 505

Chirin, Procopius, 190

Chivalry, 107

Chizhevsky, Dmitrii, 56

Cholera, 305, 413

Chosen Council, 133, 136, 138, 141

Christianity: Khazars and, 16; in Kievan Russia, 26, 28, 30–33, 46, 48–51, 52–56; in Lithuania, 32, 124; in Transcaucasia, 593, *see also* Russian Orthodox Church; specific religions

Christie, Agatha, 660

Chronicle of Novgorod, 80

Chronicles of Kievan Russia, 52–53

Chubais, Anatoly, 613, 623

Chud or Peipus Lake, 75

Chuikov, Basil, 511

Churches and cathedrals, 53–55, 80, 117–20; Cathedral of St. Sophia (Kiev), 55, 56, 118; Cathedral of St. Sophia (Novgorod), 55; Cathedral of St. Dmitrii, 55(figure), 56; Cathedral of St. George (Iuriev Polskii), 56; Cathedral of St. George (Novgorod), 56; Cathedral of the Assumption (Vladimir), 56, 118; Church of the Intercession of Our Lady, 56; Cathedral of the Assumption (Moscow), 118, 119–20; Cathedral of the Annunciation, 119–20; Cathedral of the Archangel, 119–20; Church of St. Basil the Blessed, 182, 190; Cathedral of the Novodevichii Convent, 191; Church of St. John the Baptist, 191; Church of the Prophet Elijah, 191; Kazan Cathedral, 340, *see also* Monasteries

Churchill, Winston, 462, 510, 513, 525

Church Slavonic, 51, 219

Cimmerians, 12, 16

Cinema, 437, 438, 498, 576, 579–80, 589, 662–64

Circassians, 360

Civic poetry, 424, 425

Civil rights, 285, 411, 475, 499

Civil Russian alphabet, 266

Civil service, 218, 286

Civil society, 411–13, 640

Civil War, 465, 466–69, 474, 561, 581; allied intervention in, 469; reasons for Red victory, 472–73; Stalin's participation in, 483

Class: in Kievan Russia, 42; in Imperial Russia, 241, 261–63, 397; Revolution of 1917 and, 449; Marxism on, 452–53; in Soviet Russia, 488, 559, *see also* Society; specific social classes

Classical Symphony (Prokofiev), 579

Clement, Metropolitan, 50

Clergy: Greek, 112; in zemskii sobor, 157; in Duma, 382; in Soviet Russia, 559, *see also* Russian Orthodox Church

Climate, 4–5, 8, 9

Clinton, Bill, 635, 636, 638

Coexistence policy, 502, 548, 551

Coke, Sir John, 181

Cold war, 483, 523, 526, 552, 633, 636

Collective farms (kolkhozes), 485, 486, 488–89, 490, 492, 542, 561, 562; allocation of produce in, 489; in post-war era, 519, 521; Seven-Year Plan and, 539–40; movement to dismantle, 631

Collectivism, 484, 653

College of Economy, 245

Collegia or colleges, 213–14, 284

Colonization, 102; appanage Russia and, 86–87; Imperial Russia and, 245, 257, *see also* Expansion

Cominform (Communist Information Bureau), 526, 550

Comintern (Communist International), 502–3, 526

Commissar of Enlightenment, 575

Commission for the Establishment of Popular Schools, 269

Committee of Ministers, 303

Committee of the Sixth of December, 304

Commonwealth of Independent States, 604, 637

Communism: influence on Soviet policies, 451; reasons for appeal of, 457–58; post-Lenin struggle for power and, 477–81; in China, 503–4, 527; international movement, 519; reaffirmation of orthodoxy in, 522; post-war spread of, 524–27; national, 526; Khrushchev on, 532, 534; building of, 541–42; uprising in regimes, 546–47; collapse of, 592, 598; in Russian Federation, 616, 617, 619, 620, 621–22, 624, 625, 628, 629, 637; in former Soviet satellites, 635; in post-communist Russia, 646–47, 651–54, *see also* Marxism; Marxism-Leninism; War Communism

Communist Information Bureau, *see* Cominform

Communist International, *see* Comintern

Communist Party, 451, 454–55, 567, 591, 643; domination of government, 473–74; NEP and, 476; Stalin's control of, 497; constitutional recognition of, 499; divided into two hierarchies, 540; desertions from, 550; membership of, 557; in Soviet society, 557–59; Gorbachev and, 585, 589–90, 601; abolition in former Soviet satellites, 592; in RSFSR, 596; outlawed in Soviet Union, 604; in Russian Federation, 615, 620, 624, 628, 653, 659

Communist Party Congress: Eleventh, 476; Fifteenth, 479, 482; Seventeenth, 482; Eighteenth, 482; Twenty-second, 495, 532, 533, 540, 541, 551, 570; Twentieth, 531, 546; Twenty-third, 534–35, 542; Twenty-fourth, 535; Twenty-fifth, 535, 542–43; Twenty-sixth, 535; Twenty-first, 540; Twenty-

Communist Party Congress: Eleventh, (*cont*) seventh, 587; Nineteenth, 589; Twenty-ninth, 601

Comte, Auguste, 458

Confederation of Bar, 249, 251

Confederation of Targowica, 250

Confession, A (Tolstoy), 423

Congo, 551

Congress of Berlin, 360, 371–73

Congress of People's Deputies, 589, 596–97, 600, 604, 616, 617

Congress of Vienna, 296

Congress System or Confederation of Europe, 294–96

Conquest, Robert, 484, 495

Constantine VI, Porphyrogenitus, 23, 28, 39–41, 42

Constantine IX, Monomakh, 100, 115

Constantine XI, Emperor of Byzantium, 98–99

Constantine (Nikolaevich), Grand Duke: emancipation of serfs and, 345; navy reform under, 351; resignation of, 363

Constantine (Pavlovich), Grand Duke, 304; Greek project and, 247; Decembrist movement and, 299; Polish rebellion and, 309

Constantinople, 26, 50, 100, 205, 359, 391; Rus attack on, 23; Russian invasions of, 27, 28, 29, 41; Christianity accepted from, 32; Iaroslav's invasion of, 33; sacking of, 37; trade with, 39; Turkish conquest of, 95, 98–99, 183; Russian Orthodox Church and, 112, 246; travel literature on, 116; Muscovite Russia and, 183–84, 185, 186; Greek project and, 247; French interest in, 290; Turkish-Egyptian conflict and, 310; Crimean War and, 314; World War I and, 392; Russian Civil War and, 469

Constituent Assembly, 443, 444, 445, 449; abdication of Nicholas II and, 442; Bolsheviks and, 463; disbanding of, 464, 465; Civil War and, 467; demand for reconvening of, 475

Constitutional Charter of the Russian Empire (Novosiltsev), 286–87

Constitutional Democratic party (Cadet), 389, 435–36; founding of, 378; Revolution of 1905 and, 381; the Duma and, 383–84, 385, 386; Provisional Government and, 445

Constitutional monarchy, 352, 381

Constitutional Party, 465

Constitution and constitutionalism: in Imperial Russia, 225, 285, 286–87, 298, 306, 352, 439; in Poland, 250, 293, 296, 309; in France, 293; in Soviet Russia, 473, 497, 499–500, 582, 589–90; in Russian Federation, 617, 619

Containment policy, 504

Contemporary, The (periodical), 331, 433

Continental blockade, 288, 290

Convention of Berlin, 311

Convention of Kutahia, 311

Cooperatives: in Imperial Russia, 405–6; in Soviet Russia, 561, 589

Copper coin riot, 164

Corporal punishment, state policy on, 244, 254, 351, 407

Corvée, *see* Barshchina or corvée

Cossacks, 140; first mention of, 146; in Time of Troubles, 147, 152, 155–56, 158, 160; Dnieper, 165–66, 244; Polish seizure of Ukraine and, 165–66; rebellions of, 166; Peter I and, 212, 215; Catherine II and, 240, 244; in the Legislative Commission, 240; Pugachev's rebellion and, 241–42; Ural, 241–42, 467; literature inspired by, 333; in Civil War, 466, 467; Orenburg, 467; in Russian Federation, 617; Don (*see* Don cossacks)

Cotton, 322, 361, 474, 594

[Council of Florence, 95, 112, 116

Council of Foreign Ministers, 549

Council of Mutual Economic Assistance (COMECON), 554

Council of Notables, 77–78

Council of People's Commissars, 461, 473, 500

Council of State, 286

Counterreforms, 362–65, 397, 416

Courland, Duchy of, 250

Courland, Duke of, 225

Cracow, 250, 293, 311; university of, 126

Creative freedom, 437

Crime, 586, 599, 600, 606, 616, 621, 623, 643, 648–50, *see also* Mafias; Organized crime

Crimea, 67; early cultures in, 14; Rus in, 24; Kievan Russia and, 30, 32; Mongols and, 95; Muscovite Russia and, 134, 135, 175; First Turkish War and, 246; annexation of, 247; Second Turkish War and, 247; Russian Civil War and, 469; World War II and, 511; post-World War II fate of, 522; Ukrainian sovereignty over, 595; Russian Federation and, 634

Crime and Punishment (Dostoevsky), 421

Crimean Tartars, 178; Mongol defeat and, 98; Ivan IV and, 137, 139; Polish seizure of Ukraine and, 165, 166; treaty of eternal peace and, 198; Peter I and, 203; First Turkish War and, 246, 247; republic, 471

Crimean War, 233, 307, 320, 322, 342, 344, 358, 441, 634; described, 313–16; long-range effects of, 352

Crimes and Punishments (Beccaria), 240

Critical realism, 354, 355, 428, 433

Cross, Samuel H., 59

Crusades, 37

Cuba, 552, 599; missile crisis, 533, 534, 551; Russian Federation and, 635, 638

Cui, Caesar, 428

Cult of personality, 527, 529, 531, 534, 535

Cultural autonomy, 499

Cultural revolution, 488, 564–66

Culture: of Kievan Russia, 50–57; of Pskov, 81; of appanage Russia, 111–22; of Muscovite Russia, 181–95; of Imperial Russia, 219, 264–78, 323–40, 415–38; under Peter I,

219, 264; in the 18th century, 264–78; in the 19th century (first half), 323–40; from great reforms to 1917, 415–38; of Soviet Russia, 571–81; of postcommunist Russia, 659–65, *see also* Arts; Education; Literature; Music; Popular culture; Religion

Cumans, *see* Polovtsy

Curia regis, 46

Currency: in Kievan Russia, 43; coining of, 103; debasing of, 164, 228; paper, 263; stabilization of, 306; falling exchange rates, 474; chervonets, 476; intensive printing of, 600; depletion of, 623–24; devaluation of, 630, 644

Curzon Line, 470, 513

Cypher schools, 267

Cyprian, 117

Cyprus, 360

Cyrillic alphabet, 50–51, 568

Cyril of Turov, Saint, 50–51, 52

Czartoryski, Prince Adam, 282

Czech Legion, 467, 469

Czechoslovakia, 524, 527; nonaggression pact signed by, 505; German invasion of, 506; Communism in, 525; rebellions in, 546, 549, 553; Communism collapse in, 598; Communism resurgence in, 635; Russian Federation and, 635; Slovakia secession from, 636

Czech Republic, 636

Dagestan, 288, 624

Daladier, Édouard, 506

Dallin, Alexander, 516

Dallin, David, 494

Daniel (son of Alexander Nevskii), 89

Daniel (son of Roman of Volynia), 84

Daniel, Julius, 546

Daniel, Metropolitan, 114

Danilevsky, Nicholas, 435

Danube river, 12, 30, 35, 308, 316

Danubian principalities, 290, 308, 312, 314, 316

Danzig, 250, 504, 506

Dardanelles, 311, 313

Dargomyzhsky, Alexander, 332, 340

Darwin, Charles, 419

Davlet-Geray, Khan, 139

Dead Souls (Gogol), 329, 333

Death penalty, *see* Capital punishment

Decembrist movement, 303, 334, 335, 339, 354; on serfdom, 298, 344; uprising of, 298–300

De la Gardie, Jakob, 153

Delianov, Ivan, 363, 417

Demidov Law School, 325

Democracy, 435; Marxism-Leninism on, 454–55; Soviet Russia and, 499; Russian Federation and, 616, 627, 628, 650–51, 653

Democratic centralism, 497

Democratic Centralists, 475

Democratic Party of Russia, 620

Democratic Russia, 590–91

Democratic Union, 590

Democratization, 586

Demon, A (Lermontov), 332

Denikin, Anthony, 467–68, 469, 470, 473

Denisov, Andrew, 185

Denisov, Simeon, 185

Denmark, 24; Christian conversion in, 32; Great Northern War and, 204–5, 208; Catherine II and, 252; Soviet Russia and, 503; Atlantic Defense Pact and, 525

Den and *Zavtra* (newspapers), 651

Department stores, 413

Depression of 1900, 400

Derzhavin, Gabriel, 271, 584, 607

De-Stalinization, 532, 533, 534, 546, 553

Detektivy, 660

Détente, 535, 549, 552

Deulino, truce of, 162

DeWitt, Nicholas, 571

Dezhnev, Semen, 178

Diaghilev, Serge, 425, 430, 431

Diakonov, Mikhail A., 109, 169, 174

Diakovo, 190

Diasporas, 591

Dictionaries, 270

Diet (food intake), 250, 645

Digby, Simon, 181

Dioceses, 50

Dionysus (abbot), 156

Dionysus (icon painter), 122

Directory of the Rada (Ukraine), 470–71

Dispossessed class, 645, 646

Disraeli, Benjamin, 360

Divorce, 564, 565

"Dizzy with Success" (Stalin), 488

Dmitrii (son of Alexander Nevskii), 85

Dmitrii (son of Ivan IV), 137

Dmitrii, False, *see* False Dmitrii

Dmitrii, Prince of Suzdal, 92

Dmitrii Donskoi, Grand Prince of Moscow, 67, 91, 103, 104, 112; reign of, 92–93; literature inspired by, 116

Dmitrii of Tver, Grand Prince, 90–91

Dmitrii of Uglich, Prince, 147–51; death of, 143; canonization of, 151, *see also* False Dmitrii

Dmitrii Shemiaka, 94

Dmitrov (town), 96

Dneprodzherzhinsk, 547

Dnieper cossacks, 165–66, 244

Dnieper river, 12, 21, 23, 26, 29, 33, 101; role in Russian history, 4, 8; trade and, 37, 39; role in economy, 40; as Russia-Ukraine boundary, 167; Great Northern War and, 207; Poland's partition and, 250; canals and, 320

Dniester river, 12, 82, 247

Dobb, Maurice H., 493–94

Dobroliubov, Nicholas, 354, 434

Dobrudja, 359

Dobrynia Nikitych, 52

"Doctors plot," 546

Doctor Zhivago (Pasternak), 578

Dolgoruky, Prince Ivan, 224–25
Dolgoruky, Prince Jacob, 203
Domostroi or house manager, 187–88
Don cossacks, 164, 244, 576; Azov seized by,
    162; Great Northern War and, 206; Paul I
    and, 255
Donets river, 233
Don river, 12, 14, 15, 92, 101, 165; role in Rus-
    sian history, 4; Slavic settlements near, 18;
    Sviatoslav's conquest and, 29; Mongol
    invasion and, 93; trade and, 106; Russian
    fleet in, 203; Peter I and, 215; canals and,
    218–19, 521; Civil War and, 467; World War
    II and, 511
Doroshenko, Peter, 167
Dorostolon, 30
Dorpat or Iuriev, 135, 206; university of, 325,
    327
Dostoevsky, Fedor, 333, 338, 416, 420, 424,
    435; on Pushkin, 323; work of, 324, 421–23;
    in the Petrashevtsy, 339, 421; populism and,
    355; life of, 421
Dresden, 512
Drevliane, 27, 28, 30
Dristra or Silistria, 30
Droughts, 147, 405, 474, 488
Drug abuse, 586, 632, 648, 664
Drug trade, 649
Druzhina, 27, 40, 42, 44, 46, 77
Druzhinin, Nikolai M., 284, 306
Dubcek, Alexander, 553
Dudayev, Dzhokar, 618
Dukhobory, 370
Duma, see Boyar duma; State duma
Dunlop, Douglas M., 16
Duranty, Walter, 482
Dutch, see Holland / Netherlands
Dvina river, 250, 257; Northern, 4, 135, 136;
    Western, 4, 320
Dvoeverie, 49
Dvornik, Francis, 32
Dzerzhinsky, Felix, 465
Dzhugashvili, Joseph, see Stalin, Joseph

East Berlin, 549
East China Railway, 374, 400
Eastern Europe: Soviet seizure of power in,
    523–26; rebellion in, 553; independence in,
    585, 597–99, 633; Russian Federation and,
    635, 640
Eastern Rumelia, 360, 371
East Prussia, 506; World War I and, 392;
    World War II and, 512, 513
East Slavic languages, 16, 17
East Slavs, 16–19, 26, 57; unification of, 29;
    Vladimir and, 30; agriculture in, 41–42,
    43–44; religion of, 48, 50; architecture of, 53
Economic Councils, 538
Economy: of Kievan Russia, 39–44; of
    appanage Russia, 105–6; of Muscovite Rus-
    sia, 162–64, 169–71; of Imperial Russia, 210,
    216–17, 218–19, 245, 256–61, 263, 286,
    317–22, 351, 366–67, 370–71, 396–411; under

Peter I, 210, 216–17, 218–19; development
    of national, 218–19; under Catherine II, 245;
    in the 18th century, 256–61, 263; under
    Alexander I, 286; in the 19th century (first
    half), 317–22; under Alexander II, 351;
    under Alexander III, 366–67; under
    Nicholas II, 370–71; from great reforms to
    1917, 396–411; of Soviet Russia, 474–75,
    519–21, 535, 536, 538–45, 585–89, 599–604;
    of Russian Federation, 613–16, 623–24,
    630–31, see also Five-Year Plans; New Eco-
    nomic Policy; Seven-Year Plan, see also
    Agriculture; Industry and industrialization
Edison, Thomas, 419
Editing Commission, 345
Education: in Kievan Russia, 56–57; in
    appanage Russia, 122; in Poland, 126; in
    Muscovite Russia, 191–92; Church schools
    and, 215, 267, 269, 364, 417; under Peter I,
    219, 266–68; cadet schools and, 230–31, 267;
    in the 18th century, 266–70; under Cather-
    ine II, 268–69; boarding schools and, 269,
    326, 570; under Alexander I, 284, 297–98;
    under Nicholas I, 307; in the 19th century
    (first half), 324–26; home, 325; private insti-
    tutions and, 325; of military personnel, 351;
    under Alexander II, 353; under Alexander
    III, 364; under Nicholas II, 369; Stolypin's
    policy on, 389; from great reforms to 1917,
    416–18; in Soviet Russia, 564–65, 568–71, see
    also Universities
Efrosimius, Saint, 80
Egorov, Boris, 573n
Egypt: ancient, 12; Greek War of Indepen-
    dence and, 308; Turkish conflict with,
    310–11; World War II and, 512; Suez canal
    crisis and, 550
Einstein, Albert, 572
Eisenhower, Dwight D., 525, 549
Eisenstein, Serge, 75, 580
Ekaterinburg, 467
Eklof, Ben, 417
Elba, Napoleon's exile to, 292
Elections: in Imperial Russia, 285; in zemstvo
    system, 348, 365; in the Duma, 383, 385–86,
    440; in Soviet Russia, 473, 499, 522, 589,
    590; in Russian Federation, 617, 619–20,
    621–23, 625, 626, 627, 628; in postcommu-
    nist Russia, 647
Electrification, 485
Elijah, Saint, 42
Elizabeth, Empress, 223, 224, 230, 232, 234,
    239, 240, 245, 264, 273; reign of, 226–29;
    Gentry Bank established by, 231; canals
    built during reign of, 260
Elizabeth I, Queen of England, 187
Emancipation of Labor Group, 379
Emigration: from Imperial Russia, 370; from
    Soviet Russia, 547, 559, 568, 578; from post-
    communist Russia, 646, see also Migration
Émigrés, 67, 474, 659
Empire, see Expansion
Encyclopedists, 268

Engels, Friedrich, 452, 455, 456, 457, 534
England: Kievan Russia and, 34; Novgorod and, 78; Muscovite Russia and, 135–36, 176, 193; trade with, 147, 171; Imperial Russia and, 203, 204, 215, 243, 360; culture of, 278; mortality rates in, 405; Soviet Russia and, 504, *see also* Great Britain
Enisei river, 4, 140
Enlightened bureaucrats, 345
Enlightened despotism, 213, 252, 266
Enlightenment, 8, 269, 273, 274, 334; Catherine II and, 237, 239–40, 281; Russian, 265–66; science and, 275; Alexander I and, 282; Decembrist movement and, 298; Marxism and, 452
Epiphanius the Wise, 117
Erfurt, 288
Erlich, A., 486
Ermak, 140
Erofeev, Viktor, 660
Esenin, Serge, 426, 576
Estates, *see* Pomestie
Estates General: Russian, 175; French, 176
Estonia: Novgorod and, 74, 75; Great Northern War and, 205–6, 208; acquired by Imperial Russia, 208; Treaty of Brest-Litovsk and, 464; Russian Civil War and, 467, 468; independence movements in, 470, 473, 591–92; ceded by Soviet Russia, 474; Litvinov Protocol and, 504; in Soviet Union, 507, 521; Union Treaty rejected by, 604; minorities in, 633
Eternal peace, treaty of, 198
Ethiopia, 505
Ethnic cleansing, 636
Etiquette, 267–68
Eugene Onegin (Pushkin), 329, 331, 547
Eurasian school, 9, 67–68, 69–70
Europe: Mongols in, 65, 66; Basil II and, 95; Ivan IV and, 135–36; map of at time of Peter the Great, 199(figure); map of central & eastern, 236(figure); map of central, 289(figure); map (1801-1855), 295(figure); Imperial Russia and, 357–60; Soviet Russia and, 548; Russian Federation and, 635, *see also* Eastern Europe; Western influences
European Union, 639
Euthanasia, 655
Evenings on a Farm near Dikana (Gogol), 332
Executive Committee of the All-Russian Congress of Soviets, 473
Expansion: of Muscovite Russia, 178–80; of Imperial Russia, 257, 287–88, 357, 360–61, 372, *see also* Colonization
Extraordinary Commission to Combat Counterrevolution, Sabotage, and Speculation, *see* Cheka
Ezhov, Nicholas, 495–96
Ezhovshchina, 495–96

Fables, 329, 330
Factories: in Imperial Russia, 258–60, 318, 367, 400, 407–11; manorial, 260, 319; posses-sional, 260, 319; defined, 319; in Soviet Russia, 465, 474, 475, 486
Fainsod, Merle: on Revolution of 1917, 439; on Stalin, 484, 497; on the great purge, 495–96
Fairs, 101, 261, 320
False Dmitrii I, 147–51, 152
False Dmitrii II, 152–53, 154, 155, 156
False Dmitrii III, 156
False Peter, 152
Family policy, 541, 564, 565, 566
Famines, 146, 147, 378, 405, 474, 488, 492
Fanaty, 566
Far East: Russian expansion in, 357, 360, 361; Russo-Japanese War and, 373–76, 400; Maritime Provinces of, 469; Japanese aggression in, 486; forced-labor camps in, 495; social black holes in, 649
Fascism, 504, 505, 525
Fatherland-All-Russia Party, 627
Fathers and Sons (Turgenev), 420
February Revolution (1917), 441, 447, 483
Federal Republic of Germany (West Germany), 526, 550, 598
Federation Council, 619, 628
Fedotov, George P., 48, 52, 279
Feldmesser, Robert A., 541
Fellow travelers, 575
Felon of Tushino, *see* False Dmitrii II
Feoktistov, Konstantin, 573n
Ferdinand of Saxe-Coburg, 371
Fet-Shenshin, Athanasius, 424
Feudalism, 45, 169–70, 172; development of, 42, 106–8; three defining traits of, 107; undeveloped, 145, *see also* Serfdom
Feuerbach, Ludwig, 433
Fieravanti, Aristotle, 118–19
Fifth money, 163
Fili, 190
Finland, 9; Great Northern War and, 208; Alexander I, 286, 288; university of, 325; Russification in, 366, 370, 389; Lenin's flight to, 445, 449; Treaty of Brest-Litovsk and, 464; independence movements in, 470; territory ceded by Soviets, 474; nonaggression pact signed by, 504; World War II and, 507, 508, 510, 512; territory ceded to Soviets, 521; survival as free nation, 524; treaty of friendship with Soviets, 549
Finnic-speaking tribes, 18, 22, 29, 33, 87, 152; Teutonic Knighs and, 74, 75; Ivan III and, 96; St. Sergius and, 113
Finnish Diet, 382
Finno-Ugrian speakers, 17, 28
Firebird, The (Stravinsky), 430
Fires, 133, 351, 352
First Academic Expedition, 276
First Treaty of Paris, 294
Fischer, G., 349, 435
Fitzpatrick, Sheila, 484
Five-Year Plans, 9, 459, 482–95, 563; First, 461, 481, 484–89, 492, 498, 502, 543, 559, 561, 572, 575, 581; Second, 489–92, 568; Third,

Five-Year Plans, (*continued*)
  489–92; evaluation of, 492–95; Fourth,
  519–20; Fifth, 520–21, 538; Sixth, 538;
  Eighth, 542; Ninth, 542; Tenth, 542–43, 544;
  Eleventh, 544
Flanders, 78
Flaubert, Gustave, 421
Flintlock, 212
Florinsky, Michael T., 48, 223–24
Florovsky, George V., 265, 377
Fokine, Michael, 430
Folklore, 51, 116, 272, 332
Fonvizin, Denis, 271–72
Forbes, N., 72
Forbidden years, 172
Forced-labor camps, 493–95, 546, 547, 561, 578
Ford, Gerald, 552
Foreign investment, 398, 402, 614
Foreign loans: in Imperial Russia, 263, 372,
  382, 402; in Russian Federation, 615, 624,
  630, 635
Foreign policy and relations: in Kievan Rus-
  sia, 28, 30–33, 37–38, 40–41; in Muscovite
  Russia, 135–36, 147, 187, 193; in Imperial
  Russia, 209–10, 230, 232–34, 233, 245–52,
  254, 257, 281, 287–88, 292–96, 307–13;
  389–92; under Peter I, 209–10, 232, 233;
  under Peter III, 230; from Peter I to Catherine II, 232–34; under Catherine II, 245–52,
  257; under Paul I, 254; under Alexander I,
  281, 287–88, 292–96; under Nicholas I,
  307–13; under Alexander II, 357–60; pre-
  World War I, 389–92; in Soviet Russia,
  501–8, 522–27, 548–55, 598–99; in the 1920s,
  502–4; in the 1930s, 504–6; post-war,
  522–27; in Russian Federation, 633–40, *see
  also* Trade; Western influences
Forestry regulations, 213
Forests, 5, 43, 44
Formalism, 579
Formosa, 374, 527
Fort Ross, 288
Foundations of Leninism (Stalin), 481
Fountain of Bakhchisarai, The (Pushkin), 331
Fourier, F. M. Charles, 339, 458
Four Years' Diet, 250
France, 79, 109, 176, 232, 272; early cultures
  in, 15; Iaroslav and, 33; Peter I and, 207,
  208, 209, 233; Elizabeth and, 228; Seven
  Years' War and, 234; Catherine II and, 245;
  partition of Poland and, 249, 251; Paul I
  and, 254–55; freemasonry in, 273; culture
  of, 278; Alexander I and, 282, 287, 288–94;
  Napoleonic Wars and, 288–92; Congress of
  Vienna and, 293; in Quintuple Alliance,
  294; Spanish revolution and, 296; Greek
  War and, 308; Nicholas I and, 308, 309,
  311–12; revolution of 1830 in, 309; revolution of 1848 in, 311–12, 338; Straits Convention and, 313; Crimean War and, 314, 315;
  capitalism in, 322; Polish rebellion and, 352,
  353, 357; Austria's overtures to, 357;

Alexander II and, 358; Prussian war with,
  358; war with China and, 361; Congress of
  Berlin and, 371, 372; Japan forced to cede
  Liaotung, 374; loan to Russia, 382; in Triple
  Entente, 390; pre-World War I, 390–92;
  World War I and, 392, 444; investment in
  Russia, 402; mortality rates in, 405; Russian
  Civil War and, 467, 469, 472; Polish-Russian
  war and, 470; Soviet Russia and, 503, 504,
  505, 542, 552; Munich settlement and, 506;
  World War II and, 507, 514, 519; Atlantic
  Charter and, 513; Communism in, 524–25,
  526; Atlantic Defense Pact and, 525; divi-
  sion of Germany and, 526; SEATO and, 549;
  Suez canal crisis and, 550; Russian Federa-
  tion and, 637; United States invasion of
  Iraq and, 640, *see also* French influence in
  Russia; French Revolution
Francis Ferdinand, Archduke, 391
Franco, Francisco, 505
Frank, Semen, 437
Frederick I, King of Sweden, 208
Frederick II, the Great (King of Prussia), 230,
  233, 234, 235, 250
Frederick William III, King of Prussia, 302
Frederick William IV, King of Prussia, 302
Frederikshamn, Peace of, 288
Freedom party, 447–48
Free Economic Society, 258, 268, 272
Free labor, 318, 319, 343
Freemasonry, 273–74
Free servants, 108, 109
Freeze, Gregory, 262
French influence in Russia: Catherine II and,
  235, 237, 241, 242; gentry and, 266, 324
French Revolution, 256, 269, 282, 288, 334,
  356, 444; view of Catherine II on, 245, 246,
  251, 252, 274; Decembrist movement and,
  298
Freud, Sigmund, 426
Friedland, 287
Friendship, 566
Fundamental Laws, 382–83, 384, 440
Futurists, 426, 432, 575

Gagarin, Iurii A., 573n
Gagauz people, 595
Gaidar, Yegor, 613, 616, 619, 621
Galich, 82
Galicia, 30, 61, 82, 83–85, 83(map), 86, 101,
  106, 128; Mongols in, 66, 84; Volynia united
  with, 83; Austria's acquisition of, 250, 470;
  World War I and, 392
Galkin, General, 648
Gallipoli campaign, 392
Gamsakhurdia, Zviad, 593
Gapon, George, 380
Gatchina, 255
Gathering of Russia, 62, 96, 102, 103, 104, 115,
  145
Gazprom, 630
Gedymin or Gediminas, 125

Gendarmes, 304, 305, 344
General Secretariat (Ukraine), 470
Genetic engineering, 655
Geneva conference (1922), 503
Geneva conference (1955), 549
Genoese colony, 106
Gentry, 230–32, 261–63; in Kievan Russia, 36, 44; in appanage Russia, 107, 108, 109; Polish, 127, 248, 251, 352; in Muscovite Russia, 134, 138, 171, 172, 173; in Time of Troubles, 145–46, 156, 158, 159; in zemskii sobor, 157; under Peter I, 202, 211, 217–18; under Anne, 225; under Catherine II, 240, 241, 242–45, 252, 262; incorporation of, 243–44; under Paul I, 253–54; Enlightenment and, 266; education of, 267–68, 269, 326; under Alexander I, 282, 283, 284, 285, 286; under Nicholas I, 306; in the 19th century (first half), 317–18, 321; culture of, 324; under Alexander II, 343, 344–45, 346, 351; debt accumulated by, 343; zemstvo and, 348, 349; privileges renounced in Tver, 352; under Alexander III, 362, 364–65; the Duma and, 382, 385, 386; from great reforms to 1917, 397–98; land appropriated by peasants, 445, 447; disappearance of, 559, *see also* Pomestie
Gentry Bank, 231
Gentry Nest, A (Turgenev), 324, 420, 547
George, Lloyd, 503
George, Saint, 42, 99
Georgia, 143, 308, 360, 472, 499, 567; Mongols in, 65; annexation of, 287–88; Russification and, 366; split from Transcaucasian Federation, 470; rebellions in, 547; nationalistic movements in, 591, 593–94; Union Treaty rejected by, 604; Abkhazians against, 633; Russian Federation and, 638, 640
German Democratic Republic (East Germany), 526, 546, 549, 553, 598, 625, 635
German idealistic philosophy, 334, 335, 337, 338, 339, 354, 452
German Knights, 61
"German party," 225–26, 234
Germans: in Kievan Russia, 43; in Imperial Russia, 245; in Baltic region, 257
German Suburb or *Nemetskaia Sloboda*, 100, 193(figure), 194
Germany, 232, 353, 455–56, 486, 495, 504, 533, 549; Kievan Russia and, 34, 37; Mongols in, 65, 66; Novgorod and, 74–75, 77, 78; Muscovite Russia and, 135; Peter I and, 204, 209, 216; Elizabeth and, 228–29; freemasonry in, 273; French interference in, 290; Nicholas I and, 309, 312; influence of ideas on Russia, 334–35; Alexander II and, 357, 358; unification of, 357, 598; after Congress of Berlin, 371–72; in Triple Alliance, 372, 390; Japan forced to cede Liaotung, 374; pre-World War I, 390–92; World War I and, 391, 444, 445, 464, 466; investment in Russia, 402; per capita income in, 405; Ukrainian independence movement and, 470; Transcaucasian republics and, 472; Russia invaded by, 489–90, 557; Treaty of Rapallo and, 503; Anti-Comintern Pact and, 505; Sudetenland annexed by, 506; Poland invaded by, 506–8; neutrality agreement with Soviets, 507; World War II and, 507–16, 517–19, 605; war reparations paid by, 520; in post-war era, 521–22; division of, 524, 526; in post-Stalin era, 548; Russian Federation and, 635, 638; United States invasion of Iraq and, 640, *see also* Federal Republic of Germany; German Democratic Republic
Gerschenkron, Alexander P., 413; on industrialization, 398; on peasant commune, 404; on NEP, 485; on Five-Year Plans, 486
Gierek, Edward, 553–54
Giers, Nicholas, 372
Gilels, Emil, 579
Gladkov, Fedor, 485
Glagolithic alphabet, 51
Glasnost, 546, 547, 574, 583, 585, 587, 588, 599, 607; in Imperial Russia, 344; in Soviet satellites, 598; rehabilitation of reputations and, 600; welcomed by West, 606
Gleb, Prince of Riazan, 89
Gleb, Saint, 33, 49, 120
Glinka, Michael, 332, 340, 627
Glinsky, Prince Michael, 132
Glinsky family, 131
Gnedich, Nicholas, 329
"God" (Fonvizin), 271
God-Seeking, 437
God That Failed, The, 457
Godunov, Boris, 142, 143, 150, 151, 174; accession to throne, 144, 175; death of, 145, 149; reign of, 147–49
Godunov, Theodore, *see* Theodore (Fedor) II, Tsar
Gogol, Nicholas, 329, 332–33, 338
Golden age of Russian literature, 323–24, 333, 416
Golden Horde, 67, 246, *see also* Mongols
Goldsmith, Raymond W., 398
Gold standard, 371, 399
Golikov, Ivan I., 221
Golitsyn, Prince Alexander, 297
Golitsyn, Prince Basil, 150, 154, 155, 198
Golitsyn, Prince Dmitrii, 225
Golovin, Nikolai N., 440–41
Golovkin, Gabriel, 202
Golovnin, Alexander, 353, 417
Golubinsky, Evgenii E., 48
Gomulka, Wladyslaw, 550, 553
Goncharov, Ivan, 331, 424
Goncharova, Natalie, 432
Gooch, George P., 235
Gorbachev, Mikhail, 537–38, 546, 555, 566, 573, 583, 584–93, 595–607, 610–12, 613, 618, 620; economy under, 585–89, 599–604; reforms of, 585–91; opposition to, 587;

Gorbachev, Mikhail, (*continued*)
  elected president of U.S.S.R., 589, 600;
  nationalistic movements and, 595–97; east-
  ern Europe defection and, 597–99, 633;
  Nobel Peace Prize awarded to, 599; final
  crisis, 599–605; arrest of, 604; resignation of,
  604–5; loss in presidential election, 622
Gorbitsa river, 178
Gorchakov, Prince Alexander, 357, 358, 360
Gordon, Patrick, 198, 202
Goremykin, Ivan, 385, 389, 440
Gori, 482–83
Gorky, Maxim, 416, 424, 426; quoted, 556;
  death of, 576
Gorodovye prikazchiki, 177
Gosplan, 485
Gothic wars, 19
Goths, 14–15, 17, 18
Gotland (island), 78
GPU, 494–95
Grabar, Igor F., 56, 118, 120, 420
Grachev, Pavel, 618, 619
Gradualism, 355, 356, 420
Graeco-Iranian culture, 14
Grand Embassy, 204
Granovsky, Timothy, 338
Great Britain, 455, 524; Peter I and, 208,
  212–13, 233; trade with, 233, 261; Seven
  Years' War and, 234; war with American
  colonies, 246; Catherine II and, 247, 251–52;
  Second Turkish War and, 247; Paul I and,
  254, 255; freemasonry in, 273; Alexander I
  and, 287; Napoleonic Wars and, 288, 290,
  292; at Congress of Vienna, 293; in Quadru-
  ple Alliance, 294; Greek War and, 308;
  Nicholas I and, 308, 312; Straits Convention
  and, 313; Crimean War and, 314, 315; capitalism in, 322; Polish rebellion and, 352, 353,
  357; Alexander II and, 358, 360; Turkish-
  Austrian conflict and, 360; war with China,
  361; Congress of Berlin and, 372; Russo-
  Japanese War and, 375; in Triple Entente,
  390; pre–World War I, 390–91; World War I
  and, 392, 444; investment in Russia, 402;
  Russian Civil War and, 467, 469, 472; Soviet
  Russia and, 472, 503, 504; Spanish civil war
  and, 505; Munich settlement and, 506;
  World War II and, 507, 510, 512–13, 519;
  Atlantic Charter and, 513; Atlantic Defense
  Pact and, 525; division of Germany and,
  526; SEATO and, 549; Suez canal crisis and,
  550; Russian Federation and, 638; Iraq invasion and, 640, *see also* England
Great Bulgar, 15, 29, 94
Great Northern War, 201, 204–9, 210, 211, 212,
  257, 261; countries involved in, 204; Russian military strategy in, 205–6; Russian
  low point in, 207; treaty provisions, 208
Great purge, 495–97, 504, 522, 600; prominent
  victims of, 495–96; Khrushchev on, 531, 532
Great reforms, 284, 319, 320, 321, 322, 324,
  338, 340, 343, 344, 354, 366, 378; basic goal

  of, 345; emancipation of serfs as, 346;
  description of, 348–51; reluctance to
  expand, 352; economy and society follow-
  ing, 396–414; culture following, 415–38
Great retreat, 564–66, 605
Great Russians, 61, 87, 101, 167, 197; Lithua-
  nia and, 129; Old Believers and, 186; the
  Duma and, 386; in Soviet Union, 567
Great Turn, 488
Great White Brotherhood, 657
Grebenshchikov, Boris, 641, 665
Greece, 519; Union of Florence and, 95; Turk-
  ish conflicts with, 294, 308, 391; Russian
  Civil War and, 469; formal recognition of
  Soviet Union and, 503; World War II and,
  508; United States aid to, 525
Greek fire, 27
Greek language, 51
Greek project, 245, 247
Greeks: ancient, 10–12, 14, 17; in Kievan Rus-
  sia, 43; clergy of, 112; Orthodox Church
  and, 184
Greek War of Independence, 308
Green resistance, 473
Gregorian calendar, 465
Gregory, Johann, 188
Grekov, Boris D., 41, 42, 169, 574
Griboedov, Alexander, 264, 298, 330, 333
Grigoriev, Dmitrii, 191
Grishin, Victor, 587
Gromyko, Andrei, 550, 587, 600
Grossman, Gregory, 606; on Five-Year Plans,
  492; on economic crisis, 601–4
Group of Eight (G8), 639
Grozny, 618, 632
Grudtsin, Savva, 188
Gryzlov, Boris, 627
Gubernii or governments (provinces), 214,
  243
Gubnye officials, 177
Guchkov, Alexander, 386, 389, 394, 442, 445
Guerrier, Vladimir ("Guerrier courses"), 418
Gulag, 546
Gulag Archipelago (Solzhenitsyn), 547
Gulf of Finland, 143, 162, 206, 208
Gulistan, Treaty of, 288
Gumilev, Nicholas, 426
Gusinsky, Vladimir, 622, 629, 630, 643
Gustavus II (Adolphus), King of Sweden, 162
Gutchina, 468
Gymnasia, 417
Gypsies, Nazi persecution of, 518

Hadrian, Patriarch, 200, 215
Hagiography, 116–17, 187
Hague Peace Conference, 373
Haimson, Leopold, 439
Halecki, Oscar, 123
Halloween, 654
Hangö, 208
Hanover, 208, 234
Hanseatic League, 78, 135, 147

Hapsburg dynasty, 139, 204, 232, 311, 312, 357, 358, 391
Harbin, 374
Hardenberg, Prince Karl August von, 293
Hardrada, Harold, 34
Harrison, J., 182
Hat of Monomakh, 115
Havel, Vaclav, 635
Head tax, 69, 216–17, 346, 367, 405
Hegelianism, 334, 335, 338, 452
Helen (mother of Ivan IV), 131–32
Helen, Grand Duchess, 345
Hellie, Richard, 172
Helsinki: university of, 325; agreements, 548; conference, 552
Henry VIII, King of England, 141
Henry of Valois, 139–40, 232
Herberstein, Sigismund von, 100
Heresy, 113–14, 183
Hermanric, 15
Hermogen, Patriarch, 155, 156, 158, 183
Herodotus, 5, 11–12, 13, 18
Heroine Mother award, 565
Hero of Our Times, A (Lermontov), 332
Herzegovina, 358, 359, 360, 391
Herzen, Alexander, 339, 340, 354; quoted, 235; Turkish-Austrian conflict and, 334; on intellectual emancipation, 335; philosophy and activities of, 338; Alexander II and, 345; populism and, 355, 433
Hilarion, Metropolitan, 34, 50, 52
Hippius, Zinaida, 426
Hiroshima, bombing of, 512
His Majesty's Own Chancery: Fifth Department of, 304; Fourth Department of, 304, 326; Second Department of, 304; Sixth Department of, 304; Third Department of, 304–5, 344
Historical Letters (Lavrov), 434
Historico-Philological Institute of Prince Bezborodko, 325
History of the Russian State (Karamzin), 328
Hitler, Adolf, 8, 486, 503, 504, 506, 507, 508, 510, 511, 512, 516, 519
Hohenzollern dynasty, 358
Holland / Netherlands: trade with, 171, 261; Muscovite Russia and, 193; Imperial Russia and, 203, 204, 208, 263; Belgian revolution against, 309; Atlantic Defense Pact and, 525
Holy Alliance, 280, 287, 293–94
Holy Land, 75, 80, 116, 314
Holy Roman Empire, 100
Holy Synod, 215, 230, 240, 363, 369, 417
Homelessness, 615, 646
Homer, 329
Homosexuality, 565, 655, 664
Hook, Sidney, 252
Hoover, Herbert, 476
Horowitz, Vladimir, 659
"Hot line" between U.S. and U.S.S.R., 551
Hrushevsky, Mikhail S., 165
Human rights, 628, 629, 631

Hundred-Council of 1551, 134, 183
"Hundred Days," 292, 294
Hungary, 82, 85, 537, 606; Magyars and, 28; Christian conversion in, 32; Iaroslav and, 33; Kievan Russia and, 35; Mongols in, 65, 66; Roman of Volynia and, 83; Galicia and, 84; Imperial Russia and, 312; domination by U.S.S.R, 502, 524; Communism in, 525; rebellions against U.S.S.R., 531, 546, 550, 553; Communism collapse in, 598; NATO and, 636, *see also* Austria-Hungary
Huns, 15, 18
Hunting, 44
Hypatian, 53

Iablochkov, Paul, 419
Iaguzhinsky, Paul, 202, 224
Iankovich de Mirievo, Theodore, 269
Iarlyk, 69
Iaropolk, Grand Prince (son of Sviatoslav), 30, 31
Iaropolk, Grand Prince (son of Vladimir Monomakh), 36
Iaroslav (brother of Alexander Nevskii), 76–77
Iaroslav (of Tver), 85
Iaroslav (Osmomysl, Prince), 83, 84
Iaroslav (the Wise, Grand Prince), 26, 37, 41, 46, 49, 52, 73; reign of, 33–35; succession following, 35
Iaroslavl, 96, 191, 260, 278, 325
Iaroslavna (wife of Prince Igor), 53
Iasak, 178, 180
Iatviags, 30
Iavorsky, Metropolitan Stephen, 215
Ibn-Khurdadhbih, 24
Iceland, 525
Icon painting: in Kievan Russia, 56; in Novgorod, 79; in appanage Russia, 112, 120–22; in Muscovite Russia, 190–91; in Imperial Russia, 431
Ideinost, 576, 577
Ideologies and thought: in Muscovite Russia, 187; in Imperial Russia, 334–39, 432–38; in postcommunist Russia, 650–54, *see also* specific thinkers and movements
Idiot, The (Dostoevsky), 421
Ignatius, Patriarch, 150, 151
Ignatovich, Inna Ivanovna, 343
Igor (son of Iaroslav the Wise), 35
Igor, Grand Prince, 24–25, 27–28, 31, 41
Igor of Novgorod-Seversk, Prince, 53
Iliad (Homer), 329
Ilia of Murom, 52
Ilmen Lake, 76
Imperialism, 454, 455, 502, *see also* Colonialism; Expansion
Imperialism, the Highest Stage of Capitalism (Lenin), 455
Imperial Russia, 197–449; chronological boundaries of, 197; achieves empire status, 208; official inauguration of era, 208; natural friends and enemies of, 233; culture of

Imperial Russia, (*continued*)
  (*see under* Culture); economy of (*see under* Economy); society of (*see under* Society)
India, 116, 372; trade with, 210, 261; Soviet Russia and, 549; Russian Federation and, 633, 639
Indian Ocean, 621
Indigirka river, 4
Indochina, 548, 549, 551
Indo-European language family, 12, 16, 123
Indonesia, 527
Industrial regions, 399–400
Industrial revolution, 363
Industry and industrialization: in Muscovite Russia, 171; in Imperial Russia, 219, 258–60, 319, 371, 378, 398–402, 401(map), 405, 407–11; in the 19th century (first half), 319; from great reforms to 1917, 398–402, 405, 407–11; in Soviet Russia, 465, 476, 484–85, 486–88, 490, 491(map), 492, 493, 520, 538, 542; in Russian Federation, 630–31, *see also* Factories
Informals, 589
Inheritance laws, 218, 230
Innocent III, Pope, 83
Innocent IV, Pope, 124
Inorodtsy, 361
Inspector General, The (Gogol), 333, 340
Institutions: of Kievan Russia, 45–47; of Novgorod, 76–81; of Pskov, 81; of appanage Russia, 108–10; of Muscovite Russia, 174–78
Instruction to the Legislative Commission (Nakaz), 239–41
Intellectual emancipation, 335, 339
Intellectuals, 355, 458, 547, 558, 559, 568
Intelligentsia, 231, 274, 354, 436–37, 559, 566
International Court of Justice at the Hague, 373
International Labor Organization (ILO), 549
International Monetary Fund, 623, 624, 635
International Women's Day, 441
Ionian Islands, 246, 254
Iran, 513; Soviet withdrawal of forces from, 524; Russian Federation and, 636, 638, *see also* Persia
Iranians, 18, 593
Iraq: Kuwait invaded by, 599; Russian Federation and, 635, 637, 638; United States invasion of, 640
Irbit fair, 261
Ireland, 215
Irene (wife of Theodore I), 143
Irkutsk, 261
"Iron curtain" metaphor, 457, 525, 548
Isidore, Metropolitan, 95
Islam, 57, 183, 246, 294, 567, 583, 593, 594, 639; Khazars and, 15, 16; reason for Russian rejection of, 32; Mongols and, 69, 70; Georgia and, 143; Crimean War and, 314–15; reaction to Russian expansion, 360–61; Russification and, 365; Duma representation for, 383; nationalism and, 413; women in,

566; Chechnia and, 618, 624, 631; in Kosovo, 636; in postcommunist Russia, 656, 657
Ismail, 247
Israel, 528, 547, 550, 639
Israeli-Arab wars, 551, 599
Italy, 79, 106, 506; early cultures in, 15; Kievan Russia and, 37; Imperial Russia and, 203, 204, 254, 372; rebellion and unrest in, 294, 296, 309; in Triple Alliance, 372, 390; World War I and, 392; Russian Civil War and, 469; formal recognition of Soviet Union, 503; Ethiopian conquered by, 505; World War II and, 512, 519; post-World War II treaty, 524; Communism in, 524–25, 526; Atlantic Defense Pact and, 525; Soviet Russia and, 542
Itinerants (artists), 427–28
Iudenich, Nicholas, 467, 468–69, 473
Iuriev, *see* Dorpat or Iuriev
Iurii (brother of Ivan III), 96
Iurii, Grand Prince (son of Vsevolod III), 85
Iurii, Prince (uncle of Basil II), 94
Iurii Dolgorukii (George of the Long Arm), Prince of Suzdal, 85, 89
Iurii or George (grandson of Alexander Nevskii), 85, 89–91
Ivan (son of Ivan IV), 139, 428
Ivan, Prince of Riazan, 96
Ivan I, Kalita (John the Moneybag), Prince of Moscow, 91, 96, 102, 109
Ivan II, the Meek, Prince of Moscow, 91–92
Ivan III, the Great, 62, 67, 75, 79, 102, 103, 104, 110, 114, 133, 175; reign of, 95–100; titles used by, 97, 99; architecture influenced by, 118–19, 190; views on government, 187; Western influences and, 194
Ivan IV, the Terrible, 8, 62, 128, 131–42, 143, 145, 146, 147, 151, 158, 159, 171, 175, 211, 428; childhood and early rule of, 131–36; views on government, 134, 177, 187; second part of rule, 136–40; death of, 139; explanation of, 140–42; mestnichestvo and, 174; Peter I compared with, 201, 213
Ivan V (co-tsar), 198, 209, 220; death of, 197, 213; heirs of, 224, 225, 226
Ivan VI, Emperor, 226, 239
Ivanovo-Voznesensk, 260
Izgoi, 45
Iziaslav, Grand Prince, 35
Izvolsky, Alexander, 391

Jadwiga, Queen of Poland, 126, 127
Jagiello or Jogaila, Grand Prince of Lithuania and King of Poland, 93, 126, 127
Japan, 373–76, 467, 486; Kurile islands ceded to, 361; Chinese conflicts with, 374, 504; Russian Civil War and, 469; Siberia evacuated by, 474; Soviet Russia and, 495, 505–6, 507, 599; Anti-Comintern Pact and, 505; World War II and, 507, 510, 512, 513, 519, 605, *see also* Russo-Japanese War
Jaruzelski, Wojciech, 554
Jasny, Naum, 538

Jassy, Treaty of, 247
Jefferson, Thomas, 280
Jehovah's Witnesses, 657
Jelavich, Charles, 371
Jena, battle of, 287
Jenghiz Khan, 65, 66, 69, 70, 71, 94, 477
Jeremiah, Patriarch of Constantinople, 142
Jerusalem, 185
Jesus Christ, 10, 12, 14, 41, 50, 113, 657
Jews, 583; Khazars and, 16; in Kievan Russia, 43; in Imperial Russia, 204, 366, 370, 413; Dostoevsky on, 421; Nazi persecution of, 518; "plot" against Stalin and, 528; self-affirmation, 547; United States concern over, 552; emigration by, 568; in postcommunist Russia, 654, 657, *see also* Judaism
Jihad or holy war, 360
Joachim, Patriarch, 200
Job, Metropolitan, 142, 150
Joffe, Abraham, 573
John (Ioann), Metropolitan, 655
John Paul II, Pope, 554
Johnson, Robert E., 408
John Tzimisces, Emperor of Byzantium, 29–30
Joint-stock companies, 614
Jonas, Metropolitan, 95, 112
Jordanes, 18, 19
Joseph II, Emperor of Austria, 247, 252, 269
Joseph of Volok, 114
Journey from Petersburg to Moscow (Radishchev), 274
Juchi, Khan, 66
Judaism: Khazars and, 16; reason for Russian rejection of, 32; in postcommunist Russia, 656, *see also* Jews
Judaizers, 113–14
July days, 445
Jury system, 78, 350, 628
Justification of the Good, A (Soloviev), 436

Kabakov, Ilya, 662
Kadets, *see* Constitutional Democratic party
Kadyrov administration in Chechnia, 632
Kaganovich, Lazarus, 522, 532, 550
Kalka river, 63, 65
Kaluga, 153, 155, 260
Kama river region, 15, 140
Kamchatka peninsula, 178
Kamenev, Leo, 477, 478, 495
Kandinsky, Basil, 431
Kankrin, Egor, 197, 306
Kantemir, Prince Antioch, 271, 272
Kapitza, Peter, 573
Karakozov, Dmitrii, 351, 353
Karamzin, Nikolai M., 270, 271, 333, 335; on Ivan IV, 141; sentimentalism of, 272, 329; influence on literature, 328
Karelia, 208, 507
Karelo-Finnish Republic, 521
Karpovich, Michael, 232, 256, 321, 413, 435
Kars, 315, 360
Kars-Ardakhan area of Transcaucasia, 474

Kasim (Mongol noble), 94
Kasimov, 94, 95
Katkov, Michael, 353, 435
Katyn Forest, 514
Kaufmann, Constantine, 361
Kazakhs, 499; Peter I and, 210; nationalistic movements of, 594
Kazakhstan, 594; rebellions in, 547; Russian Federation and, 633, 634, 637
Kazakov, Matthew, 277
Kazan, 67, 95, 177, 178; Basil III and, 100; fairs in, 101; Ivan IV and, 134, 135, 140, 142; peasant escapes to, 146; literature inspired by events in, 188; Pugachev's rebellion and, 241; trade in, 260; university of, 297–98, 324, 325, 327, 461; Civil War and, 467
Keep, J. L. H., 176
Keistut or Kestutis, 125, 126
Kellogg-Briand Pact, 504
Kennan, George F., 472
Kennedy, John F., 551
Kerch, 246, 510
Kerensky, Alexander: in Provisional Government, 442, 444, 445, 446; escape of, 449
Kerner, Robert J., 8
KGB, 495, 537, 624, 625–26
Khabarovsk, 361
Khakan-Rus, 23, 24
Khalturin, Stephen, 410
Kharkov: in Muscovite Russia, 192; university of, 324, 325
Khasbulatov, Ruslan, 616, 617
Khazars, 23, 28, 29; historical role of, 15–16, 18; in byliny, 52
Khitrovo, Bogdan, 191
Khitrovo Gospels, 122
Khiva, 210, 361, 472
Khlebnikov, Velemir, 426
Khmelnitsky, Bogdan or Boghan, 166, 167
Khodorkovsky, Mikhail, 629, 642
Khodsky, Leonid V., 347
Kholopy (slaves), 109
Khomiakov, Alexis, 323, 336, 337, 338
Khoromy, 189
Khristos, Maria Devi, 657
Khromov, Pavel A., 260
Khrushchev, Nikita, 8, 421, 459, 522, 527, 530–35, 536, 561, 580, 605; Stalin denounced by, 497, 531, 532, 546, 550; rise, rule, and fall of, 530–33; economy under, 538–43; foreign relations under, 548, 549, 550–51; education under, 570; religion and, 583
Khvorostinin, Prince Ivan, 152, 194
Kiakhta, Treaty of, 210
Kiao-chow, 374
Kiev, 50, 59, 101, 595; East Slavs in, 18; assigned to Iziaslav, 35; trade in, 43, 84; Mongols in, 66, 75; sacking of, 85; Moscow's replacement as religious capital, 91; Olgerd and, 125; Poland's seizure of, 128; in Muscovite Russia, 167, 183, 192; in Imperial Russia, 198; university of, 326; mass graves discovered outside, 600

Kievan Russia, 8, 12, 16, 21–57, 70–71, 80–81, 82, 86; establishment of state, 21–25; decline and fall of, 26–27, 35–36; political outline of, 26–38; rise of, 27–30; at the zenith, 30–34; reasons for fall of, 36–38; economy of, 39–44; society in, 44–45; institutions of, 45–47; religion in, 48–51, 52–53; culture of, 50–57; final days of, 59–62; inheritance claimed by Ivan III, 97–98; Lithuanian relationship with, 125–26
Kino (music group), 664
Kirchner, Walter, 223
Kireevsky, Ivan, 336
Kireevsky, Peter, 336
Kirghiz, 472, 499, 594
Kirilenko, Andrew, 536
Kiriyenko, Sergei, 613, 614, 623
Kirov, Serge, 495
Kiselev, Count Paul, 306, 322
Kishinev, 370
Kizevetter, Aleksandr A., 223, 240
Klet or srub, 117
Klin, 139
Kline, George L., 571
Kliuchevsky, Vasilii Osipovich, 8, 56, 231, 419; on northeast, 86, 87; on Moscow, 88; on Muscovite Russia, 102; on Time of Troubles, 159; on Alexis (Quietest One), 164; on boyar duma, 174; on zemskii sobor, 176; on Peter I, 202, 210; on the Legislative Commission, 240; on LaHarpe, 281
Knights of Malta, 254
Kochubey, Count Victor, 282, 303
Kohl, Helmut, 598, 635
Kokand, 361, 472
Kokovtsov, Count Vladimir, 389
Kolchak, Alexander, 467, 469
Kolchin, Peter, 232
Kolkhozes, see Collective farms
Kolomenskoe, 189
Kolyma river, 4, 178
Komanov, Vladimir, 573
Komar, Vitaly, 662
Komarov, Vladimir, 573n
Komsomol, see Union of Communist Youth
Konchalovsky, Andrei, 662
Kondakov, Nikodim, 111, 420
Konev, Ivan, 512
Königsberg district of East Prussia, 513
Konovalov, Sergei, 193
Kontsy, 76, 78, 81
Korea, 65, 527, 638–39; Trans-Siberian railroad in, 374; Russo-Japanese War and, 376
Korean War, 527, 548
Kormleniia, 177, 214, 216
Kornai, János, 606
Kornilov, Lavr, 446–47, 467
Kornilov, Vladimir, 315
Korolenko, Vladimir, 424
Korovin, Constantine, 431
Kosciuszko, Thaddeus, 250, 253
Kosovo, 636–37
Kostomarov, Nikolai I., 161

Kosygin, Alexis, 534, 536, 542
Kotoshikhin, Gregory, 194–95
Koussevitzky, Serge, 430–31
Kovalev, Sergei, 619
Kovalevskaia, Sophia, 419
Kovalevsky, Alexander, 419
Kovalevsky, Maksim, 362, 378
Kovalevsky, Vladimir, 419
Kozelsk, 68
Kozynev, Aleksandr, 633, 636
Kramskoy, Ivan, 427
Kremlin, 92, 118, 120; of Novgorod, 76; Polish occupation of, 156, 157; architecture of, 190; Napoleonic Wars and, 291
Krewo, agreement of, 126
Krishna Consciousness, 657
Kristi, Agata, 664
Krivichi tribe, 22
Krizanic, George, 194
Kronstadt, 206, 475
Kropotkin, Prince Peter, 341, 433
Krüdener, Baroness Julie de, 293
Krylov, Ivan, 329–30, 333
Kuban river and region, 244, 467
Kublai Khan, 65, 70
Kucherov, Samuel, 350
Kuchma, Leonid, 634
Kuchuk Kainarji, Treaty of, 246
Kuchum, Khan, 140
Kuibyshev, 508, see also Samara
Kukly (television program), 629, 661
Kulaks, 476, 485, 488, 493
Kulikovo, battle of, 67, 93, 98, 104, 113, 116
Kunersdorf, battle of, 234
Kuomintang, 503
Kurbanovsky, Aleksei, 662
Kurbatov, Alexis, 202
Kurbsky, Prince Andrew, 135, 138, 139, 141, 187
Kurile islands, 361, 512, 599
Kursk, 261, 511
Kursk (submarine), 632, 647
Kutrigurs, 15
Kutuzov, Prince Michael, 247, 288, 291
Kuwait, 599
Kuzmich, Theodore or Fedor, 282
Kuznetsstroi, 486
Kyrgyzstan, 637

Labor Code, 628
Labor force: in Imperial Russia, 258–60, 319, 407–11; Revolution of 1905 and, 378, 379, see also Strikes; Trade unions; Workers
Labor legislation, 367, 389, 408, 410
Ladoga Lake, 4, 76
La Fontaine, Jean de, 329
LaHarpe, Frédéric-César de, 281
Lakes, role in Russian history, 4, 8
Land: policy of Catherine II, 244; policy of Alexander I, 284; Decembrist movement and, 298; settlement for former serfs, 345, 346, 347, 352, 402; zemstvo system and, 348, 365; Duma policy on, 384; Stolypin's

suggestions on, 385, 388–90, 406–7, 440; redemption payments for, 405; Provisional Government and, 443, 444; peasant appropriation of, 445, 447; nationalization of, 465; lease of, 476; in Russian Federation, 628; of Church (*see under* Russian Orthodox Church), *see also* Pomestie
Land and Freedom society, 356
Landau, Leo, 573
Land captain, office of, *see* Zemskii nachalnik or land captain, office of
Land Code, 628
Landlords, *see* Gentry
Landsbergis, Vytautas, 592
Langer, William L., 372
Language and linguistics: in Kievan Russia, 50–53; in Imperial Russia, 270, 328; in Soviet Russia, 574
Lantzeff, George V., 169, 180
Lapidus, Gail W., 566
Lapps, 17
Larionov, Michael, 432
Lasswell, Harold D., 458
"Last Day of Pompeii, The" (painting), 340
Latvia: Novgorod and, 74; acquired by Imperial Russia, 208; Great Northern War and, 208; Poland's partition and, 250; Treaty of Brest-Litovsk and, 464; independence movements in, 470, 591–92; ceded by Soviet Russia, 474; Litvinov Protocol and, 504; in Soviet Union, 507, 521; Union Treaty rejected by, 604; minorities in, 633
Laurentian chronicle, 53
Lavrov, Peter, 355, 434, 456
Law concerning the estates, 304
Law concerning the free agriculturalists, 284
Law of 1762, 231
Law of 1897, 410
Law schools, 325
Lawyers, 350, 378
Lay of the Destruction of the Russian Land, 116
Lay of the Host of Igor, The, 53, 59, 83, 116, 271
League of Armed Neutrality, 245, 251–52
League of Nations, 504, 505
League of the Militant Godless, 582
Lebanon, 555
Lebed, Aleksandr, 619, 622
Lebedev, Peter, 419
Lednicki, Waclaw, 331
Lefort, Francis, 202, 203
Left: in Imperial Russia, 353; the Duma and, 384, 385, 386, 395; terrorism and, 389; Provisional Government and, 445–46; post-Lenin struggle for power and, 477–79; in postcommunist Russia, 651, 654, 665
Left Communists, 475
Left Hegelianism, 338
Left Opposition, 495
Left Socialist Revolutionaries, 465; in Constituent Assembly, 463; World War I and, 464; Civil War and, 466–67
Legal codes and systems: in Kievan Russia, 46; of Mongols, 70; of Novgorod, 78; of

Pskov, 81; in appanage Russia, 99; in Muscovite Russia, 177; in Imperial Russia, 231–32, 239–41, 284, 304, 306, 349–50; in Soviet Russia, 476, 500, 546; in Russian Federation, 628, *see also Russian Justice, The; Sudebnik; Ulozhenie*
Legislative assemblies or dumy, 285
Legislative Commission, 239–41, 243, 276
Leibniz, Gottfried Wilhelm, 214
Leipzig, 512; university of, 274; battle of, 292
Lemberg or Lvov, 250
Lemke, Mikhail K., 316
Lena gold field massacre, 410
Lena river, 4
Lenin, Vladimir Ilich, 434–35, 438, 447, 452, 453(figure), 454–59, 461–63, 472, 497, 534, 541, 558, 561, 647; original name of, 379; Revolution of 1905 and, 379; "April Theses," 444, 455; returns to Russia, 444–45, 449; background of, 456, 461; death of, 461; myth and reality of, 462; World War I and, 464; wounding of, 466; murder of Romanov family and, 467; as Communist Party head, 473–74; rationale behind NEP, 475–77; power struggle following death of, 477–81; opinion of Stalin, 483; interest in electrification, 485; foreign relations and, 501, 502; Gorbachev on, 585, 586; on religion, 654
Leningrad: Petrograd renamed as, 478; World War II and, 507, 508, 515; renamed St. Petersburg, 597; resistance to coup in, 625; university of, 625
Leninism, *see* Marxism-Leninism
Lenin Mausoleum, 530
Leo (son of Daniel), 84
Leo I, Pope, 15
Leonov, Aleksei A., 573n
Leontiev, Constantine, 435
Leontovich, Victor, 231, 252
Leopold, Charles (Duke of Mecklenburg), 226
Leopoldovna, Anna, 226
Le Pen, Jean-Marie, 621
Lermontov, Michael, 329, 333, 338; Pushkin's influence on, 331; life and death of, 332; work of, 332; quoted, 501
Le Sacre du printemps (Stravinsky), 430
Leskov, Nicholas, 424
Lesnaia, 207
Leszczynski, Stanislaw, 206, 233
Letters of a Russian Traveler (Karamzin), 272
Levitsky, Dmitrii, 277
Lewin, Moshe, 542
Liaotung Peninsula, 374, 376
Liapunov, Procopius, 152, 155, 156
Liapunov, Zachary, 152
Liashchenko, Peter I., 39, 399; on feudalism, 169–70; on the labor force, 260; on land settlement for serfs, 347
Libau, 261
Liberal Democratic Party of Russia (LDPR), 620, 628, 653
Liberalism: Peter I and, 221; Catherine II and, 240; Alexander I and, 282–87, 298; in

Liberalism, (*continued*)
  Imperial Russia, 334, 337, 345, 352, 435–36,
    439; zemstvo and, 349; Revolution of 1905
    and, 378; Provisional Government and, 443,
    444; in Soviet Republic, 597; in Russian
    Federation, 620, 621
Liberation, The (newspaper), 378
Liberman, Evsei, 543
Liberum veto, 248, 250
Libraries, 267, 324
Lichnost, 587
Lichud, Ioannicius, 192
Lichud, Sofronius, 192
Liegnitz, battle of, 66
Ligachev, Yegor, 587
Lilge, Frederic, 571
Limonov, Eduard, 652
Lipitsa, 74
Literacy: in Kievan Russia, 57; in Novgorod,
    80; in appanage Russia, 122; in Imperial
    Russia, 407, 418, 440; in Soviet Russia, 568
Literary criticism, 328, 338, 426, 575
Literature: of Kievan Russia, 22, 50–53; of
    Novgorod, 79–80; of appanage Russia, 112,
    116–17; travel, 116; of Muscovite Russia,
    187–88; of Imperial Russia, 270–72, 304–5,
    323–24, 328–33; golden age of, 323–24, 333,
    416; silver age of, 416, 420, 425–26, 427,
    430–31, 432, 436, 437, 575, 659; of Soviet
    Russia, 574–78; of postcommunist Russia,
    659–61, *see also* Poetry; specific writers,
    works, and movements
Lithuania, 91, 112, 123–29, 137, 138, 606;
    appanage Russia and, 61, 62; Poland and,
    79, 123, 126–28, 129, 250, 309, 310, 352;
    Roman of Volynia and, 83; Volynia
    absorbed by, 84; Tver supported by, 92;
    Mongols and, 93, 125, 126; Basil I and, 94;
    Ivan III and, 97–98; Basil III and, 100, 123;
    language of, 123, 592; evolution of state,
    123–27; role in Russian history, 128–29;
    Ivan IV and, 139; False Dmitrii I and, 147,
    149; Madeburg Law and, 177; Catherine II
    and, 250; serfdom in, 344; Treaty of Brest-
    Litovsk and, 464; independence move-
    ments in, 470, 591–93; ceded by Soviet Rus-
    sia, 474; Litvinov Protocol and, 504; in
    Soviet Union, 507, 521; Union Treaty
    rejected by, 604
Lithuanian Statute, 310
Lithuanian tribes, 17, 18, 33; Christianity
    rejected by, 32; Novgorod and, 74, 75; unifi-
    cation of, 125
Little Felon, 156, 161, 162
Little Octobrists (youth organization), 557
Little Poland, 250
Litvinov, Maxim, 502, 504, 506
Litvinov Protocol, 504
Liubavsky, Matvei K., 103, 419; on Mongols,
    106; on Lithuania, 123
Liubech, 35, 39
Liubimov, Yury, 580

Liudi, 44
Liutprand, Bishop of Cremona, 23
Living Church, 581
Livnev, Sergei, 663
Livonia, 35, 153, 205, 208
Livonian Order, 75, 98, 135
Livonian War, 137, 139–40, 141, 175
Lobachevsky, Nicholas, 324, 327, 419
Local government: in Novgorod, 79; under
    Ivan IV, 134; in Muscovite Russia, 177–78;
    under Peter I, 213, 214; under Catherine II,
    243–44; under Alexander I, 285; under
    Alexander II, 348–49; conterreforms and,
    397; in Soviet Russia, 464
Locke, John, 268
Lodz, 399
Logocentrism, 662
Lomonosov, Michael, 268, 270, 271, 275–76,
    277, 278, 324
London, Treaty of, 309, 313
Lopukhina, Eudoxia, 202, 204, 220
Lord, Robert H., 251
Loris-Melikov, Count Michael, 356–57, 362,
    363
Lossky, Nicholas, 437
Louis XI, King of France, 141
Louis XVI, King of France, 252
Louis-Philippe, King of France, 309, 312
Lovat river, 4
"Lovers of Wisdom, The" (philosophic circle),
    335, 339
Lübeck, 135
Lublin: Union of, 127–28; government of
    Poland, 513–14
Lukashenko, Aleksandr, 634
Lunacharsky, Anatoly, 575
Lungin, Pavel, 662, 664
Lunik I, 573n
Lunokhod-1, 573n
Lutheran religion, 215, 365, 567
Luxembourg, 525
Luzhkov, Yury, 627
Lvov (town), 84
Lvov, Prince George, 394, 442, 445
Lysenko, Trofim, 572, 574

Mably, Gabriel Bonnot de, 274
Macarius, Metropolitan, 133, 187
Macarius, Saint, 80
Macedonia, 360
Machine Tractor Stations (MTS), 486, 489, 540
Madariaga, Isabel de, 252
Madzhak, prince of Duleby, 19
Mafias, 614, 644, 648–49, *see also* Organized
    crime
Magdeburg Law, 177
Magnitostroi, 486
Magnitsky, Michael, 297–98, 325, 335
Magyars, 28
Main Committee, 345
Maklakov, Basil, 435
Makovsky, D. P., 142

"Malefactor, The" (Chekhov), 438
Malenkov, George, 522, 530, 531, 532, 538, 548–49, 550
Malevich, Kazimir, 431, 432, 579
Malia, Martin E., 231, 323
Maloiaroslavets, 291
Malozemoff, Andrew A., 374
Malta, 246, 255
Mamai (Mongol leader), 92–93
Manchukuo, 505
Manchuria, 506; Mongols in, 64; Russo-Japanese War and, 374, 375, 376; Trans-Siberian railroad in, 374; World War II and, 512; railroad ceded to China, 527
Mandelshtam, Osip, 426, 575, 576, 664
Manila, 549
Mao Zedong, 527
Marburg University, 275
Marchenko, Vasilii P., 540
Marie Louise of Austria (wife of Napoleon I), 290
Marinina, Aleksandra, 660
Maritime Provinces, 469
Marr, Nicholas, 574
Marriage: in Kievan Russia, 51; in Soviet Russia, 564, 565
Marshall Plan, 525, 635
Marshal of the Nobility, 244
Mars-3 probe, 573n
Martha (mother of Dmitri of Uglich), 149–50, 151, 153
Martov, Julius, 434–35
Marx, Karl, 409, 452–54, 455, 456, 457, 534, 610; quoted, 451; Stalin's acquaintance with, 483
Marxism, 108, 379, 408, 416; impact on intellectual thought, 434–35, 436; roots of, 452; tenets of, 452–54; Five-Year Plans and, 484–85
Marxism and the Leap to the Kingdom of Freedom (Walicki), 606
Marxism-Leninism, 558; tenets of, 454–56; intolerance of, 456–57; reasons for appeal of, 457–58; foreign relations and, 501–8; as official ideology of party, 601; disappearance of, 659
Mary, Empress Mother, 299, 304
Mary, mother of Jesus, 657
Maskhadov, Aslan, 619
Massacre on the ice, 75
Mass graves, discovery of, 600
Masurian Lakes, battle of, 392
Materialism, 354, 416, 433, 436, 437, 438; dialectical, 452, 457
Mathematical schools, 266
Mathematics, 327, 419
Mathewson, Rufus W., Jr., 415
Maximalists, 387, 388
Mayakovsky, Vladimir, 426, 482, 575, 576Maynard, Sir John H., 460
Mazepa, Ivan, 206–7, 215
Mazon, André, 53

Mazovia, 250
Mechnikov, Elijah, 419
Media, 627, 628, 629–30, *see also* Press
Media-MOST, 630
Medical care, 349, 419, 536
Medical schools, 267, 307
Medical-Surgical Academy, 327
Mediterranean Sea, 37, 246, 254, 290
Medvedev, Aleksei, 409(figure)
Medvedev, Roy, 547
Medvedev, Sylvester, 192
Melamid, Alexander, 662
Memoir on Ancient and Modern Russia (Karamzin), 328
Memoirs of a Revolutionist (Kropotkin), 433
Memorial (organization), 590
Mendeleev, Dmitrii, 419
Mengli-Geray, 98
Menologia, 187
Mensheviks, 379, 410, 443, 454, 557; split with Bolsheviks, 434–35; in Constituent Assembly, 463; persecution of, 465; in Georgia, 472, 593
Menshikov, Prince Alexander, 202, 220, 314; titles awarded to, 203; Great Northern War and, 206–7; Peter II and, 224–25
Menshutkin, Boris N., 276
Mercantilism, 218
Merchant marine, 218
Merchants, 162, 173, 217, 262–63, 285
Merezhkovsky, Dmitrii S., 333, 426
Merrick, Sir John, 193, 194
Mesopotamia, 12, 41, 65
Mestnichestvo, 137, 168, 173–74, 175
Metaphysics, 436–37
Methodius, Saint, 50–51
Metternich, Prince Clemens von, 293, 294, 296
Mexico, 503
Meyendorff, John, 32
MGB, 495
Miakotin, Venedikt A., 82
Michael, Grand Duke, 442
Michael of Chernigov, 117
Michael of Tver (Aleksandrovich), Grand Prince, 85, 89–90, 92
Michael of Tver (Borisovich), Grand Prince, 97
Michael Romanov, Tsar, 144, 154, 160, 167, 175, 176, 183, 190; election of, 157–58; as a pretender, 159; reign of, 161–64; Western influences and, 194
Michell, R., 72
Middle class: in Kievan Russia, 44; in appanage Russia, 106, 109; in Muscovite Russia, 173; in Imperial Russia, 217, 326, 351, 378, 398; in Soviet Russia, 465, 473, 522; in postcommunist Russia, 644, *see also* Bourgeoisie
Middle East, 261, 555, 638
Miege, Guy de, 182
"Mighty Bunch," 428

Migration: in ancient Russia, 15; in Time of Troubles, 146; to Turkey, 361; in Imperial Russia, 405–6; in postcommunist Russia, 645, *see also* Emigration

Mikhailov, Viacheslav, 662, 663(figure)

Mikhailovsky, Nicholas, 355, 434, 456

Mikhalkov, Nikita, 662

Mikoyan, Anastasius, 522

Militant atheist movement, 581

Military: in Kievan Russia, 46; Mongol influence on, 69; in appanage Russia, 107; in Muscovite Russia, 134, 173–74; in Time of Troubles, 145; in Imperial Russia, 201–2, 211–13, 217–18, 230–32, 262, 301, 350–51, 367, 370; under Peter I, 201–2, 211–13, 217–18; draft in, 211–12; under Nicholas I, 301; under Alexander II, 350–51; under Nicholas II, 367, 370; in Soviet Russia, 543, 544, 586; in Russian Federation, 632–33; in postcommunist Russia, 648, *see also* Army; Navy

Military Opposition movement, 475

Military settlements, 297

Miliukov, Paul N., 378, 419, 435; on Michael Romanov, 158; quoted, 161; on Russian Church, 186; on education in Muscovite Russia, 192; on Peter I, 210; Progressive Bloc led by, 395; in Provisional Government, 442, 445

Miliutin, Dmitrii, 350–51, 363

Miliutin, Nicholas, 345, 350, 352

Milosevic, Slobodan, 636, 637

Miloslavskaia, Mary (first wife of Alexis), 197

Miloslavsky, Prince Elijah, 164

Miloslavsky family, 197–98

Milosz, Czeslaw, 457

Mindovg or Mindaugas, 124, 125

Miniatures, 56, 122, 190, 191

Minin, Kuzma, 156

Ministries, 214, 284, 285

Ministry of Education, 305, 310, 325–26, 363, 364, 417

Ministry of Finance, 367, 370–71, 374, 398, 417

Ministry of State Domains, 304

Ministry of the Interior, 305, 363, 398, 649

Ministry of Trade and Industry, 417

Ministry of State Domains, 306

Minor, The (Fonvizin), 271–72

Minorities (national and religious): in Imperial Russia, 240, 412–13; World War I and, 392; Provisional Government and, 443, 444, 445; in Soviet Union, 464–65, 567–68, 591–97; Stalin as commissar for, 483; Russian Federation and, 633–34

Minsk, 508, 600, 634

Mir, *see* Peasant commune

Mironenko, Iurii P., 518

Mirovich, Basil, 239

Mirrlees, H., 182

Mirror for Youth, A (etiquette manual), 267–68

Mirsky (Sviatopolk-Mirsky), Dmitrii P., 111, 332, 425

Missouri (battleship), 512

Mithridates the Great of Pontus, 14

Mnemosyne (journal), 335

Mniszech, Marina, 147, 150, 153, 156, 161

Modernism, 431–32

Mogila or Mohila, Metropolitan Peter, 192

Mohammed Ali of Egypt, 310

Moldavia, 288, 622; Mongols in, 67; Lithuania and, 126; Great Northern War and, 207; First Turkish War and, 246; Treaty of Adrianople and, 308; Nicholas I and, 312; Crimean War and, 315; language of, 595; Union Treaty rejected by, 604

Moldavian Soviet Socialist Republic, 507, 521, 595

Moldova, *see* Moldavia

Molokany (religious group), 412

Molotov, Viacheslav, 497, 506–7, 522, 530, 532, 549, 550

Monasteries, 109, 183; Monastery of the Caves, 49, 50, 52, 56, 104; St. George Monastery, 56; St. Macarius Monastery, 101; Holy Trinity-St. Sergius Monastery, 104, 113, 122, 153, 156, 192, 198; Solovetskii Monastery on the White Sea, 122, 185; Monastery of St. Cyril on the White Lake, 122; Monastery of St. Macarius, 261, 320, *see also* Churches and cathedrals

Monasticism, 49–50, 115

Money, *see* Currency

Mongol Central Asian state, 70

Mongolia, 64, 506; Peter I and, 210; trade with, 321, 400; Outer, 503–4, 655

Mongols, 9, 12, 17, 27, 36, 37–38, 59, 63–71, 75, 106; Kievan conquest by, 61, 62, 75; first appearance of, 63; reasons for success of, 65–66; length of reign in Russia, 67; role of in Russian history, 67–71; Alexander Nevskii and, 74, 75; Galicia and Volynia conquered by, 84; northeast conquered by, 85, 87; in Moscow, 89–95, 101, 102, 103–4; in Lithuania, 93, 125, 126; Ivan III and, 96, 98, 99; literature inspired by conquest of, 116; decline of education and, 122; as gentry, 145, *see also* Tartars

Monroe Doctrine, 294

Montenegro, 207, 358, 359, 360, 391

Montesquieu, 237, 240, 272

Montgomery, Sir Bernard Law, 512

Moravia, 51, 506

Mordva people, 152

Mormons, 657

Morocco, 512

Morozov, Boris, 164

Morozov family, 400

Mortality rates, 405, 646, 648

Moscow, 61, 69, 88–104, 257, 273, 365, 472, 538, 590; geography impact on, 8; Tver rivalry with, 75, 89–91, 92, 93, 101; Novgorod destroyed by, 79; rise of, 86, 87, 89–95; first appearance of name, 89; Mongols in, 89–95, 101, 102, 103–4; as religious capital, 91, 104; as Third Rome, 100, 115–16, 117; reasons for success of, 101–4; architecture of, 118, 340; icon painting in, 121–22; Olgerd's siege of, 125; Lithuania and, 126, 128–29; fire of, 133; Tartar invasion of, 135; Ivan IV abandons, 138; in Time of Troubles, 147, 152, 153, 155, 157; rebellion in, 164–65; industry in, 171, 260, 319, 399, 408; university of, 228, 268, 273, 284, 325, 328, 334, 335, 338, 363; trade in, 260, 261; schools in, 266, 267; Napoleonic Wars and, 291, 292; railroad in, 320; Jews in, 366; Revolution of 1905 and, 381; conservatory of, 428; Civil War and, 467, 468–69; Kamenev's organization in, 478; World War II and, 508–10; government centralization in, 522; Popov as mayor of, 597; Yeltsin as party boss in, 610; economic situation in, 614; Chechen bombing in, 625; economic growth in, 630, 631; terrorist attacks on, 632; businesses in, 644; the arts in, 662

Moscow Art Theater, 424, 432, 579
Moscow metro, 579
Moscow Popular Front, 590
Moscow river, 89, 101, 102, 120
Mosely, Philip Edward, 311
Moses, Archbishop, 80
Moskovskie Vedomosti or *Moscow News* (newspaper), 268
Moskvitianin, Ivan, 178
Motherhood awards, 565
Motherland (party), 628
Mount Athos, 49, 115, 116, 184
Movies, *see* Cinema
Mozdok, 511
Mozhaisk, 89, 508, 510
Mstislav, Grand Prince (son of Vladimir Monomakh), 27, 36, 73
Mstislav, Prince of Galicia, 84
Mstislav of Toropets, Prince, 74
Mstislav the Brave, Prince of Tmutorokan, 33
Mstislavsky, Prince Theodore, 154
MTS, *see* Machine Tractor Stations
MTV (Russian), 664
Muir and Merrilies department store, 413
Mukden, 375
Münchengrätz, 311
Munich settlement, 506, 507
Münnich, Burkhard, 202, 226, 233
Muratov, Pavel P., 121–22
Muratova, Kira, 662
Muraviev, Nikita, 298
Muraviev-Amursky, Count Nicholas, 361
Murmansk, 469, 501, 508, 510
Muscovite or Naryshkin baroque, 190
Muscovite Russia, 59, 62, 70–71, 74, 110, 131–95; Pskov and, 81; beginning of era, 96; reasons for success of, 101–4; Lithuania and, 128–29; economy of, 162–64, 169–71; rebellion in, 164–65; society in, 171–74; institutions of, 174–78; culture of, 181–95;

religion in, 182–86; self-criticism in, 192–95
Museums, 267
Music: of Imperial Russia, 277, 324, 331–32, 340, 428–31; of Soviet Russia, 564, 579; of postcommunist Russia, 664–65, *see also* Opera, Rock Music
Musketeers, *see* Streltsy
Muslims, *see* Islam
Mussolini, Benito, 506
Mussorgsky, Modest, 143, 332, 428, 429(figure)
Mutual Defense Assistance Program, 526
Muzhi, 44
Muzhiks, 355
MVD, 495
My Past and Thoughts (Herzen), 338
Mysticism, 49, 273, 281, 297, 425–26, 437, 657

Nabokov, Vladimir, 333, 578, 659
Nagasaki, bombing of, 512
Nagorno-Karabakh, 591, 594, 633
Nagy, Imre, 550
Nakhimov, Paul, 315
Namestniki, 177
Naples, 254
Napoleon I, Emperor, 8, 255, 281, 286, 287, 288–92, 294, 298, 302, 307, 423; Polish support of, 251; abdication of, 292; attempted comeback of, 293
Napoleon III, Emperor, 314, 352, 357
Napoleonic Wars, 288–92; crises leading to, 290; Russian advantages in, 290; French defeated in, 292
Narodnichestvo, *see* Populism
Narodnost, 576, 577
Narva, 205, 206, 207, 212
Naryshkin, Leo, 200
Naryshkina, Nathalie (mother of Peter I), 197, 198, 200, 202, 203, 220
Naryshkin family, 197–98
National Bolshevik Party, 652
National Hotel, 632
National income, 520, 540, 587, 630
Nationalism: in Ukraine, 310, 366; in Imperial Russia, 353, 369; of Russian minority groups, 412–13; in Soviet Union satellites, 591–97; in Russian Federation, 620, 624, 625, 637; Putin and, 627; in postcommunist Russia, 646–47, 651–54, 657
Nationality, 302, 362–63, 367
Nationalization of industry and trade, 465, 485, 559
National missile defense (NMD) system, 638
National Salvation Front, 615, 652
Nations, battle of the, 292
NATO, *see* North Atlantic Treaty Organization
Natural gas, 543, 555, 606, 623, 624
Natural resources, 5, 8
Naval Academy, 266
Navarino, battle of, 308

Navy: of Imperial Russia, 202, 206, 212–13, 233, 308, 351, 397; in Russo-Japanese War, 375; of Soviet Russia, 543, 552; of Russian Federation, 632

Nazi organizations in Russia, 652

Near East, 390; French interest in, 290; Nicholas I and, 310–11; Izvolsky's policy in, 391; Soviet Russia and, 548

Nechaev, Serge ("Jacobin"), 356

Neglinnaia river, 120

Nekrasov, Nicholas, 338, 397, 420, 425

Nelidov, Alexander, 391

Nemetskaia Sloboda, see German Suburb

Nemtsov, Boris, 623

Neo-classical style of architecture, 276–77, 340

Neo-communist movements, 591, 615, 635

Neo-Slavophilism, 547

NEP, *see* New Economic Policy

Nepmen, 476, 485

Nepriadva river, 93

Nerchinsk, Treaty of, 178, 361

Neronov, Ivan, 183

Nesselrode, Count Karl, 307–8, 313

Nestor, 53

Netherlands, *see* Holland / Netherlands

Neva river, 75, 135, 206, 218, 320

New Academy of Fine Arts, 662

New Class, 563–64

New Economic Policy (NEP), 461, 475–77, 481, 548, 559, 561, 605; success of, 476; restrictions on, 476–77; abandonment of, 485

New Russia, 253

New Russians, 642–44, 653

Newspapers: in Imperial Russia, 222, 266, 268, 387, 407, 411, 413, 437; in Soviet Russia, 465, 499; in Russian Federation, 630

New Zealand, 550

Nezhin, 325

Nicephorus Phocas, Emperor of Byzantium, 29

Nicholas, Grand Duke, 395

Nicholas, Saint, 42

Nicholas I, Emperor, 8, 131, 212, 276, 294, 297, 301–16, 321, 322, 324, 329, 334, 338, 339, 341, 344, 357, 358, 383, 416, 432; and free thinking, 298; Decembrist movement and, 299–300, 303; character and background of, 301–2; "system" of, 303–5; reforms of, 305–6; last years of, 307; death of, 316; railroads influenced by, 320; educational policies of, 325, 326; science during reign of, 327; satire of life under, 333; Slavophiles on, 337; architecture supported by, 340; Alexander II compared with, 343, 352

Nicholas II, Emperor, 351, 362, 363, 367–76, 378, 397, 440, 441, 584; personal qualities of, 367–69; canonization of, 368–69, 655; reaction under, 369–70; Revolution of 1905 and, 379, 380–81; Fundamental Laws and, 382–83; the Duma and, 384, 385, 395; Treaty of Björkö signed by, 390; World War I and, 392–95; abdication of, 442; murder of, 467

Nicolaevsky, Boris I., 494

Nietzsche, Friedrich, 422, 426

Nightingale, Florence, 316

Nihilism, 338, 354, 355, 416, 420, 432

Nijinsky, Vaslav, 430

Nikitin, Athanasius, 116

Nikitin, Gurii, 191

Nikolaev, Andrian, 573n

Nikolaevsk, 361

Nikon, Patriarch and Great Sovereign, 167–68, 183–85, 186

Nil Sorskii or Nilus of Sora, 114

Nizhnii Novgorod, 101, 156, 260, 261, 320, 623

NKVD, 495, 496, 522

Nobility, *see* Gentry

Nolde, B., 252, 372

Nonaggression treaties, 504–5, 507

Non-conformist artists, 547

Non-Euclidian geometry, 327

Non-possessors, 114–15, 183

Non-Slavic peoples and cultures, 10–16

Normandy invasion, 512

Norman theory, 21–25

Norsemen, 21

North Atlantic Treaty Organization (NATO), 525, 526, 635–37, 638, 640

Northeast Russia, 82, 85–87

Northern accord or alliance, 245

Northern Society of the Decembrists, 299, 300

Northern Workers' Union, 410

North Korea, 527, 638–39

Norway, 61; Christian conversion in, 32; Iaroslav and, 33; Novgorod and, 75; Soviet Russia and, 503; Atlantic Defense Pact and, 525

Nose, The (Gogol), 333

Nosov, Nikolai E., 177

Notes from the House of the Dead (Dostoevsky), 421

Notes of a Madman (Gogol), 333

Novgorod, 23, 33, 37, 46, 53, 61, 62, 72–81, 82, 86, 87, 104, 110; East Slavs in, 18; Vladimir's occupation of, 30; assigned to Iziaslav, 35; trade in, 39, 43, 72, 74, 76, 78, 106; education in, 57; Mongols and, 66, 74, 75, 79; formal name of, 72; historical evolution of, 72–75; Teutonic Knights in, 74–75, 123; institutions and way of life, 76–81; Ivan III and, 96–97, 98; Moscow and, 101, 102, 103; bishops of, 112; religion in, 113; Ivan IV and, 139; land confiscated in, 145; in Time of Troubles, 145, 155, 156, 161; in Muscovite Russia, 162, 164, 192; in Imperial Russia, 257

Novgorod, Archbishop of, 77, 78

Novgorodian Chronicle, 72, 78

Novgorodian school of icon painting, 120–21

Novi Bazar, Sanjak of, 360

Novikov, Nicholas, 273–74, 334

Novikov, Timur, 662

Novocherkassk, 547

Novorossiisk, 511

Novorossiiskii University, 418
Novosibirsk, 543
Novosiltsev, Nicholas, 282, 286–87, 296
Novotny, Antonin, 553
NTV (Independent Television), 629, 630
Nuclear non-proliferation agreement, 552, 638
Nuremberg tribunal, 524
Nureyev, Rudolf, 579
Nystadt, Treaty of, 208, 210

Ober-Procurator, office of, 213, 215
Oblomov (Goncharov), 424
Obnorsky, Sergei P., 51
Obolensky, Dimitrii, 32
Ob river, 4, 178
Obrok or quitrent, 171, 257, 345, 347; defined, 109; growth of system, 258, 261, 318
Obshchina or mir, *see* Peasant commune-
Ochrid, Archbishopric of, 34
October Manifesto, 381, 382, 383, 384
October Revolution (1917), 408, 449, 454, 461, 473, 475, 485, 493, 557, 566, 571; described, 432–33; crises following, 474; Stalin's participation in, 483; destruction of old society and, 559
Octobrists, 384, 386, 389, 435
Odessa, 261, 320, 418, 469
Odoevsky, Prince Vladimir, 335
Odyssey (Homer), 329
Official Nationality doctrine, 307, 316, 328, 335, 435; tenets of, 302–3; impact on education, 325, 326
Oganovsky, Nikolai P., 397
Ogarev, Nicholas, 339
OGPU, 494–95
Oil, 5, 399, 400, 402, 543, 606, 616, 618, 624; of Middle East, 555, 638; increased prices, 630
Oil blockade, 592
Oistrakh, David, 579
Oka river, 29, 94, 96, 101
Okudzhava, Bulat, 578
Okun, Semen B., 343
Olaf, Saint (King of Norway), 34
Olbia, 11, 14
Old Belief, 168, 192, 206, 226, 400; spread of, 185; schism and, 185–86; streltsy and, 198; Peter I and, 215, 221; Pugachev's rebellion and, 241; Russification and, 365
Oldenburg, Duke of, 290
Old Sarai, 67
Oleg (son of Sviatoslav), 30
Oleg, Grand Prince, 24, 26, 27–28, 41
Olesha, Iurii, 575, 576, 577, 659
Olga, Saint, 28, 30, 31, 49
Olgerd or Algirdas, Grand Prince of Lithuania, 92, 125–26
Oligarchs, 622, 623, 625, 628, 629, 630, 631, 642, 643, 644
Olonets, 259
Omsk, 467
One Day in the Life of Ivan Denisovich (Solzhenitsyn), 578

Onega Lake, 4
On Law and Grace (hilarion), 52
On the Eve (Turgenev), 420
Opera, 277, 332, 340, 428
"Opium" (song), 664
Oprichnina and oprichniki: under Ivan IV, 138, 139, 140, 141, 142, 171; Time of Troubles and, 146
"Orchestra without a Conductor" experiment, 564
Order No. 1, 443
Ordyn-Nashchokin, Athanasius, 167
Orel, 468, 511
Orenburg cossacks, 467
Organic Statute of 1832, 309
Organized crime, 621, 648–49, *see also* Mafias
Orlov, Count Alexis, 230, 246, 311
Orlov, Prince Alexis, 305
Orlov, Count Gregory, 238
Orlov brothers, 239
Orthodox Church: in Lithuania, 125, 126, 129, 310; in Ukraine, 165, 166, 183, 186; in Greece, 184; in Poland, 248, 353; in Georgia, 593, *see also* Russian Orthodox Church
Orthodoxy, 265, 362; defined, 302; Slavophiles and, 336; Westernizers on, 337; Russification and, 366; Nicholas II and, 367
ORT (state television network), 629
Oruzheinaia Palata, 191
Oslo accords, 638
Ossetians, 14, 360, 594
Ostankino television tower, 617, 647–48
Ostermann, Andrew, 202, 226, 232
Ostrogoths, 15
Ostromirovo Gospel, 80
Ostrovsky, Alexander, 424
Otrepiev, Gregory, *see* False Dmitrii I
Ottoman Empire, *see* Turkey
Our Home Is Russia, 620, 626
Outer Mongolia, 503–4, 655
Oxford Slavonic Papers, 193

Pacification, 360–61, 386–88
Pacific Ocean, 8, 178, 327–28
Paganism, 50; in early cultures, 16; in Kievan Russia, 22, 31–32, 41–42, 48–49, 56; in Lithuania, 124, 126
Pahlen, Count Peter, 255
Pakistan, 549, 633
Pale of Jewish Settlement, 366, 370
Paleologue, Sophia or Zoe, 98
Palestinians, 639
Pallas, Peter-Simon, 276
Pamir mountains, 4
Pamyat or Memory, 651–52
Pan-Germans, 390
Panin, Nikita, 245
Pannonian plain, 28
Pan-Slav Congress, 338
Pan-Slavism, 358–59, 390, 391, 421, 435
Panticapaeum, 14
Pares, Barnard, 131

Paris: Napoleonic Wars and, 292; First Treaty of, 294; Second Treaty of, 294; revolution of 1830, 309; revolution of 1848, 311–12, 338; Treaty of, 316, 357
Parliament, 617, 619, 627, 628
Partiinost, 558, 572, 574, 576, 577
Partnership for Peace, 636
Pashkov, Philip, 152
Paskevich, Prince Ivan, 308, 309, 312
Passport system, 217
Pasternak, Boris, 426, 575, 576, 578, 659
Paterikon, 52
Patkul, Johann Reinhold, 204, 206
Patriarchate, 142, 183
Patriotism, 637
Paul I, Emperor, 131, 239, 246, 261, 262, 274, 282, 287, 296, 299; bypassed by Catherine II, 230; speculation on paternity of, 238; reign of, 253–55; deposition and death of, 255, 279, 281; architecture supported by, 276
Paulus, Friedrich, 511
Pauperization of the center, 405
Pauper's allotment, 346
Pavlov, Ivan, 419
Pavlov, Michael, 334
Pavlova, Anna, 430
Pavlov-Silvansky, Nikolai P., 45; quoted, 105; on feudalism, 106–7
Pearl Harbor, Japanese bombing of, 510
Peasant commune: obshchina or mir, 346; as moral choir, 336; Slavophiles on, 336, 339, 347; Westernizers on, 339; in Ukraine, 346; under Alexander II, 347–48; in zemstvo system, 348; populism and, 355, 433, 434; Stolypin and, 388; from great reforms to 1917, 402–4, 406–7; in Soviet Russia, 464, 561
Peasant Land Bank, 367, 389, 406
Peasantry, 8; in Kievan Russia, 36, 44–45; in appanage Russia, 107; in Poland, 128, 248; in Time of Troubles, 146, 158; in zemskii sobor, 157; in Muscovite Russia, 166; rebellions of, 166, 228, 231, 262, 343–44, 352, 474–75, 476; in Imperial Russia, 228, 239, 241, 244–45, 258, 260, 261–63, 326, 343–44, 350, 355–56, 365, 398, 402–7, 437; under Catherine II, 239, 241, 244–45; serfdom forced on, 244; in Ukraine, 251; industrialization and, 260, 398; under Alexander II, 343–44, 350; under Alexander III, 365; Revolution of 1905 and, 378; the Duma and, 383, 384, 385; Stolypin's policy and, 388–89; land appropriated by, 445, 447; in Soviet Russia, 454, 455, 465–66, 474–75, 476, 486, 488, 492, 539–40, 558, 559–62, *see also* Peasant commune; State peasants
Pechenegs or Patzinaks, 28, 29, 30, 33, 35, 37
Pechora river, 4
Peipus or Chud Lake, 75
Peking, 70, 210, 328; Treaty of, 361
Pelevin, Viktor, 641, 660, 661
Pensions and pensioners, 615, 623, 646
Penza, 260

People's Commissariat of Internal Affairs, *see* NKVD
People's Front, 592
People's *Veche,* 652
People's Will party, 356, 363, 379, 433, 456
Per capita income, 405
Pereiaslavl, 34, 35, 166
Perelog, 43
Perestroika, 562, 585, 587, 601; defined, 586; in Soviet satellites, 598; Western approval of, 606
Perestroika (Gorbachev), 585
Peresvetov, 187, 194
Periodicals, 268, 273
Perm, 96, 467; university of, 418
Perovskaia, Sophia, 356
Persia, 5; Scythians and, 8, 13; Kievan Russia and, 27; Mongols in, 65, 70; Muscovite Russia and, 164; Imperial Russia and, 210, 288, 308, 360; Russian-British conflict over, 390; trade with, 400; Litvinov Protocol and, 504, *see also* Iran
Persian Gulf, 65
Persian Letters (Montesquieu), 272
Perun (god), 22, 48, 77
Pescadores Islands, 374
Peshkov, Alexis, *see* Gorky, Maxim
Pestel, Paul, 298, 299, 300
Peter (architect), 56
Peter, Saint and Metropolitan, 91, 117
Peter and the Wolf (Prokofiev), 579
Peter I, the Great, 9, 131, 141, 162, 167, 168, 176, 178, 182, 194, 197–222, 225, 226–27, 229, 230, 231, 261, 278, 322, 328, 581; reforms of, 177, 191, 210–19, 264, 266–68, 270–71, 342; religion and, 186; birth of, 197; death of, 197, 220, 223; as co-tsar, 197–200; proclaimed tsar, 198; character, childhood, and youth of, 200–202; assistants of, 202–3; first year of rule, 203–4; Peter Mikhailov identity, 203–4; testament of, 208; titles acquired by, 208; foreign relations under, 209–10, 232, 233; colleges of, 213–14, 284; administrative reforms, 213–16; financial and social reforms, 216–18; canals built during reign of, 218–19, 260; national economy reforms, 218–19; cultural reforms, 219, 264; educational reforms, 219, 266–68; industrialization and, 219, 258; succession issues after, 220, 224, 253; evaluations of, 221–22; Catherine II compared with, 237, 239, 245, 246; long-range results of policies, 256, 257, 263; architecture supported by, 276, 277, 340; scientific expeditions under, 276; literary works inspired by, 331; Chaadaev on, 335; Slavophiles on, 336; Westernizers on, 337; military reforms (*see under* Military)
Peter II, Emperor, 220, 224–25
Peter III, Emperor, 223, 231–32, 234, 235, 238; reign of, 229–30; deposition and death of, 230, 237; Pugachev's masquerade as, 241
Petrashevsky, Michael, *see* Butashevich-Petrashevsky

Petrashevtsy, 305, 335–36, 421; philosophy and leaders of, 339; on serfdom, 344

Petrograd, 446, 472; naming of, 441; Bolshevik attempt to seize power in, 445; Soviet government established in, 449; Civil War and, 467, 468–69; renamed "Leningrad," 478

Petrograd Soviet of Workers' and Soldiers' Deputies, 442–43

Petropavlovsk (battleship), 428

Petrouchka (Stravinsky), 430

Petrov, Basil, 327

Petrushevskaia, Liudmila, 660, 661

Phanagoria, 14

Philaret, Metropolitan and Patriarch, 150, 154, 155, 158, 162, 167, 183

Philip, Metropolitan, 139

Philip, Prince, 155, 161

Philippines, 550

Philippopolis, 29

Philosophes, 237, 251, 252, 272, 281, 334

Philosophical Letter (Chaadaev), 335

Philotheus or Filofei, 115–16

Photius, Patriarch, 23

Piast family, 126

Piatina towns, 76, 79

Pilnyak, Boris, 575

Pilsen or Plzen, 549

Pimen, Metropolitan, 116

Pimen, Patriarch, 581

Pioneers (youth organization), 557

Pipes, Richard E., 297, 470

Pirogov, Nicholas, 419

Pisarev, Dmitrii, 354, 415, 432

Plague, 91

Plano Carpini, Archbishop, 68

Platonov, Andrei, 575

Platonov, Sergei F., 159, 419; on Mongols, 63; on Olgerd, 125; on the oprichnina, 138; on Ivan IV, 141, 142, 143; on Time of Troubles, 144, 146; on False Dmitrii I, 150; on Michael Romanov, 158, 161; on Peter I, 216

Plehve, Viacheslav, 369, 370, 379, 388

Plekhanov, George, 379, 461

Plevna, 359

Pliny the Elder, 18

Plough (levy), 42, 45, 46, 69

Pobedonostsev, Constantine, 363, 366, 369, 417, 435

Podgorny, Nicholas, 536

Podolia, 250

Podseka, 43

Poetry: of Muscovite Russia, 188; of Imperial Russia, 271, 329, 330–31, 332, 424–25, 426; of Soviet Russia, 575, 577, *see also* Byliny

Pogodin, Mikhail P., 37, 303, 307, 328, 335; quoted, 3; on Peter I, 222

Pogroms, 366, 370

Pokrovsky, Mikhail N., 131, 346, 574

Poland, 82, 85, 232, 233, 234, 366, 582; Galicia and, 30, 83, 84, 250; Kievan Russia and, 30, 32, 33, 34, 35; Christian conversion in, 32; appanage Russia and, 61, 62; Mongols in, 65, 66; Lithuania and, 79, 123, 126–28, 129, 250, 309, 310, 352; Roman of Volynia and, 83, 84; Ivan III and, 97, 98; Ukraine seized by, 128, 165–67, 466, 470, 474; Ivan IV and, 139–40; Theodore I and, 143; in Time of Troubles, 144, 153–57, 158, 161; False Dmitrii I and, 147, 149; Muscovite Russia and, 162, 167, 175, 187, 193; serfdom in, 172, 248, 310, 347; Madeburg Law and, 177; treaty of eternal peace and, 198; Great Northern War and, 204–6, 207, 208; Peter I and, 209; partitioning of, 233, 237, 245, 246, 247–51, 252, 253, 257, 290, 309–10; War of the Polish Succession and, 233; Catherine II and, 245, 246, 247–51, 252, 253, 257; rebellion of 1831 in, 251, 309–10; rebellion of 1863 in, 251, 351, 352–53, 357; Alexander I and, 286, 309; Napoleonic Wars and, 290; Congress of Vienna and, 293; Kingdom of, 293; Nicholas I and, 306, 309–10, 311, 312; Hungarian uprising and, 312; closing of university in, 326; serf emancipation in, 352; the Duma and, 383, 385; World War I and, 392, 394, 466; industry in, 399; independence granted by Provisional Government, 443; war with Soviets, 460, 469, 470, 471; Treaty of Brest-Litovsk and, 464; independence movements in, 470; territory ceded by Soviets, 474; Litvinov Protocol and, 504; nonaggression pact with U.S.S.R., 505; German invasion of, 506–8; incorporation into U.S.S.R., 507, 519, 524; World War II and, 507–8, 513–14; Communism in, 525; rebellions against Soviet domination in, 546, 550, 553–55; Communism collapse in, 598; Communism resurgence in, 635; NATO and, 636

Poliane, 18, 27

Poliansky, Fedor I., 260

Police, 305, *see also* Political police

Polievktov, Mikhail A., 316

Polish liberties, 248, 249

Polish reform party, 250

Politburo (Political Bureau of the Communist Party), 473, 497, 502, 504, 519, 521, 531, 535, 558; World War II and, 508; abolition of, 522; Andropov in, 537; Gorbachev in, 538, 586, 587; Russian language promoted by, 567–68; religion and, 581; decreased power of, 600

Political police, 465, 496, 500; names for, 494–95; weakening power of, 531, 546; Hungarian massacre of, 550

Polotsk, 33, 61; Ivan III and, 98; Gedymin and, 125; Polish capture of, 140

Polovtsy, 33, 35, 37, 52, 53; Mongols and, 63, 65; Roman of Volynia and, 83

Poltava (Pushkin), 331

Poltava, battle of, 201, 207, 208, 212, 221

Pomestie, 107, 108–9, 129, 134, 145, 172, 177, *see also* Gentry, Land

Poniatowski, Stanislaw (King of Poland), 238, 247, 248

Poor Folk (Dostoevsky), 421
Poor Liza (Karamzin), 272
Popov, Alexander, 419
Popov, Gavriil, 597
Popovich, Pavel, 573n
Popovtsy, 185
Popular culture, 648, 664–65
Popular fronts, 504, 505
Population: of Kievan Russia, 44; of Novgorod, 76; of Lithuania, 125; of Imperial Russia, 210, 217, 256–57, 321, 404; of Little Poland, 250; serfs represented in, 343; of Siberia (Russian), 361; peasants represented in, 402; of Magnitostroi, 486; of Soviet Russia, 559, 560(map)
Populism, 398, 416, 420, 432–34; famous adherents of, 355; failure of crusade, 355–56; Lenin's attacks on, 456; Yeltsin and, 612–13
Porkkala base, 524, 549
Pornography, 653, 659, 660
Port Arthur, 374, 527
Porte, *see* Turkey
Portsmouth Peace Conference, 390
Portsmouth Treaty, 376
Portugal, 254, 525
Posadnik, 77, 78, 79, 81, 97
Poshlost, 586
Positivism, 354, 425, 433, 434, 436, 458
Posnik (architect), 190
Pososhkov, Ivan, 276, 278
Possessed, The (Dostoevsky), 421
Possessional factories, 260, 319
Possessional workers, 260, 262
Possessors, 114–15
Postal service, 69, 194
Potemkin (battleship), 381
Potemkin, Prince Gregory, 238–39, 245, 247, 271
Potemkin villages, 247
Potsdam conference, 513
Pozharsky, Prince Dmitrii, 156
Poznan, 550
Prague, 511, 512
Pravda (newspaper), 456
Precipitation, 5
Preobrazhenskii, 201, 203, 224
Preobrazhenskoe, 198, 201
Presidential Council, 600
Presidium, 500, 522, 530, 531, 532, 535
Presniakov, Aleksandr E., 88, 104
Press: in Imperial Russia, 268, 272, 353, 363, 364, 369, 411, 440; Fundamental Laws and, 382–83; in Soviet Russia, 465, 590; in Russian Federation, 622, *see also* Media
Pretenders to the throne, 159, *see also* False Dmitrii; False Peter; Little Felon
Price controls, 613, 614
Prices, 485, 520, 536, 540, 542, 599
Prikazy, 177, 213, 214
Primakov, Evgeny, 624
Primary Chronicle, 18, 21, 22–25, 34, 56–57; on the Rus, 22–24; on Oleg, 27; on Pechenegs,

28; on Sviatoslav, 28, 29; value of, 53; on Novgorod, 72
Primitivism, 432
Primogeniture, 253
Prince Igor (Borodin), 428
Priselkov, Mikhail, 34
Prisoner of the Caucasus, The (Pushkin), 331
Prison system, 615, 648
Pritvor, 117
Private enterprise: in Imperial Russia, 260; in Soviet Russia, 476, 589; in Russian Federation, 642–44
Private property, 244, 655
Privatization, 613–14, 616, 621, 629, 642
Procopius, 18, 22
Pro eto (television program), 661
Progressive Bloc, 395, 442
Prokhorov, Alexander, 651
Prokofiev, Serge, 75, 579
Prokopovich, Archbishop Theophanes or Feofan, 203, 215
Prokopovich, Sergei N., 405, 518
Proletariat, 484, 488, 499, 563; in Imperial Russia, 351, 408–11; Marxism and Leninism on, 452, 454, 455; culture influenced by, 572; literature by, 575, *see also* Workers
Proletcult, 575
Property rights, 284
Prostitution, 648, 649, 653
Protestantism, 215, 248, 336, 365, 567, 583, 657
Protocol of Troppau, 294
Provisional Government, 441–47, 463, 470; achievements of, 443; shortcomings of, 443–44; overthrow of, 449
Prus, ruler of Rome, 115
Prussia, 347, 353; Peter I and, 204; Great Northern War and, 208; Peter III and, 230; Seven Years' War and, 233–34; Catherine II and, 248, 250–51; partition of Poland and, 248, 250–51; Royal or Polish, 250; Alexander I and, 287; Napoleonic Wars and, 290, 292; Congress of Vienna and, 293; in Quadruple Alliance, 294; Nicholas I and, 302, 309, 311–12; Straits Convention and, 313; Alexander II and, 357–58; French war with, 358, *see also* East Prussia, Germany
Pruth river, 82, 207
Pskov, 79, 91, 99, 104, 110, 164, 175; *Sudebnik,* 70; Teutonic Knights and, 75; institutions and culture of, 81; Ivan III and, 97, 98; Basil III and, 100; religion in, 113; Poland and, 140; in Time of Troubles, 145, 156
Publishing houses, 268, 282
Pugachev, Emelian (rebellion of), 237, 241–43, 262, 305, 343
Pulkovo, 468; observatory in, 326, 327
Punctuation of Olmütz, 312
Purges, 488, 557, 577; in eastern Europe, 526; in Ukraine, 567; of Yiddish intellectuals, 568, *see also* Great purge
Puryear, Vernon J., 313
Pushkin (town), 277, 320, 325

Pushkin, Alexander, 143, 203, 270, 333, 338, 547; on Mongols, 70; quoted, 197; on Peter I, 221; on Pugachev's rebellion, 241; on Lomonosov, 275; Decembrists and, 298; Third Department supervision of, 305; Dostoevsky on, 323; work of, 324, 328, 330–32; education of, 325; cult of, 329; life and death of, 330; reputation of, 330–31; on serfdom, 344

Putiatin, Count Evfimii, 352, 353

Putin, Vladimir, 610, 625–33, 648, 653, 654, 664; as prime minister, 624, 626; background of, 625; named acting president, 625; attempted coup and, 625–26; elected president, 626; beliefs of, 626–27; foreign relations under, 637–40; the Church and, 655, 657

Al Qaeda, 639

Quadruple Alliance, 293–94, 296

Quartet, 639

Quiet Don, The (Sholokhov), 576

Quintuple Alliance, 293, 296

Quitrent, *see* Obrok or quitrent

Rachmaninov, Serge, 332, 431

Rada (Pereiaslavl), 166

Rada (Ukraine), 470

Radicalism: in Imperial Russia, 334, 339, 350, 353–57, 416, 432–33, 436–37; zemstvo and, 349; Revolution of 1905 and, 378–79; of Lenin, 456; in postcommunist Russia, 653

Radio stations, 629

Radishchev, Alexander, 274, 334

Radkey, Oliver Henry, 561

Radomyslsky, Gregory, *see* Zinoviev, Gregory

Raeff, Marc, 285

Railroads, 320, 322, 367, 376, 398; Trans-Siberian, 371, 373–74, 375, 400, 467; East China, 374, 400; Berlin-Baghdad, 391; worker strikes and, 410; Chinese Eastern, 504, 505; Manchurian, 527; Baikal-Amur, 543

Rapallo, Treaty of, 503

Rashin, Adolf G., 418

Raskol, 183, *see also* Russian Orthodox Church, schism in

Rasputin, Gregory, 368, 394(figure), 395, 440

Rastrelli, Count Bartolomeo, 277

Rationalism, 334, 336, 425

Raves, 664

Razin, Stenka, 164–65, 188, 241

Raznochintsy, 354

Razumovsky, Alexis, 227–28

Razumovsky, Cyril, 228

Reagan, Ronald, 555

Realism, 354; in Imperial Russia, 329–30, 331, 332, 416, 424, 425, 427–28; critical, 354, 355, 428, 433; socialist, 426, 576–78, 579; psychological, 432

Realpolitik, 502, 637

Realschule, 417

Rechtsstaat, 285

Red Army, 520, 525; Winter Palace stormed by, 449; Civil War and, 465, 466–69; in Poland, 470; in Ukraine, 470–71; reasons for victory of, 472–73; rebellions suppressed by, 475; in Czechoslovakia, 505; in Mongolia, 506; World War II and, 507, 508, 510, 511–12, 514–15, 517–18; in Georgia, 593

Red-Brown alliance, 615

Red Cross, 394

Reformation, 68, 185, 192, 264

Reforms: of Catherine II, 239–41, 243–45; of Alexander I, 282–87, 324–25; of Nicholas I, 305–6; of Alexander II, 342–53, 362; of Stolypin, 386–89; of Gorbachev, 585–91; of Peter I (*see under* Peter I), *see also* Counterreforms; Great reforms; Legal codes and systems

Reinsurance Treaty, 371–72

Religion: of early cultures, 12; of Scythians, 14; in Kievan Russia, 48–51, 52–53; Mongols and, 69–70; in appanage Russia, 111–16; in Muscovite Russia, 182–86; in Imperial Russia, 297–98, 337–39, 365–66, 370, 411–12, 436–37; in Soviet Russia, 518, 547, 567, 581–83; in Ukraine, 595; in postcommunist Russia, 654–58, *see also* specific religions and groups

Religious-Philosophical Meetings, 411

Remizov, Alexis, 578

Renaissance, 68, 126, 192, 264

Renovationist church, 581

Repin, Elijah, 428

Rerum moscovitarium commentarii (von Herberstein), 100

Res gestae saxonicae (Widukind), 24

Reval, 207

Revolutionary Military Council of the Southern Front, 483

Revolutionary movements: under Alexander II, 353–57; Marxism-Leninism on, 454, *see also* specific groups

Revolution of 1905, 351, 362, 376, 378–82, 400, 405, 406, 410, 411, 417, 436, 439; background of, 378–79; events of, 380–82

Revolution of 1917, 386, 439–49, 590; economy and society prior to, 396–414; culture prior to, 415–38; Provisional Government and, 441–47; social, 447–49, *see also* February Revolution; October Revolution

Rheims, 512

Rhine river, 292

Riasanovsky, Nicholas, 482

Riazan, 87, 103, 108; Mongols and, 66, 68, 89, 93, 94, 116; Moscow conquest of, 92; Ivan III and, 97; Basil III and, 100; in Time of Troubles, 152, 155

Rice, Condoleezza, 638

Richter, Sviatoslav, 579

Rieber, Alfred J., 344

Riga, 592; Great Northern War and, 205, 207, 257; trade in, 260, 261; strikes in, 410; Treaty of, 470

Right: in Imperial Russia, 335, 353, 355, 435, 437; Revolution of 1905 and, 381–82; the Duma and, 383–84, 386, 395; terrorism and, 389; Provisional Government and, 446; Civil War and, 466; post-Lenin struggle for power and, 477–79; in postcommunist Russia, 651, 665

Rimsky-Korsakov, Nicholas, 332, 428

Riurik, Prince, 24–25, 72, 115

Rivers, role in Russian history, 4, 8

Roads, 320

Robinson, Geroid T., 397, 414

Rock music, 566, 664–65

Rogger, Hans, 272

Rokossovsky, Constantine, 512, 515

Roman (son of Daniel), 84

Roman Catholic Church, 32, 159, 335, 567; in Germany, 75; in Lithuania, 79; in Galicia, 84; in appanage Russia, 109; in Poland, 126–27, 128, 155, 165, 166, 249, 309, 353, 553, 554, 598; False Dmitrii I and, 147, 150; Peter I and, 215; dispute with Orthodox Church, 314; Slavophiles and, 336; Russification and, 365; Communism and, 525; in postcommunist Russia, 657

Roman of Volynia, 83–84

Romania, 391; Nicholas I and, 312; Turkish-Austrian conflict and, 359, 360; World War I and, 392; Bessarabia acquired by, 474; Litvinov Protocol and, 504; nonaggression pact signed by, 505; World War II and, 507, 508, 511, 512; in Soviet Union, 524, 553; Communism collapse in, 598; Communism resurgence in, 635

Romanov, Michael, see Michael Romanov, Tsar

Romanov, Nikita, 158

Romanov, Philaret or Theodore, see Philaret, Metropolitan and Patriarch

Romanova, Anastasia, see Anastasia (wife of Ivan IV)

Romanov dynasty: established, 144; length of rule, 157; end of male line, 225; standard of, in Russian Federation, 617

Romanticism, 329, 334, 335, 336, 339, 340, 354

Rommel, Erwin, 512

Roofs (protection rackets), 643, 649

Roosevelt, Franklin D., 513

Roosevelt, Theodore, 376

Rosenfeld, Leo, see Kamenev, Leo

Rostopchin, Count Theodore, 291, 298, 335

Rostov, 85, 86(map), 101, 150, 190; emerging importance of, 86; Ivan III and, 96; bishops of, 112

Rostov-on-Don, 508, 510, 511; university of, 418

Rostovtsev, Jacob, 345

Rostovtzeff, Mikhail I., 420; quoted, 10; on early cultures, 12, 14; on Kievan Russia, 41

Rostropovich, Mstislav, 600

Rousseau, Jean-Jacques, 268, 274

Rozanov, Basil, 426, 437

Rozhdestvensky, Zinovii, 375

Rozhkov, Basil, 317

RSFSR, see Russian Soviet Federated Socialist Republic

Rtishchev, Theodore, 192

Rubinstein, Anton, 428

Rubinstein, Nicholas, 428

Rublev, Andrew, 121–22

Rudin (Turgenev), 420

Ruffo, Marco, 118, 120

Rukh, 595

Rumiantsev, Count Peter, 234, 245, 246

Runich, Dmitrii, 297

Rural areas, 261, 561, see also Agriculture; Peasantry

Rus, 22–24, 39, 40–41, see also Kievan Russia

Ruslan and Liudmila (Pushkin), 330

Russell, Bertrand, 451

Russia and Europe (Danilevsky), 435

Russian Album, 665

Russian Association of Proletarian Writers (RAPP), 575

Russian Federation, 609–65; political life in, 616–17; foreign policy and relations in, 633–40; society in, 641–58; decay, disintegration, and disorder in, 647–50; culture of, 659–65

Russian fleet, 322; Peter I and, 203; Catherine II and, 247; Paul I and, 254; in Russo-Japanese War, 375–76

Russian idea, 610

Russian Justice (Pestel), 298

Russian Justice, The (legal code), 34, 41, 42, 44, 46, 73, 99

Russian language, 102; origins of, 16; Mongol influence on, 68–69; adaption to new needs, 270; in Poland, 352; in Soviet Union, 567–68

Russian Liberation Army, 516

Russian National Unity, 652

Russian Orthodox Church, 74, 104; in Kievan Russia, 45, 49, Mongols and, 70; in Moscow, 91; split with Byzantium, 95, 112; in appanage Russia, 109–10, 112–16; statuary banned by, 122; in Muscovite Russia, 134, 142, 167–68, 180, 182–86; landholdings confiscated / restricted, 145, 146, 239, 244, 262, 465, 581; in Time of Troubles, 145, 146, 154, 155, 159; schism in, 167–68, 182–86; in Siberia, 180; in China, 210; in Imperial Russia, 213, 215, 230, 239, 262, 365–66; excommunication from, 239; in Constantinople, 246; Crimean War and, 314–15, 316; in Peking, 328; in Soviet Russia, 465, 581–83; in postcommunist Russia, 654–58; see also Christianity; Clergy; Orthodoxy

Russian Soviet Federated Socialist Republic (RSFSR): creation of, 473–74; component units of, 499; Gorbachev and, 595–97

Russian Theater, The (periodical), 278

Russian United Workers, 591

Russia's Choice, 619, 620

Russification, 310, 363, 370, 521; in Poland, 352, 366; religion and, 365–66; Stolypin and, 389

Russo-Chinese Bank, 400

Russo-Japanese War, 373–76, 379, 390, 400, 441

Russo-Persian Bank, 400

Russo-Turkish treaty, 205

Rutskoi, Alexander, 616, 617

Rybakov, Boris A., 44

Rykov, Alexis, 461, 495

Ryndziunsky, Pavel G., 343

Ryzhkov, Nikolai, 587

Sadko, 80

Sadko (Rimsky-Korsakov), 428

Sagaidachny or Sahaidachny, Peter, 166

St. George's Day, 109, 169, 171, 172

St. Petersburg, 215, 221, 273, 345, 365; founding of, 206; Great Northern War and, 207–8; Swedish threat to, 252; industry in, 259, 260, 319, 399, 408; trade in, 260, 261; schools in, 266, 269; architecture of, 276, 277, 340; Decembrist movement in, 298; railroad in, 320; university of, 324; fires in, 352; Jews in, 366; Revolution of 1905 and, 381; strikes in, 410; conservatory of, 428; renamed Petrograd, 441; Stalin in, 483; original name restored to, 597; economic situation in, 614; businesses in, 644; decay in, 647; the arts in, 662

Saints, 49–50, 112–13, 183, 655

Sakhalin Island, 361, 376, 469, 474, 503, 512

Sakharov, Andrei N., 299, 547, 589

Salnitsa, 35

SALT II, 552, 555

Salt mining, 171

Saltykov, Michael (pseudonym N. Shchedrin), 424

Saltykov family, 161

Salyut, 573n

Samandar, 16, 29

Samara, 467, 508

Samarin, George, 336, 345, 351, 354

Samashki, 618

Samizdat, 547, 578

San Stefano, Treaty of, 359–60

Sarai, 98

Saratov, 261; university of, 418

Sardinia, 314, 315

Sarkil, 16, 29

Sarmatians, 13–14, 16

Satire, 272, 333

Saveliev, Pavel Stepanovich, 41

Savin, Sila, 191

Savinkov, Boris, 466

Saxony, 338; Great Northern War and, 204–6, 208; Seven Years' War and, 234; Congress of Vienna on, 293

Sazhin, Nikolai, 662

Sazonov, Serge, 391

Scandinavia, 21–25, 41

Schapiro, Leonard, 559

Schelling, Friedrich, 334–35

Schiemann, Theodor, 301, 316

Schilder, Nikolai Karlovich, 316

Schiller, Johann, 329, 334

Schlözer, August-Ludwig von, 21, 23, 276

Schlüsselburg, 239

Scholarship, *see* Science and scholarship

Schönbrunn, Treaty of, 290

School of Mathematical and Navigational Sciences, 219, 266

School of the tsar's icon painters, 190–91

Schroeder, Gerhard, 638

Schuman, Frederick L., 518

Schwartzmann, Leo (pseudonym Shestov), 437

Science and scholarship: in Imperial Russia, 275–76, 324, 327–28, 416, 418–20; in Soviet Russia, 572–74

Scientology, 657

Scissors crisis, 485

Scotland, 215

Scriabin, Alexander, 430

Sculpture, 56, 122, 277

Scythian policy in Napoleonic Wars, 292

Scythians, 5, 8, 12–13, 14, 16, 18, 41, 57

SEATO, *see* Southeast Asia Treaty Organization

Sech (Sich), 165, 244

Sechenov, Ivan, 419

Second Army, 298

Second Coalition, 254

Second Treaty of Paris, 294

Secretariat, 558

Sectarianism, 437

Secularism, 265–66

Security Council, 600

Seigniories, 107

Sejm or diet, 248

Selected Passages from Correspondence with Friends (Gogol), 333

Semenov, Gregory, 467

Semenov, Nicholas, 573

Semenovskii Regiment of the Guards, 201, 224, 294

Semevsky, Vasilii I., 321, 343

Senate, 226–27, 231; under Peter I, 212, 213; founding of, 213; under Catherine II, 240; University of Moscow and, 268; under Alexander I, 284, 285; under Nicholas I, 303; under Alexander II, 350

Sentimentalism, 272, 329

Serbia, 389–90; Great Northern War and, 207; Turkish conflicts with, 358, 359, 360, 391; Austria-Hungary conflict with, 390; World War I and, 391–92; Kosovo tragedy and, 636–37

Serbs: in Imperial Russia, 245; in Soviet Union, 567; Bosnian, 636

Serfdom, 70, 107, 109, 171–74, 227, 228, 256, 257–58, 324; in Time of Troubles, 146, 160; in Ukraine, 167, 244, 346; circumstances

Serfdom, (*continued*)
  fostering growth of, 171–72; dominant characteristics of, 172; forbidden years in, 172; in Poland, 172, 248, 310, 347; Siberia's escape from, 180; Golitsyn's desire to abolish, 198; Peter I and, 217; growth of, 230–32; Catherine II and, 239, 240, 241, 244, 245, 253; Paul I and, 253–54, 261, 262; in the labor force, 260; increasing exploitation of, 261–62; social criticism of, 272, 274; Alexander I and, 282, 283, 284; voluntary emancipation and, 284; in the Baltics, 296; Decembrist movement and, 298, 344; Nicholas I and, 304, 305–6; in the 19th century (first half), 317–18; increased population in, 321; Slavophiles on, 336, 337, 344; abolition of, 341, 342–48, 357, 397–98, 402; Polish abolition of, 352, *see also* Slavery
Serge, Grand Duke, 379
Sergius, Metropolitan, 581
Sergius of Radonezh, Saint, 104, 109, 112–13, 116, 117, 121
Service princes, 137
Seton-Watson, H., 396
Sevastopol, 14, 247, 315–16, 510, 634
Sevastopol Tales (Tolstoy), 316
Seven-Year Plan, 538–40
Seven Years' War, 230, 233–34
Seymour, Sir Hamilton, 313
Shadow economy, 649
Shafirov, Peter, 202
Shakespeare, William, 331
Shakhmatov, Aleksei A., 17, 24
Shakhovskoy, Prince Gregory, 151–52, 153
Shakhty coal mines, trial of engineers in, 488
Shaklovity, Theodore, 198
Shamil, 361, 618
Shanghai, 503
Shatalin, Stanislav, 601
Shatalin plan, 601
Shchapov, Afanasii P., 185
Shcherbatov, Prince Michael, 276
Shelon river, 96
Shemakha, 288
Shepilov, Dmitrii, 532, 550
Sheremetev, Count Boris, 203, 206
Shevardnadze, Eduard, 585, 587, 598, 601, 633
Shevchenko, Taras, 310
Shevtsova, Lilia, 651
Shevyrev, Stephen, 303, 328, 335
Shimonoseki, Treaty of, 374
Shipbuilding industry, 212–13
Shipka pass, 359
Shishkov, Alexander, 328, 335
"Shock therapy" for economy, 613–14, 615
Shoigu, Sergie, 627
Sholokhov, Michael, 215, 576
Shostakovich, Dmitrii, 579
Shubin, Fedot, 277
Shuisky, Andrew, 133
Shuisky, Prince Basil, 143, 154, 159, 160, 175; False Dmitrii I and, 149, 150; reign of, 151–53

Shuisky, Prince Dmitrii, 153, 154
Shuvalov, Alexander, 228
Shuvalov, Ivan, 228, 268
Shuvalov, Peter, 228
Siberia, 4, 177, 257, 276, 495, 597, 599; climate of, 5, 8; Mongols in, 64; Ermak's conquest of, 140; annexation of, 178–80; literature inspired by events in, 188; Peter I and, 210; Bironism in, 226; exile of delinquent serfs to, 232, 244; trade in, 261; exile of Raishchev to, 274; expeditions to, 327; exile of Bakunin to, 339; Russian population in, 361; Trans-Siberian railroad in, 371, 374; peasantry of, 405; exile of Dostoevsky to, 421; exile of Chernyshevsky to, 433; exile of Lenin to, 461; Civil War and, 467, 469; Japanese evacuation of, 474; uprisings in, 474; industry in, 486; exile of dissidents to, 488; World War II and, 507; science and technology center in, 543; natural-gas pipeline proposal, 555
Sicily, 512
Sigismund II (Augustus), King of Poland, 127, 139
Sigismund III, King of Poland, 153–54, 155, 156, 157
Signposts / Vekhi (essay collection), 436–37
Silesia, 66, 233–34
Siloviki, 628
Silver age of Russian culture, 416, 420, 425–26, 427, 430–31, 432, 436, 437, 575, 659
Simbirsk, 165, 461, 466, 467
Simeon, Tartar prince, 138, 142
Simeon of Polotsk, 168, 188, 192
Simeon the Proud, Prince of Moscow, 91
Simmons, Ernest J., 415
Siniavsky, Andrei, 546
Sinope, 314
Sipiagin, Dmitrii, 369, 379
Sixth Symphony (Tchaikovsky), 428
Skobeev, Frol, 188
Skobelev, Michael, 361
Skomorokhi, 56, 188
Skopin-Shuisky, Prince Michael, 152, 153, 154, 155
Skoptsy (religious group), 412
Skorina, Francis, 129
Skoropadsky, Paul, 470
Skriabin, Viacheslav, *see* Molotov, Viacheslav
Skuratov, Maliuta, 139
Slavery, 109; in Kievan Russia, 36, 40, 42, 45; in Time of Troubles, 159; in Muscovite Russia, 173, 177; in Imperial Russia, 217, *see also* Serfdom
Slavic languages, 16–17
Slavonic-Greek-Latin Academy, 192
Slavophiles, 158, 182, 221, 334, 338, 339, 340, 345, 347, 354, 421; philosophy and leaders of, 335–37; on serfdom, 336, 337, 344
Slavs: Rus compared with, 24; Balkan, 95; East (*see* East Slavs)
Sleeping Beauty, The (Tchaikovsky), 428

Slepov, Lazar A., 529
Slitte (Saxon agent), 135
Slovakia, 506, 636
Sloveni tribe, 22
Smerdy, 44–45
Smoke (levy), 45, 46, 69
Smoke (Turgenev), 420
Smolensk, 37, 61, 87, 162, 167, 257, 497; East
  Slavs in, 18; assigned to Viacheslav, 35;
  trade with, 39, 43; Ivan III and, 98; Basil III
  and, 100; Olgerd and, 125; in Time of Trou-
  bles, 153, 154, 155, 156, 161; battle of, 291;
  World War II and, 508, 514
Smolny Institute, 269, 277
Smutnoe Vremia, see Time of Troubles
Smychka, 561
Sobchak, Anatolii, 597, 625–26
Sobornost, 336
Social black holes, 649
Social criticism, 272–74
Social Democratic (SD) party, 410, 454;
  founded, 378–79; Revolution of 1905 and,
  381; Duma and, 384, 385; Lenin in, 461;
  Stalin in, 483
Socialism, 367, 440, 477–78; roots of, 339; Jew-
  ish, 413; Chernyshevsky on, 434; Provi-
  sional Government and, 442–43, 445–46;
  utopian, 452, 458; "permanent revolution"
  theory of, 481; Five-Year Plans and, 484–85;
  communism as replacement of, 541; Gor-
  bachev and, 584, 586–87; in postcommunist
  Russia, 647
Socialist realism, 426, 576–78, 579
Socialist Revolutionary (SR) party, 379, 387,
  388, 433, 434, 442, 443, 465; founded, 378;
  Duma and, 384, 385; in Constituent Assembly, 463; Civil War and, 466, 473, *see also*
  Battle Organization; Maximalists
Social security system, 615, 621
Society: of Kievan Russia, 44–45; of Nov-
  gorod, 79; of appanage Russia, 108–10; of
  Muscovite Russia, 171–74; of Imperial Rus-
  sia, 217–18, 261–63, 321–22, 411–14; under
  Peter I, 217–18; in the 18th century, 261–63;
  in the 19th century (first half), 321–22; from
  great reforms to 1917, 411–14; of Soviet
  Russia, 556–71; of postcommunist Russia,
  641–58, *see also* specific social groups
Society of the United Slavs, 298–99
Sokurov, Aleksandr, 662, 664
Solario, Pietro, 118, 120
Solidarity movement, 554, 598
Sologub, Fedor, 426
Soloveytchik, George M. de, 247
Soloviev, Sergei, 8, 101, 328, 419, 436; on colo-
  nization, 86; on Time of Troubles, 158; on
  Peter I, 221
Soloviev, Vladimir, 436, 657
Solzhenitsyn, Alexander, 494, 547, 578, 594,
  659, 660
Sophia (Regent; sister of Peter I), 198, 204
Sorokin, Vladimir, 660
Sotnia, 76

Southeast Asia Treaty Organization (SEATO),
  549–50
Southern Society, 298–99
South Korea, 527, 639
South Ossetian Autonomous Region of Geor-
  gia, 591
South Slavic languages, 16, 17, 51
Southwest Russia, 82–85, 87
Soviet of Nationalities, 499–500
Soviet Russia, 451–607; establishment of gov-
  ernment, 449; organization of new gov-
  ernment, 461–63; first months of govern-
  ment, 463–65; national independence
  movements in, 470–72; the thaw in, 546–48;
  society of, 556–71; culture of, 571–81, *see
  also* Russian Soviet Federated Socialist
  Republic; Union of Soviet Socialist
  Republics
Soviets, 381, 410, 443, 499
Sovkhozes, 489, 492, 539, 540, 542, 562
Soyuz 4 and 5, 573n
Space program, 532, 533, 539, 573
Spain, 292; Peter I and, 208; Catherine II and,
  245; Alexander I and, 287; revolution in,
  294, 296; civil war in, 505
Spark, The (newspaper), 461
Speransky, Michael, 296, 306; reforms domi-
  nated by, 284–86; attempts to counteract
  influence of, 328
Spirit of the Laws (Montesquieu), 240
Spiritual crisis, 566, 583, 586, 599, 606
Spiritualist Society, 411
Spiritual Reglament, 215
Sportsman's Sketches (Turgenev), 344, 420
Sputnik I, 539, 573n
Sputnik II, 573n
Stage painting, 431
Stagnation, 586
Stakhanov, Alexis, 493
Stakhanov movement, 493, 498
Stalin, Joseph, 8, 457, 459, 482–84, 485, 486,
  488, 490(figure), 492, 493, 495–99, 535, 538,
  540, 543, 548, 549, 559, 563, 605, 614, 625; in
  Council of People's Commissars, 461; origi-
  nal name of, 461, 482; rise to power, 477–81;
  background of, 482–83; interpreting,
  483–84; collectives criticized by, 488–89;
  Khrushchev's denunciation of, 497, 531,
  532, 546, 550; system of, 497–99; quoted,
  501; foreign relations and, 502, 503, 504;
  World War II and, 507, 508, 516; at post-war
  conferences, 513; last decade of, 517–28;
  death of, 527–28, 530; on wage equality,
  564; Russian language promoted by,
  567–68; culture influenced by, 572; Marr
  school of thought and, 574; literature influenced by, 576; religion and, 581; mass
  graves of victims discovered, 600; Chechnia and, 617, *see also* Five-Year Plans; Great
  purge
Stalingrad, 483, 511, 512, 532
Stalinism, 319, 483–84, *see also* De-Stalinization

Stanislavsky, Constantine, 432
Stankevich, Nicholas, 337–38
Stanovoi mountains, 178
Starodub, 100
Starovery or staroobriadtsy, *see* Old Belief
Starovoitova, Galina, 649
START 2 treaty, 638
Stasi, 625
State and Revolution, The (Lenin), 461
State Bank, 351
State Committee for the Management of State Property (GKI), 613
State Committee for the State of Emergency (GKChP), 604
State Council, 303, 305, 395; Polish, 310; emancipation of serfs and, 345–46; Fundamental Laws on, 382; Stolypin and, 389; great reforms and, 397
State duma, 388, 395, 436; Speransky's proposal for, 285; consultative, 381; First, 382, 383–84, 400; Second, 384–85; Fourth, 385–86; Third, 385–86, 388; World War I and, 394; labor strikes and, 410; law prohibiting abolition of, 439; limited power of, 440; Provisional Government and, 441–43, 444; Russian Federation and, 618, 619, 620, 623, 624, 625, 626, 627, 628, 629, 635, 638, 640
State Gentry Land Bank, 364, 397
State Lending Bank, 262
State of the Federation addresses, 623, 624, 635
State peasants, 173, 257, 261, 262, 322; under Peter I, 212; under Catherine II, 240; in the Legislative Commission, 240; factory work performed by, 260; under Alexander I, 284; under Nicholas I, 304, 306; under Alexander II, 346, 347
State treasury, 351
Statism, 627
Stavropol, 586
Steam power, 319
Steamships, 320, 322
Steinberg, Isaac Nachman, 377
Stender-Petersen, Adolph, 23
Stepashin, Sergei, 624
Stephen (Novgorodian traveler), 116
Stephen Bathory, Prince of Transylvania, King of Poland, 140, 143
Stephen of Perm, Saint, 113, 117
Steppe, 37; role in Russian history, 5, 9; early cultures in, 10, 11, 13, 14, 15, 16; agriculture in, 43; Ivan IV and, 134, 135
Stepun, Fedor A., 336
Stockholm: Treaties of, 208; university of, 419
Stock markets, 614, 624
Stokes, Antony Derek, 34
Stolbovo, Treaty of, 162, 193
Stoletov, Alexander, 419
Stolypin, Peter, 383, 385, 406–7, 440; policy of, 386–89; assassination of, 389
Story of the Massacre of Mamai, 116

Strabo, 13
Strait of Kerch, 14
Strait of Tartary, 4
Straits, 254, 391; role in Russian history, 8; Bering, 178; First Turkish War and, 246; French interest in, 290; Treaty of Adrianople and, 308; Turkish-Egyptian conflict and, 310, 311; Crimean War and, 314; World War I and, 392
Straits Convention, 313
Stravinsky, Igor, 332, 430
Streltsy, 134, 177, 198, 221; rebellions of, 204, 206; reform of, 211
Strigolniki, 113
Strikes, 475, 591, 599, 615; general, 381, 549; moral demands in, 410–11; February Revolution and, 441; during Civil War, 466; prohibition of, 563
Stroganov family, 140, 163, 171, 189
Stroganov school of icon painting, 190
Strogonov, Count Paul, 282
Struve, Frederick William Jacob, 327
Struve, Gleb, 105
Struve, Peter, 378, 436, 437
Subjective method in social analysis, 434
Subudey, 66
Succession issues: after Iaroslav the Wise, 35; in Kievan Russia, 37; in Muscovite Russia, 102; after Theodore I, 144, 147, 152, 175; after Alexis (Quietest One), 197–98; after Peter I, 220, 224, 253; in Austria, 233; in Poland, 233; changes made by Paul I, 253; after Alexander I, 299; after Lenin, 477–78; after Stalin, 522, 530, *see also* False Dmitrii; False Peter; Little Felon
Sudebnik, 70, 81, 99, 134, 177
Sudetenland, 506
Suez Canal, 550
Suicide, 576, 632, 664
Suicide bombers, 632
Sukhomlinov, Vladimir, 394, 440
Suleiman I, the Magnificent, 100, 232
Sumarokov, Alexander, 271
Sumgait, 594
Summer Palace, 189
Sumner, Benedict Humphrey, 8, 219, 256
Sun Yat-sen, 503
Supreme Secret Council, 224, 225, 226
Supreme Soviet, 522, 589, 616; structure of, 499–500; Yeltsin as head of, 597
Surikov, Basil, 428
Surozh, 24
Suslov, Michael, 536
Suvorov, Prince Alexander, 234, 245, 247, 250, 254, 271, 291
Suzdal, 27, 33, 66, 74, 85, 86, 87, 89, 101; trade in, 43; bishops of, 112; icon painting in, 120
Sverdlovsk, 600, 610
Sviatopolk (son of Iziaslav), 35
Sviatopolk the Damned, 33, 49, 73
Sviatopolk-Mirsky, Prince Dmitrii, 379
Sviatoslav (Iaroslavich), of Chernigov, 35

Sviatoslav (Igorevich), Grand Prince, 25, 26, 28–30, 41

Sviatoslav (Olgovich), Prince of Novgorod-Seversk, 89

Sviatoslav (Vladimirovich), 33

Sviiazhsk, 135

Swan Lake (Tchaikovsky), 428

Sweden, 23, 24, 61, 370; Alexander Nevskii's conquest of, 74, 75; Muscovite Russia and, 139, 140, 143, 162, 167, 187, 193; in Time of Troubles, 144, 153, 154, 155, 156, 161; Imperial Russia and, 204–9, 212, 213, 214, 216, 229, 232, 233, 245, 246, 247, 251, 252, 287, 288; Peter I and, 204–9, 212, 213, 214, 216, 245; Peter III and, 229; Seven Years' War and, 234; Catherine II and, 245, 246, 247, 251, 252; Second Turkish War and, 247; freemasonry in, 273; Alexander I and, 287, 288; Napoleonic Wars and, 290, 292; Soviet Russia and, 503, 524, *see also* Great Northern War

Switzerland, 254, 355

Syllabic versification, 188

Sylvester (advisor to Ivan IV), 133, 137–38, 188

Sylvester (chronicler), 53

Symbolism, 425, 426, 575

Syphilis, 413, 648

Syr Daria river, 4

Syria, 65, 310

Table of Ranks, 217, 222

Tacitus, 18

Taganka, 580

Taganrog, 205, 320

Taiga, 5

Taiwan, *see* Formosa

Tajikistan, 633, 637

Tajik republic, 499, 594

Tale about the Capture of Pskov, 116

Tale of the Town of Kitezh, The (Rimsky-Korsakov), 428

Taliban, 639

Talleyrand, 293

Tambov, 260, 474

Tamerlane, 70, 94, 102

Tanais, 14

Tannenberg or Grünwald, battle of, 126, 392

Taras Bulba (Gogol), 333

Tariffs, 46, 219, 260, 322, 391

Tarkovsky, Andrei, 662

Tarle, Evgenii V., 292

Tartars, 63, 597; Ivan IV and, 134–35; Pugachev's rebellion and, 241; Kosovo tragedy and, 636, *see also* Crimean Tartars; Mongols

Tatarinov, Valery, 351

Tatarstan, 616

Tatishchev, Basil, 276

Tatlin, Vladimir, 579

Taxes: in Kievan Russia, 42, 45, 46; Mongols and, 66, 68, 69; head, 69, 216–17, 346, 367, 405; in Muscovite Russia, 163–64, 173, 178;

iasak, 178, 180; in Imperial Russia, 214, 215, 216–17, 228, 232, 244, 263, 306, 346, 349, 353, 367, 399, 405, 406, 407; household, 216; land, 216, 306; inheritance, 367; in Soviet Russia, 476, 486; in Russian Federation, 615, 623, 631

Taxi Blues (film), 664

Tbilisi or Tiflis, 482–83, 547, 593

Tchaikovsky, Peter, 332, 428, 429(figure)

Teheran conference, 513

Telepnev-Obolensky, Prince, 132

Telescope, 335

Television, 622, 629–30, 661, 664

Teller, Edward, 552

Temir-Tau, 547

Temperley, Harold W. V., 313

Temporary Regulations, 363, 369, 370

Temuchin, *see* Jenghiz Khan

Tennyson, Alfred Lord, 316

Tenth money, 163

Tent or pyramidal churches, 118, 190

Terek area, 467

Tereshkova, Valentina, 573n

Terrorism, 356, 363, 433; Revolution of 1905 and, 379; Stolypin and, 387, 388, 389; in Imperial Russia, 440; in Civil War, 466–67; Chechnia and, 631–32; Sept. 11 attacks on U.S., 637, 639; war on, 639

Testament (Vladimir Monomakh), 35, 50, 53, 57

Teutonic Knights, 74–75, 123–24, 125, 126

Thailand, 549–50

Theater: in Muscovite Russia, 188; in Imperial Russia, 271–72, 277–78, 340, 424, 432; in Soviet Russia, 579–80

Theodore (Fedor) I, Tsar, 174; reign of, 142–43; succession problems following, 144, 147, 152, 175

Theodore (Fedor) II, Tsar, 149, 151

Theodore (Fedor) III, Tsar, 168, 194, 197

Theodosius, Saint, 49–50

Theognost, Metropolitan, 91

Theosophical Society, 411

Theosophy, 437

Third Rome, doctrine of, 100, 115–16, 117

Thirty Years' War, 205, 209, 232

Thiry-eighth parallel, 527

Thomsen, Vilhelm L. P., 23

Thor (god), 22

Thorn, 250

Three Emperors' League, 358, 371

Tibet, 390

Tien Shan mountains, 4

Tiflis, *see* Tbilisi or Tiflis

Tikhomirov, Mikhail N., 18, 176

Tikhon, Patriarch, 581

Tikhonov, Nicholas, 536–37

Tilsit, Treaty of, 287, 288

Time of Troubles, 142, 143, 144–60, 161, 163, 164, 167, 171, 176, 178, 187, 194, 328; dynastic phase, 144, 147–51; national phase, 144, 154–58; social phase, 144–45, 151–54; nature and results of, 158–60

Tito, Marshal, 512, 526, 553
Tiumen, 140
Tiutchev, Fedor or Theodore, 329, 332, 333, 357, 424–25; quoted, 3; Schelling's influence on, 334
Tkachev, Peter, 356, 456
Tobacco, 164, 173, 194, 646
Tobolsk, 140, 261
Tocqueville, Alexis de, 584
Todtleben, Count Edward, 315–16
Togliatti (manufacturing center), 649
Togliatti, Palmiro, 529
Tokhtamysh, Khan, 93, 94
Tolstaia, Tatiana, 660
Tolstoy, Alexis N., 576
Tolstoy, Count Dmitrii, 353, 363, 417
Tolstoy, Count Leo, 292, 316, 333, 370, 416, 420, 422(figure); work of, 324, 423–24; populism and, 355; life of, 423; anarchism and, 433
Tomsk, 261; university of, 418
Torgau, 512
Torture, state policy on, 78, 240, 282, 495
Torzhok, 68, 139
Totalitarianism, 483–84, 533
Town councils, 349
Towns: of East Slavs, 18; in Kievan Russia, 37, 44, 46; in Time of Troubles, 145, 156; in Muscovite Russia, 162; in Imperial Russia, 214, 261, 282, 348, 349
Townspeople, 254; in zemskii sobor, 157; in the Legislative Commission, 240; as percentage of population, 321
Trade: in ancient Russia, 13; from the Varangians to the Greeks, 26, 36, 41, 72, 76; in Kievan Russia, 29, 36–37, 39, 41, 42–43, 61; Novgorod and, 39, 72, 74, 76, 78, 106; in southwest, 82; Lvov and, 84; in appanage Russia, 106; in Muscovite Russia, 147, 171, 173; in Imperial Russia, 210, 219, 233, 260–61, 319–21, 322, 400; first modern commercial treaty and, 233; in Soviet Russia, 465, 474, 475, 476, 503, 520
Trade unions: Revolution of 1905 and, 381; in Imperial Russia, 408, 410; in Soviet Russia, 475, 493, 563; in postcommunist Russia, 647, see also Strikes
Transbaikalia, 467
Transcaspian region, 361
Transcaucasia, 143, 287, 474; early cultures in, 10; Nicholas I and, 304; agriculture in, 318; Russian expansion in, 360; Russification in, 366; industry in, 399, 400; Treaty of Brest-Litovsk and, 464; dissolution of federation, 470; Soviet republics of, 472, 499; Stalin in, 483; nationalistic movements in, 593–94
Transportation: Mongols and, 69; in Imperial Russia, 319–21, 322, 398, 441; in Soviet Russia, 476
Transrational words, 427
Trans-Siberian railroad, 371, 373–74, 375, 400, 467

Travendal, treaty of, 205
Treadgold, Donald W., 406
Trediakovsky, Basil, 270
Treml, Vladimir, 606
Trepov, Theodore, 356
Tribute: in Kievan Russia, 27, 39–40, 42; Mongols and, 67, 91, 98, 103
Triple Alliance, 372, 390
Triple Entente, 390
Tristan and Isolde theme, 188
Trotsky, Leon, 369, 475, 481, 495, 502; original name of, 449; in Council of People's Commissars, 461; World War I and, 464; Civil War and, 469; struggles with Stalin, 477, 478–79, 483; murder of, 479, 497; quoted, 556
Trubetskoy, Prince Dmitrii, 155, 156
Truman, Harry, 513, 525
Truman Doctrine, 525
Tsar: title used by Ivan III, 99; Ivan IV crowned as, 131, 133; emperor title compared with, 213
Tsaritsyn, 483, see also Stalingrad
Tsarskoe Selo, see Pushkin
Tsiolkovsky, Constantine, 573
Tskhinvali, 591
Tsushima Strait, battle of, 375–76
Tsvetaeva, Marina, 460
Tuberculosis, 408, 413, 648
Tucker, Robert C., 484
Tugor Khan, 52
Tukhachevsky, Michael, 470, 495
Tula, 152, 171, 259, 468
Tulchin, 298
Turbeville, George, 3
Turgenev, Ivan, 324, 330, 333, 338, 353, 416, 424, 432, 547; Pushkin's influence on, 331; on serfdom, 344; work of, 420–21
Turkestan, 65
Turkey, 98–99; Mongols in, 65; Ivan III and, 95; Black Sea importance to, 106, 233, 246, 247; False Dmitrii I and, 150; Muscovite Russia and, 162, 165, 166, 167, 175, 182, 183; Imperial Russia and, 198, 203, 205, 207, 209–10, 213, 232–34, 241, 245–48, 250, 252, 254, 257, 261, 288, 310–11, 312, 357, 358–60, 391; Peter I and, 203, 205, 207, 209–10, 213; Russo-Turkish treaty and, 205; Great Northern War and, 207; Catherine II and, 241, 245, 246–47, 248, 250, 252, 257; First Turkish War, 245, 246–47; Second Turkish War, 246, 247, 263; partition of Poland and, 249; Paul I and, 254; Alexander I and, 288; Georgia annexation and, 288; Napoleonic Wars and, 290; Greek conflict and, 294, 308; Egyptian conflict and, 310–11; Nicholas I and, 310–11, 312; Romanian national movement and, 312; Crimean War and, 313–16; trade with, 321, 400; Alexander II and, 357, 358–60; Balkan invasions and, 357, 358–60; Muslim migration to, 361; Alliance of the Three Emperors and, 371; Balkan conflicts

and, 391; pre-World War I, 391; World War I and, 392; Treaty of Brest-Litovsk and, 464; Transcaucasian republics and, 472; Kars-Ardakhan acquired by, 474; Litvinov Protocol and, 504; United States aid to, 525; Russian Federation and, 621Turkmanchai, Treaty of, 308

Turkmen republic, 499, 594

Tushino, 153, 154, 158, 159, 160

TV-6, 630

Tver, 103, 108; Moscow rivalry with, 75, 89–91, 92, 93, 101; emerging importance of, 86; Ivan III and, 96, 97, 98; gentry renunciation of privileges in, 352

"Twenty-five thousand" movement, 488

Twenty-year program (of building communism), 532

Tysiatskii or chiliarch, 77, 78, 79, 81, 97

Uezdy, 214, 243

Ufa, 467

Ugedey, Great Khan, 65, 66

Ugra river, 98

Ukazes, 382

Ukraine, 599, 655; climate of, 5; language of, 16; East Slavs in, 18; Polish aggression and conquest, 128, 165–67, 466, 470, 474; serfdom in, 167, 244, 346; Muscovite Russia and, 175, 176, 183, 192; Old Believers and, 186; literature in, 187; Great Northern War and, 206–7, 208; Imperial Russia and, 228, 257, 366; partition of Poland and, 250, 310; peasant uprisings in, 251; horses raised in, 320; industry in, 399, 520; strikes in, 410; Provisional Government and, 445; Treaty of Brest-Litovsk and, 464; Russian Civil War and, 468; independence movements in, 470–71, 473; as Soviet republic, 474, 489, 499; famine in, 488; Communist Party in, 497; World War II and, 507, 508, 511, 514; deprivations in, 561; purges in, 567; nationalistic movements in, 591, 594–95; independence proclaimed by, 604; Russian Federation and, 633–34, 637–38

Ukrainians, 61, 87; Lithuania and, 129; in Soviet Union, 567, 595

Ukrainian War of Liberation, 166

Ukraintsev, N., 446

Ulam, Adam, 484

Ulianov, Alexander, 456

Ulianov, Vladimir, *see* Lenin, Vladimir Ilich

Ulianovsk, 461, *see also* Simbirsk

Ullman, Richard H., 472

Ulozhenie, 165, 169, 172, 173, 175, 176, 177, 306

Ulric, Duke Anthony of Brunswick-Bevern-Lüneburg, 226

Ulrika Eleonora, Queen of Sweden, 208

Unemployment, 536, 615, 645

Uniate Church, 165, 310, 353, 582, 595, 634

Unification Church, 657

Union, Treaty of, 634

Union of Brest, 165

Union of Communist Youth (Komsomol), 547, 557, 642

Union of Liberation, 378

Union of Lublin, 127–28

Union of Officers, 652

Union of Pereiaslavl, 167

Union of Right Forces, 628, 629

Union of Salvation, 298

Union of Soviet Socialist Republics (U.S.S.R.), 451; member republics of, 474; breakup of, 584–85, 591–607, 633; official abolition of, 604, *see also* Soviet Russia

Union of Soviet Sovereign States, 604

Union of Soviet Writers, 576

Union of Towns, 394

Union of Unions, 381

Union of Welfare, 298

Union of Zemstva and Towns, 441

Union Soviet, 499

Union Treaty, 604

Unipolarity, 636

United Nations, 513, 524, 526, 527, 636, 638, 639, 640

United Nations Educational, Scientific, and Cultural Organization (UNESCO), 549

United Russia Party, 627–28, 637

United States, 5, 324, 327, 361, 371, 455, 524, 573, 586, 606, 621; Monroe Doctrine and, 294; Russian railroad industry and, 320; slavery in, 344, 346; Alaska sold to, 360; Russian immigration to, 370; per capita income in, 405; Provisional Government and, 442; Russian Civil War and, 469, 472; Soviet Russia and, 476, 492, 503, 504–5, 519, 523, 525–26, 533, 534, 535, 542, 548, 549, 551–52, 555, 585, 588, 599; World War II and, 510, 512–13; Atlantic Charter and, 513; Korean War and, 527; Cuban missile crisis and, 533, 534, 551; economy of, 538–39, 542, 544–45; SEATO and, 550; education in, 571; Russian Federation and, 609, 635–40; Sept. 11 terrorist attacks in, 637, 639

Unity Party, 625, 627, 628

Universities: in Imperial Russia, 268, 284, 307, 324–26, 328, 343, 352, 364, 416–17, 418, 440; in Soviet Russia, 558, 570

University Statute of 1835, 326

University Statute of 1863, 353, 416

University Statute of 1884, 364, 417

Unkiar Skelessi, Treaty of, 311, 313

Unkovsky, Alexis, 352

Unofficial Committee, 282–83, 284, 334

Upper class, 465, 473, 522, 574, *see also* Bourgeoisie; Boyars; Gentry

Upper Oka area, 98, 100

Ural cossacks, 241–42, 467

Ural mountains and area, 4, 8, 543, 599; Mongols in, 66; industry in, 171, 218, 258–59, 319, 399, 407, 486; trade in, 261; mass graves discovered in, 600

Ushakov, Simon, 191

Ushakov, Theodore, 254

Uspensky, Gleb, 422, 424
U-2 spy plane incident, 551
U.S.S.R., *see* Union of Soviet Socialist
    Republics
Ussuri region, 361
Ustinov, Dmitrii, 537
Ustiug, 140
Utigurs, 15
Utilitarianism, 354, 416, 433, 434, 436, 438
Uvarov, Count Serge, 302, 316, 325, 326, 417;
    resigns as education minister, 307; expedi-
    tions sponsored by, 328
Uzbek republic, 499, 594

Vasco da Gama, 116
Vasiliev (Vasilev), Aleksandr Aleksandrovich,
    24
Vasilsursk, 101
Vatican, 99
Vavilov, Nicholas, 572
Veche, 46; defined, 45; of Novgorod, 74, 76,
    77–78, 86, 97; of Pskov, 81; of Galicia and
    Volynia, 84; disappearance of, 110
Vedomosti or *News* (newspaper), 266
Vedrosha river, 98
Veliaminov, Basil, 103
Velikie Luki, 140
Venedi (designation of Slavs), 18
Venera-8 probe, 573n
Venetian colony, 106
Venevitinov, Dmitrii, 335
Venice, 118
Vereshchiagin, Basil, 428
Verkhoiansk, Siberia, 5
Vernadsky, George, 24, 34; on origins of Rus-
    sia, 9; on Kievan population, 44; on Mon-
    gols, 63, 68, 71, 95; on Dmitrii of Uglich,
    143; on Treaty of Brest-Litovsk, 464
Vernadsky, Vladimir, 573
Versailles, Treaty of, 506
Viacheslav (son of Iaroslav the Wise), 35
Viatichi, 29
Viatka, 79, 110
Viborg, 207, 208
Viborg Manifesto, 384, 385
Vienna, 293, 511, 512, 551; Imperial Russia
    and, 204; Treaty of, 309
Vienna Note, 314
Vietnam, 639
Vietnam War, 534, 548, 551, 552, 618
Vikings, 21, 24, 25
Village prose school of writers, 578
Vilna or Vilnius, 125, 128, 512, 592, 606; bish-
    ops of, 126; university of, 325, 326
Vinius, Andrew, 194
Vinogradov, Ivan, 573
Vinogradov, Paul, 420
Vinogradov, Vladimir, 642
Virgin lands project, 539
Virgin Soil (Turgenev), 420
Virgin Soil Upturned (Sholokhov), 576
Visigoths, 15

Vistula river, 17, 206, 514
Viten or Vytenis, Grand Prince of Lithuania,
    124–25
Vitovt or Vytautas, Grand Prince of Lithua-
    nia, 94, 126
Vladimir (son of Iaroslav Osmomsyl), 83
Vladimir (town), 36, 56, 61, 85, 92, 101, 115;
    Mongols in, 66; emerging importance of,
    86; capital located in, 87; Ivan Kalita and,
    91
Vladimir, Grand Prince, Saint, 26, 34, 43, 49,
    50, 73, 115; reign of, 30–33; paganism and,
    31–32, 48; in byliny, 52; chronicles of, 53
Vladimir, Prince of Moscow (son of Iurii), 89
Vladimir, Prince of Moscow (son of Vsevolod
    III), 89
Vladimir-in-Volynia, 35, 82–83
Vladimir Monomakh, Grand Prince, 27, 50,
    53, 57, 73, 85; reign of, 35–36; religion and,
    115
Vladimir of Staritsa, Prince, 137, 139
Vladimirsky-Budanov, Mikhail F., 84; quoted,
    105; on *Ulozhenie*, 172; on education in
    Muscovite Russia, 192
Vladimir-Suzdal princedom, 85, 86, 103
Vladivostok, 361, 467, 552
Vlasiev, Athanasius, 150
Vlasov, Andrew, 516
Voevoda, 178, 180, 214
Voinovich, Vladimir, 600
Volga area, 257, 352, 543; Mongols in, 67; con-
    quered peoples in, 146; rebellions in, 165,
    474; Great Northern War in, 206;
    Pugachev's rebellion in, 241; foreign
    colonies in, 245; agriculture in, 318
Volga Bulgars, *see* Bulgars
Volga-German Autonomous Republic, 521–22
Volga river, 15, 16, 101; role in Russian his-
    tory, 4, 8; Sviatoslav's conquest and, 29;
    trade and, 29, 74, 76, 106, 260, 261; canals
    and, 218–19, 320, 521; World War II and,
    510–11
Volgograd, 483, 532
Volkhov river, 76
Volkov, Theodore, 278
Volokita, 586
Volokolamsk, 114
Volost, 285, 365
Volosteli, 177
Voltaire, 235, 237, 252
Voltairianism, 272–73
Voluntary associations, 411
Volynia, 61, 82, 83–85, 86; Mongol invasion
    of, 66, 84; Galicia united with, 83; Olgerd
    and, 125; Poland's seizure of, 128
Vonifatiev, Stephen, 183
Von Laue, T. H., 413
Vorkuta, 547
Voronezh, 203, 510–11
Voronikhin, Andrew, 340
Vorontsov, Count Michael, 228
Voroshilov, Clement, 490(figure), 522, 532

Vorotynasky, Prince Michael, 135
Vorskla river, 126
Voskhod II, 573n
Vostokov, Alexander, 328
Votchina, 107, 108, 129, *see also* Land
Voyce, Arthur, 191
Vozha river, 92
Vsevolod, Grand Prince, 35
Vsevolod III, of the Large Nest, Grand Prince, 85, 86, 89, 92
Vyshgorod, 39
Vyshnegradsky, Ivan, 367
Vysotsky, Vladimir, 578

Wages: in Imperial Russia, 318, 319, 408, 409; in Soviet Russia, 486, 543, 563, 564; in Russian Federation, 615, 621, 623, 624, 630, 631, 644–45
Wales, 215
Walesa, Lech, 554
Walicki, Andrzej, 606
Wallachia, 288; Mongols in, 67; Lithuania and, 126; Great Northern War and, 207; First Turkish War and, 246; Treaty of Adrianople and, 308; Nicholas I and, 312; Crimean War and, 315
Walsh, Warren B., 383
Wanderings beyond the Three Seas (Nikitin), 116
War and Peace (Tolstoy), 292, 324, 423
War Communism, 460–61, 465–75, 476, 488; national independence movements and, 470–72; crisis and, 474–75, *see also* Civil War
War Industry Committee, 394
War of 1805, 283
War of the Polish Succession, 233
War of the Spanish Succession, 209
War of the Third Coalition, 287
Warsaw, 250, 310, 470; Grand Duchy of, 290, 293; uprisings in, 309; industry in, 399; World War II and, 514
Warsaw Pact, 553, 554, 585
Warsaw Treaty, 550
Waterloo, Napoleon's defeat at, 292
Weapons of mass destruction, 639
Weber, Max, 644
Weidle, Wladimir, 118, 264
Wenden, 140
Werälä, Treaty of, 252
West Berlin, 526
Western influences, 258, 270, 275, 278, 323, 334, 432; in Muscovite Russia, 147, 164, 192–95; self-criticism and, 192–95; under Peter I, 201, 203–4, 211, 215, 216, 219, 221–22, 262; under Catherine II, 253, 264–65; literature and, 331
Westernizers, 335, 354, 433; philosophy and leaders of, 337–39; on serfdom, 344
West Galicia, 290
West Slavic languages, 16, 17
What Is To Be Done? (Chernyshevsky), 420, 433–34, 454
Wheat purchases, 532, 542

Whistler, George, 320
Whistler, James McNeill, 320
"White House" headquarters, 617
White Russians or Belorussians, 61, 87; language of, 16; Lithuania and, 129; Old Believers and, 186; in Soviet Union, 567
White Russia or Belorussia: partition of Poland and, 250, 309, 310; Polish rebellion and, 352; Polish aggression and conquest, 466, 470, 474; independence movements in, 470; as Soviet republic, 474, 499; World War II and, 507, 514; nationalistic movements in, 595; mass graves discovered in, 600; abolition of U.S.S.R. and, 604, *see also* Belarus
Whites, 466–69, 483, 561; in Ukraine, 470; reason for Red victory over, 472–73
White Sea, 135, 315, 494
Widukind (author of *Res gestae saxonicae),* 24
Wielopolski, Marquis Alexander, 352
William II, Emperor of Germany, 390, 391
Window into Europe, 208, 257
Winter Palace, 228, 277, 356, 380, 449
Wipper (Vipper), Robert I., 141
Witte, Serge, 367, 370–71, 383, 385, 405, 417; Russo-Japanese War and, 374, 376; Revolution of 1905 and, 381, 382; industrialization and, 398–99, 400, 402
Wladyslaw, Prince of Poland, 153–55, 159, 160, 161, 162
Wladyslaw II, King of Poland, *see* Jagiello
Woe from Wit / Gore ot uma (Griboedov), 330, 340
Wojtyla, Cardinal Karol (Pope John Paul II), 554
Women, 355; Mongol influence on, 69; in early Novgorod, 78, 80; in Imperial Russia, 219, 222; education of, 269, 326, 364, 417, 418, 566; revolutionary movements and, 354; labor legislation on, 367; working-class, 411; in Soviet Russia, 541, 558, 566–67; in space, 573n; in postcommunist Russia, 644, 647; mortality rates in, 646
Women of Russia, 620
Women's rights and feminism: in Imperial Russia, 412, 436; in Soviet Russia, 547, 566–67
Workers, 488, 558; in Imperial Russia, 260, 262–63, 319, 378, 408; defined, 319, 408; Revolution of 1917 and, 447; in society, 562–63, *see also* Labor force, Proletariat
Workers' Opposition movement, 475
Working Russia, 615, 652
World Bank, 614, 635
World Health Organization, 645
World of Art (movement), 437
World of Art, The (periodical), 425
World Trade Organization, 639
World War I, 400, 416, 455, 518; foreign relations prior to, 389–92; catalyst for, 391–92; Russia in, 392–95; casualties in, 440–41; Provisional Government and, 443, 444, 445; Soviet Russia in, 463–64, 466

World War II, 500, 504, 507–16, 531, 552, 599, 605, 655; Soviet Union in, 508–12; diplomacy during, 512–14; second front in, 512, 513; evaluation of Soviet Union in, 514–16; Chechnia and, 517; human and material losses from, 517–19; reconstruction following, 519–21
Wortman, Richard, 383
Wrangel, Baron Peter, 469, 474

Yabloko (party), 619–20, 628, 629
Yagoda, Genrikh, 496
Yakovlev, Alexander, 585
Yalta conference, 513, 514
Yalu River, 374
Yavlinsky, Grigory, 619, 620, 622
Yeltsin, Boris, 599, 605, 627, 629, 630, 631, 632, 633, 641, 648, 653, 654; conflicts with Gorbachev, 587, 589, 596, 606, 610–12; elected to Congress of People's Deputies, 596–97; attempted coup and, 604, 612, 620; on visit to United States, 609; character and background of, 610; drinking of, 610; presidency of, 610–25; health problems of, 613, 622, 624; varying levels of support for, 613, 619, 621; popular referendem held by, 616–17; attempted overthrow of, 617, 620; heart surgery of, 623; resignation of, 625; foreign policy under, 634, 635–37; religion and, 655, 656
Yenikale, 246
Yuan dynasty, 65
Yugoslavia, 526, 550; World War II and, 508, 512; Soviet domination in, 524; Communism in, 525; NATO and, 636–37
Yukos oil company, 629
Yumashev, Valentin, 610

Zadonshchina, 116
Zaionchkovsky, Petr A., 341
Zakharov, Hadrian, 340
Zamiatin, Evgeny, 575
Zamiatnin, Dmitrii, 350

Zarudny, Serge, 350
Zarutsky, Ivan, 156, 161, 162
Zasulich, Vera, 356
Zechariah or Skharia, 113
Zelnik, Reginald E., 408
Zemshchina, 138
Zemskii nachalnik or land captain, office of, 365, 397
Zemskii sobor, 165, 169, 174; founding of, 133; Ivan IV and, 133, 141; in Time of Troubles, 154, 156, 157, 158; Michael Romaov and, 161, 162; Alexis (Quietest One) and, 166; influence of, 175–76; most famous, 176; Peter I and, 213; Slavophiles on, 336
Zemstvo system, 177, 353, 417, 435; reform of, 285, 348–49, 350, 416; counterreforms in, 365, 397; third element of, 378; Provisional Government and, 443
Zemstvo Union, 394
Zenkovsky, S., 186
Zhdanov, Andrew, 526, 546, 568, 574; quoted, 517; death of, 522, 527
Zheliabov, Andrew, 356
Zhidovin, 52
Zhirinovsky, Vladimir, 620–21, 622, 628, 653, 654
Zhivkov, Todor, 598
Zhukov, George, 510, 511, 512, 515, 531, 532, 598
Zhukovsky, Basil, 329, 333, 342
Zimin, Aleksandr A., 53
Zinin, Nicholas, 327
Zinoviev, Gregory, 477, 478, 495, 503
Zionism, 413
Zolkiewski, Stanislav, 154, 155, 495
Zond-5, 573n
Zorndorf, battle of, 234
Zoshchenko, Mikhail, 575
Zosima (monk), 116
Zvezdochetova, Larisa, 662
Zyriane, 113
Zyuganov, Gennady, 620, 621–22, 625, 653, 654, 655